Beyond the New Deal: Harry S. Truman
and American Liberalism

Contemporary American History Series
William E. Leuchtenburg, *General Editor*

Beyond the New Deal:
Harry S. Truman *and*
American Liberalism

ALONZO L. HAMBY

Columbia University Press
New York and London

Alonzo L. Hamby is Associate Professor of History at Ohio University.

Library of Congress Cataloging in Publication Data

Hamby, Alonzo L., 1940–
    Beyond the New Deal.

    (Contemporary American history series)
    Bibliography: p. 599
    1. United States—Politics and government—1945–
1953.   2. Truman, Harry S., Pres. U.S., 1884–1972.
3. Liberalism—United States.   I. Title.
E813.H26   973.918′092′4   73-7593
ISBN 0-231-03335-4

For Joyce

Preface

This book is a study of American liberalism in the decade or
so after the New Deal and an analysis of the relationship between the liberal movement and the presidency of Harry S.
Truman. It is not a comprehensive history of the Truman era;
rather, it is an examination of certain broad themes central to
an understanding of the period.

The concept of liberalism, while somewhat slippery, is
hardly as unmanageable as many historians seem to assume.
Fascinating semantic games may be played with the word, and
its definition has changed with the centuries. Nevertheless, in
the 1940s, contemporary observers had a fairly precise idea of
what liberalism meant, and it seems at the least antihistorical
to argue with them. The New Deal and the heritage of Franklin D. Roosevelt served as an ideological adhesive for all but
a few progressives, whatever their differences on tactics or on
some specific issues. (Following the usage of the time, the
words "liberal" and "progressive" are employed synonymously;
however, "Progressive" refers specifically to the Wallace party
of 1948.) The divisions among the liberals, including the
fundamental split on Soviet-American relations, involved dif-
fering interpretations of the Roosevelt–New Deal legacy and
the way to use it as the basis for a progressive program which
would go beyond the New Deal.

As a political phenomenon, the liberal movement encom-
passed a variety of groups so broad as to defy comprehensive
analysis—the labor unions, Negro organizations, neo-Populists,
civil libertarians, social gospel clergymen, academic intellec-

tuals, journalists, and a broad array of politicians at the local, state, and national levels. This study focuses upon a series of individuals, publications, and organizations which seem to have been most broadly representative of the liberal impulse. Their pronouncements carried great weight among middle-class reformers and gave liberalism its overall definition and tone. Functioning as intellectuals and opinion-molders, they attempted to shape the real world of diplomatic and political power, a process which inevitably led to tension with the professional politicians and to frustration as well as accomplishment. Their forging of a style of neo–New Deal liberalism occasioned bitter controversy within their own camp, and their relationship with the political "pros" was marked by mutual misunderstanding alongside mutual dependence.

In researching this project, I have attempted to draw upon a wide range of sources, both published and unpublished, but I have no illusions that I have exhausted the possibilities. The materials available to historians of the twentieth-century United States are simply too great to allow for total coverage unless one is writing the narrowest of monographs. The sources I have used are, I think, broad and representative; work in them should have established a strong foundation for judgments about the topic. Other scholars must assess the quality of those judgments.

This study was conceived more than ten years ago, and it is my first original book. These facts should suggest the extent of my obligations; in order to avoid a list so long as to be meaningless I have found it necessary to refrain from naming many people to whom I am sincerely grateful. I must thank as a group my undergraduate teachers of history at Southwest and Southeast Missouri State Colleges for their help and frequently their inspiration. My graduate professors at Columbia University and the University of Missouri provided me with a collective example of dedication to teaching and scholarship which I have tried to emulate. Librarians from Berkeley to Boston have given me assistance. Many busy people, listed in the Bibliographical Note, took time to share their recollections with me. The editors of the *Review of Politics,* the *Historian,* the *Journal of American History,* and the *American Historical Review* have kindly granted permission to use material previously published in article form. Joy Schroeder, Doris Dorr, Phyllis Tanner, and Debbie Hartley all typed portions of what must have seemed an endless manuscript.

I must give my special thanks to the Americans for Democratic Action, which quite literally permitted me to walk in off the street, rummage through its old files without restriction, and duplicate material as I wished, although I was completely unknown to its staff and its officials. Somehow one expects that the ADA will trust and assist scholars, but the organization's kindness was no less remarkable for being anticipated. Philip Brooks, Philip Lagerquist, and my other friends at the Harry S. Truman Library established a nearly perfect research climate. Their hard work and earnest cooperation vindicate the presidential library system.

Financial aid from several sources made this volume possible. The American Philosophical Society and the Ohio University Research Fund awarded me summer grants. The Harry S. Truman Library Institute supported my work on four separate occasions. The John C. Baker Fund, generously endowed by Mr. and Mrs. Edwin Kennedy, underwrote an academic quarter in which I was free to write most of Part Two. My department chairman, Robert Daniel, managed somehow to find funds to subsidize the typing of the manuscript.

Harold D. Woodman, John Lankford, and Allen Kifer subjected an earlier version of Part One to a searching and thorough reading. Davis R. B. Ross performed the same service for the semifinal draft of the entire book. James Boylan and Richard Fried kindly made their unpublished work available to me. George C. Herring, Jr., and John L. Gaddis shared their extensive knowledge of the early Cold War with me, gave me the benefit of their formidable critical powers, and tendered advice and encouragement well beyond the obligations of friendship and scholarship. Only those who have

gone through the awesome experience of having a manuscript
edited by William E. Leuchtenburg can fully appreciate his
craftsmanship, dedication, and wisdom; few historians are
greater teachers, and few give themselves so unselfishly to
their students and colleagues. My debt—intellectual and personal—to my mentor and friend Richard S. Kirkendall is
profound; his professionalism and integrity exemplify the
highest ideals of academic life.

My mother, Lila Hamby Legan, has supported me over a
longer period of time than any other individual. My wife
Joyce sustained me in ways too numerous to list; the dedication is a token of appreciation for her help and understanding.

A.L.H.

Athens, Ohio

Contents

Introduction

Many historians profess to find the concept of "liberalism" confusing, mainly it seems because the programs advocated by
liberals change from generation to generation. On the surface,
it may well appear puzzling that an eighteenth- or nineteenth-
century liberal was an exponent of laissez faire and weak, de-
centralized government, while a twentieth-century liberal has
invariably been an advocate of the mixed economy, the welfare
state, and powerful, centralized government. This apparent
paradox, however, simply indicates that the political content of
liberalism has changed along with the rest of the world over
the past two centuries. This change has overshadowed a basic
continuity in the fundamental assumptions which liberals have
held throughout modern history.

At bottom, liberalism has not been a set of programs but
rather a persuasion built around a belief in human reason and
dignity. Through the centuries, liberals have shared a commitment to freedom, equal justice, and equal opportunity. They
have rejected the argument that man is a prisoner of tradition
and have had great faith in the power of human intelligence to
restructure society. Liberals have always distrusted power and
privilege, have usually felt an emotional sympathy for the exploited and underprivileged, and have believed that enlightened social or economic policies can rehabilitate even the
lowest elements of society. Since such attitudes are to a large
extent the principles upon which America was established, it
should not be surprising that liberals in the United States have
felt a special need to achieve their goals.

The liberalism of the eighteenth and nineteenth centuries developed out of the thought of John Locke and Adam Smith. It was a reaction against powerful monarchies which oppressed the ordinary citizen and dispensed special privileges to a favored few. From Locke on, liberals believed that equal opportunity, free expression, and such fundamental rights as life, liberty, property, and the pursuit of happiness could survive only under a strictly limited government. This belief was a major presupposition of the American Revolution, of the struggle for a Bill of Rights, of Jefferson's fight against the Alien and Sedition acts, and of Jackson's destruction of the Bank of the United States. It was a natural persuasion for an individualistic agrarian society in which industrial capitalism was but a nascent force.

In response to the rapid and massive growth of industry and corporate power, liberalism began to find new definitions during the later nineteenth century. Workers, farmers, reform-minded clergymen, and social scientists all began to formulate in one way or another the idea of a powerful, activist state affirmatively promoting the welfare of its citizens. The new liberalism, as dedicated as the old to the ideals of human freedom and equal opportunity, found the most complete political expression it would reach in the nineteenth century in the Populist movement. The Populists, although rural-centered, advocated an ambitious agenda of reform which went well beyond farm grievances. An even fuller development of the new current awaited the twentieth century and the emergence of progressivism as a national political force.

Progressivism was not a single monolithic credo. For some reformers, it was just a continuation of an old struggle against the political bosses, now coupled with measures designed to "restore democracy" (the initiative, the referendum, the recall, the direct primary, the Australian ballot). For most, however, it also was an effort to curb the power of the giant corporations and to do so through the application of government power, which would either break up the trusts (the preference of most progressives) or subject them to close regulation (the program of a small but important minority). Some, but by no means all, of the trust-busters were essentially negative in their outlook, yearning for a return to a bygone atomistic competitive society, concerned only with the plight of the small businessman. Many other trust-busters, foremost among them Louis Brandeis, and most of the trust regulators, including their intellectual leader, Herbert Croly, formulated the outlines of a social welfare state which would realize the goals of human dignity and opportunity through federal intervention in labor-management relations, promotion of education, social insurance systems, and rural credit facilities. (The conventional dichotomy between the Brandeis–Wilson New Freedom and the Croly–Theodore Roosevelt New Nationalism obscures this important area of agreement.) Among the most important concrete results of the progressive movement were several important pieces of railroad regulation, the Pure Food and Drug Act, the Meat Inspection Act, the Federal Reserve Act, the Farm Credit and Warehouse acts of 1916, the income tax, the Federal Trade Commission, the Adamson Act, the federal child labor acts of 1916 and 1918, and many state and local statutes which regulated wages, hours, and working conditions, sought to improve slum housing, and provided minimum social insurance.

The New Deal was based upon the liberalism of the progressive era, and added little intellectual content to it. The New Deal's successes lay in the actual adoption of a massive body of reform legislation and in the construction of a strong, effective liberal political coalition. Its failures, in general, involved problems which the progressives had been unable to solve, especially corporate consolidation, or situations which the progressives had never faced, especially mass unemployment.

The legislative accomplishments were remarkable—the organization of agriculture to achieve tolerable price levels, laws which guaranteed collective bargaining and fair labor standards, the Social Security Act, increased regulation of the financial community, mortgage programs which prevented the liquidation of a sizable segment of the urban and rural middle classes, work programs for many of the unemployed, the Tennessee Valley Authority. The political coalition provided the most durable base yet established for reform. Early twentieth-century progressivism had drawn its political power from an uneasy and unstable alliance of reform-minded farmers and urban middle-class citizens. As reform advanced in the direction of social welfare and became more identified with the Democratic Party, it attracted increasing labor and lower-class support; but these groups had not yet been cemented into the Democratic progressive coalition when it was wrecked by World War I and the postwar reaction. It remained for the New Deal to erect a liberal coalition which drew its greatest strength from labor and the urban lower classes.

The progressive era and the New Deal demonstrated liberalism's dependence upon strong presidential leadership. This dependence was not simply a need for a chief executive who could persuade, cajole, or strong-arm a reluctant Congress, as important as such talents were. Twentieth-century liberalism required a president with the charisma to dramatize and virtually embody the cause of reform, a political leader who could mobilize a progressive coalition with the sheer force of his personality. The liberal intellectuals in particular seemed to need this sort of leadership, perhaps because their social position and professional preoccupations left them especially sensitive to political style and articulation.

By the 1940s, three great reform presidents, Theodore Roosevelt, Woodrow Wilson, and Franklin D. Roosevelt, had provided the liberal movement with the direction it needed and had compiled impressive records of accomplishment. Each for a time was the living representation of the new liberalism; each also demonstrated the fragility of a political faith so dependent upon charisma. No man had done more than Theodore Roosevelt with his forceful intellect and dynamic personality to make the new liberalism a national movement. Yet in his final years, obsessed with foreign policy and driven by hatred of Woodrow Wilson, he abandoned the Progressive Party he had so hopefully formed and ruined whatever chances his followers had to secure influence within their old Republican Party. Wilson brought the progressive movement to its zenith, but his pro-war decision in 1917, his subsequent failures at Versailles, and his tragic physical breakdown while fighting for the League of Nations were the major factors leading to the debacle of 1920 and a decade-long progressive eclipse. Franklin Roosevelt, it seemed, had avoided these pitfalls. He had held the trust and affection of most liberals in peace and war; he had made the New Deal the very definition of American liberalism. Yet FDR threatened to undermine the liberal movement in a more sub-tle way. In a very real sense, he *was* liberalism; there was no separate, organized liberal movement with an identity which transcended Roosevelt's personality and political appeal. For this reason alone, the future of liberalism beyond FDR was un-certain.

The careers of Theodore Roosevelt and Woodrow Wilson demonstrate the mercurial and frequently destructive roles of diplomacy and war in the history of American liberalism. The liberal has usually viewed war as irrational and destructive of the humane values he cherishes; war is a last resort to be con-sidered only after the failure of every constructive and nonvi-olent effort at solving diplomatic problems. Yet the liberals have also been drawn to wars justified by liberal ideals—thus the support of most Jacksonians for the war against Mexico to spread freedom and democracy to the Pacific, the support of the antislavery movement for the war to free the slaves, the support of William Jennings Bryan and many of his followers for the war to free the Cubans, the support of most early twen-tieth-century progressives for the war to make the world safe for democracy.

The liberal approach to war frequently oscillated from one extreme to another, at times recoiling from war as the antithe-sis of liberal values, at times embracing war as the means to the realization of these values. With few exceptions, the liberals had no coherent philosophy of foreign relations which might have provided a consistent approach to the use of force in di-plomacy and given them an appreciation of its occasional neces-sity as well as an understanding of its limitations. Instead, they had only shifting emotions. When they accepted war, they did so by seizing upon some justification which transcended national interest or even simple self-defense, and the greater the war, the more sweeping the justification, the more millennial the objectives—and the greater the probability of frustration and disappointment.

Reacting against the failure of the Wilsonian crusade, most liberals had favored pacifism and isolationism in the twenties and thirties. Yet the ever-increasing menace of fascism and militarism had alarmed them, and by the time France fell in mid-1940, they were ready to fight. But, as always, the conflict had to be more than a war for national security; it had to be a war for lasting peace and for the extension of freedom and democracy around the globe. The struggle against fascism became a monolithic obsession with the promise of creating a world on the verge of utopia, excluding the possibility of other threats to the national interest. Even America's totalitarian ally, the Soviet Union, had to be made over to represent liberal values.

The end of World War II and the death of Franklin Roosevelt created new problems and fears for the liberal movement. At first, the liberals assumed that there would be an essential continuity of the issues which had preoccupied them. At home, the dangers of corporate power and the possibility of mass unemployment dominated their thinking; abroad, their primary concerns were fascism and imperialism. Actually, the postwar world presented a different situation. The major domestic economic problem was inflation, not depression; the liberal need was not to provide for the unemployed but to protect the purchasing power of relatively affluent workers and middle-class Americans, and to provide them with such basic amenities of prosperity as decent housing. The postwar boom also created space for issues which had been peripheral during the depression, foremost among them the position of the Negro. As the liberals almost unconsciously shifted their priorities, civil rights became a central component of liberalism. At the same time, the development of the Cold War presented a formidable challenge to a movement which had defined its diplomacy primarily in terms of antifascism and had come to consider Communism as a part of the antifascist alliance. The postwar scene, in short, demanded a reexamination of some deeply held assumptions; it even demanded a limited redefinition of liberalism itself.

The liberal movement had the intellectual resources to make the shift, but it no longer had the leadership which could have facilitated the transition. The death of Roosevelt, coinciding as it did with unexpected new situations, threw liberalism into an identity crisis. Without direction from above, the liberals faced the difficult tasks of working out unforeseen problems by themselves, rebuilding the coalition which Roosevelt's personality had created, and reconstituting their movement as an effective political force capable of winning victories without the charisma of FDR or some other great political leader. It seemed extremely doubtful that they could succeed. The liberal demoralization and defeats of the initial postwar years appeared to be the early phase of a new period of postwar normalcy not unlike that which had followed World War I and carrying the threat of an even more disastrous culmination.

FDR's successor, Harry S. Truman, did not possess the Rooseveltian qualities of leadership which the liberals demanded. His difficulties in handling the postwar issues of domestic reconversion and foreign policy compounded his troubles and alienated the liberal movement. Truman himself was a quintessential Democrat whose own experience—as the son of Confederate sympathizers, as a young man growing up in the atmosphere of Midwestern insurgency, as an urban machine politician, and as a supporter of the New Deal—mirrored the post–Civil War history of his party. His primary allegiance was to the party, not to an ideology; but the Democratic Party was inextricably tied to the Roosevelt tradition. Thus Truman's essential political tasks were to provide leadership in the struggle against Republican conservatism and to establish a compelling liberal identity which could attract the blocs of voters who had sustained FDR. Despite the estrangement which developed between them, Truman and the liberals faced similar problems and were in fact dependent upon each other. Their fates could not be separated, and their fortunes would rise and fall together.

PART ONE

The Quest for Identity and the Struggle against Normalcy

Chapter 1

Sixty Million Jobs and the People's Revolution

Many historians believe that in the mid-1930s there was a shift in the character of the New Deal, a transition from a "First New Deal" to a "Second New Deal." The First New Deal, according to the argument, had worked for national unity and a vast cooperative effort to overcome the depression. Stemming from a school of institutional economic thought inspired by Thorstein Veblen, it stood for economic nationalism, accepted large economic units, and rejected the competitive ideal in favor of national planning and regulation. Some of its advocates hoped to restructure the American economy; yet in practice the First New Deal operated within a framework of "broker politics" and did little for the more depressed groups in American society.

The Second New Deal abandoned the goals of unity and consensus to become the program of the "common man" and the rising minority groups. It showed a greater concern for the small farmer, passed strong legislation to better the economic lot and bargaining power of labor, attempted to use taxation as a tool to redistribute wealth, and instituted a social insurance program. Its formula to combat the depression was antitrust action and government spending. For the vision of intensive national planning, it substituted the goal of a dynamic competi-

tive capitalism buffered by social security and manipulated by
government fiscal policy. Its economic ideas were Keynesian
and neo-Brandeisian. Its foreign economic policy, built around
an expanding reciprocal trade program, was internationalist in
its assumptions and objectives.[1]

The transition was hardly as neat as a brief summary suggests, and historians impressed with the disorderly character of
thought and politics during the Great Depression have questioned the utility of the First-Second New Deal approach.[2] For
all its rough edges, however, the concept provides a fairly good
key to changes which were taking place in liberal thought and
which continued even after the political stalemate of 1937–
1938 blocked reform legislation.

With the coming of international conflict, the liberals drew
upon the ideas of the late thirties as they sought to define the
purpose of the struggle in which America was engaged; the Second New Deal became the basis for the liberal vision of a
worldwide New Deal. The war may have confronted liberals
with a situation very different from that of the Great Depression, but to most the basic issues were the same—the menace of
fascism, the power of big business, the rights of labor, and,
above all, the specter of mass unemployment and economic insecurity. The New Deal had failed to provide a definitive answer to any of these problems; the war accentuated some, deferred others, but seemed at the time to resolve none. Most
liberals assumed that these would be the major concerns of the
postwar era as well.[3]

A death struggle against forces which were the antithesis of
liberalism, and an opportunity to build a new and decent
world from the rubble, the war gave liberals a sense of urgency,
militance, and determination—a feeling exemplified in the
near-millennial writings and oratory of Henry Wallace. The
course of human affairs seemed to be at a decisive turning
point; it would be directed by those with the strongest will.
"History," wrote the economist Lewis Corey, "is at another
great divide in an age that may move toward unlimited good or
unlimited evil." [4]

I

For liberals, the war was primarily a battle against fascism, and liberal hopes and plans for a new and better America derived much of their urgency from a fear which always lay behind them: the fear of a fascist United States. With the government canceling defense contracts at the end of the war and millions of returning soldiers looking for jobs, a reversion to the mass unemployment, poverty, and misery of the 1930s seemed likely. The purchasing power accumulated during the war might stave off economic collapse for a time—there might even be a spurt of rampant inflation—but disaster seemed probable. And when it came, the demagogues of the extreme right, never wholly silent during the war, would reappear, directing their hymns of hate at disillusioned, frustrated masses searching desperately both for a leader and for a scapegoat. The Gerald Smiths, the Father Coughlins, and their ilk could recruit battalions of storm troopers from among the embittered veterans. Corporate leaders, terrified by the possibility of mass revolt, desperately bargaining to retain their immense power, would provide financial backing, just as the German industrialists had turned to Hitler. Reactionaries and extreme isolationists—Burton Wheeler, Gerald Nye, Hamilton Fish, Martin Dies, and others—would rule Congress; Lindbergh might become a figurehead Führer. The nightmare of a totalitarian America, should progressivism fail to meet postwar necessities, existed constantly in the back of the liberal mind.[5]

Fear and hatred of an incipient native fascism caused many liberals to modify their views on civil liberties. How, with freedom and totalitarianism locked in a life-and-death struggle, could one condone the actions of pro-Hitler obstructionists? Even after Pearl Harbor, William L. Shirer estimated that some 95 pro-Axis hate sheets were reaching several million readers. And the great newspapers of Hearst, McCormick, and the Pattersons seemed at times to be almost fascist fellow travelers. They should be watched closely, and the obvious fifth columnists should be prosecuted. Freda Kirchwey, the editor of the *Nation,* probably spoke for a majority of liberals when she declared that, while loyal criticism merited encouragement, the pro-fascist journals were a "clear and present danger" and "should be exterminated exactly as if they were enemy machine-gun nests in the Bataan jungle." [6]

Closely linked to the specter of fascism were the images of monopoly and corporate power. "I don't like to over-use the word 'fascist,' " wrote the vigorous young head of the Office of Price Administration, Chester Bowles, "but it does seem to me the only phrase that can be applied to the kind of thinking which I ran into among some groups in business." Before the United States entered the war, liberals had attacked key industrialists who had resisted conversion to defense production; after Pearl Harbor, they placed the blame for production lags, waste, and profiteering upon the bungling of corporate executives who had moved into government positions as dollar-a-year men. Especially infuriating was the discovery that international cartel agreements with German firms were in part the reason for shortages of some essential war materials. To the *Progressive,* at that time owned and controlled by Robert La Follette, Jr., the agreements amounted to "industrial treason".[7]

Intermittent antilabor drives also aroused liberal commentators, who savagely attacked business claims that war production would be increased if the forty-hour week were repealed, if strikes and the closed shop were outlawed. "The owning classes," said the *New Republic's* columnist, T.R.B.,* "agree with Hitler about the dynamic quality of the lie." The *Progressive* called the National Association of Manufacturers a "gang of industrial privateers, who see the war only as a bludgeon with which to smash labor." I. F. Stone summed up liberal feeling toward the antiunion campaign in one blunt sentence: "This is the fifth column." [8]

The later New Deal had rested increasingly upon hostility to big business, and it is not surprising that liberals, having re-

---

New Republic columnist "T.R.B." was Kenneth Crawford during the early years of the war. In 1943, Richard L. Strout took over the column and has written it ever since.

cently experienced Thurman Arnold's antitrust drive and the investigations of the Temporary National Economic Committee, felt a deep antagonism toward monopoly and oligopoly. Monopolistic capitalism, most believed, was a system resting on artificial scarcity, fixed prices, chronic unemployment (which provided a reservoir of cheap labor), and excessive corporate political influence—a system which contained all the elements leading to fascism.

Two important books of the early forties seemed to confirm the connection between corporate power and fascism. In *The Managerial Revolution,* James Burnham asserted that the en trepreneur was being displaced by a managerial and administrative elite which would control the future all over the world. Burnham's belief that the managerial revolution was most advanced in totalitarian countries, that it probably would do away with traditional concepts of freedom everywhere, could only increase the liberal fear of the American managerial class. The California economist Robert A. Brady approached the problem more directly in his book *Business as a System of Power.* The great business associations of the free liberal-capitalist nations, wrote Brady, had approximately the same values and objectives as those powerful business groups in the fascist states who had made "the critical decisions without which the final destruction of democracy could not have taken place." Liberals running the spectrum from the young New York Social Democrat Daniel Bell to the Texas progressive Maury Maverick warned that the war against fascism must also be a struggle against monopoly.[9]

Equally vital, especially in view of the fear of a postwar depression, was a greatly expanded social security system. American liberals drew great inspiration from the British Beveridge Plan, a comprehensive scheme of social insurance based on the idea of a decent "national minimum" of security and subsistence for each citizen. In 1943, Senators Robert F. Wagner and James E. Murray and Representative John Dingell sponsored legislation for an American equivalent—a nationalized United States Employment Service, a broad national system of unemployment insurance, national compulsory health insurance, new national systems of temporary and permanent disability benefits, expansion of the old-age and survivors' insurance system. The aim, as Wagner expressed it, was to bring generous social insurance coverage to "virtually the entire national family of working Americans." The Wagner-Murray-Dingell bill had no chance of passage, but its introduction symbolized the liberal determination to enlarge even one of the signal achievements of the New Deal.[10]

More than ever, racial discrimination drew liberal attention. The New Deal had given limited benefits and recognition to the American Negro, and liberals in the thirties had displayed more concern than those of previous generations with racial injustice. But in the thirties the major problems of American liberalism had been connected with the depression, and the cause of civil rights had occupied a low priority. The war did not wholly change the situation, but the booming economy at least removed the depression as an immediate issue. The fight against fascism, moreover, seemed a mockery so long as there was outright discrimination in the armed services and black soldiers were fair game for attacks by Southern whites.[11]

The plight of the Japanese-Americans also pricked the liberal conscience, but the situation of the Negro seemed most pressing. Racial injustice and segregation in the military was matched by an almost total exclusion of Negroes from many defense industries. In mid-1941 President Roosevelt established a Fair Employment Practices Committee but its effectiveness was limited. Racial tensions increased, resulting in a few full-scale riots and innumerable smaller outbreaks. The Negro seemed increasingly bitter and militant; a racial explosion appeared to be a distinct possibility. Most liberals, aside from a few prominent Southerners, worked for a strengthened and permanent FEPC along with an end to the poll tax and all the other devices by which Southern blacks had been disfranchised. Some wanted to go farther. Carey McWilliams expressed their hopes when he advocated a "fair racial practices act" which would end Jim Crow practices in all public places and do away with discriminatory housing.[12]

Underneath these problems and solutions lay one basic realization: all else would be meaningless—even the civil rights
objectives—if America could not provide jobs for its people.
An FEPC would be a joke in a depression economy, and a nation in economic crisis was far more likely to turn toward racial
hatred than to abolish the poll tax. As James Patton, the president of the National Farmers Union, put it, "nearly all our
problems start with the possibility of mass unemployment;
nearly all our solutions must start with full employment." [13]

II

There was general agreement that full employment must be
achieved within the framework of a "mixed economy," one in
which both government and private enterprise played significant roles. But within this loose consensus there were two distinct approaches. One was close to the system of ideas identified
with the First New Deal. Deriving much of its inspiration from
Veblen and the concept of an engineer-managed economy run
for production rather than profit, it envisioned a highly organized economy functioning to a large degree under government
direction. The other approach advanced a much smaller,
though highly significant, role for government—the manipulation of tax policy and the use of government spending to raise
purchasing power and supplement private investment until the
economy reached full employment. Its goal was a competitive
capitalism freed from both excessive government control and
the ravages of the business cycle; its ideas were essentially those
of Keynes and Brandeis. [14]

One of the most thoughtful and influential expositions of the
first approach was Lewis Corey's The Unfinished Task. Corey,
a founder of the American Communist Party who had traveled
the long road to pragmatic liberalism, agreed with James Burnham that a managerial revolution was under way, but he believed that it need not erase freedom: it could be a potent tool
for the preservation of democracy. Its tendencies toward totalitarianism could be aborted by political decentralization.

The basic problem was to prevent the rise of a total state

which could wield absolute authority over the political and economic activity of the individual. The solution was to socialize and place under managerial control only large industries, organizing them as semi-independent agencies divided along regional lines after the example of the Tennessee Valley Authority. Small business and agriculture would remain areas of private enterprise. Independent consumer and producer cooperatives would be encouraged. A strong, free labor movement would be a vital autonomous social force. The resulting diffusion of power would prevent the emergence of a leviathan state.[15]

It is obvious in retrospect that Corey had written an abstract, even utopian, work. Realization of his system was hardly probable in the increasingly conservative political climate of the early forties. Yet it was an understandable product of the apocalyptic atmosphere which the war generated; the outlines of the future seemed so vague that even proposals for utopian reorganization appeared within the realm of possibility. However, there was also the increasing liberal tendency to connect the concept of managerial control with fascism. "The technician likes gadgets that work, and he is not overly concerned with what they may do to the mind and spirit of men," wrote Richard Rovere. "The political ramifications are clear." [16]

Most liberals turned toward the second approach. It attracted many advocates, but the most important was a brilliant Harvard economist who was doing more than anyone else to make the essentials of Keynesian economics intelligible and plausible to noneconomists, Alvin H. Hansen. As a prolific writer and consultant to the Federal Reserve Board and the National Resources Planning Board, Hansen had a great impact upon the liberal mind. Government spending and tax policy were his key tools. It was necessary to topple the idol of the balanced budget; regardless of the deficits which might be necessary, the goal of public policy must be to maintain high consumption levels, to stimulate investment, especially in new and risky ventures, and to create jobs for everyone. In a depression-prone economy, these objectives could be achieved with low taxation and high government spending. Conversely, although it did not seem that this would be an immediate problem in the postwar world, an inflation-prone economy could be cooled off by high taxes, low government spending, and budget surpluses. In either case, government participation in the economy, as important as it might be, was a supplementary, compensatory participation, easier to manage and less of a threat to freedom than in the first approach. Hansen did not object to public regulation or to some public ownership, but his system was essentially an attempt to preserve private enterprise.[17]

Hansen's recommendations for government spending made him a liberal leader. Federal fiscal policy could rebuild America through urban redevelopment, rural rehabilitation, low-cost housing, express highways, transportation facilities, electrification, flood control, reforestation, public health programs, hospitals, adequate old-age benefits, higher educational standards, improved cultural and recreational facilities. The objective should be "an enrichment of the material and spiritual resources of our American way of life."

At the same time, Hansen stressed the dangers of overcentralized planning. "We do not want a totalitarian state," he wrote. "We want freedom of enterprise . . . freedom for collective bargaining . . . freedom for cooperative action . . . freedom of choice of occupation." He believed that his limited kind of planning could preserve these freedoms. But they would not survive without any planning; the result would be a new depression, "social disintegration, and, sooner or later, another international conflagration." [18]

Within the government, Hansen and the economic thought he represented were especially influential in the National Resources Planning Board, an agency established during the New Deal and along with the Office of Price Administration, one of the last refuges for liberal economists who wanted to stay within the government. The board's 1943 report, a landmark in wartime liberal thought, envisioned an expanding, democratic postwar economy freed from monopolistic restrictions. Keynesian and Brandeisian in its economic methods, sweepingly progressive in its social ideas, the document called for a "new Bill of Rights," not simply the traditional rights of civil liberty and legal equality but also the right to work, the right to adequate food, clothing, shelter, and medical care, the right to security against old age, sickness, and unemployment, the right to education, and "the right to live in a system of free enterprise, free from compulsory labor, irresponsible private power, arbitrary public authority, and unregulated monopolies." Urging a vigorous antitrust program, the report was unmistakably committed to free enterprise, especially to small business. The *New Republic* celebrated its issuance with a special supplement, and the *Antioch Review* commented that its ideas opened "a new frontier in which both initiative and adventure may be reinstalled to their high place in American life." Liberals everywhere praised the manifesto.[19]

A hostile Congress destroyed the Planning Board, but the report's influence lived on. It became the basis for an "Economic Bill of Rights" enunciated by President Roosevelt in early 1944, and, although FDR refused to commit himself to anything as specific as the Wagner-Murray-Dingell bill, liberals took heart as his rhetoric seemed increasingly closer to their hopes. In a stirring speech at Chicago near the climax of his fourth-term campaign, Roosevelt reaffirmed the Economic Bill of Rights, attacked corporate monopoly, promised opportunities to small business, and called for a permanent Fair Employment Practices Committee. He not only used the phrase "full employment," he set a goal: sixty million jobs.[20] With this goal, Roosevelt expressed a fundamental objective of American liberalism. The liberal vision, however, extended beyond the reconstruction of American life; its scope included the entire world.

III

During the 1930s, many liberals, even those who embraced the general idea of the Popular Front or who displayed pro-Russian sympathies, had refused to support the idea of collective

security or to advocate active American intervention in the
struggle against fascism. After the fall of the European continent to the Nazis in mid-1940, however, liberals increasingly
moved in the direction of interventionism. There were some
notable exceptions—many liberal churchmen, some confirmed
pacifists, thinkers such as Stuart Chase and Charles A. Beard
who believed that America could be militarily and economically self-sufficient, a few Midwestern politicians—but they
were quite obviously becoming isolated from the main current
of liberal thought. By mid-1941, two important liberal newspapers, the New York *Post* and *PM*, were calling for a declaration
of war; so was the *New Republic*. The *Nation*, which long had
advocated collective security, refrained from doing so only out
of a belief that American sentiment was not yet strongly
enough in favor of war. When the *New Republic* polled its
contributors in the fall of 1941, it found most in agreement
that war would be necessary sooner or later.[21]

Phrases such as "war to end war" and "make the world safe
for democracy" may have been conspicuously absent from liberal rhetoric. Yet in truth they would have described liberal
war aims fairly accurately. The liberals of this era may have
been, as some historians argue, tougher minded than their
counterparts of the age of Woodrow Wilson. At bottom, however, most were equally Idealist* in their approach to international relations. The purpose of American foreign policy, they
were convinced, must be realization of the quest for freedom,
justice, and human dignity. The war must do more than simply
restore some precarious balance of power or even place America in a position of world hegemony; it must create a new international order characterized by peace, cooperation, democracy,
prosperity, and stability. And just as the fear of American totalitarianism lay behind the liberals' hopes for the United States,
the specter of resurgent militarism and a third world war lay

---

*The term "Idealist" refers to a specific type of foreign policy thought built
around concepts of morality. Conversely, the word "Realist" indicates an approach to foreign policy mainly concerned with factors of national power and
self-interest.

behind their international program. "Only a New Deal for the world, more far-reaching and consistent than our own faltering New Deal, can prevent the coming of World War III," wrote Freda Kirchwey.[22]

As most progressives saw it, the major problem was the revitalization of democratic government, which had failed the common people in much of the world during the twenties and thirties and had thereby paved the way for fascism, the direct cause of the war. Recent history could be viewed as a great worldwide revolution in which the masses everywhere were rising in search of security and belief. If democracy could not give them these things, no matter what the outcome of the present military conflict, they would turn to fascism or something very much like it. Only a new democracy which could identify itself with the aspirations of the people and establish itself all over the globe would be able to prevent a resurgence of authoritarianism and perhaps the destruction of civilization itself. Fundamentally, the war was not a conflict between military forces; rather the struggle was between political systems and ideas. Democracy had to prove that it could provide jobs and stability for the peoples of America and Europe.

Democracy also had to demonstrate that it could end political and economic imperialism in Asia, Africa, and Latin America. The imperial nations had to free their subject populations, and the great international cartels, which had exploited peoples in underdeveloped areas and gouged consumers in the industrial nations, had to be broken up. Indeed, the economic imperialism of the cartels probably represented a greater threat to the world than the political imperialism of the Western European governments. The cartels were international monopolies, and, like all monopolies, they fixed prices, restricted production, created unemployment, and sowed the seeds of totalitarianism and war.

The worldwide success of democracy required a social and economic revolution in what a later generation would call the Third World. Using economic-technical assistance and the political leverage which accompanied it, America and a rebuilt

Europe had to promote industrial development, which alone could lay the basis for decent minimum standards of living, and encourage reforms to break the power of selfish, entrenched oligarchies. Some worldwide controls would be necessary—international currency stabilization, for example—and governments everywhere would assume increasingly important roles; but the liberal goal was an open international economy. Protectionism and economic nationalism had helped cause the war; an approximation of free trade and equal access to important raw materials might prevent another conflict.[23]

World reconstruction depended upon a peaceful atmosphere, and the liberals hoped for the establishment of some sort of world order which would replace the old anarchy of conflicting nationalisms and power politics. Wendell Willkie's vision of One World inspired them all. Some hoped for a full-blown world government and a substantial reduction of national sovereignty Most realized that such hopes were not feasible, but they supported the only slightly less utopian objective of a strong new international organization possessing its own police force and protecting the rights of small nations. Many liberals experienced some disappointment and disillusionment when after the Dumbarton Oaks conference in the fall of 1944 it became clear that the successor to the League of Nations would fall short of their dreams. By and large, however, they were prepared to extend their optimistic support to an imperfect beginning.[24]

Liberals committed to the unconditional establishment of freedom and democracy would have found it necessary, one might think, to face another major problem: Communism. There were two aspects to this problem, quite distinct and separate to some liberals but completely intertwined to others— Communism in America and American relations with the Soviet Union.

During the 1930s, probably most liberals in one way or another had accepted the general idea that the American Communist Party could function as a partner in a Popular Front against fascism. After the Nazi-Soviet pact of 1939, however, the prestige of both the Soviet Union and American Communism, which now worked to cripple defense production, reached a low ebb. Even after the German invasion of the Soviet Union changed the Party line, many liberals did little more than tolerate the Communists. Commenting on the idea of a United Front, the *New Republic* declared: "We hope the Communists will exercise a unilateral united front, by keeping their mouths shut." [25]

Yet if liberals had little respect for the Communists, they were willing to use them and work with them. The wartime alliance with Russia and the menace of fascism encouraged a resurgence of the Popular Front attitude—"a very serviceable coalition," commented the liberal attorney general of California, Robert Kenny. So long as the war continued, and so long as progressives and Communists seemed to be working for similar objectives, most liberals frowned on "Red-baiting." [26]

The Union for Democratic Action, the smallest and weakest of the liberal pressure groups by the end of the war, was the only progressive organization with strong bars against Communists and fellow travelers. But even the UDA refrained from criticizing the Communists during the war, and in the 1944 election it worked with the National Citizens Political Action Committee, which did have Communist members. Only in New York, where a group of anti-Communist liberals left the American Labor Party to form the Liberal Party, did the tension between Communists and liberals reach a breaking point. Significantly, however, the first Liberal Party platform contained no attack upon the Communists.[27]

Moreover, despite the disgust which most liberals had felt for the pact with Hitler, all favored aiding the Russians against the German invasion. And as the Soviet Union, fighting alone on the Continent, stubbornly resisted the German advance, liberals increasingly lapsed into a sentimentalism which refused to apply to the Soviet state the moral judgments implicit in an Idealist view of international relations. For most liberals, outraged by the inhumanity of fascism, the Soviet Union acquired a large measure of moral legitimacy simply by being a member of the antifascist coalition. Single-minded concentration on the utter destruction of fascism easily led one to the assumption that fascism was the only danger to peace and freedom in the world. The magnificent resistance to the Nazis seemed, in addition, to indicate that the Russian people supported the Soviet system. Russia was a totalitarian state, wrote Max Lerner, but all the same it had given the people "a sense of participation in a process of social and economic construction." Even Roger Baldwin, the national director of the American Civil Liberties Union, was able to discover "a form of industrial democracy" within the USSR. There were, it is true, some important dissenters, including the literary critic Granville Hicks and the great liberal philosopher John Dewey. "It is not only unnecessary but dangerous," Dewey commented, "to present the totalitarian despotism of Stalin in any but its true light." Baldwin and Lerner, however, almost certainly typified a majority of liberals.[28]

Much of this wishful thinking stemmed from some basic facts of power. "The war cannot be won unless America and Russia win it together," wrote Lerner in mid-1943. "The peace cannot be organized unless America and Russia organize it together." Liberal hopes for the postwar world hinged in large measure on some sort of understanding with the Soviet Union, and many liberals with their Idealist attitude toward foreign relations were intellectually unprepared to face the imperfections necessarily involved in agreements with an expansionist, totalitarian dictatorship. Few wished to admit that even flawed compromises might be impossible.

Some very plausible considerations seemed to lend support to the hopes for Soviet-American accord. Russia would probably need American aid to rebuild after the war. Stalin was reputed to be primarily a defender of Russian interests and an advocate of "socialism in one country," not an apostle of world revolution. The Soviet Union had a historic and ideological suspicion of the Western world, but most liberals hoped that the Russians could be won over by demonstrations of sincerity and by reasonable agreements which would protect Soviet interests without seriously compromising the ideals for which the war was being fought. America and Britain must miss no opportunity to demonstrate their friendliness; they must recognize Russia's historically justified claims to the Baltic states and eastern Poland; they must guarantee "peaceful, democratic governments" around the Soviet frontiers in Eastern Europe.[29]

Even as tough-minded a thinker as Reinhold Niebuhr was within the liberal consensus.* A preacher and theologian of rare spiritual and intellectual power, Niebuhr was becoming increasingly prominent as a progressive social thinker. His neo-orthodox philosophy was built around an understanding of the elements of tragedy in human history and the persistence of imperfection in human nature and institutions. More than most liberals, Niebuhr realized that nations were motivated in large measure by self-interest, and he never believed that the war would produce any sort of world government. Yet where the Soviet Union was concerned, he was in agreement with most liberals.

Niebuhr had no illusions about democracy in the Soviet Union. Nor did he feel that the USSR was likely to be the most cooperative of partners in the postwar world. Of the three great powers, he wrote in 1944, "Russia will have the greatest difficulty in establishing inner moral checks upon its will-to-power." He had nothing but contempt for the Communist parties of Europe and America and even expressed the hope that the Soviet Union could be persuaded to disband them. His name on the letterhead of an organization, William E. Leuchtenburg has observed, constituted a guarantee that the group was non-Communist.

*Niebuhr's philosophical differences with many liberal intellectuals and his tendency to express these differences in a polemical manner have obscured the fact that he rarely had real substantive differences with liberals who did not adhere to his theology. Arthur Schlesinger, Jr., has written of his political thought in the 1930s: "Reinhold Niebuhr, the most searching critic of the rationalism and utopianism of the official liberal tradition, had himself a political position indistinguishable from the utopians and the rationalists." Schlesinger, *Politics of Upheaval* (Boston, 1967), p. 157. See also Schlesinger's admiring interpretation in Charles Kegley and Robert Bretall, eds., *Reinhold Niebuhr: His Religious, Social, and Political Thought* (New York, 1961), pp. 126–50.

Nevertheless, during the war, Niebuhr essentially agreed with most liberals on the matters of Communism and Soviet-American relations. Perhaps he was more acutely aware that the American Communist Party was an instrument of Soviet foreign policy, but he was willing to work with Popular Front organizations, and, like many of his UDA associates, became affiliated with the National Citizens Political Action Committee in 1944. At the same time, he seems to have been somewhat hesitant about joining the New York Liberal Party. Like many liberal intellectuals, moreover, he preferred to discuss the more benign aspects of Communist theory and even indulged in some sentimentalism about Soviet life.

"Though communism uses dictatorship brutally, it does not exalt it as an end in itself," he wrote in early 1943. "Nor does it worship either race or war." Its ultimate moral goals were the same as those of the liberal-democratic states, even if the Communist belief that the Soviet dictatorship, along with the state, would wither away was "the most pathetic of utopian illusions." In fact, there were valuable elements in the Russian political experience. If Americans enjoyed more liberty, Russians had more equality. "Whether democracy should be defined primarily in terms of liberty or equality is a source of unending debate. But history proves fairly conclusively that if we subordinate one too much to the other, we shall end by losing them both." Perhaps collaboration would lead both nations toward a synthesis of the two extremes.

Niebuhr agreed also that the Soviet Union was not aggressive and even asserted that the USSR had been driven to the pact with Hitler in 1939 by the refusal of the Western democracies to accept the Russians as partners in a collective security system. As for the postwar era, "Russia's desire to rebuild its own land in peace and security will be the dominant motive of all its policies, and that task will absorb its resources for a long time to come." Difficulties in Soviet-American relations were likely to arise only if the American State Department attempted to install actively anti-Communist governments throughout Europe. This was a very real possibility, he feared, and one which would lead to inevitable Soviet efforts to dominate the Continent. By the spring of 1945, he was willing to accept the Russian push for dominance in Eastern Europe as a tolerable and legitimate, if imperfect, safeguard for Soviet security; underneath this acceptance was the assumption that Russian objectives went no further than security precautions: "Russia is not driven by the mania of world conquest, though it obviously has residual fears of the Western world."

Niebuhr was never as optimistic as most liberal thinkers. "We are living in a tragic age in which the available moral and political resources are not sufficient for the task in hand," he wrote during a period of pessimism at the beginning of 1945. "We can only hope for an approximation of the needed solution." Even so, he hoped for a semblance of world order and stability. In common with most liberals, moreover, he assumed that the USSR would behave in a rational manner and that its international objectives were strictly limited. It was natural to move from these propositions to the belief that the liberal task was to restrain those anti-Communist forces in the Western world whose policies might goad the Russians into aggression. Conversely, it seemed that the USSR would respond to demonstrations of friendship and good will. Niebuhr had devoted much of his career to an effort to awaken naïve liberals to the prevalence of evil and irrationality, but he had come close to accepting the optimism and rationalism he professed to abjure. Most liberals, caught up in the atmosphere of the war and the enthusiasm of their common cause with the Soviet Union, seem to have given little attention to his precautions and qualms even as they wholeheartedly agreed with the major thrust of his writing.[30]

The liberal foreign policy with its Idealism, its essential optimism, its near-utopian goals, its sentimentalism about the Soviet Union, may seem remarkably innocent. It had little room for factors of national self-interest, an insufficient appreciation of the importance of power in international relationships, little understanding of the fallibility and irrationality of human beings and their institutions, virtually no premonition that the defeat of fascism, instead of initiating an era in which the world would solve most of its problems, might create new dilemmas. Yet the liberal viewpoint had much to recommend it so long as the war continued. Defining the conflict as an apocalyptic struggle of good against evil, it helped to focus American efforts upon the defeat of the great immediate threat to the interests of the United States, the fascist powers. Its goals for the postwar world were, perhaps, utopian, but they revealed a remarkable comprehension of the revolutionary forces which the war had unleashed. And, of course, the progressives were hardly wrong in their insistence upon preservation of the wartime alliance; their intellectual weakness stemmed from the fact that so many of them had nothing to fall back upon if the attempt failed.

The formulation of an international plan was one thing; gaining its acceptance was quite another. The most critical area was the Asian theater, where only the people of the Philippines, who had a promise of postwar independence, seemed willing to fight the Japanese. America had to support the nationalistic revolution which was gathering force in Asia and guide it along democratic reformist lines. Failure to do so would spell an end to American influence in the Far East. The *New Republic* called for "a clean sweep of the forces in London that have so long and so stupidly clutched an outdated imperialism." Instead, there was Winston Churchill's frustrating declaration that he had not become the King's first minister in order to preside over the dissolution of the British Empire. Most liberals doubtless agreed with Milton Mayer's outburst that Churchill "has told . . . all of us, that he is fighting, and that we are fighting alongside him, for human slavery and not against it." [31]

Moreover, the American government coddled the fascist governments of Spain and Vichy France; it made agreements with Admiral Darlan in North Africa and Marshal Badoglio in Italy. Except for Sumner Welles, the State Department seemed old, tired, and reactionary. Even the Atlantic Charter and the Four Freedoms were too vague as statements of war objectives.

The charter itself was unacceptable to some, who felt that its emphasis was on restoration rather than revolution. President Roosevelt, observed the *Nation* in 1944, still appeared "singularly blind to the revolutionary forces that are determining the shape of the postwar world." [32]

Liberalism, however, still had spokesmen within the administration. Welles in the State Department and free-wheeling Milo Perkins in the Board of Economic Warfare were especially conspicuous among those who advocated new departures at home and abroad. And there was the most visible and courageous advocate of the liberal cause, the vice-president—Henry Wallace.

IV

Wallace was, as the liberal columnist and commentator Frank Kingdon observed, an uncommon man. "He is shy, ill at ease in public places, sloppy in his dress, tousled of hair, and completely incapable of small talk." He rarely drank, and did not smoke, "play cards, gamble, swear or tell off-color stories." As a political campaigner, he was tireless and effective; yet there was a mutual antipathy between him and professional politicians. "It's hard to be a politician and be honest with yourself," he said after he had left public life. Often called a dreamer, he had nevertheless served brilliantly in one of the most difficult Cabinet positions. His career—as a scientist who had done valuable work in plant genetics, as a successful businessman, as a leader in farm journalism, and as an able public administrator—seemed to be that of an eminently practical man. But Wallace's deepest yearnings took him beyond the world of practical affairs. He was a deeply religious man.[33]

Wallace's religion, combining the concrete ethical concerns of the social gospel with an ethereal mysticism, defied classification. His mysticism found orthodox expression in the ritual of High Episcopalianism and, during the 1930s, a less orthodox outlet in his relationship with a White Russian guru. The other side of his faith consisted of an intense belief in the dignity of the individual and a vision of human brotherhood and solidarity. The ultimate solution in a time of crisis, he seemed to believe, was a regeneration of human nature and a great co-operative effort.[34] Perhaps the bond which united these two elements was the inspiration which he derived from the Old Testament prophets.

Wallace admired and strove for the intense conviction of the prophets, whom he seemed to consider the social reformers of their era. His special model was Isaiah, who "knew something of the arts of the politician as well as having the vision of a statesman and the fervor of a prophet." In 1934 he wrote of the need for "a modern Isaiah" who "would go to the people of the different nations and call for a New Deal among nations." His attempts to commune with the Almighty and capture the prophetic commitment of an Isaiah may at times have led him to believe that he talked *for* God as well as *to* Him. Certainly it encouraged a self-righteousness, which in turn probably led to stubborness and inflexibility and which left him more vulnerable to criticism than the average politician if he did change his position on an issue. Yet in a time of deep world crisis and even deeper liberal hopes, Wallace's religious strivings may have strengthened his appeal, even among those whose outlook was normally secular. During the war years he appeared as a prophet at Armageddon.[35]

For all of Wallace's appeal and personal power, there was a dangerously weak side to his character. He was shy, introverted, almost incapable of close human relationships. Even his closest aides felt that they did not understand him, and many eventually were hurt by his apparent lack of gratitude for their service and loyalty. He championed the common man in the abstract; yet he seemed incapable of relating to individuals. "I like Henry," remarked his friend and biographer Russell Lord, "but he certainly makes it hard to do so." Wallace himself told a friend that when he met with small groups of people he felt as if a cold snake were curled up within him. One means of escape, which he employed often, was simply to doze off—even in the middle of an important conference. Such a man was not likely to have multiple lines of communication. Throughout his career, Wallace seems to have drawn on only a few advisers, who enveloped him, established a climate of opinion which influenced his thinking, and to a large extent made his decisions for him.

During the years he was vice-president, his relationship with the Senate was frigid and uneasy. "If he had given a little party now and then, and showed he was trying to get along, to be a good fellow, that would have been all they wanted," one of his former subordinates, Samuel Bledsoe, has commented. "But the people around him encouraged him. They said, 'These damned Southern reactionaries, sons-of-bitches,' and what not." Wallace himself came to feel that he had let Milo Perkins push him into his disastrous dispute with Jesse Jones in 1943. He was too much an introvert in an extroverted profession, too easily led; in the end, his keen intelligence and his ability to inspire others could not surmount these personality flaws.[36]

Wallace had begun his public career in the 1920s as a remarkably provincial farm editor whose concept of progressivism did not go beyond agriculture. During his years as a Cabinet officer, he did not always take the side of the liberals. In 1935 he "purged" several reform-minded intellectuals from the Department of Agriculture. There are indications that his attitude toward government spending was equivocal as late as 1938. He backed conservative Iowa Senator Guy Gillette for reelection even as Roosevelt was attempting to beat down the Democratic right wing. Yet he also worked closely with liberal-minded advisers such as Paul Appleby and Mordecai Ezekiel, became increasingly acquainted with Keynesian ideas, and moved toward the assumption that rural and urban poverty were indivisible. He developed an intense concern with foreign policy and by 1940 had become a militant antifascist convinced that war with Germany was inevitable. He had, in short, outgrown his earlier provincialism. Ranging beyond agricultural affairs, he was beginning to think of himself as a national political leader. In the late thirties, he permitted Appleby and a few others to promote him for the presidency or vice-presidency.

There are indications that he already saw himself as a man of destiny.[37]

Wallace did not really emerge as a liberal leader until May 1942, when he delivered a widely noted speech which he called "The Price of Free World Victory." Employing the rhetoric of evangelical religion, but calling for a secular millennium, he interpreted the war as a struggle to the death against demagogues, who, backed in the beginning by entrenched wealth, defying God and turning Satan loose upon earth, had cast spells over inexperienced masses and were trying to lead the world into slavery and darkness. The goal of the democratic nations must be the fulfillment of the "people's revolution," a movement based upon Christian ideals which had found expression in the revolutions of the American and Latin American colonies, of France in 1789, of Germany in 1848, and of Russia in 1917. A just and enduring peace, ending imperialism and exploitation, developing the old colonial areas, could complete the long march of the people toward liberty. The greatest challenge was securing freedom from want; a prime object of the war should be to give everyone in the world the privilege of drinking a quart of milk a day. "The century on which we are entering—the century which will come of this war—can be and must be the century of the common man," he declared. "The people's revolution is on the march, and the devil and all his angels can not prevail against it. They can not prevail, for on the side of the people is the Lord." [38]

The speech, with its sweepingly democratic statement of war aims, its commitment and resolve, its millennial sense, captured the liberal imagination. The vice-president, said the *New Republic,* had proven himself "a statesman capable of the grand conceptions for which the world has never had a greater need." His "lonely, eloquent words," wrote Marquis Childs, had expressed "the vague aspirations and desires that are in men's hearts everywhere." [39]

In subsequent speeches and writings Wallace showed that his "world-wide new democracy" mirrored the liberal program. Based on concepts of global full employment and decent minimum standards of living, it included the destruction of cartels, the removal of trade barriers, equal access to raw materials, a world investment fund, industrialization, and a vast system of public works, including transportation facilities and TVA-style reclamation and development projects. "A 'new order,' " he wrote, "is truly waiting to be created." [40]

Wallace's attitude toward Russia was equally representative of liberal views. He praised the Soviet Union for its "ethnic" and "educational" democracy, and for its extension of equal economic opportunity to women. He asserted that Marxism had "never preached international war as an instrument of national policy," and that the Russian actions of the 1930s had sprung from a fear of Germany. The Russian people were fundamentally religious, and the Soviet system was moving toward greater political democracy. But if the United States "double-crossed" Russia, lasting peace would be impossible.[41]

Wallace also attacked "American fascism," which he seemed to identify largely with corporate power and those, he once said, "who believe that Wall Street comes first and the country second." Many monopolists were willing to sacrifice democracy, just as they had in Germany, he warned, in order to stamp out economic opportunity and preserve their power and privilege.[42]

In the 1920s Wallace had been deeply influenced by the writings of Thorstein Veblen, and in the 1930s he had talked vaguely at times of the need for some sort of a "central clearing-house" which would maintain high production during depressions. But the economic theory which emerged from his wartime writings was Keynesian* and Brandeisian. Not only

*Wallace was perhaps prepared for Keynesian theory when in the 1920s he enthusiastically read *The Road to Plenty* by William T. Foster and Wadill Catchings, the controversial economists who anticipated many of Keynes's basic ideas. Arthur M. Schlesinger, Jr., *The Crisis of the Old Order* (Boston, 1956), p. 136. Wallace did not recall Hansen as a major source of his economic ideas, but it may be noteworthy that even before the United States entered the war Hansen wrote to Wallace, outlining a liberal postwar program and urging the administration to adopt and advocate it. Wallace interview; Hansen to Wallace, May 6, 1941, Wallace MSS, FDRL.

did he accept the framework of competitive capitalism, he seemed more than most liberals to draw upon the past for inspiration. He hoped, for example, that rural redevelopment, inexpensive automobiles, and adequate roads and highways would "hasten the march of the common man back to the country and nature" and thereby "restore to the family much of the significance which it had a hundred years ago." Even closer to the ruggedest American traditions was a talk entitled "Horatio Alger Is Not Dead" which praised "the driving force of self-interest" and the virtues of hard work and initiative, warning that social insurance must only supplement, not replace, these qualities. An advocate of private enterprise and economic opportunity, tempered always with a sense of Christian responsibility, he spoke for a humanitarian capitalist democracy rather than a proletarian social order.[43]

V

It would be easy—and probably accurate—to criticize the dominant liberalism of the war years as too optimistic and rationalistic. Not comprehending the difficulties of a relationship with Russia, it failed to grasp the depth of Communist hostility toward the capitalist powers and the paranoia of Stalin. The Keynesian economics which Hansen and others popularized would be usable only if the expected postwar depression materialized; instead, it was to become apparent that Keynesian principles were much more difficult to apply in an inflationary situation. The link-up of big business and fascism was at best a half-truth, and progressives who talked of promoting small business were naïvely glorifying one of the most illiberal elements in American life. The economic conditions which would follow the war would demonstrate that corporate power, if always in need of restraint, was not quite the fundamental problem which many liberals had expected it to be.

Yet many of the liberal hopes and visions demonstrated an essential grasp of the demands of the present and the requirements of the future. A liberal movement which in the previous decade had restricted itself simply to deploring fascism and to providing only moral support to antifascists was now dedicated to active participation in the urgent task of destroying it. Keynesian economics, whatever its weaknesses, constituted the best method yet devised for bringing the business cycle under control. The steadily increasing liberal commitment to the cause of civil rights demonstrated an awakening to a fundamental injustice which past reformers had too long ignored. Assistance to the underdeloped areas of the world would indeed be a postwar imperative. As the New Deal, and especially the ideas connected with its later phase, reached an intellectual zenith, however, liberals found themselves increasingly at bay in the most hostile political climate since the 1920s.

Chapter 2

Wallace, Truman, the Liberals, and the Politics of World War II

Even as the liberals formulated visionary war objectives, they fought a defensive political battle. With Congress more hostile than ever and President Roosevelt preocupied with the war effort, progressives had to struggle to maintain their position within the Democratic Party, the very basis of their national political strength. Henry Wallace, courting political martyrdom, provided the leadership they needed.

As the war neared an end, the liberals, despite some setbacks, could look to the future with a degree of hope. Independent liberalism had established a vigorous and promising organizational base. Wallace, although unable to retain the vice-presidency, remained in the administration as secretary of commerce. The Yalta Conference, a dramatic demonstration of antifascist unity, gave encouragement to the liberal dream of international cooperation in the postwar world. Roosevelt seemed to have resumed the fight for progressive objectives.

FDR's death aborted the hopeful mood. The liberals knew only that his successor was a different and less exciting personality with an ambiguous political record. The accession of Harry S. Truman to the presidency was not in itself cause for despair, but it was no longer certain that the progressive movement could seek aid and comfort from the White House.

I

After a stunning victory in the 1942 elections, Congressional conservatives had undertaken an offensive against the remnants of the New Deal. The National Resources Planning Board and the National Youth Administration were abolished; the Farm Security Administration survived only by sacrificing its director.[1] The future of American liberalism seemed gravely uncertain, not simply or even primarily because of the dominance of reaction within the Republican Party, but more because of the growing power of conservative forces within the Democratic Party. If these forces were triumphant, the liberal movement would be left without an effective political vehicle and would have to face the dreary choice of turning to a third party or beginning anew the struggle to gain ascendancy among the Democrats.

The battle for control of the party came to be symbolized in the personal struggle between Henry Wallace and Jesse Jones. Jones, a Texas banker whom Herbert Hoover had called to Washington to serve on the Reconstruction Finance Corporation, had become head of the RFC under Roosevelt, and had succeeded Harry Hopkins as secretary of commerce. His influence with the Senate was as great as Wallace's was small, and when he entered the Cabinet he had been allowed to retain control over the important federal lending agencies. A millionaire Southern conservative, he was the antithesis of Wallace and all that Wallace represented.[2]

With Jones at their head, the Department of Commerce and the Federal Loan Administration were rallying points for conservatives within the Roosevelt administration. Conversely, the Board of Economic Warfare, under Wallace, was a leading center of New Deal liberalism. The administrative structure of wartime Washington almost guaranteed a conflict, for in order to fulfill its mission of acquiring vital war materials, the BEW had to rely upon Jones and the lending agencies for financing. For months, Wallace and BEW staffers seethed quietly over Jones's insistence upon cautious, "businesslike" procedures and his apparent reluctance to fund BEW projects. By mid-1943, Wallace had reached the limits of his patience; defying a presidential order against public squabbling, he issued a public statement which charged that Jones was hampering the economic defense program. The Texan, in turn, scathingly denounced Wallace. The angry charges and countercharges which followed laid bare the emotional tensions between the conservatives and the New Deal Democrats.[3]

The incident weakened Wallace politically but strengthened him as a liberal leader. Roosevelt apparently had already been disillusioned by his vice-president's inability to penetrate the Senate power structure, and, furious at a display of public disunity, he impartially rebuked both men and relieved them of their economic warfare responsibilities. The episode may have dealt a fatal blow to FDR's confidence in Wallace, but it increased the vice-president's stature among progressives. Enveloped by an aura of martyrdom for the sake of principle, his hold on the liberal imagination was greater than ever. "Almost alone," wrote J. Donald Kingsley in the *Antioch Review,* "he has kept faith with the common man and the future; and the tattered mantle of the New Deal is now wrapped securely about his shoulders." [4]

In the months which followed, Wallace consolidated his strength among the liberals and seized every opportunity to display his loyalty to the president. "The New Deal is Roosevelt," he told a Jackson Day dinner. "Roosevelt has never denied the principles of the New Deal and he never will. They are a part of his very being." As the 1944 Democratic convention assembled, Wallace enjoyed nearly solid liberal-labor support and still could reasonably nourish the hope that the president would compel his retention upon the ticket.[5]

Roosevelt remained silent, but Wallace nevertheless displayed remarkable personal strength. Appearing before the convention to deliver one of the seconding speeches for FDR, he nearly stampeded the delegates with a fervent call for racial reforms and economic democracy. He led the first ballot for the vice-presidential nomination and might have won it all had not

the convention managers frantically secured an adjournment of
the proceedings. With Roosevelt's secret connivance, the party
leaders were able to put over the nomination of a candidate acceptable to the Southerners, the city bosses, and the labor
unions—Harry S. Truman of Missouri.[6]

Few liberals could find anything especially wrong with the
victor, but the defeat of their leading spokesman within the administration seemed nonetheless a major triumph for reaction.
"The Chicago convention almost broke my heart," wrote Jo
Davidson, the renowned sculptor and liberal leader. "I was terribly distressed about Chicago, and felt that we had come to a
very bad time," Charles Bolte, the leading organizer of the new
American Veterans Committee, told Wallace. "I only hope that
you will stay active in public life somehow. You speak the
hopes of too many people to be retired." To the liberals, Wallace's stature was greater than ever. "Next only to the President, you are the strongest man in the Democratic party," Harold Ickes told him. He was, said the *New Republic,* "the first
Democrat of prominence to stand entirely on his own feet as a
leader of progressive liberalism within the party." Once again
he was a martyr to liberal principles.[7]

Wallace was surprised and hurt by the action of the convention, but at the end of August Roosevelt called him to the
White House and offered him a place in the Cabinet after the
election. He came to believe that FDR had been duped, and he
stumped the country tirelessly, telling liberal groups that the
Democratic Party was the only possible vehicle for American
progressives, that the first goal of the liberal movement must be
a Democratic victory in November, that the second must be the
triumph of liberalism within the party.[8]

Wallace accurately expressed the liberal mood. Thomas E.
Dewey and the Republicans presented no alternatives; to most
liberals, the GOP campaign with its attacks on the CIO and Sidney Hillman, antisemitic attacks some believed, seemed permeated with reaction. And, despite some criticism of Roosevelt,
the majority of liberals probably retained an almost transcen-

dent faith in him. He was still the outstanding symbol of
domestic reform, a great war leader, and a world statesman who
could deal with Stalin and Churchill. Admitting that FDR had
not carried the cause of reform as far as it would have wished,
the *New Republic* commented that he nevertheless "came
closer to it than any other President in our history"; despite his
foreign policy mistakes, moreover, he was "a great symbol of
democracy, the first figure of hope to enslaved peoples throughout the world." As the campaign progressed, liberals took
heart; Roosevelt's pronouncements, especially the "sixty million jobs" speech, seemed to justify their faith, their belief that
at heart he was with them.[9]

II

There were many groups in 1944 who were interested in one
reform cause or another—world government, civil liberties, racial justice—but the liberal movement found its direction and
definition mainly in five organizations, two of them aligned
with specific economic interest groups, three of them drawing
their membership mainly from those portions of society which
can be designated only as "middle-class" and "professional" or
"intellectual." The differences between them did not seem
great in that wartime year. They all shared the general liberal
consensus on domestic policy and international relations, and
they all strove for the immediate objective of all liberals—the
reelection of Roosevelt. It was only natural, therefore, that
there should be talk of establishing a consolidated liberal front
which could carry on the struggle for progressive policies when
the magic appeal of FDR was gone from American politics.

The oldest of these organizations was the National Farmers
Union. Drawing its membership mainly from the mountain
and plains states, the NFU saw itself as a representative of the
small farmer and drew upon a neopopulist ideology which celebrated the virtues of agrarian life and the fundamental social
importance of the small landholder. Its dynamic young presi-

dent, James G. Patton, warned that the demise of the family farm could lead only to the establishment of a "rural fascism" which would inevitably spread to the rest of the nation.

The NFU was the most militant supporter of the Farm Security Administration and its efforts in behalf of the little farmer, but the organization also possessed an intense concern with city politics and economics. For all its rural fundamentalism, the NFU had adopted the assumption that rural prosperity and the survival of the small farmer were dependent upon a healthy urban economy. Patton worked closely with liberal and labor groups, striving for the establishment of a reform coalition built around a union of the producing classes—a farm-labor party. By 1944, the NFU was playing a leading role in the development of full employment legislation for the urban workers, who presumably would pass along the benefits of their prosperity to the farmers through increased consumption.[10]

Under the leadership of Sidney Hillman, the CIO Political Action Committee was establishing itself as the most powerful election-day vehicle of American progressivism. Founded in 1943 as a response to the antiunion Smith-Connally Act, it effectively mobilized the most important segment of the New Deal coalition, the labor vote in the urban centers. Working with nonlabor groups, supporting a broad range of reforms, the PAC could serve as the major vote-getting machine of the liberal movement, but as a labor organization it could not provide a home for middle-class liberals.[11]

Closely affiliated with the PAC and receiving financial support from it was the National Citizens Political Action Committee. Established to bring nonlabor reformers into the CIO effort, the NCPAC gained a broad and impressive membership —NFU president Patton; leaders in the fight for racial integration, such as Clark Foreman, Mary McLeod Bethune, and Channing Tobias; a few liberal businessmen, among them James H. McGill and Morris Rosenthal; important journalists, including Freda Kirchwey, Bruce Bliven, and Max Lerner; politicians such as California Attorney General Robert Kenny and

former Minnesota Governor Elmer Benson; notable independent progressives, including Barley C. Crum of California
and Frank Kingdon of New York. Originally devised as a temporary committee to promote a fourth term for FDR, the
NCPAC was organized after the election on a permanent
basis.[12]

The driving force behind the NCPAC was its executive
vice-chairman, Calvin B. "Beanie" Baldwin, who had become
an increasingly important figure in the Department of Agriculture during the New Deal. Appointed head of the Farm Security Administration in 1940, Baldwin had become the target of
increasingly bitter attacks by Congressional conservatives. In
1943 he had been forced out of office, given the assignment of
planning the economic rehabilitation of Italy, and sent into a
humiliating eclipse when opponents in the State Department
undermined his authority. Offered a position with the
NCPAC, he left the government a bitter man, bent on destroying the conservatives who had driven him from public service.
Originally sponsored for his new job by the pro-Communists
Lee Pressman and John Abt, Baldwin worked closely with
them, becoming, Gardner Jackson believed, "a mere echo of
Lee." Baldwin's personal bitterness, his association with pro-
Communists, and perhaps the leftist leanings of his wife all left
him and his organization vulnerable to Red influence.[13]

The most spectacular group working for Roosevelt was the
Independent Voters Committee of the Arts and Sciences, reor-
ganized after the election as the Independent Citizens Committee of the Arts, Sciences, and Professions. Its national chairman was the esteemed sculptor Jo Davidson; its national
director, Hannah Dorner, a New York theatrical agent. An organization of scientists, writers, artists, and show-business people, the ICCASP could draw on enormous talent and had great
fund-raising potential. It was the most heavily Communist-infiltrated liberal group; much of its membership was politically
naïve, and its leadership showed no concern about the Stalin-
ists and their fellow travelers. "We ask no one what their polit-

ical affiliations are," declared Davidson. "We know no more who are communists than who are Republicans and Democrats." [14]

The Union for Democratic Action was the weakest and the smallest of the liberal organizations. Founded in 1941 to work for a strong antifascist foreign policy, it had spent the years after Pearl Harbor as a participant in the struggle for liberal war goals. It differed from the other liberal groups mainly in its exclusion of Communists; tolerating the concept of the Popular Front during the war, it nevertheless balanced its antifascism with an anti-Communist, or at least non-Communist, stance. Eleanor Roosevelt gave the group the prestige of her name, and Bruce Bliven, the editor of the *New Republic,* occasionally provided its leaders with a journalistic outlet. But the UDA's two most important and active leaders were James Loeb, Jr., and Reinhold Niebuhr, former right-wing Socialist Party members who had broken with the party over the issue of resistance to fascism. Loeb, the UDA's executive secretary, was a former teacher of Romance languages who had been drawn into politics through the Spanish Civil War. Tolerant and humane, he won the respect and affection of his coworkers, one of whom has described him as a "Lincolnian personality." A skillful administrator and a tireless worker, he was dedicated to the cause of liberal unity. Niebuhr served as chairman and gave the UDA and its successor, the Americans for Democratic Action, a kind of spiritual leadership which drew its power more from personal example than from theology. His emphasis on the sinfulness of man and the imperfection of human institutions influenced Loeb and several young progressives, but it was too conservative for most liberals. The UDA's rejection of Communist utopianism may have been in line with Niebuhr's philosophy, but the UDA was not a mirror of his thought.

The UDA had made an important contribution to American politics with its *New Republic* voting charts, the first liberal effort to assess the record of every member of Congress on a broad range of issues. But despite this innovation, and despite the talent of its leadership, the organization was barely a going concern. It had only a few active chapters and a relatively small membership (it claimed 5,000 in 1944) composed mostly of "middle-class intellectuals." It had reeled from one financial crisis to another, unable at one point to pay its first Washington director, Tom Amlie. Partly because of its policy of excluding Communist members, but mostly because of the strength and dynamism of the NCPAC and ICCASP, the UDA was becoming increasingly isolated and unimportant.[15]

In early 1943, before the passage of the Smith-Connally Act, Loeb and the UDA had attempted to establish what Niebuhr described as "a general alliance to support the New Deal." The proposed new organization, a federation of the UDA, the NFU, and various labor organizations, was to be led by George W. Norris. The project collapsed when CIO President Philip Murray decided against it, citing the AFL's refusal to cooperate. The passage of the Smith-Connally Act changed Murray's mind about political action, but the CIO's decision to establish its own middle-class affiliate suggests that Murray never wished to become involved with the UDA. His reasons are not clear, but they probably stemmed from the UDA position on Communism, which, muffled as it was during the war, still must have been unacceptable to Lee Pressman and the sizable Popular Front faction within the CIO.

The rise of the PAC, the NCPAC, and the ICCASP added strength and vigor to the liberal movement, but it also led to a lack of unity and a diffusion of effort. Since these groups, along with the UDA and the NFU, seemed in general to be pursuing common objectives, many liberals hoped they could unite to establish a well-organized progressive force with a solid popular and financial base. Loeb continued his own efforts. He joined the NCPAC but thought of it as only a temporary campaign committee, considering it too close to labor to attract middle-class liberals. He also had unspoken doubts about Communist influence within it. Arguing for a new liberal organization, probably to be built around the UDA, he gained the backing of the *New Republic,* which advocated a "National Progressive Federation." Freda Kirchwey, while less specific, urged the establishment of "a popular front in America—a solid union of progressive forces," which might be headed by Henry Wallace. Loeb won over some influential members of the NCPAC, including Gifford Pinchot, Jim Patton, Railway union leader A. F. Whitney, and, Loeb thought, Philip Murray himself. The NCPAC National Board, however, refused to dissolve the organization and never invited Loeb to another meeting. The lines which would divide postwar liberalism were already beginning to form.[16]

In February 1945, Loeb and Jim Patton discussed the problem of liberal solidarity in a long article published as a supplement to the *New Republic*. The liberal coalition which had triumphed during the 1930s, they warned, possessed no coherence other than that given it by the appeal of Roosevelt, who would surely retire at the end of his fourth term. Repeating the call for a National Progressive Federation, they warned that unless a strong liberal movement with a political base independent of FDR's charisma were built, American liberalism in the post-Roosevelt era would disintegrate and lapse into futility.[17] There was, of course, a fatal flaw in their plans—the assumption that there was time to carry them out, that FDR would remain as a unifying symbol until 1948.

III

Roosevelt's fourth term started well for liberals. By March Wallace was back in the president's official circle, and the chances for continued Big Three unity seemed better than ever. There were some defeats, but progressives could look to the future with hope.

The first triumph was the surprising ouster of Jesse Jones from the Cabinet on Inauguration Day, 1945, and the appointment of Wallace as secretary of commerce, the post Wallace had chosen in response to the president's preelection offer. Once again Wallace became the central figure of American liberal politics as Southern Democrats and Republicans joined in a determined effort to block his nomination. Jones himself appeared before the Senate Commerce Committee, engaging in friendly repartee with the Southern senators and delivering a broadside attack against Wallace.

Then Wallace came before the committee, called for an investigation of the RFC, and unfolded a broad domestic reform program. Using Roosevelt's Economic Bill of Rights as a point of departure, he advocated a Keynesian economic policy to maintain full employment, use of the lending agencies to give strong support to small business, governmental maintenance of wage stability, an eventual guaranteed annual wage, federal aid to education, continued agricultural price supports, stronger federal crop insurance, a tough antitrust effort, a large-scale housing program, and compulsory federal health insurance. He spent five hours on the stand, debating with his conservative questioners and defending his business experience.[18]

At the end of January, the UDA and the *New Republic* sponsored a testimonial dinner for Wallace. Almost every important liberal leader either spoke or sent words of praise. Discussing his fight for confirmation, Wallace spoke of the struggle as part of the larger battle for full postwar employment and prosperity. It was also, he asserted, another episode in the continuing struggle for control of the Democratic Party, and, warning against "the futility of a third party," he called on liberals to continue this fight at all costs. Predicting that the existing liberal groups would join in a federation some time in the future, he urged them to begin preparations for the 1946 campaign, which he believed would determine the fate of the Roosevelt reform proposals and the future of postwar America. "We must organize and keep organized, ready for action every month of every year. The 'Economic Bill of Rights' must be made to live. Those who fight this issue must be defeated in 1946."

The UDA–*New Republic* gathering symbolized the depth and solidity of Wallace's progressive support. Prominent liberals from around the country lobbied for his confirmation or otherwise registered their support. "I am doing all that I can," wrote the young mayor of Louisville, Wilson Wyatt. "I am gratified by your superb performance," Paul R. Porter told Wallace. "Your appointment to become Secretary of Commerce was one of the most encouraging moves in many months," declared Chester Bowles. "I want you to know once more how great a privilege it was for the Union for Democratic Action to have been connected with the dinner," James Loeb assured the former vice-president, "and also, how privileged I felt personally, in being able to work with you." New York Liberal Party leader Dean Alfange urged Wallace to assume the leadership of a national third party movement.

The effort to bring Wallace into the Cabinet continued all through February. On March 1, he won Senate confirmation, but only after the vital federal lending agencies had been separated from the Commerce Department. To the extent that this outcome was a defeat for liberalism, Wallace was again something of a martyr, for once more he had been the central protagonist in a struggle for liberal principles. But all in all, the result was a qualified victory. The man whose name had become almost synonymous with the New Deal had come back from defeat to occupy a post in the Cabinet.[19]

Meanwhile, liberal hopes had received another boost with the news of the Yalta Conference. Yalta seemed to be a dramatic demonstration of Big Three unity and good will, characterized by concession and compromise on both sides. Especially notable were the decisions relating to Eastern Europe. The Polish problem apparently was on its way to an equitable solution with the designation of the Curzon line as the new Polish-Russian boundary and the agreement to establish a coalition government which would include representatives of all factions. The Declaration on Liberated Europe seemed to commit the Big Three to work in concert for the establishment of antifascist democracies. The call for a conference to establish a new international organization appeared to indicate that the Big Three would continue to cooperate after the defeat of fascism and gave hope to those who believed that the world was at the dawn of a new era. The statesmen in the Crimea apparently

had given life to the principles of the Atlantic Charter. The
conference, the *New Republic* believed, meant that there
would be no division of Europe into spheres of influence, no
return to power politics, and no more wars. It was too early to
say for certain, but Yalta might well have been "a turning
point in world history." There was a good chance, commented
the St. Louis *Post-Dispatch*, "that this time the world will not
miss its opportunity to create peace and security for future
generations." [20]

The achievements of Yalta, together with the nomination of
Wallace, provided further proof to most liberals that their faith
in Roosevelt had been well placed. Whatever FDR's compromises, asserted I. F. Stone, "Mr. Roosevelt's course clearly remains charted toward the two major objectives of an enduring
peace abroad and full employment at home. This is what we
voted for." [21] Most liberals realized that the road ahead was not
easy either at home or abroad, but they could look to the future with renewed optimism. Then on April 12, 1945, came
the stunning news of Roosevelt's death and the accession of a
new and largely unknown figure to the presidency. The future
of American liberalism was enveloped in a fog of uncertainty.

IV

Harry S. Truman's past provided no sure indications of the
directions he would take. He was, above all, a professional politician, for whom party regularity was a way of life; his associations and friendships extended to all factions of the Democratic
Party. His earlier career had given him the outlook of a small
businessman, a viewpoint which was increasingly less congenial
to reform. Yet he also had grown to political maturity in the
progressive Democracy of Bryan and Wilson and had absorbed
the protest spirit of Midwestern progressivism. His subsequent
association with the Pendergast machine, black mark though it
was to liberal intellectuals, had brought him into contact with
city minority groups and urban politics, giving him a breadth
of view and necessitating a tolerance which most politicians

with a rural entrepreneurial background never achieved, and placing him squarely in a situation which was creating new definitions of liberalism.[22]

"I was a New Dealer from the start," Truman has written in his *Memoirs*. "In fact, I had been a New Dealer back in Jackson County." Perhaps so. Certainly, in his years on the Jackson County Court he must have been one of the most effective local administrators in the United States. The admirable road system for which he was largely responsible, the honesty and efficiency which he brought to the county government gave him a national reputation in his field. He became interested in metropolitan planning, organizing the Regional Plan Association of Greater Kansas City, subsequently presiding over a state agency, the Missouri Planning Association. In 1930 he became a director of the National Conference of City Planning and a member of the American Civic Association. Local civic reformers admired and supported him even as they vainly fought to destroy the Pendergast organization.

Yet it is doubtful that Truman was really a New Dealer in any meaningful sense. He was, no doubt, a "progressive" county judge, but his progressivism does not appear to have gone beyond honesty, efficiency, interest in road building, and a general belief in coordinated urban growth. He, like many Democratic politicians of the 1920s (including Franklin D. Roosevelt), seemed to accept the conventional wisdom of the Republican New Era. Certainly, he won no reputation as an advanced social reformer, although his position brought him into close contact with urban problems of all kinds. Two years after the beginning of the Great Depression, when Truman made an unsuccessful effort to secure the Democratic nomination for governor of Missouri, his supporters still depicted him as a "clean, conscientious businessman who would render unto the people a real business administration." [23]

Once the New Deal got under way, however, Truman was one of its vocal supporters. As Federal Re-Employment Director for Missouri, he coordinated the early New Deal relief programs within the state and established good working relation-

ships with Harry Hopkins and Frances Perkins. As a candidate
for the Senate in 1934, he, like many Democrats around the
country, depicted himself as a New Deal liberal and his opponents as conservatives unwilling and unable to meet the economic crisis. Most progressives, however, were aware only of
his affiliation with the Kansas City machine, which many believed had secured Truman's nomination in the primary by
dishonest means. The *Nation* pictured the new senator as a
puppet of Tom Pendergast, an obscure little man who had
gone to the Boss to ask for the county collectorship and had received the Senate seat as a consolation prize.[24]

As a senator, Truman gave faithful support to New Deal
measures, even the most controversial ones. He burned thirty
thousand letters and telegrams which urged him to oppose the
Wheeler-Rayburn Holding Company Act. "I was personally
opposed to the monopolistic practices which were squeezing
the consumer to death," he recalled years later. "I knew that
the 'wrecking crew' of Wall Street was at work behind the
scenes." New Dealers who had discounted the Missouri senator
in advance began to change their thoughts about him. Truman
also went down the line for the Court-packing plan, at first
using Roosevelt's argument that the heavy work load and the
age of the justices made a larger Supreme Court necessary, but
later more frankly asserting that the scheme was "the easiest
and simplest so far proposed to meet a situation where the
court had assumed legislative powers which in no sense it constitutionally possesses." [25]

Truman's basic agreement with the antimonopoly, Brandeisian tone of the later New Deal became apparent when he directed an investigation of railroad financing in the late 1930s.
Despite frantic appeals from his home state, he subjected the
Missouri Pacific Railroad to a devastating scrutiny and won the
admiration of the liberal committee counsel Max Lowenthal.
Through Lowenthal, Truman met Justice Brandeis and became a regular visitor to the Justice's Sunday afternoon open-
houses. "The old man would back me into a corner," Truman
has recalled, "and pay no attention to anybody else while he

talked transportation to me." [26] These discussions confirmed a bias which Truman already had. His first major Senate speech, expressing his anger at the financial manipulations which he had uncovered during the railroad investigation, revealed the type of liberalism for which he stood:

No one ever considered Carnegie libraries steeped in the blood of the Homestead steel workers, but they are. We do not remember that the Rockefeller Foundation is founded on the dead miners of the Colorado Fuel & Iron Co. and a dozen other similar performances. We worship mammon; and until we go back to ancient fundamentals and return to the Giver of the Tables of the Law and His teachings, these conditions are going to remain with us.

It is a pity that Wall Street, with its ability to control all the wealth of the nation and to hire the best law brains in the country, has not produced some financial statesmen, some men who could see the dangers of bigness and of the concentration of the control of wealth. . . . they are still employing the best law brains to serve greed and selfish interest. People can stand only so much, and one of these days there will be a settlement. . . .

I believe the country would be better off if we did not have 60 percent of the assets of all the insurance companies concentrated in four companies. I believe that a thousand insurance companies, with $4,000,000 each in assets, would be just a thousand times better for the country than the Metropolitan Life, with $4,000,000,000 in assets. . . . I also say that a thousand county-seat towns of 7,000 people each are a thousand times more important to this Republic than one city of 7,000,000 people. Our unemployment and our unrest are the result of the concentration of population in industrial centers, mass production, and a lot of other so-called modern movements.[27]

The speech, probably as revealing of Truman's deepest feelings as any public utterance he ever made, epitomized the Midwestern populist-progressive tradition. Its mild Christian fundamentalism and its surprising antiurbanism were products of a bygone age. But the great corporate interests were as much the enemies of FDR as of Bryan or Wilson, and Truman's militance matched the spirit of the later New Deal.

Truman was, however, hardly a liberal crusader. Most of his

best friends were the moderates and conservatives of the Senate "Establishment"—J. Hamilton Lewis, Carl Hayden, Tom Connally, John Nance Garner. Among the progressives, his closest friend was the anti-Roosevelt maverick, Burton K. Wheeler, who by the end of the thirties was rapidly losing his reputation for liberalism. On the other hand, Truman had been hurt by the attitude of more distinguished and genuine progressives such as George Norris and Bronson Cutting, who he felt "looked upon me as a sort of hick politician who did not know what he was supposed to do." His own relationship with Roosevelt was cool, and he seems to have grown increasingly angry at the way the administration took his vote for granted. His general conduct during his first term won him little liberal attention. He accepted the Establishment rule that a junior senator should keep quiet and prove himself by hard committee work; his major interest, transportation policy, involved some of the less spectacular issues of the 1930s. Despite his liberal voting record, moreover, he supported Pat Harrison of Mississippi for Senate majority leader and voted for James F. Byrnes's resolution condemning sit-down strikes. By 1940, he was even declaring his opposition to a third term for Roosevelt.

Worst of all, so far as most liberals were concerned, was Truman's vehement opposition in 1938 to the reappointment of anti-Pendergast U.S. District Attorney Maurice Milligan. He did not attempt to invoke Senatorial courtesy against Milligan, but he did deliver a blistering attack upon him. Since this was only his second speech from the floor of the Senate, it established more firmly than ever his image as the tool of the Kansas City machine.[28]

When Truman ran for renomination in 1940 the administration and liberals in general displayed either hostility or indifference and tended to favor anti-Pendergast Governor Lloyd Stark, who had become increasingly friendly with Roosevelt. Harold Ickes probably was typical. He refused to give Truman any help and wrote in his diary, "I favor Governor Stark, although Truman has made a good New Deal Senator."[29]

Yet Truman's campaign was notable for the backing he received from labor and Negroes. Especially crucial were the help of the Railway Brotherhoods, whose interests he had always backed, and the aid of A. F. Whitney, the most liberal of the railway union leaders. Despite Truman's vote on the sit-downs, few senators had compiled stronger pro-labor records.[30]

Truman also worked hard for the black vote, and the opening speech of his campaign, delivered at Sedalia, Missouri, contained a strong statement on racial issues:

In all matters of progress and welfare, of economic opportunity and equal rights before law, Negroes deserve every aid and protection.

I believe in the brotherhood of man; not merely the brotherhood of white men, but the brotherhood of all men before law. I believe in the Constitution and the Declaration of Independence. In giving to Negroes the rights that are theirs, we are only acting in accord with our ideals of a true democracy.[31]

Truman subsequently made it clear that his concept of racial equality did not extend to social mixing—"The Negro himself knows better than that, and the highest types of Negro leaders say quite frankly that they prefer the society of their own people. Negroes want justice, not social relations." Nevertheless, his attitude was an advanced one for a border-state senator, and much of it doubtless stemmed from his affiliation with the Pendergast machine, one of the first Democratic organizations to enjoy substantial Negro support. If not a leader in civil rights struggles, Truman nevertheless gave backing to antilynching and anti–poll tax bills and efforts to end discrimination in the armed forces. And on the most important of all civil rights issues, fair employment, Roy Wilkins has commented: "He came out for FEPC at a time when a lot of other fellows were straddeling the fence." [32]

While Truman's first term was not especially distinguished, one might suppose that his chairmanship of the important war investigating committee would have established him as one of the most important liberal leaders. On some vital issues his mind seemed almost perfectly in tune with the liberal mood.

He was one of the few Congressional leaders who demanded early planning for peacetime reconversion; his committee even submitted a report on the subject. Especially notable were his blasts at big business—attacks on Alcoa's monopolistic practices in the aluminum industry, on cartel agreements with German industry, on the use of substandard materials in aircraft production, on firms which used cost-plus government contracts to underwrite advertising. He criticized Jesse Jones, though not as severely as liberals had hoped he would, indicated a distrust of dollar-a-year men, worked to carve out opportunities for small business. He was a leader in the attempt to save the National Youth Administration. And while he criticized strikes which hampered the war effort, few liberals seemed to identify more strongly with labor.[33]

Truman's stature certainly increased among liberals within the government who understood the pressures which were brought to bear upon him. When the investigation of Alcoa's government contracts was under way in the fall of 1941, Harold Ickes invited the senator to lunch and praised his efforts. Yet Truman, perhaps because of his self-effacing manner and his insistence on committee unanimity, did not gain the attention and prestige among liberals which one would expect. Liberal journals invariably referred to the good work of "the Truman Committee" but seldom singled out Truman. Many apparently felt that if any single person deserved credit it was committee counsel Hugh Fulton.[34]

At the start of the war, Truman's ideas on international relations seemed somewhat less than liberal, but he came more and more frequently within the progressive consensus. He attracted great attention when after the Nazi invasion of Russia he tossed off a comment that the United States should work for a military deadlock between the two powers by aiding whichever nation seemed to be losing. The remark drew criticism even from many conservatives. Yet Truman gradually won recognition as an advocate of postwar international cooperation and collective security. He cosponsored a Senate resolution calling for postwar economic collaboration among the members of the

United Nations; he spoke of the need for "a powerful international police force." In the summer of 1943, he undertook an arduous tour through the Great Plains states to carry the message of internationalism, and near the end of the year the *New Republic* listed him on an "honor roll of fighting Senators" who were working for a liberal postwar world.[35]

By now he was one of the most popular and important members of the Senate. When he came out for a fourth term for President Roosevelt, a New York *Times* news story commented that the prestige of his endorsement would be an important boost for FDR.[36] But to many progressives, especially those who observed him from a distance, he remained a dull, uninspiring politician who had taken on a difficult assignment and done a good job, but who was not the vigorous, independent leader behind whom they could unite.

The liberal reaction to Truman as vice-presidential nominee was ambivalent. Certainly most progressives had nothing against the senator himself. The New York *Post*'s evaluation was typical: "A liberal and a convinced servant of the war effort." But he was not Henry Wallace, and, as most liberals saw it, Wallace's defeat was a victory for conservatism. Truman's record entitled him to the support of liberals, wrote Freda Kirchwey. "But let us not fool ourselves with the idea that the choice of Truman almost compensates for the defeat of Wallace. In spite of this forced concession, the convention ended with the combined reactionary forces in the Democratic Party, North and South, more firmly in control than at any time since 1932." [37]

Not all liberals, moreover, had a favorable impression of Truman. An article in the monthly journal *Common Sense* depicted him as a mediocre machine politician, a representative of the small-town middle-class viewpoint, a racist, and a non-ideological broker who lacked a grasp of the fundamental issues facing America and the world. He was an honest and devoted public servant, no doubt, but if he should become president, "he would tend to drift with events and follow the path of least resistance." [38]

Those who had a better opinion of Truman could not

achieve the sense of identification with him that they felt with Wallace. At a reception held in honor of the vice-presidential candidate, neither Frank Kingdon of the NCPAC nor Jo Davidson of the ICCASP, both friends and admirers of Wallace, could bring themselves to approach the senator. Finally the bearded artist Davidson came over to Kingdon to say: "Frank, one of us simply *has* to go over and shake hands with that man." [39]

Yet Truman's campaign was strongly in accord with the liberal viewpoint. Time and again, he praised Roosevelt's leadership in both foreign and domestic affairs. He attacked Dewey as a tool of reaction and isolationism, charging that the Republican candidate, "like Hearst and McCormick . . . lumps all liberals in with the Communists," and asserted that the Republican campaign was pervaded by "racial and religious bigotry." [40]

His speeches included militant calls for a liberal postwar economic program. Especially prominent was his emphasis on the conversion of government-owned war plants to civilian production and their sale to new, independent enterprises which would use their productive capacity to the fullest. He also stressed measures which would maintain mass purchasing power during the reconversion period, including a national system of unemployment insurance. He came out for a Missouri Valley Authority and for a similar project in the Pacific Northwest. In Illinois, he defended the New Deal farm policies and accused the Republicans of attempting to "drive a wedge between the farmer and the workingman." In New York he called for civil rights legislation. "No repudiation of the principles of Henry Wallace was made by the Democratic party in my nomination," he said in another talk. "The Democratic party will always be the liberal party." [41]

Late in the campaign, the Hearst newspapers carried a charge that Truman had been a member of the Ku Klux Klan, but the senator's swift and convincing denial doubtless carried weight with most liberals. The *New Republic* dismissed the accusation as another example of the "unparalleled and sweeping mendacity" of the Republican campaign. [42]

Despite Truman's rhetoric, it was apparent at the end of the campaign that he had not replaced Wallace in the hearts of the liberals. The two men made a joint appearance at a Liberal Party rally in New York a few days before the election. The crowd gave Truman a warm greeting but went wild when the vice-president was introduced, and cries of "Wallace in 1948" rang above the ovation. Truman appealed to the mood of his audience by generously lauding Wallace who, when he spoke, conspicuously failed to return the praise.[43]

If the liberals could not identify with Truman, they did react favorably to his campaign and after the inauguration hoped that he would be an effective vice-president; generally, however, they were disappointed. Truman's most discouraging act was his referral of the Missouri Valley Authority bill to a hostile Senate committee. Russell Smith of the Farmers Union, the organization which had spearheaded the struggle for the MVA, commented: "Whatever his reasons, the fact remains that the Vice President took the most effective possible course to throttle the bill for this session." There was also adverse reaction to a report, probably false, that Truman had urged Aubrey Williams to give up his losing struggle for confirmation as head of the Rural Electrification Administration. Some, but not all, liberals disagreed with Truman's apparent concept of the vice-presidency as an office which should emphasize personal and social contacts; the *Progressive* deplored his emergence as a Washington "social butterfly." [44] Truman's performance as vice-president had simply increased the ambiguity which characterized the liberal picture of him. When he assumed national leadership, liberals might hope for the best, but they could be certain of nothing.

Truman's view of the liberal movement was equally ambivalent. He had been a New Dealer; he clearly had been influenced by the Midwestern progressive heritage. Whatever his liberal biases and policy preferences, however, his public career was not built around an ideology or a highly systematized social philosophy. In no sense an intellectual, he was essentially a shrewd professional politician who reached the presidency by aligning himself with important sources of political power: in

Missouri, the Pendergast machine, the rural courthouse rings, the St. Louis bosses, labor, and Negroes; in Washington, the Senate Establishment. A man whose position sprang from such sources could have little rapport with doctrinaire reformers who refused to compromise and had scant actual experience in the political and legislative processes. Truman seems instead to have respected the practical liberal politician, the man who fought and won election campaigns, who knew how to get along in Washington, who met the opposition halfway when necessary, and who got things done. Such a man, he apparently believed, was Harry Hopkins. Hopkins "had horse sense and knew how to use it," Truman commented in his diary. He was "a noted and advanced 'Liberal' but not a professional one (I consider the latter a low form of politician)." [45]

In April 1945, the liberal movement and Truman each held serious reservations about the other. Given favorable circumstances, these reservations might easily have evaporated; in the chaotic world of 1945, they would degenerate into mutual suspicion and hostility.

Chapter 3

Truman, the Liberals, and the Politics of Alienation

The liberals were convinced that the postwar situation at home required a revival and enlargement of the New Deal. Roosevelt's political course in 1944 and 1945 had confirmed their conviction and had encouraged them to believe that the postwar years could become a new era of reform. Yet the New Deal actually had been engaged in a holding action since 1938. It had come into being largely as a result of the emergency created by the Great Depression and had been stalemated even before that emergency had ended. Given the antiliberal mood which dominated Congress, the chances for a New Deal revival rested upon the possibility of a new domestic emergency, the long-feared postwar depression.

The political and economic situation which did develop was quite the opposite. Characterized by severe inflationary pressures, it was inimical to reform and indeed to almost any sort of successful political management. Harry S. Truman could not master it, nor could he deliver the reform results for which the liberals had hoped. The progressives might have forgiven him for these failures, as they had forgiven Roosevelt for the years of domestic deadlock. But Truman failed in another respect also. Roosevelt had given the liberals inspiration, excitement, identity, unity; he had preserved the spirit of the New Deal

long after the New Deal's demise. Truman, as the progressives
saw him, stumbling from one problem to another, and surrounding himself with drab, conservative advisers, could not
even maintain the appearance of dynamic liberalism in the
White House. Increasingly, the nation seemed to be slipping
into an era of "normalcy" with all that Hardingesque word
implied—incompetence, corruption, reaction, economic disaster.

I

Americans generally have displayed a tendency to give a new
president a "honeymoon," especially if he enters office under
difficult circumstances, and in the weeks after Truman assumed
the presidency most liberals were determined to be optimistic
about him. Truman's New Deal voting record was reassuring.
He was popular in Congress and reputedly a skillful political
manipulator; he combined humility and decisiveness. When he
addressed Congress after Roosevelt's funeral and declared allegiance to his predecessor's policies, the New York *Post* commented: "He stood before the country as the President in the
fullest sense." A few days later, Max Lerner wrote: "No man in
the history of the Vice Presidential succession has grown in
stature so fast or so visibly."

Yet from the start there were doubts. David E. Lilienthal,
upon hearing of Roosevelt's death, felt "consternation at the
thought of that Throttlebottom, Truman. 'The country and
the world doesn't deserve to be left this way. . . .'" New Deal
voting record or not, Truman was a regular Democrat, not an
independent progressive. His tenure in office might well be
one of Cabinet government, not strong presidential leadership,
and it was doubtful that he would fight the conservative coalition to the limit. His cultural heritage, moreover, was that of
the small-town Midwestern middle class, a heritage, commented the *New Republic,* that was not "well attuned to the
future of a world in depression, war and revolution." It seemed
unlikely that he possessed the vision to go beyond the Roose-

velt program with bold departures of his own—as did, for example, Henry Wallace.

There was special concern over the president's relationship with the party bosses and professional politicians. "Can a man who has been associated with the Pendergast machine be able to keep the panting politicians and bosses out of the gravy?" asked Max Lerner. "Harding became their prisoner after Wilson's death." The new president had been in office only six weeks when California Attorney General Robert Kenny received a harsh report from a liberal friend:

You get this stuff every place you turn: "Truman is a nice man, but no superman; he is surrounded by a bunch of 'regular' party hacks who are going to drive every decent person out of important administrative positions. We should start developing Wallace . . . or Douglas or some piece of driven snow for President in '48. There will be another Teapot Dome and the Missouri gang will go to the penitentiary."

These were doubts which had roots deep in the American progressive tradition. Liberals long had tended to connect party regularity with corruption and had searched for forceful, independent leadership which transcended parties and politics. From the first, there were strong fears that Truman could not provide this type of leadership, that his character was not distinguished by the stubborn individualism of a Robert La Follette or George Norris, a Harold Ickes or a Henry Wallace.[1]

The simplest way of evaluating the new president—and one which had great impact upon liberals during the early months of the Truman administration—was to judge him by the men he gathered about him and named to responsible posts. Liberals were by no means universally dissatisfied, but they were cool and increasingly pessimistic. Truman retained some of the most prominent New Dealers, but his own appointees, with the possible exception of his old friend Charley Ross, could not be characterized as "intellectuals" or "independent progressives."

Many of Truman's early appointments, as the liberals viewed them, were perfectly acceptable and occasionally outstanding.

The president retained the New Dealers Samuel I. Rosenman
and David K. Niles as White House assistants. For his press secretary, he chose Charles G. Ross, a widely respected Washington correspondent for the St. Louis *Post-Dispatch*. He designated the able and liberal-minded Paul Herzog as chairman of
the National Labor Relations Board and the capable, well-
liked General Omar Bradley as head of the Veterans Administration. Over the opposition of Tennessee Senators Tom Stewart and Kenneth McKellar, both powerful and patronage-
hungry, he reappointed as chairman of the Tennessee Valley Authority perhaps the foremost representative of New
Deal idealism, David Lilienthal. Lilienthal himself, certain that he had been called to the White House to be
dumped, came away from his first meeting with Truman with
respect for the president's straightforwardness and desire to
protect the integrity of the TVA.[2]

The new secretary of labor, Lew Schwellenbach, had been a
militantly liberal senator during the New Deal. Fred Vinson,
the new secretary of the treasury, was moderately progressive
and commanded great respect from all quarters in Washington.
Congressman Clinton Anderson, having headed an investigation of food production, seemed a logical choice for secretary of
agriculture and a distinct improvement over his weak predecessor, Claude Wickard. Robert Hannegan as postmaster general
looked neither better nor worse than the politicos who had
held the job in the past. The new attorney general, Tom
Clark, did not appear to be an improvement over the outgoing
Francis Biddle, but he was believed to be an antitruster and a
man of respectable qualifications. (Biddle, who was more familiar with Clark's record, privately opposed his nomination.[3])

Other appointments, however, had a negative impact. Truman made the inept Wickard head of the Rural Electrification
Administration and appointed the conservative W. H. Wills to
the Federal Communications Commission. His first judicial
nominees—for three vacancies on the District of Columbia
Federal Court of Appeals—were hopeless mediocrities.[4] The
president seemed to surround himself with crude "cronies"

such as Harry Vaughn, Ed McKim, and Jake Vardaman. Especially distasteful and even dangerous, many progressives believed, was George Allen, a jovial Mississippian who had served Roosevelt mainly as a court jester but appeared to be a trusted and important adviser to Truman. In early 1946, the president appointed Allen a director of the Reconstruction Finance Corporation. A conservative, back-slapping "fixer" with some unsavory connections, Allen became a symbol of all the administration's bad impulses—in style as well as in policy.[5]

Another crony who drew much criticism was John W. Snyder. A Missouri banker and long-time friend of Truman, Snyder worked in the RFC during the war, had been appointed federal loan administrator by the new president a few days after Roosevelt's death, and had succeeded Fred Vinson as head of the Office of War Mobilization and Reconversion. Snyder had been involved in a dispute with Jesse Jones, but any belief that he would pursue progressive policies soon dissolved. The new OWMR director brought in a conservative general as one of his aides, undertook an offensive against economic controls, and obtained the abolition of the more liberal-oriented Office of Economic Stabilization.[6]

Equally disturbing was the naming of oilman Edwin Pauley as ambassador to the Allied Reparations Commission, displacing New Dealer Isador Lubin, who had been slated for the job by Roosevelt and who now gamely agreed to stay on as Pauley's lieutenant. The leader of the Democratic right wing in California, Pauley had been one of the most prominent figures in the movement to push Wallace off the party ticket. There were rumors that his eventual reward would be a Cabinet post, perhaps Harold Ickes's job as secretary of the interior.

As the cronies, conservatives, and party regulars seemed to become more entrenched and influential, a political Gresham's Law appeared to be driving important liberals out of the government. In September, Truman abruptly dumped the respected William H. Davis, director of the Office of Economic Stabilization, and merged the OES into John Snyder's OWMR. The merger probably had been planned anyway, but the president had acted precipitately after reading a newspaper story which misquoted Davis's views on wage policy. Subsequently, he felt compelled to write Davis a public letter of apology.[7]

In December Robert Nathan, a dynamic young economist who had been a key figure in the war production effort and had become deputy director of OWMR, left the government without bothering to conceal his disgust with John Snyder. Lubin was soon fed up with Pauley and quit the Reparations Commission in February 1946. Samuel Rosenman apparently had worked well enough with Truman, but when he resigned to practice law, his departure also indicated the declining influence of the New Dealers. "President Truman is more desperately in need of sound counsel, of experienced aides than even President Roosevelt at the peak of the war crisis," Bartley C. Crum told Rosenman. "I have kept my confidence in his integrity of purpose. You can understand, however, that each resignation—top-side—makes the task of convincing others more difficult. It makes, in brief, for dissolution of the coalition of progressive forces." [8]

T.R.B. commented as early as September 1945 that the mediocrity of the men around Truman was "beginning to show like the mid-day sun." By December, the *Progressive*'s Washington column was reporting that John Snyder and George Allen were said to be the last men the president consulted before making important decisions. In February 1946, Thomas L. Stokes compared the administration to a "county courthouse crowd passing the jobs around among friends" and warned: "Past experience has shown that too much of this sort of thing has proved an unwise course." At about the same time, Beanie Baldwin privately predicted to Henry Wallace that the Truman administration would be one of the most corrupt in American history.[9]

In early 1946 a prominent progressive, still in the government, granted *PM* journalist James A. Wechsler an anonymous interview. "Truman keeps lamenting that good liberal men won't take top posts in his Administration. . . . Who wants to work in a set-up where you have to go through this forward wall of politicians?" The president was surrounded by "a lot of second-rate guys trying to function in an atom bomb world"; by contrast, "even FDR's bad appointments were first team." And, while Truman's own honesty was beyond question, "it may be tough to keep track of corruption if he continues to make this Administration a party field day. Sometimes things get out of control." [10]

By early 1946 Truman's appointments had given his administration an image which alienated many liberals. The dynamic, imaginative, independent progressives who had served Roosevelt were being replaced, it seemed, by mediocre party men of dubious ethics. However, the two most important representatives of the New Deal and the spirit of independent liberalism remained—Secretary of the Interior Harold Ickes and Secretary of Commerce Henry Wallace. They were important symbols; if they left the president's official circle, they would probably carry the allegiance of the great body of liberals with them.[11]

II

Liberals, however, were concerned with more than Truman's cronies and questionable appointments; increasingly, they doubted his qualities of leadership and his commitment to the cause of progressivism. As World War II came to an end with surprising rapidity, economic matters overshadowed all else. The immediate need was to cushion the shocks and dislocations which would inevitably accompany the transition to a peacetime economy. The fear of postwar depression and resultant fascism remained alive. The *Progressive* warned of a revival of nativism and attributed the situation to "the deep-going insecurity felt by the great mass of our people as they face the postwar era." Charles Bolte, the chairman of the American Veterans Committee, feared that management would try to use jobless returning soldiers to break unions. The *Nation* compiled a list of a half-dozen new fascist-type veterans' organizations, one of them sponsored by Father Coughlin.[12]

Truman soon gave indications that he would work for government stabilization of the economy. He displayed a concern with inflation by issuing a statement of praise for the Office of Price Administration. Conversely, he recognized the problems of displaced workers by asking Congress for higher unemployment benefits and wider coverage.[13] Liberals took heart from these actions; but their long-range hopes for stability focused upon a daring new piece of legislation, the Full Employment Bill.

Fundamentally, the bill was an attempt to write into law the economics of Keynes and Hansen by requiring enough compensatory government spending to wipe out unemployment. It demonstrated the way in which Keynesianism had captured the allegiance of the liberals during the war. The enormously successful military effort had rested upon deficit spending, the progressives realized, and so if necessary must the peace. The bill was sponsored by an impressive group of liberal senators, led by Robert F. Wagner of New York, and by 116 members of the House, most of them from urban, industrial districts. The National Farmers Union and the Union for Democratic Action spearheaded the movement for its adoption. More than any other measure, this bill seemed essential to the future of postwar America. "Given full employment," Stuart Chase wrote with remarkable optimism, "nearly every other economic and social problem becomes manageable." "The fate of this bill will be decisive for American prosperity and world peace," declared the *Nation*. Administration leaders issued strong endorsements, and Truman declared that the bill was on his "must" list.[14]

Yet liberals were far from content with Truman's stance. There seemed to be too little thought within the administration about the difficult transition period. In July, Walter Reuther demanded concrete implementation of Truman's 1944 campaign pledges to make war plants available to new enterprise. A dozen liberal senators, led by Harley Kilgore of West Virginia and Claude Pepper of Florida, called for a sweeping reconversion program. But John Snyder's statements and policies were noticeably to the right of Truman's, and the important War Production Board seemed to be staffed by men close to big business. Above all, there were doubts about Truman's tenacity. "He has got to choose sides," wrote T.R.B. in August, "he has got to stop writing nice notes to Congress on crucial domestic issues that divide conservatives from liberals, and begin throwing his weight around." [15]

Only slightly less urgent was the racial problem, especially the future of the Fair Employment Practices Committee. When Truman entered the presidency, two bills were pending; one would provide funds to prolong the temporary wartime agency which Roosevelt had set up, the other would establish the FEPC on a permanent basis. The first measure was receiving a drastic financial trimming; the second was bottled up in the conservative-controlled House Rules Committee. Progressives urged the president to work to get the second measure on the floor of the House. "A word from him" would bring the signatures necessary for a discharge petition, asserted the *Nation*.[16]

On June 5, Truman gave the word. In a public letter to Congressman Adolph Sabath, the chairman of the Rules Committee, the president condemned job discrimination as "un-American," urged release of the FEPC bill, and declared that "The principle and policy of fair employment practice should be established permanently as a part of our national law." Progressives hailed Truman for defying the Southern bloc of his party. A White House staff analysis of mail reaction concluded: "The letter established him as a liberal." [17] Actually, as events would demonstrate, fleeting reactions to a public statement could establish nothing. Liberals would demand more both in results and in the exercise of leadership.

Truman seemed to make his intentions clear with a long and important message to Congress on September 6. A broad declaration of administration reconversion policy, the document specifically cited Roosevelt's Economic Bill of Rights as its basis. To meet the fear of depression, the president called for extension and enlargement of unemployment benefits; continuance of the federally operated U.S. Employment Service to facilitate the placement of war workers in new jobs; continued price and rent controls to avoid the boom-and-bust cycle which had occurred after World War I; "an immediate and substantial upward revision" of the minimum wage to help maintain purchasing power; passage of full employment legislation; and a vast program of public development similar to that outlined during the war by Hansen and Wallace—highways, airports, hospitals, regional development authorities. Truman urged a permanent FEPC, "broad and comprehensive housing legislation," government aid for small business, the continuation of agricultural price supports, and a stronger system of crop insurance. He promised plans for a national health program and expansion of the social security system.[18]

"I wanted to let the Hearsts and McCormicks know that they were not going to take me into camp," Truman told Jonathan Daniels a few years later. And for a while it seemed that the president had made his point. "The message was solid, detailed, a conscientious implementation of every point in President Roosevelt's Economic Bill of Rights," said the St. Louis *Post-Dispatch,* and Thomas L. Stokes declared that "Franklin D. Roosevelt never said it more clearly or explicitly or more eloquently." [19]

However, it soon became apparent that the administration's legislative program was encountering great difficulty in Congress. Doubts about Truman's ability and tenacity seemed justified as the administration backed down from its strong stand on unemployment compensation and went along with a weak Senate substitute; the use of George Allen as the White House agent made the deal even less palatable. At about the same time, the Office of War Mobilization and Reconversion lifted restrictions on building materials, thereby diverting construction activity from family housing to more lucrative commercial enterprises, among them resorts, race tracks, and cocktail lounges. The controls were restored after it became apparent that vitally needed housing could not be built without them. But John Snyder's temporary victory over the protests of New Dealers such as Chester Bowles was disturbing.[20]

Such incidents destroyed whatever standing the September 6 message had given the president. Surrounded by cronies, "shooting from the hip" at press conferences, and projecting a sense of inadequacy, Truman was not meeting liberal expectations. The president's course appeared to be one of drift and indecision. "A curious uneasiness seems to pervade all levels of the Government," declared the *Progressive*'s Washington column. "There is a feeling at times that there is no hand at the wheel." Since the turn of the century—perhaps even since the days of Jefferson and Jackson—liberals had relied heavily upon strong, aggressive presidential leadership. Their evaluation of Truman rested heavily upon the assumption that a president with ability and eloquence could force a recalcitrant Congress to act. Truman, wrote Thomas L. Stokes at the beginning of October, was "expected to become the mouthpiece for the people, to be their voice, to give them direction." [21]

The president seemed to give progressives what they wanted on October 30 when he made a radio speech urging the appropriate Congressional committees to release the unemployment insurance, U.S. Employment Service, and full employment bills. "HARRY TRUMAN HAS BEGUN TO FIGHT," exulted the *UDA Congressional Newsletter*. "From now on, it is —or should be—a ding-dong battle against the bipartisan coalition that puts property and profits above people." But the mood of jubilation did not last long. Results failed to materialize, and most liberals blamed the White House. Perhaps Truman had spoken out, but he lacked the ability to do so effectively. "Truman has one means, and one alone, of blasting the program loose, that is to appeal over the heads of Congress to the public," T.R.B. wrote in early December. "Always in history that is what strong Presidents have done. . . . Alas for Truman, there is no bugle note in his voice." [22]

The crucial Full Employment Bill, which already had passed the Senate, remained stalled in a House committee headed by the conservative Carter Manasco of Alabama; and with one economist predicting an unemployment high of 12 to 18 million during the postwar transition period, the liberal movement continued to fear the specter of armies of jobless men. Progressives were stunned when the administration decided that the only way to get the measure out of committee was to acquiesce in a new version so weak that Washington wits said it had been "Manascolated." On the floor of the House, a bloc of liberals attempted to fight for the original strong version, but administration forces vigorously quashed the rebellion. On December 14, the Manasco bill passed the House, and discouraged progressives watched the measure upon which they had staked so much move toward a highly uncertain fate in a Senate-House conference committee. "Who said the Truman administration didn't know how to fight?" asked the *UDA Congressional Newsletter* ruefully.[23]

Liberals received yet another disappointment in early December when one of the Negro members of the FEPC, Charles Houston, resigned in protest against administration refusal to let the committee issue an order banning discrimination in the District of Columbia Capital Transit Company, which had been seized by the federal government. The administration claimed, perhaps validly, that a knotty legal question was involved, that Congressional legislation prohibited any changes in the employment policy of a company under government seizure. But the White House refusal to consider the FEPC's argument understandably angered the committee and undermined Truman's position. In his letter of resignation, Houston hotly asserted that the committee's position had become "intolerable" and sharply added:

The failure of the Government to enforce democratic practices and to protect minorities in its own capital makes its expressed concern for national minorities abroad somewhat specious, and its interference in the domestic affairs of other countries very premature.

The entire committee was on the verge of following Houston's example until Truman issued an executive order affirming the FEPC's continuance and sent an accompanying directive on fair employment to all executive agencies. The incident dealt another blow to liberal confidence in the president's civil rights policies.[24]

Actually, there are indications that, however he may have

hedged on the FEPC issue, Truman sincerely cared about minority rights. In December 1945, Eleanor Roosevelt sent the president a copy of a letter she had received concerning several instances of violence and discrimination against Japanese-Americans. Truman replied with what appears to have been genuine indignation: "This disgraceful conduct almost makes you believe that a lot of our Americans have a streak of Nazi in them." In a memorandum to Attorney General Clark, Truman asked: "Isn't there some way we can shame these people into doing the right thing?" Clark replied that in most instances the federal government had no jurisdiction and the Justice Department could only investigate and turn evidence of any crime over to state and local authorites. Observing, however, that during the war Roosevelt had directed the Justice Department to investigate all lynchings, the attorney general suggested that the president might issue a similar order to apply to cases of violence against Japanese-Americans. Truman did so.[25]

The president's rather weak indication of concern was typical of his approach to minority problems during the early phase of his tenure in office. Like most liberals, he considered economic reconversion the most important issue. In early 1946, he made no strong public denunciation of a Senate filibuster which was destroying the permanent FEPC bill; subsequently, he refused to work for an anti-poll tax bill. "The program has been almost ruined by one filibuster and I think that is enough for a season," he told Irving Brant. Truman attempted to balance his inaction by appointing the eminent Negro, Judge William Hastie, governor of the Virgin Islands, but such tokenism, welcome as it was, could not satisfy liberals who hoped for more fundamental moves. All the same, the president had displayed a belief in elementary justice for minority groups. He could easily give civil rights a more urgent priority whenever it seemed necessary or expedient.[26]

Truman's relations with the labor movement also deteriorated badly. As early as June 1945, Sidney Hillman was privately expressing worry over the conservatism of the president's advisers. William Green of the AFL and Philip Murray of the

CIO let it be known they were annoyed because of the lack of regular contact with the White House. In September, Murray publicly criticized the president for failing to fight for the administration program, and a CIOPAC handbook commented: "We do not have the support and leadership in Washington that we enjoyed when President Roosevelt was alive."

Labor was reacting to more than the snapping of its once-close ties to the White House. The end of the war had brought both the fear of mass unemployment and the actuality of a sharp cut in take-home pay as many industries reverted to a standard 40-hour week without the abundant overtime of the war years. The cut in purchasing power often amounted to 30 percent or more, and union leaders, who felt that their men had made substantial wage sacrifices during the war, resolved to restore as much of the slash as possible. A wave of strikes followed, widening the rift between the president and the labor movement.

A strike led by Walter Reuther against General Motors dramatized the problem. Reuther demanded a 30 percent increase in wages, unless GM was willing to open its books and publicly demonstrate that higher prices would be necessary to meet the union demand. The company declined, and a bitter stalemate developed, epitomizing the gap between labor and management. Refusing to open its books, GM nevertheless insisted on higher prices as a condition of any wage hike. Management, as most liberals saw it, was attempting to starve the auto workers into submission, smash organized labor, and wipe out price controls, even at the risk of a depression.[27]

Truman seemed to back labor's argument in his radio speech of October 30. He said that the economy could not afford the loss of purchasing power involved in a return to the 40-hour week and declared that substantial wage increases could be effected without raising prices, although he refused to endorse a 30 percent boost. In early November, a general labor-management conference called by the White House met in Washington. The administration hoped the conference would develop a wage formula which would win wide approval, but it was too late. The meeting was a failure, and the strikes continued.[28]

On December 3, the president sent a surprising message to Congress requesting new labor legislation. Patterned after the Railway Labor Act, his proposal contained two salient features: fact-finding boards which would investigate disputes and make recommendations, and cooling-off periods in which workers would return to their jobs while the fact-finding investigation was under way. At the same time Truman, using his executive authority, appointed a provisional fact-finding board for the General Motors strike and asked for a voluntary return to work. He likewise requested the postponement of an impending steel strike. Philip Murray took to the radio to protest. Accusing Truman of "a very serious departure" from the Roosevelt policies, Murray characterized the proposals as an effort "to weaken and ultimately destroy labor union organizations" and the first step in a campaign of "savage legislative repression." The Auto Workers indignantly rejected the back-to-work request, calling it a "retreat from economic democracy as furthered under the courageous leadership of Franklin D. Roosevelt." [29]

Few liberals were as vehement as Murray; some even defended Truman's message as an attempt to head off antiunion legislation, which was taking shape in Congress. To most, however, the recommendations seemed unfair; the fault lay with management, not labor; and the right to strike, which Truman wanted to curb, was labor's major defense. Few believed that absolute reaction was rampant in the White House, but the incident seemed to be another Truman blunder. "To charge the President with crass incomprehension may, indeed, be worse than to accuse him of willful labor-smashing," commented the *Nation,* "but it seems a more accurate indictment." Roosevelt, the journal pointedly added, would have at least consulted with labor leaders before sending such a bill to Congress.[30]

Yet some of Truman's actions impressed liberals as praiseworthy. On December 12, he announced a new emergency housing program to be headed by the respected former mayor of Louisville, Wilson Wyatt. On December 20, he urged the

Senate-House conference committee on the Full Employment Bill to recommend legislation similar to the original strong Senate version. The same day, he put himself on the side of Reuther and the United Auto Workers by making it clear to a press conference that the labor fact-finding boards he had proposed should have the power to look into company books and consider profit margins. On December 23, he released a tough veto of an appropriations bill which carried a rider returning the U.S. Employment Service to the states. On January 3, he made another strong radio appeal for his program.[31]

By this time, however, the adverse liberal impression of Truman was well developed. Essentially, this impression consisted of a belief that the president was a little man caught in a job he did not want, simply another politician incapable of providing aggressive and inspiring leadership. As late as November 1 Eleanor Roosevelt, distressed by the way in which the Full Employment Bill was stalled in Congress, felt it necessary to suggest that "a group of people, such as those who worked for instance for special legislation in the past, might be formed within Mr. Snyder's office." Apparently believing that only George Allen handled legislative problems, she advised the president that "no one man can possibly do all the work that needs to be done." (Actually a special committee had been formed to lobby for the employment bill, although its efforts were sporadic and generally ineffective.) That Mrs. Roosevelt felt that Truman needed such elementary advice indicated a rather low opinion which even her customary politeness could not altogether conceal.[32]

Newbold Morris, who had run for mayor of New York with the support of Fiorello La Guardia, publicly compared "Harding normalcy" to "Truman futility." The New York *Post* commented that the administration's difficulties sprang "not necessarily from a lack of idealism or good intentions, but from a lack of realism and of day-to-day competence." Max Lerner saw in Truman the inadequacy of the Midwestern, middle-class mind; the president could not grasp "real social cleavages and struggles," thought solely in personal terms, and naïvely attempted to win over Congress by handshaking. "It is difficult to find anyone who is strongly opposed to Mr. Truman, but even more difficult to find anyone who is violently for him," wrote Robert Sherwood at the beginning of January 1946. "Those most antipathetic are those who were the most ardent and militant supporters of F.D.R. and the New Deal." [33] By now, there was also what the *UDA Congressional Newsletter* called "desperate talk" of a third party, with a few liberals beginning to speculate half-seriously about the establishment of a new political force built around the CIO, the Farmers Union, and the middle-class organizations, led, perhaps, by Henry Wallace.[34]

The dissatisfaction continued throughout early 1946. At the beginning of February, the Full Employment Bill finally ended its journey through Congress. The final version, called simply the Employment Act, omitted the government commitment to full employment and the mandatory spending provisions; it did assert that the government should attempt to maintain *maximum* employment, and it established a potentially influential Council of Economic Advisers. At best, the act was a qualified victory. Much would depend upon Truman's appointments to the council, and liberals hoped that he would name such figures as Alvin Hansen, Robert Nathan, or Harold D. Smith, the dynamic director of the Bureau of the Budget. But there were no exciting or dramatic nominations; in fact, by mid-July, the council seats were still vacant. Russell Smith of the Farmers Union, who had helped draft the original bill, had worked for its adoption, and had been considered as a possible council member, wrote that Truman's delay had "given a serious setback to the chances that the act can work to avoid a future terrible deflation and bust following the present inflation." [35]

As the Employment Act cleared Congress, economic stabilization became imperiled by a drawn-out steel strike and a controversy over its settlement. John Snyder, backed by Civilian Production Administrator John Small, advocated a substantial price increase to compensate the companies for the expense of a wage hike. Chester Bowles, who had become increasingly alienated from Snyder, led the opposition. Bowles argued—and most liberals agreed with him—that inflated corporate profits could absorb higher wages with only moderate price increases. A crisis developed as Bowles privately sent the president his resignation and leaked news of his imminent departure to the press.

Among progressives, Bowles had enormous prestige as the strongest fighter in the administration for price controls and economic stability. He was, moreover, a Roosevelt man fighting for progressive policies against Truman appointees. His conflict with Snyder appeared to demonstrate his increasing isolation from the conservative, uninspiring men Truman was bringing to Washington. "Mr. Bowles is beginning to look like a man who got into government by parachute, and is trying to defend a small clearing against the enemy," commented Samuel Grafton.[36]

Truman's feelings toward Bowles were ambivalent and probably typical of his attitude toward the type of liberal the OPA chief exemplified. The president was a professional politician who had come up through the ranks; he had won the respect of his Senate colleagues by quiet, hard work. Bowles was a political amateur who had never run for office; he had an impressive record of accomplishment, but his background as an advertising executive led him to give much attention to public relations. Since the price control effort rested ultimately upon popular support, Bowles was probably wise, but he annoyed Truman. "Bowles is a grand guy, but he makes me mad as the devil at times," the president told Harold Smith. "He has a headline in every Monday morning paper, and I think that he makes entirely too many speeches." [37]

The outcome was a compromise. Steel received a price rise, twice the amount Bowles had recommended, driving a serious "bulge" in the price line. Bowles, however, was persuaded to stay in the administration as director of economic stabilization, and a Kentucky liberal, Paul A. Porter, became the new head of the OPA. Progressives at first felt that they had won a

major victory and that Snyder was on the way out, but Truman
soon made it clear to a press conference that the power relationship between Snyder and Bowles was ill-defined, that at
best the two men were equals. Bowles and Porter were clearly
upset; no one was talking for publication, James Wechsler reported, but "bitter off-the-record comments were being freely
voiced." Bowles not only privately protested but sent out letters making it clear that the president had promised him full
backing, that he would not have taken the job otherwise; but
in the following months he was far from satisfied with the administration. With Bowles in a more strategic position to carry
on the battle against inflation and with a reliable successor at
the OPA, liberals might view the episode as a gain, but Snyder's continued authority seemed another case of Truman's tendency to put personal ties above the public welfare.[38]

While Truman was keeping one New Dealer in the administration, he was losing another. An old Bull Mooser, a
Republican who had supported FDR and had served as secretary of the interior throughout his administration, Harold
Ickes was the very embodiment of militant, independent progressivism. Irascible, petty, suspicious, vindictive, he was in
many ways the model of the grasping bureaucrat. Rather than
accept an independent Missouri Valley Authority, he had
played a key role in sabotaging the MVA bill; he distrusted the
TVA and worked against David Lilienthal. Yet Ickes's integrity and ability were unquestioned; liberals universally regarded him as a great public servant. Moreover, he had been a
fighting campaigner for the New Deal; few men were so closely
identified with the legacy of Roosevelt.[39]

Soon after becoming president, Truman had declined Ickes's
resignation, but in February 1946, a break developed over an
issue on which Truman could expect no sympathy from
liberals—the president's nomination of Ed Pauley to be undersecretary of the navy. Truman had a high opinion of Pauley and big plans for him. James Forrestal, the president believed, was ready to return to private life. Pauley would
succeed him as secretary of the navy, and, with the unification

of the armed forces, would become secretary of defense. "I don't agree with all Pauley's policies," Truman remarked a few years later, "but he is a tough, mean so-and-so who might make sense of this defense policy." The president somehow thought that Ickes agreed with his estimate. Actually, Ickes shared the general liberal view of Pauley—"a man who mixed business and politics, public and private interest, with no apparent scruples," as the Chicago *Sun* put it. The thought of Pauley with disposition over the naval oil reserves led at once to memories of the Harding administration and Teapot Dome. The nomination was a scandalous disregard of public trust, charged the *New Republic,* another indication that Truman put "personal friendship before everything else in selecting governmental officials." [40]

Whatever Ickes had told Truman about his opinion of Pauley, in testimony before the Senate Naval Affairs Committee the secretary delivered a scathing denunciation. He asserted that in 1944 Pauley had delivered the "rawest proposition ever made to me," a suggestion that the Democratic Party could raise several hundred thousand dollars if suits to bring the tidelands oil fields into the federal domain were dropped. Truman stood behind Pauley and told reporters at a press conference: "Mr. Ickes can very well be mistaken the same as the rest of us." A few days later, February 13, Ickes responded with a long letter of resignation. "It was the kind of letter sent by a man who is sure that he can have his way if he threatens to quit," Truman has written. "But I was not going to be threatened." The president accepted the resignation.

Perhaps Ickes expected Truman to ask him to stay on, as Roosevelt had done so often. Perhaps, as the president believed, he was ready to leave the administration and wanted to go out with a bang. If so, his dreams were realized. Speaking to a packed press conference a few days before his seventy-second birthday, he charged that Truman, by asking him to "be as gentle as you can with Ed Pauley," had indirectly requested him to commit perjury. Speaking to a national radio audience that evening, he said: "I could no longer, much as I regret it, retain my self-respect and stay in the Cabinet of President Truman." When the president asserted that Ickes would not dare question his integrity, the Old Curmudgeon responded that Truman was "neither an absolute monarch nor a descendant of a putative Sun Goddess" and attacked "what I regard as the President's lack of adherence to the strict truth." [41]

Progressive opinion sided almost unanimously with Ickes. Detecting the "unsavory odor of oil politics," Freda Kirchwey wrote: "The greater intelligence and probity of Mr. Truman does not suffice to wipe out an unhappy resemblance to Mr. Harding." Truman, said the St. Louis *Post-Dispatch*, "has now raised distressing doubts whether he considers public office as sacred and inviolate." The Chicago *Sun* summed up the liberal view: "Here is the old struggle between the machine politician and the independent; between those who hold office for its own sake and those who see it as a means to public ends; between expediency and progressive principles." Ickes was not the first liberal to leave the administration out of disgust or disillusionment, but he was the first to proclaim his feelings publicly. The incident was, Marquis Childs observed, "the first open break between the Democrats of the New Deal wing and the Democrats of the city machines and the Old South." [42]

In an attempt to regain liberal support, Truman offered the Interior Department to Supreme Court Justice William O. Douglas, but Douglas was not interested in saving the administration from embarrassment. After the justice turned down the appointment, Truman passed over another liberal favorite, Undersecretary Oscar L. Chapman, and named Julius Krug, who as head of the War Production Board had been too friendly to big business for most liberals. [43]

Ickes subsequently accepted lucrative offers to serve as executive chairman of the Independent Citizens Committee of the Arts, Sciences, and Professions and to write a nationally syndicated column for the New York *Post*. For the next two years he would subject Truman to almost unrelieved denunciation. Yet he never closed the door on possible support of the president. He had not questioned Truman's attempt to follow the Roosevelt policies, and he had made it clear at the time of his resignation that he was not foreclosing the possibility that he would back the president in 1948.[44]

Other factors contributed to the increasing liberal alienation. The administration continued to show little interest in civil rights. On April 6, Truman touched off a flurry of protests by remarking to a press conference that the poll tax was a matter for the Southern states "to work out themselves." A few days later at another press conference, he had to eat his words and read a prepared statement reaffirming his support of anti–poll tax and other civil rights measures. On June 21, Attorney General Clark made a speech which seemed to criticize lawyers who confined their practice to representing labor unions and minority groups. The National Lawyers Guild, headed by Robert Kenny, replied with a strong condemnation of Clark's civil rights record.[45]

There was restlessness, too, over Truman's failure to challenge big business. To most liberals, corporate arrogance had reached a peak when General Motors had refused to open its books to the president's fact-finding board and when big steel had rejected compromise settlements which would have held prices down. Yet Truman refused to denounce the corporations. "He was still seeking to avoid a showdown," wrote James A. Wechsler at the beginning of February, "still fearful that direct language would upset the boat, still unwilling to carry his case to the country." [46]

The administration seemed to do little to foster competition against the great industrial complexes. The efforts of Surplus Property Administrator Stuart Symington to encourage competition in the aluminum industry won praise, but progressives felt that in critical instances the administration had failed to come through on its promises to make war plants available to new enterprise. The most glaring example was the sale of a large steel plant in Geneva, Utah, to U.S. Steel, rather than to Kaiser. In fact, the administration did frequently sell war facilities to small business, but these instances passed unnoticed. "The government is actually doing little or nothing at the mo-

ment to encourage free competition and strengthen independent enterprise," commented the *Progressive* in May.[47]

By the spring of 1946, the once-cordial relationship between
the administration and the National Farmers Union had deteriorated also. Truman, who apparently had little interest in or
time for agricultural problems,* had delegated responsibility to
his secretary of agriculture, Clinton Anderson. It soon became
apparent that Anderson's policies were designed to appeal to
the conservative power structure in American agriculture.† He
seemed too close to the Farm Bureau Federation and the ferti-
lizer and packing interests, hostile to price controls, indifferent
to the terrible threat of a worldwide famine.[48]

The Farmers Union protested reports that Anderson would
back a return to the old policy of acreage allotments. "This
country no longer will stand for the destruction of food or the
restriction of its production while people are hungry and un-
dernourished," James Patton told Anderson. The secretary pro
ceeded to emasculate the liberal-oriented Bureau of Agricultural Economics, an agency with close ties to the Farmers
Union. He displayed little interest in a bill to establish the
Farm Security Administration on a permanent basis and in December 1945 appointed a Georgia conservative to head the
FSA. Patton called the nomination "a bitter betrayal of millions of small farmers." Subsequently, Anderson recommended
an increase in the interest rates on FSA loans. In March 1946

---

*Observing that Truman was "the first president since Ulysses S. Grant to
work part of his adult life as a farmer," Allen F. Matusow seems a bit puzzled
by his lack of interest in farm problems. Matusow, *Farm Policies and Politics in
the Truman Years*, (Cambridge, Mass., 1967), p. 1. Actually, Truman's early life
as well as that of his speculator father consisted of one effort after another to
escape from the farm. John Truman did not return to the land until his financial ventures failed, and Harry was investing in zinc mines and oil fields even
during the prosperous years of 1916 and 1917. For the Trumans the farm was a
symbol of failure; their idea of success was business or financial achievement.
For HST's lack of interest in agriculture as a senator, see Paul Appleby, Oral
History Memoir, pp. 357–59, COHC.

†Anderson's own account of his tenure as secretary of agriculture makes it
clear that the liberal diagnosis of his objectives was substantially accurate. Anderson, *Outsider in the Senate* (New York, 1970), ch. 3.

his liberal undersecretary, John B. Hutson, resigned; no conflict with Anderson was involved, but Hutson's departure cut another tie between the liberals and the Department of Agriculture.

On May 2, 1946, Patton wrote a long, angry letter to Truman demanding Anderson's ouster from the Cabinet. The president bluntly refused: "I think he is as able a Secretary of Agriculture as the Country has ever had and I intend to keep him." At midyear, the Farmers Union expressed its frustration by virtually closing down its Washington office. The NFU, Patton said, had lost confidence in Truman, although it had not made a complete "break" with the administration.[49]

The greatest shock to liberals, however, grew out of the railroad strike of 1946. The relationship between Truman and labor had become increasingly strained after the president's call for fact-finding and cooling-off legislation in December. If the unions had recoiled at Truman's legislative proposals, the president had come to blame labor for the strikes which were wrecking the reconversion program. Both he and Secretary of Labor Schwellenbach believed, for example, that Walter Reuther had prolonged the General Motors strike in order to advance his ambition to be president of the United Auto Workers. The unions, Truman privately told Henry Wallace, had become grown-ups with legal recognition and needed to assume the responsibility which went with their status.[50]

In May 1946, when two railway unions went ahead with strike plans despite a government seizure of the railroads, an angry, frustrated president was driven to the breaking point. The strike meant rejection of a compromise accepted by 18 other railway brotherhoods, threatened to wreck the American economy, imperiled relief shipments to Europe, and openly defied federal authority. The president's reaction was one of sheer rage.

Truman drafted an incredible speech calling for "Volunteers to support the Constitution," condemning "effete union leaders" and their followers, who received "from four to forty times the pay of a fighting soldier," and throwing out accusations of

Communism and lack of patriotism at the labor movement. "Come along with me and eliminate the Lewises, the Whitneys, the Johnsons, the Communist Bridges and the Russian Senators and Representatives and really make this a government of by and for the people." It is hardly conceivable that Truman even in his most furious moments actually planned to deliver such an address. The hand-written pages that he dashed off probably represented a release of long-accumulated frustrations. There can be little doubt, however, that the document represented Truman's deepest feelings, and it showed a degree of estrangement from the labor movement which was deeper than anyone had suspected.[51]

Truman instructed Charley Ross and his able young political adviser, Clark Clifford, to redraft the speech, almost certainly expecting them to soften it. Even so, the president's words and actions were explosive. On May 24, he condemned the strike in a radio address, warning that it could lead to economic disaster at home and mass starvation abroad. On May 25, he went before Congress and requested power to draft the strikers into the army.[52] The president's antistrike legislation contained some safeguards, but it horrified most liberals. A few who were especially unsympathetic toward labor endorsed the bill, but the vast majority considered it a species of fascism.

The proposal was similar, said Max Lerner, to "what happened when Hitler came into power and drafted workers into the labor battalions of the party." "In his angry determination to get the trains running on time again," wrote Helen Fuller, "Truman made the mistake of taking a leaf from the book of another man who made railroad history, Benito Mussolini." "The bill, for the first time in American history, proposes to use guns to coerce free citizens to work," said James Patton. Harold Ickes, speaking for the ICCASP, called the Truman proposal "the heaviest blow ever struck in America against the fundamental rights of labor and the democratic traditions of our country" and added that Truman had "opened the door for the striking down of much social legislation enacted under President Roosevelt." Sidney Hillman made his first public attack upon Truman. Eleanor Roosevelt came out against the scheme and privately warned the president against military advisers. The overwhelming majority of the liberal movement clearly agreed with the *Nation's* characterization of Truman as a "weak, baffled, angry man." [53]

For a brief period it appeared that Truman had almost completely lost the support of liberals and the labor movement. A. F. Whitney, head of the Brotherhood of Railway Trainmen and one of the union leaders Truman had attacked, threatened to spend the Brotherhood's entire treasury to defeat the president. The consensus among labor and liberal leaders, Helen Fuller reported, was that Truman had "killed any chance of his being elected President in 1948." In New York the American Labor Party told Truman it would not support him in 1948, while Liberal Party leader David Dubinsky called for the formation of a labor-based third party. [54]

The final test of Truman's estrangement from the liberals would be his decision on the Case bill, a piece of permanent antiunion legislation making its way through Congress. On June 11, Truman sent the Case bill back to Congress with a strong veto message, and the *Nation* admitted that, "Mr. Truman rather ably reconciles his desire for emergency anti-strike powers with his opposition to permanent legislation designed solely to weaken labor." The president had not regained the enthusiasm of labor and liberals and he remained privately bitter toward the union leaders, but he had at least avoided a complete break. [55]

His relations with the labor movement remained shaky. He was privately contemptuous of the CIOPAC's political know-how and clout and would not even give Jack Kroll, its new director after the death of Sidney Hillman, a 15-minute appointment. The PAC did little to improve the situation by interfering in one of Truman's pet projects, the "purge" of a right-wing Democratic congressman, Roger Slaughter, who represented the president's home district. As Truman heard it, the PAC had offered Enos Axtell, the candidate of the remnants of the Pendergast machine and the White House, $15,000 to withdraw in favor of a labor candidate. After Axtell won the primary, the Kansas City CIOPAC sent Truman a telegram which rather brashly claimed partial credit for the victory. The president authorized a cordial reply, signed by correspondence secretary William Hassett, but penciled in his personal feelings at the bottom of the telegram: "Made no contribution whatever." [56]

Two weeks after the Case veto, Truman took up a cause which promised for a time to regain every ounce of prestige he had lost among the liberals, the continuance of a strong OPA. For months, a bill to extend the agency's life had dragged through Congress with crippling amendments being attached at almost every turn. Progressives, who almost universally saw the OPA as the major barrier against ruinous inflation and eventual depression, had criticized the lukewarm attitude of John Snyder and had demanded stronger presidential leadership. As the bill became a clear sham, they desperately called for a veto.[57]

On June 28, the OPA bill passed the Senate, and Chester Bowles abruptly resigned, apparently believing that Congress would be more amenable if he left the government. Truman accepted the resignation with "deep regret" and pledged to carry on the battle against inflation. The next day the president released a strong veto message.

I wish it were possible to tell you exactly how many billions of dollars the American people would eventually have to pay. . . . To attempt to do so, however, would be like trying to estimate the cost of a fire about to sweep a city before the first building had started to burn.

That night he made a strong radio appeal for public support. He had called a spade a spade, he said. He was fighting "shortsightedness and impatience, . . . partisanship and greed." He was working for "an era of the greatest opportunity and prosperity in our history." [58]

To elated liberals Truman had become a hero. "Every American family should be grateful to the President for his courageous action," commented Fiorello La Guardia. Tris Coffin, one of Truman's strongest liberal critics, compared the radio speech to "the fighting talks of Franklin Roosevelt." Truman's bold and decisive action had defined the major issue of the November elections, said the *New Republic*. "The President's action breathes new life into the campaign and perhaps will save him and the whole liberal movement from a major political disaster." But after three weeks without controls Truman signed a second bill which was only somewhat less objectionable than the first one. Some liberals, such as La Guardia, had wanted another veto; others reluctantly admitted that the legislation was the best Truman could get and might be of some value. In any event, a once clear-cut issue was now blurred, strong price controls were a thing of the past, and Truman's aggressive veto was soon forgotten.[59]

While Truman was waiting for the second OPA bill, he shocked liberals by endorsing Burton K. Wheeler in the Montana Senatorial primary. For the president, it was an act dictated by loyalty to an old friend. In the 1930s Wheeler had treated the junior senator from Missouri with generosity, had been a teacher of sorts to him, and had given him his first major responsibility, the railroad investigation. Their viewpoints were now far apart, but Truman felt compelled to stand by Wheeler. To progressives, who hated Wheeler with the vehemence reserved for one who deserts a cause, Truman's endorsement of the increasingly conservative Montana isolationist was yet another indication that the president placed friendship above the public interest and, as *PM* writer Saul Padover commented, had not "measured up to the size required for the job of Chief Executive." [60]

Even the successful purge of Slaughter failed to enhance Truman's reputation among the liberals. Agreeing with the objective, most progressives were unhappy with the means. Enos Axtell was so obscure and lackluster that the president could not recall his first name when asked for it at a press conference; the CIO choice, by contrast, was a reliable liberal. Axtell's subsequent nomination seemed at best a draw to the *Na-*

tion. It began to appear somewhat less when an investigation revealed that Axtell had been the beneficiary of large-scale voting irregularities.[61]

In June 1946 the president designated Secretary of the Treasury Vinson chief justice of the United States, named John Snyder as Vinson's successor at the Treasury, and nominated former Republican Senator Warren Austin U.S. ambassador to the United Nations. "All these appointments lack brilliance and imagination—as do the appointees—and tend to stress the increasingly sober conservative complexion of the Truman administration," wrote Thomas L. Stokes. Commenting on Snyder, the *New Republic* was even blunter: "It is cruel to plunge a man of this caliber into the duties of Secretary of the Treasury." Nor was there much satisfaction with the men Truman finally named to the Council of Economic Advisers. Only Washington lawyer Leon Keyserling was noted as a solid liberal. John D. Clark, a businessman who had been dean of the University of Nebraska's business school, and Council Chairman Edwin Nourse, a former vice-president of the Brookings Institution, seemed to be, if not outright conservatives, at least unexciting moderates. All in all, the summer appointees left most liberals inclined to agree with Helen Fuller's judgment that Truman was "a man who is afraid of his job, and therefore is also afraid of the kind of man it takes to do the job." [62]

Liberals even found themselves looking not to Truman, but to Hannegan—Boss Bob Hannegan!—for communication. It was Hannegan who seemed most interested in preserving the Democratic Party's ties with Sidney Hillman and the CIOPAC, Beanie Baldwin and the NCPAC. By early 1946, Hannegan had assembled an informal brain trust of aggressive young liberals, including Leon Henderson, Paul A. Porter, Robert Nathan, Wilson Wyatt, Ed Pritchard, Josiah DuBois, Jr., and Gael Sullivan. The group advised on reconversion policy, and, for a time there was hope that it might have strong influence upon the president. Sullivan, the "generalissimo" of the group, was a protégé of Chicago boss Ed Kelly, an advocate of "bread and butter liberalism," and Hannegan's close lieutenant. He and his chief seemed more aware than were Truman or most members of the administration where the power base of the party lay.[63]

Truman's own outlook was even more contradictory than his policies and reflected the sharply contrasting forces which had shaped his political career. He had been born and raised among Southern Democrats, had gone into politics as a member of an urban machine, and had adopted New Deal liberalism when he moved from Jackson County to the U.S. Senate. "As he had developed," Richard Kirkendall has observed, "he had not switched from one type of Democrat to another; he had added one to another, layer by layer, as he moved along." [64] Moreover, he still had much of the outlook of the small businessman. His efforts as a senator to secure war contracts for small entrepreneurs, his long and close friendship with John Snyder, his admiration for Ed Pauley, his increasing irritation with the labor movement were among the indications that he was still the man who in earlier years had committed his resources to zinc mining, oil drilling, the haberdashery, and banking.

In addition, as a member of the Senate for ten years, he had developed a sensitivity to what that body considered its prerogatives. As a senator who on occasion had felt pushed around by the White House, he could not avoid sympathy with congressmen who resented executive pressures. And on a more practical level, he must have felt that the sort of bitterness which had developed between Congress and the White House during the last years of the Roosevelt era was self-defeating. Many of his early appointments represented an attempt to conciliate Congress—Clinton Anderson, the popular representative from New Mexico, Tom Clark, who "was strongly endorsed by the whole Texas delegation," Lew Schwellenbach, the former senator from Washington, George Allen, the lobbyist with friends on the Hill, Fred Vinson, the widely respected former Kentucky congressman, James F. Byrnes, the former South Carolina senator.[65]

A professional politician, Truman had a temperamental aversion to "intellectual" or "nonpolitical" liberals. Shortly after Clark Clifford began to work closely with him, he told Clifford that most of the people who had been close to Roosevelt were "crackpots and the lunatic fringe," expressed an intention to "keep my feet on the ground" and asserted: "I don't want any experiments; the American people have been through a lot of experiments and they want a rest from experiments." As late as the end of 1948, Clifford was convinced that Truman disliked the words "liberal" and "progressive," preferring instead the less ideological and more ambiguous term, "forward-looking." [66]

Yet such attitudes were not necessarily incompatible with the programs Truman offered in 1945 and 1946. If for no other reason, his background as a businessman whose enterprise was wrecked in the boom-and-bust economy which followed World War I would have inclined him toward the liberal ideas on reconversion. There are firm reasons to believe that he sincerely wanted a measure as drastic as universal health insurance; certainly, there was little political capital in his endorsement of the proposal.[67] In his own way, the president probably saw himself as a legatee of the New Deal, and despite Clark Clifford's memory, he doubtless considered himself a liberal of sorts. "There should be a real liberal party in this country and I don't mean a crackpot professional one," he wrote in his diary in September 1945. "The opponents to liberalism and progress should join together in the party of the opposition." These private jottings were not the words of a man who wanted to put an end to reform; as much as anything they probably represented the feelings of a man alienated from the *style* of American liberalism.[68]

If Truman's impulses were confused and contradictory, the liberal critique of the president was often ill-considered and shallow. The progressives were on solid ground when they attacked some of the men around Truman, but there was more to their viewpoint than attacks upon questionable appointments or a few bad legislative recommendations. The liberals proceeded from a theory of presidential leadership which was naïve, even adolescent, in its content and expression.

In essence, the liberals believed that an eloquent, fighting president could force Congress to action, if necessary by arousing public opinion. Truman had to demonstrate "a willingness to slug it out with the opposition," said the *Progressive* in October 1945. He had to "continue to lay down the law to Congress," Richard L. Neuberger told Charley Ross at the beginning of 1946. The very phraseology demonstrated the frustrated simplicity of this viewpoint. Few, if any, of his critics, had they paused to consider their position, could really have believed that a president could dictate to Congress and run the government in the manner of a Dutch uncle; yet such was the essence of their argument.[69]

Equally unrealistic was the assumption that there existed across the nation a public opinion waiting to be roused so that it might force an unregenerate Congress to act. Essentially, the liberals believed that "the people"—the ordinary people at any rate—would heed rational, persuasive arguments and would force their representatives to do so. Given the right leadership, the people could become disinterested arbiters of the public interest. Such a viewpoint was remarkably unrealistic. It ignored the ways in which the complexities of the representative system and the very organization of Congress itself allowed "veto groups" to block the will of even a numerical majority. It wildly overestimated both the political attention span of the ordinary person and his capacity to transcend his own interests. The liberal assumptions, for all the veneer of sophistication and tough-mindedness which American reform had acquired since the early twentieth century, were remarkably similar to those of progressive reformers who had believed the direct primary, the initiative, and the referendum to be the indispensable prerequisites to the remedy of any and all social problems. When Truman's radio addresses failed to bring results, the liberals refused to reexamine their fundamental beliefs. Truman, stumbling and inept as a public speaker, *had* to be at fault.

"The country needs to be electrified, not bored," wrote I. F. Stone.[70]

The assumption that a strong, eloquent president could achieve their objectives revealed also the almost pathetic dependence of the liberals upon FDR. "President Roosevelt encountered blockades in Congress," wrote Thomas L. Stokes, "but, once he took his case to the people and once they had spoken at the polls, he would hammer more and more of his program through Congress." Stokes's history was at best only partially accurate, but the comment summed up the great faith liberals had placed in Roosevelt, their dependence upon him to break down all barriers. Much of the liberal feeling about Truman stemmed from the president's personality and style, from his inability to assume Roosevelt's image of omnipotence and provide personal inspiration. In a candid moment, Max Lerner admitted that Truman's appointments probably were no worse than FDR's, that Truman's policies probably were about the same that FDR would have pursued. "What one misses in it is the confident sense of direction that Roosevelt gave, despite all the contradictions of his policy." [71]

A few liberals still defended the president. In December 1945, the Philadelphia *Record* asserted that Truman had become a "scapegoat" for the failures of Congress, that it was "a kind of national game" to criticize him simply because he did not possess Roosevelt's extraordinary qualities. In the summer of 1946, however, as the Seventy-ninth Congress was destroying price controls despite the president's ineffective opposition and as Truman was endorsing Burton Wheeler, most liberals were ready to agree with Robert Kenny, who had just been defeated in the California gubernatorial primary. When reporters asked if Truman would "take care" of him with a federal appointment, Kenny replied that he no longer considered himself a Truman supporter and added: "I'm not the one who needs taking care of. If anybody needs taking care of, it's the administration." [72]

Chapter 4

Truman, the Liberals, and the Origins of the Cold War

The liberal hopes for the postwar world rested upon a continuation of the antifascist alliance, which in turn would allow the victorious Allies, especially the United States, to concentrate upon constructive programs for international democratization and economic development. In 1945 and 1946, these hopes steadily disintegrated. Failing to maintain the alliance, unable to offer vision and leadership, stumbling from one diplomatic problem to another, Truman increasingly appeared to be a little man who lacked the qualities of his predecessor, who was forsaking the objectives for which the war had been fought and might even be leading the nation toward disaster.

I

Truman's initial acts encouraged the progressives. He promptly announced that the San Francisco conference to draw up the United Nations Charter would begin, as originally scheduled, at the end of April, and he persuaded Stalin to send Foreign Minister Molotov to the meeting. He declared his support of the Bretton-Woods proposals for international monetary stabilization and economic development, reaffirmed his backing of reciprocal trade, and signed legislation extending Lend-Lease.

However, liberals also had their misgivings. Not familiar with the high-level wartime meetings and decisions, Truman would have to rely heavily upon Secretary of State Edward R. Stettinius, whom progressives generally considered a weak and conservative figure, dependent upon the reactionaries who dominated the State Department. Above all, the president's policy toward Russia was uncertain.[1]

The San Francisco conference developed into a discouraging brawl between the USSR and the United States. The Russians were stubborn on some issues, such as the future of Poland, but they appeared to have a good case on many contested matters. It was the Soviet Union which led the opposition to admitting Argentina's fascist-type government to the United Nations, attempted to put the "right to work" and the "right to an education" into the charter, attacked imperialism, and advocated guarantees of independence for colonial peoples. Thomas Stokes observed that the United States was apparently turning away from the hopes which first Woodrow Wilson and then Franklin Roosevelt had aroused in the common peoples of the world, and, paradoxically, the authoritarian Russians were moving to assume the moral leadership of the world. Such developments appeared to stem from a lack of presidential leadership. Roosevelt, most liberals believed, had kept firm control of foreign policy and had never lost sight of the fundamental objective of Big Three unity. "With his death, this keen sense of direction seems to have departed from our diplomacy," wrote Samuel Grafton, "there is a kind of slackness; matters which used to be delicately but firmly negotiated, are now thrown out as free-for-alls."

It appeared that Republican Senator Arthur H. Vandenberg was the strong man of the American delegation at San Francisco, and, as he filled the vacuum left by FDR's death, he seemed bent on wrecking Soviet-American relations. With the atmosphere worsening, Truman sent Harry Hopkins to confer with Stalin, and after a dramatic meeting the break was at least temporarily healed; but serious doubts now existed about the new administration.[2]

The progressives cheered the conference's success in drafting a charter for a new United Nations organization. Most, it is true, would have preferred a U.N. which came closer to a genuine world government, which made stronger and surer provisions for collective security, and which gave less authority to the great powers. Nevertheless, the new body could focus the moral sentiment of the globe upon an international transgressor; its establishment was a giant step toward the creation of the world order for which American liberalism hoped. Conceding the U.N.'s limitations, Freda Kirchwey wrote that all the same it was "the best possible expression of the present level of world opinion" and warned that those who attacked its imperfections were in reality working for the only alternative, "a return to unrestrained international anarchy." The St. Louis *Post-Dispatch* called the U.N. "our greatest stake in security for the future," and the Chicago *Sun* ranked the charter "among the greatest documents of all history." [3]

At the end of the San Francisco conference, Truman appointed James F. Byrnes secretary of state. A Southern moderate respected as an administrator and negotiator, Byrnes seemed to be an improvement over Stettinius, but progressives doubted that he had the imagination and vision to grasp the social and political revolutions which were sweeping the globe. Nevertheless, he chose as his undersecretary Dean Acheson— "the man around whom progressives in the Department have rallied," commented T.R.B.—picked the prominent New Dealer Benjamin V. Cohen as department Counselor, and put Latin American affairs under the staunch antifascist Spruille Braden. Other changes were less exciting, and the liberal confidence in Byrnes remained strictly limited. Progressives agreed, however, that the new foreign policy team was actually stronger and more progressive than that which had operated under Roosevelt.[4]

For a brief time in the summer of 1945, the apprehensions of April and May faded, and liberal foreign policy aspirations seemed well on their way to fulfillment. The success of the San Francisco conference, the reorganization of the State Department, the amicable, if inconclusive, Big Three meeting at Potsdam, the overwhelming Senate approval of the United Nations Charter, the ratification of the Bretton-Woods agreements—all gave hope for the future. However, as the postwar world became a reality, the progressives received one jolt after another.

No issue penetrated to the core of the liberal conscience more deeply than America's unwillingness to give adequate food supplies to the famine-stricken areas of the world. "The amounts Truman reports we are planning to send to Europe are the merest trifle in terms of our resources," wrote Helen Fuller as the fall of 1945 began. Inside the administration, Chester Bowles urged increased food shipments. However, the U.S. appropriation for the United Nations Relief and Rehabilitation Administration lingered in Congress. Moreover, the president told a delegation which met with him to ask for a greater effort that some of the Europeans were waiting like birds to be fed. The *New Republic* replied that the appropriations delay was "condemning thousands of men, women and children to death every day it continues." Truman endorsed the appropriation, but his declaration seemed inadequate. "Here is a question of the President's leadership in Congress." wrote Marquis Childs at the end of October. "Words are not enough, no matter how earnest and sincere the words are." [5]

Even after the bill went through, the United States was unable to meet its food commitments to UNRRA, and the organization's director, Herbert Lehman, resigned in frustration. Most progressives favored a resumption of meat rationing, a step which would halt the diversion of grain to livestock feeding. Administration measures—voluntary food conservation, the designation of Herbert Hoover to head a Famine Emergency Committee, and assurances that the worst was over, or at least nearly over—stung liberals to a mood of fury bordering on despair. A. Powell Davies, the prominent churchman, scathingly commented that Secretary of Agriculture Anderson was "able, it seems, to be buoyant, high-spirited and optimistic in all circumstances, even in the face of a record of incompetence that it would be hard to equal in United States

history." Oddly enough, Davies added sarcastically, all
Anderson's mistakes seemed to have the side-effect of favoring
the food processors and the larger agricultural interests.

Progressives generally believed that the American public
would have responded to the threat of mass starvation if there
had been leadership from the White House. The country, said
T.R.B., was "listening for a clarion call, but maybe the man
who could give it is dead." "Mr. President, it's definitely up to
you," commented the *Nation*. "You have recently promised to
stand in the tradition of Franklin Roosevelt. . . . In this crisis
we know what line he would have taken."

By mid-1946, the desperate food situation was easing, largely
because of the energetic, if belated, efforts of Secretary Anderson. Yet Anderson, who had been justly castigated for initial
policy blunders, now received little praise. "What the liberals
and their allies really wanted," Allen F. Matusow has perceptively commented, "was a man to lead a moral crusade against
hunger, to raise an earnest and eloquent voice on behalf of national sacrifice." Neither Anderson nor Truman was capable of
assuming such a role; consequently, their eventual success in
coping with the food shortage made little impact upon the progressive mind.[6]

II

The war was hardly over before the United States appeared to
abandon one of the fundamental objectives for which it had
been fought. The liberals had hoped that the war would spell
the end for imperialism and reactionary government; instead,
America seemed to align itself with these forces. The Dutch in
Java and the French in Indochina used American weapons
against nationalist insurgents; the State Department simply requested that U.S. identification be removed from the arms.
The United States did exert pressure for negotiated settlement
of the Asian uprisings, but all the same its role, Morris Rubin
commented, had been similar to that of a murderer concealing
his fingerprints.[7]

Equivocation over the plight of the displaced European Jews seemed even more serious. Most liberals, feeling a close sense of identification with a people who had suffered so terribly from fascist persecution, adopted the cause of Jewish immigration to Palestine as their own and considered it a matter of elementary justice.

Truman's first moves in this area won praise. In August 1945, he called for the admission of as many Jews as possible to Palestine. At the end of September, he sent a strong public letter to General Eisenhower demanding an end to the practice of billeting Jewish refugees in former concentration camps, ordering the requisition of German homes if necessary. In mid-October, he told a press conference he was urging the British government to allow 100,000 Jews to enter Palestine. But praise turned to criticism when the president announced in November 1945 that he had agreed to a British proposal for an Anglo-American Committee of Inquiry which would study the problem. Most liberals agreed with Freda Kirchwey that the president had "walked into a trap" designed to delay action, and there was general disappointment with the Americans he named to the committee.

In late April 1946, the Anglo-American Committee issued a report advocating the immediate admission of 100,000 Jews to Palestine, but the British government now declined to follow its recommendations. Bartley Crum, the most liberal and pro-Zionist member of the committee, expressed the view of a majority of progressives when he charged that the British were concerned only with protecting their Middle Eastern oil interests and were appeasing pro-fascist Arabs. Moreover, he asserted, Truman's sincere pronouncements in favor of the Jewish cause were being sabotaged by antisemitic middle-level State Department officials who also placed oil above humanitarianism. The White House continued to advocate large-scale Jewish settlement in Palestine, but displaced Jews remained stranded and homeless.[8]

If the Palestine situation appeared to many progressives to indicate a lack of concern for the victims of fascism, American policy in Europe often seemed to encourage the remnants of fascism. In Germany the American military government, instead of seeking out and extending recognition to democratic elements, worked with people and groups once close to the Nazis. By contrast, the Soviet Union's actions in the months after V-E Day seemed liberal and enlightened. The Russians announced—and appeared to be putting into effect—a policy of restoring all antifascist political parties and trade unions. "It would not be surprising if sooner or later the German people in the Western zones of occupation came to regard Russia as the real guarantor of their freedom, political and economic," commented the *New Republic*. Even the strongly anti-Communist *Progressive* called the Anglo-American policies "disappointing" and asserted that the USSR was "reaping a harvest of good-will and support." [9]

The United States refused to push for any action against the Spanish fascist government stronger than a refusal to maintain diplomatic relations at the ambassadorial level. The toleration of the Franco government, even at arm's length, repelled most liberals. The Nation Associates took the unique step of submitting a memorandum condemning the Spanish rulers to both the White House and the United Nations. Signed by nine liberal groups ranging from the UDA to the ICCASP, the document impressively demonstrated a deeply felt progressive consensus. Most liberals attributed the American inaction to State Department fears that a reconstituted Loyalist government would have Communist representation. Perhaps so, admitted the *New Republic,* but a Loyalist government also would work for "agrarian reform, the right of men to learn to read and write, separation of Church and State, nationalization of heavy industry." Was fascism preferable to such a program? [10]

American tolerance of imperialism and of reactionary elements not only appeared to betray the cause for which the war had been fought; in some instances it seemed to endanger the antifascist alliance itself and propel the United States toward a confrontation with Communism. As full-scale civil war developed in Greece, the United States supported the right. Many progressives criticized Communist aid to the guerrilla insurgents,* but all were more disturbed by American-British backing of the monarchist-fascist groups, whose eventual defeat seemed both desirable and certain. In the fall of 1946, an obviously fraudulent plebiscite produced a vote for the return of King George. The St. Louis *Post-Dispatch*, although it had become sharply critical of Soviet expansionism, commented that the United States by propping up British imperialism was supporting "doubtful friends and certain enemies of democracy, virtually inviting from the right the tyranny we hope to prevent from the left." When there was an announcement that planes from the new aircraft carrier *Franklin D. Roosevelt* would celebrate the King's return by skywriting the letters FDR over Greece, Roosevelt's former press secretary, Jonathan Daniels, called the plan "the first forgery by air power." [11]

Soviet forces which had occupied northern Iran during World War II now refused to withdraw and aided a secessionist movement. However, British forces, stationed in southern Iran, provided encouragement for a feudalistic government. Most liberals, consequently, found it impossible to feel any special moral indignation against the Soviet Union. The situation seemed to be just another episode in the long history of conflict between Russian and British imperialisms. To some, the Soviet brand of imperialism seemed desirable. "Russia has encouraged the variously named left party, in and out of its sector, and has offered the people hope of reform and a decent life," commented Freda Kirchwey.

Others were not so certain. "No one seems to be considering with much concern . . . the pitiful lot of the people of Iran," asserted the St. Louis *Post-Dispatch*. About all agreed that the only solution to the problem involved Big Three negotiations,

*Most Americans, including the liberals, assumed that the Soviet Union was masterminding the Greek insurgency. Actually, the USSR apparently had little interest in the Greek guerrillas and felt that their slim hopes of victory did not justify a substantial military investment. Such aid as the Greek rebels received came from Balkan Communist nations which exacted promises of Greek territorial concessions in return. Richard J. Barnet, *Intervention and Revolution* (New York, 1968), ch. 6.

supplemented perhaps by a U.N. investigation, the eventual withdrawal of all foreign troops, and the establishment of some sort of a plan for internal development and democratization. Far from being exercised about Soviet aggression, a majority of progressives appeared to believe that all sides to the Iranian dispute enjoyed a degree of legitimacy, that a solution which would be equitable for all was possible and desirable, and that the preservation of Big Three unity remained paramount.[12]

In China, full-scale civil war resumed between the Kuomintang government of Chiang Kai-shek and the Communists. American forces gave logistical support to Chiang's reactionary and corrupt regime, and American Ambassador Patrick J. Hurley made no effort to conceal his sympathy with the Nationalists. Most progressives were outraged, and the *Nation* expressed a common sentiment in an editorial entitled "Get Our Troops Out of China." Charging that, even during the war, Chiang had been friendlier toward the Japanese enemy than toward the Communist ally, the young radio commentator Eric Sevareid observed: "the United States government has taken sides, supporting the side which controls by far the greater territory and population, against the side which, by the overwhelming testimony of visitors there, has by far the more democratic regime."

Near the end of 1945, the situation seemed to improve. Ambassador Hurley resigned, vaguely attacking Communist influence in the State Department, and Truman named the respected General George Marshall as a special envoy who would try to settle the Chinese conflict. In an important statement on December 15, the president defined American policy. The United States would continue to recognize the Kuomintang government but would not intervene in the civil war. Marshall would work for a cease-fire, a national conference of all political parties, and a broadly based coalition government. Large-scale economic aid to China would be conditional upon the achievement of these objectives. The new policy seemed to be an enlightened reversal.[13]

During the early months of 1946, it appeared that General

Marshall's efforts might be successful, but by spring the negotiations were collapsing. As the arrangements for a coalition
government fell apart, most liberals were convinced that, as
Elmer Davis put it, "the responsibility lies chiefly on reactionary elements in the Kuomintang." And, as the Kuomintang
began to resume the civil war with American military supplies
which had been intended for the coalition government army,
progressives were increasingly convinced that total withdrawal
from China was the best policy.

Some, failing to grasp the nature of Chinese Communism,
were perfectly willing to accept a Red victory. The Chinese
Communists, Irving Brant wrote, were no more communistic
"than the farmers of Minnesota and North Dakota." The respected old liberal Congressman Adolph Sabath told Truman
that the Red uprising appeared to be "a genuinely spontaneous
and democratic movement of the agrarian, peasant, and submerged urban classes to rescue themselves from their hopeless
economic condition." He added: "There is competent testimony, as you know, that the term 'Communist' as applied to the
Armies of North China is a misnomer." Colonel Evans Carlson,
the former Marine hero and West Coast left-wing leader, declared that only an end to American aid could force the Kuomintang reactionaries "to form a bona fide coalition government,
which alone can assure peace and establishment of democratic
reforms." Even many who had more doubts about the Communists agreed, hoping for a coalition government in which a
third force, the genuinely liberal elements inside and outside
the Kuomintang, would hold the balance of power.

Others, not yet willing to abandon Chiang, nevertheless condemned his corrupt military dictatorship and argued that the
United States had a duty to force him to clean up his regime,
"Isn't it our right as well as our obligation to insist upon fundamental reforms in the Nationalist Government?" asked the
St. Louis *Post-Dispatch*. The hopes of all went unfulfilled; consequently, almost all progressives could agree that Truman's
China policy was a failure. When on December 18, 1946 the
president issued a statement asserting that the United States

would continue to work for a peaceful, democratic solution to China's problems the *Nation* dismissed the declaration as "a long-winded defense of American policy." [14]

The China situation illustrated a fundamental irony of the relationship between Truman and the liberals. In this instance at least, the administration proceeded from about the same assumptions as many liberals and worked for virtually identical objectives, failing simply because the assumptions and objectives were unrealistic. Both the progressives and the administration wanted a genuinely democratic government with all parties represented and with Chinese liberals holding the balance of power; the objective was admirable but virtually foredoomed. Both the progressives and the administration shared the untenable assumption that perhaps with a little pressure Chinese politics could be subjected to the American process of compromise and conciliation; they had little understanding of the violent traditions and the harsh polarization of forces which Marshall would face. The liberal image of Chinese Communism (which incidentally was also held by many conservatives) was naïve and inaccurate, as was the belief that Chiang would give in with some prodding.

The point is not that the administration and the progressives overlooked some more promising alternative. China presented no promising alternatives. What is remarkable is the liberal optimism, the conviction that a rational solution was possible in China, and the indictment of an administration which shared this optimism and tried to achieve a liberal solution. The failure of the Marshall mission was, among other things, a failure of liberalism; yet few liberals realized this. It was much easier to assume that only a failure of technique was involved, that a tougher policy toward Chiang would have compelled a solution. On the China issue, at least, the administration became a scapegoat for the inadequacy of the progressivism it had attempted to practice. [15]

The most serious of all diplomatic problems in the last half of 1945 was the growing tension between the West and the Soviet Union. Big Three unity was the indispensable cornerstone of an effective United Nations and a constructive peace; the collapse of that unity could only bring the antithesis of the world for which the liberals had hoped. The essential difficulty was Soviet consolidation of power in Eastern Europe. Few liberals defended Soviet actions without reservation; most conceded that the Russians often behaved clumsily. However, most also felt that the extension of Soviet influence into Eastern Europe was motivated by a legitimate desire for security. They tended to view the Soviet Union much as if it were an individual who had been gravely injured by an assailant and was attempting to build a fence around his home to safeguard against his attacker's return.

Moreover, Russian power in Eastern Europe did not yet seem absolute, even if it was heavy-handed. The experience of the war provided a basis for the belief that the Soviet Union would tolerate nonhostile and antifascist democratic groups. In the fall of 1945, the Hungarians elected a non-Communist government. Subsequently, the Bulgarian voting was postponed in response to protests against Russian manipulation. So long as the Eastern European nations retained a measure of independence, a majority of the liberals could accept Soviet influence in the area.[16]

Many were convinced that another key problem of Soviet-American relations was the unilateral U.S. control of the new atomic bomb. By giving the United States overwhelming military power, the bomb, they felt, had provoked the Soviet Union to a defensive aggressiveness. Virtually all liberals, whether or not they agreed entirely with this thesis, believed that the destructive new force of atomic energy must be controlled by some sort of international authority. While plans were being developed, American-British atomic knowledge might be shared with Russia, up to and including the bomb itself. The basic scientific knowledge which had gone into the bomb was no secret, and the USSR could develop its own atomic weapons in a few years. It would be far better to improve the international climate and prevent a nuclear arms race by voluntarily letting the Russians in on Western techniques.

Within the administration, the matter received vigorous discussion at a Cabinet meeting on September 21, 1945. Outgoing Secretary of War Henry L. Stimson proposed that the U.S. offer Russia full partnership in atomic development and immediately share some, although not all, atomic knowledge with her. Several of those present backed Stimson, the strongest support coming from Henry Wallace. On October 8, however, Truman flatly stated that the United States would not give information on the bomb to other powers.

Many progressives dissented. "I cannot say that I am too happy about the way the atom bomb is being handled," Harry Hopkins told Eleanor Roosevelt in November. "In fact, I think we are doing almost everything we can to break with Russia which seems so unnecessary to me." "That Russia should be given full information about the atomic bomb is so evident that the question no longer seems arguable," wrote Freda Kirchwey at about the same time. Speaking to a forum on atomic energy sponsored by the Nation Associates in December, Walter Millis called the Truman statement a disastrous pronouncement that had led to a serious deterioration of East-West relations and suggested a "pooling" of Russian and American military secrets. There were, to be sure, liberals who had their doubts about giving atomic information to the Soviets, but even they were critical of the administration's failure to produce a plan for international control by the end of the year.[17]

Meanwhile, throughout the last half of 1945 Soviet-American relations moved farther away from cooperation. At the beginning of October, a meeting of the Big Three foreign ministers held in London broke up with no accomplishments and with angry recriminations. While conceding that the Russians had been truculent and belligerent, most liberals were critical of the "tough line" which the United States had taken. To many, the position of the U.S. was no more commendable than that of the Soviet Union. If the Russians wanted dominance in Eastern Europe, America expected dominance in Japan; if the Russians wanted overseas bases, so did America. "There is little moral difference—and none in our favor—between Russia's demand for control of Tripoli and the United States' assumption of control of Okinawa and Iwo Jima under the thinnest possible veneer of internationalism," commented the *New Republic*. It reminded its readers that the Soviet Union might understandably be worried by the exclusive U.S. possession of the atomic bomb, the still-large American military establishment, and the Pacific bases so close to the Asian mainland.[18]

At the same time, progressives were becoming increasingly concerned with the president's pronouncements. Truman urged universal peacetime military training, and even appeared before Congress to ask for its adoption. Most liberals believed that atomic weapons had made mass armies obsolete, that universal training could only teach militarism and regimentation at home, and that it would drastically worsen the international climate. Elmer Benson, speaking as chairman of the National Citizens Political Action Committee, called the proposal "an invitation to an arms race" and an indication that the United States had "embarked on a program of power politics." [19]

On October 27, 1945, just four days after he had called for universal training, Truman delivered a Navy Day address in New York after a massive display of U.S. sea power. Billed in advance as a major foreign policy declaration, the speech probably seemed balanced to the administration. The talk did contain a pledge to work through the United Nations, a strong plea for Big Three unity, and a declaration, obviously aimed at Russia, that the United States would seek to understand the interests of other nations, especially their desires for security. But most liberals felt these points were overshadowed by near-jingoistic passages celebrating U.S. power, proclaiming America's everlasting righteousness, and reiterating the refusal to share A-bomb secrets. The St. Louis *Post-Dispatch* called the speech a "dreary recital of pious platitudes," and observed that the president had given only passing mention to the U.N. instead of establishing it as the "very cornerstone" of American foreign policy. The address in fact created an impression of belligerence. "Are we planning war?" asked the *Nation*.[20]

On November 29, Truman told a press conference that he planned no more Big Three meetings, that none would be nec-

essary if the United Nations functioned as expected. The declaration struck many liberals as a repudiation of the concept of
Big Three cooperation. "One can imagine what a shock would
have swept this country if Russia had bluntly announced that
she was not interested in meeting with the United States and
Britain again," commented Samuel Grafton. Increasingly, Truman appeared to be under the influence of military leaders and
conservatives, drifting away from the wartime alliance toward
disaster.[21]

On December 4, a Madison Square Garden "crisis meeting"
held by the Independent Citizens Committee of the Arts, Sciences, and Professions expressed the disillusion which so many
liberals felt. The gathering adopted resolutions criticizing
American failure to move toward international control of
atomic energy, U.S. involvement in China, the use of American
weapons in Java and Indochina, and the refusal to move
against fascism in Spain, Greece, and Argentina.

We won the war against Fascism, but as victors we are falling into
the trap prepared by the vanquished; the unity of the United Nations is disappearing, heading toward the dangerous path of a
third world war. This is the period of crisis. This is the period of
decision. . . .

The present administration has shown, by a series of unmistaka
ble actions that it is departing from the tested and successful foreign
policy of the late President Roosevelt, based on the unity of the Big
Three. . . .

Henry Wallace, who as a featured speaker had made a strong
plea for international control of atomic energy, sat on the platform as a crowd of twenty thousand cheered the declaration.[22]

By the end of the year, however, it appeared that Big Three
unity had been restored. The United States had asked for another Big Three conference after all, and the foreign ministers,
meeting in Moscow, reached agreements on the principle of international control over atomic energy, on the occupation of
Japan, on the need for an end to the fighting in China and the
unification of that country, on peace conferences for Bulgaria,

Rumania, Finland, and Italy. Relieved liberals praised the accords. "We have returned to the machinery of international collaboration, and checked the fatal trend to divide the world into exclusive zones isolated from each other by the deadlock of the great powers," commented the New York *Post*.[23]

III

It soon became apparent, however, that the new amity was an illusion. In subsequent weeks the United States became increasingly resistant to Russian demands, and the USSR responded with rhetorical belligerence. On March 5, 1946, at Fulton, Missouri, Winston Churchill—still the representative of Tory imperialism to many liberals—delivered his famous "iron curtain" speech attacking Russian policy in Eastern Europe and virtually calling for an anti-Soviet alliance. President Truman sat on the platform in apparent approval.[24]

Churchill, declared a *Nation* editorial, had "talked like a man committed to war." Senators Claude Pepper, Glen Taylor, and Harley Kilgore issued a joint statement: "Mr. Churchill's proposal would cut the throat of the United Nations. It would destroy the unity of the Big Three, without which the war could not have been won and without which the peace cannot be saved." In the weeks after the Fulton speech a genuine war scare developed among liberals. "If somebody doesn't call a halt, the interests in this country who seem hell-bent on a war with Russia—and soon—will get their way," Thomas L. Stokes commented privately. "Lots of people seem to have gone completely mad." [25]

One of the most important indications of the new liberal fears was a meeting called the Win-the-Peace Conference which assembled in Washington in early April. The conference demonstrated the continuing appeal of the wartime alliance and the Popular Front. It was initiated by Jo Davidson, singer Paul Robeson, United Electrical Workers Secretary-Treasurer Julius Emspak, and the California liberal Bartley Crum. Davidson, Robeson, and Emspak were widely considered fellow travelers of Communism; Crum's independence, on the other hand, was beyond question. In all, there were some 250 sponsors, ranging from avowed Communists such as Benjamin Davis and Frederick Field to reputed fellow travelers such as Lee Pressman, Vito Marcantonio, and Hugh DeLacy to important independent liberals such as James G. Patton, Helen Gahagan Douglas, and Harley Kilgore. Many of the officers of the ICCASP and the NCPAC were on the list. The UDA, reacting against the Communist influence, remained aloof and tried to spike the meeting; however, it could persuade only four Congressmen to withdraw as sponsors. Among the featured speakers were Claude Pepper, the foremost Southern liberal, and the venerable Adolph Sabath, who subsequently told Congress: "Critics of the Win-the-Peace Conference stand self-convicted, if not of sympathy with the Nazi blight, then certainly of opposition to a just and permanent peace." [26]

The conference adopted a declaration which asserted that American foreign policy was in danger of being dominated by "the economic royalists, the old enemies of peace to whom Roosevelt gave battle more than once." "President Roosevelt, who led the Nation to victory in the anti-Fascist war, charted the road to just and enduring peace," asserted the document. "His policy of Big Three unity was and is the policy of the American people." The statement called for the destruction of the remnants of fascism, an end to colonialism, no interference with "the new democracies of Europe," withdrawal of American troops from "all friendly lands" in order that "the peoples of those lands may achieve democracy and unity," and cession of control over atomic energy to the U.N. Security Council, "which lives by the unity principle." "We call on the Americans whose hearts are turned to peace . . . to join with us in a common cause. Together we can and will prevent a third world war." The declaration's rather obvious pro-Communist, anti-British implications were to the left of the views of even many of the conference sponsors. However, the invocation of the memory of FDR, the calls for a renewal of Big Three unity, the militant antifascism, the fear of a new world conflict all

accurately reflected the sentiments of a large group of progressives, probably a majority.[27]

A rather large number of progressives were arriving at the
conclusion that United States foreign policy had become the
tool of British imperialism and American monopoly, of the
"Churchills and Hoovers," as Washington Congressman
Hugh DeLacy expressed it. A military clique, including presidential aide Admiral William Leahy, Ambassador to Moscow
General Walter Bedell Smith, and General Marshall, wielded
great influence with the president and was pushing the country
toward war. The strength of this view is uncertain, but it extended beyond Communists and Party-liners. In August 1946,
the Farmers Union newspaper devoted a large spread to an ex-
position of it by Congressman Charles Savage: "Together with
the big trusts and monopolies who wish to strengthen and extend their control over the life of the American people, and to
expand it to every corner of the earth, these military men are
forming an unofficial war party which is leading our country to
disaster." In October, Max Lerner discussed military-monopoly
influence in a series of *PM* columns: "The partnership between a military caste and an industrial caste spell fascism in
Japan and in Germany both. Can it in the end spell anything
less in America?" [28]

Perhaps the most conspicuous and consistent advocate of the
extreme anti–Cold War viewpoint was Senator Claude Pepper of Florida. Loquacious and energetic, Pepper long since
had established himself as the most militant and vocal of Southern progressives. After a trip to Europe which included personal interviews with Stalin and Tito, he began to speak out
more strongly than ever on foreign policy. Perhaps, as some
critics charged, he did so because such a course seemed the
most promising way of capturing the leadership of the liberal
movement and, if Truman continued to falter, a possible presidential nomination in 1948.[29]

In his speeches, Pepper lashed out at the "sinister forces"
which were trying to supplant antifascism with anti-Commu-

nism. "We have absolutely nothing to fear from the Soviet Union as long as the Soviet Union has nothing to fear from us," he told a meeting of the NCPAC. "The struggle against fascism is not yet over—let us all remember that." In his address to the Win-the-Peace Conference, he attacked the selfishness of British Tories, represented by Winston Churchill, arguing that they had subjugated the war effort to the preservation of the Empire and now were trying to initiate an anti-Communist crusade for the same objective. Referring to the Iron Curtain speech, Pepper said: "Mr. Churchill was the spokesman of all those who wish to make America the great defender of that imperialism. Although it was built in British blood, they want to secure it with American blood." Moreover, the United States with its control of bases around the world, its diplomatic intervention in China, its exclusive dominance of Japan was in danger of becoming "the newest and most dangerous imperialist."

By contrast, Russia could not even secure acknowledgement of its request for a postwar loan, was falsely accused of manipulating Communist parties around the world, and faced condemnation if it talked about a need for strategic bases close to its homeland—in the Dardanelles or Tripolitania. The postwar American leadership, he argued, was losing perspective and indulging in a specious universalism which was quite naturally leading to tension with Russia. "If the Soviet Union had as much confidence in the American Government of today," Pepper commented, "as it had confidence in the real friendship of the American Government headed by Franklin D. Roosevelt, there would still be the unity of the Big Three." [30]

Some Soviet actions, it is true, disturbed many liberals. Canadian authorities exposed a Russian spy ring. The Russians systematically stripped machinery from plants in Manchuria. At the United Nations, the Soviet delegate Andrei Vishinsky clashed with Eleanor Roosevelt over the question of free speech in the refugee camps. Intent upon protecting their U.N. veto power, the Russians even blocked the General Assembly from considering moves against Franco Spain. *PM* writer Alexander Uhl, usually among the most consistent defenders of the USSR, bitterly charged that the Soviet Union had "sacrificed the interests of the Spanish people." [31]

For most, the greatest shock was the Soviet attitude on the all-important question of atomic energy. Liberals had worked hard for civilian authority over this new force and for an international control plan. At first, Truman had drawn great criticism by apparently renouncing the idea of international control and apparently endorsing a bill which left domestic jurisdiction in the hands of the military. The president, however, quickly reversed himself on domestic control, and endorsed legislation for civilian supremacy sponsored by Senator Brien McMahon. The administration also moved to provide an answer to the liberal demands for international control. A committee headed by Dean Acheson and David Lilienthal reported a plan in early April, and in June Bernard Baruch presented a modified version to the U.N. Some liberals, including Lilienthal, felt that Baruch dwelt too much on the need to eliminate the veto in atomic affairs. In general, however, they praised the plan, hoping that it would remove the major cause of Russian suspicion and serve as a persuasive demonstration of American good will. The Soviet rejection of the Baruch plan, largely because it required abandonment of the veto, left progressives shaken. "Gromyko's reasons for rejection defy comprehension and invite the most disturbing conclusion about Russia's intentions for bonafide control," said the *New Republic*. The *Nation* called the Russian substitute, which retained the veto, "no plan at all." At the same time, however, it urged continued negotiation, and Freda Kirchwey argued that Russian assent might be achieved by rearranging the phases of the Baruch plan so that the Soviet Union would not be forced to divulge its scientific progress before the actual imposition of international control. In the hope that the Russians could be convinced that the United States would respect their security, that the Soviets would be amenable to patient reasoning, Miss Kirchwey and the *Nation* probably reflected the nearly desperate hope of the bulk of American progressives.[32]

The strongest—and least representative—criticism of the Soviet Union and Communism came from the *New Leader,* a weekly tabloid magazine published in New York. Affiliated with the Social Democratic Federation, an organization of dissident Old Guard Socialists who had split with the party, the paper served as an outlet for a tough, uncompromising, and rather shrill variety of anti-Communism. Although it characterized itself as America's leading liberal-labor weekly, it appears to have had few subscribers outside metropolitan New York and, as its scathing attacks upon so many other liberal journals, organizations, and writers indicated, it existed on the fringes of the progressive movement.

The *New Leader* was motivated by an absolutist social-democratic idealism more consistent than that of most liberals, but its rhetoric, which frequently anticipated the later outpourings of right-wing extremists, tended to demonstrate the way in which absolutist idealism could degenerate into destructive and unrealistic scapegoating. The Yalta and Potsdam conferences drew vehement condemnation as sellouts of democratic principles with no reference to the realistic alternatives open to American leaders. (Yalta became a positive obsession with one of the magazine's editors, William Henry Chamberlain, who for years would seize every opportunity to denounce the meeting.) The journal supported Chiang Kai-shek's Chinese government and pictured it as moving toward democracy on the assumption that any regime was preferable to the Communists, but its writers appear to have given little consideration to the impossibility of maintaining Chaing's crumbling authority. Convinced that American democracy and Soviet totalitarianism were engaged in an "irrepressible conflict," the *New Leader* was prepared to wage the fight without restraint.

Because its commitment to an anti-Soviet policy ran so far ahead of the rest of the liberal movement and indeed of the Truman administration, the *New Leader* was quick to detect Communist influence in important places. Its writers pilloried the *Nation,* the *New Republic,* and *PM,* and denounced the ICCASP as a Communist front. As early as 1945, the *New*

Leader was charging that Communism was scoring successes because of the presence of pro-Communists within the government—Dean Acheson (regularly called the "Dean of Appeasement" by Washington correspondent Jonathan Stout), Alger Hiss, Owen Lattimore, John Carter Vincent. The journal's motives were doubtless pure, but its style and method of accusation did little credit to the values it sought to advance.[33]

The *Progressive,* the personal organ of Robert La Follette, Jr., until its reorganization as an independent monthly at the end of 1947, was also firmly anti-Communist but less strident than the *New Leader,* less prone to hurl accusations of pro-Communism at those who disagreed with it, and less likely to imply that the threat of force was required against the USSR. La Follette and his editor, Morris Rubin, represented a dying Midwestern pacifist-isolationist tradition; their editorials frequently betrayed the frustration of progressives who, having failed to stave off international entanglements, were now demanding a perfect peace and the total fulfillment of all the neo-Wilsonian values which had been employed to justify World War II.

Other *Progressive* contributors had different perspectives. Kenneth Crawford, a top-notch Eastern journalist who had once written the "T.R.B." column for the *New Republic,* had clashed repeatedly with pro-Communists during his tenure as Washington correspondent for *PM.* James A. Wechsler and Louis Fischer were talented writers and commentators who, having gone through disillusionment with Communism themselves, thoroughly understood the cynicism and deceit which pervaded the movement in America and elsewhere. Fischer resigned as a contributing editor to the *Nation* in mid-1945 as a protest against the journal's friendly attitude toward the USSR. "All imperialists and aggressors have pleaded security as their motive," he declared.

Yet even these observers often shrank from the consequences of their views. At their best and most constructive, they advocated American encouragement of democracy abroad and U.S. participation in economic development. The adminis-

tration, Fischer commented, "can only 'stop Russia' by building a new world, a free world, a truly democratic world, a better world." In general, they did not advocate military
containment. La Follette, for example, opposed the draft and
advocated drastic cuts in defense expenditures. Fischer admitted that if the Russians expanded into the Mediterranean and
the Near East, an Anglo-American alliance against them would
be inevitable; but he also commented that "No decent person
wants such competition; it is fraught with grave dangers for all
humanity." In mid-1946, he could only advocate the establishment of a world government, with or without the Soviet
Union, as the best way to preserve peace.

With the exception of some of the *New Leader* writers, the
anti-Communist liberals had no desire to employ the possibility of force as a tool of American diplomacy. Yet they wanted
the American government to oppose Soviet expansionism in
areas where the Russians could command overwhelming power.
Constructive in their calls for economic development and the
encouragement of democracy, they had not formed an understanding of the place of power in diplomacy. America might
preserve its moral position by denouncing the imposition of
Communism in Eastern Europe, but only at the cost of intensi-
fying the Cold War, which even the anti-Communist liberals
wished to avoid. Military power might be the least important
part of an affirmative anti-Communist policy, but to ignore it
so completely could lead only to drift and futility.[34]

Much of the fuzziness about how to counter the Soviet
Union stemmed from the fact that even most anti-Communist
liberals were uncertain about the scope of Soviet ambitions.
Elmer Davis, for example, detested Soviet totalitarianism and
viewed the USSR with suspicion but had to admit in early
1946 that Russian objectives were foggy: "The Russians are not
yet looking as far as the Atlantic seaboard; but their present
policies raise some doubt as to just where they intend to stop.
The doubt may be unwarranted; but it is the Russians alone
who can remove it." Until the USSR presented a clear threat to
the balance of power in Europe, the bulk of the anti-Commu-

nist progressives could not bring themselves to advocate measures which would destroy for once and for all the hopes they had nurtured during the war.[35]

The New York Liberal Party, led by former Socialists who had spent much of their lives clashing with Communists, was vehemently opposed to domestic Communism but more cautious in its approach to the Soviet Union. Its 1946 platform took only the most indirect swipes at Russia, calling for an end to all imperialism, colonialism, and spheres of influence, urging the United States to insist upon observance of the principles of international morality embodied in the United Nations Charter. The declaration probably was primarily aimed at the Soviet Union, but it could as easily have been directed at Great Britain or France.[36]

The UDA provided a national basis of sorts for anti-Communist liberalism, but the Soviet section of its foreign policy platform, adopted in the spring of 1946, contained only a mild, almost apologetic slap at Russian expansionism and stressed the need for Soviet-American agreement and cooperation. A typical passage declared:

We must continue to seek for mutual agreements with Russia. The progressive movement in America must find a solid position between those who regard Russia as the fixed point of international virtue and those who hate and fear Russia to the point of supporting every policy which widens the gulf between Russia and the West. It is essential to develop a positive democratic program on which mutual understanding can be developed among all nations of both the eastern and western worlds.

The strongest "condemnation" of the Soviet Union was an assertion that: "We must make it clear to Russia and the world, by opposing any American imperialist policies or those of other nations, that our opposition to Russian imperialism is because it is imperialism, not because it is Russian." [37]

Individual UDA leaders were equally equivocal. Eleanor Roosevelt, despite relatively frequent clashes with the Russian delegation at the U.N., refused to give up all hope of Soviet-

American cooperation. UDA Chairman Reinhold Niebuhr was often vehement in his denunciation of Popular Fronters, and in an attack on the Win-the-Peace Conference, he blasted its condemnation of British policy "without a suggestion of criticism for a Russian policy which has brought the whole of Eastern Europe under Russia's sway." But as late as September 1946, Niebuhr was writing in the *Nation* that the United States should end its "futile efforts to change what cannot be changed in Eastern Europe, regarded by Russia as its strategic security belt."

Western efforts to change conditions in Poland, or in Bulgaria, for instance, will prove futile in any event, partly because the Russians are there and we aren't, and partly because such slogans as "free elections" and "free enterprise" are irrelevant in that part of the world. Our copybook versions of democracy are frequently as obtuse as Russian dogmatism. If we left Russia alone in the part of the world it has staked out, we might actually help, rather than hinder, the indigenous forces which resist its heavy hand.

Niebuhr made it clear that the U.S. must oppose Soviet expansionism if it started to move toward Western Europe, but like many of the other anti-Communist liberals he was still receptive to accommodation and hardly ready to threaten Russia with force.[38] During 1946, the St. Louis *Post-Dispatch* became increasingly critical of Soviet expansionism. Yet in May it called for a Truman-Stalin meeting, and in mid-June, while strongly condemning Russian belligerence, it expressed the hope that the Soviet Union might be induced to meet the West halfway.[39]

Many progressives found themselves somewhere between the strong anti-Soviets and the pro-Russians. Robert Lasch, the chief editorial writer of the Chicago *Sun,* argued that while Big Three cooperation was probably not feasible, an era of peaceful ideological competition was possible and preferable to war. The Soviet Union, he felt, was seeking "not indefinite expansion of power, but the same degree of strategic security which the other great powers, including the United States, already possess." It was not necessary for the United States to acquiesce in Soviet bad behavior, as in Manchuria or Iran, but the American government had to "accept Russia as an equal partner in world affairs." Such an attitude would put America in a "much stronger position to make effective protest against any treaty violations, and to insist that all decisions at the points of friction be made by agreement, inside the United Nations." If America treated the Russians as an aggressor, then the Soviet Union surely would act like one and all hope of accommodation, even of peace, probably would be lost.[40]

University of Chicago historian Walter Johnson, writing in *Bell-Ringer,* the organ of Independent Voters of Illinois, decried the growth of anti-Soviet hysteria and charged that the United States was applying a double standard to the USSR. America was too prone to overlook British sins and to accept its own broad spheres of influence while criticizing the USSR. The U.S. had to back the United Nations, and should become the mediator between England and Russia rather than a country which sided automatically with England. The right to national security must not become a justification for land-grabbing. Soviet behavior was "admittedly a disturbing question," but American policy had to steer between the extremes of "the professional Russian-haters" and the "professional pro-Soviet advocates." The United States had to be "frank and firm and consistent . . . playing no favorites and rattling no atomic bombs," and Americans should remember that "although we may not understand or even like what Russia is apparently doing in certain instances, none of these Russian acts involve threats to American security." [41]

To Helen Gahagan Douglas, the popular, idealistic congresswoman from California, the major task of American policy was to assume the initiative in rebuilding Big Three mutual understanding. She was convinced that nations which had gone through the holocaust of World War II were unwilling to risk a new conflict. Unlike many of the critics of U.S. diplomacy, she was sympathetic toward the British and understood that their reluctance to abandon their political and economic em-

pire derived largely from their wartime suffering and grim
postwar situation. By the same token, the Russians were obsessed with their security. The growth of anti-Soviet feeling in
America and the continued manufacture of atomic bombs had
created a situation in which the USSR might return to belligerent isolation and begin an atomic arms race. Yet since the
1930s, she believed, the Soviet Union had been "willing and
eager to cooperate in the building of world security" and
"would be relieved if she could stop worrying about danger of
attack from without and get on with the building up of her
country for the good life." The United States had to provide
the friendship, understanding, and assistance which would help
Russia meet her legitimate security needs and allay Soviet suspicion.[42]

Lasch, Johnson, and Mrs. Douglas probably represented the
feelings of most progressives. Not necessarily regarding the Soviet Union as a model of international virtue, they nevertheless
found it hard to believe that the USSR would embark upon a
dangerous imperialist course immediately after having experienced the devastation of the war. Their thinking as they tried
to cope with a changing situation was perhaps muddled and
naïve, but they were surely correct in realizing that the success
of the U.N. rested upon some sort of peaceful Big Three relationship, that the Soviet Union did have real security requirements, and that these requirements posed no serious danger to
the United States. So long as the Truman administration followed a futile and negative policy of carping at Russia and
doing little constructive, it could attract few liberals. Conversely, it was easy to believe that a greater effort to understand
and reassure the Soviet government might end the tragic split
which had developed between East and West.

IV

Truman's own impulses led him quickly toward a policy of
"toughness" with the Soviet Union. In his early months as president, however, toughness meant little more than rhetorical

bluntness, to a large extent an adaptation of the Soviet style of diplomatic blustering which was apparently based upon the assumption that America could have its way simply through rough talk. On April 20, 1945, the president told Averell Harriman that he did not fear the Russians and that the Soviet Union needed the United States more than the U.S. needed the USSR; perhaps America could not get 100 percent of its objectives, but certainly firmness could achieve 85 percent. Talking with other advisers on the same day, he tore into the Soviet Union and remarked that if the Russians disapproved of American plans for the establishment of the United Nations, "they could go to hell." On April 23, he met with Soviet foreign minister Molotov and outraged the Russian diplomat by firmly opposing the USSR's drive for dominance in Poland.[43]

Near the end of May, Truman granted an interview to NCPAC officials Elmer Benson and Beanie Baldwin. As they recalled it, the president literally banged his fist on the desk as he declared: "We have got to get tough with the Russians. . . . We've got to teach them how to behave." Yet when Benson protested that the United States had to get along with the Soviet Union, Truman vigorously agreed.[44] Truman may well have seen verbal toughness as the sort of discourse which the Russians understood, as a means of reaching agreements. There is strong evidence that in his early months as president he appreciated the vast Russian capacity for suspicion and wanted to preserve the Big Three alliance. He drew upon Joseph Davies and Harry Hopkins, both strong believers in Soviet-American accord, for advice and in late May sent Hopkins to Moscow for talks with Stalin which settled the Polish question, largely on Russian terms, in return for Soviet concessions at the San Francisco conference. He refused to meet separately with Churchill before the Potsdam conference, fearing that Stalin would believe that the two Western leaders were "ganging up on him." The Russians "evidently like their country or they would not die for it," he commented in a diary entry dated June 7. "I like ours, so let's get along." [45]

Yet other portions of his diary condemned totalitarianism in general and Communism in particular. Totalitarian states were

all alike, based on "the old disproven formula that the end justified the means." American Communists were disloyal hyphen-
ates. The Soviet Union had not achieved a just society:
"There's no socialism in Russia. It is the hotbed of special privilege." By mid-June, the president was writing: "Propaganda
seems to be our greatest foreign relations enemy. Russians distribute lies about us." [46]

Truman then was hardly in a pro-Soviet mood when he went
to Potsdam, but there are many indications that both before
and after the conference he was optimistic about the chances of
good relations with the USSR. Before leaving for Potsdam, he
told Burton K. Wheeler "that he wasn't afraid of Russia, that
he was more afraid of England and France." In his *Memoirs*
Truman comments that he and the American delegation believed that the Soviet Union, because of the enormous losses of
the war, "would join wholeheartedly in a plan for world
peace." His response to Stalin was quite favorable: "I was impressed by him and talked to him straight from the shoulder.
He looked me in the eye when he spoke, and I felt hopeful
that we could reach an agreement." Near the end of the conference Truman declared to Secretary of the Navy Forrestal that
"he was being very realistic with the Russians and found Stalin
not difficult to do business with." Years later, Truman claimed
that he came home from Potsdam deeply disillusioned with the
Russians. At the time, however, he remarked to an associate
that Stalin was "as near like Tom Pendergast as any man I
know." He subsequently explained to Wheeler that Stalin was
"all right" and that the Politburo was responsible for the problems in Soviet-American relations. [47]

Truman's erratic, apparently paradoxical, attitudes and behavior actually proceeded quite consistently from his background and personality. His approach to diplomacy was all too
American. He was convinced of American innocence and altru-
ism. He saw international problems as moral problems, international relationships as matters that could be handled in the
same way as personal relationships. It was natural for him to be
outraged by the Russian presence in Eastern Europe, to mistake the rhetoric of diplomacy for substance, to feel an upsurge

of optimism after meeting with Stalin, who seemed like a tough but reliable political boss. He was inexperienced in diplomacy and a bit frightened of it; indignantly rejecting the classical concepts of *Machtpolitik,* he believed that America must stand for the new democratic world order embodied in the United Nations. In many respects his assumptions were identical to those of the liberals, but they led him in a different direction.

There is little evidence that he related his Eastern European objectives to American interests or even to the power resources available to the United States. Whenever his mind moved from diplomatic principles to national power, he seems to have assumed (as in the Navy Day speech) that American might was overwhelming. Perhaps he initially expected that the atomic bomb would give the United States great leverage; Byrnes certainly thought so. If so, Truman soon realized that he was wrong.* "I am not sure it can ever be used," he told Budget Director Harold Smith in early October 1945.[48]

*Gar Alperovitz, *Atomic Diplomacy: Hiroshima and Potsdam* (New York, 1965), selectively uses circumstantial evidence to argue that Truman adopted a systematic anti-Soviet strategy almost immediately upon taking office and part of this reversal of Roosevelt's policy was the needless use of the atomic bomb against Japan.

The book fails to deal convincingly with the contradictions in Roosevelt's policies in the weeks before his death (see esp. Appendix I). It ignores the disorder in the early weeks of the Truman administration as an unbriefed and inexperienced president attempted to develop a grip on foreign policy. It is unable to cope with the crucial distinction between a simple assumption (widely held in the administration) that the bomb would make the USSR more tractable and a decision to use the bomb primarily to intimidate the Soviet Union (never demonstrated).

If Truman had indeed at once adopted a systematic anti-Russian strategy, then the oscillations in his attitude toward the USSR are difficult to comprehend, especially his optimism after Potsdam. Until firm evidence to the contrary appears, it still makes more sense to assume that Truman, like so many Americans, held contradictory attitudes toward the Soviet Union, was puzzled by its behavior, and was uncertain of its intentions. The use of the bomb followed naturally from the momentum behind its development and from the universal wartime hatred for the Japanese.

Truman's realization that the bomb might not be a feasible threat persisted into the spring of 1948, when, during the "war scare" which followed the Czech coup, he directed Admiral Leahy to prepare a plan for resisting a Soviet attack without atomic weapons. Leahy, Diary, May 6, 1948, Leahy MSS, LC.

Truman nevertheless refused to abandon the American resistance to Communist domination in Eastern Europe. In addition, he became increasingly concerned with Soviet ambitions in Iran and Turkey. By the end of 1945, he was apparently convinced that the Russian encouragement of separatism in northern Iran and push for control of the Turkish straits represented the first phase of a design to gain control of the Mediterranean and the Middle East. The results of the Moscow conference, hailed by so many liberals, outraged him; he felt that Secretary Byrnes had conceded Russian control of Bulgaria and Rumania and had gained nothing in return. Angered also by Byrnes's independence, Truman prepared a memorandum on January 5, 1946. The document began with a firm demand that Byrnes should adequately consult with and brief the president; then it moved on to a long denunciation of Soviet foreign policy:

Iran was our ally in the war. Iran was Russia's ally in the war. Iran agreed to the free passage of arms, ammunition and other supplies [without which] . . . Russia would have been ignominiously defeated. Yet now Russia stirs up rebellion and keeps troops on the soil of her friend and ally—Iran.

There isn't a doubt in my mind that Russia intends an invasion of Turkey and the seizure of the Black Sea Straits to the Mediterranean. Unless Russia is faced with an iron fist and strong language another war is in the making. Only one language do they understand—"how many divisions have you?"

I do not think we should play compromise any longer. We should refuse to recognize Rumania and Bulgaria until they comply with our requirements; we should let our position on Iran be known in no uncertain terms and we should continue to insist on the internationalization of the Kiel Canal, the Rhine-Danube waterway and the Black Sea Straits and we should maintain complete control of Japan and the Pacific. We should rehabilitate China and create a strong central government there. We should do the same for Korea.

Then we should insist on the return of our ships from Russia and force a settlement of the Lend-Lease debt of Russia.

I'm tired of babying the Soviets.[49]

Truman has called this document "the point of departure" in Soviet-American relations. Apparently he had reached a solid conviction that cooperation with the USSR was impossible and that the Soviet Union was in fact an enemy. On February 22, George Kennan sent the State Department his influential "long telegram" from Moscow urging a strong and constructive policy to contain Soviet expansionism. Churchill's "iron curtain" speech followed in March. Byrnes, under pressure from the White House and the Congressional leadership, adopted a policy of "firmness and patience." On September 6, Byrnes, in Europe for yet another foreign ministers' conference, delivered a major address at Stuttgart, Germany. The speech, widely interpreted as a bid for German support against the USSR, pledged a continued American presence in Europe, committed the United States to work for the political and economic unification of Germany, and even extended the hope of restoration of some of the German territory which had been ceded to Poland.[50]

At about the same time, Clark Clifford was finishing a long memorandum on Soviet-American relations for Truman. A synthesis of reports from the State Department, military officials, Reparations Ambassador Pauley, the Central Intelligence Agency, and the Justice Department, the document pictured the USSR as a nation bent on the imperialistic expansion of Communism, ready to break any diplomatic agreement, engaging in vast espionage and subversive activities against the United States, continuing with a military program which could be directed only against its former allies. While stopping short of predicting an imminent attack from Russia, the memorandum underscored the Soviet military threat to American security. It advocated an unyielding diplomatic position, military preparedness, and determination to fight in response to any serious challenge.[51]

The Clifford memorandum represented the culmination of a hardening process which had begun in early 1946. American policy by now had found a consistency and sense of purpose. At the same time, however, it was enjoying few successes. The

Russians did withdraw from northern Iran, but they would not budge from Eastern Europe, and the escalation of American rhetoric bore little relation to the objectives which might realistically be achieved. Truman and those around him had steeled themselves to turn back future Communist expansion, but it was futile to hope that they could undo the Russian fait accompli in Poland and the Balkans.

The liberal critique was strongest in its realization that tough talk could accomplish nothing but the worsening of Soviet-American relations, and that the United Sates had to adopt constructive democratic policies. With the exception of a few dissenters, the liberals were weakest in their assumption that the Soviet leaders viewed the world rationally, wanted only peace after the terrible ordeal their nation had experienced, and simply sought defensive security. This assumption, often accompanied by the parallel idea that fascism still existed as a menacing force in the world, led naturally to the conclusion that the West must be responsible for the erosion of a wartime alliance which had to be preserved. Specifically, British and American imperialists, monopolists, and militarists had to be responsible, and they were using the unimaginative little man in the White House.

The liberals had invested great emotional capital in the war. They had supported its enormous carnage and destruction in the hope that it would bring worldwide reconstruction, reform, and justice on an unprecedented scale. In addition, for more than a decade the progressive view of the world had begun with the necessity of halting the demonic trust of fascism; it was impossible for most to break with the idea of antifascist unity in a matter of months, especially when the break would entail acceptance of a new era of international tension, expensive and dangerous arms races, and the possibility of atomic war. Even most anti-Communist liberals shrank from the thought.

Until the liberals could redefine their world view, however, the creative element in their criticism of the administration would remain hidden. Events in the fall of 1946 presented no evidence that a redefinition was under way.

Chapter 5

Demoralization and Defeat

I

"How I wish you were at the helm," the young Minnesota politician, Hubert Humphrey, wrote to Henry Wallace upon hearing of FDR's death. A few days later, Eleanor Roosevelt told Wallace: "I feel that you are peculiarly fitted to carry on the ideals which were close to my husband's heart." Such was the instinctive response of most liberals. From April 12, 1945, Wallace was the central figure of the American left, a displaced heir in the court of those who had overthrown him. As the progressives grew disenchanted with Truman, as Chester Bowles and Harold Ickes left the administration, Wallace became the only major symbol of the New Deal in high office.[1]

Wallace, hoping that he could transform the Department of Commerce into an agency larger and more powerful than had existed under Herbert Hoover or Jesse Jones, had expected to use the office to establish ties with the business community. The separation of the lending agencies from the department during the struggle over Wallace's confirmation made it plain that Commerce would never become the influential Cabinet post which its new secretary had wanted; Wallace nevertheless made a show of working for business interests by striving for increased foreign trade, larger small-business programs, and expanded Commerce Department services. On occasion, he won grudging praise from the business establishment, but he was too politically typecast to make the effort work. Distrusted by his department's constituency, he remained the chief spokesman of the liberal cause.[2]

His pronouncements aligned him conspicuously with non-business progressives. In speeches and Congressional testimony he strongly supported reciprocal trade, American-Soviet friendship, civilian authority over atomic energy and its international control. He spoke out for the OPA, generous wage hikes within the existing price structure, full employment, and racial integration. In September 1945, his book, *Sixty Million Jobs*, appeared, and progressives praised his Keynesian program for full employment. Alvin Hansen called the volume "an education in applied economics" which should be read and reread by every voter. "Wallace has a human touch, a world view, a sense of tolerance and a dramatic idea of what America can be," wrote the Minnesota liberal Howard Williams.[3]

In his speeches and writings Wallace constantly rejected the idea of a third party, hammering home again and again the theme that only the Democratic Party could be the vehicle of American liberalism. Yet his own political path was erratic. In the 1945 New York mayoralty election, he endorsed the regular Democrat William O'Dwyer. But in February 1946, he intervened in a special Manhattan Congressional election to support the American Labor Party candidate Johannes Steel, a local radio commentator generally believed to have Communist connections, although Steel's Democratic opponent, backed by the Liberal Party and the New York *Post,* had a solid progressive record. Then, a month later, Wallace delivered a speech which called for rigid party discipline. The talk drew wide criticism, especially from the small coterie of Republican liberals who had regularly broken with their party to support the New Deal. President Truman indicated some sympathy with the idea of party discipline but hastened to add that he would welcome all the Republican votes he could get. Wallace backed down to the extent of saying that he did not believe in "purges." [4]

The relationship between Wallace and Truman was superficially cordial, but there was no rapport between the two men. Personally ill at ease with Wallace, Truman respected Wallace's ability and especially his political following. In the fall of 1945, the president told James Byrnes that there were two people he had to keep in the administration—Wallace and Eleanor Roosevelt. Truman supported Wallace's effort to put new life into the Commerce Department, but he had little regard for the secretary as a practical operator and thought him incapable of steering his department budget through Congress. Wallace, for his part, may have believed that Truman had good intentions, and he seized opportunities to say something nice about the president; but he also considered Truman a "little man" and must have felt a suppressed resentment against the person who had edged him out of the White House.[5]

The new president had hardly taken office when liberals began to speculate on his relationship with Wallace. Early signs encouraged them, but by late 1945 there were recurrent rumors that Wallace, overshadowed by the White House gang, was disillusioned with the administration and about to resign. Actually, Wallace appears to have been relatively satisfied. He disregarded suggestions from Eleanor Roosevelt and others that he should leave the Cabinet and establish himself as the spokesman of the independent liberals, discouraged attempts to form "Wallace in '48" clubs, worked with the president on such matters as full employment legislation, and gave strong support to Truman in his speeches. It was only after the president asked for power to draft the rail strikers that public coolness appeared. Wallace made it clear that he was against the request and warned against fascist techniques; asked by reporters if he still favored Truman for president in 1948, he replied with a crisp "No comment." [6]

By then, however, neither the rail episode nor domestic economic developments were as important to Wallace as the state of Soviet-American relations. Even before V-E Day, Wallace had displayed great concern over the preservation of the Big Three alliance, and by early 1946 this concern was becoming an obsession. He met with other liberals worried about the

direction of American foreign policy—among them Congressmen Mike Mansfield, J. William Fulbright, and John Carroll,
Senators Claude Pepper and Harley Kilgore, and Assistant Secretary of the Interior Oscar Chapman. Determined to push for
his ideas in public as well as in private, perhaps recalling that
during the 1930s Roosevelt had given Cabinet members great
latitude, Wallace formulated a theory of Cabinet irresponsibility. "The Cabinet of the President was never meant to be—
and never can be—a meeting of closed minds," he said in June
1946. "No President has ever found strength in the blind acquiescence of members of his Cabinet. And no President worth
his salt—or the people's salt—wants blind acquiescence."
Deeply influenced by the atomic scientist J. Robert Oppenhei-
mer, Wallace was especially motivated by his fear of an atomic
arms race and nuclear war; with some justification, he believed
that his own scientific experience enabled him to grasp more
fully than any other Cabinet-level official both the destructive
power and constructive potential of atomic energy.

He assumed great freedom in publicly discussing foreign policy and did not hesitate to appear before groups such as the
ICCASP which criticized the administration. Calling for friendship with Russia but criticizing Communism, denouncing
British imperialism and the Iron Curtain speech but supporting the important $3.75 billion loan to England, he undoubt-
edly felt his diplomatic recommendations were balanced and
moderate. In March 1946, he engaged in a friendly debate with
Averell Harriman at a Russian relief gathering, replying to
Harriman's condemnation of the Soviet government with the
argument that the USSR was trying to defend itself against capitalist encirclement. Two days later he made a speech criticizing U.S. negotiations for a permanent base in Iceland as unnecessary and provocative. Secretaries Byrnes and Forrestal
expressed outrage to the president over the Iceland declaration, but Wallace would give them neither a retraction nor a
promise to refrain from further critiques of administration policy.[7]

Privately, he virtually appointed himself an unofficial adviser to Truman on foreign policy and tirelessly advocated measures which he felt would reassure the Russians and establish an international climate of cooperation and interdependence. Strongly supporting Secretary Stimson's proposal for cooperative atomic research with the USSR, he warned against the dangers of "useless secrecy" and competition in the building of nuclear weapons and asserted that the best way to maintain good relations with Russia was to "keep in the closest possible touch with her scientific, agricultural, business, and cultural development." This, he believed, was the best way to protect American security and "gain a true friend." [8]

In March 1946, as the new ambassador to the Soviet Union, Walter Bedell Smith, prepared to leave for Moscow, Wallace advocated the dispatch of a special economic delegation to negotiate long-term trade agreements.* "We know that much of

*Ronald Radosh and Leonard P. Liggio in their article, "Henry A. Wallace and the Open Door," Thomas G. Paterson, ed., Cold War Critics (Chicago, 1971), pp. 76–113, argue that Wallace's emphasis on foreign trade was primarily motivated by the belief that American capitalism was dependent upon international expansion for survival and that, moreover, Wallace hoped for American domination of the Soviet economy. To my mind, this interpretation misreads Wallace's economic thought and distorts his fundamental impulses.

Wallace believed that foreign trade could contribute significantly to American prosperity and may have felt it absolutely vital in the twenties and thirties; his advocacy of foreign trade in the postwar period naturally stressed American advantages. Yet it also appears that Wallace, like many another liberal thinker, had awakened to the domestic potential of the American economy during World War II and had come to consider foreign economic relationships as a relatively small component of national prosperity. Sixty Million Jobs stresses opportunities for economic development at home and devotes scant attention to international trade. In his correspondence, Wallace estimated that foreign trade might account for four or five million jobs, a substantial figure but hardly the margin of survival for a sixty-million job economy.

In common with most liberals, Wallace advocated stepped-up American trade because he felt it would foster economic growth and prosperity on all sides and because he believed that economic interdependence—not U.S. dominance—would contribute to international peace. His central motivation was liberal moralism rather than any calculation of national advantage. He himself years later recalled the atomic bomb as his major concern, not the American economy. Wallace interview.

On international trade in general, see Wallace to F. J. Challinor, April 10, 1945, and several similar letters, and Wallace to Irving Fisher, May 11, 1945, Wallace MSS, Iowa.

the recent Soviet behavior which has caused us concern has been the result of their dire economic needs and of their disturbed sense of security," he told Truman. The events of early 1946 had reawakened the specter of "capitalist encirclement" and were convincing the Russians that "the Western world, including the U.S.A., is invariably and unanimously hostile." The United States could "strengthen the faith of the Soviets in our sincere devotion to the cause of peace by proving to them that we want to trade with them and to cement economic relations with them." The task was to carry on discussions in a rational, understanding manner which would demonstrate the fallacies of the Communist world-view and lay the basis for a long-term, large-scale economic relationship. Truman thanked Wallace for the suggestion but did nothing about it.[9]

On July 23, Wallace sent the president a long letter which warned that "in our earnest efforts to achieve bipartisan unity in this country we may have given way too much to isolationism masquerading as tough realism in international affairs." There were, he argued, "reasonable Russian grounds for fear, suspicions and distrust." Throughout its history Russia had been the victim of successive invasions. Since the Bolshevik Revolution it had endured a struggle for existence against Western hostility. It was natural for the Soviet Union to fear the American military program and to react in a hostile fashion to "our resistance to her attempts to obtain warm-water ports and her own security system in the form of 'friendly' neighboring states." The United States must concede to the Russians "reasonable . . . guarantees of security" and attempt to counter the "irrational fear" of the Soviet Union which was being spread by American right-wingers.

Agreement on the control of atomic energy was especially crucial. The American plan for U.N. control, Wallace asserted, was weighted against the Soviets because it called upon them to reveal the extent of their atomic resources and their scientific progress before the United States had to commit its atomic monopoly to international control. As he saw it, the plan required the Russians to give up their only negotiating cards and to run the risk that the United States might not "want to continue to play the game." It was possible, he conceded, that the Russians might not want an atomic control pact, at least not until they had developed their own bombs; but he was optimistic about the possibility that they would agree to a treaty in which the United States made a few concessions on the timing of international control.

He again urged strong economic ties with Russia. "The reconstruction program of the USSR and the plans for the full development of the Soviet Union offer tremendous opportunities for American goods and American technicians." There was a basis for mutually profitable trade, and an American loan, made "on economic and commercial grounds," would demonstrate that the United States sought peace and friendship.

Essentially, Wallace argued that only relatively limited concessions and gestures were needed to reestablish the wartime alliance—reasonable guarantees of security, official disapproval of anti-Soviet publicists, a few mechanical changes in the atomic control plan, a development loan, and increased trade. These approaches, he believed, would create "an atmosphere of mutual trust and confidence" which would be the foundation for One World. It is at the least debatable that Wallace's recommendations would have secured such happy results, but his position was hardly unreservedly pro-Soviet.

Truman again thanked the secretary, made a show of sending his letter along to Byrnes, but did nothing. Discouraged and frustrated, Wallace apparently decided to resign from the Cabinet after the November elections. By now peace was becoming an obsession with him.[10]

II

Early that summer, Wallace accepted an invitation to speak at a major political rally sponsored by the ICCASP and NCPAC and scheduled for New York on September 12. Since the meeting was to provide a major kick-off for the liberal effort in the Congressional campaign, Wallace initially planned to attack the way the conservatives had blocked domestic progress in the Seventy-ninth Congress. However, one of Wallace's junior aides in the Commerce Department had leaked his July 23 letter on Soviet-American relations to Beanie Baldwin. Pleased and excited by the document, Baldwin persuaded Wallace to switch his topic to foreign policy and base his speech on the letter.

Baldwin shrewdly warned Wallace that such a pronouncement could never get State Department clearance and advised him to go directly to Truman. Wallace met with the president on September 10 to discuss the address and at least two other topics. Subsequently, Truman claimed that they talked for only a few minutes while Wallace asserted that they carefully examined the speech for "over an hour." (The White House appointment book scheduled Wallace for only fifteen minutes, but it is possible that his stay ran overtime.) There can be no doubt that Truman, always a bit nervous with Wallace, did not give the address his close attention. It is equally certain that Wallace engaged in a bit of salesmanship which was less than candid. He especially emphasized the innocuous sentence, "I am neither anti-British nor pro-British, neither anti-Russian nor pro-Russian." When Truman expressed emphatic agreement—"By God, Henry, that is our foreign policy!"—Wallace quickly secured his permission to mention their accord in the speech. He would do so in a way which made it appear that Truman subscribed to the entire document. When he returned to his offices at the Commerce building, he told his assistants that he had the president's approval but doubted that Truman had understood the speech. His public relations men promptly put out the word of Truman's endorsement, thereby leading some observers to believe that Wallace was going to call for a tough policy toward the Soviet Union. On the afternoon of the twelfth, surprised reporters who had seen advance copies of the speech asked Truman if he had approved it; the president declared unequivocally that he had.[11]

The motives of both Baldwin and Wallace are hard to understand. Baldwin was already moving rapidly toward the idea of a third party and may have seen his suggestion as a method of prying Wallace away from the Democrats; yet he later denied any such intention. Perhaps he thought Wallace's enunciation of principles of Soviet-American friendship could reverse American foreign policy. Wallace must have had some hope that he could have some such effect; it seems certain that he still wanted to help the Democratic Party, not undermine it. He could have had no idea that he had started on the road to political disaster.

The rally, held at Madison Square Garden, was an antiadministration meeting. It adopted a resolution charging that the "aims of President Roosevelt have been placed in jeopardy by the 'get tough with Russia' policy, the refusal to withdraw American armed forces from China and support for British imperialism." Claude Pepper eulogized Roosevelt, urged a return to a policy of friendship with the USSR and accused the administration of appeasing "the imperialists in the Republican party." Wallace's speech was probably the most moderate statement of the evening.

American foreign policy, he declared, must be independent, following neither Britain nor Russia, and it must be built around a program of massive worldwide economic assistance and development. Its ultimate goal should be "a functioning, powerful United Nations and a body of international law." But the realization of this goal lay far in the future. "Realistically, the most we can hope for now is safe reduction in military expense and a long period of peace based on mutual trust between the Big Three." American policy, however, was being influenced by "numerous reactionary elements which had hoped for Axis victory—and now profess great friendship for the United States." The "get tough policy" they advocated could accomplish nothing constructive. "The tougher we get, the tougher the Russians will get."

He asserted that the United States must drop its concern over Soviet penetration of Eastern Europe and concede the Russians a *political* (not economic) sphere of influence there. But America could not tolerate Soviet expansion beyond Eastern Europe, not even through the technique of "stirring up native communists to political activity." In addition, Eastern Europe must remain open to American trade. Nor could the United States tolerate any foreign sphere of influence, political or economic, in China. An understanding containing these elements could be the basis for a long period of peaceful competition between democratic capitalism and authoritarian communism. Eventually, Wallace argued, the differences between the two systems would blur as the capitalists moved toward more socialism and the Communists granted greater civil liberties.

Wallace's speech seemed to have been formulated within an intellectual framework which had been odious to most liberals. Progressives generally assumed that international relations should be based upon international morality; they were Idealists in their approach. Wallace spoke of spheres of influence and seemed to advocate power politics; he sounded like a hard-boiled Realist who accepted the amoral exercise of power as the dominant aspect of international life. However, it is doubtful that Wallace had given much thought to such implications. Neither a pure Idealist nor a pure Realist, he was making an effort to come to grips with the world as it was. Essentially, he still looked toward the Idealist's utopian goal of peace with meaningful international law, but he now believed that its realization was far in the future. His call for free economic relations between the United States and Eastern Europe underscored his fundamental adherence to the principle of One World and grew from his belief that economic intercourse could overcome political differences. Indeed, he failed to realize that the Russians would not allow economic penetration to undermine their political control and thereby revealed the superficiality of his conversion to Realism. By advocating spheres of influence, Wallace had departed significantly from the unalloyed Idealism with which so many liberals viewed world politics, but he had not executed a complete reversal. He sought only new means for the same Idealistic ends.

The reaction of his audience was remarkable. Perhaps prepared to heckle by the advance speculation about the speech, a significant segment hooted and jeered as he asserted that the

Russians were suppressing civil liberties in Eastern Europe and had displayed an unwarranted intransigence which was partly to blame for the Cold War. The next day, the early editions of the Communist *Daily Worker* contained a strong condemnation.[12]

However Realist (or realistic) the Madison Square Garden speech may have been, it was undeniably moderate. Wallace offered the Soviet Union only the most limited concessions. The United States, he observed, claimed the entire Western Hemisphere as a sphere of influence. Was then Eastern Europe so great a concession to the USSR? Yet Wallace was still publicly urging a drastic shift in American foreign policy and doing so just six days after Byrnes had spoken at Stuttgart. With Truman's inadvertent endorsement, Wallace had thrown American foreign policy into doubt even as Byrnes was presenting an unyielding resistance to Soviet treaty demands at the Paris peace conference.[13]

Anti-Soviet progressives and their supporters the chieftains of the Liberal Party, the *New Leader,* the *Progressive,* the St. Louis *Post-Dispatch,* Elmer Davis, Reinhold Niebuhr— roundly criticized the Wallace speech. Davis charged that Wallace had committed "a blunder gravely injurious to the national interest" and had ignored the Soviet record of broken promises. Niebuhr, who just a few weeks earlier had talked of allowing the Russians an Eastern European sphere, returned from a trip to Europe overwhelmed by the fear and loathing of Soviet Communism which he had encountered in social-democratic circles everywhere. He was now convinced that the Soviet Union was determined to dominate all Germany and then all Europe. An anti-Soviet policy was a necessity quite in line with the desires of the European people. Wallace and other liberals had to face "the tragic fact that there is no real peace in the world," stop complaining about firmness toward the USSR, and start working for the constructive economic development of Western Europe.[14]

Many other liberals were disturbed by the sphere-of-influence proposal. It was, said the New York *Post,* "surprisingly enough, like isolationism, two-worldism and a repudiation of the hopeful principles of the Atlantic Charter and the United Nations." The *Nation* called it "a brutally realistic position, demanding a new orientation on the part of most liberal thinkers," and commented: "A division of the world into 'zones' dominated by great powers has so many obvious dangers that it must be accepted, if at all, reluctantly and as a bad second best."

Yet Wallace had presented a concrete plan for solving the Soviet-American crisis; he offered the liberal movement more than the formless hope that somehow the principle of One World might prevail. Gilbert Harrison, the anti-Communist vice-chairman of the American Veterans Committee, told Wallace that he had given encouragement to those who felt that peace between the United States and Russia was still possible. Thomas L. Stokes felt that the speech charted a valid course between pro- and anti-Soviet extremes; *PM* reprinted it as an editorial. The *New Republic* called the address "a reaffirmation of America's moral leadership" and "a contribution to the search for peace." [15]

Meanwhile, Truman was attempting to repair the damage. On September 14 he called reporters into his office and read them a statement "clarifying" his September 12 remark approving the speech. He had not intended, he said, to indicate his personal approval of Wallace's words. He had meant only to endorse Wallace's right to deliver the speech. At the same time, White House sources were telling the press that Truman had taken time only to thumb through the address and, not having read it, could not have approved its content. The people around Wallace were countering with the assertion that the president had gone over the speech in detail. Liberals, whether they favored Wallace or not, denounced Truman's latest move. "Surely this has been one of the sorriest performances in the history of the Presidential office," wrote the pro-Wallace Max Lerner, asserting that the incident proved that Truman was in the grip of a war party, "the new united reactionary front of the press, the diplomats, the monopoly kings, the army." The overwhelming consensus in Washington, wrote I. F. Stone, was that Truman simply did not know what he was doing in foreign policy. Truman's statement, said the *Nation*, had left a "general impression of fumbling irresponsibility." No president, said Elmer Davis, had been in such an embarrassing position since Harding had been forced to admit that he did not know the contents of an important treaty.[16]

Thereafter events moved quickly. On September 17, Wallace's letter of July 23 was released to the press, adding fuel to the controversy. On the eighteenth, Wallace conferred with the president for two and a half hours, finally agreeing to make no further speeches until the adjournment of the Paris conference. Truman was angered and disillusioned by the discussion; a diary entry indicated his growing estrangement from Wallace, Wallace's followers, and the Soviet Union:

I am not sure he is as fundamentally sound intellectually as I had thought. . . .

He is a pacifist 100 percent. He wants us to disband our armed forces, give Russia our atomic secrets and trust a bunch of adventurers in the Kremlin Politbureau. I do not understand a "dreamer" like that. The German-American Bund under Fritz Kuhn was not half so dangerous. The Reds, phonies and the "parlor pinks" seem to be banded together and are becoming a national danger.

I am afraid they are a sabotage front for Uncle Joe Stalin. They can see no wrong in Russia's four and one-half million armed force, in Russia's loot of Poland, Austria, Hungary, Rumania, Manchuria. They can see no wrong in Russia's living off the occupied countries to support the military occupation.

On September 19 Truman received a message from an angry Jimmy Byrnes, declaring in effect that the president must choose between him and Wallace. Already simmering from a belief that Wallace had broken his agreement of silence by answering questions from reporters and telling aides what had happened, Truman angrily asked for Wallace's resignation. That evening, Wallace, a private citizen for the first time in thirteen years, went on the air to explain his stand. He declared his opposition to "all types of imperialism and aggres-

sion, whether they are of Russian, British or American origin,"
his belief in world unity and justice for all nations. He ended
by saying, "I intend to carry on the fight for peace." [17]

Only a few liberals supported Truman; to a majority the
firing was clearly a shock. Even the UDA, for all its disagreement with Wallace's foreign policy, called the resignation "a
great loss to progressive forces in the country. . . . we cannot
align ourselves with the conservative and reactionary forces
which have made such enormous political capital out of the
whole episode." Most liberal responses were less equivocal.
"You have thought profoundly and in my judgment you are
profoundly right," William H. Davis told Wallace. "Clear-
thinking Americans who abhor the thought of another world
conflict will join Mr. Wallace in the fight for world peace,"
said Jack Kroll. Fiorello La Guardia called Wallace, "the champion of liberty and minorities. . . . A humble, little man who
has lived the Sermon on the Mount bigger than any man in his
Party." The *New Republic* called upon "every progressive
American . . . every American who holds misgivings for the future in this atomic age" to enlist behind Wallace.[18]

To many liberals the episode was an indication that Byrnes,
Vandenberg, and the other makers of American foreign policy
were attempting to cut off all discussion and criticism. And it
was something more, something which transcended substantive
matters. The last and greatest symbol of the Roosevelt years
had left the government. The Chicago *Sun* declared: "The
New Deal, as a driving force, is dead within the Truman
administration." [19]

III

With Wallace out of the Cabinet, demoralized liberals faced
the final weeks of the Congressional campaign. The primary
elections had been encouraging. The Republicans, it was true,
had rejected some outstanding liberal congressmen, including
Robert La Follette of Wisconsin and Charles La Follette of In-

diana. But the trend within the Democratic Party was clearly in favor of the progressives. Truman's purge of Representative Slaughter and the defeat of Senator Wheeler were only the most spectacular indications. By mid-August 9 incumbent conservative Democrats had been defeated while only 2 liberal Democrats had lost bids for renomination. Even in the South, there were liberal victories, the most notable being John Sparkman's triumph in the Alabama Senatorial primary. "The great wave of conservatism that was supposed to sweep the country after the war is a delusion," wrote Alexander Uhl in *PM*.[20]

After the firing of Wallace, however, the campaign developed into a disaster. The former secretary remained in the headlines and became the focus of a disruptive split within the Democratic Party. The Democratic campaign speakers' bureau at first refused to schedule engagements for him or for Senator Pepper but reversed itself after discovering that there was strong demand for them. Wallace engaged in a public controversy with Bernard Baruch over the American plan for international atomic control and won a large segment of the liberal movement to his view that the U.S. proposal was too rigid. In the middle of October, he announced that he had accepted the editorship of the *New Republic* and embarked upon a national speaking tour in behalf of liberal Democratic candidates.[21]

Republicans, who were already hurling charges of pro-Communism at their opponents, seized upon the Wallace issue. Branding Wallace and the large element in the Democratic Party which supported him pro-Communist, GOP candidates dared their Democratic opponents to come out flatly against Wallace's foreign policy statements. In the large urban states where Wallace had a mass following, Democrats frantically tried to avoid the issue. California Democratic Chairman James Roosevelt, for example, invited Wallace to come into the state but refused either to endorse or repudiate his views. In New York, Senatorial candidate Herbert Lehman found himself caught between the anti-Wallace Liberal Party and conservative Democrats on the one hand, and the pro-Wallace American Labor Party and left-wing Democrats on the other. Wallace's rallies drew huge crowds, but right-wing Democrats denounced him. The party seemed to be falling apart.[22]

While progressives were coming to grips with the Wallace ouster, they were watching the administration's handling of a growing meat shortage. The results contributed to their demoralization and loss of confidence in Truman. In an attempt to force an end to price controls, livestock producers were holding their stock off the market. In early September, the administration allowed a moderate increase in meat price ceilings, but the producers demanded total abolition. Liberals opposed any concessions and applauded when Truman strongly defended controls on September 26 and expressed determination to preserve them.

On October 14, however, under heavy pressure from Democratic leaders, Truman went on the air to announce a new policy. He denounced the producers and the anti–price control block in Congress, but he gave in and abolished ceilings. The tottering price control system had suffered a mortal blow. Some liberals, including Chester Bowles, conceded that Truman had had no choice, but others were sharply critical. Any special interest, said Fiorello La Guardia, could now feel free to "dislocate the economy of the entire country, or impair the health of the people, or jeopardize the life and safety of a community" until its demands were met. Many felt that the episode had provided yet another example of the president's weak and erratic leadership. He should have carried the fight to the country, declared the *New Republic*. He should have firmly exposed the producers' conspiracy, used all his powers to break it, and called upon the people to back him. At least he would have placed responsibility where it belonged, and he might have won.[23]

This impression of weak leadership was confirmed by the president's failure to participate in the campaign. Truman did not make a single speech. Democratic Chairman Hannegan even tactfully vetoed an election eve radio address, and the party put old Roosevelt recordings on the air. The Democrats, commented Thomas L. Stokes, had needed "someone to speak out strong and clear on the vital issues," but Truman had evaded his duty. "In trying to please everybody, in trying to be everything to all men, he came in the end to stand for little to anybody." [24]

The election was a liberal disaster by almost any measurement. The Democrats lost control of Congress for the first time since 1930. Of the 77 congressmen who had a rating of at least 80 percent liberal from the *New Republic*, only 36 were reelected. Of 98 congressmen who had formed a committee under George Outland of California to work for the Full Employment bill, 43 lost, including Outland himself.[25]

Progressives who examined the wreckage agreed that the defeat did not constitute a repudiation of Roosevelt and the New Deal. Most saw two key reasons for the rout—first, a vague but powerful and widespread discontent with government controls, consumer goods shortages, and labor disturbances; second, the failure of the administration to follow the Roosevelt example and provide the strong, liberal leadership which could have overcome these irritations. "The Democratic Party, when it recovers the forthright liberalism it had in the days of Franklin Roosevelt, will be called again to power," wrote the liberal Tennessean Jennings Perry. "And until then, it matters little to me whether it is in power or not." The New York *Post* concisely expressed the progressive consensus:

The men who gave the New Deal its vitality have been brushed out of Washington. They have been succeeded by Cabinet members and White House advisers too often possessing little vigor and less vision. Small wonder that so many voters preferred a Republican flag flying at the top of the pole to a New Deal standard at half mast.[26]

As for Truman, his prestige had reached its nadir. The Missouri returns illustrated the totality of his personal defeat. His hand-picked candidate for the House, Enos Axtell, and his friend and successor in the Senate, Frank Briggs, both lost to conservative Republicans. Most liberals could no longer take the president seriously. After Truman terminated what was left of price controls and issued a statement pledging cooperation with the Republicans, Tris Coffin wrote: "The President is only too glad to dump all the responsibilities on a Republican Congress." J. William Fulbright suggested that Truman restore unity to the government by conferring with Republican leaders, appointing their choice secretary of state, and then resigning the presidency in his favor. Marshall Field, publisher of the Chicago *Sun* and *PM,* and Harold Ickes endorsed the idea. For most liberals, a divided and deadlocked government with Truman was preferable to a unified and reactionary government without Truman, but this attitude implied little respect for the president. The New York *Post* refuted Ickes by stressing Truman's incompetence: "Holding against Truman his proven inability to make good appointments, in all logic how can Ickes then urge that Truman be allowed to make a more important appointment than any man has ever before in the history of this country—that of the next President?" [27]

At the start of December, another event reinforced the liberal opinion of Truman. More perhaps than any other person the president had brought into the government, Housing Administrator Wilson Wyatt had captured the imagination of progressives. Wyatt was advocating a daring crash program of prefabricated housing, but the new pre-fab companies would require enormous federal assistance. George Allen, Truman's personal representative on the RFC Board, strongly opposed loans in this new and unproven area. Truman decided in favor of Allen, and Wyatt bitterly submitted his resignation. Another important liberal had left the administration, and the housing problem seemed farther from solution than ever. [28]

Two distinct third-party movements indicated the depth of liberal discontent with Truman. One, organized in May 1946, was the National Educational Committee for a New Party. It included some powerful forces of native American radicalism and liberalism. The great old philosopher, John Dewey, gave the effort his blessing. The militant civil rights leader, A. Philip Randolph, was chairman. James G. Patton of the Farmers Union, Samuel Wolchak, president of the United Retail,

Wholesale and Department Store Workers, Walter Reuther, the newly elected president of the Auto Workers, the New York Liberal Party, Norman Thomas and his Socialists—all were involved. Clayton Fountain of the Auto Workers, Daniel Bell of the New York Social Democrats, and Lewis Corey, who was teaching economics at Antioch College, drafted a "Provisional Declaration of Principles" which was published in the *Antioch Review*.

The National Educational Committee stood for a collectivist social democracy which would go beyond the New Deal, and its economic program owed much to Corey's *The Unfinished Task*. Most of its members were Socialists or former Socialists, and its delcaration of independence from the major parties ("Liberals in the Republican party are frustrated, while the New Deal is a spent force in the Democratic party.") was more an exhortation to others than a promise of action by its drafters. Its foreign platform embraced the ideals of worldwide democracy and economic development. It pointedly and explicitly extended its strictures against imperialism to the Soviet Union, rejected the spheres-of-influence doctrine as a "thinly disguised form of colonial and political domination" which could only lead to future wars, and called upon the United States to support "the liberal democratic rights of people anywhere in the world, and to insist that other nations respect those rights."

The National Educational Committee represented the last effort of an indigenous American radicalism to change the structure of American politics and thereby open new vistas of reform. But its leadership, although impressive, could muster little in the way of the numbers which are the ultimate power in democratic politics. Jim Patton, for example, symbolized a tradition of agrarian radicalism which was no longer a viable force on the plains; he could deliver few votes. The Auto Workers represented a different tradition, but the union was to a great extent a creation of the New Deal, and most of its members probably felt an intense identification with the party of FDR. The others—Thomas, Randolph, the New York Liber-

als, the academicians—had only very small constituencies. Jack
Kroll firmly excluded the CIOPAC from the committee's councils, and most of the major unions had no interest whatever in
it. The committee had little political influence and virtually no
power; it could succeed only if the Democrats continued on the
path to disintegration.

The other third-party movement, informal and less distinct,
came from the extreme left wing of the liberal movement.
Since the end of 1945, the Communists had advocated a new
party. Vito Marcantonio and the American Labor Party had
joined the drive. Important elements in the NCPAC and the
ICCASP—Beanie Baldwin the most vocal among them—
favored the move. By November, this group seemed to be gaining a new recruit. Speaking in New York the day before the
election, Henry Wallace hinted at a third party, saying that
"new currents will be forming" and that events would determine their direction.[29]

Most liberals who held office or possessed serious political
ambitions and most labor leaders who had to deal with the
major parties in working for the practical needs of their constituencies were not yet prepared for a quixotic foray into the
unknown. However, if the discontent with Truman continued
to mushroom, the new-party sentiment would grow accordingly, and liberal leaders might be swept into it.

IV

An integral part of the liberal attitude toward Truman was a
belief that the president was betraying the memory of Roosevelt and the New Deal by his personal inadequacy, by throwing the New Dealers out of the administration, by departing
from Roosevelt's policies. After his death, FDR became a secular Christ symbol who had given his life to save America from
the hopelessness of depression and the grinding authoritarianism of fascism. In the progressive mind, he seemed possessed
of superhuman powers which could overcome any obstacle, put
America back on the path of reform, and restore international
harmony. Fiorello La Guardia exemplified this attitude in a

fervent broadcast from Roosevelt's Hyde Park study on January 26, 1947:

Pilgrimages will be coming to this shrine for centuries and centuries. They will be coming here as long as man reads history.

We cannot think of President Roosevelt as one who is gone. He is here. Every hope, yes, the peace of the world, requires his constant spiritual presence. . . .

President Roosevelt had the faculty of putting the beauty of poetry, the hope of life, the theories of better life, into actual daily practice. He gave so much to our people and translated into action all that had been written, but never tried before for a better, a richer, a fuller life.

How we miss him. Hardly a domestic problem or an international situation today but what we say 'Oh, if F.D.R. were only here.' [30]

Liberals who were disillusioned with Truman's inability to lead seemed to forget that Roosevelt had lost control of Congress long before his death. What the progressives missed was the power of FDR's *style,* not necessarily his ability to achieve liberal goals. A brilliant orator, a natural leader, a politician who had inspired and electrified the liberal movement with the force of his unique personality, Roosevelt had always seemed in command of a situation, ever moving, if at times deviously, toward the fulfillment of broad progressive accomplishments. Few men could have stood the contrast, and Truman, as he neared the end of his second year in office, was especially vulnerable. A colorless, bespectacled little man unable to make a decent speech, he seemed increasingly incapable of measuring up to the presidency.

The type of man Roosevelt had brought to Washington was disappearing also. Ickes had left in disgust; Wallace had been kicked out; Bowles and many others had exited quietly. At the start of the year, rumor had it that Truman was attempting to appease Congress by bringing into the administration only people who had not been connected with Roosevelt. A few New Dealers remained in inconspicuous places—Ben Cohen in the State Department, David Niles as a White House assistant, James M. Landis as chairman of the Civil Aeronautics Board

—but the new Washington climate did not seem congenial to bright, idealistic young lawyers of the type who had come into the administration in the 1930s. "It is more important to have a connection with Battery D, 129th Field Artillery, than with Felix Frankfurter," wrote one observer. The men around Truman appeared to exemplify the new mood. "Gentle, worldly-wise, sensitive Harry Hopkins has been replaced by ebullient, slap-on-the back George E. Allen as chief White House confidant and confessor," wrote James Wechsler. "Hopkins was a deep citizen with a vast range of political, social and human interests. Allen is an amiable drugstore cowboy, splashing joyously about in a big pool."

The departures ran beyond the top offices. "Hundreds on the lower levels have slipped out unnoticed," wrote labor journalist Henry Zon, "and thousands of others are eying the door." This was perhaps an exaggeration, but certainly many prominent lower-level officials did leave. It is hard to say how many of them did so in sorrow or in anger; many were simply physically and financially exhausted by arduous wartime jobs. Yet as the astute journalist Cabell Phillips observed, they were more willing to depart an administration headed by Truman. FDR had served as "a sort of spiritual anchor" holding them to government service; his successor could play no such role. The exodus of the New Dealers, however large, whatever its reasons, became another symbol of the inspirational vacuum the liberals found in Washington.[31]

For many liberals, the most catastrophic development of the Truman administration was the growing rift with Russia, a rift which they believed Roosevelt, through the wisdom of his policies and the magic of his personality, would have prevented. On the first anniversary of FDR's death, Samuel Grafton expressed a widely held conviction:

It is because he is gone that the West, squealing legalisms, is now forlornly on the defensive, whereas if he had lived, blessed bad lawyer that he was, we might now be trying for a new level of international understanding.

For he, more than any other, was the coalition, he, who could deal with Mr. Churchill as a country squire, and with Mr. Stalin as a commoner. Somehow, in him, the two currents had met, but not in a whirlpool; and the fact that these two contrary streams could produce a man so much at peace with himself and at ease with his world, made hope feasible for others.[32]

This conviction seemed even more credible in the fall of 1946 after the appearance of Elliott Roosevelt's *As He Saw It,* an account of most of the top-level conferences of World War II by one of FDR's sons. The 250 pages of breezy prose depicted the late president as a leader determined to undermine the great imperial systems and promote popular democracy throughout the world's underdeveloped areas. Churchill was the major antagonist, the personification of the Tory imperialism which Roosevelt despised. "Don't think for a moment, Elliott, that Americans would be dying in the Pacific tonight, if it hadn't been for the shortsighted greed of the French and the British and the Dutch," Elliott quoted his father as saying. "Shall we allow them to do it all, all over again?" By contrast, Stalin appeared simply as the leader of a nation which was waging a valiant battle against the fascist enemy and which seemed ready to cooperate with the United States.[33]

Postwar policy, Elliott believed, had taken a ghastly turn away from his father's plans. The United States was supporting reaction and imperialism; guided by the State Department and the military, it was blindly backing the British and abandoning the principle of Big Three unity, refusing to recognize Russia's legitimate fears and interests. "If a Churchill could talk about an iron curtain in Europe, a Stalin could point to the reasons for its necessity." But the United States no longer listened to both sides, no longer attempted to be the honest broker.

A small group of willful men in London and Washington are anxious to create and foster an atmosphere of war hatred against the Russians, just as though the Russian people had not borne the brunt of the military force of Nazism, borne it, overthrown it, and thereby demonstrated for all time their importance to the coalition for peace.[34]

Strongly anti-Communist liberals denounced the book. "It is a passionate perversion of the truth to try to picture President

Roosevelt as leading a Russian party as against a British party," wrote Adolf A. Berle, Jr., of the Liberal Party, asserting that Elliott had left the impression that FDR "was fighting the war against Great Britain and that his main object was to agree with any claim that the Soviet Union put forward." [35]

But among that large center group of liberals who were neither firmly pro-Russian nor firmly anti-Russian, who still hoped for an agreement with the Soviets, the book stirred a different reaction. In an important review, Jonathan Daniels said, "There are living men who, without knowledge of the details Elliott reports, can testify to the basic truth of his report of the workings of his father's mind and his father's clear purposes and plans." What was happening after Roosevelt's death, he feared, was similar to what had happened after Lincoln's death —small-minded men had seized control of policy and were using a late president's name for a course which he would have disapproved. Truman had good intentions, but not only did he lack FDR's diplomatic skill—"Nothing is so obvious as that the warm, human, smiling, face-to-face dealings Roosevelt made famous and effective have disappeared"—but he had failed to grasp basic foreign policy issues. He was being pushed toward a final break with the Roosevelt tradition by a coalition of State Department reactionaries, newspaper publishers, "Irish politicians and Claghorn senators." "He was—and I believe is— eager to fulfill the hopes Roosevelt delivered to him. But Mr. Truman is not Roosevelt." Daniels' last sentence doubtless expressed much of the frustration and disillusion which progressives felt. [36]

For some liberals the memory of Roosevelt was the best hope for the revitalization of the progressive movement. In 1946 there were at least two projects based on this concept. John L. Nichols, a transportation consultant with an interest in Democratic politics, proposed the establishment of an elaborate system of National Roosevelt Clubs which would attempt to identify the Democratic Party with the spirit of the New Deal. Claude Pepper, Chester Bowles, and Oscar Chapman planned a national pressure group tentatively called the Roosevelt

Forum. Like Nichols's clubs, the Forum would have state and local chapters as well as a national headquarters and would work for a rebirth of liberalism within the Democratic Party. It might also provide a boost to Pepper's hopes for the 1948 vice-presidential nomination. The plans were ambitious—a Washington office with a full-time national director, a regular radio series, a legislative bulletin. Pepper, Bowles, and Chapman obtained the blessings of Eleanor Roosevelt and hoped to obtain some of the country's outstanding progressives as sponsors, among them Henry Morgenthau, Robert Kenny, James Folsom, Senators Joseph Guffey, Glen Taylor, and Harley Kilgore. The Forum idea rested explicitly upon the assumption that the Truman administration had abandoned the heritage of FDR. A memorandum outlining the project said:

[I]t is obvious that throughout the country there is being expressed sharp dissatisfaction with the present Democratic administration. The dissatisfaction comes out of the fact that the leadership of the Democratic Party has turned away from the Roosevelt program and policies. . . .

[A] real effort must be made inside the Democratic Party to revert to the Roosevelt foreign and domestic program and to restore to the people a feeling of confidence in the party's desire and ability to put this program across.

Neither the Nichols plan nor the Roosevelt Forum idea reached fruition. One reason was the hostility of the Democratic National Committee. Another was the intense activity under way on other fronts to rebuild the progressive movement. There would be a final and futile attempt to achieve the dream of progressive unity; then the liberal movement would undergo a process of polarization and sharp division over the issues of Communism and Russia. There would be no room for groups in the middle.[37]

Frustrated, beaten, and demoralized, the liberal movement was about to embark upon a searching reexamination of some of its basic assumptions and a difficult quest for identity.

Chapter 6

The Polarization of the Liberal Movement

The discouraging political events of 1946 revealed to many liberals the fact that the progressive movement, so dependent upon FDR, had never quite achieved the ability to stand by itself. The liberals might find inspiration and conviction in the memory of Roosevelt, but they also realized that something more would be necessary to bring them back from serious defeat. Many believed that their major problem was organizational, and that the road back to power had to be based upon liberal solidarity. To others, however, the liberal difficulty was moral and ideological; it centered upon the refusal of so many progressives to disassociate themselves strongly from Communists and pro-Communists. From this perspective, the paramount urgency was the reestablishment of American liberalism as a movement in the native progressive tradition. By mid-1946, these two lines of thought and action were already struggling for dominance; by 1947, they formed two poles, with most progressives being drawn toward one or the other.

I

The advocates of progressive unity generally thought in terms of perserving the Popular Front and displayed an obsession with the dangers of fascism. They were powerful in most liberal organizations. Under the leadership of Beanie Baldwin, the NCPAC remained committed to the Popular Front. Dynamic and well-financed, the NCPAC had set up branches in all the important industrial states, and planned to have offices in 25 states by November 1946. The Southern Conference for Human Welfare, whose director, Clark Foreman, was an ardent Popular Fronter, acted as an unofficial Southern affiliate and also drew support from the CIO. Despite the accusations of pro-Communism thrown at him and the NCPAC, Baldwin remained an influential figure who enjoyed ready access to Democratic chairman Hannegan. The ICCASP, with its talent and fund-raising potential, appeared equally formidable. It secured the services of both Harold Ickes and James Roosevelt, FDR's eldest son, who spent a few months as its chief organizer before resigning to become California Democratic chairman. The ICCASP and NCPAC seemed for most of 1946 to be the vigorous and expanding groups to whom the future of the liberal movement belonged.[1]

The Popular Front approach had an extremely able advocate within the CIO in the person of Lee Pressman, widely regarded as a pro-Communist but nevertheless a close adviser to CIO President Philip Murray. Murray himself was a devout Catholic who leaned toward anti-Communism, but he was genuinely fond of Pressman. More importantly, he realized that strong manifestations of anti-Communism might seriously split the CIO at a time when the future of American labor was uncertain. Many state and local CIO councils were under the control of Popular Front factions so dedicated to the USSR that they occasionally attempted to knife anti-Soviet politicians who had prolabor voting records. Popular Fronters also controlled the United Electrical Workers and a few lesser national unions.

Anti-Communism nevertheless grew rapidly within the labor movement after the conclusion of the war. CIO Secretary-Treasurer James B. Carey, who had been ousted from the presidency of the Electrical Workers by a Popular Front faction, provided a focus of leadership at CIO national headquarters. In the spring of 1946, Walter Reuther won election as president of the United Auto Workers; his victory, throwing control of a major union to militant anti-Communists, was a turning point in American labor history. Successful anti-Communist movements developed within several local CIO councils, and in the fall of 1946 a group of labor leaders headed by Jack Altman of the Retail, Wholesale and Department Store Workers established the Committee for Democratic Trade Unionism to fight Communists and fellow travelers. At the CIO convention that November, Murray had to use all his power and prestige to avoid a wide-open debate between Popular Fronters and anti-Communists.[2]

Popular Front advocates even amassed considerable influence in the National Farmers Union. The NFU's bent toward agrarian pacifism naturally inclined it against policies which might lead to war with the Soviet Union. Moreover, it was financially dependent upon a foundation controlled by Popular Fronters for the maintenance of its active Washington, D.C., operations. Most of its important national and state officials were tolerant toward the Communists, and the head of its small Eastern division was an ardent Party-liner. In mid-1946, Gardner Jackson, a militant anti-Communist progressive, was dismissed from the NFU staff, and Benton Stong, the editor of the *National Union Farmer,* was transferred to another position. Both moves, Jackson charged, stemmed from the growing influence of pro-Communists around NFU president James Patton.

In the fall of 1947, Patton fired James Elmore, Stong's successor, because, Elmore asserted, the *National Union Farmer* had run anti-Soviet features. The St. Louis *Post-Dispatch* gave some credence to Elmore and criticized Patton for failing to deliver a satisfactory rebuttal. In 1948, Elmore continued his attacks with a charge that 5 of the 6 men on Patton's personal staff were pro-Communist. There was at least a bit of truth to Elmore's accusations. Patton himself, however, was an independent radical born and raised in the tradition of Debsian socialism. He was also close to Beanie Baldwin and Henry Wallace. He was erratic, willing to use the Communists, and perhaps susceptible to being used by them, but he felt no identification with the Soviet Union and was determined to preserve his own autonomy. The NFU president was also a smooth political operator. He had resigned from the NCPAC when charges of Communist influence within it had become embarrassing, and was careful to keep a line open to the Truman administration. He doubtless realized, moreover, that Popular Fronters were influential in only about half of the 15 state organizations which claimed 90 percent of the NFU membership and wielded most of the NFU's effective political power; they had practically no rank-and-file support. Despite some Communist influences, the Farmers Union remained essentially independent, ready to move with events or political imperatives.[3]

The American Veterans Committee was another major battleground. The only veterans organization with a liberal orientation, the AVC had been established by a group of young progressives caught up in the idealism which had accompanied World War II. Its leading members were prominent and capable non-Communists—Charles Bolte, the founder and chairman, Franklin D. Roosevelt, Jr., Robert Nathan, Richard Bolling, Oren Root, Chat Patterson, and Gilbert Harrison. By 1946, the AVC had 80,000 members and appeared capable of becoming a major force in American politics. That January, however, the Communist Party, which at first had attempted to infiltrate the American Legion and the Veterans of Foreign Wars, began to encourage its members to join the AVC. Soon several local chapters were under the control of Communist or Popular Front factions.

At the AVC's first annual convention in June 1946, the Popular Front faction made no attempt to challenge Bolte's hold on the chairmanship but did offer a candidate for vice-chairman, NCPAC official Frederick Borden, against Gilbert Harrison, who had the support of the leadership. When it became apparent that Borden could not muster a majority, the Popular Fronters made an effective, if false, gesture of compromise by turning to a so-called "unity candidate." Harrison still won the vice-chairmanship, and the leadership was able to win a majority of the National Planning Committee, which subsequently issued a scathing denunciation of the Communist Party. At the time, the outcome seemed to be a major victory for anti-Communist liberalism. However, the Popular Fronters, by representing themselves as a unity caucus, secured the election of 7 members to the National Planning Committee and continued to control key locals. For the next three years, the AVC would go from one paralyzing factional fight to another. Anti-Communists would retain control of the national offices, but the organization's appeal and effectiveness was destroyed. By early 1949, it could claim only 40,000 members. To many liberals, the AVC's difficulties demonstrated that if the Communists and their allies could not rule an organization, they would not hesitate to ruin it.[4]

During 1946, Communist participation in the liberal movement, taken for granted during the war, developed into an issue which seriously divided liberals. "The traitors and knaves within the walls are always much more dangerous than those without," warned Robert La Follette, Jr. Marquis Childs condemned the Communist Party as a "fifth column" whose adherents had obtained "positions of power and influence in the labor movement and in organizations allied with it." The Philadelphia *Record* declared that the liberals were "permitting Communists who 'came along for the ride' to climb into the driver's seat." In June James Wechsler and four other journalists in the Washington bureau of *PM* resigned with a charge that the paper was hewing too closely to the Communist line. A month later, the gifted young historian and publicist Arthur M. Schlesinger, Jr., published an article in *Life*, condemning the Communists as authoritarians who worked for the interests of the Soviet Union, wielded great influence within the CIO and the ICCASP, and helped the American right wing by "dividing and neutralizing the left." At a West Coast liberal conference in September, Professor Harry Girvetz, an authority on the history of liberal thought, urged the establishment of a progressive organization which would emphatically disavow the Communists.[5]

The Union for Democratic Action provided a focus for anti-Communist liberalism. With the Employment Act through Congress, the organization no longer had a cause which could draw money and support or which necessitated work with Popular Front liberals. In May, the UDA's National Board decided to undertake an all-out expansion effort, organized largely around its long tradition of anti-Communism. Jim Loeb kicked off the drive with a letter published in the *New Republic,* attacking the Communist penetration of American liberalism. The *New Republic* had solicited the letter and promised its readers that it would take a stand on the issue; despite pressure from Loeb, however, the journal never did so.[6]

Responses published in subsequent issues revealed the depth of liberal disagreement. Even Jackson Valtair of Dallas and Stanley Isaacs of New York, both active UDA leaders, disagreed with Loeb. They recalled the Spanish Civil War, argued that the Popular Front was still workable because liberals and Communists had the same objectives, and asserted that a policy built around anti-Communism was negative, disruptive, and self-defeating. Isaacs, a highly respected politician, expressed an attitude prevalent among liberals: The Communist menace was phony; the fascist menace was real. Therefore, one could not attack the Communists, as obnoxious as they were; to do so would simply strengthen fascism and divide its opponents. Others expressed even more extreme views. To Clark Foreman, a Communist was a left-wing liberal, and the liberals had to achieve unity. Curtis MacDougall, a leader of the Popular Front group within the Independent Voters of Illinois, argued that the Communists and their associates were "doers" and activists, unlike the "old time liberals" who had failed to progress beyond the issuance of manifestoes and the writing of magazine articles.[7]

Other letters, although not a majority of those the *New Republic* printed, agreed with Loeb. Los Angeles progressive Art Arthur and the young political scientist Stephen K. Bailey both warned that the Communists followed orders from Moscow, often managed to take over groups in which they gained a foothold, and would not hesitate to sabotage an organization if such tactics suited their purposes. Arthur pointedly observed that in the recent California primary "the so-called old-time liberals got their candidates elected; it was the Communists who showed themselves incompetent when the key men on whom they concentrated their support went down to defeat under that handicap."

The stir caused by Loeb's letter was scarcely over when another UDA official, Alfred Baker Lewis, published a communication in the *Nation*, attacking the NCPAC and ICCASP for failure to exclude Communists. "Communists are obviously not liberals but fanatical supporters and defenders of the Russian totalitarian dictatorship and its foreign policy, whatever that policy may be." [8]

The UDA was attempting to reverse the trend of liberal thought, to convince progressives that fascism was no longer a danger which dwarfed all else, that liberals must no longer divide the world between fascists and antifascists but rather between authoritarians and anti-authoritarians. Perhaps during the era of the anti-Hitler coalition liberals and Communists had shared some important objectives, but they were no longer on the same side. Fundamentally, the anti-Communists argued their position in terms of libertarian morality. However, one aspect of their persuasion grew out of simple expediency. This was the assertion that the Communists were discrediting the liberal movement by their very presence, and alienating masses of voters. After the November elections, this argument would be especially effective.

The Oregon journalist Richard L. Neuberger illustrated the divided and confused attitudes within the liberal mind. A hard-fought Democratic primary in Seattle, Washington, had pitted incumbent Democratic Congressman Hugh De Lacy against Howard Costigan, an anti-Communist liberal who emphasized De Lacy's Communist associations and alleged adherence to the Party line. It was symbolic of the doubts within the progressive movement, Neuberger observed, that FDR's family had divided on the election, with James Roosevelt endorsing

De Lacy while his sister, Anna Boettiger, supported Costigan. Neuberger's first instinctive reaction was to deplore the "Red-baiting" which had entered the campaign; yet after some thought he had decided that the issue was legitimate and had opted for Costigan. "I do not want men in public office in America whose decisions appear to be decided by the interests of Russia." [9]

But many others, as the replies to Loeb had shown, did not feel that the issue was legitimate. A majority or near-majority of the liberals still felt it was possible to work with Communists and feared that efforts to exclude the Communists could lead only to Red-hunting negativism. This was the essential mood of the last major attempt to reconstruct the Popular Front.[10]

I I

In mid-May, the leaders of the CIO, the NCPAC, and the ICCASP formed a joint committee to coordinate liberal activity in the fall Congressional campaign. The establishment of the coordinating group seemed to be a significant step toward the long-sought objective of liberal solidarity. The committee soon took another important stride by issuing a call for a general Conference of Progressives to meet in Chicago at the end of September.[11] One of the widest and most representative assemblies of liberals ever brought together, the meeting convened a few days after the firing of Henry Wallace. In addition to representatives of the sponsoring organizations, James Patton, Philip Murray, A. F. Whitney, Clark Foreman, NAACP Secretary Walter White, Claude Pepper, Henry Morgenthau, and many other prominent progressives attended. Wallace did not come, but his close aide Harold Young was present. Only the UDA was conspicuously absent.

The conference adopted resolutions on domestic policy with which few liberals could disagree—condemnation of the conservative coalition in Congress; opposition to antilabor legislation; support of price and rent controls, a housing program, civil rights, welfare legislation, resource development programs, antimonopoly action, aid to small business, and tax reform to increase purchasing power. But the foreign policy program, while by no means blatantly pro-Communist, was more debatable.

It began by urging "a swift return to the progressive global thinking of Franklin Roosevelt." Many of its planks—opposition to fascism, militarism, and imperialism, support of the Four Freedoms, of "a free, united and independent China" with an end to intervention by all foreign powers, of the Jewish cause in Palestine, of a redoubled famine relief drive, of a worldwide economic development program—could command general assent among progressives. But other planks assumed that Big Three unity was still possible. They called upon America, not Russia, to "exert every effort" to recapture the mutual trust of the war period and asserted that fascism was still the major danger to the world, that Russian demands for huge reparations were justifiable, that spheres of influence existed and must be accepted, and that the American plan for control of atomic energy was defective in its refusal to destroy the U. S. atomic stockpile until an international inspection plan was functioning. Moreover, a special resolution praised Henry Wallace:

Carry on in your fight for the fullest, freest discussion of that basic problem of our day—international cooperation.

Carry on with confidence that you have the support of the millions upon millions of Americans who believe in the program of Franklin Delano Roosevelt.

Despite frantic efforts by some of the convention's managers, the Communist issue broke into the open. Philip Murray added an off-the-cuff attack against "damn American Communists" to his speech. Harold Ickes withstood strong pressure and delivered an address attacking Russian as well as American and British policy, warning that progressives who advocated free elections in Spain or Greece must also advocate them for Poland, Bulgaria, and Rumania.

The anti-Communist declarations, especially Murray's, received applause, but the acclaim, coming as it did from many seasoned Popular Fronters, must have been a bit ritualistic. Some observers, in fact, detected skullduggery when the conference mimeograph machine suddenly broke down just as Ickes's speech was brought to it, thereby making it impossible to distribute copies and hampering press coverage. Perhaps they were a bit too suspicious, but the episode demonstrated how pervasive the concern over Communism was becoming.[12]

All the same, the movement toward a new Popular Front proceeded. A continuations committee, representing all the major participants in the conference, was established, and after its first meeting in mid-October, Philip Murray announced that it had taken the first step toward the construction of "the most powerful liberal and progressive organization brought together in the history of the country."

The consequences for the UDA and its own expansion effort were all-important; no large-scale liberal organization could survive against a competitor financed and encouraged by the CIO. James Loeb worked closely with Jack Altman and James Carey to discredit the Chicago conference by showing that the ICCASP and NCPAC were Communist-infiltrated. Eleanor Roosevelt, after much difficulty in obtaining a hearing, personally carried the UDA case to Murray.

There are indications that Murray was already acutely worried about the political liabilities of Communist infiltration and a pro-Soviet foreign policy; he may have never had a serious interest in continuing the Conference of Progressives. By the middle of December, he had dropped any commitment to the continuations committee. An expanded UDA was assured, and there was no longer a possibility that the liberal movement would come under the domination of a single large group, based on the Chicago conference and containing pro-Communist elements.[13]

III

The disaster of the elections handed the anti-Communist liberals a new and convincing argument. "The Communist party gave the kiss of death to Democratic candidates in many parts of the country," declared the Philadelphia *Record,* warning that the Democratic Party must repudiate the Communists who had seized its coat-tails. Marquis Childs, Elmer Davis, and James Wechsler all agreed. Richard Neuberger attributed the defeat of the progressive Washington Senator Hugh Mitchell to the sweeping vote against Hugh De Lacy in Seattle. The liberal Indiana Republican Charles La Follette charged that the Communists had been responsible for many of the liberal defeats and asserted that they were trying to sabotage the liberal movement. [14]

Some independent liberals who had not been conspicuously anti-Communist seemed to be won over. "The plague of Communism," wrote Thomas L. Stokes, had become a serious problem within many progressive organizations. There was only one way to deal with the difficulty: "unmask the Communists and vote them out and root them out of the key spots as a matter of internal government and policing." In a series of editorials for *PM,* Max Lerner asserted that the Republicans had won "largely on the basis of a Red scare" and called for the reconstruction of the progressive movement. He still believed that the great enemy of American democracy was the reactionary right, but "that enemy can be fought effectively only by a liberal-labor coalition which has replaced Communist influence by a militant non-Communist leadership." The Communists might not be an immediate menace but neither were they to be treated as allies; their solutions and tactics were alien to American radicalism. The central problem of liberalism for perhaps the next decade would be the building of "a trade-union and political progressive movement which is clearly non-Communist but does not spend its best energies in Communist-hunting." [15]

The Communist controversy surfaced most noticeably within the ICCASP. As early as June 1946, Harold Ickes, the organization's biggest political name, was offering to resign as Executive Director. His reasons were complex. The Old Curmudgeon did not get along well with Director Hannah Dorner and the rest of the staff, who apparently felt that his high salary entitled the ICCASP to more than token services and the use of his name. In addition, the organization was $100,000 in debt by mid-1946 and in July Miss Dorner had to ask Ickes to forego two months of his salary. ("I am sure that his Scotch blood froze cold at the thought of it, but he gave in," she told Jo Davidson.) Even as these problems were developing, Kenneth Crawford and others were trying to persuade Ickes that the ICCASP was Communist-dominated.

Ickes agreed to withhold his resignation until after the Congressional elections, but during the fall he found himself in further conflict with the organization. He opposed the ICCASP protest over the firing of Wallace, probably more out of his dislike for Wallace than for reasons of policy, and he refused to go along with the group's opposition to the American plan for international control of atomic energy, although he did harbor doubts about the Baruch plan. Six days after the election, the ICCASP announced Ickes's resignation, and Ickes did nothing to discourage a widespread belief that his departure was an anti-Communist protest.[16]

At about the same time, Nobel prize–winning chemist Harold Urey of the University of Chicago also resigned, charging that the ICCASP had failed to live up to its professions of independent liberalism. The New York *Times* reported that many other Chicago scientists were following Urey's example, leaving the organization's technological division with "only a handful of active participants." [17]

Another important defection was that of the ICCASP's Philadelphia chairman, Morris L. Cooke, a highly respected 74-year-old progressive who had served as head of the Rural Electrification Administration during the New Deal. He warned that the organization would have to undertake "some housecleaning—part of it painful." He agreed with the argument that the Communists had hurt the liberal movement in the elections and that they were essentially tools of the USSR. "American liberalism seeking to regain its dominance in American political affairs can have no traffic of any kind whatsoever with *American* Communism or *American* Communists." When his call for a staff housecleaning went unheeded, Cooke resigned; his departure deprived the ICCASP of yet another figure with political experience and standing.[18]

Shaken by its internal difficulties, the ICCASP prepared to dissolve its identity, but not its principles.

IV

During the fall, the leaders of the NCPAC and the ICCASP decided to merge their organizations. The move was natural enough. The two groups shared common ideals and had often cooperated in the past; in addition, they were both in debt and tired of competing with each other for money. Sidney Hillman, who had opposed the merger, reputedly out of fear of undue Communist influence, was dead. The new combination would be an impressive organization of nonlabor progressives capable of playing a major role within the continuations committee of the Conference of Progressives.[19]

On December 28, the two groups, along with some smaller state and local progressive organizations, met in New York to establish the Progressive Citizens of America. Many of the delegates clearly saw themselves as the nucleus of a new party. They cheered Fiorello La Guardia's strong criticism of the Truman administration, but La Guardia was perceptibly less in tune with his audience when he warned against a third party. The next day, Henry Wallace appeared, and it was immediately apparent that he was the leader of the PCA in spirit, if not in title. According to the New York *Times,* he received only "unenthusiastic applause" when he declared his neutrality between Soviet-haters and pro-Communists, but the audience was with him as he declared that planned prosperity at home

was the first step toward world order, condemned the administration program of "imperialism and heavy armament," exhorted the PCA to "repel all the attacks of the plutocrats and
monopolists who will try to brand us as Red," lambasted the
organization's foes as "neo-Fascists," and hinted at a new party.

The PCA's "Program for Political Action" declared that the
Democratic Party—"notoriously tainted by jim-crow reaction
and machine greed"—had abandoned the Roosevelt tradition.
"We cannot, therefore, rule out the possibility of a new political party, whose fidelity to our goals can be relied upon." Its
domestic program was an unexceptional statement which denounced monopoly and racial discrimination and expressed
support for welfare legislation, civil rights bills, the rights of
labor, protection of the family farmer, benefits for veterans,
and equal opportunity for youth. Its foreign program was an
equally standard expression of progressive goals, but many liberals were prepared to disagree with its omissions and emphases. It stressed the danger of fascism—in Spain and
Argentina—but made no mention of Communism or the Soviet Union. In some respects it was virtually a duplicate of the
Russian line: it urged worldwide disarmament without the
slightest mention of a specific plan; it met the enormously difficult problem of atomic energy simply by calling for the immediate and total destruction of all nuclear weapons.

The PCA constitution prohibited discrimination within the
organization because of political beliefs, and the leadership
made it clear that the provision extended to Communists. The
group would not even reply to criticism on that point, said co-
chairman Frank Kingdon. "This, of course, is the way in which
the Communists traditionally invite themselves into the house
and make it illegal for their critics to do anything about it
while they take over the furniture," commented James Wechsler.

Nevertheless, the PCA had respected leadership and strong
possibilities. Jo Davidson shared the chairmanship with Kingdon, and, when he left the country in mid-1947 for an extended stay in France, the popular Californian Robert Kenny

took his place. Beanie Baldwin, as executive vice-chairman, was a capable and experienced national director. Among the vice-chairmen were Bartley Crum, Colonel Evans Carlson, Clark Foreman, Philip Murray, Jack Kroll, and A. F. Whitney. Most of the important figures from the Roosevelt era stayed out of the PCA, but the organization had identified itself with the most charismatic of the New Dealers, Henry Wallace.[20]

Many of the Roosevelt people were nevertheless itching to return to public life; * they simply considered the expansion of the UDA a more attractive alternative. A week after the founding of the PCA, an impressive group of liberals convened in Washington to form Americans for Democratic Action. Among the old New Dealers in attendance were Leon Henderson, Richard Gilbert, Chester Bowles, Paul A. Porter, David Ginsburg, Carl Auerbach, Ed Pritchard, and John Kenneth Galbraith, all from the OPA; Elmer Davis, who had headed the Office of War Information; Gardner Jackson, who had fought for the rights of the sharecropper. Isador Lubin and William H. Davis would be prominent at a second meeting in March. Benjamin V. Cohen, upon leaving the government in the fall, would work with the new group. Eleanor Roosevelt was there with her great name and enormous moral authority. Presiding over the initial meeting, Elmer Davis commented that they looked like a "government-in-exile."

Other names filled in a broad spectrum of a newly emergent anti-Communist liberalism. A delegation of labor leaders—James B. Carey, Walter Reuther, David Dubinsky, Emil Rieve, and Hugo Ernst—needed a successful ADA to exemplify the

*Isador Lubin's experience probably was representative of the eagerness with which the New Dealers sought to return to public service. Lubin quickly became bored with private business, toyed for a time with the idea of establishing a volunteer committee on economic stabilization, practically begged the Truman administration for a job, and was extremely happy to receive an appointment to the United Nations Reconstruction Commission. Lubin to William H. Davis, April 25, 1946, and Davis to Lubin, May 1, 1946, Davis MSS, State Historical Society of Wisconsin; David E. Lilienthal, *The Journals of David E. Lilienthal—The Atomic Energy Years, 1945–1950* (New York, 1964) p. 527; Lubin to Matthew J. Connelly, July 29, 1946, HST MSS OF 481.

appeal of anti-Communist progressivism, and the nascent organization needed them as a bridge to organized labor and a source of financial support. Other founders were rising young political figures wary of old Popular Front dogmas and sensitive to the necessity of removing any Communist taint from the liberal movement: Franklin D. Roosevelt, Jr., Wilson Wyatt, George Edwards of Detroit, Richardson Dilworth of Philadelphia, and a group which was reaching for control of the Minnesota Democratic-Farmer-Labor Party, Eugenie Anderson, Arthur Naftalin, and Minneapolis Mayor Hubert Humphrey. Several influential journalists attended: Joseph and Stewart Alsop, Marquis Childs, Barry Bingham, who published the Louisville *Courier-Journal,* James Wechsler, who had joined the New York *Post,* Kenneth Crawford, and Robert Bendiner of the *Nation.* Another founder was Arthur Schlesinger, Jr., the activist-scholar. An especially important force was Joseph L. Rauh, a dynamic Washington, D.C., attorney who had served as deputy to Wilson Wyatt before Wyatt's ejection from the Truman administration and was beginning a practice in which he would fight (all too often unsuccessfully) for one good cause after another. Somewhat overshadowed was the old UDA itself, represented by Loeb, Niebuhr, and other long-time members.[21]

The expansion meeting began on January 3, 1947, with a dinner at which Chester Bowles, the main speaker, launched strong attacks upon Republican reaction and Communist totalitarianism. Establishing a temporary organizing committee, the ADA issued a statement of principles calling for extension of New Deal welfare programs, protection of civil liberties, stabilization of the American economy, support of the U.N., efforts for democracy and reform all over the world. A key sentence stated: "We reject any association with Communists or sympathizers with communism in the United States as completely as we reject any association with Fascists or their sympathizers." From the start it was apparent that this was the issue which divided the ADA and the PCA.[22]

Loeb made this point even clearer in a letter to the *New Re-*

public. Deferring to the sensibilities of many liberals, he deplored the press emphasis on a liberal split over Communism; he said that the ADA did not stand for "an inflexible and doctrinaire 'anti-Sovietism'" nor did it "offer a blueprint for American-Russian relations." But at the same time he called the establishment of the ADA "a declaration of liberal independence from the stifling and paralyzing influence of the Communists and their apologists in America." And he added: "No movement that maintains a double standard on the issue of human liberty can lay claim to the American liberal tradition." [23]

At the end of March another ADA meeting elected permanent officers and drafted long platforms on domestic and foreign issues. A glance at the new leadership indicated the transformation from the UDA—Wilson Wyatt, national chairman; Leon Henderson, chairman of the Executive Committee; Hubert Humphrey and Franklin D. Roosevelt, Jr., vice chairmen; New York businessman Louis Harris, treasurer; Joe Rauh, secretary of the board; Jim Loeb, executive secretary, the only officer who had been a prominent member of the UDA. Able to call on considerable talent and energy, the ADA began an ambitious nationwide organizational campaign.

Perhaps its greatest triumph thus far had been its success in attracting the New Dealers, an enterprise which at times had required a great deal of effort and persuasion on Loeb's part but which would pay enormous dividends. Their mere physical presence in the ADA was a strong counter to the PCA's close ties with Wallace; moreover, they were a group whose pronouncements, testimony before Congressional committees, and speeches could command considerable attention. Capitalizing on its links with the New Deal and the memory of FDR, the organization instituted a series of "Roosevelt Day" fund-raising dinners to be held every year about the time of FDR's birthday. FDR, Jr., seemed to be one of the most promising young politicians in the country and was much in demand as a speaker at organizing affairs. Eleanor Roosevelt was an invaluable asset, although she refused to accept any office and wanted the organization run by the younger liberals. When Henry Wallace seized upon her relatively inactive role to argue that she was not really a member of the ADA, Jim Loeb replied with a stinging rebuke. She alone could match Wallace's appeal to the liberal community. Beyond her the ADA had a vast pool of talent which the PCA could not equal.[24]

V

Jo Davidson best expressed the PCA's reaction to its new rival. In the wake of the 1946 defeat, it was imperative for liberals to work together. Instead, reactionaries who had screamed "Communism" had been able to divide the left. It was an old, familiar technique:

I saw how it was used by Hitler to divide and confuse the progressives in Germany. . . . We must not let it happen here.

Those who make anti-Communism the sole basis for organization will find themselves so busy witch-hunting that they will have little energy left to work on the important issues.

. . . when you become effective you're sure to be called Communist. And if you're not, then you're not effective. You and I expect the word Communist to be used by reaction. We don't expect it to be used by liberals. Because when liberals use it to divide and split themselves it spells doom. They play straight into the hands of reaction.[25]

Few independent progressives accepted Davidson's argument. The Chicago *Sun,* while refuting suggestions that the PCA was a Communist front, called the split "an honest division over principle" and went on to say: "The time has come to realize that Communist aims are one thing and progressive aims another." Harold Ickes did not join the ADA because he felt that it was too close to the Democratic Party, but he sympathized with the organization in his columns and bitterly attacked the PCA, commenting that it consisted of "the same names and the same faces that under ever-changing labels, have offered themselves, time without number, as volunteer leaders of the liberals." He sharply attacked Frank Kingdon's assertion that members of any "minority" could join the PCA. The Communist Party, he warned, was not a racial or religious minority; it was the vehicle of a nonassimilable political ideology which was alien to American liberalism.[26]

Jim Patton and the Farmers Union, on the other hand, while officially uncommitted, leaned toward Wallace and the PCA. The *New Republic,* with Wallace as editor, scarcely bothered to conceal its wrath toward the ADA. Throughout 1947, the *New Republic*'s young publisher Michael Straight and its editorial director Bruce Bliven engaged in acrimonious private debates with such ADA figures as Schlesinger and Loeb. "The one over-riding issue in the world today is to prevent war with Russia," Bliven told Loeb in October 1947, adding that "red-baiting in the United States moves toward war rather than the contrary."

Other liberals, for one reason or another, maintained a position of neutrality. The respected Georgian Ellis Arnall argued that national liberal organizations did not understand Southern problems. Robert M. La Follette, Jr., rather pathetically hoping for a resurgence of progressivism within the Republican Party, thought the ADA was too closely identified with the Democrats. Former Congressman Jerry Voorhis, privately sympathetic toward the ADA, felt that his new position as executive director of the Cooperative League prohibited a formal affiliation. Most of the individuals affiliated with the National Educational Committee for a New Party agreed with the need to root the Communists out of the liberal movement, but considered the ADA tied to the old party structure and doubted that its economic programs could pave the way for the new collectivism they wanted. Many liberal congressmen, as a matter of necessity, refused to affiliate with either group. Helen Gahagan Douglas, for example, represented a marginal district in Los Angeles and needed support from both sides. Her husband, Melvyn Douglas, was a West Coast ADA leader, but she remained independent.

No politician was more ardently recruited by both groups than Chester Bowles. He seemed to lean toward the ADA. His presence at its founding session and his subsequent participation in its efforts to develop an economic program identified him with the organization. Throughout 1947, however, he refused to become a dues-paying member; his wife, meanwhile, was an officer in the Connecticut PCA. Although anti-Communist, he sympathized with much of Henry Wallace's critique of American foreign policy and felt that the ADA was too prone to engage in negative Red-baiting. On the other hand, he would not join the PCA because he considered it too Communist-influenced and too third-partyish in outlook. His own political ambitions committed him to the Democratic Party and to the maximization of his progressive constituency. Until events would force a decision, he was determined to keep a foot in both liberal camps and even maintain his ties with the Truman administration, however much he might criticize it to his friends.[27]

Some liberals, including Henry Morgenthau and Elliott Roosevelt, impartially criticized both the PCA and the ADA for dividing the liberal movement. There might be too much Communist influence in the PCA, but would not the ADA with its principle of excluding Communists and fellow travelers find itself diverting its energies into a futile internal Red-hunt? In asking Chicago *Sun* editor Robert Lasch for a report on an ADA organizational meeting scheduled for that city, Marshall Field expressed a special interest in knowing "how much emphasis Loeb and other speakers put on red-hunting and quarreling with other progressive groups." Field must have been relatively satisfied, but his initial doubts were representative of the caution with which so many progressives regarded anti-Communism.[28]

Max Lerner expressed the feelings of those who had misgivings about the whole situation. He still wanted a non-Communist liberal movement, but he feared that the ADA was developing an obsession with anti-Communism. The major enemy remained the right, and the liberal movement must concentrate on that enemy. To equate Communism with fascism was "an atrocious reading of history." The ADA, moreover, should have tried to recruit Wallace, his close association with the PCA notwithstanding; if it did not consider Wallace a progressive, it was guilty of "a paralyzing provincialism." The PCA, for its part, had failed to show "clarity and courage" on the Communist issue; it needed to "get away from its 'Red-baiting' bogey and declare itself independent." Not yet prepared to abandon the goal of progressive unity, Lerner declared: "If the leaders of both groups show themselves flexible enough, they can find a common ground on which to unite all the progressive forces of the Nation." Freda Kirchwey agreed with Lerner; in general, the two organizations shared common goals, and their rivalry was "as unnecessary as it is unfortunate." She impartially blamed "fringe" elements—Communists and fellow travelers in the PCA, those who equated Communism and fascism in the ADA—for dividing the liberal movement.[29]

One position which mattered strongly to all segments of the liberal movement was that of Philip Murray and the CIO. Murray was a vice-chairman of the PCA, but many prominent CIO leaders were backing the ADA. With the need to avoid a division in the CIO probably uppermost in his mind, he decided to follow a policy of neutrality. He withdrew from the PCA and asked other leaders to refrain from affiliation with either group. The ADA, left only with the firm support of David Dubinsky's International Ladies Garment Workers Union, believed it had been dealt a heavy blow, since most of the major CIO leaders had sided with it.

The PCA felt about equally hurt. The CIO withdrawal meant that A. F. Whitney of the Railroad Trainmen would be the only major labor leader left in the organization. Beanie Baldwin implored Murray to encourage Whitney to remain with the organization, and, whether on Murray's advice or not, Whitney did so. On March 14, the CIO Executive Board adopted a neutrality resolution and called for liberal solidarity. "The CIO appeal to the liberal movement to drop its differences and unite can only be based on the theory that unity with communists is possible," replied the ADA. "The ADA will continue to build an independent, non-Communist movement and to welcome all progressives who accept its program." [30]

In the spring of 1947, both the ADA and the PCA moved forward with definite advantages and equally definite handicaps. Hurt by the Communist issue, the PCA had Henry Wallace and a clear stance of independence from the unpopular Truman administration. The ADA, conversely, benefited greatly from its strong stand on Communism. The affiliation of Mrs. Roosevelt and most of the old New Dealers was also a great help, canceling out to some extent Wallace's presence in the other camp. But the ADA's program was bringing it, literally against its will, into an identification with the administration. Nothing demonstrated the president's lack of popularity and respect among liberals more strongly than the ADA's subsequent refusal in the face of ever-clearer facts to admit that its fortunes had become unavoidably intertwined with Truman's.

Chapter 7

The Politics and Diplomacy
of Containment

At the beginning of 1947, both the president and the liberals were defeated and uncertain about a future course of action. It seemed to many that Truman and the progressive movement had come to a final parting of the ways. The president appeared to be moving in the direction of conservatism at home and abroad, convincing a large number of liberals that he had made the ultimate decision to junk the heritage of FDR. By midyear, however, Truman was beginning to emerge as a militant defender of the New Deal and an advocate of an enlightened, constructive foreign policy. The president had arrived at a policy of containment—both of Soviet expansionism and of a right-wing opposition Congress—and he managed that policy in a manner that brought the bulk of the liberal movement to his side.

I

The abandonment of price controls, the firing of Wilson Wyatt, the apparent predominance of conservative advisers in the White House all seemed to indicate that Truman would fight no battles on behalf of liberalism with the new Republican Eightieth Congress. The president's January legislative messages

—the State of the Union address, the economic report, the budget—while liberal in their thrust, were drab and uninspired. Commenting critically that the economic message prescribed only voluntary remedies for inflation, T.R.B. wrote: "There is no ringing challenge to instant action; it was written for history and its tone is as dull as a leaden bell." To Samuel Grafton, Truman was standing for a "new centrism"—"a strange combination of conservatism without animus and liberalism without the glow." [1]

Truman's first show of strength came when he moved to smash a coal strike which John L. Lewis had called in violation of a contract with the government. Few progressives could give Lewis positive support. Marriner Eccles even privately warned the White House that if Lewis succeeded in his power play, he might regain control of the entire labor movement and initiate a series of strikes and wage demands which would wreck the economy. All the same, Truman was going after a labor union. and when the administration went to court, many progressives feared for the sanctity of the anti-injunction provisions of the Norris–La Guardia Act. In addition, the decision to put all the pressure of government power on the miners seemed inequitable to those who believed that Truman had conspicuously failed to take strong measures against corporations which had flouted government price recommendations. When the Supreme Court upheld the injunction against the union, Max Lerner called the decision "labor's Dred Scott Case." [2]

Even more alarming was the administration's reaction to the growing anti-Communist hysteria that was sweeping the country and was stimulated by the enunciation of the Truman Doctrine. When in March Secretary of Labor Schwellenbach urged the outlawing of the Communist Party, he shocked liberals as anti-Communist as Elmer Davis. The Constitution, Davis observed, might have been written in an era which was innocent of modern techniques of subversion, but it was still "too good a barn to burn down just to get rid of a few rats."

A couple of weeks later, the president established a loyalty program designed to root Communists and their sympathizers out of the government. The program, unprecedented in American history, had been thrown together by a committee of sub-Cabinet officials in the wake of Canadian spy revelations. It hopelessly confused the difficult but manageable problem of security in sensitive areas with the general problem of the loyalty of all government employees. It failed to provide elementary procedural safeguards for those accused of disloyalty and practically included a presumption of guilt. Truman had some qualms about implementing the program, but they were directed at the wrong target. The president, for some reason, had an intense suspicion of the FBI, feared that its investigators might act as a "Gestapo" terrorizing the bureaucracy, and attempted to minimize its role. Actually, the main problem in the administration of the loyalty program was the judgment of the boards set up to examine investigative data and rule on accusations of disloyalty. The White House grossly underestimated the seriousness of this difficulty and believed that through careful supervision it could prevent injustices.

A few liberals accepted the loyalty program as an unwelcome necessity. The *New Leader* hailed it as a broom which would sweep the totalitarians out of Washington, and the New York *Post* called it a logical response to attempts at subversion by antidemocratic forces. Most progressives, however, were strongly critical, among them some of the strongest anti-Communists. The St. Louis *Post-Dispatch* recalled the Red Scare. The *Nation* warned that the program contained broad "opportunities for malicious gossip, character assassination, and the settlement of private grudges." Speaking for the PAC, Frank Kingdon and Jo Davidson compared it to "the infamous sedition laws of 1798." The anti-Communist James Wechsler accused Truman of creating "an artificial uproar" to establish his credentials as a militant anti-Red. Philip Murray wrote to the president condemning the lack of due process and commenting that the nation had managed to survive World War II without such a drastic departure from its traditions. Helen Gahagan Douglas declared that the country was accepting totalitarian practices which it professed to despise. Thomas L. Stokes wondered if the next step would be book-burnings in front of the Capitol.[3]

The administration also disappointed progressives with its failure to produce a constructive solution for the growing problem of inflation. As prices rose sharply, many liberals feared that the economy was in the first phase of a boom-and-bust cycle. The president called for voluntary price reductions, but he proposed no concrete steps. On April 22, Chester Bowles met with him and suggested that he establish a price board composed entirely of businessmen to study the price structure and recommend voluntary reductions. Truman took no action.[4]

On May 15, an ADA Committee for Economic Stability, headed by Bowles, offered a comprehensive economic program to stem the price tide, buffer a possible recession, and stimulate the consumer purchasing power necessary to a healthy economy. It included voluntary price reductions averaging 10 percent, extension of rent controls, more assistance to housing construction, continued farm subsidies, greater unemployment compensation coverage with higher benefits, a higher minimum wage, a general wage increase of 15 cents per hour, and a worldwide program of economic reconstruction. Leon Keyserling privately protested to Jim Loeb that the administration already stood for all these measures, but to most liberals the ADA report was an activist manifesto, implicitly indicting an apathetic and ineffective administration.[5]

One revealing indication of Truman's low stock among progressives by the spring of 1947 was the increasingly bad relationship between him and the New York Liberal Party, despite the Liberal Party's support of his foreign policy. At their state convention in May, party leaders accused the president of repudiating the domestic programs of FDR and warned that the White House could not take their support for granted in 1948. A month later, John L. Childs, a former Liberal Party chairman, publicly remarked that progressives might face a sad choice in 1948: "a Truman on the one hand and a Bricker, a Taft or a Dewey on the other. . . . a choice of the lesser evil, certainly not a choice of the greater good." [6]

In May, Tris Coffin, a Washington correspondent and talented writer who had long since given up on Truman, published *Missouri Compromise,* an account of the president's first two years in office. The book expressed what had become for many liberals the conventional view of Truman as an affable small-town politician who was trying hard but was not big enough for the presidency, moving from blunder to blunder, allowing admirals and generals to shape policy, surrounding himself with incompetent cronies, swinging toward conservatism after the 1946 defeat.[7] The book, however, had scarcely hit the market before events began to reshape the president's image.

II

Truman's foreign policy during the early months of the year was disquieting. The Palestine question, referred to the United Nations, hung fire and the United States could not get a solution. In China, negotiations for a coalition government collapsed, and most liberals agreed with General Marshall's condemnation of both sides. The appointment of Marshall as secretary of state, however, drew a mixed reaction. No liberal questioned the general's integrity and good intentions, but he was yet another military man in high office. "The principle involved is vastly important," commented the *Progressive,* "for Marshall is a professional soldier whose entire adult life has been devoted to preparing for war rather than planning for peace." Marshall's Latin American policy confirmed fears that he would not engage in any liberal departures. In June, Spruille Braden resigned in protest against American conciliation of the Argentine dictator Peron.[8]

However, U.S. policy toward the Soviet Union had become the all-absorbing question, with the focus now in the Middle East. The USSR was continuing to press for control of the Dardanelles, issuing vituperative attacks upon the Turkish government, and holding military maneuvers close to Turkish borders. In Greece, the situation of the right-wing regime was desperate; only the British military presence staved off a victory for the Communist-led insurgents. Both Truman and the State Department found the authoritarian and inept Greek and Turkish governments distasteful and exasperating. Yet both were also acutely aware of the strategic and economic importance of the Middle East and convinced, perhaps mistakenly, that Greece and Turkey were the first objectives of a Soviet grand design to control the entire region. (Actually, Stalin's interest in Greece was disputable, but the Russian ambitions in Turkey and, earlier, in Iran were open and indisputable.) With Great Britain on the verge of economic ruin and no longer able to prop up the Greek government, there was little doubt within the administration that the United States would move into the impending power vacuum.

In a discussion with Congressional leaders, it quickly became obvious that the only sure way of selling a Greek-Turkish aid program to the Congress and the public was the ideological argument—Western democracy had to block the relentless drive of Soviet Communism. It was an appeal, moreover, which Truman and most of the administration found emotionally satisfying because it provided much-needed moral reinforcement for their strategic calculations. This sweeping sense of national mission, however, soon overshadowed America's specific objectives in Greece and Turkey even in the minds of such hardheaded presidential advisers as Clark Clifford and Dean Acheson. It emotionalized the Cold War and made rational discourse between the U.S. and the Soviet Union still more difficult.

Truman appeared before Congress on March 12, 1947, to ask for $400 million in aid to Greece and Turkey. Both nations, he asserted, were fighting for their national freedom against outside forces. Devoting most of his attention to Greece, the president admitted that its government was not perfect but argued that it was essentially a democracy and capable of making progress. Only the United States could preserve Greek independence; the U.N. was incapable of providing the rapid, large-scale assistance which the country needed. The United States would carefully supervise the use of the aid, and the major objective would be the creation of economic stability.

Truman explained the "broad implications" of his proposal at length. The imposition of totalitarian regimes upon free peoples by direct or indirect aggression would threaten world peace and thereby endanger American security. Totalitarianism was already being inflicted upon Poland, Rumania, Bulgaria, and "a number of other countries." The world was being forced to choose between democracy and dictatorship. The United States should support—"primarily through economic and financial aid"—those "free peoples who are resisting attempted subjugation by armed minorities or by outside pressures." Such a policy would vindicate the principles of the United Nations. Failure to act would mean the disappearance of Greek independence, the probable spread of "confusion and disorder" throughout the Middle East, and even the possible collapse of free institutions in Western Europe. "The free peoples of the world look to us for support in maintaining their freedoms," Truman concluded. "If we falter in our leadership, we may endanger the peace of the world—and we shall surely endanger the welfare of this Nation." [9]

The speech marked the end of a long foreign-policy process. At last, the United States was openly committed to the containment of Soviet expansion. To some liberals—those still dedicated to the Popular Front—the very declaration of the new American objective was a shock and a challenge. To many others, including some anti-Communists, the specific method of implementing the U.S. objective was an affront to liberal goals and aspirations. *PM* headed its report of the speech with the words "Truman Scraps FDR Policy on Russia" and in a sharp editorial Max Lerner accused the president of a demagogic appeal to the anti-Communist right. The PCA asserted that Truman had renounced the policy of One World, assumed the burdens of British imperialism, divided the globe into two hostile camps, and invited an atomic arms race which would inevitably result in nuclear destruction. Asserting that the new Truman Doctrine stood only for a negative anti-Communism, Freda

Kirchwey wrote sarcastically: "This is the Great Crusade—the one, you will remember, that Hitler invited us to join long ago." [10]

Far more important to most liberals than the Popular Front impulse was the nature of the program itself. It supported reactionary, fascistic governments and consisted primarily of military assistance despite Truman's rhetoric to the contrary. An effort to keep the Middle East and its oil reserves in the Western orbit, it was tinged with imperialism. It ignored the possibility that the Soviet Union might be entitled to some greater control over the strategic Dardanelles. Worst of all, it wholly bypassed the United Nations.

Glen Taylor charged that "economic royalists" had returned to power and were setting out to exploit the world, and Claude Pepper reminded the Senate that the Greek insurgency had developed from deep and legitimate domestic grievances. In the House, Helen Gahagan Douglas and a few other progressives sponsored legislation to bring the United Nations into the aid programs. Aubrey Williams condemned the administration proposal and asserted that Roosevelt would have sponsored constructive economic development based upon the example of the New Deal. Fiorello La Guardia commented that it was not worth the life of a single American soldier to keep the Greek king on his throne. "We cannot stop the spread of Communist ideology by bolstering a corrupt and reactionary regime," warned Charles Bolte as he spoke to a Congressional committee for the AVC.

The Chicago *Sun* charged that by supporting a fascist Greek government the United States was practicing "naked imperialism" and that American Turkish policy was ignoring legitimate Russian security problems. *Sun* editor Robert Lasch, after attending a background briefing with high administration officials, expressed his fears to Marshall Field:

I believe our foreign policy is now dominated by military advisers, by men with big business backgrounds, and by small-bore politicians of the Missouri clique. It appears to be actuated almost entirely by the narrowest considerations of national interest and blind fear of communism. There is no vision or understanding in it, and above all no real interest in working toward a strong United Nations organization based on reconciliation of our interests with Russia's. It is not surprising that such a policy, formulated by such men, should be repugnant to progressives. The Roosevelt policy is dead.

Almost every critic, including Jim Patton, Elliott Roosevelt, Samuel Grafton, and Thomas L. Stokes, attacked the decision to bypass the U.N.; some feared it might amount to a death warrant for the world organization. Even Eleanor Roosevelt, who still represented the administration at the U.N., expressed grave doubts in her newspaper column. The *Progressive,* as anti-Communist as it was, refused to support the Truman program unless it were administered by the U.N. and made conditional upon democratic reforms. "It was only five years ago that we were being implored to help Communism stop Fascism," wrote Morris Rubin. "Now, in effect, we are being urged to help Fascism stop Communism." [11]

Truman, however, was not totally without liberal support. Some anti-Communist progressives accepted the need to contain the Soviet Union and considered the Truman Doctrine a fundamentally moral policy. "Further appeasement of injustice and coercion would surely lead to war," declared the *New Leader.* "Our new policy of positive democracy offers at least a chance of maintaining peace." Arthur Schlesinger, Jr., recalls the move as a welcome and overdue indication that the president was capable of decisive action. Hubert Humphrey argued for an unequivocal endorsement by the ADA National Board. The New York *Post* argued that the Administration was attempting to preserve freedom of choice for the Greek people.

Most progressives who supported the administration, however, did so with qualms and doubts, only after convincing themselves that the national interest dictated the Truman Doctrine, that the United Nations was too weak to be effective, that the president's program was the least evil of several unpleasant alternatives. Correctly predicting Truman's course at the beginning of March, the St. Louis *Post-Dispatch* commented: "It adds up to a nasty job which has nothing to recommend it except that the alternative is nastier." Louis Fischer argued: "The UN has no money and no arms, and Greece and Turkey need both urgently." Harold Ickes wrote a reluctant endorsement. Most of the ADA leaders declared in favor of the program. Elmer Davis expressed the equivocal attitude which many of them felt. The Greek government was hopelessly reactionary, he told his radio listeners, but at least the United States could work for something better and stave off the imposition of a permanent Communist tyranny. America, he had decided, could not avoid the responsibility of blocking totalitarian expansion: "History moves, whether we move with it or not. We had better not let it move past us; still less move over us."

The ADA's first national convention, meeting only two weeks after the president's address to Congress, adopted a resolution of only qualified support. It asserted that the United States must work for the development of genuinely free institutions in Greece and take steps to strengthen the U.N. "If we continue to allow the ragged and hungry people of Greece to be exploited, we shall only fan the fires of Communism," warned Wilson Wyatt. "But if we assume the burdens of guarding national independence and supervising economic reconstruction, we will give the democratic alternative to Fascism and Communism new strength and vitality throughout the world." Even a good many ADA members, however, regarded the Truman Doctrine with skepticism, and a majority of the liberal community rejected the organization's lukewarm endorsement.[12]

A considerable number were not even prepared to admit that the USSR was tightening its grip on Eastern Europe. In January, the editor of *PM*, Ralph Ingersoll, covered the Polish elections. He sent back reports of an honest and orderly balloting, described the Communists as independent of Moscow, and called them "the ablest and most vital bloc" in the government. Upon returning, he declared that the major difference between

Polish and American politics was that freedom was steadily developing in Poland while repression was constantly increasing in the United States.[13]

On May 30, Ferenc Nagy, the anti-Communist premier of Hungary, fled the country after a pro-Soviet coup d'etat. Truman told a press conference that the incident was an outrage, and some progressives who had opposed aid to Greece and Turkey joined in the president's condemnation, among them the editors of the Chicago *Sun*. Others, however, including the two most influential liberal journals, the *Nation* and the *New Republic*, gave credence to assertions that the coup had been necessary to block a right-wing takeover.

In any event, Truman's angry denunciation provided little hope of a positive foreign policy. The Chicago *Sun* probably expressed the dominant liberal mood:

Clearly, we have got to find a more creative principle for our foreign policy—one that will permit peoples genuinely free self-determination, that will remove the economic conditions which breed Communism, that will build peace instead of hardening the divisions between the two blocs. Otherwise, we can expect more Hungaries.[14]

In California, Truman's diplomacy had become a key factor in a three-way party split. Pro-Wallace Democrats, led by Robert Kenny, were in open revolt against the president. An important group of liberal Democrats, headed by Jimmy Roosevelt and George Outland, was involved in a struggle for party control with more conservative regulars, led by Ed Pauley. When the Roosevelt-Outland liberals mildly criticized the Truman Doctrine, Pauley persuaded John Snyder and Gael Sullivan, the executive director of the Democratic National Committee, to withdraw from the program of a Los Angeles Jackson Day dinner at which young Roosevelt presided and Eleanor Roosevelt was the guest of honor. Angry Roosevelt Democrats considered the incident an insult and began to talk of running their leader as a favorite son candidate in the 1948 presidential primary. "Pauley with a Truman ticket next year will get licked by a Jim Roosevelt ticket," warned a glum Truman backer.[15]

III

Truman's conservative appearance was deceptive. During the first half of 1947, he was formulating policies and awaiting opportunities which would rebuild his public image. By midyear, he was beginning to look like a fighter for progressive principles. The most important factor in this metamorphosis was the new Republican Congress and the presidential attitude toward it.

Truman's experience as a senator who had made friends in all camps may have disposed him a bit toward compromise, and shortly after the 1946 election he met with one conservative Republican senator to discuss areas of agreement on farm policy. From the very beginning, however, he was determined to preserve the independence of the presidency and his freedom of action. "I shall fight for what I think is the public interest first last and all the time," he wrote in a draft statement a day or two after the election. As rewritten by his staff, his public comments on the election were somewhat more conciliatory than his own notes—and a bit deceptive. In fact, he was already formulating a strategy. In a letter to Eleanor Roosevelt on November 14, he observed, "I think we will be in a position to get more things done for the welfare of the country, or at least to make a record of things recommended for the welfare of the country, than we would have been had we been responsible for a Democratic Congress which was not loyal to the party." The White House moved toward implementation of the concept by undertaking an in-depth exploration of the problems and techniques involved in dealing with an opposition Congress.

Perhaps the most important product of the White House inquiry was a paper produced by the talented Washington attorney and political operator James Rowe, Jr. The document was

a remarkable exercise in political analysis, running some 27
pages of single-spaced typescript, beginning with a lengthy quo-
tation from *The Federalist Papers* and ranging over the whole
of American political history. It was impossible, the paper asserted, for a president to have a meaningful cooperative relationship with an opposition Congress; the likely result of an effort to do so would be a virtual abdication. It was both
constitutionally and politically imperative for the president to
maintain his autonomy as the representative of all the people.
The Republicans believed that they had won an antiadministration mandate and smelled victory in 1948; they would cooperate only on their own terms. The president should make
meaningless gestures of cooperation in order to avoid the appearance of partisanship, but he had to steel himself for conflict. He should follow a strategy of speaking out vigorously in
behalf of the public interest, making strong and dramatic appointments to important posts, and using his most effective
weapon, the veto, to mobilize support. No one can say whether
Rowe "influenced" Truman; it is very possible that the president would have moved as he did anyway. In its main outlines,
however, the paper amounted to a remarkably accurate forecast
of presidential strategy.[16]

Truman and those around him still faced the necessity of defining the substantive positions which the White House would
advocate. If the administration was committed in a general way
to the Democratic heritage of the past fourteen years, its position on some important matters—labor relations, housing, civil
rights, economic controls—was ambiguous. Moreover, several
people close to the president, most notably John Snyder, were
working to discourage any vigorous steps forward in these
areas. It was politically impossible for Truman to turn toward
stark reaction and anti-New Dealism, and there is no indication
that he had any impulse to do so. It was possible that he might
decide against new initiatives, seek the "middle of the road,"
and even countenance some small steps backward from the
more "extreme" New Deal measures. The bland generalities of
his January messages to Congress indicate that he probably

gave some thought to such a strategy. (An initial middle-of-the-road approach to Congress also had the virtue of avoiding an image of undue partisanship, and, as it worked out, giving the Republicans the rope with which they eventually hung themselves.) [17]

There were still several individuals within the administration who were convinced that Truman's political future and the welfare of the country demanded an aggressive liberalism. A few weeks after the election, they appointed themselves an informal strategy board and began a series of weekly meetings. The regular members of the group were Oscar Ewing, director of the Federal Security Agency and a vigorous exponent of welfare legislation; Leon Keyserling, generally considered the most progressive voice on the Council of Economic Advisers; C. Girard ("Jebby") Davidson, assistant secretary of the interior, a militant defender of civil liberties and an ardent advocate of government manipulation of the economy; David A. Morse, assistant secretary of labor; White House aide Charles Murphy; and presidential counselor Clark Clifford.

This progressive caucus hammered out a consensus on the specific domestic issues and sought to sway the president. Its key member was Clifford, who had direct and continuous access to Truman, was free to make suggestions on practically any issue, and enjoyed the president's trust and confidence. Clifford was not an ideologist, but he was, like Truman, a Democrat by inheritance and sympathetic toward the New Deal tradition. An uncle for whom he was named, a former editor of the St. Louis *Post-Dispatch,* had influenced him in a liberal direction. He identified his fortunes with Truman's and laced his arguments heavily with considerations of political advantage. A persuasive advocate and a shrewd political analyst, he was more than a match for any of the mediocre moderates or conservatives in the administration. Clifford and the other progressives did not overwhelm Truman or control him, but they did present him with clear policy options which pointed out the advantages, both moral and political, of a liberal course and the disadvantages of a gray centrism. They did not prevail because

Clifford had mystical powers of persuasion, but because his recommendations generally appealed to Truman's inclinations and political astuteness.[18]

Perhaps the most important determinant of Truman's strategy was the Republican Congress itself. The president's critics could no longer hold him responsible for legislative leadership with the opposition party in control; he was free to make maximum demands without having to worry about results. Moreover, the Congress was so conservative in its aspirations that the president could distinguish himself from it only by following a liberal line. If he were to follow Rowe's advice and accept the inevitability of conflict, he would have to do so as a progressive battling a reactionary Congress.

An incident in early 1947 foreshadowed the future. Most of the Republicans in the Senate, led by Robert A. Taft, joined with Tennessee's vindictive old Senator McKellar in an attempt to block the appointment of David Lilienthal to head the new Atomic Energy Commission. Truman stood firm. When a discouraged Lilienthal went to Clark Clifford with an offer to withdraw, Clifford relayed a message from the president: "he was in this fight to the finish . . . he was in it if it took 150 years with all the effort and energy he had . . . if they wanted to make an issue of this matter, he would carry the issue to the country." After a two-month struggle, the Senate confirmed Lilienthal.

The GOP increased its already considerable discredit among progressives with a program which included exemption of the railroads from the antitrust laws, a tax cut designed to give most of its relief to higher income brackets, a bill which would weaken rent controls, strong antilabor legislation, and elimination of the school lunch program. The Republicans were, moreover, formulating cuts in appropriations for rural electrification, public power projects, conservation programs, and the Farmers Home Administration. They were refusing to act on housing, civil rights, aid to education, revision of immigration laws, a higher minimum wage, monopoly, and inflation. "No Congress since the ill-starred days of Warren G. Harding has yielded so completely to big business pressures," declared Jim Patton. "This Congress brought back an atmosphere you had forgotten or never thought possible," wrote T.R.B. that summer. The representatives of the worst special interests, the Neanderthal Men, had come out of their hiding places and were growing bolder by the day, questioning victories which seemed to have been won long ago. Suddenly, declared the *New Republic* columnist, the liberal accomplishments of a decade and a half were in jeopardy.[19]

By June, Truman was ready to do battle in earnest. On June 5, he opened a press conference with a strong denunciation of Senator Taft's opposition to foreign aid and domestic price reductions: "Senator Taft's economic philosophy follows the old idea of boom and bust. . . . I utterly reject this defeatist economic philosophy, and I believe in maintaining a full employment and full production economy." On June 16, he vetoed the Republican tax cut, arguing that any reduction would be inflationary and that the Republican bill was especially objectionable because of its concentration upon relief in the high-income levels.[20]

On June 20, he sent the Republican labor bill, the Taft-Hartley Act, back to Congress with a stinging veto message which asserted that the legislation "would reverse the basic direction of our national labor policy" and "conflict with important principles of our democratic society." That night, he went on the radio to declare: "We do not need—and we do not want—legislation which will take fundamental rights away from our working people." [21]

Other blasts at the Republicans followed in rapid succession. On June 26, Truman vetoed a bill to increase the tariff on wool, warning that it would have been a first step on the disastrous road to economic isolationism. On June 30, he reluctantly signed the Housing and Rent Act, but sent a sharp message to Congress, calling the bill a "most unsatisfactory law" which he had accepted only to prevent the expiration of rent control. Damning the real estate lobby ("It has displayed a ruthless disregard of the public welfare"), he demanded far-reaching housing legislation. On July 18, the president vetoed a second Republican tax cut, nearly identical to the first, charging that it was "at complete variance with the fundamental requirements of a good tax bill." On August 6, he vetoed a bill to remove newspaper vendors from the Social Security system: "We must not open our social security structure to piece-meal attack and to slow undermining." [22]

Truman had solidly aligned himself with the principles of the New Deal and the priorities of the liberals. On June 10, the ADA had urged vetoes of the Taft-Hartley and tax bills and a strong presidential declaration in behalf of rent controls; Truman had delivered on these requests and had added to them. The Taft-Hartley veto, although overridden, was especially important. It brought almost the entire labor movement back behind him and drew acclaim from middle-class liberals, most of whom still passionately identified themselves with labor.* "Let's come right out and say it, we thought Truman's labor veto message thrilling," wrote T.R.B. "Mr. Truman has reached the crucial fork in the road and turned unmistakably to the left," commented James Wechsler. "He has given American liberalism the fighting chance that it seemed to have lost with the death of Roosevelt," said the *Nation*.[23]

The administration also effected a dramatic shift in foreign policy. On June 5, Secretary of State Marshall delivered his epoch-making speech at Harvard calling for a vast, cooperative effort, supported by U.S. aid, to rebuild the economy of all Europe—East and West, the Soviet Union included. Some liberals were critical of Marshall's avoidance of the United Nations, but his proposal seemed to point toward a constructive new diplomacy which might unite Europe rather than further divide it. Certainly, it appeared to be a reversal of the military negativism of the Truman Doctrine, and many who had fought

---

*A few liberal voices, especially the editorials of newspapers which had labor problems, favored Taft-Hartley, but they were a distinct minority. More intriguing is the disclosure that the administration liberal group was at first not certain of its position; eventually, it decided to work for a veto. *SLPD,* June 27, 1947; Cabell Phillips, *The Truman Presidency* (New York, 1966), pp. 164–65.

the earlier program supported the new Marshall Plan. "There shines in Marshall's speech the recognition that we are engaged in a struggle for the souls of men, and not for the possession of mountain passes," wrote Samuel Grafton. The Chicago *Sun* praised the new departure, and Max Lerner defended the Marshall policy against Communist denunciation. The *Nation* called the plan an indication that the United States was "going to make at least one more effort to prevent the development of two irreconcilable worlds." The *New Republic* commended the program and asserted with some satisfaction that the administration was turning to the ideas of Henry Wallace.[24]

The PCA, however, ventured a tentative and cautious criticism. Near the end of June, its national board adopted a policy statement declaring that it would support any plan for European reconstruction "provided that the policy upon which this is predicated is consistent with the principles of the United Nations and the unity of the Great Powers." But it went on to assert that "any plan conceived or administered in such a manner as to encourage the creation of a Western Bloc, a divided Europe or a divided world cannot serve the ends of peace or economic recovery." The Truman Doctrine, it believed, was still the basis of American foreign policy; the Marshall Plan could not be considered in isolation. The organization had stopped short of an outright rejection, but the tone of its position was negative. By stressing geat-power unity above all other considerations, the PCA was declaring that it would oppose any Marshall Plan unacceptable to the Soviet Union. If the USSR refused Marshall's invitation, the PCA would find itself conspicuously following the Russians and facing the formidable task of mobilizing the progressives against the program.[25]

For most liberals, the Marshall Plan was an affirmative departure from the Truman Doctrine and held the enormous promise of reuniting and rebuilding Europe. The new policy went far toward rehabilitating the administration's image, and if the Russians rejected it, many progressives were already prepared to blame them, not Truman and Marshall.

IV

In order to maintain his new reputation, Truman had to deal decisively with two problems—the necessity of emergency foreign aid to prevent some European governments from collapsing before the Marshall Plan could begin and the need to control the increasingly serious inflation at home. By fall, liberals were urging Truman to call a special session of Congress and advance strong, effective programs to manage the dual crisis.[26]

For a time, it appeared that the administration was again lapsing into passivity. Truman's housing expediter handled rent control with even greater leniency toward landlords than most progressives believed the weak law required. The president then told a press conference that economic controls were "police state methods." The context of the remark indicates that he probably was trying to be sarcastic and certainly was not condemnatory. Newspaper accounts, however, concentrated on his words without analyzing his intentions, and liberals reacted with indignation. "The great man has now given us a definition," wrote Frank Kingdon. "When you safeguard the many against the greed of the few, this is 'police state methods.'"[27]

Just a week later, however, Truman called a special session of Congress to deal with the inflation and foreign aid problems, warning that inaction would cause economic disaster at home and the spread of totalitarianism abroad. On the first day of the session, November 17, Truman appeared before Congress to request emergency aid to Europe and a surprisingly strong anti-inflation program. The economic proposals, a victory for administration progressives, included rationing and price controls for key commodities. Truman and his advisers had no illusions that Congress would act; in fact, they felt that it was impossible to clamp real controls back on the economy and would have been flabbergasted if presented with the authority to do so. The proposals were hardly radical—many progressives felt they were inadequate—but they drew the line and defined the is-

sues between president and Congress. From the administration's point of view, the program was, as Oscar Chapman commented privately, right not only morally but politically. The
Republicans, led by Senator Taft, inadvertently contributed to
Truman's strategy by unreservedly denouncing his economic
bills while refusing to advance any credible alternatives. The
St. Louis *Post-Dispatch* condemned the "bankruptcy" of the
GOP leadership while Max Lerner praised Truman for having
"risen magnificently to the occasion." [28]

Meanwhile, the Marshall Plan was in the final stages of preparation, and although the Soviet bloc had withdrawn from participation, most liberals continued to back it with enthusiasm.
"We are playing for big stakes—a free Europe, a democratic
world, and peace," declared Helen Gahagan Douglas. On December 19, Truman sent a long special message to Congress de-
tailing the plan, and even a Popular Fronter like I. F. Stone
could acclaim it as "big in conception and magnanimous in
inspiration." "Nations have not often pursued their self-interest
with such foresight and generosity," commented the Chicago
Sun.[29]

Truman had also moved to establish himself as a friend of
the Negro. At the end of 1946, he had quietly appointed a special committee on civil rights. It was headed by the corporate
executive Charles E. Wilson but dominated by several outstanding liberals, including James Carey, Morris Ernst, Franklin D. Roosevelt, Jr., Boris Shiskin, and Channing Tobias. The
prestige of the committee alone guaranteed that its recommendations could not be ignored. As Truman waited for the
committee's report, he confined his legislative requests to a routine advocacy of a permanent FEPC. In May, his civil rights record was blotted, indirectly when his appointees to the District
of Columbia Court of Appeals formed the majority in a decision upholding restrictive land covenants; the lone dissenter,
the *New Republic* observed, had been put on the bench by
Roosevelt. But on June 30, the president, speaking to an
NAACP rally at the Lincoln Memorial, advocated positive government action against discrimination and expressed confi-

dence that the civil rights committee would produce "a sensible and vigorous program for action by all of us." "I was very proud," commented Eleanor Roosevelt in her newspaper column. Truman's decision to make a strong pronouncement—he had thrown out an earlier innocuous speech draft prepared by David Niles—was yet another indication that he was seeking to present himself as an aggressive liberal.[30]

At the end of October, the civil rights committee issued its report as a book-length publication entitled *To Secure These Rights*. Among its most important recommendations were an antilynching law, abolition of the poll tax, legislation to prevent discrimination in voter registration, an end to segregation in the armed services, a cutoff of federal funds to recipients practicing segregation, and prohibition of Jim Crow practices in interstate public transportation. Reviewing *To Secure These Rights* for the *New Republic,* James R. Newman expressed the feelings of most liberals outside the South: "For those who cherish liberty, freedom and forebearance; for those sickened by the sight of reaction riding the land; for those who feel alone and for those who are afraid, here is a noble reaffirmation of the principles that made America." [31]

The administration quietly began to prepare a legislative message on civil rights, although in public Truman refrained from any definite commitments; it also decided to take important executive action. In early December the Justice Department intervened as an *amicus curiae* in the restrictive covenant decision, which was being appealed to the Supreme Court. In a precedent-making brief, the department urged the Court to overrule the lower courts. The move followed one of the less-noticed recommendations of the civil rights committee. Subsequently, Solicitor General Philip Perlman made it clear that the restrictive covenant brief represented the beginning of a new policy of intervention in important civil rights cases.* By

*Barton J. Bernstein, "The Ambiguous Legacy: The Truman Administration and Civil Rights," Bernstein, ed., *Politics and Policies of the Truman Administration* (Chicago, 1970), pp. 296–97, 311–12, obscures the significance of the *amicus* policy by taking pains to demonstrate that the drafting of the briefs was

1950, the department would be attacking the "separate but equal" principle itself. It was not certain by the end of 1947 just how far the administration was willing to go, but no one could doubt that it was moving in a more liberal direction on Negro rights.[32]

Nevertheless, as the year drew to a close, liberals still had serious doubts about the president. The loyalty program was especially disturbing. In July, ten State Department employees had been dismissed without even being told the charges against them; James Wechsler characterized the incident as a "purge" whose victims had been "deprived of minimum democratic protections." By the end of the year, there were rumors that some loyalty investigators were actually questioning civil servants about their attitude toward the Taft-Hartley Act, with the implication that those who opposed it, i.e., agreed with Truman's position, were dangerously radical. Others apparently considered the ADA subversive. Within the administration, Jebby Davidson complained that the program was "sacrificing the basic civil rights of government employees and . . . creating an atmosphere of fear and intimidation that will undermine the effectiveness of the Government." Most liberals agreed. The American Civil Liberties Union adopted a stiff condemnation. Freda Kirchwey called the program "an organized system of thought control," and the St. Louis *Post-Dispatch* described it as a "star chamber business." Old New Dealers such as Benjamin V. Cohen and Abe Fortas publicly attacked it as offensive to libertarian principles. The administration established a review board to hear individual appeals, but the program continued to be riddled with abuses. In the fall of 1948, the NAACP complained that many loyalty investigators were questioning government employees on their attitudes toward racial integration.[33]

---

done in isolation from the White House. During the Truman era, the White House rarely, if ever, participated in the drafting of legal briefs; it established a general policy and allowed the Office of the Solicitor General to implement it. The *amicus* policy had been advocated by a presidential committee and had, at the very least, the acquiescence of the White House.

There was some disappointment when Truman passed over the popular Gael Sullivan and named the phlegmatic party regular, Senator J. Howard McGrath, to succeed Bob Hannegan as chairman of the Democratic National Committee. McGrath had a liberal voting record, but, as the *New Republic* commented, a real crusading spirit was as important as a good viewpoint. Many progressives still doubted the administration's zeal and unity. It was difficult to miss the lack of enthusiasm which such key officials as John Snyder, Clinton Anderson, and Averell Harriman displayed for the anti-inflation program. Thomas L. Stokes observed that most of the dynamic liberalism within the Democratic Party was outside the administration, embodied in men who had either left the government in disgust or had been "given as actual hostages in the retreat that the President himself maneuvered on the counsel of conservatives in his Cabinet and among his close advisers." [34]

Yet Truman's tough vetoes, the formulation of the Marshall Plan, the advocacy of the anti-inflation program, the civil rights activity—all were creating a positive new image. The special session of Congress obliged him with programs that were diplomatically and politically happy. It authorized the badly needed European relief, but enacted a meaningless anti-inflation bill which Truman signed but ostentatiously criticized as "pitifully inadequate." Eleanor Roosevelt congratulated the president on the courage and political shrewdness of his program. Truman was succeeding in putting across his dual containment policy.

A majority of the liberals could endorse a European containment which was a by-product of the Marshall Plan and which had developed out of the Soviet rejection of a constructive American initiative. At home, they could whole-heartedly back Truman's struggle with Congress, especially when the president followed through with affirmative programs of his own. Many, as the events of 1948 would demonstrate, still had doubts about Truman's greatness of character and qualities of leadership, but he had gone far toward redefining the progressive impression of his administration. "The President has fought hard in the past few months," wrote the young California politician Pat Brown at year's end, "and it is beginning to be felt throughout the United States." [35]

V

One might have expected the ADA and the PCA to encourage Truman's new leadership. Instead, they moved farther apart, the PCA becoming more anti-Truman than ever, and the ADA firmly supporting most of the president's policies but not the president himself. The Truman Doctrine gave the PCA a popular cause, and the organization launched a nationwide campaign against it. Henry Wallace and Elliott Roosevelt headed a list of speakers at a Madison Square Garden "crisis meeting," and Wallace toured the country under PCA auspices. The organization staged a letter-writing campaign, ran full-page advertisements in major newspapers, and sponsored nationwide radio broadcasts featuring such figures as Robert Kenny, Claude Pepper, and Jim Patton.[36]

The ADA wisely refrained from countering with a similar campaign in behalf of the Truman Doctrine. Instead it concentrated on the inflation problem, an issue on which it could best utilize the broad range of talent available to it. Headed by Chester Bowles, its Committee for Economic Stability was a formidable team of New Deal economists—Leon Henderson, Paul A. Porter, Lauchlin Currie, William H. Davis, John Kenneth Galbraith, Richard Gilbert, David Ginsburg, Joe Rauh, and Robert Nathan—whose recommendations gained favorable attention throughout the liberal community. The PCA subsequently developed a program of its own, similar in many respects to the ADA proposals but going beyond them by calling for nationalization of the coal mines, the steel industry, the railroads, and the electrical utilities. But the PCA did not have a single prominent economist and could not attract the attention and respect which the ADA enjoyed. Even a collectivist such as Lewis Corey, who feared that the ADA was too tied to the piecemeal approach of the New Deal, criticized the PCA program as a shallow collection of agitational cliches.[37]

By mid-1947, criticism of the administration was built into every PCA position. When Truman vetoed the Taft-Hartley Act, the PCA had not a word of praise. Rather it charged that he had opened the way for labor repression by attempting to draft the rail strikers the year before, and it attacked his failure to mobilize the Democrats to sustain his veto. After the Russians and their satellites had rejected the Marshall Plan, the PCA denounced the plan as a variation of the Truman Doctrine, continuing the division of Europe into Eastern and Western blocs, attempting to forestall the growth of socialism in the West. The PCA alternative—a U.N. world reconstruction fund "with no political strings attached"—received surprisingly little support.[38]

For the ADA, on the other hand, the Marshall Plan became an all-important rallying point, worthy of unreserved support on its merits and also a means of isolating the PCA. "The divergence between ADA and PCA on the Marshall Plan should serve to clarify a difference which may have seemed obscure to some progressives," observed the *ADA World,* charging the rival organization with subservience to the Communist line. In December, the ADA issued a foreign policy pamphlet entitled *Toward Total Peace* which urged support of the non-Communist left as the constructive alternative to European collapse and a Red takeover. The Marshall Plan, it said, could be the keystone of such an approach and was "the highest point U. S. foreign policy has reached since the death of Roosevelt." On this issue, the ADA could carry most of the liberal movement.[39]

Toward Total Peace also brought the ADA into a close identification with the president's foreign policy. "It establishes the ADA's position as the left wing of the Truman Administration," commented the *New Republic.* On domestic matters also, the same relationship was developing. The organization had little direct influence on the White House, although it maintained contacts with David Niles, Leon Keyserling, Jebby Davidson, and other administration progressives. Many observers nevertheless perceived a confluence of policy positions. In the fall of 1947, Paul A. Porter temporarily joined the White House staff to help formulate Truman's anti-inflation program. The administration proposals were so close to the ADA agenda that Senator Taft attacked them as the work of "Leon Henderson and his crowd." In December 1947, Wilson Wyatt accepted the chairmanship of the 1948 Jefferson-Jackson Day dinners and called for Truman's reelection. The spectacle of the national chairman aligning himself so firmly with the administration bothered some ADA members, but it was genuinely symbolic of the relationship which seemed to be developing.[40]

The Taft remark and the Wyatt appointment gave the ADA an appearance of influence and recognition which enhanced the group's prestige,[41] but they also created problems. Truman was still less than a liberal hero, but the ADA was more firmly identified with him than ever. The PCA had the dual advantages of independence from the administration and a close relationship with Henry Wallace. Throughout the year Wallace and the PCA had acted informally as a third force in American politics. By the end of December, they were ready to formalize this arrangement.

Chapter 8

Toward a Gideon's Army

I

As the editor of the *New Republic* and the most prominent, articulate liberal critic of the administration, Henry Wallace continued to have a wide following. His first *New Republic* editorial revealed perhaps not a messianic complex, as his enemies charged, but certainly a sense of mission, a conviction that he must be the leader in the struggle for peace, democracy, and justice for the common man. "My field is the world," he wrote. "If I have importance, it is because of the ideas that I have come to represent. They are major ideas, indestructible and on the march." He appealed to liberals who were not yet willing to give up the near-millennial hopes of the war years, who still believed, as Wallace put it, that "jobs, peace, and freedom can be attained together and can make possible One World, prosperous and free, within our lifetime." [1]

Wallace made no effort to control the operations of the *New Republic*. "He lived in his own little world," Michael Straight has recalled. "He rarely read through the magazine, took little interest in the editors, frequently forgot their names." Yet by his very presence he exercised a remarkable domination over the journal's staff. Meeting with the *New Republic* editors in February 1947, Arthur Schlesinger, Jr., found them completely under Wallace's influence, obsessed with the fear that the United States was provoking Russia to the point of war, and determined to avoid any appearance of Red-baiting. The young publisher, Michael Straight, was just 29 years old, and until September 1946 Wallace had been a distant hero whom he had never met. In addition, Straight had not yet worked out a coherent approach to the Communist problems, domestic and foreign, in his own mind. He opposed Communist involvement in liberal organizations and was at times critical of the USSR. Yet in 1947 he still hoped for the reconstitution of the wartime alliance. He reacted strongly against the Truman Doctrine and the Cold War, and was in any case too awe-struck by Wallace to disagree with him. Straight may have initially favored the ADA, but he soon followed Wallace's lead. As late as the end of 1947, he wrote a stiff critique of *Toward Total Peace* and the idea of containing the Soviet Union.[2]

The week Wallace became its editor, the *New Republic,* invoking the symbolism of Roosevelt, began a series of articles entitled "A New Deal with Russia," defending the wartime Soviet annexations as a return to Russia's 1917 boundaries, calling for economic aid to the USSR, agreeing with Russian demands for joint control of the Turkish straits and a share of Iranian oil. The journal added a list of "Wall Streeters"— Secretary of Commerce Harriman, Secretary of Defense Forrestal, Undersecretary of State Robert Lovett, Ambassador to Great Britain Lewis Douglas—to the admirals and generals who were exercising a negative influence on U.S.-Soviet relations. Conceding that all these men had come into the government under Roosevelt, *New Republic* writer William Walton argued that nevertheless FDR alone had made the great decisions; under Truman, the financial barons had become "the movers and shakers." [3]

Wallace himself strove for greater balance in his declarations. Concentrating on Soviet-American relations and the Communist question almost exclusively, he coupled his attacks on British imperialism and U.S. diplomacy with refusals "to underwrite to the full" Russian policy. On rare occasions, he might reveal a feeling of bitter disillusionment—"I, myself, didn't realize how far the United States had gone on the road

to imperialism until after I made my speech of September 12,"
he told a British supporter—but his calls for conciliation and
peaceful coexistence with the USSR seemed constructive and
continued to draw strong liberal support.

His opposition within the liberal community, while vocal,
was a distinct minority. In January, when Wallace announced
plans for a trip to England, the *New Leader* collected 70 signatures for a cablegram to the British foreign minister asserting
that Wallace had the support of only a splinter group of Communists, fellow travelers, and "totalitarian liberals." The Wallace forces countered by collecting 125 signatures for a "scroll
of greeting" to the progressives of Great Britain, depicting
Wallace as an embodiment of "the spirit and faith of the democratic tradition of our two countries." Among the signers were
Senators Harley Kilgore, James E. Murray, Claude Pepper,
Glen Taylor, and Elbert Thomas; Fiorello La Guardia, Elliott
Roosevelt, Helen Gahagan Douglas, Freda Kirchwey, James G.
Patton, Rexford Tugwell, Aubrey Williams, and A. F. Whit-
ney.[4]

The loyalty order and the Greek-Turkish aid program gave
Wallace two causes that had wide appeal to liberals. He had already feared "a lot of witch-hunting," and he denounced the
president's order as a directive which, by its disregard of proce
dural rights and by the power it placed in the hands of many
department heads who "on a basis of past record and public utterance, have certainly not been conspicuous for their sympathy with the ideals of freedom of thought and expression," vio-
lated "the fundamental principles of Anglo-Saxon justice." The
new program would not keep out Communists, he warned.
Rather it would "tend to drive from public service the man
who has ever read a book, had an idea, supported the ideals of
Roosevelt or fought fascism." [5]

In a series of eloquent speeches and editorials, Wallace denounced the Truman Doctrine and advanced an appealing alternative. "How does support given to the undemocratic governments of Greece and Turkey aid the cause of freedom?" he
asked, characterizing the Greek aid as a military subsidy which

would be used to wipe out democratic opposition and recalling that Turkey had been close to the Axis during the war. Truman, moreover, was undercutting the U.N. "If we took the matter to the United Nations and the Russians exercised their veto, the moral burden would be on them. When we act independently . . . the moral burden is on us." America was pursuing a fundamentally amoral and dangerous policy concerned with neither the preservation of democracy nor the suffering of the Greek people but simply with keeping Communist influence out of the Mediterranean and preserving a Middle Eastern oil pipeline. Truman's course was aiding Communism and would lead to "generations of want and war."

The way to defeat Communism and advance American interests was not by supporting reaction and repression; U.S. leaders had to think on a Rooseveltian scale. The United States should assume that its conflicts with the Soviet Union were as susceptible to compromise as most disputes between powerful nations. American leaders should supplement a conciliatory Russian policy with a program of worldwide economic development under U.N. administration. The United States could give the common man all over the world something better than Communism, "but President Truman has not spoken for the American ideal." Truman was asking for a "Century of Fear" rather than a century which would fulfill the American dream. "The world cries out, not for an American crusade in the name of hatred and fear of communism, but for a world crusade in the name of the brotherhood of man." [6]

In early April, Wallace left for a speaking tour of England, Sweden, Denmark, and France. Continuing his attacks on the Truman Doctrine, he called for peace with Russia and restated his program for global reconstruction. In America, conservatives charged treason and demanded the revocation of Wallace's passport. Shocked by the right-wing blasts, even the former secretary's liberal opponents defended his right to speak, and few among them could wholly disagree with his pleas for a more constructive foreign policy. [7]

Returning to the United States, Wallace embarked on a

coast-to-coast speaking tour which ended on June 16 with an address in Washington, urging a personal meeting between Stalin and Truman to work out Soviet-American differences. Surprisingly large crowds paid admission to hear him at PCA-sponsored rallies. In Chicago, he drew 20,000; in Los Angeles, 27,000. In Portland—"the most conservative community west of the Continental Divide," according to Richard L. Neuberger—more people bought tickets to hear him than had attended a free rally featuring Harold Stassen the week before. The New York *Post*, at that time still critical of Wallace, conceded that the crowds were "an eloquent demonstration of the widespread thirst for affirmative idealism in public life; a thirst which has been virtually unslaked since the death of President Franklin Delano Roosevelt." "Wallace has identified himself with a deep longing for peace that is worldwide," admitted Marquis Childs. "All he is doing, it comes to you as you listen to him, is expressing what is in the minds and hearts of so many people," wrote Thomas L. Stokes. "The success of the Wallace tour points up the tremendous potential strength of PCA," wrote a jubilant Beanie Baldwin. "It has shown that there are millions of Americans who believe in our program." [8]

The large crowds which greeted Wallace on his return to the United States led to talk of a new political party, and he did nothing to discourage the speculation. Before leaving for England, he had avoided attendance at a Democratic Jefferson Day dinner at which Truman had been the featured speaker. Throughout his subsequent speaking tours, he tossed out hints of a third party and even made a couple of indirect overtures to Claude Pepper. Speaking in North Dakota on May 30, he warned that he might "take a vacation" in 1948. Then he added: "If the cause of peace can be helped, I shall do more than take a vacation. The day is coming when labor will agree on a real labor party." [9]

The administration, for its part, tried, not always successfully, to control its anger. At the beginning of April, Gael Sullivan told a radio interviewer that Wallace and Claude Pepper probably would not campaign for the Democrats in 1948 because of their differences with the administration. Truman, however, quickly sent private apologies to Pepper and saw that the senator and Wallace received prominent seats at the Jefferson Day dinner which Wallace decided to skip. "I have no desire to read anybody out of the Democratic Party," Truman told a press conference.

While Wallace was in Europe the White House declined comment on his trip, but on April 15, Attorney General Clark, who, everyone assumed, was speaking for the president, declared that anyone "who tells the people of Europe that the United States is committed to a ruthless imperialism and war with the Soviet Union tells a lie." Several weeks later, syndicated columnist Robert S. Allen claimed that Truman, in a letter to the commander-in-chief of the Veterans of Foreign Wars, had called Wallace a "publicity hound" and had compared him to Aaron Burr. Actually, Truman's letter to the VFW commander had done neither (unless the president added a handwritten postscript which the White House copy did not record); rather it defended Wallace's right to travel and express his opinions. Nevertheless, Allen's report doubtless contributed to the rift between Wallace and the administration.[10]

By midyear Wallace appeared formidable to Democratic strategists. His supporters had temporarily captured the party machinery in Oregon and were threatening to do the same in Washington. Robert Kenny was organizing a drive to capture the California delegation to the 1948 Democratic national convention and, because of the Pauley-Roosevelt split in that state, seemed to have a fair chance of success. Colorado state chairman Gene Cervi admitted to the national party leadership that he had decided to stay with Truman only after "a great deal of soul searching." Wallace forces appeared to have an even chance of controlling the Minnesota Democratic-Farmer-Labor Party and displayed strength in Wisconsin. In New York, the American Labor Party provided a strong power base for the former vice-president. By the beginning of June, Gael Sullivan was warning the White House that Wallace was mobilizing a vast

amount of antiwar sentiment. He was being shrewdly managed
and was gaining strength. The president had to explain the
Truman Doctrine more clearly and persuasively and needed to
decide quickly whether to take some steps to bring Wallace
back into the fold. A month later, Joseph and Stewart Alsop
predicted that there would probably be a sizable minority bloc
of Wallace delegates at the 1948 convention and that after
being beaten they would walk out and set up a third party.
"They will certainly succeed in wrecking the Democratic party,
at least temporarily. They will also succeed in electing the most
stodgily conservative Congress in a great many years." [11]

II

By mid-1947, William Harlan Hale has written, Wallace "was
seeing more and more of fewer and fewer people." As in the
past, his introverted personality was leading him to draw on
only a small circle of advisers, almost all of them ardent Popular Fronters. The two most influential were Beanie Baldwin
and Lew Frank; beyond them were Harold Young, Robert
Kenny, Lee Pressman, John Abt, Jo Davidson, and Hannah
Dorner. Young, who had been with Wallace for several years,
was a nonideological political manager, and Kenny's Popular
Frontism coexisted uneasily with a commitment to the Democratic Party. The others were either radical independents,
yearning for the excitement and moral uplift of a third party,
or conscious fellow travelers of the Communist Party. Wallace
was too preoccupied with foreign policy to worry about political problems, and Baldwin, whose association with him went
back to the 1930s, was gradually easing out Young as his political decision-maker. Intelligent and persuasive, a leader of the
Popular Front faction in the American Veterans Committee,
Frank was constantly at Wallace's side and served as chief
speech writer. Frank, Baldwin, and the others formed a tight
circle around a shy and essentially lonely man, creating a climate of opinion which was certain to influence him. [12]

Increasingly, Wallace embraced a radical critique of American politics, and his arguments had some force among liberals because he appealed to the fears of the war years. He depicted an America going through the final phases of a nightmarish political-economic process. At home, monopoly capitalism was ever more firmly in the saddle, unleashing an offensive against labor which was exemplified in the Taft-Hartley Act, relentlessly pursuing profits at the risk of catastrophic inflation, following the economics of scarcity, as demonstrated by the steel industry's refusal to expand in order to meet domestic demand and by the reluctance of business as a whole to put enough of its huge profits into wages. "Scarcity economics, high prices, and huge profits," he warned, "inevitably breed depression." And out of a fear of depression the business powers which ruled America had embarked on an anti-Communist crusade, marked by acts of repression at home—the loyalty program, the smears and slanders of Congressional investigators, the removal of liberal voices from the airwaves—by large and wasteful armament programs, by calls for universal military training, by alignment with the reactionary right abroad. The result would be economic collapse, war, and eventually fascism.

More and more, he was convinced that there was no difference between the two major parties. The Republican Congress was a "sell-out," but the Truman administration was equally bad. The administration had promoted war-mindedness, had instituted the loyalty program, had made, Wallace believed, only a half-hearted effort to sustain the Taft-Hartley veto. "The Administration's own record is in many instances an attempt to outdo the Republicans at their game." Indeed, the Democrats might be worse than the Republicans. "Under the Republicans Wall Street ran America," Wallace told a Madison Square Garden rally, "under the present administration Wall Street is all set to run the world." By mid-December, he was even saying that he would rather see Taft in the White House than Truman.[13]

Nothing was more indicative of Wallace's new course than his shifting attitude toward the Marshall Plan. To many liberals, the plan was a constructive fulfillment of the valid criticisms which Wallace had made of American policy. At first Wallace himself called it "a great advance over the Truman Doctrine" and asserted that Marshall "said many of the things that I have been saying." After Russia refused to participate, however, he began to waver. The Marshall Plan had become a containment device, and despite Marshall's initial offer of aid to all Europe, Wallace began to fear that the Truman Doctrine containment philosophy had been the basis of the proposal all along. Soon he was writing that "without Soviet participation the Marshall program may further divide the world." By October, with the Soviet bloc undertaking a vociferous offensive against the Marshall proposal, Wallace had come to the conclusion that, while he favored aid for hungry populations, he had "absolutely no faith in any kind of Marshall Plan which sets up Western Europe against Eastern Europe." By now he was convinced that the Marshall Plan was simply the Truman Doctrine in disguise, not really a constructive economic program originally designed to unite Europe but an extension of the counterrevolutionary effort to prop up fascists and incipient fascists. "We are not loved in Europe, and the more we use economic pressures to intervene in European affairs, the worse we are hated," he said. Marshall's fine words were only a cover for the Wall Street–military control of foreign policy; the real plan was a "martial plan." [14]

Wallace's thinking from the war years to the Marshall Plan contained many continuities. His overriding concerns were always peace and worldwide economic development. He consistently believed that fascism was the major threat to peace and freedom and that maintenance of the antifascist Popular Front was thus imperative. Although he had dropped his illusions about the internal nature of Soviet society, he continued to believe in the essential diplomatic good will of the Russians.

His Realism of 1946—provisional and never deeply held—contrasted sharply with his views of a year later. In the Madison Square Garden speech, he had recommended only limited concessions to the USSR; he had talked of spheres of influence, of accepting a politically divided Europe, of blocking further

Soviet expansion if that became necessary. By the end of 1947, Wallace had fallen back into a sentimentality which was a product of the war years, refusing to accept the division of Europe and opposing the one policy which might peacefully block the spread of Soviet influence beyond what Wallace himself had once carefully defined as the Russian sphere. Using a crude conspiracy theory as his point of departure, he rendered harsh moral judgments against U.S. foreign policy while he increasingly tended to depict the USSR as an injured and provoked party. No longer able to advance a plausible or constructive alternative to the Truman's administration's course, he could only invoke the ideals of One World and the United Nations and make vague generalizations about the need for good will, democracy, and peace. While he was moving in this direction, the bulk of the liberal movement was passing him, going in the other direction.

III

At the beginning of June, third-party sentiment, fueled by the crowds which Wallace drew on his speaking tour, was reaching a peak. Two events, however, gave it a severe setback. The first, the announcement of the Marshall Plan, made administration foreign policy once again attractive to many liberals. The second, the Taft-Hartley veto, had a devastating organizational and financial impact upon new party ambitions. The PCA tried to pin responsibility for the Taft-Hartley Act on Truman and asserted: "The failure of the Democratic Party to defeat the Taft-Hartley bill may well mark a turning point, not only in the history of American labor, but in the history of American political parties as well." But the organization was whistling in the dark. Almost all important labor leaders took Truman's veto at face value and rallied around him. The Amalgamated Clothing Workers, the major union component of the ALP, served notice that it was ready to support the president in 1948. Equally dramatic and stunning was the personal and political reconciliation between Truman and A. F. Whit-

ney, the most prominent labor leader in the PCA. A few
months later, Jack Kroll foreclosed any possibility that the
CIOPAC would help a political insurgency. After the Taft-
Hartley veto, it was apparent that a third-party effort would
not have the money and manpower of the important unions.[15]

Meanwhile, a special Congressional election in Washington
raised doubts about Wallace's appeal. Former Congressman
Charles Savage, who was identified with Wallace's foreign policy views, had won a hard primary fight from a "Truman Democrat" in mid-May. Many observers interpreted Savage's victory
as a triumph for Wallace. Actually, Savage had avoided discussing foreign policy and had managed to win the support of such
anti-Communists as Richard Neuberger and Oregon ADA
leader Monroe Sweetland. Nevertheless, he was unable to escape his reputation. Wallace came into his district to campaign
for him and some of his workers were stamped, probably accurately, as pro-Communists connected with the Popular Fronter
Hugh De Lacy. On June 8, Savage lost the general election to
his Republican opponent. Anti-Communist liberals blamed the
loss on Wallace and the Communists. Asserting that the Republicans had won by stressing Savage's Communist support,
Sweetland wrote: "His campaign furnished one more illustra-
tion of why the Communists . . . [must be] rebuffed at every
appearance, if progressives hope for success in this generation."
Marquis Childs saw the incident as an indication of Wallace's
"negative power"—"the power to disconcert, to dismay, to confuse and divide." Once again the anti-Communist liberals
could use election results as a practical argument.[16]

Other liberals registered agreement. Speaking to the American Veterans Committee, Wilson Wyatt warned that a new
party could benefit only "the Communists and the NAM." Liberal Party leader Alex Rose endorsed the president for reelection and asserted that the Communists had received "the number one assignment of defeating Truman in the 1948 election
and all their resources are bent in this direction." Claude Pepper, who had consistently turned back third-party feelers,
emerged from a mid-August meeting with Truman endorsing

the president for reelection and calling him "the salt of the earth." Could the senator be thinking of a Salt and Pepper ticket? asked the *New Republic*.[17]

All the same, the third-party boosters were ready to go ahead. At the end of June, the PCA charged that the Democrats and Republicans had, in effect, merged into "one Reactionary Party" and called for "a new party if necessary, to have [a] clear choice between Progressive and Reactionary candidates for President." Although Robert Kenny was laying the groundwork for a Wallace effort in the California presidential primary, Beanie Baldwin gave the go-ahead for the establishment of a California Independent Progressive Party, which began a petition campaign to secure a place on the state ballot. In Illinois a Chicago group calling itself the Cook County Progressive Party not only got on the ballot but rolled up a stunning 313,000 votes in a judicial election. In New York, the left wing of the ALP still favored a national third party, and Vito Marcantonio was having the Library of Congress look up ballot requirements state by state. The Communist Party and the Popular Front unions were ready to provide some national organizational support.[18]

Wallace continued to travel and speak tirelessly in his drive to establish himself as an important political force. In the fall, he flew to Palestine, visited *kibbutzim* and issued a strong call for a Jewish state. Returning to the United States, he toured the South, attacked Jim Crow laws, and refused to speak at segregated meetings. Time and again he mentioned the possibility of a new party. "If the Democratic party is a war party, if my party continues to attack civil liberties, if both parties stand for high prices and depression," he told a PCA rally in September, "then the people must have a new party of liberty and peace." [19]

By the beginning of December, time was forcing a decision. Field workers in California and Ohio warned that Wallace must commit himself by the first of the year or efforts to get his name on the ballot would collapse. Democratic Chairman

McGrath made a final bid, saying that the party would welcome Wallace's support. On December 12, however, Wallace declared that he could not back Truman unless the president abandoned universal military training. He did not expect such a concession, he admitted. It was obvious that he had all but made his decision.[20]

As one delegation after another, representing union locals and citizen groups, urged Wallace to declare his candidacy, several prominent liberals attempted to dissuade him. Some agreed with Wallace's critique of the administration but feared the divisive and disruptive impact a new party would have on the liberal movement. Others warned him of Communist manipulation. Michael Straight, Helen Fuller, Helen Gahagan Douglas, Aubrey Williams, Max Lerner, J. Raymond Walsh, and Charles Bolte were among those who failed to change his course. Frank Kingdon found him thoroughly insulated from reality, determined to go ahead, and confident of polling 12 million votes.[21]

On December 16, the PCA executive committee endorsed a third party; events which followed demonstrated the bitterness of the liberal split. Kingdon, who was seeking the Democratic Senatorial nomination in New Jersey, promptly resigned, charging Communist control of the organization. Bartley Crum followed him out. Speaking for the Liberal Party, Alex Rose charged that the PCA call was part of the Communist campaign against the Marshall Plan and asserted that Wallace had "accepted the viewpoints of Vishinsky and Molotov." Walter Reuther leveled a scathing attack: "I think Henry is a lost soul. . . . Communists perform the most complete valet service in the world. They write your speeches, they do your thinking for you, they provide you with applause and they inflate your ego." [22]

Wallace officially revealed his decision in a nationwide radio broadcast on December 29. The Truman administration, he declared, was leading America toward fascism. "We are not for Russia and we are not for communism, but we recognize Hitlerite methods when we see them in our own land." He knew that he did not have a massive organization, but he had, he believed, "assembled a Gideon's Army, small in number, powerful in conviction." [23] Armed with little more than a belief in the righteousness and urgency of his cause, Wallace moved into the next phase of his crusade.

Chapter 9

Truman and the Liberal Quest for Leadership

The Wallace challenge, as hopeless as it was, underscored Truman's weakness as a candidate. The liberals might find themselves increasingly in accord with the bulk of the president's program, but Truman could provide them with neither inspiring leadership nor, it seemed, the promise of victory. Throughout the first half of 1948, the progressive movement became increasingly alienated from a president who was more liberal than ever. As the Democratic convention approached, the liberals desperately looked for a compelling new leader who might save them from disaster.

I

In the summer of 1947, Clark Clifford secured Truman's approval for the preparation of a document which would analyze the 1948 political situation and make recommendations on campaign strategy and organization. On November 19, Clifford submitted a 43-page memorandum to the president. Far-ranging and frequently astute, it was essentially a rationale for continuing the same course which the administration had perceptibly adopted by mid-1947; in addition, it was shrewdly designed to increase the influence of the administration liberals.

His sole concern, Clifford declared, was the political advantage of the president, and he wrote from the perspective that in general "the policy that is politically wise is also the best policy for this country." He accurately predicted that Truman would face a tough dual challenge in 1948. The probable Republican nominee was Governor Thomas E. Dewey, with an efficient organization and valuable experience from 1944—"he will be a resourceful, intelligent and highly dangerous candidate." Henry Wallace would almost surely run as a third-party nominee and, although manipulated by the Communists, would have wide appeal to idealists, pacifists, isolationists, and the "lunatic fringe." If he drew 5 to 10 percent of the vote in a few important states, he could throw the election to the Republicans.

In order to prevail against such opposition, the president would have to rally the enthusiastic support of the heterogeneous Democratic coalition—the Southern conservatives, the Western progressives, and the overlapping big-city constituencies of labor, the political machines, and religious-ethnic minority groups. The administration could ignore the South. The Dixie states were safely Democratic in presidential elections, and there was no need to make concessions to the powerful Southern leaders in Congress, because there was no hope of getting the administration's domestic program through Congress. The president must therefore concentrate on the other major elements of the party.

The "Winning of the West" should be the first priority. The administration should underscore its interest in the region's problems—flood control, reclamation, agriculture—and emphasize the failures of the Republican Congress. Most importantly, in the West and elsewhere, the administration could not rely upon the moribund Democratic machines to turn out the vote. The White House should attempt to reinvigorate the party organization wherever possible, but always with the realization that the only way to win the election was to appeal to the independent voting groups which held the balance of power. In general, the basis for such an appeal would have to be a strongly liberal program which would remind farmers and workers of the benefits the Democrats had given them, make convincing appeals to the Negroes, promise generous displaced persons legislation to the ethnic groups, and support the embattled Palestinian Jews. There were some exceptions—the Italian-Americans were most concerned with the Italian peace treaty and the Catholics were most receptive to a simple anti-Communism—but a militant progressivism was the essential common denominator for a successful strategy.

The liberals themselves constituted one of the important groups whose loyalty the administration had to capture. Clifford realized that most of them had lost their enthusiasm for Wallace but warned that they felt cut off from the administration. He observed that they could be as important to the Democrats as the large financial contributors were to the Republican Party. "The 'right' may have the money, but the 'left' has always had the pen." Because they were intellectuals and articulate "idea men," the liberals were far more important than their numbers would indicate. The administration needed them.

Clifford listed the major domestic issues: high prices, housing, tax revision, conservation and development of Western resources, civil rights. On each one the administration had to be prepared to fight a no-compromise battle with Congress with the objective of seizing the liberal position while pinning the conservative tag on the Republicans. Real accomplishment would be impossible in the highly charged partisan setting of an election year; the White House could only maneuver for maximum political advantage.

Finally, Clifford recommended the establishment of a small committee of Truman supporters not tied to any government agency or department, able to devote full-time effort to the assembly of facts, the analysis of political fortunes. Truman agreed and authorized the establishment of a "Research Division," financed by and nominally a part of the Democratic National Committee but actually under Clifford's supervision. To head the Research Division, Clifford chose William L. Batt,

Jr., a young Philadelphia liberal who had run unsuccessfully for Congress in 1946 and was prominent in both the ADA and the AVC. Batt in turn recruited a staff of dynamic and intelligent progressives: Kenneth Birkhead from the AVC and NAACP, Johannes Hoeber from the Philadelphia reform movement, John Barriere, a graduate student in economics who had studied under Paul Douglas, Frank Kelley, a talented journalist and writer, Phil Dreyer, an AVC leader from the Pacific Northwest and a natural resources expert, David Lloyd, the former legislative director of the ADA and the author of *Toward Total Peace*. The Research Division was actually an extension of the liberal caucus within the administration, serving essentially as its staff, and held the same essential conviction that progressivism represented the road to victory.[1]

The 1948 State of the Union message marked the effective beginning of the campaign. Largely the work of the administration liberals, it was so bold that Truman had to overcome some qualms before approving it. Appearing before Congress on January 7, the president advocated expansion of unemployment compensation and social security with higher benefits, national health insurance, federal aid to education, a large-scale housing program, stronger rent controls, an increase in the minimum wage, "the integrated development of our great river basins" by TVA-style projects, and tax legislation which would provide substantial cuts for low-income families while increasing the levy on corporate profits. He promised a special message which would make civil rights recommendations based on the report of the civil rights committee.[2]

Some liberals expressed doubt that Truman would back up his words with action, but most reacted favorably, many enthusiastically. New York *Post* editor T. O. Thackrey had become increasingly critical of administration foreign policy, but he praised Truman's domestic program as "little short of inspiring." Max Lerner commented that the address possessed "a large measure of Roosevelt's fighting liberalism." The *Nation* called the speech one of the president's best. Jim Loeb remarked that it sounded like the ADA program.[3]

Yet a few days before the State of the Union address Truman had upset many liberals by dropping James Landis as chairman of the Civil Aeronautics Board and appointing an air force general to replace him. Angry and bitter, Landis made no secret of his belief that he was being punished for his attempts to block monopolistic control of the airlines and to obtain stronger safety measures. Most progressives agreed. The ouster of Landis also had an important symbolic significance, for Landis's government service had begun in the early days of the Roosevelt administration. He was, said the liberal journalist Robert Estabrook, "the last of the brain trusters." One reaction went unnoticed. Senator Glen Taylor later revealed that upon hearing of the Landis firing he threw away a draft statement rejecting Henry Wallace's third party and began a long process of reconsideration.[4]

Liberals had hardly recovered from the Landis incident when Truman asked another old New Dealer, Marriner Eccles, to step down as chairman of the Federal Reserve Board in favor of a Republican banker. That the president asked Eccles to stay on the board made little difference to progressives, who were stunned by the unceremonious dumping of one of the most distinguished advocates of liberal economic policies within the government. Eccles did not complain in public, but privately he was convinced that he had been done in by John Snyder and by powerful California banking interests which had persuaded Truman to dump him in return for assurances of campaign support. "The President has given new proof that his program is a lot better than his appointments," said the *ADA World*.[5]

The dumping of Landis and then Eccles, along with the drab conservatism of their replacements, reawakened all the feelings which had followed earlier departures of New Dealers. "While Truman stands for liberal ideas," remarked Chester Bowles privately, "he continues to *do* reactionary things." "You are making it very difficult for me to remain a good Democrat," a liberal California woman wrote the president, adding that most of her friends were already working ardently for Wallace. "Please, Mr. President, no more military or banking men!" [6]

Yet whatever the meaning of Truman's appointments, his program continued to move to the left. On February 2, he sent Congress a long message on civil rights requesting antilynching legislation, an FEPC, prohibition of discrimination in interstate transportation, an anti–poll tax law, and other measures to protect the right to vote. In addition, he promised an executive order to end discrimination in the civil service and steps to do away with segregation in the armed forces.[7]

The message carefully avoided implications of social equality, but it did commit the administration more firmly than ever to the advancement of equal opportunity and legal rights for Negroes. It went well beyond any position Roosevelt had ever taken. The program almost immediately touched off a Southern revolt within the Democratic Party, and, according to subsequent public opinion polls, was a major factor behind a sharp drop in Truman's popularity. Liberals, however, hailed the civil rights manifesto. It was, commented the *Progressive,* "a daring and distinguished effort which merits the militant support of every progressive-minded American." The *Nation* called it "a genuine and highly admirable document," and the Chicago *Sun-Times* described it as "a noble deed." [8]

Somewhat embarrassingly, however, Truman began to display signs that he was shaken by the vehemence of Southern denunciation. The administration refrained from introducing an omnibus civil rights bill in Congress, and the promised executive orders failed to materialize. Having taken the South for granted, Truman, Democratic Chairman J. Howard McGrath, and even some members of the administration liberal caucus were stunned by the prospect of rebellion; by April, the president and his advisers apparently had decided on an indefinite postponement of executive action. Yet the decision to conciliate the South led to the threat of a mass black defection from the Democratic Party. The NAACP pressed Truman to deliver on his promises, and New York black ward leaders warned Oscar Ewing that as much as 75 percent of their constituents might vote for Wallace. Somewhat painfully, the administration was discovering that the civil rights issue could not be filed and forgotten.[9]

Meanwhile, U.S. policy toward Palestine was causing almost as much bitterness and anger. Near the end of 1947, the United Nations had decided upon a plan, supported by the United States, to partition Palestine into Jewish and Arab states. When the Arabs prepared to fight, however, the United States began to hedge. Instead of expressing determination to enforce the U.N. decision through the creation of an international police force, American diplomats began to talk of the need to find some new solution, and the U.S. placed an embargo upon the shipment of arms to the Middle East, in effect aiding the Arabs, who were obtaining weapons from England. More than ever, progressives believed that anti-Jewish elements in the State and Defense departments were teaming up with British diplomats whose only concerns were influence in the Muslim world and access to Arab oil. These officials, many liberals thought, were prepared to wreck the U.N. and sacrifice the lives of Jewish refugees. Most progressives felt that Truman's sympathies were with the Palestinian Jews, but few had much confidence in his ability to resist the military and diplomatic pressures for what I. F. Stone described as "a cynical policy of swapping Jewish blood for Arab oil." [10]

Palestine exemplified Truman's difficulties at the beginning of 1948. He and his advisers might privately be laying the basis for a liberal reelection campaign, but in public he appeared weak and erratic, at best a leader of good intentions unable to withstand the conservatives within his own administration. His zigs and zags underscored his personal weakness and dismayed liberals who looked to the White House for guidance and inspiration.

II

While liberals alternately praised and criticized the administration, Wallace's new party was establishing an organization. The PCA dissolved and became the basis of a National Wallace-for-President Committee headed by Elmer Benson, Rexford G.

Tugwell, Jo Davidson, and Paul Robeson. Wallace appointed Beanie Baldwin his campaign manager. The party had quickly established basic campaign machinery, but it still faced formidable difficulties, the most important being the opposition of a clear majority of the liberals.[11]

The progressive anti-Communists—the ADA, the Liberal Party, almost all liberal congressmen—quickly rejected the Wallace movement, most of them characterizing it as a Communist-inspired effort to undermine true liberalism and throw control of the government to reactionaries. A. Philip Randolph, speaking for the National Educational Committee for a New Party, said: "Mr. Wallace is performing a distinct disservice to the cause of a peaceful world and a democratic America." The entire Roosevelt family came out against the third party, and Eleanor Roosevelt wrote unusually sharp attacks that were given wide distribution by the ADA, characterizing Wallace as a naïve politician being manipulated by the Communists.[12]

Many progressives who had been somewhat sympathetic with Wallace's critique of the Truman administration also refused to support him. Thomas L. Stokes wrote that Wallace had played a constructive role inside the Democratic Party, but could only hurt the liberal movement as a third-party candidate. The Chicago *Sun* warned that he was encouraging the Republicans to nominate one of their worst conservatives. Max Lerner called Wallace "a potentially great leader who . . . has allowed himself to become isolated from the large mass of independent progressives." Freda Kirchwey wrote that the new party could only lead to the triumph of Republican reaction and the defeat of the Marshall Plan.[13]

The Wallace effort forced the CIO to abandon its equivocal position on Communism. The organization assumed a tough anti-Communist, anti-Wallace stance and cracked down upon state and local councils which resisted the national policy. Philip Murray ousted pro-Communists from the national staff, a move symbolized by the forced resignation of Lee Pressman, whom he replaced with an anti-Communist Chicago labor lawyer, Arthur J. Goldberg. The CIO president warned his membership that Wallace's candidacy could throw the election to the Republicans and thus lead to higher prices, more antilabor legislation, an intensified attack upon civil liberties, continued inaction on housing, and eventual depression. By the end of April, he was publicly condemning the Wallace candidacy as a Communist plot.[14]

Wallace did receive support from several state and local leaders of the National Farmers Union, including Fred Stover, president of the Iowa NFU, but Jim Patton, who had never favored a third party, adopted a position of neutrality and seemed cool. The *New Republic* continued to feature a column by Wallace, but Michael Straight took over the editorship, refused to commit the journal to the new party, and quickly displayed misgivings about the venture. The American Labor Party provided Wallace with a ready-made place on the New York ballot, but only at the cost of losing its most important union component, the Amalgamated Clothing Workers. Even the PCA had suffered the defection of at least a dozen members of its national board after endorsing Wallace. The new party did gain one prominent recruit. Rexford G. Tugwell, the great New Deal thinker who had worked with and admired Wallace in the 1930s, resigned from the ADA, declaring: "I must support the only great voice now being lifted for friendship to all men and against the exploitation of any." Still, Wallace's backing clearly did not run the broad gamut of progressivism. Composed mainly of the Communist Party and organizations dominated by Communists, fellow travelers, and Popular Fronters, obsessed with a fear of domestic fascism, it was not a promising basis for an appeal to the democratic and increasingly anti-Communist American left.[15]

Wallace was nevertheless optimistic and uncompromising. The United States had reached a turning point in its political history, he told Louis Bean in January. The Democratic Party was disintegrating, and the new party would take its place, just as the Republicans had replaced the Whigs. As for the liberals in Congress who accepted anti-Communism and stayed with the Democrats, he was as ready to work for their defeat as for Truman's. At the beginning of January, Wallace listed three key issues as a basis for judgment—universal military training, the Taft-Hartley law, and the Truman Doctrine. If the Democratic liberals were "bad on more than one of these three things, out they go into the total darkness," he told an old associate. "I am more worried about appeasing native born fascists than I am about appeasing Russia. Those who call me an appeaser today are the same breed of people as those who initiated the Anti-Comintern in the late thirties." When a wealthy and influential supporter of Wallace tried to arrange a reconciliation between him and Paul Douglas, the new party leader replied: "I am certain it is impossible to get together with Douglas as long as I believe that peace is the all-important issue, and as long as he believes that hatred of Russia and Communism is all-important." Such attitudes might lead to defeat not just for Truman but for many prominent liberals.[16]

The Wallace movement's first test of strength was an unusual four-cornered special Congressional contest in the Bronx. The American Labor Party was running a talented New York state assemblyman, Leo Isacson; the Democrats had put forth a relatively unknown figure, Karl Propper; because of Democratic boss Ed Flynn's refusal to deal with the Liberal Party, the popular Dean Alfange was on the Liberal ticket; there was an unheralded and generally ignored Republican candidate, Joseph DeNigris. The district normally delivered a strong ALP vote, second only to Vito Marcantonio's East Harlem bailiwick; and it had a large Jewish population restive over the administration's Palestine policy. The ALP, moreover, had always run well in special elections, situations in which it could bring its zealous and able workers from all over the city into a single district. Unlike the other parties, it had been able to bring out about the same vote in a special race as in a general election. But observers tended to discount all these factors and generally pictured the election as an indicator of Wallace's popularity.

Wallace, who was calling for a U.N. police force to carry out the Palestine partition plan, came to the Bronx to wage an effective campaign. At one rally, he was reported as saying that "Truman still talks Jewish and acts Aryan." He later insisted that he had said "Arab" instead of "Aryan," but in either case he was hitting the administration at a very vulnerable point. The Democrats attempted to counter the ALP effort by bringing in outside workers of their own, and Eleanor Roosevelt campaigned for Propper. But as many as 7,000 ALP workers blanketed the district, far outnumbering Flynn's men as well as outperforming them. On February 17, Isacson creamed his three opponents, polling almost 56 percent of the vote and running 10,000 ahead of Propper.[17]

The election gave an enormous boost to the Wallace effort all over the country, and it practically sent Democrats into fits of hysteria. Political analysts wrote that the vote seemed to indicate that Wallace's candidacy would throw New York, California, Michigan, Illinois, and Pennsylvania to the Republicans. Chester Bowles believed Wallace would take 80,000 to 110,000 votes in Connecticut. There was even a report that Wallace might *carry* three urban Congressional districts in the president's own state of Missouri. Nervous Democrats and anti-Communist liberals began to wonder aloud if someone other than Truman might be secured to lead the Democratic ticket in the fall.[18]

Less than a week after the Isacson election, the Wallace party obtained an important recruit. The folksy, popular senator from Idaho had finally made his long-deferred decision. He would support the new party and would be Wallace's running-mate. "I am not leaving the Democratic party, it left me," said Glen Taylor. "Wall Street and the military have taken over." With an able and effective vice-presidential candidate, the Wallace campaign moved into the spring.[19]

III

Although the Isacson victory was in large part a protest against the administration's Palestine policy, it brought no changes. Military and diplomatic officials within the administration stressed the difficulty of actual armed intervention in the Middle East, warning that the Russians could use a U.N. police force to gain a foothold in the area and emphasizing the great importance of Arab oil. With the support of Secretary Marshall, whom Truman respected above all other men, they won the president over to a policy of delay. At the White House, Clark Clifford frantically tried to change the president's mind, arguing that the national interest required strong support of the U.N., that the alternative to partition was a Middle Eastern chaos which would provide ample opportunity for Soviet intervention, that there was no danger to Western oil supplies. (Significantly, he did not discuss political considerations: he realized that Truman was determined to approach the issue as a nonpartisan diplomatic problem.) However, even Clifford found it impossible to prevail over Marshall's monumental presence and rectitude.

On March 19, the United States abandoned partition and called for a U.N. trusteeship over Palestine pending some new settlement. Truman had completely lost control of policy and had not even realized that the shift was planned; nevertheless, he sustained the State Department. Liberals reacted in anger and amazement. "We have been vacillating and dishonest," declared Helen Gahagan Douglas. "The record adds up to the story of an inglorious muddle," commented the Chicago *Sun-Times*. Eleanor Roosevelt offered her resignation from the American delegation to the U.N. and withdrew it only after Truman urgently requested her to stay and assured her she was free to express her disagreement in public. Leon Henderson said that the policy switch had betrayed "the hope of peoples everywhere that this nation is prepared to place world order ahead of power politics." [20]

On May 14, with the British withdrawing from Palestine, Truman secured State Department acquiescence to immediate de facto recognition of the newly proclaimed state of Israel, but the United States did not extend aid or lift the arms embargo. Fighting continued, the British still backed the Arabs, and liberals still protested American policy. "It is a shameful and disgraceful record," wrote T. O. Thackrey, by now so alienated from the administration that he was preparing to back Henry Wallace. In a letter to Truman, Freda Kirchwey assserted: "It is inconceivable that you are aware of this policy or that it would meet with your approval." Bartley Crum's New York *Star,* the short-lived successor to the defunct *PM,* urged de jure recognition, military aid, and a loan for the new state. In the minds of most progressives Palestine remained a moral issue, not an economic or strategic problem. "The Jews, bearing the wounds of the Hitler decade upon their bodies and souls, have been again grievously wounded," wrote Reinhold Niebuhr.[21]

In the central area of American foreign relations, however, lib-erals moved closer to the administration position. At the end of February, the Communists staged a shocking coup d'état in Czechoslovakia. Czechoslovakia had been a functioning democ-racy. It had subordinated its foreign policy to that of the Soviet Union, and had hoped to serve as a bridge between East and West. Czech leader Jan Masaryk, who died mysteriously, a sui-cide according to the Communists, had been Eastern Europe's greatest symbol of democratic nationalism. Communist charges of a right-wing plot were clearly fraudulent. "All the Czechs asked was to be allowed to rule themselves," commented Elmer Davis. "But this is a privilege the Kremlin seems determined not to allow." [22]

Far more significant than Davis's reaction was that of liberals who in the past had been less disposed to condemn Russian tac-tics in Eastern Europe. Expressing his belief that the coup had been dictated by Moscow, Chester Bowles called it "the most disheartening event since the beginning of the Cold War" and asserted that "the Soviet Union today is moving the world rap-idly towards disaster." Freda Kirchwey criticized American pol-icy this time for failing to give energetic support to the Czech democrats, called the coup a betrayal of an honest attempt to work with the Communists, and warned that the Marshall Plan must stop Communist expansion by supporting the democratic left in Europe. Having initially backed the European Recovery Plan as a device to unite Europe, Miss Kirchwey was now embracing the ADA approach by accepting the division of the Continent and advocating a reformist ERP as a containment measure. Michael Straight, through a more circuitous reasoning process, brought the *New Republic* unequivocally behind the Marshall Plan: "There is a lot to criticize. . . . But, given this congress, it's a great achievement and a major source of hope." He condemned the Czech coup and reprinted a eulogy of Masaryk by Edward R. Murrow.

Many liberals nevertheless felt the administration reaction was alarming. Truman went before Congress, belligerently denounced the Soviet Union, and reiterated his request for universal military training. It seemed that the U.S. and the USSR might be at the brink of total war. "Now we have a military foreign policy proposed," wrote Thomas L. Stokes. "There it is, naked as a bayonet." The United States, most liberals were still convinced, could stem the Communist tide only with a positive economic policy. America, moreover, should always attempt diplomatic negotiations; indeed, the prospect of war made negotiation all the more necessary. "Is it appeasement to stand up as the defender of the world's peace, to put the onus on the other side for turning down reasonable proposals?" asked Samuel Grafton. Even Reinhold Niebuhr expressed a belief that to some extent the administration was adopting "the stupidity of meeting political peril by military threats." The Chicago *Sun-Times,* while expressing general support of Truman, warned of the need for coolness and willingness to negotiate. The American Veterans Committee urged Truman to propose a personal meeting with Stalin. The St. Louis *Post-Dispatch* called upon the president to send General Eisenhower to Moscow "to do all that can honorably be done to halt the drift toward war." For all the criticism of administration aggressiveness, however, more liberals than ever before were convinced that the Soviet Union represented a threat to Western Europe. They were simply arguing in favor of political and economic modes of containment.[23]

Truman combined his anti-Communism with an attempt to present himself as the advocate of a positive liberal program and a defender of the New Deal. He publicly lashed out at Henry Wallace only twice before the conventions, both times departing from prepared texts. "I do not want and I will not accept the political support of Henry Wallace and his Communists," he declared on March 17. On March 29, he suggested that Wallace "ought to go to the country he loves so well and help them against his own country if that's the way he feels." But such outbursts could only hurt Truman's image and direct even more attention toward Wallace, who demanded and received free radio time to answer the first blast. The president and his advisers seem to have decided to avoid any public mention of Wallace and concentrate on the development of an affirmative liberal record. In a more typical pronouncement, Truman told a Jefferson-Jackson Day dinner that his administration represented "the forces of positive, progressive liberalism" as opposed to "those forces of conservatism which believe in the benefit of the few at the expense of the many." [24]

Truman continued his militant legislative leadership with messages to Congress advocating a far-reaching housing program, stronger rent control, a sweeping enlargement of social security coverage with higher benefits, and federal aid to education. He rebuked Congress at every opportunity, criticizing the rent control measure it passed as hopelessly inadequate and, as in 1947, vetoing—unsuccessfully this time—both a Republican-sponsored tax bill and an act which removed newspaper and magazine vendors from social security.[25]

In the meantime, the administration had gone far toward achieving a reconciliation with the Farmers Union. The new relationship had begun to develop in the spring of 1947 when the Department of Agriculture had adopted a long-range policy plan which advocated maximum agricultural production with markets provided by a full-employment economy at home and large exports abroad. The document had been prepared under the supervision of Undersecretary of Agriculture Charles F. Brannan, an old friend and ally of Jim Patton and the NFU. Patton called the recommendations, which dovetailed neatly with NFU policy, "a statesmanlike performance." Subsequently, Patton supported the Marshall Plan, although he had serious reservations about the failure to utilize the U.N. and allowed the Farmers Union paper to feature strong criticisms of administration foreign policy. Truman ignored the criticism and took another step toward attaching Patton to the administration by appointing him to a special Marshall Plan advisory committee. In the spring of 1948, Clinton Anderson resigned from the Cabinet to run for the Senate, and Truman named Brannan to replace him. Patton declared that the choice merited "the gratitude of all true friends of agriculture." [26]

Truman worked toward a liberal identity in other ways. He gave strong backing to David Lilienthal and other members of the Atomic Energy Commission when Congress balked at approving five-year appointments for them. He conspicuously brought Roosevelt's old aide, Sam Rosenman, back into the White House circle.[27] Since the middle of 1947, the president had committed himself and the Democratic Party to progressivism. With his civil rights program he had gone beyond the New Deal. The keystone of his foreign policy, the Marshall Plan, had clearly won the support of the great majority of liberals. Yet the anti-Wallace liberals not only failed to unite behind him during the first half of 1948, they became progressively more alienated from him. Despite their commitment to Truman's program, they were more opposed than ever to Truman.

IV

Many progressives still disliked Truman, doubted his sincerity, or felt he was too small for the presidency. The ADA convention, meeting the last week in February, seethed with rank-and-file feeling against the president. The organization's grass roots, wrote Jim Loeb, "almost erupted in an anti-Truman explosion." The Bronx election added a practical and objective dimension to this emotional and subjective resentment. It was the crucial factor in touching off a liberal drive to deny the president the Democratic nomination.[28]

By March, liberals and labor leaders all over the country, convinced that Truman would pull the entire Democratic ticket under, were frantically searching for a new Roosevelt. Chester Bowles, who was trying for the Democratic gubernatorial nomination in Connecticut, wrote to Leon Henderson that he saw little chance of winning in November with Truman at the head of the slate. "I might be able to run as much as 40,000 ahead of the national ticket. But if the polls are right, that wouldn't be enough." Both Walter Reuther and David Dubinsky, talking to Loeb on March 15, agreed that Truman's condidacy would be a disaster for the Democratic Party and the liberal movement. "We not only face defeat in November," Hubert Humphrey told Loeb, "we face a disintegration of the whole social-democratic block in this country." "We cannot compete with the Wallace crowd unless and until we have a national Presidential figure to crusade for," Loeb remarked. "Harry Truman is ADA's great frustration." [29]

Writing in the March 13 issue of the *Nation,* Freda Kirchwey called on Wallace to make a deal with the Democratic leaders, to offer to withdraw from the campaign in return for the dumping of Truman and the nomination of a candidate acceptable to all liberals. On March 27, Franklin and Elliott Roosevelt urged the Democrats to nominate the new president of Columbia University, Dwight D. Eisenhower. The Liberal Party seconded the call. Harold Ickes wrote in his newspaper column that Truman could either follow the "patriotic" course of retirement with dignity or face the prospect of being driven out of office by a "disillusioned and indignant citizenry." Michael Straight was quoted as favoring Wallace over Truman, and in early April the *New Republic* featured a front-page editorial by Straight: "AS A CANDIDATE FOR PRESIDENT, HARRY TRUMAN SHOULD QUIT." Despite the Marshall Plan, and despite Truman's good intentions, the president's blundering leadership was leading America toward war. "On issue after issue the President has surrendered, first to one group, then to another, taking no stand or reversing his stand, robbing America of morality and consistency." There would be no easy way of achieving a settlement with the USSR, but Straight believed it could be done by a president who could think in the broad terms that overall negotiations with the Soviets would require, who had the stature and ability to deal with the Soviet chiefs and to assume the leadership of democratic forces all over the world—in short, a president like Franklin Roosevelt.[30]

On April 11, the ADA National Board emerged from a special meeting with a statement calling for "an open Democratic convention" and saying, "this Nation has the right to call upon men like Dwight D. Eisenhower and William O. Douglas if the people so choose." On April 12, a Jackson Day dinner in Los Angeles turned into an anti-Truman demonstration. Keynoter Jimmy Roosevelt drew prolonged applause when he mentioned Eisenhower. Democratic Chairman McGrath attempted to counter with strong praise of Truman, saying rhetorically, "Can you ask for more than this in leadership?" "Yes!" shouted members of the crowd. Top labor leaders came out for Eisenhower, including Emil Rieve, Hugo Ernst, and CIO Secretary-Treasurer James B. Carey, who many observers rightly believed was speaking for Philip Murray. At the end of April, Gael Sullivan resigned from the Democratic National Committee to indicate his displeasure with the president.[31]

While the liberals perceived practical reasons for getting Truman off the Democratic ticket, they were also moved by less pragmatic impulses. The president's record, James Wechsler conceded, was not bad, and his intentions were good. The grievances against him were not concrete. His *personal leadership* was inadequate. Neither reactionary nor corrupt nor wholly incompetent, Truman had the misfortune to occupy the White House in an era of unparalleled insecurity and fear, "a time when . . . democracy is crying for daddy." It was a time for a greatness which the president could not provide. "Mr. Truman's place in history may be written in Mike Gonzales' ageless remark about a rookie ballplayer: good field, no hit." [32]

Virtually all liberals were turning away from Truman in the spring of 1948, but they all were not stampeding toward Eisenhower. Neither the *Nation* nor the *New Republic* ever came out for the general, and the *Progressive* vehemently opposed him, observing that it knew his stand on only one issue—he favored universal military training. Thomas L. Stokes wrote indignantly that there was already too much military influence in the government; throwing the presidency to a general hardly seemed an appropriate remedy. David Lilienthal was privately outraged by the "lynch-law atmosphere" which seemed to be dominating the progressive movement: "Did F.D.R. ever stand up for public development of power, or human rights, or labor, essentially any more firmly than Truman? And who knows what Eisenhower would do on any of these issues! Bah!" Many prominent ADA leaders opposed support of a military man whose views were largely unknown. Lester Granger of the Urban League resigned from the ADA National Board because Eisenhower had defended segregation in the armed forces. Richard L. Neuberger, the ADA's Oregon chairman, also left the organization, charging that it was abandoning its principles. Marquis Childs was against Eisenhower or any other general. Elmer Davis criticized the Eisenhower movement in broadcast after broadcast. "If he runs, eventually he's going to have to say something and then a lot of people might be surprised," he told his radio audience at the end of March. Reinhold Niebuhr was firmly opposed to the Eisenhower boom. Eleanor Roosevelt and Wilson Wyatt would have nothing to do with it. Eugenie Anderson told Loeb it was "a little silly." ADA's legislative director, Andy Biemiller, who was planning to run for his old seat in Congress, rejected the Eisenhower coattails and brashly asserted, *"Truman is still within striking distance of a majority."* One ADA member summed up the difficulties of supporting the general by asking the perfectly valid question, "Why are we against MacArthur and for Eisenhower?" [33]

But Eisenhower was an appealing personality,* and most of

*Truman himself, for reasons which remain obscure, offered the Democratic nomination to Eisenhower in the fall of 1947 and pledged to act as his running mate. Perhaps he was entirely serious, although at that time his standing in the his public declarations exuded a good will and humaneness which could be taken for liberalism. John Gunther reportedly assured his ADA friends that Eisenhower was a liberal, albeit an ignorant liberal. He would keep the presidency in the Democratic Party and carry a liberal Congress with him. Elected on a progressive platform, given a progressive Congress, Eisenhower, many ADA'ers reasoned, would be carried along by the thrust of the situation and would naturally move the country back toward the New Deal. In any event, Eisenhower with a liberal Congress was clearly preferable to a Dewey or a Taft —or someone worse—with another Congress like the Eightieth.[34]

As reports of Truman's dwindling stock came in from all over the nation, the liberals, who felt no personal loyalty to him, were more convinced than ever that he had to go. James Wechsler even reported from California that some political experts were convinced that the president would poll fewer votes than Wallace in the state. Writing to an ADA dissenter, Jim Loeb outlined the consequences that would follow a Truman candidacy:

[I]t will, of course, mean a Republican Presidential victory. . . . This is the opinion of every competent newspaperman, commentator, and rank-and-file liberal all over the country. . . . perhaps more seriously, it means disaster in terms of our Congressional races. The wonderful liberal ticket of Adlai Stevenson and Paul Douglas in Illinois has no chance with Truman. . . . Confidentially, Paul Douglas practically admits it. Truman's nomination probably means the defeat of Hubert Humphrey in Minnesota, of Helen Douglas in California, of Chester Bowles, if he is nominated for the Governorship in Connecticut, of Congressman Jackson in Washington, of Senator Murray in Montana. . . . I could name outstanding potential candidates, from coast to coast, who simply will not file because they know that they will be defeated on the Democratic ticket if

---

public opinion polls was high. Perhaps he wanted to maneuver Eisenhower into an early refusal before a group of ambitious president-makers could surround the general. Cabell Phillips, *The Truman Presidency* (New York, 1966), pp. 196–97.

Truman heads that ticket. This is a tragic situation, but it is a fact.[35]

If Eisenhower was the practical favorite of the liberals, Supreme Court Justice William O. Douglas was the sentimental favorite. One of the dynamic young men of the New Deal, a militant defender of civil liberties, Douglas was a non-Communist alternative to Wallace. Privately he was critical of the Truman administration, feeling that its appointees had emasculated the regulatory agencies and that there were too many conservatives around the president. His differences with the Truman policies, however, were largely matters of style. His conception of Soviet Communism as inherently expansionistic and bent on world domination differed little from Truman's; he even told Robert Lasch that the Greek aid program might be an unpleasant necessity. Yet Douglas's public addresses carried the promise of a more inspiring, positive, and democratic foreign policy, oriented toward the common people of the world and seeking, as he put it, to win the Cold War in the ricefields rather than on the battlefields. An eloquent Memorial Day eulogy at FDR's grave went far toward establishing him as the true claimant to the Roosevelt mantle.

Douglas may have had some interest in the Democratic nomination, although he admonished some progressives who, admitting that they knew nothing of Eisenhower's values, asked him if he would be the general's running mate. (According to one report, he told them he was not interested in entering what might turn out to be a political whorehouse.) All the same, he did nothing to foreclose any movement in his behalf. Douglas had a personal appeal to progressives which even Eisenhower could not match and Truman could not approach. Perhaps he could not win in November, but he would wage a better campaign than Truman, would draw many votes which otherwise would go to Wallace, and in defeat would be a vigorous opposition leader around whom the liberal movement could unite. As the Wisconsin ADA leader Carl Auerbach put it, "we would rather lose with Douglas than lose with Truman." [36]

V

As the liberals surveyed their presidential prospects with a mixture of gloom and desperation, Henry Wallace traveled across the country, charging that monopolists and military officials controlled the government, that they were pursuing a policy of imperialism and counterrevolution abroad while repressing workers and dissenters at home. He seemed to be holding his fervent mass following. At the end of February, 7,000 people went out into a Minneapolis blizzard and paid admission to see him. Morris Rubin said the *Progressive* had never received so much mail in opposition to an editorial policy as it did after its condemnation of Wallace. "Jesus was misunderstood and crucified too," wrote one subscriber. "Much as I hate to admit it," Rubin conceded, "I must say that there are tens of thousands of good American progressives who aren't even faintly fellow travelers who are lined up with Wallace." "When Wallace speaks of Wall Street and the Army in government, when he warns of imposing our will on neighbor nations, when he taps the burning American desire for peace," observed Richard Neuberger, "millions of people at their radios will nod in agreement." [37]

But Wallace's campaign received a stiff blow from the Communist takeover in Czechoslovakia. He was at first inclined to blame the coup on the Truman Doctrine, calling the seizure of power part of a Soviet "get tough" policy in reaction to the American "get tough" policy. Then at a press conference two weeks later, he made the amazing charge that the U.S. ambassador had been involved in a right-wing plot, but evaded demands for evidence. (Subsequently, he argued that the American diplomat had committed a serious provocation by expressing the hope that the Czechs might still be able to participate in the Marshall Plan.) He also remarked that Masaryk might have been driven to suicide by cancer or by depression about the state of the world. "To many of his earlier sympathizers," Karl Schmidt writes, "his remarks indicated that the extreme leftists among his advisers had gained his ear too well."

There seems to be no reason to quarrel with Schmidt's judgment: "Numbers who had already joined now left the third party; many who were previously undecided now stayed away." [38]

Wallace also hurt himself by accepting Communist backing, although he was unaware of the extent to which the Communists were penetrating his party. Louis Bean, Tugwell, and others warned him of the infiltration, but Beanie Baldwin always persuaded him to discount such charges. "He was relying on his management, which of course is what you would normally do," Bean comments. "But in this case, it was a misplaced confidence." It was indeed, for Wallace's speeches were being put together by a "research team" with strong Communist connections. Moreover, Wallace believed that the Communist Party was not a subversive group. At the beginning of February, he called on all presidential candidates to renounce individuals or organizations which were antilibertarian. Declaring that this demand was not inconsistent with his acceptance of Communist backing, he said, "I find nothing criminal in the advocacy of different economic and social ideas, however much I may differ with them." Ironically, he felt that, so long as he made it clear that he "believed in God and progressive capitalism," the Communists were behind him at *their* peril not his, that they were his tools and not he theirs. "If the Communists want to support me, they must do it on my terms," he said. "If the Communists are working for peace with Russia, God bless 'em. If they are working for the overthrow of the Government by force, they know I'm against them." [39]

Although he remained hopelessly naïve on the matter of Communist involvement in the new party, Wallace moved back toward the center of the American progressive tradition with his strong attack on the indictments of top Communist leaders under the Smith Act. His charge that America had taken another step toward fascism was perhaps farfetched, but most liberals agreed with him that "Defense of the civil rights of Communists is the first line in the defense of the liberties of a democratic people." [40]

Perhaps the outstanding incident of the Wallace campaign between the Isacson victory and the new party convention occurred in mid-May. At a Madison Square Garden rally on May 11, Wallace read an open letter to Stalin calling for an agreement between the U.S. and the USSR. More than any pronouncement he had made in months, the document seemed to distribute blame for the Cold War equally, perhaps because Wallace himself, rather than his speechwriters, had produced it. The basic points of his proposed settlement were: (1) a general arms reduction and the outlawing of weapons of mass destruction; (2) a worldwide embargo upon the export of weapons; (3) a free flow of individuals, goods, and information between the two power blocs; and (4) a U.N. agency for international relief.[41]

A few days later, Radio Moscow broadcast a statement by Stalin saying that Wallace's proposals were "a good and fruitful basis" for discussion. Receiving the news in the form of a bulletin while he was making a radio talk, Wallace was overwhelmed. "I am humble and grateful to be an instrument in this crisis, in having been able to bring about this offer for a settlement." The main effect of the incident seems to have been the sharp hike it gave to the morale of Wallace and his group. It did not make the strong impression among liberals which one might have expected, although there was a great deal of progressive criticism when the administration refused to accept vague Soviet overtures for peace talks as genuine.

Freda Kirchwey somewhat surprisingly rejected Wallace's formula for a settlement, saying it was "heavily weighted in favor of Moscow," and expressed disagreement with his call for an "open, fully-reported conference" on all matters of dispute. "Not through staged, floodlit assemblies but through day-to-day negotiations in a hundred normal contacts, will the reality of the recent peace maneuvers be tested." The *New Republic* not only failed to show enthusiasm but virtually foreclosed support of the new party. In early July, the journal announced that Wallace would no longer contribute his weekly column.[42]

On one matter, Wallace and his team scored heavily. This

was civil rights, an issue which was becoming increasingly important to liberals. A tour through the South by Glen Taylor dramatized the new party's concern for the Negro. Almost everywhere he went, Taylor refused to speak to segregated audiences and in Birmingham was even thrown in jail. Wallace called on Truman to take civil rights action in areas where congressional assent was unnecessary; as commander-in-chief, for example, the president could issue an executive order desegregating the armed forces. "If the President's message was more than an attempt to woo votes with lip service, he will issue that executive order, and he will issue it without further needless delay." [43]

VI

Instead, Truman devoted much of the spring to the development of a new asset. The president's speech delivery both over the radio and in front of large crowds had been humdrum and uninspiring; if he were to provide strong leadership for a national campaign, he had to master new techniques. As early as mid-1947, Gael Sullivan was suggesting important departures to Clark Clifford:

We have not been able to capitalize fully on the President's impact on the people.

Sometime before the National Convention in 1948 the President should show himself to the Nation via the back platform of a cross-country train.

The easy manner of speaking when speaking informally has been lost in translation to the people via radio and speaking tours.

The entire approach to the President's speeches should be changed. It would be well to gain more natural delivery, even if some rhetorical effects are lost.

Clifford and some of the other people around Truman quickly picked up the idea (if indeed they had not already thought of it). After some urging, the president agreed to attempt an "off-the-cuff" talk in April at the end of a prepared speech to a group of newspaper editors. The attempt worked beautifully. Using only an outline, Truman discussed Soviet-American relations off the record. "He spoke fluently, with deep feeling, almost passion, and courageously," wrote David Lilienthal. "He took the editors quite by surprise, and by storm, and everyone said: Why wasn't that on the record? That is what the whole country should hear." Truman used the technique on the record several other times during the spring, once even over the radio, always with greater success than reading a prepared text. By the beginning of June, he was ready to adopt Sullivan's other recommendation, to "show himself to the Nation via the back platform of a cross-country train." [44]

On June 4, the presidential train left Washington on the beginning of a "non-political" tour which took Truman to the West Coast to receive an honorary degree from the University of California. In the next fourteen days the president made a half-dozen full-scale addresses and about five dozen whistle-stop speeches. There were some mistakes and blunders. A bad publicity job left the stadium at Omaha more than half empty; Truman made a flippant remark about Stalin—"I like old Joe! He is a decent fellow."—which would be used against him for years. But vastly more important was the crystallization of the style and substance of his campaign. In his folksy rear-platform talks and his prepared speeches, he tore into the Eightieth Congress and advanced an affirmative liberal program of his own.

In Chicago, he devoted most of a major address to a call for legislation which would allow a substantial number of displaced persons to enter the United States with no discrimination on the basis of race or creed. He ended by listing an ambitious agenda of reform legislation as the best answer to Communism. At almost every junction he recalled his efforts to save price control and Congress's refusal to accept his anti-inflation recommendations. In Omaha, he delivered a major speech on agricultural policy, identifying the Democratic Party with agrarian prosperity and outlining a comprehensive agenda for the farmer—price supports, soil conservation, extension of markets at home and abroad, and rural welfare programs in housing, education, health, and electrification.

In the Northwest he emphasized his support of reclamation, river valley development, and public power; and he charged that the Republican Party had no interest in the development of the West. In California, he stressed the need for increased irrigation in the great Central Valley. All along the line he lashed into Congressional inaction on these matters. At the same time, he ripped away at the Republican record on housing and rent controls, at the Taft-Hartley Act, the refusal to raise the minimum wage, the slashes in the services and appropriations of the Labor Department. He must have sensed that his message was going over well; on the way back to Washington, he was swinging harder than ever.

Albuquerque, New Mexico: "The issue in this country is between special privilege and the people."
East St. Louis, Illinois: "I think they are hunting for a boom and bust."
Richmond, Indiana: "They have emasculated the housing bill in the interest of the real estate lobby."

Shrewd observers realized what Truman was doing. "On just about every important public issue the President has decided to carry the banner of Franklin Roosevelt," wrote Scripps-Howard correspondent Charles Lucey. "The new deal—its preservation, perpetuation and completion is what Harry S. Truman is pinning his hopes on," wrote Barnet Nover in the Denver Post. "He has begun to make an impression." [45]
Even before his return to Washington, moreover, Truman was striking directly at Congress with a series of rebukes and vetoes. On June 12, he vetoed the Bullwinkle bill to exempt railroads and other interstate carriers from the antitrust laws, asserting that the antimonopoly statutes needed to be strengthened rather than weakened. Congress overrode the veto. On June 14, he vetoed legislation which would exclude more groups of workers from social security. "If our social security program is to endure, it must be protected against these piecemeal attacks." Congress passed this bill over the veto, too. On June 15, he vetoed a transfer of the U.S. Employment Service from the Labor Department to the Federal Security Agency,

noting that Congress had already taken the Conciliation Service away from the department and had slashed its funds, charging that the bill was "another in a series of legislative actions stripping the Department of Labor of essential funds and functions." Congress overrode the veto.[46]

At the end of the month, the president faced several bills which Congress had passed just before adjournment. He signed all but one, not, however, without making strong protests. He savagely tore into the Displaced Persons Act, calling it antisemitic and anti-Catholic, asserting that its provisions formed "a pattern of discrimination and intolerance wholly inconsistent with the American sense of justice." He said that Congress had thrown American foreign commercial policy into doubt by extending reciprocal trade for only one year. He scored a failure to appropriate funds for a new TVA power plant as "reckless and irresponsible" and defended the TVA as "a demonstration of the ability of a democracy to conceive and execute large plans for the public welfare" and "an inspiration and example to the rest of the world." On the same day, he issued a sharp protest against an Interior Department appropriation act which contained cutbacks in reclamation and public power, and he asserted that provisions which attempted to eject two prominent New Dealers from the Bureau of Reclamation were designed for the benefit of special interests.[47]

On July 3, he criticized agricultural measures which would extend price supports as stopgap legislation and called for the enactment of the comprehensive program he had outlined at Omaha. The same day, he attacked the Congressional decision to extend the terms of the Atomic Energy Commission members for only two years, declaring that Congress had injected partisan politics into atomic energy, and calling the action another indication of "the refusal of the Republican leadership to put the public interest first." [48]

Truman's blasts at Congress squared with the liberal view. The Farmers Union newspaper suggested that it might be well for the voters to " 'plow under' most of the present 'stand' of representatives and try a new 'crop.' " The Chicago Sun-Times commended Truman and remarked that the Congress had "turned its back on the individual American citizen." The New York *Post* asserted that the Republicans had failed to pass a single progressive or constructive piece of legislation. Leon Henderson said that Congress's record was "the story of selfish interest triumphant over the general welfare." The *Nation* declared that the Congressional performance, if not quite as bad as Truman charged, "was surely bad enough to be the Number One issue of the 1948 elections." [49]

By the end of June, the White House was indeed arriving at a decision which would insure that Congress would be the major issue. "Should the President call Congress back?" asked an unsigned memorandum prepared by some of Truman's campaign strategists.* Many liberals were urging such a move, and the document aggressively endorsed their arguments: he should, it said, bring the Republicans back to Washington and push for every point in his liberal program, including civil rights. "The election will be won or lost in the Northern, Mid western and Western states."

It concluded: "This Congress cannot meet the critical needs of the country. It is tied up by the rich interests which expect to make a killing after the Republican victory—if they get that victory." [50] There was, of course, no chance that Congress would upset the strategy by accepting Truman's demands.

VII

Despite the president's increasingly militant leadership, liberals were more determined than ever to find someone else to head the Democratic ticket. By the end of May, the ADA was

---

*The authorship of this document is one of the minor historiographical mysteries of the Truman era. R. Alton Lee attributes it to Samuel Rosenman since the only copy thus far discovered is a carbon in the Rosenman MSS. However, the wording seems to indicate that it was a group project, and Rosenman did not claim authorship. The Research Division might have produced it; William L. Batt thinks so. However, Batt was advising against a special session while Truman was on his Western trip. The importance of the document, in any event, probably has been overstressed. So many people were suggesting the idea of a special session that it appears impossible to isolate a single source as a determinative influence. (See note 50 for documentation.)

trying to set off a revolt in California's Democratic convention delegation, which was pledged to Truman, and was mapping a full-scale effort to draft Eisenhower, with Douglas as a second choice. "The Connecticut delegation," Chester Bowles told Loeb in early June, "will be uninstructed and more than willing to follow the slightest sign of leadership." In mid-June, Hubert Humphrey and the ADA won a stiff battle against the Wallace faction for control of the Minnesota Democratic-Farmer-Labor Party. Humphrey announced his support of Eisenhower or Douglas; the state convention put through a pro forma resolution praising Truman, but sent an unpledged delegation to the Democratic national convention.

The ADA released at least two analyses purporting to show that Truman could be dumped easily. If the president were allowed to run, Leon Henderson warned, he would drag scores of liberals to defeat. "Roaring reaction would ride the rails. The awful pattern of polarity, so tragic in Europe, would repeat itself leaving liberals helpless and unrepresented." By the end of the month, even Reinhold Niebuhr was behind the dump-Truman effort. "We are sunk now and Eisenhower is the only possible candidate who could defeat the Republicans. I would support almost any decent man to avoid 4 years of Republican rule." [51]

Even Truman's Western trip failed to convert many liberals. T.R.B., who was along on the train, was an exception—"when Truman tears up prepared speeches and talks naturally on a subject he knows something about, he is surprisingly good." Thomas L. Stokes also pronounced the tour a success: "He has established a kinship with average folks. And, behind the friendly surface, he has shown himself as a scrapper with considerable punch . . . in behalf of the common people." But most liberals, including some who were on the spot, depicted a failure. Ancil Payne, the ADA's Northwestern organizer, called the president's Seattle appearance "a first class flop." "He was just a little man in a big stadium." Liberal journalist David Karr characterized Truman's speeches as cliché-laden and felt they demonstrated that he did "not yet completely grasp the many issues he is tackling." Other liberal critics, the *Nation* among them, were upset by the blasts at Congress while the Marshall Plan appropriation was being debated in the House. As important as any factor, perhaps, was the pronounced distaste for the president's style, even among down-to-earth progressives such as Elmer Davis and James Wechsler. Davis disapprovingly compared Truman's free-swinging tour to Andrew Johnson's disastrous swing around the circle. Wechsler condemned the president's crudeness: "On his lips the sentences sounded like small-boy sniping." [52]

On the eve of the Democratic convention, the anti-Wallace liberals, spearheaded by the ADA, were more estranged from Truman than ever and determined to push him off the ticket, despite a strong commitment to the Truman program. The brave and hopeful words of 1944 about constructing a progressive movement which could function without dependence upon personalities were forgotten. The liberals were desperately seeking a charismatic leader.

Chapter 10

Campaign for Liberalism

The political conventions and the presidential campaign discouraged most progressives. Truman, for all his new vigor, still failed to rouse most liberals and seemed headed for certain defeat. The Wallace campaign, despite the essential courage and integrity of its leader, appeared hopeless, hollow, even fraudulent. The progressives with very few exceptions braced themselves for a Republican victory, hoping only to retain a foothold in Congress; some, convinced that the end had come for the Democratic coalition created by Roosevelt, began to work toward the fundamental political realignment which had to follow.

I

It was appropriate, wrote Max Lerner as he observed the power-hungry GOP delegates preparing to descend upon Washington in 1949, that the telephone number of the Republican convention headquarters was in the Locust exchange. Lerner and other liberals watched glumly as the convention chose Thomas E. Dewey. Calling Dewey "the nominee nobody loves," Robert Bendiner attributed his victory to "years of compromise and strategic silence." The Chicago *Sun-Times* characterized it as "a triumph in the art of political synthetics." Dewey might not be an ultraconservative, but the liberals regarded him as smooth, slippery, and unprincipled, a political technican devoid of personal appeal who had taken the convention with a ruthless and well-oiled political machine. Walt Kelly, the creator of *Pogo* and at that time a political cartoonist for the New York *Star,* perfectly expressed liberal feelings by depicting the Republican candidate as a pint-sized robot-computer with a human head.[1]

In the days before the Democratic convention, the liberals continued their quest for a leader who could beat Truman. "He lacks the greatness of mind and character which America needs so much in the years ahead," said the *Progressive.* "Douglas or Disaster," warned T. O. Thackrey. In an editorial entitled "Truman's Big Chance," the *Nation* urged the president to withdraw in favor of a stronger candidate. The *New Republic* warned that Truman's big chance was also the Democratic Party's *last* chance. Walter Reuther issued an endorsement of Douglas, and Hubert Humphrey indicated that he was ready to make the nominating speech. Reuther, Leon Henderson, and Chester Bowles openly solicited funds for a last-minute Douglas blitz. "In order to find itself," wrote Max Lerner, "the Democratic Party must first shake off the burden of Harry Truman." The Independent Voters of Illinois assured Truman that history would vindicate a decision to step down in favor of Douglas. Jimmy Roosevelt moved to organize an anti-Truman caucus. Of the labor leaders only A. F. Whitney seemed willing to lift a finger for Truman. The Chicago *Sun-Times* endorsed Eisenhower. Southerners of all stripes, influential big-city bosses, labor leaders, and liberals all frantically attempted to draft the general. The ADA, headquartered a few blocks from the convention, stockpiled Douglas signs and buttons against the probability that Eisenhower would refuse to run.[2]

The attempt was futile. Eisenhower replied with two firm refusals. Douglas was equally adamant, both with the liberals and with Truman, who wanted him for the vice-presidential nomination. Then, just before the convention opened, Claude Pepper announced his candidacy. Despite his closeness to Wallace on foreign policy and his opposition to Truman's civil rights program, Pepper picked up some liberal backers, including T. O. Thackrey and Joe Rauh. But the senator could unite neither the diverse factions of the party nor the progressives; his candidacy simply added a comic touch to the dump-Truman effort. Rauh's attitude notwithstanding, the ADA refused to touch Pepper. "We have already had two dark horses shot from under us," said Henderson. "Why the hell should we get up and ride on a red roan?" [3]

Humiliated and discredited by the dump-Truman fiasco, the liberals, led by the ADA, came back to stun the convention by demanding and achieving, against the wishes of the administration, the most sweeping civil rights plank ever written into a Democratic platform. The ADA planning had been careful and complete; as early as mid-March, the organization had decided to make an all-out effort. Hubert Humphrey quietly circulated a statement urging that all the recommendations of the President's Committee on Civil Rights be written into the platform. By the start of July, he had the backing of 50 important liberals and urban politicians.

When Truman, in an effort to appease the South, pushed a vague civil rights plank through the platform committee, the ADA carried the fight to the floor with a substitute declaration praising the president's efforts for civil rights and specifically urging the enactment of every recommendation he had made. The big-city bosses and the labor leaders provided the support necessary for a close victory, but the ADA, led by the eloquent Humphrey, headed the struggle. After first looking ridiculous, the organization gained new prestige. "Chunky, cigar-chewing Henderson, the butt of cynical convention jokes for 48 hours, was suddenly being greeted with mingled awe and astonishment," observed the New York *Post*'s Washington column. The victory electrified progressives and facilitated allegiance to the Democratic ticket. The Liberal Party, which might have sat out the campaign had the plank been defeated, was now firmly behind the Democrats, and independent progressives were heartened. "Some observers believed they glimpsed a preview of a brighter Democratic future," wrote James Wechsler.[4]

The platform adopted, old party wheel-horse Alben Barkley chosen for the vice-presidency, Truman appeared before the convention at 2:00 A.M. on July 15 to accept its unenthusiastic nomination. Weary spectators awaited the president's usual uninspired oratory. Instead they found the fighting, two-fisted candidate who had toured the country the month before. He recalled all the issues he had taken stands on—price controls, housing, the Taft-Hartley Act, aid to education, a national health program, civil rights, the "rich man's tax bill." All were vital matters; the Republican platform promised action on several of them. He was going to call Congress back to deliver on these promises. Predicting that the Republicans would "try to dodge their responsibility," he declared: "The battle lines of 1948 are the same as they were in 1932 when the Nation lay prostrate and helpless as a result of Republican misrule and inaction."

The address brought the convention back to life. "It was a great speech for a great occasion, and as I listened I found myself applauding," commented Max Lerner. "It was fun to see the scrappy little cuss come out of his corner fighting . . . not trying to use big words any longer, but being himself and saying a lot of honest things," wrote T.R.B. "Unaccountably, we found ourself on top of a pine bench cheering." "The feeling of apathy—the sense of inevitable defeat—is gone," said the New York Star. The call for a special session, said Michael Straight, was "a stroke of bold and liberal leadership." A Democratic rank-and-filer, who had urged Truman to withdraw just the week before, was now full of enthusiasm for his "forceful and courageous manner" and his attempt "to make the Democratic party the party of the New Deal, of liberalism, of labor." David Lloyd, writing in the *ADA World,* praised the special session as yet another phase of Truman's path-breaking effort to mitigate the hardships of a peacetime inflationary boom: "No other President of the United States has ever made such a proposal, even once." Truman's speech, together with the civil rights victory, wrote Robert Bendiner, at least had "breathed into the party the hope of immediate survival." [5]

Soon after the Democrats had gone home, the new party's convention met; few national political gatherings have hurt their candidate so much. From the beginning of the platform deliberations to the adoption of the final document, the issue of Communist domination was increasingly in the public eye and increasingly obvious. "The New Party has separated itself from the American democratic tradition," said Jim Loeb in a dramatic appearance before the platform committee. "It has done so, not only by admitting to its ranks Communists and fellow-travelers, but by lending itself to the support and extenuation of Soviet totalitarianism and Soviet aggression."

The platform, which rather disingenuously asserted that the United States "has vastly greater responsibility for peace than Russia because it has vastly greater power for war," appeared to confirm Loeb's charges. The most disastrous event of the convention came when a delegate from Vermont, observing that the failure to criticize Soviet as well as American policy might be misunderstood, offered an innocent amendment which declared: "It is not our intention to give blanket endorsement to the foreign policy of any nation." Hugh De Lacy and Lee Pressman were among those who spoke against it, and the delegates voted it down by an overwhelming margin. By the end of the convention, Rexford Tugwell, who had chaired the platform committee, was disillusioned and worried. Noting that the new party had officially adopted the name Progressive, he urged Wallace to repudiate the Communists as had the Progressive candidate of 1924, Robert M. La Follette, Sr. Wallace, who by this time automatically recoiled from any hint of "Red-baiting," refused: "If they want to support me I can't stop them."

The party's domestic platform of "progressive capitalism" was in many respects appealing and by no means Communist: strong civil rights measures, greater protection of civil liberties, regional development authorities patterned after TVA, nationalization of monopolistic industries, repeal of the Taft-Hartley Act, a $1.00 minimum wage, extension of the Fair Labor Standards Act to all workers, continued agricultural price supports, measures to raise food consumption, maintenance of the family farm, promotion of small business, a vast housing program, aid to education, enlarged social insurance programs. This portion of the platform, Elmer Davis commented, was "in the tradition of American radicalism—an old and honorable tradition." Yet the new party's progressive capitalism made little impression. Hardly original, it was largely an extravagant version of the New Deal tradition with a bit of American socialism blended in. Many of its planks appeared lifted from the administration agenda. Others, such as an old-age pension plan which won the endorsement of Dr. Francis Townsend, gave the party something of a crackpot tinge. Most importantly, Wallace himself, almost totally obsessed with foreign policy, devoted little attention to his domestic program. Nearly forgotten by the leading Progressives themselves, "progressive capitalism" never became an important campaign issue.

The majority of those at the convention were doubtless sincere and well-intentioned people, many of them idealistic youths, seeking a world of peace and abundance, greeting Wallace with revivalistic fervor. As James Wechsler observed, it took more than intense rank-and-file emotion to demonstrate the validity of a cause. Yet it was hard to be unimpressed. "The elements of birth and vitality are present here in abundance," wrote Max Lerner. Conceding that the Communists had controlled the proceedings, Howard K. Smith suggested that "American liberals might consider abandoning the effort to recapture the Democratic party and start trying to recapture the Progressive party."

However, the dominant impression, even among liberals, was one of Red domination, especially after Wallace called for American abandonment of beleaguered Berlin in his acceptance speech. "It is surprising and disturbing that no honest advocate of a radical, non-Communist program could be found among the assembled Gideonites," said the *Nation*.[6]

II

The civil rights struggle at the Democratic convention and its outcome increased the pressure upon Truman for action. The problem of the armed forces was especially crucial. Bitter and militant Negro leaders, headed by A. Philip Randolph, were threatening resistance to the draft. Wallace was demanding an end to segregation in the military, and anti-Wallace liberals were urging Truman to seize the issue from his Progressive opponent.

On July 26, Truman issued two executive orders, one setting up a Fair Employment Board to work for equal treatment in the civilian federal service, the other establishing a policy of "equal opportunity" in the armed services, "having due regard to the time required to effectuate any necessary changes without impairing efficiency or morale." After the Progressive Party attacked the failure specifically to abolish segregation and after General Omar Bradley indicated that Jim Crow would continue, the president told a press conference that the order envisioned the end of segregation. Praising Truman's action as "a long and bold step forward," the New York *Star* observed that it also represented a challenge to the Republican Congress.[7]

On July 27, Truman went before the special session with a broad legislative agenda. His two priority measures were sweeping anti-inflation legislation, including price controls, and a comprehensive housing bill. He also urged action on a long list of other proposals—aid to education, a $.75 minimum wage, extension of social security and higher social security benefits, revision of the Displaced Persons Act to eliminate its discriminatory provisions against Eastern and Southern Europeans, Senate ratification of the International Wheat Agreement to give American farmers an expanded export market, increased appropriations for federal power projects, enactment of his civil rights program.[8]

After two weeks, Congress adjourned, having passed only bills to provide for some controls on credit and some assistance for housing construction. Taking full advantage of this record,

Truman caustically lashed out at the Republicans, saying that the Housing Act was "an emasculated housing bill," asserting that Congress had met for "a 'do nothing' session." Liberals agreed. "A lost fortnight," said the St. Louis *Post-Dispatch*. "Congress Quits; Does Nothing to Mar 'Worst-of-All' Record," declared a headline in the *National Union Farmer*. "Republican strategy was based throughout on the assumption that the voters are stupid and have short memories," asserted the Chicago *Sun-Times*.[9]

By the first of September, Truman was ready to begin a series of tours patterned after his June trip to carry his denunciations of Congress to the country. His campaign team consisted essentially of the administration liberals, the Research Division, and a few individuals friendly to their viewpoint. Oscar Chapman performed admirably as an advance man. Jonathan Daniels and Samuel Rosenman gave the campaign a New Deal aura. Charlie Murphy supervised the writing of prepared speeches in Washington, heading up a group which included the young David Bell, on loan from the Bureau of the Budget, David Lloyd, Leon Keyserling, David Noyes, Albert Carr, and the newspaper columnist John Franklin Carter (Jay Franklin). Noyes and Carr, who had a long-standing relationship with Truman, regarded themselves as more liberal than the administration liberals, and pressed with frequent success for aggressive, neo-populist phrases. On the train itself, Clark Clifford advised on strategy and tactics, and his brilliant young aide George Elsey hammered out one outline after another for whistle-stop talks. The public and the liberal community realized from the start that while there were a few political technicians aboard the train, there were no John Snyders or George Allens.[10]

Truman made an initial tour west of the Mississippi, then several swings east of the great river, and in every major address, in every whistle-stop talk, there was the same objective— to arouse those who could not find a house in which to live, those who felt the pinch of inflation, those who felt that the future of their region depended upon federal projects, those whose prosperity rested upon federal farm programs, those who felt that their unions were imperiled by the Taft-Hartley Act, those who felt the sting of discrimination and bias, those who worked for broad reforms which would realize the promise of American life. The times and many of the issues were different, but Truman was trying to identify himself and the Democratic Party with the heritage of Roosevelt. He claimed that the Republican Party was attempting to repudiate this heritage and attacking the interests of the common man.

Fresno, California, September 23: "I am not asking you to vote for me alone. I want you to vote for yourselves. Vote for your own interests."

Akron, Ohio, October 11: "The Republican politicians don't like the New Deal. They never have liked the New Deal, and they would like to get rid of it—repeal it—put it out of existence.

". . . Now, they have tasted blood, and they are waiting eagerly for the time when they can go ahead with a Republican Congress and a Republican President and do a real hatchet job."

He was, in short, attempting to mobilize the groups which either out of conviction or self-interest had voted for Roosevelt.[11]

Throughout the West, he warned that the Republicans would cut back on the reclamation and power projects which had brought increased prosperity to that region. "They will turn the clock back to the day when the West was an economic colony of Wall Street," he said in Denver. "You have been crudely and wickedly cheated by the power lobby in Washington, operating through the Republican 80th Congress," he told a crowd in Salt Lake City.[12]

Speaking in agricultural areas, Truman continued to advance a comprehensive farm program, but increasingly he concentrated on gut issues which were developed by Secretary of Agriculture Brannan. Opportunistically twisting a statement which Harold Stassen had made about high food prices just after a conference with Governor Dewey, Brannan charged that Stassen had been detailed the job of sending up a trial balloon against price supports. He also lashed at the failure of the Republican Congress to provide sufficient storage facilities for the Commodity Credit Corporation and observed, quite correctly as it turned out, that many farmers would have to sell their grain at prices below the support level because the CCC would be unable to store it. Brannan campaigned tirelessly through the Midwest with these themes, and Truman quickly picked them up. "Stassen had made it very plain that they want to revise the price support program down to the point where the farmer won't have a chance," he said in Shawnee, Oklahoma. The Republicans had crippled the Commodity Credit Corporation "at the request of the grain speculators who wanted to force farmers to sell their grain at low prices so they could make a killing," he asserted in Tipton, Indiana.[13]

Speaking to labor audiences, he lashed at the Taft-Hartley Act, asserting that it was but the first step in a grand design of repressive labor legislation, supporting his argument by quoting from a book by Representative Hartley. At a New York rally:

This is what he says now: "The Fair Labor Standards Act is typical of the New Deal legislation enacted to combat the depression. Such legislation failed to affect the depression one way or another, and it has definitely outlived the usefulness it was supposed to have had."

They want to repeal the Fair Labor Standards Act. I have been trying to get a bigger floor under the minimum wage. You know, the Republican candidate said the other day that he was for the minimum wage. He didn't say how much, but I came to the conclusion that the smaller the minimum, the better he would like it.[14]

His appeals to minority groups were equally strong. "Dangerous men, who are trying to win followers for their war on democracy, are attacking Catholics, and Jews, and Negroes, and other minority races and religions," he told a rally in Chicago. "Some of these demagogues have even dared to raise their voice of religious prejudice in the 80th Congress. We need only remember the shocking displaced persons bill." Governor Hastie of the Virgin Islands returned to the United States in October to campaign vigorously and effectively before Negro audiences.

Truman himself went into Harlem to defend his civil rights record and to attack Congress for failing to adopt his program.[15]

At virtually every stop, he brought out the issues of inflation and housing. "The Republicans don't want any price control for one very simple reason: the higher the prices go up, the bigger the profits for the corporations," he said in Reading, Pennsylvania. "The real estate people have one of the most powerful, best organized, and most brazen lobbies in Washington," he told a rally in Buffalo. "And the Republican Party has proved to be its faithful servant." [16]

Time and again, he recalled the Republican record on social security, contrasting his calls for extension of the program with Congress's cuts. "The Republican firemen . . . actually set fire to a couple of buildings, just for fun," he said in Indianapolis. "They struck nearly a million Americans off the social security rolls; and their fire chief now says he is proud of that Congress." He attacked the Republican tax bill, calling it an inducement for the wealthy to give large campaign contributions. "That's what they mean: 'We've lined your pockets. Now see that we get some of that so we can debauch the country by buying the election,' " he said in Clarksburg, West Virginia.[17]

He struck back belligerently at Republican charges that he was soft on Communism. In a nationally broadcast address from Oklahoma City, he sought to reassure Midwesterners of his anti-Communism by invoking his anti-Soviet foreign policy, his loyalty program, and the investigative work of the FBI. But he also appealed to liberal values, charging the Republicans had "trampled on the individual freedoms which distinguish American ideals from totalitarian doctrine" with their unfounded smears. He directly attacked the House Committee on Un-American Activities. "With reckless disregard for the Bill of Rights, this committee has injured the reputations of innocent men by spreading wild and false accusations." He reminded his listeners that the Communists were supporting the third party, not the Democrats, and asserted they were doing so in an attempt to throw the election to the GOP. "Could it be that they are counting on a Republican administration to produce another economic crash, which would play into the hands of world communism?"

Dewey, for his part, hoped to avoid any debates with Truman, and his speeches usually skirted specific issues. Occasionally, however, he made a slip. When he declared that the time had come to remove the " 'dead hand' of government" from the development of atomic energy, Truman lunged at the opening. In an effective speech, broadcast across the country from Milwaukee, he condemned Dewey for playing politics with atomic power and characterized his opponent's comments as yet another indication of the influence of selfish special interests among the Republicans: "Atomic energy cannot and must not be another Teapot Dome for private exploitation." [18]

Although Truman was privately bitter at the liberal condescension toward him, his speeches included appeals to those who thought of themselves first and foremost as liberals or progressives. Arguing that a vote for the third party would be wasted, he told a rally in Los Angeles, "The Democratic Party is the party which truly expresses the hopes of American liberals, and which has power to fulfill those hopes." Warning that a vote for the third party would be an indirect vote for the Republicans, he concluded: "This is the hour for the liberal forces of America to unite. . . . Together we can rout the forces of reaction once again." In St. Paul, three weeks later, he returned to the theme:

Now, I call on all liberals and progressives to stand up and be counted for democracy in this great battle. I call on the old Farmer-Labor Party, the old Wisconsin Progressives, the Non-Partisan Leaguers, and the New Dealers to stand up and be counted in this fight.[19]

Every pronouncement contained a vehement denunciation of the Republicans and the Eightieth Congress. "Wall Street expects its money this year to elect a Republican administration that will listen to the gluttons of privilege first, and to the people not at all," he said at Dexter, Iowa. "They took you to the cleaners in 1929. They want to do it again," he said in Gary,

Indiana. He lashed at Dewey's bland refusal to discuss the issues. "He is having such a high-level tea party with the voters that he is horrified whenever anybody mentions the facts of life," Truman said at Cleveland. "He has given 'G.O.P.' another meaning," the president declared at Framingham, Massachusetts. "It now means 'Grand Old Platitudes.' " [20]

Truman seemed to think of himself as the tribune of the people, the *vox populi,* the quintessence of the common man. "I am on a crusade for the welfare of the everyday man," he said in Trenton, Missouri. "All over the country," he told a crowd in Ardmore, Oklahoma, "they call me Harry. I like it. I believe when you speak to me like that you really do like me —and I want you to like me because I'm trying my best to serve you with everything I have." [21]

Truman's image, now so clear and sharp in domestic affairs, remained ambiguous in foreign policy. Throughout the summer and fall, the U.S. and the USSR appeared to be on the verge of war as the Russians employed a blockade of Berlin in a desperate effort to prevent the establishment of a West German republic. Many progressives were uneasy over the prospect of a renascent Germany—Samuel Grafton commented that the new state ranked "about 214th on the list of things the world badly needs right away." But aside from the Progressive Party, which defended the Soviet position recklessly, most liberals supported the administration's determination to stay in Berlin by airlifting supplies over the blockade. "We must not give in to Moscow's threats and blackmail," said the Chicago *Sun-Times.* The United States government, moreover, took the problem to the United Nations and displayed a conciliatory attitude. "Everybody concerned has been eager to give the Soviet Union an opportunity to achieve a settlement, if that is what the Communist leaders want," commented the *Nation.* "To abandon Berlin at this moment would be to accept finally the division of Europe and of the world," said the *New Republic.*

Yet the danger of war also increased the pressure for some dramatic new effort at negotiation, no matter how slight the chances of success. As Grafton observed, "the worst that could happen is that we'd be back where we are now, playing games with C-54's." Meeting with Truman in July, Jim Patton urged the president to make some direct approach to Stalin and left believing Truman was considering the idea. A few days later, Bill Batt suggested that the president send General Eisenhower to Berlin as his personal representative to engage in negotiations with the Russians. By the end of September, David Noyes and Albert Carr were advocating some similar gesture.[22]

In early October, Truman was ready to act. The drawing power of the Progressive "peace issue" worried him, and he allowed his associates to persuade him that a dramatic exercise in personal diplomacy would be an act of high statesmanship, not a political ploy. He prevailed upon his trusted friend and counselor Chief Justice Vinson to undertake direct conferences with the Russian leaders in Moscow and had his staff arrange for radio time to announce the decision. Only then did the president inform Secretary of State Marshall, who was in Paris at the U.N. General Assembly meeting; Marshall was so strongly and firmly opposed that in the end Truman found himself practically forced to scrap the idea. By then, however, news of the plan had leaked to the press.[23]

To many liberals, the incident was a fiasco which underscored Truman's ineptitude. "It was a blunder which would have diminished, rather than increased, the chances of any satisfactory settlement," said Elmer Davis. The St. Louis *Post-Dispatch* observed that Truman had been on the verge of bypassing the U.N., his European allies, his own State Department. Even the *Nation* agreed that such headline plays could accomplish little, and Max Lerner called the cancellation of the mission further proof that reactionaries and military men still controlled U.S. foreign policy.[24]

Yet even an abortive gesture impressed many others. "Truman was acting as an honest President striving for a great goal—peace," commented the *New Republic*. The New York *Star* compared the plan to earlier missions to Moscow by Joseph Davies and Harry Hopkins, recalling that those trips had been successful. "It would have been a bold stroke in the right direction," wrote Jennings Perry. "President Truman's mistake was not in the idea, which was excellent, but in failing to go through with it," wrote Thomas L. Stokes. Perhaps, conceded the Chicago *Sun-Times,* the president had handled things badly, but "Whether Mr. Truman's motives were political or not, he was on the right track."

Truman himself was convinced that he had made a telling point by demonstrating a willingness to take extraordinary measures in the pursuit of peace. Subsequently, he conspicuously defended the Vinson plan in a speech to the national convention of the American Legion: "I want to make it perfectly clear that I have not departed one step from my determination to utilize every opportunity to work for peace." On balance, the Vinson mission probably helped Truman's standing among the progressives. "If there was any reaction to the incident," George Elsey observed several months later, "I think that people said to themselves, 'Harry Truman is trying to do something for peace, but the State Department has blocked him again.' " [25]

American policy toward Palestine, however, continued to draw strong liberal fire. On September 12, Eleanor Roosevelt warned Truman that U.S. indifference might drive the Israeli government into the arms of the Soviet Union. On September 23, Chester Bowles, who was running for governor of Connecticut, told Clark Clifford that the Palestine issue was hurting the Democrats and suggested that the president might at least issue a statement promising support for Israel as soon as elections were held there. Clifford himself continued to work hard for de jure recognition and economic assistance. At the end of September, however, with the Jews and Arabs still fighting, Secretary Marshall and the State Department indicated approval of a new partition proposal, which had been recommended by the assassinated U.N. mediator, Count Folke Bernadotte. The Bernadotte plan would have greatly reduced the territory allotted to the new Jewish state, and once again progressives lashed out at the State Department's Middle Eastern experts. "They are having an undreamed-of success in politically assassinating . . .

President Harry S. Truman in the city of New York" declared Bartley Crum.

Truman, however, was soon convinced that the Bernadotte plan was unacceptable, and he moved to assume control of Palestine policy. On October 17, he confidentially directed Marshall and the American delegation to the U.N. to refrain from any statement or action on the issue which did not have White House clearance. A few days later, Dewey charged that the president was betraying his earlier promises on Palestine, and Clifford quickly persuaded Truman that his integrity had been questioned. On October 24, the president issued a statement reaffirming his commitment to the original partition plan and pledging de jure recognition as soon as Israel held elections. He promised an eventual lifting of the arms embargo and stated that the United States would give sympathetic consideration to Israeli applications for economic aid. Speaking in New York on October 28, he repeated his position and praised the pioneering spirit of the Jewish settlers. Such declarations, however, came too late to convince many. "Truman's record on Palestine becomes increasingly more reprehensible as Election Day approaches," wrote Dorothy Thackrey in the New York *Post*. "Under his administration every platform pledge has been broken." [26]

III

Many progressives, although they tended to discount Truman's chances, were won over by his effort. The New York *Star* moved behind him before Labor Day; its editorial cartoon, depicting the president as a battered but undefeated figure holding aloft the flickering "liberal torch of F.D.R.," indicated its rationale. Eleanor Roosevelt, although she possessed serious private reservations about the president, squelched rumors that she favored Dewey and told Truman in a letter which she allowed the White House to release: "I am unqualifiedly for you." Even pro-Wallace columnist Jennings Perry praised Truman's fighting liberal campaign: "He has made himself the symbol of the real virility of his party." The Chicago *Sun-Times* gave the president its endorsement, and its backing, lukewarm at first, increased in enthusiasm as election day neared.[27]

Several liberal journalists who went along on the campaign train left impressed. Truman, wrote Marquis Childs, was saying things that needed saying "in the political vacuum that is created by Candidate Dewey's bland assurance that he will take over in January and that he will tell the people as much as is good for them to know." Other liberals praised the president's uncompromising indictment of the Eightieth Congress, his strong identification of the Democratic Party with the cause of progressivism, his invigoration of the state and local Democratic organizations by his hard-hitting appearances. He had, wrote Willard Shelton, "overcome almost unbearable obstacles to prove himself a Chief Executive of personal dignity and a party leader who understands his present function." He had "breathed life into the Democratic campaign, not only improving his chances . . . but definitely helping the state tickets," Alexander Uhl commented in mid-October. "It was a great educational drive," wrote T.R.B. at the end of the campaign, adding that, while Truman had not been a great president, "he may some day, not far off, become a great Senator." [28]

One by one, the liberal organizations threw their weight behind the president. The Farmers Union, following its tradition of formal nonpartisanship, made no endorsement, but its state and local structure seems in general to have worked for Truman, picking up the attacks on Stassen and the Eightieth Congress. The CIO endorsed Truman, and by early September the former Eisenhower booster, James B. Carey, was praising the president as an even greater liberal than FDR. The Liberal Party initially showed little enthusiasm for the president, but it eventually came out for him and even sponsored a Madison Square Garden rally when the New York Democrats decided against picking up such a heavy tab in a losing cause.[29]

The ADA also endorsed Truman, praising his liberal stand on domestic issues and his work for the Marshall Plan, calling

the Democratic platform "the most forthright and liberal document of its kind ever offered the American people by a majority party." The organization established liaison with the White
House, but the ADA effort in the presidential contest was
against Wallace rather than for Truman; it consisted mainly of
a widely distributed mimeographed document blasting the Progressive candidate and of a public denunciation of the third
party by 37 prominent New Dealers. Despite a sharp internal
financial crisis, moreover, the ADA was able to undertake a
positive effort in some key Congressional and gubernatorial
races, including those of Hugh Mitchell and Henry Jackson in
Washington, Richard Bolling in Missouri, Hubert Humphrey
in Minnesota, Paul Douglas and Adlai Stevenson in Illinois,
and Chester Bowles in Connecticut. In doing so, the organization was making a marked contribution to the reconstitution of
a politically powerful liberal movement.[30]

Many of the liberals who worked for Truman did so in the
spirit of Harold Ickes. His former Interior Department associates, Oscar Chapman and Michael Straus, realized that Ickes
was aching to get into the campaign; Truman, for his part, recognized the value of the Old Curmudgeon's endorsement.
With some trepidation Chapman arranged a personal meeting
between the two old antagonists; it went beautifully. "They
were like two bulldogs who had fought and were making up,"
Chapman has recalled. Yet when Ickes endorsed the president,
he managed to do so with hardly a single unqualified word of
praise. "As between Thomas Elusive Dewey, the Candidate in
Sneakers, and President Truman, I prefer the latter, who is
straightforward and sincere, if at times more unpredictable
than I would wish." The old man went on the radio to launch
a withering blast at Dewey, and gave a real lift to the Democratic campaign. However, he was convinced that he was backing a loser, and he had little respect for Truman. "I am supporting as my candidate for President a man who is as fully
equipped for that office as would be Adam's off ox," he remarked privately.[31]

The *New Republic* displayed somewhat the same attitude.

"No paper has exposed more outspokenly than the NR the personal shortcomings of Harry Truman," it said in the editorial which came out for the president. "The great argument for the President has no reference at all to Truman," commented Gerald W. Johnson. "It is simply this: take a look at the others!" "Mr. Truman is a poor vehicle for . . . liberal aspirations, but his victory would at least indicate that they existed," said Samuel Grafton. "I am going to vote for him for strictly negative reasons," declared Frank Kingdon.[32]

Much of the liberal coolness toward Truman was personal, a distaste for his style, a questioning of his sincerity. "We doubt that a President of the United States helps his cause by referring to the Martin-Halleck-Taber cabal as 'predatory animals,' " said the *Nation*. His blasts at Wall Street, said I. F. Stone, "were transparent forays into a ludicrous demagogy." Commenting that Truman's speeches "were more frantic than factual," the *Progressive* said, "Certainly he fought courageously, but it was a courage that was born of desperation, not conviction." Even David Lilienthal had to stave off a last-minute impulse to vote against the president who had supported him so steadfastly. Elmer Davis called the campaign the dullest in his memory. Reinhold Niebuhr dismissed the president as a political and diplomatic bungler, proclaimed the collapse of the Roosevelt coalition, and remarked: "We wish Mr. Dewey well without too much enthusiasm and look to Mr. Truman's defeat without too much regret." [33]

The *Nation* refused to endorse anyone, and Freda Kirchwey wrote, "This is a year when independents would be happier if they could vote against rather than for the candidates." A poll of the Nation Associates gave Truman 431 votes; Wallace, 430; Dewey, 121; Norman Thomas, 116; 176 had no choice. If this was a representative sampling of liberal sentiment, it indicates that progressives were scattered and divided, that the liberal movement was still fragmented and leaderless.[34]

A few liberals even swallowed hard and moved behind Dewey. Dorothy Thackrey, alienated from the administration mainly by the Palestine issue, called the president "incompetent and inconsistent" and urged progressives to jump on the Dewey bandwagon in the hope of influencing the Republican's policies. The St. Louis *Post-Dispatch* admitted that Dewey apparently disagreed with its editorial policies on a dozen or so issues and was "not the ideal candidate for President." Nevertheless, it argued, Truman was not big enough for the presidency.[35]

A few liberals stayed to the end with Wallace as a symbol of peace and democracy, among them Jennings Perry, I. F. Stone, and editor T. O. Thackrey, who engaged in a running debate in the New York *Post* with his wife and publisher. "A vote for Wallace can be clearly counted as a vote for less militarization and more civilization at home and abroad," declared Thackrey on his half of the editorial page.[36]

IV

As Truman stormed up and down the land, an increasingly dispirited Henry Wallace embarked upon the last phase of his campaign. Moving across the country on a tour fully as arduous as Truman's, he argued as strenuously as ever that Wall Street and the military were pushing America toward fascism and war. The Vinson mission, he said, had been aborted by "the real masters of our foreign policy—the big brass and the big gold." [37]

The most spectacular episode of his campaign occurred in late August and early September as he moved into the South. In Virginia, there were calm, orderly, racially integrated meetings. But in North Carolina, one violent scene followed another—loud, angry hecklers, volleys of eggs and tomatoes. In Durham, a Wallace supporter was stabbed; only in Chapel Hill and Asheville could the Progressive candidate make himself heard. When he moved into Alabama, an uncontrolled Birmingham mob almost turned over the cars in his motorcade. Yet he managed to hold a dozen unsegregated meetings, and he set an example of courage and moral determination which even his bitterest liberal opponents found hard to denounce. "He was a genuinely distinguished figure," wrote James Wechsler. "His journey," said the *Nation,* "may well turn out to have been the redeeming feature of an otherwise ill-advised candidacy." [38]

Truman, speaking through his press secretary, Charley Ross, denounced the Southern violence as "a highly un-American business . . . contrary to the American spirit of fair play." Yet it was but one incident in a pattern of repression which the Progressive Party faced. In several colleges and universities — Evansville, Bradley, Northwestern, Georgia, Miami of Florida, New Hampshire—pro-Wallace professors found themselves out of a job, or at least under heavy pressure to withdraw from active participation in the third party. At times, there was violence—gunplay and auto chases in West Virginia, kidnappings in Georgia. One of the worst incidents happened in the southern Illinois mining town of West Frankfort, where Progressive Senatorial candidate Curtis MacDougall and his party were mobbed and stoned while the police refused to provide protection. One of the members of the MacDougall group said that he had experienced fascism, and for once the new party's use of the word rang true.[39]

From the start one of the most telling arguments against the Progressive Party was the assertion that it would not only throw the presidency to the Republicans but would also split the vote for liberal congressmen. "You may think this Congress is pretty conservative; but it is nothing to what the next one will be if the Wallaceites have their way," Elmer Davis had commented earlier in the year. When the American Labor Party, the New York branch of the Progressive Party, announced that it would run Lee Pressman for the Brooklyn House seat held by the liberal Abraham Multer, the New York *Post*'s Washington column said: "Multer has been steadily identified with the small progressive House bloc on both domestic and foreign issues. His only offenses, it appears, are his refusal to play ball with the Communists and his support of ERP." By the fall, such attacks were beginning to hurt.

On September 21, an open debate on the problem broke out

between Wallace and Beanie Baldwin. Speaking at a fund-raising dinner, Baldwin observed that some Progressives had already withdrawn from races against liberal Democrats, and he defended the withdrawal policy. Wallace followed him, and, to the surprise of all, strongly disagreed, saying that he would be unwilling to support any Democrat who favored the Marshall Plan. Moreover, his remarks indicated that he had not yet given up the dream of a new mass party. "We've got to build a party, Beanie, we've got to build a party," he said in what New York *Times* reporter Warren Moscow described as a tone of "sorrowful reproof." But Baldwin prevailed, and on September 30 the Progressive Party announced that most of its candidates who might take votes away from liberal Democrats had withdrawn.[40]

The decision to pull out of the Congressional races, virtually forced upon the Progressives by liberal opinion, underscored the continuing vitality of liberalism within the Democratic Party and the increasingly obvious weakness of the new party. Perhaps the most stunning example of the failure of the Progressive appeal had come in Minnesota, where Elmer Benson, who had represented the state in the Senate and served as its governor, had considered running against Hubert Humphrey and Joseph Ball in the hot Senatorial campaign. A poll had indicated that he would receive perhaps 3 percent of the vote, and he had decided that his health would not permit him to enter the race. Three percent might be enough to make the difference in a close contest, but it was not a foundation for a new mass party.[41]

As the campaign drew to a close, Wallace's crowds were falling off badly, and it was evident that his apparently large support had evaporated. He had attempted to identify himself with the Midwestern progressive tradition, but the lineal descendant of *La Follette's Weekly,* the *Progressive,* continued to repudiate him: "The Wallace venture sullies the word 'progressive' and damages the prospects for building a genuine progressive party." In California, New Mexico, Nevada, and Colorado, key party officials resigned in protest against the increasingly obvious Communist influence, and thousands of others, David Shannon believes, left the new party without publicity.

Perhaps the most dramatic attack upon Wallace came from John Dewey. "In the Wallace candidacy," declared the 89-year-old philosopher, "I see no hope for progressives." A party capable of promoting fundamental reform had to possess a genuinely new program; its leadership had to be responsible and consistently democratic; its structure had to be broadly rooted in the trade union movement. The Wallace party failed each test; to Dewey it was no more than a tool of the Communists, advocating in their behalf an amoral and reprehensible international program. "There can be no compromise, no matter how temporary, with totalitarianism," he wrote. "Compromise with totalitarianism means stamping an imprimatur on the drive for a pax Sovietica." [42]

The only important New Dealer who had followed Wallace, Rexford Tugwell, was publicly voicing uneasiness over the Communists by August and urging that those close to them be removed from high party positions. Tugwell was still devoted to Wallace and stayed in the party, but he did not campaign and made no effort to conceal his disillusion. In October, Robert Kenny jumped off the rapidly sinking Progressive ship. Even the Communist-dominated Electrical Workers, fearing a right-wing secession, failed to endorse the Progressive Party.[43]

In the beginning Wallace had seen himself as the leader of a movement which would be remembered as a turning point in American history. He had talked of 12 million votes or more. In the spring, he had revised his estimate down to 4 million; by the end of October, even this seemed optimistic. He had believed that many of his old liberal supporters would return to him after the conventions, but as election day approached he knew they had left him forever. "I had hoped they would come back after Truman was renominated," he said, hurt and baffled. "Sometimes I think their only governing motive is that they hate Henry Wallace." [44]

V

Some liberals, including Max Lerner and the editors of the *Progressive,* endorsed Norman Thomas. For this group, alienated from both Truman and Wallace, support of the perennial Socialist candidate was the first step toward a larger goal—a basic political realignment.[45]

The National Educational Committee for a New Party had made few headlines since its establishment in 1946, and even some of its founders had despaired of any accomplishment. But with the apparent disintegration of the Democratic Party in 1948—the Wallace secession on the left, the Dixiecrat rebellion on the right—there was renewed talk of a political reshuffle after the election. Lewis Corey urged Norman Thomas to spend the 1948 campaign working for "a new party of the people with a program that would tie in with the liberal democratic and social democratic forces of Europe." In his own pronouncements Thomas made no effort to conceal his hope for the establishment of a social-democratic coalition which might even shed the designation "Socialist."

In mid-July, the New York *Star* reported that at least two important labor leaders, unnamed, were planning to establish a National Liberal-Labor Party. The United Auto Workers was at the center of the effort. The Amalgamated Clothing Workers expressed interest, and even the stodgy leadership of the AFL seemed ready to lend support. The Liberal Party and the Socialists were prepared to join in, and the Farmers Union probably would have maintained at least a sympathetic interest.

Many liberals, including most of the ADA leaders, were not yet sold on the idea. The new party "would be led by some of the best people in the CIO and the AFL," said Jim Loeb, "and would have all the right principles and the best of intentions; but it would never elect anybody to public office." Whether the skeptical liberals would have continued to work within a shattered Democratic Party after a disastrous election, however, was questionable. And there seemed to be little doubt that there would be an election disaster and that the Democratic Party might fly apart. Reuther worked for a Truman victory, making hard-hitting speeches for the president, but he did not expect to win. That fall, the UAW scheduled a conference on political realignment for January 19, 1949, just one day before Thomas E. Dewey was to be inaugurated president of the United States.[46]

Chapter 11

The Quest for Identity and the Struggle against Normalcy

I

Truman's victory amazed and electrified the liberal movement. It was clear at once that the president had succeeded against enormous odds in reestablishing the old New Deal coalition. He had successfully rallied labor and the liberals. In several Midwestern states, his astute employment of agricultural issues had brought a sizable farm vote back into the Democratic Party. Most of those who voted for him did not do so out of an altruistic desire for a broad reform program, but for narrower reasons of self-interest and, in many cases, out of simple fear that the Republicans would try to repeal some aspect of the New Deal. Yet Truman's appeals to self-interest and fear were based squarely upon the achievements of the Roosevelt years. The individual motivation behind a vote for Truman was often enough a hope of saving a slice of the New Deal, and the sum of these motivations was in fact a vindication of the Roosevelt heritage.[1]

The liberals in their elation devoted little attention to the limitations of such a mandate. Their near-unanimous impulse was to proclaim the result of the election as not only an endorsement of the New Deal but also a popular demand for the entire Truman program, an agenda which went well beyond the New Deal in its breadth and ambition if not in its basic philosophy. "We have in the White House a man with the most radical platform in Presidential history," wrote T.R.B. "Nothing less than a new era of reform has been demanded by America and nothing less will Americans accept," declared the *New Republic.* "Damn the torpedoes. . . . Full speed ahead!" [2]

The election signaled the beginning of a new relationship between the president and the liberals. Freda Kirchwey praised Truman's "pugnacious and stout-hearted campaign," and I. F. Stone pronounced the victory "a magnificent display of moral courage." Thomas L. Stokes wrote that Truman had emerged "as a kind of Andrew Jackson character, a plain man of the people against those who would exploit them." The president had not eclipsed the memory of Roosevelt, but he had succeeded in identifying himself with it. Most progressives could never quite achieve a sense of personal identification with him nor accept the White House "cronies"—Joe Rauh noted with disgust that John Snyder, who had been conspicuously absent from the campaign, was back in the inner circle at the victory celebration—and in the future, the liberals would criticize Truman on many issues, but never with the intense alienation, pity, and even contempt which had characterized their feelings before the election.[3]

The election produced much more than a presidential victory. Many promising figures won important offices for the first time—Governors Chester Bowles, Adlai Stevenson, and G. Mennen Williams, Senators Hubert Humphrey, Paul Douglas, and Estes Kefauver, Representatives Richard Bolling, Eugene McCarthy, Sidney Yates, and Abraham Ribicoff. Several liberals who had lost in 1946 returned to Washington; almost all who had survived the 1946 debacle won reelection. Some had strong local appeal which helped Truman, but others benefited greatly from the enthusiasm which his aggressive campaign created. Many were identified with the ADA, which had played a strong role in some states, most notably Massachusetts and Minnesota. The work which had gone into so many campaigns seemed at last to be fulfilling Jim Loeb's dream of moving the liberal movement onto an organized basis away from dependence upon a charismatic personality.[4]

For some liberals the election ended hopes of a new departure in American politics. "Where does all this leave us independent progressives who supported Norman Thomas because we wanted to encourage the forces working for a new progressive party and a basic political realignment?" asked the *Progressive*. "Frankly, it leaves us high and dry for the moment." Reluctantly, Thomas admitted that "any plan for a new party must be put in cold storage," although he continued to hope that the project might be revived. There was still some emotional sentiment within the UAW for a new party, but it was tempered by a realization that most of the labor movement would not, indeed could not, take leave of the administration it had helped elect. With Truman pledged to work for Taft-Hartley repeal and a broad progressive program, and with an unexpectedly large number of liberal Democrats in important offices, even the most independent-minded liberal and labor forces found themselves tied to the Democratic Party, and simply strove to maintain some degree of autonomy.[5]

The Progressive Party fared badly. Even in New York, where it polled a half-million votes, it was unable to send Lee Pressman to Congress or even reelect Leo Isacson; only Vito Marcantonio was victorious. Nationally, the party registered less than one and a quarter million votes. Party leaders claimed with some justification that many Progressive ballots had gone uncounted; even so, the new party had made a bad showing.[6] Wallace and other Progressive leaders still believed, however, that they had played a decisive role in forcing a reluctant Truman to the left at home and abroad. "Compare the despair in the winter of 1947 with the hope in the winter of 1948," said Beanie Baldwin. "We upset the plans of the warmakers," he declared. "It is we who forced the Democrats to don the Roosevelt mantle and promise the people a return to the New Deal."

Such claims were ludicrously inflated. Truman's impulses had always been in the direction of liberalism, and the political situation in which he had found himself since 1945 had dic-

tated an effort to reconstruct the liberal-oriented Roosevelt voting coalition. His own political survival and the survival of the
Democratic Party—both more important to him than any ideological predisposition—depended upon his ability to effect
such a reconstruction. Whatever his compromises, and however
inadequate his leadership may have been, the president had attempted to establish himself as a liberal from the beginning.
He had enunciated a comprehensive progressive program in
the fall of 1945, appointed the liberal-dominated civil rights
committee in late 1946, vetoed the Taft-Hartley Act in June
1947.

By campaigning to the left of the administration, Wallace
provided some insurance that it would stay on its course, and
he may have pushed Truman into moving faster on civil rights.
The Wallace candidacy, moreover, was probably the major factor behind the aborted Vinson mission, although the value of
this gesture was surely questionable. At best, however, the Progressive candidate's success in advancing the liberal cause was
marginal. He had fought the Marshall Plan, he had naïvely become involved with the Communists, and he had nearly
thrown the election to Dewey. Had his candidacy been more
"successful," it is hardly probable that Baldwin would have
been acclaiming a new climate of hope at the end of 1948. As it
was, the greatest loss to liberalism was Wallace himself, now a
pathetic and hopelessly discredited figure. A man of the most
humane instincts, an individual who possessed genuine elements of greatness, he had destroyed himself politically.[7]

II

During the years immediately following World War II Truman and the American liberal movement faced similar problems. Both were committed to a difficult fight against the
emergence of a reactionary period of "normalcy" similar to that
which had followed World War I. In order to win this struggle, both had to establish identities which could lead them to
political power.

In 1944 and 1945, the liberal movement seemed to be regaining vitality and coming back from earlier wartime defeats. The death of Franklin D. Roosevelt and the events which followed, however, precipitated crises of leadership, of organization, of the collapse of excessive hopes, of the disintegration of a fundamental assumption. By the end of 1946, the progressive movement was racked by internal differences, fragmented, demoralized, and defeated. It was doubtful that it could be a serious force in the foreseeable future, and the preservation of its past accomplishments was questionable. Conservatism, even reaction, seemed dominant for the first time since the 1920s. In 1947 and 1948, liberalism made important strides back toward power; but as late as November 2, 1948, when the American people trooped to the polls to elect, everyone believed, Thomas E. Dewey president of the United States, it still appeared lost and scattered.

In large part, the story of the liberal movement in the postwar years involved the discarding of a fundamental assumption —belief in the Popular Front and in the unity of the antifascist left. In domestic politics the Popular Front meant liberal-Communist cooperation in the struggle against reaction. In 1945 only a small group of progressives was willing to argue that Communists should be excluded from liberal groups and projects. Gradually, however, liberals came to perceive a wide gulf between themselves and the Communists; partly as a matter of moral integrity, partly as a matter of practical necessity, they redrew a line that had been clear in the days of the elder La Follette but had become blurred in succeeding decades. At the beginning of 1947, the effort to exclude Communists from the liberal movement found a powerful focus in the Americans for Democratic Action. By the end of 1948, Communism was no longer a significant force in American politics.

The belief in antifascist solidarity meant that American foreign policy had to rest on the keystone of the unity of the wartime alliance—more explicitly, that it had to maintain good relations with Russia. Instead, relations with the Soviet Union became more hostile and at the same time American policy, as many liberals saw it, seemed to support reaction and imperialism. Ignoring or even justifying Russian expansionism, liberals tended at first to place most of the blame for the breakup of the Big Three upon U.S. and British policy; even those who were anti-Soviet from the start neither agreed with much of American policy nor offered a realistic formula for preventing Soviet imperialism. Not until the Marshall Plan did most of the liberal movement swing behind the administration, many liberals doing so because they saw the plan either as an affirmative attempt to reestablish Big Three solidarity on the basis of an economically united Europe or as a constructive blueprint for European rehabilitation with neither pro- nor anti-Soviet overtones. And it was not until the Communists overthrew Czechoslovakian democracy that the liberal movement began to arrive at a commitment to contain Russian expansion.

The postwar years also saw the collapse of liberal hopes for a new period of domestic advance. As progressive programs bogged down in Congress and the liberal movement suffered a stunning defeat in the 1946 Congressional elections, progressivism, though it never abandoned its plans for the future, found itself more than ever forced to continue waging a holding action. Liberals developed new strength in the ADA and achieved a moment of real victory at the Democratic convention in 1948, but all the way up to the election of that year they remained divided and dispirited, hoping more for triumphs in later years than for immediate success.

Yet the ADA was leading American liberalism toward the new identity it needed. By moving liberal thought away from a simple antifascism to a more genuinely liberal opposition to all forms of totalitarianism, the organization was restoring the moral integrity and political appeal of progressivism. The ADA's role in the campaign and the vigorous new leaders it produced seemed to show that the liberal movement had finally shaken off the paralyzing demoralization which had followed the death of Roosevelt and was beginning to stand on its own, less dependent upon great personalities.

The career of Harry S. Truman during the years 1945–1948 significantly paralleled the course of the liberal movement, thereby demonstrating how closely their fortunes were intertwined. Coming to the presidency with widespread sympathy and a distinguished, if not spectacular, career behind him, Truman's prospects for a moderately successful administration appeared good. By the end of 1946, like the liberals, he seemed to have been utterly defeated and overwhelmingly repudiated. By election day, 1948, he, again like the liberals, had clearly come a long way from this low point; but few observers believed he had won over a majority of the voters.

The successor to Roosevelt, Truman nevertheless did not automatically inherit Roosevelt's strongest supporters, the progressives. Indeed, throughout the years 1945–1948, many liberals were convinced that the collapse of their hopes and assumptions rested squarely upon the inadequacy of Harry S. Truman. By the end of 1946, they saw him as a fumbling little man incapable of leadership, a courthouse politician who had repudiated the progressive heritage of Roosevelt in both foreign and domestic policy, at best a decent citizen with good impulses but without the ability to translate these impulses into action or even to understand the direction in which his administration was moving.

In part, this conviction was a result of the liberal movement's dependence upon Franklin Roosevelt. In part, it was the result of a natural search for a scapegoat as optimism turned to frustration. In part, it rested on hard evidence—the rail labor draft bill, the fiasco of the Wallace firing, the loyalty program, the appointments of men such as John Snyder, George Allen, and Ed Pauley, the dropping of prominent New Dealers. Yet from the start Truman generally held to a liberal program at home. By mid-1947, after a period of uncertainty in the wake of the 1946 election results, he was exercising a stronger and more militant leadership than ever; at the same time his administration introduced the Marshall Plan. By the last half of 1948, he was storming up and down the land, identifying himself with and defending the liberal cause. He regained some progressive support, but, in the main, the estrangement between him and the liberals persisted, partly for practical reasons—he was certain to be defeated in 1948 and would pull liberals down with him—but also because of the progressive movement's inability to find in him the charisma it was seeking so desperately. Having relied so long upon the magic personality of Roosevelt, liberals could not identify with an unobtrusive party regular who was unable to present an appearance of forceful, independent progressive leadership. Truman's lack of Roosevelt's great leadership qualities combined with a liberal failure to achieve a sense of personal identification with the president, and these elements formed the most persistent and important facet of the progressives' alienation.

Truman's victory in 1948 marked the success of his personal search for a political identity. It was triumph for both the president himself and for the liberal movement. Progressivism had been on the verge of another period of fragmentation and futility; Truman's election unified it and infused it with a new sense of purpose and determination. The president had established himself as a forceful liberal leader. He would receive plenty of criticism from progressives in the future, but so had Roosevelt. The important thing was the new respect which the liberals felt for him.

The Truman victory surely hastened the demise of the Progressive Party, and it aborted the National Educational Committee's plan to establish yet another new party—an effort which might never have gotten off the ground but which would have drained important strength from the Democratic Party and further fragmented the liberal movement. Instead, progressives were more united than at any time since the end of the war, and they were united within the party of FDR. Truman, Elmer Davis commented, had "made himself the successor to Roosevelt." [8] For the first time since that terrible afternoon in April 1945, the liberals felt that they had a leader in the White House.

PART TWO

The Fair Deal and the Vital Center

Chapter 12

The Vital Center

The 1948 victory vindicated the ADA's style of progressivism. Refusing to make major distinctions between fascism and Communism, the new liberalism conceived of itself as a "vital center" midway between the two poles of totalitarianism. By rejecting Communism the vital-center approach returned American liberalism to its historic mainstream and saved it from the repudiation which the Wallace movement had endured. However, as the experience of the ADA would demonstrate, the new progressivism lacked the strength and organization to become the dominant force in American politics. The ascendancy of the vital center was at best a moral triumph which helped keep the cause of reform alive in a difficult era.

I

Implicit in the new liberal self-image were a slight tendency toward moderation, a decline of utopian hopes and aspirations, a somewhat stronger suspicion of powerful government, increasing doubts about the goodness of human nature. It was no coincidence that four significant expressions of this viewpoint appeared in 1949: *Target: You* by Leland Stowe, *The Power of Freedom* by Max Ascoli, *Strategy for Liberals* by Irwin Ross, and *The Vital Center* by Arthur Schlesinger, Jr.

Stowe, a widely read foreign correspondent, addressed himself to "John Between" or "Mr. American Middle Man," the target of Fascist and Communist totalitarianism, of monopolistic "Big Capitalism" and Communist Marxism. He argued that for all its weaknesses, the American middle class represented the last bulwark against the authoritarianism which had overwhelmed European democrats before World War II. Americans had to find "a strong political Center" which would counter both domestic Communism and right-wing extremism by providing economic security and civil liberty under the rule of law.

Perhaps the preservation of American democracy will depend largely upon how clearly and persistently American citizens—particularly those of the great middle class—keep in mind that the cross fires of totalitarianism come from *both* the extreme Right and the extreme Left; that they will continue, in one guise or another, throughout our lifetime; that free men must comprehend and combat *every* assault upon their freedoms from every direction.[1]

Max Ascoli, an Italian journalist and political thinker who had fled Mussolini's Italy, had experienced totalitarianism personally. In *The Power of Freedom* he depicted the earth as caught up in a "worldwide civil war" with one side struggling to maintain freedom and the other attempting to achieve "the total subjection of men on a world-wide scale to the mechanisms that their technological and political ingenuity has devised." He did not distinguish between different types of totalitarianism; freedom had to defeat them all, and it could do so only by finding a middle way between the old laissez-faire capitalism and total socialization of property.

Ascoli stressed the limitations of human nature. Freedom had to be carefully defined and exercised with discipline. Total freedom was likely to lead only to totalitarianism; utopias were unattainable. Man did not even have natural rights; his rights varied from one culture to another and developed from the history of his particular civilization.

No state or super-state can legislate for all men the identical enjoyment of basic rights or freedoms, any more than it can guarantee them the same degree of happiness or well-being. . . .

There is one and only one right to which all men have an absolute and identical claim. It is the right to earn rights.

Ascoli unabashedly admitted that he was a disciple of such thinkers as Edmund Burke, Alexander Hamilton, and Alexis de Tocqueville. Yet he saw no inconsistency in declaring: "I am a liberal, and I don't want to add any qualifying adjective." [2]

In *Strategy for Liberals,* the political journalist Irwin Ross called upon progressives to take a tough-minded view of politics. In the past, he argued, liberals had naïvely assumed that the political process was mainly educational, that conservative interests would cease their obstruction as soon as they realized that liberal programs were in the general welfare. In the first place, the assumption was false—a really thorough reform program would hurt the wealthiest and most powerful classes, and rightly so. Moreover, progressives had given little attention to the reality of the greed and desire for authority which characterized entrenched interests. The liberal movement could be successful only if it prepared itself for the possibility of another depression and a consequent crisis which only a raw struggle for power could resolve.

Strongly influenced by Lewis Corey, Ross advanced an ambitious reform program for a "Mixed Economy," including government ownership of most big business. But Ross believed that the mixed economy could not be achieved until a depression crisis had materialized and been mastered by a strong progressive movement. He took special pains to distinguish the mixed economy not simply from fascism and Communism but even from socialism, which with its complete control of industry, detailed planning, massive bureaucracy, and domination of communications, contained within itself "if not the seeds of decay, certainly the seeds of totalitarianism." One might protest that Ross himself had come closer to socialism than he realized, but his approach was characterized by a rejection of old dogmas and a militant affirmation of the middle way.[3]

The most acclaimed book was *The Vital Center* by Arthur M. Schlesinger, Jr. *The Vital Center* displayed not only Schlesinger's own thought but to a large extent popularized the political ideas of Schlesinger's friend and philosophical mentor, Reinhold Niebuhr. Indeed, the publication of *The Vital Center* probably represented the point at which Niebuhr's ideas, as well as his personality, began to have a significant impact upon the liberal community. At once an exercise in political philosophy and an exhortation to American progressives, the volume won an impressive reception. "It seemed to me one of those books which may suddenly and clearly announce the spirit of an age to itself," wrote Jonathan Daniels.[4]

Schlesinger argued that until recently the American left had failed to realize that, whatever the differences in blueprints and rationale, fascism and Communism were essentially the same. Both used all the power of the state to suppress freedom; if necessary, both worked together against the democratic center. Yet in the past many American liberals had been sentimental believers in progress and human perfectionism, yearning for utopias, seduced by the surface idealism of Communism, captivated by the Russian Revolution and the Soviet Union. Awake only to the evils of fascism, they had sympathized with at least some aspects of the Soviet experience and had accepted the Communists as allies in a common struggle. They had not understood that such a tactic could lead only to self-destruction.

The "restoration of radical nerve" had come with the rise of a non-Communist left in Europe and the United States after World War II, largely through the efforts of younger liberals whose impressions of the Soviet Union stemmed from the Stalinist purges of the 1930s rather than the idealism of the revolution. The "revival of American radicalism" had come with the election of Walter Reuther to the presidency of the United Auto Workers, the founding of the ADA, the dismissal of Lee Pressman from the CIO.

The new liberalism (or "radicalism," as Schlesinger preferred to call it) unconditionally rejected all varieties of totalitarianism. It consisted of "a belief in the integrity of the individual, in the limited state, in due process of law, in empiricism and gradualism." It was acutely aware of the weaknesses of human nature and of the dangers of excessive concentrations of power. It was devoted to the furtherance of individual liberty. It stood for a mixed economy, featuring partial government planning and ownership, antitrust action to discipline private big business, and welfare programs to provide a minimum of security and subsistence to all.

Applied to foreign affairs, the new liberalism stood for a dual policy of vigilantly containing Communism and encouraging democratic elements through a policy of economic reconstruction. Schlesinger dismissed the argument that the Truman Doctrine had been negative and militaristic while the Marshall Plan had been affirmative and democratic. "The record on balance justifies the Administration's insistence that, far from being contradictory, the Truman Doctrine and the Marshall Plan are complementary. Each is essential to the success of the other." The vital center must not shrink from the threat of force; if not the sole instrument of foreign relations, force nevertheless provided the necessary support for democratic diplomacy.[5]

The vital center was not a new liberal *program;* it was essentially a new *mood.* Its most important economic manifesto, a collection of essays edited by the eminent Keynesian Seymour Harris and entitled *Saving American Capitalism,* added little to the broad outline of liberal thought which had emerged during the New Deal and had been consolidated during World War II.[6] The vital center's greatest achievement was in giving the liberal movement a truer perspective, providing it with a moral integrity and consistency which had been absent during the Popular Front era.

The conception of liberalism as a sort of centrism had significant symbolic ramifications. One who thought of himself as in the center of the political spectrum was inevitably more disposed to accept the virtues of moderation. Schlesinger, for example, found it natural to identify with "responsible conservatives" such as Charles Evans Hughes and Henry L. Stimson, suggesting that liberals might frequently find a common cause with this group, especially on matters of civil rights and civil liberties.[7] Doubtless, Schlesinger was correct; yet it was all too easy to move from his qualified acceptance of the conservative tradition to uncritical adulation of it. Even the responsible conservatism of a Stimson or a Hughes provided few answers for the problems which preoccupied the liberal movement, but it was tempting, after militantly rejecting the revolutionary totalitarian ideology of Communism, to conceive of liberalism as a species of conservatism, as an effort to preserve humane, democratic values. But unfortunately, it was only a short step from the salutary perspective of the vital center to the superficialities of the "New Conservatism" in the 1950s.

I I

There were other indications that liberalism was taking a new direction. In April 1949, Dorothy Schiff Thackrey announced the dismissal of her husband as editor of the New York *Post.* It is difficult to say how much of the estrangement between these two independent individuals was personal and how much was ideological. Nevertheless, it is significant that Mrs. Thackrey defined the break in terms of attitudes toward Communism, arguing that the Communists posed "new threats to democracy" and asserting that henceforth the paper would fight with equal vigor "all totalitarianism, whether Fascist or Communist." The editorship passed to the militant anti-Communist James A. Wechsler. Columnists I. F. Stone and Alexander Uhl, whom Mr. Thackrey had brought to the *Post* after the New York *Star* had folded, soon left the paper. Thackrey became editor of the New York *Compass,* a new daily which attempted to carry on the tradition of *PM;* during its short life, however, the *Compass* never approached its goal of becoming a national organ of American radicalism.[8]

Of even greater importance was the shift of tone in the *New Republic.* By early 1949, Michael Straight was actually undertaking a speaking tour on behalf of the ADA. "The *New Republic* has divested itself of all its Wallace atmosphere and is now pretty much an ADA house organ," observed Jim Loeb with great satisfaction. By midyear, the journal was denouncing the Communist Party as an organization akin to "a secret society" seeking to manipulate liberals for illiberal ends. "The non-Communist liberals must stand on their own feet, and fight solely, and without entangling alliances, for liberal ends." [9]

In 1949, Max Ascoli established the *Reporter* magazine. Not a "journal of opinion" in the classic sense of the *New Republic* or the *Nation,* the *Reporter* stressed in-depth interpretation. Ascoli wrote regular editorials on foreign affairs, the area in which he believed "the liberal values need to be thoroughly cleansed of triteness and smugness." And even the "straight" features, if they did not assert a viewpoint, reflected the attitude of the vital center, or as the magazine defined it, "Liberalism without tears." [10]

The vital center also won acceptance in the labor movement. During 1949, the rift between pro- and anti-Communists in the CIO became irreconcilable. Unchastened by the Progressive Party experience, the Popular Front unions continued their vociferous dissent from the CIO's support of the Truman administration and frequently indulged in intemperate attacks upon Philip Murray. In turn, the CIO leader abandoned the remnants of his neutrality. "We in American labor will fight totalitarianism from the right or from the left," Murray declared in January 1949. "We regard the human welfare state as America's middle way. It should be neither right nor left, but liberal, progressive, openminded and daring." That November, in an emotion-packed atmosphere, the CIO convention expelled the left-wing unions, charging them with subservience to the Soviet Union, internal disruption, and, in some instances, ineffective labor organization. [11]

The liberals had mixed feelings about the CIO action. Some held grave reservations about the crushing of any political dissent and feared that the CIO might develop into a monolith with no room for diversity. "To brand the Communists with the scarlet letter of political adultery, and stone them out of the fold of the decent, is not the course of trade-union militancy," wrote Max Lerner. "Beat them inside their own unions." But most progressives reluctantly concluded that the CIO leadership had little choice. The *New Republic* called the expulsion "a dangerous precedent" but asserted that the left-wing unions had constituted "a present danger and not a future threat" to the integrity and very existence of the CIO. Robert Bendiner, writing in the *Nation,* argued that the left-wingers were being ejected because they had engaged in "bitter opposition, disruption, threats, and an abuse of the leadership that no organization can countenance." In the labor unions as elsewhere the vital center was incompatible with Communism.[12]

III

The organizational expression of the vital center, the ADA, now seemed to be firmly established as the major focus of American liberalism. In the weeks after the 1948 victory, ADA leaders began to plan for the establishment of a liberal bloc in Congress, for local conferences to support the Fair Deal, and in general for the liberalization of the Democratic Party. "The truly progressive element has come into its own as a factor in national politics," commented the Chicago *Sun-Times* as the ADA met for its annual convention in April 1949. The election of Hubert Humphrey as national chairman symbolized the organization's appeal to the younger liberals as well as to older New Dealers. The success of prominent ADA members such as Humphrey, Paul Douglas, and Chester Bowles demonstrated the triumph which the vital center had won in 1948. During 1949, the Students for Democratic Action, an ADA affiliate, managed to establish chapters on 175 college campuses and recruit some 5,000 members. The ADA itself grew from 27,500 to 32,000 members, with chapters in well over a hundred cities, and appeared to be a strong and growing force in American politics.[13]

Yet for all its surface dynamism the ADA faced serious difficulties, which were frequently entwined with the problems of the liberal movement as a whole. The most obvious problem was inadequate financing. Labor unions contributed about one-third of the ADA budget, and the leadership feared that a greater percentage would imperil the independence of the organization. Thus, most of the budget had to come from membership dues, chapter quotas, fund-raising events, special appeals, and relatively small contributions. The organization had no really big "angels" who could donate large sums of money when needed, and efforts to interest Marshall Field in assuming such a role were unsuccessful. The ADA's income was not enough for an organization which sought to exercise substantial influence upon American politics. It could do little more than pay its own office staff. It needed a large force of field organizers but could maintain only a very few and frequently could not even support them adequately. Conservatives often charged that the ADA had unlimited resources; but Jim Loeb, wryly commenting on an assertion that the ADA had pumped a million dollars into the 1950 California primary, stated the case fairly: "We would settle for five cents on the dollar." The reform-oriented middle class simply could not provide the money which an independent liberal organization needed if it were to function at peak effectiveness.

Nothing indicated the fragility of the ADA—and the problems of independent liberalism—better than its failure to maintain active chapters in some of the areas of the most spectacular ADA success. Many liberal politicians who had allied themselves with the ADA during the bleak days of 1947 and 1948 were now in office and able to construct their own organizations. The ADA was no longer an important asset for them; in fact, it was something of a liability because of its independence and its "controversial" nature. Despite the substantial ADA assistance he had received in his race for Congress, Richard Bolling discouraged formation of a chapter in Kansas City. In Minnesota, the ADA organization which had captured control of the Democratic-Farmer-Labor Party virtually disappeared into it. Admitting that the Minnesota situation might be the logical outcome of the near-total ADA victory, Jim Loeb was nevertheless disturbed by "the continued rumors that some of our old friends talk of the bad reputation that ADA has there." The situations in Michigan and Connecticut were somewhat similar. The problem was obvious. If the ADA locals disintegrated in areas of success, the ADA as a national group could not have a solid power base. It could provide assistance for liberals seeking power and serve as a haven for those who had been ousted from office, but it could not lead a reform movement at a time of liberal triumph. Success meant integration into a party organization, and it was questionable that independence could survive under such conditions.[14]

In fact, the ADA was suffering from an identity crisis, since it had never successfully resolved the question of whether it should be entirely independent or connected in some way with the liberal wing of the Democratic Party. Hubert Humphrey, during his term as national chairman, was personally anxious to tie the ADA to the Truman administration and the Democratic Party, and most of the ADA's office-holding politicians agreed. But among the rank and file there was a strong sentiment for independence. At the 1949 ADA convention it took a fervent plea by Humphrey to secure adoption of a rather innocuous platform resolution affirming support of the Fair Deal and pledging cooperation with the liberal element of the Democratic Party.

To many liberal Democrats, this resolution was somewhat disappointing. David Lloyd, who had moved from the 1948 Democratic Research Division into the White House as a presidential assistant, commented: "The liberal movement, as such, rebels against party discipline and refuses to seize the fruits of political power which are within its grasp if it would work long and hard within the party framework." Yet others felt that the ADA's integrity had been destroyed. The chairman of the central Ohio chapter resigned in protest against domination by "professional politicians." Harold Ickes adamantly rejected membership overtures from the ADA, calling the group "a Democratic faction" which could only become strong by acting as an independent power balance between the two parties.

Within the organization, Joe Rauh generally concurred: "The ADA is strong when it is independent of the Democratic Party and weak when it toadies to it."

Yet, as Rauh also observed, the road to independence was not easy. Most ADA politicians and labor leaders were firmly committed to the Democrats. At the same time, there were few Republicans liberal enough to be interested in ADA affiliation. Jim Loeb, who had little enthusiasm for independence from the Democrats, observed that in 1948 the ADA had found only two Republicans who had seemed worthy of endorsement for Congress. After both were elected, one immediately began voting with the conservatives. With a new party out of the question, the options open to independent liberalism were extremely limited; but for most of those liberals not running for office the need to preserve independence was terribly important. Independence was a test of integrity, of forthrightness, of refusal to compromise on ideals.[15]

As liberal frustration grew during 1949, the independents' position gathered support. In New York, the ADA endorsed the futile mayoralty campaign of the independent Newbold Morris. "As merely a wing of the Democratic Party, A.D.A. has little bargaining power," commented Marquis Childs in early 1950. "Its position must often seem humiliating and a little absurd." At the ADA convention that year a floor revolt secured the deletion of references to the Democratic Party from the platform drafted by the leadership. Humphrey had resigned as national chairman because of the pressure of Senatorial duties and perhaps also because of the difficulty of wearing two hats. His successor was a staunch independent and non-officeholder, Francis Biddle. Most liberals greeted the convention decisions with enthusiasm. Arthur Schlesinger, Jr., thought the episode had shown the administration that the ADA could not be taken for granted, and the New York *Post* congratulated the organization for demonstrating that it was "not the property of any political party." [16]

Yet the gesture of independence could not change the reality that the ADA had no home outside the Democratic Party.

Within the ADA, moreover, the independence issue did not involve servile party regularity, for none of the leaders, Humphrey included, wanted to change the organization into a cog in the party machinery. Essentially, the question was whether or not to recognize that the Democratic Party was the best available vehicle for liberal reform at the national level and consequently to determine that the major ADA effort should be to make this vehicle more serviceable. The advocates of independence offered no logical alternative. Their position essentially was other-worldly. They did not want to be contaminated by association with a political party which, even if it did offer the best hope for liberalism, was a most imperfect instrument of reform. The split between the progressive as moral critic and the progressive as politician represents one of the oldest themes of American liberalism, the one side fearlessly exposing the flaws of American society and creating forceful programs for its reconstruction, the other side operating in the realm of power, forging compromises, settling for piecemeal progress, both sides fulfilling vital and complementary functions yet frequently suspicious and hostile toward each other. The ADA could not produce a strategy to reconcile these forces.

Another difficulty, endemic to the history of American progressivism, was the apparently insurmountable problem of building a unified liberal coalition. The ADA worked for a broad range of liberal causes, but it could not obtain an equally wide view from most of the groups whose interests it helped advance. Labor might provide financial support but was determined to retain its independence. The unions, moreover, frequently gave only lip service to many liberal causes. In 1950, the ADA attempted to enlist labor support for a challenge to the demagogic, Red-hunting Nevada Senator Pat McCarran. The organization discovered that the AFL and the Machinists Union had already endorsed McCarran and that the CIO, if less enthusiastic, was not disposed to fight him. "Senator McCarran voted right on the Taft-Hartley Act; and, unfortunately, that seemed to be the only criterion with the labor unions," Jim Loeb explained to McCarran's disappointed opponent. The National Farmers Union, anxious to preserve its own tradition of autonomy, remained at arm's length. As late as 1950, the only farm leader of note who was affiliated with the organization was Murray Lincoln, the maverick head of the Ohio Farm Bureau. In 1951, Jim Patton joined the ADA and served on its National Board, but the Farmers Union retained its independence. Labor, the NFU, the NAACP, the ACLU— any of the organizations which might be described as "underdog, single-interest groups"—could generally take ADA cooperation for granted. They were willing to give the ADA some support or engage in loose affiliation, but they would gain little by actual fusion or tightly structured unity and perhaps lose much in freedom of action and concentration of effort. With a constituency consisting essentially of reform-minded liberals, the ADA naturally worked on all sorts of reform causes; the other groups had more cohesive constituencies and had to determine their priorities accordingly.

The situation was especially frustrating to the Indiana Republican progressive, Charles La Follette, who served as ADA national director from mid-1949 to mid-1950. In a meeting with President Truman in July 1949, La Follette advanced the idea of building some sort of a unified coalition to fight for the Fair Deal programs. As soon as news of the conversation leaked to the press, however, Democratic Party leaders and labor officials recoiled. At the end of the year, La Follette tried to achieve his objective by reverse action. In a half-sarcastic, half-serious public letter to James F. Byrnes, by now a bitter critic of Truman and the Fair Deal, he argued that Byrnes should attempt to formalize the conservative coalition and should become the recognized leader of a new conservative bloc or party. Of course, the conservatives, already quite successful in their operations, were hardly likely to be more disposed toward formal unity than the liberals. The goal of rationalizing American politics upon an ideological basis, of destroying the political blurring which worked in favor of the status quo, was unattainable.[17]

Finally, the ADA ran up against another of the historic barriers to American liberalism, the South and the emotions of race. Despite some ambitious efforts, the ADA could gain little more than a toehold in a few cities on the periphery of the deep South. The reason was clear to everyone; it was the same issue which had smothered the liberal side of early nineteenth-century Southern agrarianism, had wrecked and embittered Southern Populism, had corrupted Southern progressivism, and had managed to snuff out one reform movement after another in the region. The ADA's identification with civil rights, so indelibly impressed in the public mind by the 1948 Democratic convention, was an insuperable burden in the South. Even those Southern liberals who supported the movement for Negro equality were convinced that they could make headway only by camouflaging their position. The leaders of the struggling Chattanooga chapter asked if it were really necessary to begin the ADA platform with the civil rights plank. Couldn't it at least be inserted in a somewhat less conspicuous place?

Other Southern liberals went farther. A Miami ADA member expressed a mixture of doubt and frustration about civil rights that doubtless reflected the thinking of many Southern progressives. "I am not one of those who insist that Negroes do not want civil rights," he explained. "But I have worked with Negroes . . . and I do know that they are afraid of FEPC." Moreover, civil rights served only as a roadblock to other reforms in the South: "I have seen the issue defeat good candidates. . . . I have seen Calhounism run rampant over the South, trampling out all expressions of liberalism wherever it trod." The issue, in fact, had reduced the Miami ADA to futility: "According to ADA national policy, we could hold no segregated meetings. According to local laws, we could hold no unsegregated meeting, as much as we might have liked to. So, we cannot meet."

Faced with monolithic racial attitudes which stood more solidly than ever before against the main current of American liberalism, the ADA could accomplish little in the South, despite the expenditure of a relatively large amount of time and effort. In one experiment, the ADA's only full-time field organizer, Alden Hopkins, spent eight months in North Carolina. She had accomplished little by January 1950, and the organization could no longer support her. A few months later, the state's respected liberal senator, Frank Graham, was defeated in a vicious primary dominated by the racial issue. Graham was a member of the ADA National Board; yet, as Jim Loeb observed, "Obviously, the ADA as such could have no part in the campaign."

After meeting with the Chattanooga chapter in early 1950, Arthur Schlesinger, Jr., suggested that the ADA draw up a liberal program for the South, addressing itself primarily to "economic and political problems," although there would be some subordinate mention of civil rights. Such a program, he argued, could draw support from leading Southerners and serve as a basis for an organizing campaign. But the suggestion and the hope behind it were ill-founded. They seemed to rest upon the assumption that civil rights was essentially a matter of diplomacy, that the issue could be put over or at least tolerated in the South if it were not overly flaunted. The problem, of course, ran much deeper. Conversely, even the mild compromise Schlesinger suggested would have been unacceptable to many ADA members. Civil rights had become an integral part of the ADA's identity, and for most non-Southern liberals it was an issue of increasing importance involving an irrevocable moral commitment. The ADA and the liberal movement in general could make significant headway in the South only by condoning illiberal policies of segregation and discrimination; such a move was unthinkable. By the spring of 1951, the ADA had given up hope of organizing local chapters throughout the South and initiated a policy of seeking enough Southern national members to provide a base for local organization at some unforeseeable point in the future. Liberal morality had fared badly in its collision with the irrationality of racism.[18]

American liberalism had established a new identity and forged a new sense of purpose, but as the euphoria of 1948 dissipated, the liberal movement still faced many of the obstacles of the past. The experience of Harry S. Truman and the Fair Deal provided an impressive measure of the barriers which lay between progressive aspiration and accomplishment.

Chapter 13

The Political Economy
of the Fair Deal

"Every segment of our population and every individual has a right to expect from our Government a fair deal." With this declaration in the 1949 State of the Union address, Harry S. Truman gave his program an identity of its own. The political expression of the vital center, the Fair Deal included virtually the entire list of liberal goals: an impressive list of anti-inflation measures, a fairer and more progressive tax structure, repeal of the Taft-Hartley Act, a 75-cent minimum wage, a farm program based on the concepts of abundant production and parity income, resource development and public power, expansion of social security, national medical insurance, federal aid to education, extensive housing programs, and civil rights. The president even requested authority to expand plant facilities in basic industries, such as steel, if they failed to meet the demands of the economy. He spoke in tones of determination which excited most progressives. The *New Republic* called the proposal for government financing of industrial expansion "probably more significant for the future of our economy than any message since Roosevelt proposed the TVA," and the liberal movement eagerly anticipated a new era of reform.[1]

Most liberals now recognized Truman as a leader of sorts—not a masterful figure with the electric personality of FDR, but a genuine democrat who epitomized the aspirations of the common man, even if in a somewhat plodding and inarticulate manner. "Without eloquence or command of speech, he lights fires among crowds who sense that Roosevelt was for them and that Truman is of them," wrote Michael Straight. Roosevelt would have made the Fair Deal a crusade, commented T.R.B. It was Truman's gift "to be able to make the Revolution sound as casual as shopping at the Safeway." [2]

A new cordiality developed between the president and the ADA. Liberal White House advisers, including David Niles and David Lloyd, went to some effort to impress Truman with the work the ADA had done in the 1948 election and with its potential as an administration ally. Beginning in 1949, Truman sent greetings to the ADA conventions and established what appears to have been a genuinely warm friendship with Hubert Humphrey. The president had achieved a rapport with the vital center. "Between the reactionaries of the extreme left with their talk about revolution and class warfare, and the reactionaries of the extreme right with their hysterical cries of bankruptcy and despair, lies the way of progress," he declared in November 1949.[3]

I

The ties between Truman and the independent liberals remained loose, but no one doubted that the Fair Deal was part of the main current of American progressivism. Just as the vital center differed a bit from the older liberalism, the Fair Deal had special emphases and approaches which distinguished it from the New Deal. The New Dealers had frequently gloried in accusations of "liberalism" or even "radicalism"; the Fair Dealers tended to shrink from such labels. The New Dealers had often lusted for political combat; the Fair Dealers generally opted for low-keyed rhetoric. Election campaigns demanded a militance which would arouse the Democratic presidential party, but the continued strength of the conservative coalition dictated accommodation in the postelection efforts to steer programs through Congress. Such tactics reflected Truman's personal political experience and instincts. In the past he had frequently employed fiery speechmaking to win office, but always with the assumption that solid accomplishment rested upon accomodation and compromise. The problems of prosperity and inflation, moreover, rather naturally produced a different style of political rhetoric than had the crisis of economic depression. In addition, the Fair Deal, although a child of the New Deal, acquired a separate identity from the belief of its formulators that some New Deal nostrums had been inadequate.

The Fair Deal reflected Truman's policy preferences and approach to politics; however, it was no more the president's exclusively personal creation than the New Deal had been Roosevelt's. Just as the Brain Trust had formulated much of the New Deal, a group of liberals developed much of the content and tactics of the Fair Deal — for the most part, the men who had formed the liberal caucus within the administration during the bleak days of 1947, Clark Clifford, Charlie Murphy, Jebby Davidson, Oscar Ewing, and Leon Keyserling. Others who now worked with them included Charles Brannan, economist Louis Bean, Dewey Anderson of the Public Affairs Institute, and Leland Olds, the most liberal member of the Federal Power Commission. Of this group, the key men were Ewing, Keyserling, and Brannan.[4]

Ewing best exemplified the lineage from the New to the Fair Deal. Even as a young man in turn-of-the-century Indiana, Ewing had possessed a consuming interest in Democratic politics and social welfare problems. At the age of sixteen, he had worked for the state Democratic committee, and for a time he planned to become a social worker. Instead, after graduating from Harvard Law School, he settled in New York and pursued a highly successful practice as a partner first of the elder and then of the younger Charles Evans Hughes. By the 1940s, he had also become one of the most prominent Democrats in the state and was frequently mentioned as a possible candidate for high office. During Bob Hannegan's tenure as chairman of the Democratic National Committee, Ewing was vice-chairman and, as Hannegan's health collapsed, acting chairman. Appointed administrator of the Federal Security Agency in 1947, he began a drive to revitalize the agency and secure Cabinet status for it. At the same time, he was mobilizing the liberals within the Truman administration for the crucial struggles of 1947 and 1948.

Ewing's advocacy of comprehensive social welfare legislation —a popular magazine described him as "Mr. Welfare State himself"—was the end result of a tradition which had begun with the social workers of the earlier progressive era, found partial realization during the New Deal, and was now struggling for complete fulfillment. Ewing also represented a type of Democrat who had developed during the New Deal—the staunch, partisan regular who was nevertheless committed to, and identified his party with, social welfare liberalism. The strongest fighter for expanded welfare programs within the administration, he did not shrink from debate with the opposition. "It is the fate of the American liberal to be a scrapper," he remarked. Accepting the Sidney Hillman Award in March, 1950, he defined the key to America's future as "the protection and extension of equal opportunity for all our people— opportunity to live, to advance, to think, to achieve." Especially in 1949 and 1950, he engaged in lusty verbal combat with his conservative opponents ("the League of Frightened Men," he called them).

Ewing demonstrated the way in which the New Deal, and indeed the whole progressive social welfare tradition, provided a solid basis for the Fair Deal; but his ideas did not give the administration program its claim to a separate identity. His style, as it turned out, was not especially productive; someone doubtless had to speak out against the bitter-end opponents of social welfare reforms, but Ewing only exposed himself to defeat by doing so. His militant advocacy of national health insurance created a backlash and caused Congress to reject an administration reorganization plan which would have created a Cabinet-level Department of Welfare with Ewing as its first secretary.

His personal defeat on this issue exemplified many of the difficulties the Fair Deal encountered when it adopted the militant tones of years past.[5]

While Ewing expressed the continuing thrust of New Deal liberalism, Leon Keyserling of the Council of Economic Advisers gave the Fair Deal much of its distinctive approach. Keyserling was, it is true, a product of the New Deal. Educated at Columbia University (where he was deeply influenced by Rexford Tugwell) and the Harvard Law School, he had gone to Washington in the early days of the Roosevelt administration to work for Jerome Frank in the Agricultural Adjustment Administration. In a few months, he had attracted the attention of Senator Robert F. Wagner, who made him an administrative assistant. During the next several years he participated in drafting some of the most important legislation of the 1930s, including the National Labor Relations Act. Subsequently, he served as general counsel to the U.S. Housing Authority, later the National Housing Agency. In 1944, he took second prize in an essay contest on how to achieve postwar prosperity with a paper urging expansion of the economy to provide jobs for all. In 1945, he was active in the struggle for full-employment legislation. With Senator Wagner's backing, he was a natural choice for the new Council of Economic Advisers.[6]

A valuable member of the administration liberal caucus during 1947 and 1948, he also gained a reputation for being the most imaginative and articulate economist in the government. When Edwin Nourse resigned as chairman of the Council of Economic Advisers in October 1949, Keyserling automatically became the liberals' candidate for the post, and the ADA spearheaded an intensive lobbying campaign in his behalf. After a long delay, the president gave him the appointment in the spring of 1950.[7]

Although he had won formal appointment as the chief economic spokesman of the administration and had long been valued by the ablest members of the president's staff, Keyserling appeared rather insecure. Academic economists were cool toward him because he lacked the appropriate pedigree of a Ph.D.

in economics. (In mobilizing support for his promotion, the ADA found most liberal economists willing to support him not as the best man for the job but simply as the best available.) Within the administration, he had to live down his reputation as an Ivy League liberal ideologue. (He seized opportunities to remind listeners that he had been born in South Carolina and could produce a letter of commendation from Robert A. Taft.) Perhaps such difficulties were responsible for his enormous vanity and stuffy manner. Yet his brilliant mind transformed Truman's style and aspirations into a program.[8]

In line with the mood of the Fair Deal, Keyserling assiduously avoided labels for his ideas more specific than "forward-looking" or "the middle way." He noted on the first page of his contribution to *Saving American Capitalism* that he rejected "classification within any 'school of thought' or endorsement of any 'general theme' or 'purpose' which this collection may be deemed by some to represent." Adamantly refusing to be typed as a Keynesian, he would frequently criticize New Deal economics: "Neither those 'liberals' who betray nostalgia for the New Deal of the thirties which accomplished much but not nearly enough, nor those 'conservatives' who would reincarnate the brutal and reckless economic philosophy of the twenties should be allowed to say the last word." [9]

On the surface, his ideas and advice seemed an odd mixture of liberalism and conservatism. Writing to Clark Clifford in December 1948, with suggestions for the State of the Union message, he sounded like a conservative: "I am particularly concerned about the discussion of the economic program, which seems to imply that the Government is going to do the whole job. . . . [T]he first responsibility for employment and production rests with business." Yet a few days later he was advocating more ambitious public housing schedules than those proposed by the National Housing Authority. He sounded like a conservative when he emphatically disclaimed responsibility for Truman's controversial proposal to expand basic industries. He sounded like a New Dealer when he urged delegates to the

Meat Cutters Union convention to push for higher wages and declared that "accruals of fat earnings" justified such demands. Shortly thereafter, however, he was reassuring business: "Nobody in Washington has ever taken the position that the American economy could expand without profits." [10]

Keyserling's critique of New Deal economics had several themes. First of all, the New Deal had failed to grasp the virtual impossibility of the task it had undertaken, the lifting of the nation out of the depression. Those who argued that the New Deal would have been successful with a more massive spending effort were probably wrong. Government alone simply could not solve great economic crises, and if the New Deal could not be blamed for its failure, the New Dealers could be blamed for not learning the lessons of that failure.

The New Dealers also had become too dogmatic in their adoption of the antitrust position. "Today some industries which are organized on a large, integrated basis are charging prices under the limit of what the traffic will bear," Keyserling wrote in 1948. By contrast, home-building, the most fragmented industry in the country, "has been notoriously inefficient, highly resistant to technological change, and periodically prices its product out of the market." The antitrust laws should be used to prosecute monopolistic wrongdoing, but "we cannot re-create the pre–Civil War pattern." The liberals needed instead to ask if there were not instances in which monopolistic concentration might be "used to stabilize rather than to exploit the economy." Conversely, they needed to undertake a more searching analysis of the problems which competition presented to economic stability. Some degree of economic coordination, as voluntary as possible, would always be desirable and, during times of economic difficulty, essential.

The adoption of Keynesianism by the New Dealers had not provided American liberalism with an economic panacea. Keynesianism might be useful during a depression, but it raised more problems than it solved by its remedies for inflation. Higher taxes and interest rates bore most heavily upon the lower and lower-middle classes. Cutbacks in government spending meant the sacrifice of "national objectives which we should not forego merely because we are prosperous."

Finally, Keyserling argued, the New Dealers had lost faith in the potential of capitalism. Considering the system pathologically unstable, even if for some reason worth saving, they awaited the inevitable onset of a major depression armed with vast government programs which probably would be no more successful than the New Deal itself. They had failed to address themselves to the potential of the American economy; they had not formulated theories for the maintenance of prosperity. "The people of America need to be electrified by our limitless possibilities, not frightened into action by prophets of disaster."

As Keyserling envisioned it, American capitalism had virtually unlimited opportunities for growth; an ever-expanding economy could produce undreamed-of abundance and material gain for all classes. The liberals should concentrate not on re-slicing the economic pie but rather on enlarging it. Business could expect higher profits, labor better wages, farmers larger incomes, and, above all, those at the bottom of the economic scale could experience a truly decent life. The federal government should publicize these possibilities; it should educate those private forces whose responsible cooperation would be imperative. Keyserling recommended the initiation of a "National Prosperity Budget," in which the government would lay down targets for employment and production, indicate priority needs, and sketch out price and wage recommendations. It would be purely advisory, depending upon the cooperation of the private sector for implementation.

The government would not be passive. It would continue to police the economy against monopolistic abuses, dictate minimum wages, use Keynesian fiscal and monetary techniques, and even impose selective controls if conditions so demanded. It would provide important programs and services—low-cost housing, social insurance, education, resource development—which were outside the realm of private enterprise. The government, however, could not keep the economy growing by itself. Expansion demanded voluntary cooperation: "The widening of this area of voluntary cooperation, through common study of common problems, is the only way that our highly industrialized and integrated economy can steer between the danger of periodic collapse and the danger of excessive governmental centralization of power."

To those who feared that expansion meant the inflation inherent in the boom-and-bust cycle, Keyserling replied that the growth years 1927–1929 had constituted an era of remarkable price stability. Economic policy should concentrate less on prices as such and more on the relationship between wages, prices, and profits; it should work for the optimum balance between consumer purchasing power and corporate income in order to maintain full employment and expansion. The New Dealers, he believed, had turned too frequently toward controls to fight inflation. Selective controls might be necessary at times, but the way to deal with inflation was to enlarge productive capacity to meet demand. Fundamentally, although he did not admit it, Keyserling was willing to trade a mild inflation for growth. Such an alternative was greatly preferable to the achievement of price stability via a "downward 'correction' " or recession. Higher unemployment and lower production solved few problems and worsened many more. "The idea that we can protect production and employment by reducing them 'a little bit' is about as safe as the ancient remedy of blood-letting." [11]

During the first half of 1949, Keyserling transformed his vision of abundance to solid figures. Assuming an annual growth rate of 3 percent and constant dollar values, the gross national product could rise from $262 billion in 1948 to $350 billion in 1958, and national income from $226 billion to $300 billion. In 1948, almost two-thirds of all American families had lived on incomes of less than $4,000 a year; by 1958, $4,000 could be the minimum for all families. It would require only about half of the GNP increase to attain this goal, leaving a substantial sum for government programs and the enhancement of private incomes at other levels. Poverty thus could be eliminated without a redistribution of wealth. Progressive reform did not necessarily mean social conflict; rather it required intelligent cooperation.[12]

Truman adopted Keyserling's figures and rhetoric. Speaking to a Kansas City audience in the fall of 1949, he acclaimed the nation's history of economic growth and increasingly higher standards of living and declared his determination to continue the process. He talked of the $300 billion national income and the $4,000 family minimum. "That is not a pipe dream," he asserted. "It can be done." [13]

Keyserling had not discovered the idea of economic growth, although he seemed at times to imply that he had. It was true that the early Keynesians assumed that American capitalism had matured, in fact had reached a point of stagnation, but the growth levels of World War II had awakened them. Alvin Hansen and Henry Wallace, for example, had come to conceive of capitalism as a dynamic force with great growth potential. Nor was Keyserling fair in his assertion that the New Dealers really accepted the business cycle, that their remedies could not be put into effect until a depression had already hit the economy. The Keynesians sought at the least to smooth out the business cycle so that depressions would be eliminated altogether, at best to maintain a constant growth without periodic recessions.

If some of Keyserling's polemics rested on artificial assertions, his broad conception of economic expansion was nevertheless inspiring and enormously constructive. The major difficulties in the program he advocated were his reliance on voluntarism, his faith in education, his belief that group conflict could be mitigated through alluring vistas promising gain for all. His dream of an ever-prosperous society based on voluntary cooperation was, in its way, almost as utopian as nineteenth-century anarchism. Yet Keyserling was neither naïve nor inexperienced, and his ideas resembled those of many other liberals—most notably Henry A. Wallace in *Sixty Million Jobs*. It was neither politically realistic nor in tune with the spirit of vital-center liberalism to advocate government domination of the economy; voluntary cooperation was inherent in the concept of the middle way. But liberals who understood this were less prone to admit the imperfections of voluntarism. Like most of them, Keyserling never fully came to grips with the problem of executing his own ideas, and very possibly he realized he never could fully achieve the ideal-type he had constructed. Nevertheless, he had defined important goals for the administration—there were many ways of promoting economic growth—and had captured the friendship and admiration of the president.[14]

II

If Keyserling gave the Fair Deal an overall economic philosophy, Charles F. Brannan gave it a political strategy and formulated its clearest departure from the New Deal. No man, not even the elder or younger Henry Wallace, had come to the office of secretary of agriculture with clearer credentials as an aggressive liberal. He had begun his career in Colorado politics as a disciple of the old progressive, Edward Costigan, and as an associate of the young Oscar Chapman. During the Roosevelt era, he had worked as an attorney for the Resettlement Administration and had been a regional director of the Farm Security Administration. Long close to the National Farmers Union, he was a friend of Jim Patton. He had come to Washington as assistant secretary of agriculture in 1944 and had quickly established himself as a loyal and capable lieutenant. By 1948 he could move into the secretary's office with both the blessing of his old chief, Clinton Anderson, and the enthusiastic endorsement of the Farmers Union.

That fall, his advice on political strategy and his vigorous campaigning won the attention of Truman and brought him into the White House inner circle. Brannan had grasped the potential Democratic strength on the farms, had defined the issues, and had stumped the country areas for the administration. Truman's unexpected successes in the rural Midwest made the secretary one of the major figures of the administration and also suggested new political strategies to liberals both inside and outside the government.[15]

Many progressives believed that the farm results represented a new trend in liberal politics. To Samuel Grafton, 1948 had been "a year of deep and quiet decision" for farmers; the election indicated that they had overcome their conservative biases in favor of their practical need for government support and would turn increasingly to the Democratic Party.[16] If this were the case, then the liberal task would be to encourage and consolidate the trend. The ultimate result would be a new Democratic Party with a more solidly liberal base than ever before, a liberalism which would fuse the outlook and voting power of labor with an apparently reborn Midwestern agrarian insurgency. The liberal cause would be greatly strengthened, and the conservative forces proportionately weakened. Within the Republican Party, the number of Midwestern reactionaries would decline, and within the Democratic Party, Southern conservatives would have less leverage.

The first imperative was to establish lines of communication between the farmers and the liberal-labor forces. The ADA began the process by calling a conference of about 30 farm and labor leaders in Chicago at the end of February 1949. The farm leaders included Jim Patton from the Farmers Union, Murray Lincoln and some other progressive dissenters from the Farm Bureau, Jerry Voorhis and others from the cooperative movement, and several local Grange officials. Among the labor delegates were representatives of the Railway Trainmen, the Textile Workers, the International Ladies Garment Workers Union, and the United Auto Workers. The meetings amounted simply to an exchange of views; the conference made no effort to hammer out a legislative program or to draft a call to action. Yet Jim Loeb found the sessions "an exciting experience." The discussions were friendly, despite some disagreements, and many of the participants favored more conferences at the state and local levels. "The farm and labor groups are moving, slowly but definitely, in the direction of mutual understanding," declared Loeb. "The encouragement of this process can have a lasting effect on the future history of America." [17]

The administration took the next step in April with the introduction in Congress of a new farm program which had been drawn up under the direction of Secretary Brannan. The Brannan Plan was complex in detail, but essentially it was an effort to maintain farm income at the record-high level of the war and immediate postwar periods while letting market prices fall to their natural supply-demand level. Brannan thus proposed to continue the New Deal policy of subsidizing the farmers, but he broke dramatically with the New Deal technique of restricting production and marketing in order to achieve artificially high prices.

Many agrarian progressives, including Henry Wallace, had long been troubled by the price-support mechanisms and had sought methods of unleashing the productive capacity of the farms. Brannan seemed to be showing the way. He proposed the maintenance of farm income through direct payments to farmers rather than through crop restriction. Moreover, in order to encourage and protect the family farm, he recommended supporting a maximum of about $26,100 worth of production per farm. He promised to the consumer, for example, milk at 15 cents a quart, and to the dairy farmer a sustained high income. To the Democratic Party, he offered an apparently ingenious device which would unite the interests of farmers and workers.[18]

Liberals generally were enthusiastic over both the principles and the politics of the Brannan proposals. "The new plan lets growers grow and eaters eat, and that is good," commented Samuel Grafton. "If Brannan is right, the political miracle of 1948 will become a habit as farmers, labor and consumers find common political goals," wrote agricultural columnist Angus MacDonald. Jim Patton called the Brannan Plan "a milestone in the history of American agriculture," and the *Nation* asserted that the average consumer should devote all his spare time to support of the program.[19]

However, the plan immediately encountered difficulty in

Congress. It was vehemently opposed by Republicans, who feared that the political coalition it attempted to build would perpetuate Democratic rule, by the influential Farm Bureau Federation, and by many Southern Democrats responsive to the needs of large cotton producers, who would suffer from the subsidy limitation. Most conspicuous of all was first the silence, then finally the opposition of the freshman senator from New Mexico, Clinton Anderson. By June, it was obvious to most observers that there would be no Brannan Plan passed in 1949. But the administration and a majority of liberals were far from discouraged. The issue seemed good, the alignment of interests logical and compelling; enough political education and campaigning would revive the plan.[20]

The CIO and the Farmers Union agreed. Both organizations undertook campaigns to spread the message of farm-labor unity. An article in the *National Union Farmer* typified the effort:

Workers today are in a tough spot, just like farmers.

Production has been steadily declining, and that means fewer jobs and lower wages. And that means smaller markets for farm products.

This worries everybody but Big Business, but these advocates of scarcity still rule the roost.

Monopoly wants less production, less employment, lower wages, fewer family farmers, less collective bargaining, lower farm prices and less competition except for jobs. . . .

There is little basic difference between the labor fight against the Taft-Hartley law, and our fight against attempts to tax cooperatives out of existence. . . .

Labor's strong objections to 40¢ an hour as a minimum is no different than our equally strong objections to 60% of parity.[21]

Brannan campaigned extensively for his program. "Farm income equals jobs for millions of American workers," he told a labor gathering in a typical effort. "Together, let workers and farmers unite in achieving a full employment, full production economy." The administration sponsored regional farm-labor conferences around the coutnry. The one attracting the most attention was held at Des Moines, Iowa, in June and featured prominent labor leaders, important Democratic congressmen, and Vice-President Barkley. Other such grass-roots meetings were organized as far east as upstate New York, and the Democratic National Committee prepared a Brannan Plan pamphlet for mass distribution. On Labor Day, the president devoted two major appearances, one in Pittsburgh, the other in Des Moines, to the Brannan Plan and farm-labor unity. "Those who are trying to set these two great groups against each other just have axes of their own to grind," he told his Pittsburgh audience. "Price supports must . . . give consumers the benefits of our abundant farm production," he said in Des Moines.[22]

Many liberals and Democratic politicians remained convinced that they had an overwhelming political strategy. "I believe the meetings we held in Des Moines have set a new pattern in politics," J. Howard McGrath told Jack Kroll. "In 1950 and '52, the Brannan Plan will be the great issue in the doubtful states," wrote journalist A. G. Mezerik. "After that, Congress will enact a new farm bill—one which is based on low prices for consumers and a high standard of living for family farmers." In early 1950, the Brannan Plan seemed to be gaining popular support. Liberals inside and outside the administration continued to hope for vindication at the polls in November. They could not, of course, foresee the Korean War and the ways in which it would change American politics.[23]

Even without the Korean War, however, and even without the disruptive impact of McCarthyism, it is doubtful that the Brannan Plan would have worked the miracles expected of it. The liberals who had created or worked for it assumed that urban and rural groups could be united simply on grounds of mutual self-interest. They failed to understand that these groups were not overly concerned with *mutual* self-interest; both sides had practiced with some success methods which had taken care of their own self-interest. The rhetoric about urban-rural interdependence was incredibly superficial, and not deeply felt. Most farm and labor leaders, even those progressive in their outlook, had hardly any basis for communication. The

ADA conference of February 1949 included some of the best-informed figures from the unions and the farms. Yet one of the labor leaders had to ask for an explanation "in simple language" of the concept of parity. One of the farm leaders then admitted that he had no idea what the dues check-off was or how it worked. The farm leaders also frankly commented that their constituents were strongly against such things as a minimum wage applied to farm workers, the extension of Social Security to cover farm labor and farmers in general, and especially the reestablishment of any sort of price controls.

The situation at Des Moines seems to have been much the same. Even some of the Farmers Union officials at the conference were annoyed by the presence of the labor people. "Some farmers wondered if they weren't being sucked in to help the forces of labor fight the Taft-Hartley Act," reported journalist Lauren Soth. (Such ideas, of course, were not entirely fanciful.) Most of the observers at Des Moines sensed the artificiality of the whole affair, but they continued to hope that with further contact the union of city and country could be consummated.[24]

If farm leaders harbored a provincial suspicion of labor, the reverse was true in the cities. "While labor has given general support to the Brannan plan, I have had the suggestion made, almost ironically, that labor might be given a guaranteed income if such were to be granted to farmers," remarked Jim Loeb in November 1949. Many liberals felt that the Brannan Plan, as proposed by the administration, was too generous. The Chicago *Sun-Times* and the *Nation* agreed that the principles and machinery of the Brannan system were excellent, but both protested Brannan's intention of maintaining rural income at record heights. "The country as a whole should not undertake to support farm income at a higher level than is fair and just," warned the *Sun-Times,* adding that it would always be easier to raise supports than to lower them. Chester Bowles went a step farther and proposed that the whole matter of agricultural subsidies be tied to urban employment, with no supports at all during periods of full employment. Such ideas were hardly the cement of a new urban-rural coalition.[25]

Many urban liberals found the plan itself difficult to grasp and could not work up much enthusiasm for it. "Most of us do not understand it completely," admitted Jim Loeb a month and a half after its introduction. A group of ADA leaders had a cordial meeting with Brannan in June 1949 and pledged their support. Actually, however, the ADA did little to promote the program. In the spring of 1950, a Philadelphia liberal wrote to the organization asking for information on the issue, but Legislative Director Vi Gunther replied that the ADA had published nothing other than an endorsement in the platform, nor could she think of any group other than the Farmers Union which might have something available. The *Nation* and the *New Republic* gave the plan only occasional mention. Most liberals could heartily endorse, even get excited about, the political objectives of the Brannan Plan. But understanding and identifying with the plan itself was quite a different matter.[26]

The Brannan Plan, it is true, was to a large extent a victim of circumstances. Had there been no Korean War and no McCarthyism, it might have been enacted. For a while in early 1950 declining farm prices seemed to be generating an upsurge of support for it. Even if it had become law, however, it is far from certain that it could have created the dreamed-of farmer-labor-liberal coalition. Most leading agricultural economists, including progressives, were convinced that the plan would be unworkable and prohibitively expensive. Some progressive economists especially deplored its failure to give the rural poor at least as much aid as the middle-class family farm.[27]

Even assuming that the economists were wrong, there is no guarantee that a perfectly functioning Brannan program could have united the very different cultures of urban liberalism and rural insurgency; such a feat probably would have required more than mutual economic benefits. The down-to-earth, church-social, 4-H ethos of the Farmers Union would not homogenize with the sophisticated, intellectual progressivism of the city liberals or the wage-and-hour, union-shop reformism of labor.

Despite administration hopes to the contrary, the 1950 election was not fought on the basis of the Brannan Plan, and the Democrats suffered reverses in the Midwest. The farm-labor unity concept was soon forgotten. In the fall of 1951, the popular cartoonist Herblock expressed the new liberal viewpoint when he drew an unfortunate citizen attempting to protest high food prices and rural legislative gerrymandering only to be run over by a large tractor. At the wheel was a "farm politician" weeping crocodile tears about the iniquity of big city machines. With characteristic overstatement but fundamental accuracy, Truman privately summarized the problem to Aubrey Williams a few days after the 1950 elections: "The main trouble with the farmers is that they hate labor so badly that they will not vote for their own interests." [28]

Chapter 14

The Fair Deal:
The Anatomy of Stalemate

The fate of the Brannan Plan was that of much of the rest of the Fair Deal. As the promise of a new era disappeared into the jungle of the legislative process, the exhilaration of victory became the frustration of stalemate. At times, the liberals were unhappy with Truman's leadership, but now they began to search beyond him for the causes of their problems. Their analyses, however, never reached the root difficulty. Convinced that their cause was right and their political strategy sound, the progressives never perceived that the public might be indifferent to their program.

I

In the glow of the 1948 triumph, most liberals looked forward to an age of reform. "The President can get most of his program, and without too much compromise," wrote Thomas L. Stokes in December 1948, "if he constantly calls upon the great public support manifest for him in the election . . . and uses his political skill to organize the progressive forces." Even Jim Loeb expected "relatively easy Congressional agreement" on most liberal measures.[1]

At the beginning of January, the liberals won their first big

victory when administration Democrats secured adoption of a
measure which virtually ended the House Rules Committee's
power to bottle up legislation. This institutional change
seemed to assure that reform bills would come to a vote and
cheered progressives who had attributed their frustration to
minority obstruction rather than majority indifference. Robert
Bendiner called the episode "the worse Confederate defeat
since Appomattox" and asserted that it marked the beginning
of the end for the conservative coalition: "What Roosevelt
tried to do on a piecemeal and personal basis, through the
doubtful medium of the purge, Truman has attempted by chal-
lenging the whole rotten structure of Southern bigotry." [2]

The Rules Committee success and then Truman's uncompromising State of the Union proposals created a feeling that at
last the barriers had fallen. "Truman is likely to get most of his
program adopted and within a deadline of six months," wrote
Marquis Childs. Elmer Davis believed there was "a fair prospect that a good deal of the President's program will eventually
become law"; T. O. Thackrey asserted that Congress was "completely under the control of the administration"; and T.R.B.
predicted the emergence of "a Truman 'steam roller.'" As late
as the end of January, Samuel Grafton could mention casually
that national health insurance was as good as enacted, and a
few days later Thomas Sancton could write of the administration's "mastery of the art of politics." [3]

Six weeks after he had enunciated the Fair Deal, Truman
himself appeared cocky and confident. He avoided any verbal
prods at Congress as an institution, but at a Jefferson-Jackson
Day dinner he lashed out at the Republicans, "special interests," and "diehard reactionaries." Urging the proposals of the
Democratic platform, he issued a warning which recalled the
success of 1948: "I may even get on the train again and make
another tour around the country. If I get on that train, I am
going to tell the people how their Government is getting along.
And I know how to tell them." [4]

Yet the Democratic platform was already in trouble on the

fundamental issue of civil rights. Few liberals questioned Truman's sincerity on the matter, even after Alabama Congressman Frank Boykin claimed that the president had confided to him a lack of belief in the civil rights program. Realists knew that the passage of an FEPC would be difficult, but they had real hope for success. They were confident that at least an antilynching or anti–poll tax bill would become law. In early February, the inevitable Senate filibuster began to develop, not over the FEPC bill itself but over an effort to change the cloture rules to make it easier to shut off debate. The new Democratic leader in the upper chamber was Scott Lucas of Illinois, an easygoing moderate who had been handpicked by the Southern conservatives. Lucas talked of offering only token opposition to the filibuster. "To those who supported your Party and its platform it will seem strange indeed that a great victory was the signal for surrender," declared Joe Rauh in a letter to the Illinois Democrat.

Truman called for an effort to beat the filibuster and even endorsed a rule which would allow cloture by a simple majority of senators present and voting. The New York *Post* praised him for his refusal to make "dreary after-hour deals with the Southern Democrats," and observers such as T.R.B. and Thomas L. Stokes professed elation at his forthright, even reckless honesty. Lucas still failed to make a vigorous effort and refused to call the Senate into round-the-clock session. Nevertheless, the White House left him the job of lining up votes. In March, Truman and several of his aides departed for a vacation in Key West, Florida, apparently optimistic that the filibuster could be overcome. Instead, the administration lost the key cloture vote by the narrow margin of 41 to 46.[5]

The outcome revealed the hollowness of the 1948 victory and plunged most liberals into deep gloom. "It is hard to recall a more discouraging, a more complicated, or a more fantastic legislative picture," said Jim Loeb. Even as the administration lost on civil rights in the Senate, its strong rent control bill was seriously diluted in the House. "Any illusion that the liberal Democrats dominate either the House or the Senate has been conclusively blasted," admitted Loeb. Soon it was apparent that the entire Fair Deal was in serious trouble, perhaps hopelessly blocked.[6]

Truman denounced the "Dixiecrats" at a Florida press conference. Subsequently, he warned that presidential patronage would be reserved for loyal party members. "However sordid this procedure may be, it is the raw stuff of politics," said the *Nation*. "If it forces a showdown with the states-rights crowd, the country can only be the gainer." In August, the Democratic National Committee expelled Southern members who had endorsed Strom Thurmond the year before, and Truman in a brief talk to the Committee proudly observed that the Democrats had won the 1948 election without the industrial East or the solid South. Although he carefully balanced his geographical sections, his key remark seemed especially aimed at the South: "The Democratic Party is a national party, and not a sectional party any more. The tail no longer wags the dog." Liberals applauded the ouster of the Dixiecrats— "a bolder step, in party terms, than any ever taken by Franklin Roosevelt," said the *New Republic*.[7]

However, Truman still carefully avoided attacks upon Congress as an institution. "Basically the Congress and the President are working together," he told a mayors' conference after returning from Key West. "And when the final score for this Congress is added up, some of the selfish pressure groups are going to be pretty badly disappointed." The White House, moreover, piled new programs onto the already considerable Fair Deal requests. In April, Secretary Brannan unfolded his new farm program, and Truman sent special messages to Congress recommending the establishment of a Columbia Valley Authority and the initiation of a national health insurance system.[8]

Progress on the domestic program was slow, almost imperceptible, but nevertheless near the end of May Senator Lucas emerged from a White House conference with the announcement that Congress would try for a July 31 adjournment and that repeal of the Taft-Hartley Act would be the only "must" objective on the domestic reform list. Again Joe Rauh expressed the reaction of the ADA, calling the statement "a flat betrayal of the Democratic Party platform," and warning: "The majority of the people will not tolerate compromise or equivocation on the part of politicians." [9]

Lucas's statement had all the earmarks of a trial balloon floated by an administration hoping to score one big success during the first session of the Eighty-first Congress, and then to use election-year pressure to get more of its program in 1950. Few in the administration really expected passage of health insurance, although there was hope for other medical programs; civil rights and the Brannan Plan seemed good campaign issues. Nevertheless, after an outpouring of criticism similar to Rauh's, Truman repudiated his majority leader, declared that he wanted all of his program enacted, had no priorities whatever, and expected Congress to remain in session for as long as it would take to do the job. Such declarations, however, could neither erase the impressions of administration disorganization nor still the cynical joke that the difference between the ADA and the Democrats was that the ADA believed in the Democratic platform. [10]

II

Disappointed and discouraged, many liberals blamed the president for the wreckage of their hopes. There was special criticism of his role in the cloture fight. To some, his declaration in favor of ending debate by a simple majority vote—"one of those careless off-the-cuff remarks for which he is noted," said the St. Louis *Post-Dispatch*—was a blunder which had foreclosed any chance of a reasonable compromise. Most were appalled by his absence from Washington during the crucial days. "This was referred to a number of times on the floor [of the Senate], and it was devastating," said Jim Loeb. "American history is singularly lacking in instances of Presidents who have started fights, gone fishing, and won," commented the *New Republic*. [11]

A large number of liberals seemed to assume that there was a progressive majority in Congress; the president simply did not have the talent or determination to organize it. Truman was "a good, perhaps a great campaigner," admitted Frank Kingdon, but Congress knew that despite his conscientiousness and good intentions, "he had no stomach for a last ditch, gruelling, ruthless fight." As early as February, the *New Republic* called upon the White House to assume direct management of the legislative program by appointing "a traffic manager over legislative business so that some one person knows at every moment the status of every item, knows where and when presidential intervention is required, and sees that it is forthcoming." Marquis Childs agreed, fondly recalling the operations of FDR's old lieutenant Tommy Corcoran. There were complaints from some of the young liberals in Congress, who had organized a group called the Eighty-first Club. Leading administration progressives met with the club at weekly breakfast-discussion meetings, but Truman himself saw the group only once. Feeling alienated from the presidency, many of the new congressmen lost what liberal zeal they had. "This Administration—and this means Harry Truman primarily—should pull itself together, decide what it wants and go to work for it in earnest," asserted the St. Louis *Post-Dispatch*.[12]

At their best, the liberal suggestions on the techniques of dealing with Congress were constructive and intelligent (although the complaints of the freshmen Democrats were probably an excuse for their own lack of drive). Far more dubious were the comments which seemed to rest on the assumption that presidential leadership was somehow a matter of rhetoric and inspiration. "A dramatic address to the nation, a return to Washington—and a flood of mail from home—these would have made a profound difference to wavering Senators," declared the *Nation* just after the cloture struggle. Samuel Grafton expressed the same sort of viewpoint as he resorted to the inevitable example of Roosevelt:

[Mr. Truman] is vastly concerned with being right; he does not seem sufficiently concerned with getting the right things done. The great thing about Mr. Roosevelt was his sense of urgency, his sure, uncanny instinct that the moment had come. One misses this in Mr. Truman, one has the feeling that whereas Mr. Roosevelt used to greet the suggestion for an overdue reform by saying "Now!" Mr. Truman greets it by saying "Good!"

. . . . One can hardly tell, in the Washington of today, which issue is "hot" at a given moment; they all kind of run on simultaneously, all supported by the President, and none of them set on fire.

One wonders if Mr. Truman realizes just what Mr. Roosevelt's fireside chats used to mean—that they were not merely set occasions on which a President explained his stand to the people, but that they were actual mobilizations, and adult education, and the exquisitely judged culminations of movements in time and the minds of men.

There is no similar sense of time in Washington today, which is why we are again settling down into the doldrums.[13]

Yet, for all the continued complaints about Truman's leadership, few liberals viewed their problems in strictly one-dimensional terms. For one thing, Truman's mistakes were clearly overshadowed by the weakness and ineptness of the Senate leadership. Perhaps, wrote the *Nation's* Congressional correspondent, Thomas Sancton, the filibuster could have been licked if the Senate liberals had been led by "a man of Mr. Truman's determined temperament" rather than the vacillating Scott Lucas. "Lucas," said Max Lerner at the end of May, had displayed "the deftness of the dinosaur and the backbone of a housefly." [14]

The cloture struggle also laid bare the naïveté of some central liberal assumptions about the political process—that there was a two-party system in Congress, that the Democratic Party, pledged to the Fair Deal, was the majority, and that hence with a little leadership from the president a new era of reform would be at hand. The Southern Democrats held separate formal caucuses, and their leader, Georgia Senator Richard Russell, appeared at press conferences on an equal footing with Lucas and the Republican leader Kenneth Wherry. Many progressives suddenly realized that they did not after all have a majority.

Few had fully grasped the difficulties in translating what they considered an electoral mandate into Congressional action. The filibuster battle seemed to demonstrate that, rather than a two-party system, there was a three-party system, and the Fair Deal Democrats, when stacked up against both the Southern Democrats and the Republicans, were a numerical minority. Actually, the Fair Dealers could pick up a sizable total of Dixie votes on issues other than civil rights, and the Southerners themselves were not about to secede from a party within which they possessed great leverage. All the same, the cloture episode demonstrated that the liberal program faced institutional obstacles far more formidable than any problem of personal leadership from the president.[15]

Even the *Progressive,* which had long been suspicious of the president's sincerity, admitted that the one overriding reason for legislative disappointment was "the all too obvious fact that, while the Democratic Party is in control of Congress, Mr. Truman and his Fair Deal philosophy are not in control of the Democratic Party." The *Nation,* at the same time that it criticized Truman for failing to make a great speech on the filibuster issue, conceded that the Democrats seemed hopelessly split. Thomas L. Stokes, in contrast to his former critiques of the president, now observed that even Roosevelt had encountered much the same difficulties in Congress and concluded that liberals had to find some way to counter the pressures which organized special-interest groups could impose upon the legislative process. "Truman is stuck with a new and weighty reality—the open and systematic betrayal of the majority party by its disciplined minority," wrote Thomas Sancton.[16]

Perhaps the most extensive analysis of the Congressional blockage was conducted in the *Reporter,* in its own editorial articles and in essays by James MacGregor Burns and Arthur Schlesinger, Jr. All agreed that the basic problem was the breakdown of the two-party system. Schlesinger asserted that conservative interests, because of flaws in American electoral machinery, were overrepresented in Congress and had gained a veto power. The result was similar to the concurrent majority system which John C. Calhoun had once advocated. Truman's leadership was adequate, although not inspired. He did not have the creative dynamism of Andrew Jackson, but he might justly be compared to James K. Polk, an ordinary man of modest talents, who had perceived the necessities of his time and acted upon them. The fault lay elsewhere. "The 'veto' of minorities, by preventing the government from doing necessary things, can endanger the prestige of free government," Schlesinger warned. Burns was in essential agreement. "A majority of the voters endorsed the Democratic platform and candidates," he asserted. "But for six months now the will of that majority has been thwarted. Behind our democratic facade the minority rules in Congress." [17]

III

Some progressives indulged in the quixotic hope that a liberal insurgency could restructure the Democratic Party. The Congressional liberals, wrote Samuel Grafton, had to restage the stirring performance of the 1948 convention, when they had defied the party bosses and written a rousing civil rights plank into the platform. "The liberal forces took over effective, if not formal, direction of the party then, and they can do it again." The Nation drew on the same example: "Once again, the Humphreys will have to save the party from its Lucases." But the Nation also observed that "such a rebellion will have to go beyond the mavericks if it is to mean anything," tacitly admitting that a successful revolt might be possible in a Democratic convention but was hardly conceivable in Congress, which had a much different structure and constituency.[18]

Most liberals turned to another answer. "The solution for this mess is to find some means of strengthening party discipline," commented T.R.B. in September. "We can't see any other way out." But how? The liberals could only fall back on presidential leadership. Burns produced as a model the tight, unified Democratic-Republican party of Thomas Jefferson. The building of a responsible, disciplined party would be an enormous effort to be undertaken from the ward level up, but the role of the party leadership, headed by the president, would be decisive. "Everything would depend on how they wielded several weapons at their disposal—party funds, patronage, party machinery, the President's prestige." By the spring of 1950, the *New Republic* was urging Truman to intervene against conservative Democrats in the primary elections. "The fact that Franklin D. Roosevelt failed miserably, largely because of poor planning, to purge the New Deal's enemies . . . is no reason why diplomatic intervention in the few crucial Southern primaries yet to be held could not succeed now." [19]

The liberals overestimated the powers of the presidency and the discretion presidents enjoyed in employing the weapons they possessed. Truman even found it difficult to withhold patronage from important conservative legislators whose support was vital on important foreign policy questions. Antiadministration Democratic senators, moreover, could and did invoke courtesy to block federal appointments for their local opponents. The expulsion of the Dixiecrats from the national party machinery did little more than provide the liberals with a symbolic gratification which may have compensated slightly for real defeats but could not erase them. Presidential prestige was a fragile commodity which would lose what power it had if it were invoked too often and in any event would have little effect on a determined and secure opposition. And surely it was questionable whether Burns's Jeffersonian model, drawn from the dawn of the American party system, could be applied in the mid-twentieth century.

The liberal analysis stemmed from an even more basic miscalculation. "Never was a mandate given by voters more unmistakable than the one handed down last November," declared the *New Leader* in the spring of 1949. Burns expressed the same assumption, common to most progressives, when he asserted: "A majority of the voters endorsed the Democratic platform and candidates. . . . the will of that majority has been thwarted." [20] But had it?

It seems more likely that the liberals had failed to under-

stand the meaning of the 1948 election. If the voters had delivered a mandate, it was essentially a hold-the-line mandate,
perhaps a go-ahead on some issues which were vital to a wide
spectrum of the population, such as housing and inflation control. Public opinion polls taken in 1949 provided little evidence that the Democratic majority had been activated by a desire for programs as advanced as FEPC or national health
insurance or even an objective as modest as Taft-Hartley repeal.[21] The liberals, of course, supported the Fair Deal as a
whole, but the Truman majority was made up primarily of
groups with a much narrower view and much more limited
goals. Only the Negroes and the liberals had any real commitment to civil rights. Labor wanted little more than a return to
the Wagner Act and an updating of the Fair Labor Standards
Act. Farmers who had swung Democratic in 1948 had done so
because their declining income had successfully been blamed
on the Republicans. It mattered little to them how their well-
being was safeguarded, and of course the Brannan Plan had not
been a campaign issue.

The "Fair Deal majority" then was actually an election year
conglomerate, not a coalition which felt a degree of unity and
had a broad ideological base. Primarily concerned with its own
objectives, each group within the conglomerate functioned
without a deeply felt attachment to the entire Fair Deal. Near
the end of the antifilibuster effort, the *New Republic* complained: "valuable weeks, which should have gone into organizing local pressures for a majority-cloture bill, have been lost
while the liberal lobbies delayed the decision to put constitutional liberties ahead of their own special interests." [22]

The middle-class liberals attempted to provide the ideological cement which the conglomerate needed in order to become
a coalition; their lack of success was probably less a matter of
ineptness than an indication that the other Democratic groups
felt no need for ideological cement. The progressives never
fully grasped that no unified, coherent "Fair Deal mandate"
had emerged from the 1948 campaign.

About equally unrealistic were the calls for party discipline. If the liberals at times overestimated the possibilities of enforcing discipline in the chaotic American party system, they also interestingly enough forgot their own attachment to independence. The ADA had feared that association with the Democratic Party might lead to an irreversible taint. Most of the politicans who had strong followings in the liberal community —men such as Hubert Humphrey, Paul Douglas, Estes Kefauver—were mavericks. The ideal of party discipline was best embodied in the machine politician who generally was distrusted and often thoroughly disliked by progressives.

In defending Hubert Humphrey against an ADA dissenter who thought the Minnesotan was a "cheap politician," Jim Loeb promptly pointed to Humphrey's ostentatious refusal to be bound by the Democratic caucus and his other deviations from political regularity. "It is absolutely impossible to imagine that anyone could be more independent than Hubert Humphrey has been," Loeb asserted with pride. It was true that independence could be a virtue on many occasions, but the question presented many progressives with the age-old dilemma of the little boy who wanted to both eat and keep his piece of cake.[23]

The liberals thus had found no real solutions to the problems they faced, and neither had the Truman administration. Its strategy was to employ the Brannan Plan and farm-labor meetings to strengthen the Democratic Party in the Midwest and to elect more Fair Dealers to Congress. For all their surface rationalism, such tactics rested upon precisely the same misreading of 1948 which had been done by liberals outside the government. There might still be tension between the progressives and the president, but he had adopted much of their political viewpoint—including their mistakes.[24]

IV

The liberals sought to overcome the legislative stalemate by investigating and exposing the forces which were blocking reform legislation. Well-financed lobbyists who represented powerful special interest groups had long occupied a prominent position in liberal demonology, and the use of investigation and indignant exposure had frequently been a tactic of twentieth-century progressivism. During the progressive era, the Pujo committee had sensationally revealed the workings of the "money trust," and, within the memory of all liberals, Congressional committees led by Ferdinand Pecora, Hugo Black, and Robert M. La Follette, Jr., had effectively castigated Wall Street manipulations, the utility lobby, and antiunion forces. It was only natural to believe that a similar investigation might clear away the obstacles to passage of the Fair Deal.

Shortly after the 1948 election, the *New Republic* had called for an investigation of the lobbies. At about the same time, the Machinists Union convention adopted a resolution urging an inquiry. Thomas L. Stokes supported the idea and listed several groups which needed to be probed—utilities, the real estate lobby, the large oil corporations, the railroads, the American Medical Association. Upon receiving a copy of the Machinists' resolution, Truman responded with a public endorsement and let it be known that he and Attorney General Clark were investigating ways of tightening the lobbying statutes.[25]

The administration, however, was apparently too preoccupied with launching the Fair Deal and perhaps too optimistic in the early weeks of 1949 to give much attention to the problem. As it became evident that Truman's program faced a difficult future, the situation changed. Shortly before the president left for Key West in early March, Walter Reuther urged him to work for an investigation of the "special interest lobbies":

a vigorous investigation, armed with subpena power, will reveal a well planned, well financed conspiracy to defeat the legislation which you have proposed and which is vital to the welfare and safety of the nation.

Such an investigation would arouse an outraged public opinion which as in the case of the La Follette, Pecora and similar inquiries in the past, will create an atmosphere in which progressive and essential legislation for the advancement of the national interests can be enacted.

By the time Truman returned from Florida, he had been beaten on the cloture issue, and the entire Fair Deal was in serious trouble. He began to press the Congressional leadership for an investigation.[26] The results demonstrated all the difficulties which plagued the Fair Deal.

First of all, a resolution for a joint House-Senate investigation was blocked in the upper house. Then Representative Frank Buchanan of Pennsylvania sponsored a House inquiry, but his proposal won approval only after it was modified to include a probe of "governmental lobbying." It was not until September that the Buchanan measure was approved and the machinery for an investigation established. Despite the delay, progressives continued to hope that a tough, hard-hitting investigation might give the administration program the extra push it needed. "Only this searchlight of exposure and publicity can protect the American people's common interest from perversion by self-seeking special interests," the St. Louis *Post-Dispatch* had declared near the end of July.

In the White House, Charlie Murphy urged Truman to make certain that Speaker Rayburn would appoint an able and vigorous Democratic membership to the investigating committee. "As you know so well, the chief danger to most of the measures which you have supported for the good of the people comes from the organized campaign of misrepresentation about them," asserted Murphy.[27]

As was customary, Representative Buchanan, having sponsored establishment of the committee, was named its chairman. His three Democratic colleagues were consistent supporters of the administration: Clyde Doyle of California, Carl Albert of Oklahoma, and Henderson Lanham of Georgia. The committee counsel, Louis Little, was a labor lawyer who had handled many cases for the CIO, and the staff director, Lucien Hilmer, was an experienced investigator who had won a reputation as a militant advocate of civil liberties by defending the right of Communists to hold government jobs. The committee had adequate funds and strong powers. Yet, in terms of the objectives which had been established for it, it was a miserable failure.

As was so often the case with the Fair Deal Congressional delegation, the Democratic members lacked the will to conduct a strong partisan expose. Buchanan, for example, had a firm liberal voting record, depended heavily upon labor support for his congressional seat, and had even been irritated by the pressure tactics of the real estate lobby. However, in proclaiming his intention of conducting an "objective and impartial" investigation, he declared that he was not opposed to lobbying as such, only to the malpractices in which some lobbyists engaged. "We were not out to be sensational," he later told the House. He sincerely wanted to advance the progressive cause, but as Robert S. Allen and William V. Shannon have observed, he was not a Ferdinand Pecora or a Hugo Black.

The Republicans hampered the committee by naming three of their sturdiest conservatives— Charles Halleck of Indiana, Clarence Brown of Ohio, and Joseph O'Hara of Minnesota—as representatives. Throughout the inquiry, Halleck and Brown, accomplished hatchet-men that they were, conducted a campaign of sniping at the "left-wing" sympathies of the committee staff, denounced the whole investigation as an unwarranted attack upon free speech and the right to petition, and sabotaged any move designed to embarrass conservatives. They were more than a match for the liberal majority, which spent much of its time refuting charges of unfairness and rearranging its plans to meet Republican objections.

Public hearings did not get under way until April 1950, a year after the administration had first begun to push the inquiry. Then the only substantial group to be investigated was the real estate lobby; the sessions devoted to it were by and large polite and unsensational. Moreover, Buchanan felt compelled to balance the investigation of the forces against public and low-cost housing with an investigation of the forces in favor of these objectives, especially the CIO National Housing Committee. The result was to dilute to the vanishing point any unfavorable publicity which the real estate lobby might have received.

Under pressure from the Republicans, the committee investigated alleged improper activities by Oscar Ewing and Charles Brannan; it examined such liberal groups as the ADA and the Farmers Union; it even moved into the field of the House Committee on Un-American Activities by staging a hostile investigation of the Civil Rights Congress, a Communist-front group whose influence with Congress was, needless to say, rather limited. On the other hand, the committee did probe ultraconservative organizations headed by Edward Rumely, Merwin K. Hart, and Joe Kamp, revealing that they had received millions of dollars from large corporations as payment for anti–Fair Deal propaganda. Even these disclosures fell flat.

In the fall of 1950, the Buchanan investigations came to an end. The committee staff produced a scholarly and worthwhile report on the nature of lobbying and suggested some amendments to existing statutes, but the liberals had failed to pillory their opponents and advance the president's program.

If Buchanan and his fellow liberals were reluctant crusaders, hamstrung by a tough opposition, there were nevertheless more fundamental reasons for the failure of the investigation. The liberal assumptions upon which it was based were shallow and ill-conceived. Most progressives assumed that the conservative lobbyists engaged in illegal activities or at least employed methods widely regarded as illegitimate. The activities which the Buchanan committee uncovered, however, consisted essentially of various forms of propaganda and persuasion, peddled at times by unsavory characters, often consisting of downright misrepresentation, supported by huge sums of money, but perfectly legal. The "interests" may have resorted to criminal tactics during the progressive era, but life was different in the mid-twentieth century. As subsequent events would demonstrate, outright bribery was far more likely to be practiced within the executive branch than the Congress. Liberals who began the attack upon the lobbies with the assumptions of a Henry Demarest Lloyd ran into unforeseen difficulties.

Even the *Nation* had to admit that "the scope and procedures of the committee raise some extremely difficult questions." How could the liberal congressmen attack efforts to influence the public without endangering the constitutional freedoms of speech and press? This, ironically, amounted to an admission that Halleck and Brown were right. The weakness of the investigation may have stemmed from a realization on the part of the liberal majority that their attack against the lobbies was undermining values in which they deeply believed.[28]

The investigation did not have to uncover any outright criminal activity to be a success. Its objective was to arouse and outrage public opinion, but the facts it uncovered —that large and respectable corporations had ties to some of the shadiest right wingers in the United States, that staggering amounts of cash had been thrown into the fight against the Fair Deal—stirred hardly a ripple of indignation. There were several causes for the failure. A tougher, more partisan inquiry might have put more heat on the conservative forces, but it also would have risked charges of sensationalism and irresponsibility. The rise of McCarthyism and then the Korean War eclipsed the Buchanan committee just as they overshadowed most of the Fair Deal. Perhaps most fundamental, however, was the mistaken assumption that a frustrated public opinion was only waiting for the information it needed to rise up against the special interests. Proceeding from the illusion that the Fair Deal enjoyed a broad popular mandate, the Buchanan investigation developed into a demonstration of liberal weakness.

Chapter 15

The Fair Deal:
Promise and Performance

By mid 1950, the relationship between Truman and the liberals was oddly ambiguous. The president persisted in habits of political cronyism which rankled most progressives. He was unable to get most of his program through Congress and not altogether successful at some tasks, such as desegregation of the army and management of the economy, for which the executive branch already had extensive authority. Nevertheless, the administration had identified itself with the mainstream of American liberalism. Liberals still found it difficult to achieve rapport with the president and still had many criticisms of him; yet he was not only with them but was perhaps their most effective advocate. So long as he utilized his formidable talents as a campaigner in behalf of the Fair Deal, the liberals could follow him and hope for future victories.

I

At the beginning of 1949, Truman, his economic advisers, and liberal commentators had all been obsessed with the danger of inflation. It had seemed natural, even necessary, for the president to ask for higher corporate taxes and for authority to impose selective economic controls. Small warning signs began to appear—price declines in some areas, slowly but steadily rising unemployment—and the administration was well aware of them. But the economic indicators were conflicting and uncertain; until the White House could be surer of the direction of the economy, the best course would be to avoid any public displays of concern.[1]

"I do not attach too much significance to the very short-line swings in prices from month to month," Leon Keyserling told a Congressional committee in February. "I do attach much significance to the fact that the cost of living is still hovering within about 2 per cent of its all-time peak, has shown no pronounced trend downward, and is now about 74 per cent above June, 1939." [2] Two months later Keyserling admitted that there were signs of a slump but also many signs of economic growth— continued industrial expansion, overall high consumer income, actual higher civilian employment than in early 1948, despite the parallel rise in unemployment. "Sensational overplaying of a few soft spots in the economy and of some recent increases in unemployment should not be permitted to distort judgment or to produce a 'fear psychology,' " he asserted in the *Progressive*. "The outlook for 1949 is still bright, and optimism combined with the right course of action can keep it bright." Crash programs against a depression which did not exist were unnecessary. All that was needed was a long-range effort to encourage economic growth.[3]

Progressives outside the administration were not so certain, but most of them, even as they noted the danger signals of winter and spring, continued to focus on the threat of inflation. As late as the beginning of March, the *Nation* commented that Truman probably was still justified in seeking a budget surplus; yet at the same time it expressed the fear that he might regard a balanced budget as sacred, "the error of Mr. Hoover." This rather contradictory commentary, expressing worry over inflation but also recalling the depression, probably typified the puzzled analyses of most liberals.[4]

It was not until June that real progressive concern over an economic collapse began to appear. Leon Henderson predicted a sharp recession, criticized Truman and John Snyder for an obsession with inflation, and characterized the president as "a budget balancer at heart." The Public Affairs Institute, headed by Dewey Anderson, called for a tax cut and the initiation of public works and other government employment programs. Walter Reuther suggested a conference of leaders from government, business, labor, and agriculture to make plans for averting a slide into depression. "Nineteen hundred and twenty-nine can happen again in 1949," he warned. The *Nation* expressed concern that the downward spiral had continued so long and urged the federal government to step up plans for public projects. The *New Republic* commented sarcastically at the end of June that Truman and the Council of Economic Advisers were "about to take official notice of the growing deflation which lesser mortals perceived months ago." (Ironically, this was the first time the *New Republic* had taken notice of it.) After blasting the Council, the journal praised the economic growth approach, which it identified with Keyserling and Brannan, and advocated a wide range of antidepression measures, including those publicized by the Public Affairs Institute. Robert Nathan under the sponsorship of the CIO issued a similar analysis. Chester Bowles wrote to Truman and Edwin Nourse urging federal spending, repeal of excise taxes, and special aid to depressed regions. On June 12, the ADA National Board released a statement asserting that the nation was "on the thin ice of a recession, and unless we act quickly and effectively, we may plunge through into disaster." [5]

Fair Dealers in the administration worked with Congressional liberals to formulate a far-reaching measure, the Economic Expansion Bill. Seen as a logical follow-up to the Employment Act of 1946, the bill embodied the economic philosophy of Keyserling. It proposed the establishment of a National Economic Cooperation Board, whose members, appointed by the president, would represent all segments of the economy. The board would oversee government studies of consumer purchasing power; it would examine and publicize proposals for promoting full employment and economic expansion; it would be strictly an advisory body, but, the bill's sponsors hoped, a very influential one. The bill contemplated the promotion of private investment and production through a tightening of the antitrust laws in areas where monopoly represented an economic bottleneck, through positive government aid to new enterprise, and even through government construction in critical economic sectors. It provided for long-range federal and state planning of resource development and public works, including a ready backlog of projects for periods of economic distress. It authorized special government aid programs to depressed areas. Introduced in Congress by a large number of prominent liberals led by James Murray in the Senate and Wright Patman in the House, it won wide acclaim from progressives. Yet it never received administration endorsement and eventually died in committee.[6]

Truman advanced a somewhat more modest set of proposals in his midyear economic report to Congress and in a nationally broadcast speech. He acknowledged a "moderate downward trend," expressed the objective of economic expansion, and abandoned his effort to raise taxes. He vigorously rejected arguments that the government must retrench in order to prevent a budget deficit. "We cannot expect to achieve a budget surplus in a declining economy. There are economic and social deficits that would be far more serious than a temporary deficit in the Federal budget."

Truman recommended repeal of the federal tax on transportation of goods, passage of some corporate tax benefits, an extension of the time limit for repayment of Reconstruction Finance Corporation loans to business, and encouragement of American investment abroad through technical assistance programs and extension of reciprocal trade. He called for increases in unemployment compensation, veterans benefits, and social security. He advocated a higher minimum wage and "an improved program of farm income supports." He asked Congressional authorization for long-range public works planning and "a broad study of investment and development needs and market opportunities in an expanding economy." In a keynote, doubtless written by Keyserling, the president declared: "We cannot have prosperity by getting adjusted to the idea of a depression—by cutting investment or employment or wages or essential Government programs."

Truman's approach was cautious, but by abandoning the balanced budget, by stressing economic growth, Truman indicated that he had adopted the liberal expansionism of his most articulate economic adviser. If the situation worsened, it was logical to expect the president to enlarge his program.[7]

Most liberals nevertheless wanted stronger action. An ADA "Full Employment Conference" urged enactment of the Economic Expansion Bill, total federalization of unemployment compensation, and repeal of all wartime excise taxes. The conference also admitted that it was working from the same frame of reference as Truman, commended his proposals as a worthwhile beginning, and called for the application of pressure to Congress, not the White House.[8]

The anti–Fair Deal coalition in Congress blocked most of Truman's recommendations, but by fall it was clear that the recession was passing. A transitional phenomenon, occasioned by the overbuilding of inventories, it had marked the end of the postwar inflationary spiral. The basic strength of the economy, the "stabilizers" built into it by the New Deal, and the administration's tolerance of a budget deficit all had prevented a serious setback. Income and production began to increase, but unemployment remained disturbingly high and underscored the need for economic expansion. Throughout early 1950, Truman pursued a dual policy of boasting about economic recovery while advocating a faster rate of economic growth. That spring the administration introduced a comprehensive bill for aid to small business, designed in part to promote growth.[9]

One casualty of the recession was Edwin Nourse, the economically orthodox chairman of the Council of Economic Advisers. Nourse had long been unhappy within the Truman administration and had made several half-hearted attempts to resign. Truman's antirecession policy especially disturbed him, and in mid-October he spoke out publicly against deficit spending. Asked at an off-the-record press conference to comment on Nourse's qualms, Truman declared: "I am very certain that Dr. Nourse didn't know what he was talking about. Although he is an economist, he knows absolutely nothing about Government financing." The same day, the White House announced Nourse's resignation. Shortly thereafter the president met with Keyserling and John Clark and purportedly remarked: "Well the Doctor was a very nice old gentleman, but he wasn't very practical." [10]

II

As the recession ended, the liberals had another cause for concern. Truman had won much praise for his decision to reappoint Leland Olds to the Federal Power Commission. During his ten years on the FPC, Olds had developed a reputation as its staunchest champion of consumer interests. When Truman submitted his name for a third term to the Senate, progressives acclaimed the president's defiance of the oil and natural gas interests. However, the nomination remained in committee for months. Oil senators exhumed radical articles which Olds had written twenty years earlier and waved them about with charges that he was a Communist. "The sort of campaign that has been made against him is an excellent recommendation for him," commented Elmer Davis.

Somewhat belatedly, the White House realized the seriousness of the situation, and Truman made what seems to have been a genuinely strong effort to save Olds. He contacted leading liberals, including Eleanor Roosevelt, and asked their help. He sent a public letter to the Senate asserting that Olds was a vigorous and fair-minded representative of the public interest and that the opposition to him came from powerful corporations seeking to dominate the commission which had been established to regulate them. The president had the new chairman of the Democratic National Committee, William Boyle, publicly urge state and local party leaders to use their influence with their senators. At a press conference, he strongly defended this tactic: "It is customary, and it is proper, and it should be done, and Bill Boyle is doing it because I asked him to. . . . You have got to have party discipline if you are going to transact the business of the Government."

"The Administration is certainly pulling out all the stops," reported Jim Loeb's ADA lieutenant, John Tucker. "Mr. Truman deserves applause for his vigorous fight," remarked the *Nation*. The result, however, indicated the limitations of presidential leadership. On October 12, 1949, the Senate voted to reject Olds by the incredible margin of 53 to 15. A leading Fair Dealer had been drummed out of the government, and the administration had received a stinging defeat.[11]

Most liberals felt that Truman had performed with credit in the Olds episode. They were further encouraged in November when the president accepted the resignation of Julius Krug as secretary of the interior and designated the able, jovial Fair Dealer Oscar Chapman as his replacement. "President Truman could not have done better," commented Harold Ickes in a concise summary of the progressive reaction. (Chapman, who knew how to protect his Congressional flank, was easily confirmed.)

There was an equally warm reception of the designation of Charlie Murphy as successor to Clark Clifford when Clifford left the administration for private legal practice. "All of us here are sorry to see Clark go, but are delighted that the President has seen fit to appoint you as his successor," CIO General Counsel Arthur J. Goldberg told Murphy. "I am sure it will make all the Fair Deal Democrats on the Hill very happy, as we know the staunch and fearless position you will take on our program," wrote Andy Biemiller.[12]

However, other presidential appointments seemed less inspired. In early 1949, Truman attempted to name as chairman of the National Security Resources Board Mon Wallgren, an old Senate crony who had been defeated for reelection as governor of Washington. Most progressives considered Wallgren a complete mediocrity and were shocked by his appointment to head a vital defense agency. Even Richard L. Neuberger, who

liked Wallgren and attempted to defend him, admitted lamely
that "he might be a misfit in many other posts" and that he
would not be "one of the outstanding appointments made by
Harry Truman." The Senate Armed Services Committee was
not so charitable, and apparently motivated by no consideration other than the national welfare, it took the unprecedented
step of refusing to report the nomination of a former senator to
the floor for a vote. After three months, Truman withdrew
Wallgren's name.

In October after Leland Olds had been beaten by the Senate, Truman nominated Wallgren, this time successfully, for
Olds's seat on the FPC. "No doubt the President feels that Mr.
Wallgren has to be taken care of," remarked Elmer Davis, "but
it is a pity that in the present disturbed state of the world he
can't be taken care of, as he could have been in the past, by
making him Ambassador to Tibet or Afghanistan." [13]

Wallgren, for all his fumbling and lack of competence, at
least had a rather liberal record. Progressives could not say the
same for the new secretary of the navy, Francis Matthews.
Matthews, an Omaha lawyer, was quickly revealed to be an extreme right-wing Democrat who, as a leading member of his
local Chamber of Commerce, had overseen the preparation of a
political pamphlet which charged that the Roosevelt and Truman administrations had been heavily infiltrated with Communists. Even after being named to his new post, Matthews declared that he still backed those charges. (Ironically, Truman's
first choice for the job had been the progressive North Carolin-
ian Jonathan Daniels.) "It passes understanding that a man associated with unfair criticism of the Administration . . .
should be invited to become a part of it," commented the St.
Louis *Post-Dispatch*.[14]

Truman's appointments to the Supreme Court seemed even
worse. In July, the president named Attorney General Tom
Clark as successor to the greatly admired defender of civil liberties, Frank Murphy. In September, after the death of an
equally devoted libertarian, Wiley Rutledge, Truman nominated his friend and former Senate colleague, Federal Circuit

Judge Sherman Minton of Indiana. The designation of Clark especially drew protests. "His choice at this juncture is a bitter disappointment," said T.R.B. "In all calmness and candor we submit that it indicates Truman does not have an intellectual grasp of the difference between conservatism and liberalism in the judicial sense." The St. Louis *Post-Dispatch* compared Clark's record on civil liberties to that of A. Mitchell Palmer. "Tom Clark will have to prove himself to a skeptical public," declared the Chicago *Sun-Times*. "President Truman has not 'elevated' Tom C. Clark to the Supreme Court," snarled Harold Ickes, "he has degraded the Court." [15]

There was less protest over Minton, whose record both as a senator and a judge had been weighted on the liberal side. Still, he was hardly a distinguished choice, and in one sense his appointment was similar to Clark's. "Both are lawyers, have done the party's work faithfully, and are Presidential cronies— presently the basic requirements for elevation to the nation's highest court," commented the *Progressive*. Thomas L. Stokes criticized Truman for making appointments "after the manner of a Missouri politician with whom personal and political loyalty are guiding influences." The *New Republic* commented: "The tragedy of Truman's Fair Deal has been that first-rate intentions have constantly been dissipated through second-class people." The progressives, not so far removed from the late nineteenth-century mugwumps, expected Truman to appoint the *best* people to important positions, even if they had no close ties to the president. Minton might be a decent enough liberal, a fairly capable judge, and an administration stalwart, but that was hardly enough. "What was needed was an appointment on a higher level of politics, one that would assure the country of an intellect and a will devoted to the constant refreshening of the Constitution in the light of current social demands and yet jealously protective of the freedoms laid down in that document," asserted Robert Bendiner.[16]

The early actions of the new "Truman Court" added to the sense of dismay. In November, the St. Louis *Post-Dispatch* observed that the new appointees were voting against even hearing appeals involving vital civil liberties issues. An important decision in February 1950 reversed earlier rulings restricting police powers of search and seizure. All four Truman appointees—Vinson, Burton, Minton, and Clark—were in the five-man majority; the dissenters were all Roosevelt appointees. "This case should remind all citizens that their rights . . . can be whittled down a little at a time," warned the Chicago *Sun-Times*. The *New Republic* commented that the decision "increases fears that basic freedoms are in jeopardy." The major historical importance of Minton and Clark, said the New York *Post,* probably would be to remind liberals of the terrible loss they had suffered with the deaths of Rutledge and Murphy. By June 1950, Harold Ickes was observing that the Court might adopt as a motto: "Leave all hope behind, ye who enter here to seek the civil rights that once were yours." In early 1952, the *New Republic* featured an article by labor attorney Joseph Finley on Truman's appointments to the lower U.S. courts. The president, Finley concluded, had "drifted back from the high standard set by President Roosevelt" and, by naming so many political hacks, had "weakened the federal judiciary and lowered its prestige." [17]

The most conspicuous example of Truman's political cronyism was Harry Vaughn. In mid-1949 a Senate investigating committee revealed that Vaughn had used the considerable influence attached to his White House position to help friends who were having difficulties with various government agencies and had accepted expensive gifts from them. The disclosures, coming as part of a general investigation of Washington influence peddlers, only angered Truman, who had long since convinced himself that any attack on Vaughn was an indirect personal slap at the integrity of the presidency.

Not surprisingly, liberals disagreed. Few believed that Vaughn was actually dishonest, but all were repelled by his lax sense of public propriety. Most admitted that he had only done the sort of services which congressmen generally performed as a matter of routine, that the real corruption in Washington existed outside the White House. Nevertheless, the power, prestige, and symbolism of the presidency presented a special case. "The White House is quite different from a city hall, a state house or a Senate office building," declared the Chicago *Sun-Times*. "The General's performance, by his own testimony, was so redolent of the morality of a wardheeler, so scandalously lacking in a sense of his position, so raw in its misuse of influence, that there is no question of his unfitness for further service," said the *Nation*.[18]

Truman of course thought otherwise and Vaughn remained in the White House. The president, moreover, engaged in other distressing acts of cronyism. In early 1950, he endorsed Missouri State Senator Emery Allison for the Democratic U.S. Senate nomination. A party man, Allison doubtless would follow Truman's orders, but his record demonstrated that when he thought for himself he was a hopeless reactionary and a strong foe of even the mildest civil rights measures. In addition, many observers doubted that he could defeat the Republican incumbent, Forrest Donnell. (As it developed, Missouri voters saved Truman from probable long-term embarrassment by nominating the highly qualified progressive, Thomas Hennings, Jr., in the Democratic primary.) Shortly after the Allison endorsement, Truman further upset many liberals by issuing a pardon to the roguish old Boston politician, James Michael Curley, who was serving a federal prison term. "By this act he surely exhibited careless indifference almost amounting to contempt for the standards of public service in this country," commented Arthur Schlesinger, Jr. Marquis Childs summarized the attitude of many liberals in the spring of 1950:

If ever there was an Administration that needed the corrective of vigorous and persistent criticism on both performance and principle it is the Truman Administration.

In large areas it is shabby, threadbare and specious, or worse. It is lacking in vigor and resolution. Far too many misfits and hacks are in important positions. Political appointments have lowered the standards of the judiciary.

For a real and a forceful opposition the opportunity would seem to be unparalleled.[19]

III

Despite such complaints, the liberals had by no means given up
on Truman. The first session of the Eighty-first Congress approved a long-awaited housing bill, increased the minimum
wage, and progressed on several other measures. It was possible
to have a limited sense of achievement and hope that the second session would bring some victories. Most progressives were
willing to admit that Truman deserved much of the credit. He
was personally unimpressive, and hardly an overpowering
leader. Yet, as Thomas L. Stokes said, he had gotten results,
which once would have been possible only during emergencies.
T.R.B. described the president's technique with mingled respect and bafflement:

Truman would ask Congress for about 120 percent more than he
expected. Congress, with a great show of indignation, would slash it
down to 75 percent. Truman would smile his little-man smile and
bounce back with something else. It's a funny way to run a country.
It's not the Roosevelt way. But at the close of the session there the
score is. It's been creeping up. It's impressive.[20]

The off-year elections provided more encouragement, although in fact they were too few and too scattered to indicate a
national trend. The most publicized contest was a special senatorial election in New York between John Foster Dulles, basing his campaign on opposition to the "welfare state," and
Herbert Lehman, who in general supported the administration. Lehman's victory, along with several other triumphs
around the country, seemed to indicate a sweeping endorsement of the Fair Deal. "Unquestionably, the progressive tide
was running even stronger this year than when Harry Truman
was elected last November," asserted the *New Republic*. "The
outstanding feature of the day was the success of what would be
called in Europe the third force, the anti-Communist left,"
commented Elmer Davis. "Everything points to a deep under-
current of feeling in the direction of some kind of Fair Deal,"
wrote Max Lerner. Commentators could not overlook the role
of the man who had defined the Fair Deal and become its chief

advocate. "Mr. Truman has worked hard in the New Deal vineyard. And he has gathered in the votes," said the Chicago *Sun-Times*. There seemed more reason than ever to agree with the *New Republic* that "the present Truman coalition is capable of growing into a revitalized Democratic Party strong enough to guide us for years to come." [21]

The administration's victory at the polls might convince Congressional waverers; moreover, issues such as Taft-Hartley repeal, civil rights, and the Brannan Plan would be harder to dodge in an election year. In fact, there seemed no way the administration could lose politically. "Those [bills] that are passed will strengthen the Democrats; those that are beaten will be cited to illustrate the mischievous influence of the Republican-Dixiecrat coalition," commented the *Nation*. Prospects seemed especially good in the rural Midwest if the Brannan Plan could be sold to the farmers, and at the end of 1949 most liberals still believed it could be. "The Brannan plan, which ties farm prosperity directly to full employment, is on the way to creating a farmer-labor coalition," commented the *New Republic* just after the elections. "The Democratic Party, which stands for an expanding economy, is on its way to becoming a farmer-labor party." [22]

The president's State of the Union message, delivered at the beginning of 1950, reflected this optimism. It called for enactment of the whole list of Fair Deal measures, contained the strongest and most positive endorsement yet of the Brannan Plan, promised a list of recommendations to encourage small business and new enterprise, and included a request for a new housing program to meet the needs of middle-income groups. It glowingly depicted America's economic growth potential and called for policies which could triple the real income of the average family by the year 2000. It asserted that the government must play a key role in fostering this expansion and that a balanced budget must take second place to "the essential needs of economic growth, and the well-being of our people." [23]

As usual, Truman received plenty of praise from progressives. "We congratulate you on your magnificent statement of the principles of democratic liberalism," Joe Rauh telegraphed for the ADA. Yet, in contrast to early 1949, there was also a general realization that Congress would not accept many of the items on the presidential list, that there might be some modest accomplishments, but that the administration was already planning for the elections. Some liberals were uneasy about this course. The *Nation* warned that the president must fight hard, no matter how hopeless some of his causes, for a meek surrender to the conservatives might alienate rather than arouse the public. The *Progressive,* still pursuing the will-o'-the-wisp of party realignment, agreed. But to many the strategy of stockpiling issues for the election seemed necessary and virtually inevitable. The Republican leadership, ignoring the 1949 election setbacks, hastened to condemn Truman as a "socialist" and, if anything, intensified the GOP attack upon the "welfare state." When one considered the shallowness and negativism of such opposition, contrasted with the vast coalition of interests to which the Fair Deal logically appealed, it was easy to be optimistic about the administration strategy.[24]

Truman himself gave no sign of pessimism. "I believe that a party platform means what it says, and I am doing everything I can to carry out the platform of the Democratic Party . . . and I am going to keep fighting for that as long as I live," he declared to a group of Democratic congressmen a week after the State of the Union message. In mid-February, he delivered a partisan, fighting speech to a Jefferson-Jackson Day dinner gathering, condemning the Republicans for having dragged out "the same old moth-eaten scarecrow of 'socialism.'" Praising the reform accomplishments of the New Deal, he promised that the Democrats would "meet the needs and carry out the aspirations of the American people." [25] It soon became apparent, however, that little had changed, and that for the Fair Deal, performance remained more difficult than promise.

IV

Nothing exemplified liberal difficulties more vividly than the frustration which accompanied the administration's civil rights efforts. Throughout 1949, a special committee headed by former Solicitor General Charles Fahy worked for implementation of Truman's executive order establishing a policy of equal opportunity in the armed services. The navy and the air force soon satisfied the Fahy committee, but the army, which contained by far the largest percentage of black personnel, threw up one roadblock and objection after another. The new secretary of defense, Louis Johnson, seemed inclined to confine his support of integration to rhetoric.

On October 1, 1949 an impatient ADA issued a public letter to Truman calling for action. Truman reiterated his commitment to military integration, and continued to speak in favor of his civil rights program. "In view of the fundamental faith of this country and the clear language of our Constitution, I do not see how we can do otherwise," he declared in a speech to the National Council of Christians and Jews in November. Many liberals apparently were convinced of his basic sincerity. "The man from Independence deserves a salute for this persistence on the side of justice and fair dealing," said the St. Louis Post-Dispatch.[26]

The Fahy committee continued its negotiations with the army, at times appealing to the White House, at times threatening to go to the public. Strongly supported by Clark Clifford, the committee won the backing of the president. By mid-January 1950, the army had committed itself to integration, but clearly in a gradualistic manner; moreover, it refused to abandon its 10 percent enlistment quota for Negroes. Many liberals and black leaders remained unsatisfied. A. Philip Randolph called the new policy "ineffectual lip service to the problem of racism in America." However, following Clifford's recommendation, the president rejected a Defense Department request for termination of the Fahy committee. The committee now pressed for abolition of the racial quota. Truman personally intervened and secured army acquiescence in mid-March, although he did sign a secret agreement that the quota might be reinstituted if the new policy resulted in an unspecified "disproportionate balance of racial strength." Clifford had hoped that the Fahy committee would continue to function as a watchdog body, but by now he had left the administration. In mid-1950, a few days after the beginning of the Korean War, Truman gave in to the demands of the Defense Department and ended the Fahy committee, reserving the option of forming another committee if it seemed necessary in the future. Nearly two years had passed since the executive order of July 1948. The army was committed to integration in principle, but implementation was far from certain.[27]

Even the appointment of William Hastie as a federal circuit judge, at that time the highest judicial position ever awarded to a Negro, encountered great difficulty in the Senate Judiciary Committee and got to the floor for confirmation only after a strong lobbying effort by the ADA and the White House. The favorable impact of the Hastie appointment, moreover, was to some extent cancelled out when Truman put a racial bigot on the Loyalty Review Board—"one of the worst appointments that could possibly be made," commented Charles La Follette privately.[28]

Despite the efforts of its proponents, the FEPC suffered about the same fate as in 1949. In mid-January, some 4,000 civil rights advocates came to Washington to stage an intensive three-day lobbying campaign. Truman met with a delegation from the group, telling them that he was making every possible effort and that Vice-President Barkley and Senator Lucas had assured him "that they will eventually get a vote, if it takes all summer." [29]

At the end of January, the Southerners offered a compromise —a voluntary FEPC accompanied by a weak antilynching law. Some liberals were prepared to go along, feeling that a compromise was the best which could be obtained and that a voluntary FEPC if properly administered might be a valuable educational agency. Most, however, probably were unwilling to accept a halfway measure, and Truman voiced their desires when he told a press conference: "My compromise is in my civil rights message." The only result of this all-or-nothing attitude was the eventual House passage of an FEPC bill even weaker than the original Southern compromise.[30]

The developments which followed in the Senate were, if anything, even worse. As in 1949, Senator Lucas was unwilling to force round-the-clock debate or apply any sort of determined pressure. Moreover, it quickly became apparent that other measures were more important to the administration. In mid-April, the FEPC issue had to be deferred to allow Senate action on a European assistance appropriation, and Truman endorsed the delay: "Every effort will be made to pass FEPC promptly without starting a filibuster against an international matter that is of vital importance to the whole world." It was hard to argue with the need for Marshall Plan appropriations, but an exasperated New York *Post* commented that Lucas had adopted a new version of an old slogan—"for 'we have just begun to fight' he has substituted: 'We may begin to fight if we ever get around to it.' " There followed an off-and-on filibuster as Lucas allowed other business to be brought up. "FEPC is being postponed to death," declared ADA Chairman Francis Biddle in early June.[31]

For all practical purposes, FEPC was already dead. The first attempt at cloture lost badly on May 19. (White House administrative assistant Stephen Spingarn privately complained: "I was working with the pressure groups but was unable to make any contact with Senator Lucas to coordinate our efforts with his.") The administration pushed for a second try, but with no real expectation of victory. All that was at stake at this point was the image of the president and the morale of the civil rights forces. Liberals outside the administration as well as officials within it were seriously worried that disillusioned Negroes might leave the Democratic Party in large numbers, returning to the GOP or transferring their allegiance to the still-functioning Progressive Party. More then than the fate of the Truman administration was involved; the future of the vital center was also at stake.

By the spring of 1950, the attempt at strong civil rights legislation had become a charade. Probably no one in the White House was more committed to civil rights than Spingarn, whose father and uncle had been among the founders of the NAACP. Yet after the first cloture defeat, he admitted matter-of-factly: "We cannot win the FEPC cloture fight in *this* Congress, but . . . it will be pretty important in November *how* we lost it." With no illusions of victory, the administration and the liberals began to work not for a winning vote, but for a showing respectable enough to keep the Negro in the Fair Deal coalition. Advocates of civil rights could only hope for gains in the Congressional election and a breakthrough in the Eighty-second Congress.[32]

V

It was against this record that Truman faced a serious challenge to his progressive reputation. In April 1950, Congress passed a bill sponsored by Senator Robert Kerr of Oklahoma to exempt producers of natural gas from regulation of the prices they might charge to pipelines. The Kerr bill had the powerful backing of Southwestern oil interests which had contributed heavily to the Democratic campaign. It was pushed through the House by Speaker Sam Rayburn; in the Senate, Scott Lucas made no effort to organize an opposition and was conveniently absent when the final vote occurred. The bill's proponents claimed the support of the Democratic National Committee and asserted that the president had agreed to sign it.

To liberals, the bill was yet another step in the drive for power which the gas and oil interests had begun with the ouster of Leland Olds. Ostensibly an effort to protect "independent producers," it actually would deliver large benefits to some of the largest and wealthiest corporations in the country. "It will enable the big oil and gas companies to charge what the traffic will bear," warned the *New Republic,* estimating that consumers would be forced to pay hundreds of millions of additional dollars for gas. In the Senate Paul Douglas rallied Fair Dealers with a three-day attack on the bill that inspired and galvanized the liberal opposition. Kerr and Rayburn argued that the bill would not lead to higher prices, but if such were the case, asked Harold Ickes (who called the measure an "asphyxiation bill"), why had they gone to such lengths to force it through Congress? [33]

By the time the Kerr bill reached Truman's desk, it had become a *cause célèbre* for the progressives. On the other hand, the powerful congressmen who had put it over were insistent that Truman honor his commitment to approve it. The result was a classic demonstration of the conflicting forces which acted upon the president and constricted the Fair Deal. The ADA, holding its national convention just as the bill was clearing Congress, passed a unanimous resolution urging a veto, and its national director, Charles La Follette, in a three-and-a-half-page letter to Truman, condemned the measure as an attempt to rob the consumer, assured the president that Kerr and his allies had practiced duplicity, and warned that presidential signature could mean disaster in the 1950 elections. Within the administration, Oscar Chapman worked hard for a veto, arguing to Truman that the Kerr advocates had misrepresented the bill, even persuading the conservative secretary of commerce, Charles Sawyer, to oppose the measure because it would increase the power costs of many industries.

In his own dispassionate suggestions, Charlie Murphy summarized the president's dilemma. First of all, it was impossible to argue that the bill served the public interest—"It seems to me that the bill has no merit whatever." Yet, despite the fears of the liberals, it seemed doubtful that its passage would lead to substantial price increases in the near future; in a few years, general regulation of natural gas prices probably would be necessary, but not immediately. The economic effects of the bill therefore would be insignificant. Moreover, while presidential approval "would take some of the shine off of the Fair Deal," the consequences for the 1950 elections probably would be slight; after all, the Republican leadership had supported the bill also. On the other hand, a veto "would seriously impair relations between the President and the Speaker," thereby placing important segments of the administration program in jeopardy. Murphy could only suggest that the president might try to smoke out the bill's backers by sending a public letter to Kerr asking if he and his cosponsors would support repeal in the event gas prices did rise unreasonably. "If the President received a reply which was not clear-cut one way or the other, which I think is most likely, I do not believe that the situation would be worse than it is now." [34]

Truman, however, opted for a firmly worded veto. "To withdraw entirely from this field of regulation . . . impelled only by imaginary fears, and in the face of a record of accomplishment . . . would not be in the public interest." Most liberals realized that Truman probably would have approved the bill had they not mounted a strong campaign against it, but they were willing to give him credit for bucking the Congressional leadership. "We suspect that Mr. Truman's instincts would have been on the side of a veto in any case; we think the liberal thunder gave him the courage of his convictions," commented the New York *Post.* The *New Republic* said that Truman had wisely "put votes before dollars" and congratulated him. "The President's decision was not easy," said the St. Louis *Post-Dispatch,* "but he made it, as he said, 'in the national interest.'" "One man who can feel that he has been vindicated," observed Elmer Davis, "is Leland Olds." [35]

VI

In May, Truman left Washington for a ten-day whistle-stop tour which took him into the Pacific Northwest. Officially a "non-partisan report to the people," the trip was designed to explain and defend every aspect of the administration's program. The president carefully avoided attacks upon the Republicans, but as Chicago *Sun-Times* writer Carleton Kent observed, "Anyone over the age of ten knows whom a Democratic President refers to when he speaks blandly of old fogies, mossbacks, penny-pinchers, economic isolationists, acorn minds, prophets of gloom, the lunatic fringe, robber barons, diehard reactionaries, men of little faith, calamity-howlers, the timid minority." In ten-minute rear-platform talks and major prepared speeches, Truman discussed such general principles as the need for sustained economic growth, the interdependence of the urban and rural economies, and the wisdom of government spending for projects which constituted an investment in the nation's future. He spoke of specific benefits which the Democrats had given or were attempting to give the people, such as reclamation, flood control, public power, social security, minimum wages, the Brannan Plan, a Columbia Valley Authority, health insurance, aid to education. On his return trip, he addressed a large Democratic gathering in Chicago as an unofficial kickoff for the drive to capture Congressional seats in the Midwest. Rejecting "the delusions of the extreme left" and "the prejudices of the extreme right," he declared: "The Democratic Party, today, is the party of the mainstream of American life. It is the party of progressive liberalism." [36]

The tour appeared to be a rousing success. The large, friendly crowds and the strong presidential rhetoric boosted liberal morale. "If there's any one reason why you've endeared yourself to so many millions, it's because you have identified yourself with the people," the *Sun-Times* told Truman as he arrived in Chicago. "Mr. Truman has set a high tone for his party," said the *New Republic*. "The man the Democrats tried to shake off two years ago has become their hope and their salvation," declared the *Nation* with a trace of wonderment. "Mr. Truman has again tapped the wellsprings of American idealism that were the source of Roosevelt's strength." [37]

Success on the road, however, did not translate into success on Capitol Hill. The middle-income housing program was dead with no hope of revival. Taft-Hartley repeal was no longer a possibility. The administration had some hope for an aid-to-education bill, but the issue already had been crushed to death by the pressures of race and religion. The effort to secure an improved unemployment compensation program was going nowhere. Health insurance, of course, had no chance, and Truman found himself unable to pry even a badly needed aid-to-medical-education bill out of a House committee although he spent forty-five minutes trying to persuade its members.

It was true that the outlook was not entirely dark. A more liberal and humane displaced persons bill was nearly through Congress. A greatly improved and updated Social Security program was close to passage. There seemed to be a good chance that Congress would approve a significant tightening of the Clayton Antitrust Act. And the president's broad program for aid to small business, submitted at the beginning of May, had won an encouraging reception.[38]

In June, Truman registered another important veto when he disapproved a bill to legalize "basing point" price policies (the practice of calculating the delivered price of a product by adding the freight rate from a "basing point" which was usually more distant than the actual point at which the shipment originated). The veto message, a strong defense of the antitrust laws and an assertion of the need to protect small enterprise from "ruthless price discrimination," cheered the liberals. Along with Truman's action on the Kerr bill, it provided proof of the administration's commitment to a firm antimonopoly policy. The basing-point veto was also an implicit rebuke to John Snyder and other administration conservatives who had favored the bill. "The President must be given credit for solicitude for the welfare of the people as against a few industrialists seeking special advantage," commented the St. Louis *Post-Dispatch*.[39]

Like so many other victories, the basing-point veto was negative. Truman had achieved some results from the Eighty-first Congress—as Richard Neustadt has observed, it was the most liberal Congress since 1938—but for the most part the objectives which distinguished the Fair Deal from the New Deal, which attempted to break new ground, had failed of passage.[40]

Nevertheless, by mid-1950, a partnership, uneasy though it was at times, still existed between Truman and the progressives. For all its futility, the Fair Deal was the expression of the vital center, and Truman, whatever his inadequacies, was the foremost spokesman of American liberalism. The blockage of the Fair Deal, most progressives realized, could not be attributed primarily to the president. Rather, it was partly the result of the complex mechanics of the American political system;

this the liberals understood. What they did not understand was that the reform stalemate also had developed quite logically out of the ambiguous nature of the Truman mandate of 1948. They still hoped that Truman might succeed in mobilizing a majority, but in fact defeat was near. McCarthyism and the Korean War together would in the end overwhelm the Fair Deal.

Chapter 16

Truman, the Vital Center, and American Foreign Policy

The events of 1948 largely destroyed the Popular Front attitude. Only the inconsequential remnants of the Progressive
Party continued to argue that the United States was mainly responsible for the Cold War. The triumph of the vital center,
however, did not mean a monolithic liberal endorsement of aggressive anti-Sovietism. The vital center was not a specific program; rather it was a broad attitude which disassociated liberalism from Communism and advocated a foreign policy which
would encourage democracy and economic development
abroad. It had room for different emphases, frequently coexist-
ing within the same individual. One emphasis was in the direction of hard-line *anti*-Communism, accepting the Cold War as
a power struggle likely to continue for decades and recognizing
the threat of force as one of its inevitable aspects. The other
emphasis was toward a *non*-Communist liberalism which
shrank from the power implications of the Cold War and desperately hoped for a diplomatic breakthrough which would
lead to a peaceful settlement.

By and large, the Truman administration stood within the
vital center, finding its characteristic mode of expression in the
hard-line anti-Communist emphasis. Indeed, the president and
his subordinates celebrated American superiority, engaged in

self-righteous stubbornness toward the Soviet Union, and clothed even their most constructive proposals in the garments of American mission and destiny. The non-Communist liberals tended to find such rhetoric grating and self-defeating; they also found it frustrating that, as with the domestic Fair Deal, the administration's promise far outdistanced its performance. The liberals might agree with the general thrust of Truman's diplomacy, but they still found plenty of specifics to criticize. Moreover, in a tense world dominated by the steadily growing fear of atomic war, the tone and attitude of the policy-makers could seem as important as their concrete policies.

I

Truman's inaugural address—a major foreign policy statement —exemplified both the elements of his diplomacy which appealed to the vital center as a whole and the rhetoric which disturbed its non-Communist element. He lashed into Communism as a false, warlike philosophy characterized by "deceit and mockery, poverty and tyranny," irreconcilably at odds with democracy and threatening "the efforts of free nations to bring about world recovery and lasting peace." He proclaimed four basic points for American foreign policy: (1) "unfaltering support to the United Nations and related agencies," (2) continued efforts in behalf of foreign economic recovery via the Marshall Plan and encouragement of reduced trade barriers, (3) the negotiation of a North Atlantic mutual defense treaty to "strengthen freedom-loving nations against the dangers of aggression," and (4) "a bold new program for making the benefits of our scientific advances and industrial progress available for the improvement and growth of underdeveloped areas."

The president dwelt longest on the fourth point. The technologically advanced peoples had a duty to help the submerged, impoverished half of the globe. "Our aim should be to help the free peoples of the world, through their own efforts, to produce more food, more clothing, more materials for housing, and more mechanical power to lighten their burdens." The

United States and other freedom-loving nations should work cooperatively, through the U.N. whenever possible, in "a worldwide effort for the achievement of peace, plenty, and freedom." What he advocated, Truman declared, was not an exploitative imperialism but "a program of development based on the concepts of democratic fair-dealing." The advanced nations would profit from new markets, but not at the expense of underdeveloped populations. Most importantly, by raising living standards, the program would advance freedom and establish America's moral leadership. "Democracy alone can supply the vitalizing force to stir the peoples of the world into triumphant action, not only against their human oppressors, but also against their ancient enemies—hunger, misery, and despair." [1]

The liberal reaction demonstrated the divergent impulses of the vital center. Few progressives were enthusiastic about the militant and simplistic anti-Communism which occupied so much of the speech; for some, it wholly overshadowed the "bold new program." The *Progressive* stiffly criticized the inflammatory rhetoric and its military implications in an editorial which made no mention of Point Four. Thomas Sancton feared that the address reflected the influence of primitive "Pentagon mentalities" and might have been "a moment of high tragedy for the nation and the world." Freda Kirchwey called the speech " a new declaration of cold war, the more distressing because it was cloaked in the language of peace and democratic self-determination." [2]

Many others, including the editors of the *New Republic,* took a more mixed view. "The plan for aid to the backward nations of the world is a proposal magnificent in purpose and breathtaking in scope, the sort of thing Franklin Roosevelt would have loved and to which he certainly would have turned," declared the journal. Yet Truman appeared also to advocate a "holy crusade" against world Communism which could only end in war. Genuine development of the backward world, genuine extension of democratic principles were incompatible with a driving anti-Communism which would impel the United States to support any dictator who professed hatred for the USSR. If Truman had really meant his rhetoric, then the outlook was dark indeed.[3]

A substantial number of liberals, however, accepted or at least overlooked the hard-line segments of the speech and focused on its constructive aspects. The Chicago *Sun-Times* declared that Truman had become "the heir to Franklin Roosevelt's world leadership" and praised him for moving away from the negativism of containment to a "positive and dynamic program." An elated David Lilienthal saw the inaugural as a statement of his own aspirations. The St. Louis *Post-Dispatch* asserted that the president's words had "soared to heights that will lift up the spirit of men everywhere." [4]

Truman's initial foreign policy and defense appointments provided hope that he would follow the constructive side of the inaugural. General Marshall and Robert Lovett resigned their posts as secretary and undersecretary of state. The president's designation of Dean Acheson and James E. Webb, a former director of the Budget Bureau, as their successors appealed to most liberals as a symbolic move away from Wall Street–military influence in foreign policy.

No one believed that Acheson would be "soft" toward the Soviet Union, but he had a reputation as an intelligent and progressive-minded diplomat. Elmer Davis called him a "left-of-center liberal," and the Chicago *Sun-Times* depicted him as a believer in democracy "aware of the forces at work for social and political change in the world." Jim Loeb expressed gratification at his appointment. The *New Republic* believed that the new secretary would strive for a political settlement of the Cold War.[5]

At first, progressives were much less enthusiastic about the new secretary of defense, Louis Johnson. Johnson was a former commander of the American Legion, and it was an open secret that the appointment was a payoff for his crucial fund-raising activities during the 1948 campaign. Some liberals, however, remembered Johnson's record as assistant secretary of war in the dark years before Pearl Harbor when he had crusaded for military preparedness against the Axis. Even the *New Republic* was able to commend him as a tough administrator who might bring genuine unification to the armed services.[6]

The optimists seemed vindicated when Johnson threw himself strongly behind an administration effort to cut back military spending. Most liberals viewed the Pentagon as a Babylon of extravagance and heartily endorsed the economy drive. The move also represented a restoration of civilian control and was another indication that the United States was moving away from an emphasis upon military power. The program had been planned and begun before Johnson's appointment, but his hard work for it drew much favorable comment.[7]

II

The first major foreign policy development of 1949 was the negotiation of a historic military alliance with the nations of Western Europe. The vital center's response to the North Atlantic Treaty and the closely related issue of military aid to the European allies demonstrated its divided mind.

Predictably, Henry Wallace and his old supporters opposed the treaty, but others who had refused to back the Progressive Party also fought the pact. Many feared that the treaty would undermine and perhaps destroy the U.N. The world organization, asserted the liberal Minnesota congressman, John Blatnik, was fighting for its life against power politics and the division of the world into two armed camps. The alliance might well divert Marshall Plan money away from constructive economic recovery and into armament programs. Far from offering a way out of the Cold War, it committed the West more deeply than before and focused on a military approach. Thomas L. Stokes expressed the feelings of many non-Communist progressives with his comment that the United States should have "taken the leadership boldly on a positive program, instead of falling back on this negative, defensive alliance."

Since even the administration conceded that the Soviet Union had no immediate plans for military aggression against Western Europe, many liberals quite logically considered the pact an unnecessary move which could only increase Cold War tensions and touch off an escalation of the arms race. Of course, the treaty was defensive, remarked the *Progressive,* but "we certainly can't kid ourselves into believing that the Russians share our own view of that purity of purpose." The leadership of the Farmers Union depicted the treaty as a triumph of militarism. Other liberals, alarmed especially by the inclusion of Portugal in the defense system, feared that the pact would strengthen the European right and possibly ignite class warfare. Freda Kirchwey predicted that Europe would experience "a period of economic dislocation, strikes and demonstrations, severe repression, and growing political reaction." [8]

While advocates of the treaty rejected such apocalyptic prophecies, most of them shared some of the opposition fears and came out for the pact only after a period of self-questioning. The Chicago *Sun-Times,* for example endorsed the alliance but voiced practically every argument which might be made against it. The *New Republic* conceded that the pact could encourage a foredoomed effort to defeat Communism simply by military treaties and admitted the danger that American arms might bolster undesirable governments. The pact, moreover, did not eliminate the need for renewed efforts to achieve Soviet-American agreement and to strengthen the U.N. The alliance was justifiable, the journal reasoned, because it was a step toward European unity, and Europe had a right to self-defense.

The ADA overcame similar doubts. The delegates to the 1949 national convention, Reinhold Niebuhr remarked, "tore their souls" before deciding to support the treaty. In testimony before congressional committees, Charles La Follette stressed that "economic and political aid must be our first line of defense." ADA leaders sought to identify the treaty with FDR's prewar advocacy of quarantining the aggressor. No less a figure than Eleanor Roosevelt argued that the pact was in harmony with the U.N. Charter. The St. Louis *Post-Dispatch* somewhat less legalistically dismissed complaints that the treaty split the world by arguing that, far from creating divisions, the North

Atlantic alliance simply recognized those which already existed.

Many liberals asserted that instead of increasing the chances for war, the alliance would add a vitally needed degree of stability and certainty to the diplomacy and politics of Western Europe, thereby discouraging Soviet aggression and enhancing the prospects for peace. "Our ratification of the North Atlantic Pact serves notice on the Kremlin," declared Paul Douglas. Helen Gahagan Douglas, whose conversion to anti-Communism was much more recent, agreed. The Russians probably were not planning any immediate attack upon Western Europe, she admitted, but they had "deliberately created an atmosphere of fear and danger." The Czech coup, moreover, had demonstrated the effectiveness of Communist subversion when it could be supported with the threat of Soviet military power. Economic aid had started Western Europe on the road to freedom and self-respect; now military aid was necessary. "To do nothing is to sow the seeds of war. The plain facts of history demonstrate that."

Liberals who supported the pact argued that it would reassure the democratic forces of Europe. "Most of our European friends feel safer now," declared Jim Loeb. "This is certainly true of our friends in liberal and labor circles in Europe. And it seems to me that should be the touchstone of judgment for most American liberals." "The treaty is not designed to contain Communism but to promote freedom," asserted the *Reporter*.

For these progressives the North Atlantic Treaty encouraged freedom by extending a sense of security to Western Europe, but few saw the treaty as the primary means of combating Communism. To them military security was not an end in itself, but rather a prop for economic recovery. "Our primary purpose must be to prevent war," commented Reinhold Niebuhr. "Yet we do not contribute to the ultimate objective, except negatively, by ratifying the pact. Therefore, we must not expect too much of it or sacrifice more important strategies to it." Probably a majority of the liberal movement was willing to support the treaty, but only with these qualifications.[9]

A related issue, almost as important as the treaty itself, was the future of Germany. By now, the Western powers were preparing to establish a West German republic, and the logic of the Cold War pointed toward a rearmed, resurgent Reich. Such a possibility was especially frightening because of the policies of the American occupation. Since the end of the war, liberals had protested an apparent U.S. inclination to work with the conservative and reactionary elements of German political life. In early 1949, as West Germany prepared for autonomy, these protests, at times almost hysterical, increased.

Charles La Follette resigned as director of the Military Government of Württemberg-Baden, charging that American military authorities were returning control of German industry to former Nazis and undermining democracy. Max Lerner wrote that the German economy was once more in the hands of the men who had backed Hitler, the financiers and cartelists "whose aim is to help neither America nor Russia but to prepare to run Europe again for Germany." In one column after another, Thomas L. Stokes condemned the generals and Wall Street bankers who shaped German policy and warned that the new Germany probably would be undemocratic and more likely to side with Russia than with the West. Elmer Davis agreed that it was foolish to assume that the Germans would realize it was in their interest to side with the peaceful, democratic nations. Frank Kingdon concisely expressed the widespread progressive belief that the Germans were almost by nature authoritarian and untrustworthy: "Germany needs no revolution to be Nazist. It needs a revolution to go democratic." As was frequently the case, Freda Kirchwey expressed the greatest alarm: "Under cover of a democratic set-up a tight reactionary regime is crystallizing, with the promise of outright fascist developments in the early future." [10]

Some liberals expressed the hope that Germany might be united and neutralized under an agreement which would give security to both East and West—the Chicago *Sun-Times* commented that such an arrangement should be the major objective of U.S.-Soviet negotiations. But most progressives saw little hope for a settlement so ideal. Reluctantly, a majority of liberals accepted the creation of West Germany, continued to urge the encouragement of democracy, and hoped that the new state would make an important contribution to Western European economic recovery. "The present power struggle is too dynamic, Germany too rich a prize for either side, to permit the country to become a second Switzerland," said the St. Louis *Post-Dispatch*. The imperatives of the Cold War had overwhelmed the qualms of the greater portion of the vital center.[11]

The Cold War also dictated and sustained other unhappy situations. In January 1949, the St. Louis *Post-Dispatch*, which in 1947 had supported military aid to Greece, ran a series of articles condemning the brutality and corruption of the Greek right-wing government, and editorially characterized the Greek prime minister as "a political racketeer." Marquis Childs warned that American policy-makers might "find themselves receivers for a bankruptcy that cannot be contained." Such warnings were in vain. The Greek right wing remained in power, the protests of vital center liberals notwithstanding, secured by the enemies it had made rather than by any accomplishments it had wrought.[12]

Powerful conservative congressmen used the Cold War as an excuse to press for closer ties and economic assistance to fascist Spain. The progressives presented a solid front in opposition. Jim Loeb had been drawn into liberal politics by the Spanish Civil War and had worked with relief efforts for exiled Loyalists. Many anti-Communist liberals doubtless perceived the Spanish issue as a test of their devotion to a true vital center.

Truman had no use for Generalissimo Franco, and in mid-1949 bluntly opposed an effort to divert some Marshall Plan funds to him. "We are not on friendly relations with Spain," he told a press conference. In early 1950, however, Secretary Acheson intimated that the United States might be ready to accept Spain as a legitimate member of the international community. Loeb wrote to the secretary that any belief that Franco represented the West's only alternative was "a gross insult to the Spanish people and a misreading of history." The ADA produced and distributed a pamphlet attacking Franco, and in April its national convention adopted a resolution expressing shame for "those American politicians who have lately discovered great virtue in Franco's fascism." In June, Francis Biddle wrote to Truman that a loan to Spain would undermine the cause of democracy and identify the United States with authoritarianism. The president apparently agreed fully, and even after the beginning of the Korean War attempted to avoid an alignment with the Spanish dictatorship.[13]

The North Atlantic Treaty, West Germany, Greece, Spain —all were by-products of the central issue of the Cold War, Soviet-American relations. After the inaugural address, Truman refrained from fiery declarations of anti-Communism; in fact, he made no public statements on foreign policy at all until June. The president's subsequent speeches and messages generally emphasized the constructive aspects of U.S. foreign policy.[14] Yet the administration remained tough and unyielding, and Dean Acheson proved to be unexpectedly rigid.

Privately, Truman still believed that the USSR was bent on expansion. In early February, he told David Lilienthal that only the atomic bomb had prevented the Russians from taking over all of Europe. During the spring, he became optimistic about the possibilities of negotiation, but only because he was convinced that the Soviet empire faced serious internal difficulties. He jotted down some notes in early June on his impressions of the history of U.S.-Soviet diplomacy. At the end of World War II, the United States had had only peaceful, friendly intentions toward Russia. The Soviet Union had responded by taking aggressive actions and breaking every agreement it had made with the West. Peace depended essentially upon American firmness and a strong defense. "There is only one language they understand, force." At an off-the-record press conference in October 1949, the president declared that the only way to "settle" the Cold War would be to hand over most of the non-Communist world to the USSR.[15]

Soviet-American diplomacy reflected Truman's tough attitudes. Early in 1949, Stalin had told an American journalist that the Russians were ready to engage in negotiations on the Berlin blockade and the entire range of East-West difficulties. The first American reaction was to dismiss the unconventional overture as a propaganda move. Liberal reactions exemplified the split between the confirmed anti-Communists and the non-Communists, who still hoped for a way out of the Cold War.

The anti-Communists backed the administration. Elmer Davis characterized Stalin's ploy as an insincere attempt to block the North Atlantic Treaty. The St. Louis *Post-Dispatch* commented that since the Cold War was mainly the product of Soviet policy, Stalin could end it unilaterally. When the Soviet government sponsored mass peace rallies, the New York *Post* called the gatherings part of a Hitler-like effort to create anti-Western hysteria within the USSR, break up the Western alliance, and leave the free world "defenseless and disunited before the Soviet power." By the end of March, even the *New Republic*, which had swung to tough anti-Communist liberalism, was arguing that only a successful liberal democratic policy at home and abroad carried through over a period of years could settle East-West tensions: "There is no longer a 'settlement' to be reached with Russia. Negotiation of every dispute must be pressed; but the cold war is frozen so hard that its thaw has become more a consequence than a precondition of a stable world." [16]

The non-Communist liberals, however, believed that no Soviet initiative should be summarily rejected. Admitting that Stalin had to do more than make a general invitation during a newspaper interview, the Chicago *Sun-Times* nevertheless hoped for genuine negotiations and urged Truman to make a counterproposal. Thomas L. Stokes called upon the president to respond with the "forthrightness and down-to-earth simplicity" which characterized his approach to domestic problems. "The United States cannot afford to put itself in the position of refusing to talk peace, even with a nation whose motives it suspects," wrote Freda Kirchwey. [17]

Such attitudes stemmed neither from trust of the Soviet Union nor a belief that the USSR was still a potential ally.

Most of the non-Communist liberals still clung to the belief that rational men sitting around a conference table could arrive at reasonable compromises which might at least mitigate the Cold War. They felt an almost desperate emotional need for gestures at negotiation, for symbolic affirmations of the U.S. commitment to peace. "All that is required is a *will* to negotiate, a *will* to accept honorable compromise, a *will* to reach a live-and-let-live peace settlement," declared the *Progressive*. "There may not be such a desire in the Kremlin, but, the stakes being what they are, it's worth trying all over again." [18]

In May, Russia and the Western powers reached an agreement to end the Berlin blockade and hold a foreign ministers' meeting. The conference, which assembled in Paris, developed into a month-long wrangle which could claim only the limited success of having caused the resumption of East-West contact. Most of the anti-Communist liberals had expected little more. Others, however, despairingly criticized the spectacle. The Russians, Freda Kirchwey wrote, had engaged in propaganda, but the Western powers had "failed to counter with a constructive plan, offering terms which would persuade the world of their desire for peace." The West, in short, had demonstrated that it was no more sincerely interested in a peace settlement than the Russians; the United States had failed to establish its moral superiority. [19]

The *New Republic* demonstrated the divided impulses of the vital center by backing away from its early hard line and joining in the criticism. Perhaps after all the Russians had been ready for some limited resumption of four-power cooperation in Germany; perhaps there had been a real chance for a degree of East-West cooperation. The administration had shown no interest in any sort of a deal; it was determined to press ahead with the creation of a West German state which would be economically, and possibly militarily integrated into the anti-Communist alliance. The Truman-Acheson approach to diplomacy thus apparently rejected without serious investigation any chance of moderating the Cold War. The journal's editors found such a course morally unacceptable. [20]

Increasingly, non-Communist progressives tended to criticize both sides in the Cold War. At the end of 1949, Freda Kirchwey described Soviet foreign policy as "stupid and ill-conceived" and commented that Moscow had "managed to alienate many persons who in the past have strained their emotions and their credulity to the limit." But she also attacked the Truman administration for presenting the world with "a confused foreign policy, largely anti-democratic in its effect, coupled with an attitude of calculated hostility to Russia in the U.N." The *Progressive*, despite its hostility to Communism, called U.S. policy "provocative" and urged more genuine efforts at disarmament. Glenn Talbot of the Farmers Union condemned the "suicidal march" toward war.[21]

The anti-Communist portion of the vital center, however, was confident that the United States was moving in the right direction. Proceeding from the assumption that the Russians respected only strength and would not engage in rational negotiations, the anti-Communist progressives believed that the chances for peace were greater at the end of 1949 than at the beginning of the year. Yet they also considered the Cold War primarily an ideological conflict, not a military face-down. As they prepared for a long struggle, the anti-Communist liberals more consciously than ever adopted what the St. Louis *Post-Dispatch* called an "informed pessimism" based on the realities of power yet essentially grounded in idealism. Ironically, they frequently criticized George F. Kennan, still popularly considered an exponent of Bismarckian *Machtpolitik*. (Actually, Kennan had privately argued against the North Atlantic Treaty.) In January 1950, the *Post-Dispatch* devoted a long editorial to an attack upon Kennan's apparent views, arguing that American foreign policy had to rest not upon power politics and self-interest but upon the vigorous advocacy of democracy. Reinhold Niebuhr, increasingly visible as the major philosopher of anti-Communist liberalism, asserted that while the West could not ignore military power, its appeal had to be primarily moral, political, and economic, "the total strength of a body plus the psychic vitality of the soul."

Truman and Acheson might be criticized on some specifics, but the anti-Communist liberals could usually support them. The ADA pressed Acheson to speak at any Roosevelt Day dinner of his choice, telling him that his appearance would make the occasion "an overwhelming success." "We stand behind what you have been trying to accomplish and can promise you a rousing reception and continued support," wrote National Director Charles La Follette. At the end of 1949, Reinhold Niebuhr congratulated the State Department for resisting military pressures and forging a realistic and successful European policy. "The chances of avoiding a conflict are brighter than they have been for a long time," he declared.[22]

The liberals remained divided as to whether the administration was pushing Europe toward security or toward disaster. Truman and Acheson had not alienated the vital center, but neither could they claim its united support.

III

Liberals found it easier to arrive at a consensus on developments in the Far East, where political situations were less ambiguous. All agreed that the United States should take the most drastic measures against Dutch efforts to subjugate the Indonesian Republic, even cutting off Marshall Plan aid if necessary. All felt that the United States had seriously erred in establishing the tyrannical Syngman Rhee as ruler of South Korea. Early in 1950, after the administration had applied mild pressure, the Netherlands recognized Indonesian independence. In South Korea, on the other hand, Rhee consolidated his authority.[23] But both South Korea and Indonesia were increasingly overshadowed by the massive problems of China.

By 1949, Chiang Kai-shek's regime was doomed, and the liberals agreed that it was not worth saving. "It has been interested primarily in maintaining a corrupt bureaucracy and a static social and economic system which serves landlords and warlords rather than the people," commented the Chicago Sun-Times. The impending fall of China presented a grim prospect, wrote Samuel Grafton, but perhaps it would provide a lesson for those who wanted to support every anti-Communist leader in the world, no matter how reactionary or authoritarian.

Few progressives expected the new Chinese government to be liberal in the Western sense, but they believed that it would do more than had Chiang for the people. Many hoped that it would not follow an orthodox Marxist-Leninist line and might be disposed to establish friendly political and economic relations if the United States abandoned Chiang, recognized the Communists, and made conciliatory gestures. Here as elsewhere in Asia, they believed, America had to accept, even promote, nationalism and revolution.* The result could be a China independent of Soviet domination in which there was a substantial U.S. moderating influence. Reinhold Niebuhr expressed the attitude of even most anti-Communist liberals:

[A] Communist China is not as immediate a strategic threat as imagined by some. The Communism of Asia is primarily an expression of nationalism of subject peoples and impoverished nations. We still have a chance to espouse their cause and help them to achieve independence and health. . . . It may take a long time to prove that we are better friends of China than Russia is. But if Russia should prove as heavy-handed in dealing with China as she has been with the Eastern European nations it may not take as long as it now seems.[24]

Truman privately agreed with the liberal analysis. Chiang's government, he told David Lilienthal in May 1949, was a group of "grafters and crooks" who had stolen at least a billion dollars in American aid and had no interest in the hungry Chinese masses. The insurgents were not real Communists— "Joe Stalin says that people of North China will never be Com-

---

*A notable exception to the liberal consensus on China was the *New Leader*. David J. Dallin, one of its regular columnists, consistently advocated greater assistance to Chiang, depicted Mao as a puppet of Stalin, and condemned "fellow travelers" such as Owen Lattimore and Edgar Snow for influencing State Department policy in a contrary direction. After Chiang's flight from the mainland, the *New Leader* opposed recognition of the Communists. (See note 24 for documentation.)

munists and he's about right." Truman clearly hoped that the United States could have a working relationship with the new regime. "The dragon is going to turn over," he told Lilienthal, "and after that perhaps some advances can be made. . . ." In August, the administration released a "White Paper" which strongly indicted the Chinese Nationalists and defended the administration's refusal to become more deeply involved in the Chinese conflict. Liberals generally endorsed the document.[25]

Assuming that the White Paper signaled the beginning of disengagement from Chiang the progressives impatiently awaited the next logical step—recognition of the Communists. When recognition did not come, partly because of pressure from right-wing Republicans who had adopted Chiang, partly because of violent Communist demonstrations of anti-Americanism, progressives became impatient with administration caution. The liberals thought essentially in terms of the impact of U.S. policy upon nationalistic and revolutionary Asians, not upon anti-Communist American voters. From such a perspective, the break with Chiang had to be swift and decisive rather than gradual and reluctant. Moreover, Chiang's savage imposition of Nationalist rule upon his island sanctuary of Formosa further discredited him. The administration had not completely disavowed the Nationalists by the end of the year, and General MacArthur was arguing for a U.S. pledge to defend Formosa. The St. Louis *Post-Dispatch* warned that such a commitment would stamp the United States as an imperialist nation. Freda Kirchwey asserted that U.S. China policy was in danger of being composed of "blunder upon blunder," and the *New Republic* criticized the "China muddle." [26]

Truman relieved some fears by announcing on January 5, 1950, that the United States would not defend Formosa; subsequently he refused to spend $75 million which Congress had appropriated for aid to Chiang. "I have still got that $75 million locked up in the drawer of my desk, and it is going to stay there," he told an off-the-record press conference. The president, declared the *New Republic,* had shown "great courage and common-sense." The New York *Post* praised the administration for refusing to be stampeded. On January 12, Dean Acheson summarized American policy in an encouraging speech to the National Press Club. The secretary defined an Asian defense perimeter which excluded Formosa. He argued that the United States must align itself with the forces of progress in Asia and concentrate on economic aid. An elated *New Republic* praised the address as signaling the death of the negative Truman Doctrine and the birth of a hopeful new approach. Nonintervention, insistence upon tolerance, encouragement of dissent, patience, constructive aid—all would create "a Third Force in Asia, of nations not democratic and not dictatorial, not bound to the West, and not satellites of Russia." Eventually the Third Force would be alienated by Soviet imperialism and align itself with a friendly and sympathetic West.[27]

The enunciation of affirmative principles was one thing; putting them into practice was another. The liberal calls for relations with Communist China continued—in April 1950, the ADA convention advocated diplomatic recognition—but the administration refused to move from its attitude of watchful, uneasy waiting. Moreover, the United States began to extend military aid to the French and their puppets in Indochina, who were struggling against the insurgency led by Ho Chi Minh. Few doubted that Ho had close Communist ties and support, but the unrepresentative French-dominated rulers presented an impossible alternative. The *New Republic* commented that France had no popular support in Indochina and was "holding on from old-fashioned imperialistic greed and nothing else."

There was little questioning, however, of the need for an effort to block Communist expansion. "It seems pretty clear that if the Communist movement, both military and political, cannot be stopped at the northern border of Indochina, it cannot be stopped anywhere in Asia," said the *New Republic* in an amazing declaration. The liberals did not strongly oppose American interference; they simply wanted it to be affirmative. The alternative to supporting reaction, wrote Frank Kingdon, was "to create a genuinely democratic force." The United States, said the Chicago *Sun-Times,* had to give Indochina economic as well as military assistance and move against French as well as Communist imperialism. The *New Republic* called for a multifaceted aid program involving the U.N.[28]

The liberal plans for the Far East were constructive, but also naïve and wildly optimistic. The liberals, by and large, were correct in the negative aspects of their analysis, in their condemnations of Syngman Rhee and Chiang Kai-shek, of Dutch and French imperialism. They were less perceptive in their belief that liberal democracy could eventually dominate or exercise a substantial influence within the region. Liberal democracy was essentially a Western concept tied to capitalism and not easily grafted on to Asian nationalism. The dogmatic, xenophobic Leninism of Mao could not conceive of conciliatory Western liberalism. In Indochina, the people's war being conducted by Ho moved inexorably toward its goal, convinced that only military victory could destroy foreign imperialism and create a Vietnamese national identity. The progressive solutions of conciliation and economic aid were more realistic than a blind anti-Communism, but hardly likely to produce the happy results which so many seemed to think possible.

IV

The liberals hoped to build an American appeal to Asia and the rest of the underdeveloped world around the Point Four program. As the *Reporter* observed, Point Four could disprove the Marxian dogma that imperialism was the final outgrowth of capitalism; it could provide a revealing contrast to the Russian subjection of Eastern Europe. If the government did not rapidly implement the program, Communism might well sweep over Asia.[29] Yet Point Four had been a general idea inserted in the inaugural address at the last minute. The process of transforming the concept into a program was more difficult than the progressives had imagined.

They were aware of some possible pitfalls. Thomas Sancton expressed the fear that Point Four might be "taken over at the administrative level and turned into a government-subsidized colonialism by the same reactionary forces that have commandeered American foreign policy and turned it into the cold war." In order to be successful, the *New Republic* believed, the program would have to be administered by an agency directly responsible to the White House, not the unimaginative State Department, and run by "men of great energy and vision, unhampered by the preconceptions of the ordinary engineer or diplomat." [30]

Most liberals felt also that for both practical and idealistic reasons, Point Four should be developed in cooperation with the United Nations. Mordecai Ezekiel, who had joined the Food and Agricultural Organization of the U.N., argued that only the world body could provide the cosmopolitan understanding and diverse technical skills that the enterprise required. But more important to many progressives was the feeling that under the U.N. Point Four would take on greater integrity. A U.N. affiliation, declared the Chicago *Sun-Times,* would indicate a clean break with the old imperialism, a sure divorce from sordid national ambition. [31]

Truman, who had great enthusiasm for Point Four, wanted it to be essentially an American program. It fit perfectly into his aspirations for benevolent world leadership by a powerful United States. It would block Communism but in a constructive way, replacing old systems of colonial exploitation and acting as a stimulus to the American economy. In February 1949, during a conference with David Lilienthal, the president, as Lilienthal expressed it, "talked in as dramatic and 'visionary' a way as Roosevelt ever did":

I have been dreaming of TVAs in the Euphrates Valley to restore that country to the fertility and beauty of ancient times; of a TVA in the Yangtze Valley and the Danube. These things can be done, and don't let anyone tell you different. When they happen, when millions and millions of people are no longer hungry and pushed and harassed, then the causes of wars will be less by that much. [32]

Many of the men around the president were equally enthusiastic. If Point Four were applied properly, J. Donald Kingsley told Clark Clifford, "I think it will be the judgment of history that—while Roosevelt created the New Deal in America—Truman extended it to the world." Clifford, George Elsey, and David Lloyd, the White House group responsible for including Point Four in the inaugural, felt an almost fatherly devotion toward the idea. In June 1949, the president submitted recommendations to Congress, but no legislation materialized. The State Department moved slowly on planning, failed to mobilize outside support, and did not present the concept effectively. Several liberal groups that had established a Point Four Information Service received neither help nor encouragement from the department. As late as July 1950, the administration discovered with dismay that no one had persuaded the labor organizations to work for the program, that labor in fact considered one of its aspects—guarantees for overseas private investment—a handout to big business. "Point IV is never going to reach the expectations that you and I had for it at its inception, so long as initiative for the program remains in the Department of State," Elsey told Clifford in April 1950. "It seems to me that a 'bold new program' is necessary to get our bold new program out of the mud." [33]

Congressional approval and a small appropriation finally came in the summer of 1950 after strenuous effort had overcome determined Republican opposition. Elsey and Clifford tried to persuade Truman to place the program under a special agency or individual directly responsible to the White House. At first the president seemed to agree with them, but in the fall of 1950 he formally established Point Four under State Department jurisdiction. [34]

Point Four as it developed was salutary in purpose but modest in accomplishment. By the end of 1952, it could point to many specific projects in the impoverished nations—technical education, irrigation, disease control, increased agricultural yields. Yet compared with the need, the achievements were miniscule. The program which Truman and the liberals had envisioned, comparable in scope to the Marshall Plan, had hardly gotten off the ground.

The disappointment was nearly inevitable. The idea's drama and the fanfare which accompanied its enunciation generated an optimism which obscured staggering difficulties. The problems of the underdeveloped areas were enormous; yet the United States had to supply economic and military assistance to Western Europe and after mid-1950 had to meet the demands of Korean mobilization. Moreover, it was far more difficult to aid the underdeveloped areas than to extend help to a down-and-out but highly skilled European civilization. Point Four did succeed in giving American foreign policy a constructive and idealistic aspect which most liberals had rightly demanded. By early 1950, however, the bright hope of the "bold new program" had been eclipsed by a grim and terrifying escalation of the Cold War.

V

In the fall of 1949, the White House announced with elaborate calm that the Soviet Union had exploded its first atomic bomb, thus initiating a new and frightful era in the history of the arms race. A few anti-Communist liberals who accepted the Cold War saw only one feasible response—a reversal of Secretary Johnson's defense economy drive. The atomic bomb, wrote Arthur Schlesinger, Jr., at the end of the year, was "both strategically inadequate and morally repugnant." The United States needed to build a varied and flexible defense which would give the nation realistic alternatives to a suicidal nuclear war. Undertaking an effort to bring the ADA behind such a program, he told Jim Loeb: "This is really the most important issue. Next to it such questions as the welfare state are pretty secondary." [35]

Most progressives rejected the Schlesinger viewpoint. Economy drive or not, the U.S. military budget was still the highest in peacetime history. Military expenditures were essentially wasteful, depleted natural resources, and strained the economy. "Defense outlays must be kept within the capacities of a stable peacetime economy so long as peace rather than war is the goal of our foreign policy," commented the Chicago *Sun-Times* in March 1950. Even many progressives who had been conspicuously on the anti-Communist side of the vital center felt that an enlargement of the defense program would be more likely to contribute to the possibility of war than stave it off. The largest segment of American liberalism stressed the urgency of new initiatives toward a settlement with the USSR, no matter how small the chances. The United States had to strive in all sincerity and earnestness to avoid atomic war.[36]

The Soviet A-bomb, however, was but a mild prelude to Truman's announcement on January 31, 1950, that the United States was proceeding with the development of a hydrogen bomb, a superweapon with destructive power far beyond that of the devices which had leveled Hiroshima and Nagasaki, one blast capable of incinerating hundreds of thousands of people. The decision threw many liberals into a state of outrage and despair. "One of the great moral battles of our time has been lost," wrote Max Lerner. To move always toward the ultimate weapon could mean only an ever-escalating arms race, the possible decay of democracy in a garrison atmosphere, and the probability of unimaginable horror. "The men in charge of policy have decided that a third world war is inevitable and that it will be fought in terms of mass slaughter and torture," said Frank Kingdon.[37]

Some of the anti-Communist liberals reacted with less alarm, treating the H-bomb as a regrettable necessity but not a prelude to the apocalypse. "It is I think highly creditable to the common sense, as well as the moral sense, of the American people that there seems to be a practically universal desire not to use it unless we have to," said Elmer Davis. Reinhold Niebuhr quoted a European friend who expressed the fear that the American conscience would renounce the H-bomb and thereby leave Europe helpless before a Russia which would develop one regardless. "Does morality ever require a society to expose itself to the threat of absolute destruction?" asked Arthur Schlesinger, Jr. The New York *Post* expressed confidence that

Truman had ordered construction of the bomb with the prayer that it would never be used.[38]

Yet most of the vital center was at least divided in its attitudes. The *Post,* for example, coupled its expression of confidence in Truman with a warning that his decision required "a dramatic restatement of our quest for international atomic control and reiteration of our readiness to seek agreements," and the St. Louis *Post-Dispatch* agreed. Senator Brien McMahon spectacularly captured the liberal imagination by proposing a crusade for peace in which, after the conclusion of a general disarmament treaty, the United States would contribute $10 billion a year for 5 years to a world development fund.[39]

McMahon's proposal represented the kind of leadership for which the liberals yearned, and even those who questioned its feasibility found themselves caught up in admiration for the impulses behind it. "America would gain for itself moral supremacy in the world, and recapture leadership for peace in the eyes of the world," Hubert Humphrey declared. Other progressives brought forth even larger plans. Jim Patton suggested annual U.S. contributions to world development of $10 billion a year for 15 years, Walter Reuther talked of $13 billion a year for 100 years.[40]

Truman, however, brusquely dismissed the idea of new initiatives and asserted that the United States had already made its offer to the Russians—the old, long-dead Baruch Plan of 1946. Acheson talked ominously of the need for a military buildup, "negotiation from strength," and "total diplomacy." By the spring of 1950, the president had secretly approved, in principle, a drastically increased military program.[41]

For the non-Communist liberals especially, American foreign policy had become depressingly negative. The *Progressive* said that Acheson's "total diplomacy" represented "total sterility," warning the secretary that "The revolutionary ferment of peoples everywhere will not be satisfied with your doctrine of peace through strength." The *Nation* asserted that Acheson was rejecting compromise with the USSR and practicing a "diplomacy of repisal." "Merely hurrying on to a higher level of destructiveness is a policy so despairing as to amount to sheer nihilism," it declared.[42]

The liberals demanded affirmative moral leadership. Thomas L. Stokes wrote that the president "could rally the people of the world for another attempt to get a solution." T.R.B. complained that in announcing the H-bomb Truman "had the ear of mankind if he wanted it, but contented himself with a mimeographed handout." Harold Ickes called upon the president "to undertake the principal task for which he was elected, that of aggressive leadership in the cause of peace," and "to fight like a flaming evangel" to save the world from destruction.[43]

Nothing perhaps was more revealing than the latest shift in the most sensitive barometer of liberal feeling, the *New Republic*. After breaking with Henry Wallace, the journal had become increasingly sympathetic toward the administration, if always detached and somewhat critical. Its response to the H-bomb, however, was a radical and often brilliantly argued editorial agreeing with those who asserted that the nuclear arms race was destroying democracy and leading to war, that America was returning to the rigidity and military-mindedness of the Truman Doctrine. Warning that the United States could not dominate the earth, the editorial declared: "We are not the keeper of the world's conscience; the arbiter of its morals; the helmsman of its course; the judge of its errors. We hold no monopoly of its resources, of its wisdom or of its weapons."

Quoting from no less a source than George F. Kennan's celebrated article, "The Sources of Soviet Conduct," the journal argued that the Communists, unlike the Nazis, felt no irresistible compulsion toward war, would negotiate, would even make strategic retreats if it seemed necessary. The national interest and simple sanity demanded a new effort to deal with the Russians and to do so on a more realistic basis than the Baruch Plan: "Once America gives up her active search for peace, we lose all hope of reaching the peoples of Communist countries; we lose our ties with friendly and allied nations which cannot willingly accept war; most grave of all, we lose the basic moral purpose that forms a nation from this continent of many races and faiths." Throughout the spring, the New Republic persisted in its cry for negotiations. Its shift indicated the growing alarm within the liberal community and demonstrated that most of those within the vital center would support anti-Communism only when it was constructive and conciliatory.[44]

The more convinced anti-Communists among the liberals, however, directed their criticism more at the aggressive and negative tone of administration diplomacy than at its substance. It was especially hard to attack Acheson after he had refused to turn his back on Alger Hiss and had come under vicious attack from the Republican right wing. The New York Post admitted that the secretary was not always inspiring but nevertheless characterized him as "a figure of major dimensions in a time of small men." The Chicago Sun-Times praised him for making the relatively innocuous concession that peaceful coexistence with the Soviet Union might be possible and at the same time expressed agreement with his demand for withdrawal of Russian troops from Eastern Europe. By late April, after a Soviet fighter had shot down an American plane over the Baltic sea, the paper was ready to support a military expansion program. The St. Louis Post-Dispatch rather quickly reverted to its old line that the USSR could easily end the Cold War on its own by abandoning totalitarianism and imperialism; it praised Acheson for his courage and determination. The ADA national convention saw no inconsistency in coupling a plea for new efforts at atomic disarmament with a resolution commending Acheson. By and large, the anti-Communist liberals wanted gestures at negotiation and compromise, but as the shock of the H-bomb wore off, they returned to the assumption that agreement was nearly impossible, that, as Max Ascoli put it, "the world civil war" was an irrepressible conflict in which the United States and democratic liberalism faced an implacable foe.[45]

The administration might have moderated its inflexibility in time. Within the White House, George Elsey and Charlie

Murphy—sensitive not only to the liberals but to general public uneasiness—were advocating the establishment of a special advisory board to explore atomic disarmament proposals.[46] Neither Truman nor Acheson were so dogmatically anti-Communist that they would have rejected Soviet peace feelers which had a ring of sincerity. Both expected the Cold War to continue for a long time, but neither felt an interest in prolonging it. Truman found more appeal in the vision of a benevolent America leading a constructive effort to raise living standards in the underdeveloped world. Given different circumstances than those which prevailed in the last years of his presidency, he might have been able to emphasize this vision and unite the vital center behind him. Instead, the Korean War would unite the liberals in a very different way.

Chapter 17

The Vital Center and the Politics of Anti-Communism

By 1949 the American confrontation with the Soviet Union had provoked steadily mounting public concern with domestic Communism. The Truman administration's loyalty program, far from allaying popular fears, seemed to concede at least a possibility that Red subversion existed within the government. The fall of China, the Soviet A-bomb, and discoveries of Russian espionage created a climate of apprehension in which accusations of disloyalty could flourish. Conservatives quickly perceived that anti-Communism was a powerful political issue; especially after the rise of Senator Joe McCarthy, it served as an effective bludgeon against the Fair Deal and the liberal movement. Conceiving of politics as a rational exercise, neither the Truman administration nor the vital center could devise a strategy against McCarthyism. By mid-1950, the president and the liberals were unsuccessfully fighting an irrational Red scare with little more than a forlorn faith in the ultimate reason and libertarianism of the American public.

I

Since late 1945, the FBI had been investigating Communist subversion. At that time, Elizabeth Bentley and Whittaker Chambers had confessed to having engaged in espionage for the

Soviet Union and had implicated several persons who had held government positions during the Roosevelt administration. A few held strategic offices, but most were obscure and no longer in federal service. The three who drew the greatest attention in later years were, however, still in the government when Truman took office. William Remington in the Commerce Department filled an important foreign trade post. Harry Dexter White in the Treasury Department had been one of Henry Morgenthau's most trusted subordinates and was in line for the directorship of the International Monetary Fund. Alger Hiss in the State Department had traveled to Yalta with President Roosevelt, had organized the San Francisco conference, and possessed a secure place near the top of the department bureaucracy until he left the government in 1947.

The initial investigations of the Bentley-Chambers charges yielded little hard evidence. Truman, after conferring with James Byrnes and Fred Vinson, saw no reason to rescind White's nomination to the International Monetary Fund directorship. (He was confirmed by the Senate in February 1946, held the post for a year, and resigned to go into private business.) The FBI continued its probe, but neither the facts which it discovered nor the assertions of Bentley and Chambers impressed a special federal grand jury in New York.* By the summer of 1948, after hearing months of testimony, it had returned no indictments.[1]

At this point, a Senate subcommittee gave Miss Bentley a public forum, and the House Committee on Un-American Activities began a series of hearings with Chambers as the principal witness. Their disclosures, especially the accusations against Hiss, White, and Remington, created a sensation. White, although critically ill, appeared at his own request before the Un-American Activities Committee to deliver a strong and apparently forthright denial; three days later, he was dead. Rem-

*The statute of limitations would have prohibited the grand jury from issuing espionage indictments. However, there remained the possibility of a perjury indictment or a bill of presentment making public the facts as the grand jury understood them.

ington also issued a convincing rebuttal, and when Miss Bentley repeated her charges in a radio interview, he sued her for libel. Hiss, thus far accused only of Communist Party membership during the 1930s, demanded a confrontation with Chambers, and dared him to repeat his charges outside the protection of Congressional immunity. When Chambers did so, Hiss also instituted a libel suit.

Many of the other people named by Miss Bentley and Chambers, however, resorted to the Fifth Amendment or took refuge in evasion. At least one, Julian Wadleigh, a minor State Department official, confessed to passing information to the Soviets. There clearly was a core of truth to the Chambers-Bentley allegations, but the two turncoat Communists appeared emotionally unstable and quite capable of embroidering their stories. The unequivocal refutations thrown back at them by White, Remington, and Hiss looked genuine to most liberals.

In mid-November, a new development startled the country—Chambers accused Hiss of espionage and produced documents, most of them typed, a few in handwriting, which he claimed to have received from Hiss in 1937 and 1938. The New York Grand Jury indicted Hiss for perjury on December 15, 1948. Other sensations followed. In 1949, the FBI arrested Judith Coplon, a Justice Department clerk who had passed documents to Russian agents. In 1950, the government apprehended the atomic spies Harry Gold, David Greenglass, and Julius and Ethel Rosenberg.

To the average citizen, the pattern of all these accusations, indictments, and arrests must have been puzzling. There were many variables involved: some individuals were accused of adherence to Communism during the era of the Popular Front, others of continuing their Party commitment into the Cold War; some may have been guilty only of bad judgment, others of premeditated malice; some, either the accusers or the accused, had committed massive perjury. The careful observer might well wonder where verifiable fact merged into improvisation and innuendo. A baffled and frighened public knew only that China had gone under, the Russians had an atomic bomb, the Cold War seemed interminable, and people in influential places had been accused of disloyalty.

The problem of Communist espionage had a long history by 1949; so did the use of anti-Communism as a political issue. Political attacks against alleged radicals and subversives, going back at least as far as the Alien and Sedition acts, had found expression in the frenzied fear of anarchism, proletarian violence, and labor unionism which was so prevalent in the late nineteenth century, and had surfaced anew during the post-World War I Red Scare. Since the 1930s many angry conservatives had asserted that the New Deal was in one way or another un-American and tied in with Communism. Charges of pro-Communism against liberal Democrats in the 1946 elections had given extra impetus to the establishment of the ADA.

By 1948 even the more "respectable" or "moderate" Republican leaders were engaging in Red smears. In April, Thomas E. Dewey casually lumped the Communist Party with the CIO, the New York Liberal Party, and the Democrats, calling them all allies in a common cause. In August, after the Bentley-Chambers testimony, it appeared that Communism might become a major factor in the presidential campaign. At a press conference President Truman denounced the investigations as a "red herring" designed to divert attention from the real issues of the campaign. Others in the White House were worried that the Republicans had found a strong appeal which could seriously damage the administration. Truman attempted to deal with the problem in late September with a speech at Oklahoma City defending his own programs for handling Communism and striking out at conservative smear tactics. But the issue hurt the Democrats little in 1948, given the undeniable fact that the Communists were supporting Henry Wallace. Wallace served as a lightning rod, attracting all the accusations of subversion and leaving Truman free to define the quarrel between himself and Dewey as one of reform against reaction. In 1949, neither the administration nor the vital center was as lucky.[2]

Almost all liberals, whether they were strongly anti-Communist or simply considered themselves non-Communist, reacted very much alike to the charges of Communism or pro-Communism, the circus tactics of Congressional investigators, the calls for repressive legislation, and the excesses of Red hunters within the executive branch. With very few exceptions, they adhered strongly to the liberal tradition of individual rights, placed the burden of proof upon the accuser, and demanded fair hearings for anyone charged with disloyalty. They opposed legislation directed against the political activities of the Communist Party, not out of any belief in a Popular Front but out of a faith in the open society. Few saw any real danger of internal subversion, and most feared the Red smears as a menace to American freedom. In addition, they passionately identified themselves with those accused by demagogic right-wing congressmen or turncoat Communists. When Harry Dexter White appeared before J. Parnell Thomas's Un-American Activities Committee to deny the charges of Whittaker Chambers and Elizabeth Bentley, he had nearly unanimous support from the liberal community. When he died most progressives considered him a martyr. William Remington was able to secure the services of Joe Rauh as his attorney and could number among his journalist defenders no less an anti-Communist than James A. Wechsler.[3]

All the liberal feelings found expression in the epic and traumatic case of Alger Hiss. The fact that charges against Hiss had originated in the partisan, sensation-charged atmosphere of the Un-American Activities Committee, the dubious character of the accuser, Hiss's own record of hitherto unquestioned public service within the Roosevelt and Truman administrations— these factors left most liberals confident that he would be vindicated. A few were willing to admit a possibility that Chambers had told the truth—James Wechsler remarked that the despair of the Spanish Civil War and the sellout at Munich had led other sensitive and patriotic men to believe that only the Soviet Union could stem the fascist terror. The *New Leader* was firmly convinced of Hiss's culpability. Most progressives, however, felt outrage at the procedures of Congressional Communist-baiters and had faith in the still-youngish intellectual who was struggling to preserve his reputation. The Chicago *Sun-Times* condemned the methods of the Un-American Activities Committee—the leaks to right-wing newspapers and columnists, the "secret" hearings accompanied by more leaks, the public hearings replete with accusations based on only the shakiest evidence, all overwhelming the victim's protestations of innocence and establishing a public presumption of guilt. Marquis Childs observed skeptically that Chambers had waited ten years before producing his evidence. Eleanor Roosevelt declared: "I am going to believe in Alger Hiss' integrity until he is proved guilty." [4]

Most progressives attempted to be balanced and restrained in their public comments on Hiss's trials for perjury. But their empathy for the defendant, their revulsion at the way right-wingers were twisting the episode into a condemnation of the New Deal tradition, their belief that the accused was entitled to the benefit of reasonable doubt—all inclined them toward Hiss. After the first trial ended with a hung jury in the summer of 1949, the *Progressive* commented that the prosecution had produced impressive circumstantial evidence, but it also noted that Chambers had already confessed to earlier perjury, was a former Stalinist, and "a man curiously lacking in balance, stability, and consistency, to put it cautiously." Elmer Davis, discussing one of the crucial points of the trial, observed: "If my hope of staying out of jail depended on my remembering correctly what I did with a typewriter I owned twelve years ago, I think I'd wind up behind the bars."

Liberals also recoiled from the way that conservatives had used the case to indict the Roosevelt tradition, thereby stirring up emotions which made a calm judicial proceeding nearly impossible. "The ritual of justice cannot be exposed to tests like this one," asserted Max Ascoli and Robert K. Bingham. When Richard Nixon and other conservative congressmen attacked the first trial judge and declared that the 8-to-4 split among the jury amounted to a guilty verdict, the Chicago *Sun-Times* reacted in anger: "This isn't justice. Alger Hiss has a right to a second trial, and one must hope that it will be conducted in a calmer atmosphere." The *New Republic,* while confessing bafflement about the fact of Hiss's guilt or innocence, condemned Nixon and the conservatives for "seeking to discredit the process of justice." Even Richard Rovere, who believed Chambers was probably telling the truth, commented privately that if he were a juror he could not vote for conviction simply on the basis of Chambers's word.[5]

The guilty verdict in the second trial settled the issue for some. Bruce Bliven of the *New Republic* had been convinced by Chambers's testimony; so had Arthur Schlesinger, Jr. James Wechsler asserted that Hiss had been found guilty not simply on Chambers's word but because he had failed to explain the documents Chambers had produced, and charged that the liberals who still defended him betrayed a lingering nostalgia for the Popular Front.[6]

Others, including Robert Bendiner in the *Nation* and Merle Miller in the *New Republic,* admitted that the evidence was impressive but urged compassion for a man who, if actually guilty, had acted essentially from a desire to aid the cause of antifascism, not to subvert the U.S. government. Dean Acheson announced that he would not turn his back on Hiss and won support from liberals as anti-Communist as Thurman Arnold, Paul A. Porter, and Joe Rauh.[7]

A sizable group of liberals simply could not accept the outcome. "There is a difference between the legal verdict of a jury and the moral verdict each of us must render to himself," wrote Max Lerner. "I should feel clearer in my own mind if the machinery for getting at the legal guilt or innocence of Hiss had functioned under circumstances of greater fairness." To Eleanor Roosevelt the case still rested essentially upon Chambers's word, and with rare public bitterness she lashed into his character. The Chicago *Sun-Times* believed that "even if the verdict is sustained there remain important factors that are yet to come out." The St. Louis *Post-Dispatch* still rejected Chambers's story and argued that the evidence he had presented had not even warranted prosecution. Marquis Childs wrote that "there will be a persistent doubt whether Hiss received a fair trial in the present atmosphere when guilty accusers seek to unload their burden of guilt by public accusation." [8]

The evidence against Hiss, while not overwhelming, was stronger than some liberals liked to admit. Nevertheless, they were correct in contending that justice had not been served by the circumstances of his trial, and justice was their fundamental concern, not their personal sympathy with Hiss. The progressives believed deeply in certain principles of fair play, and it was because of these principles that so many of them could not accept the verdict. Unfortunately, these beliefs, which no real liberal could abandon, had become a trap. In the Buchanan investigation, they prevented the scathing indictment of the "special interests" which progressives had emotionally desired. In the Hiss case, they led the liberals into a position of identification with an agent of what the right wing was now calling "the Communist conspiracy."

II

The Hiss controversy represented only one aspect of a frightening venom which had infected American politics and threatened to eradicate traditions of individual liberty. The fear of Communism led to a wide demand for repressive legislation. Karl Mundt and Richard Nixon sponsored a bill to require registration of Communists, and the leaders of Communist-front organizations, bar them from government employment, and fine or imprison anyone conspiring to establish a Communist dictatorship. Opposed to any sort of sedition act as a matter of principle, the liberals also feared the vagueness of the Mundt-Nixon legislation. Harley Kilgore warned that a prejudiced prosecutor or administration might use it to attack organized labor. The *New Republic* observed ominously that many of the Mundt-Nixon advocates were strong supporters of the theory that democratic socialism was actually the first stage of Communism. The ACLU condemned the bill's provisions as "police-state tactics." [9] But Mundt-Nixon represented only a potential danger. The administration opposed it, and not until the spring of 1950 did the proposal threaten to break out of committee. Far more urgent were the problems being created by the Truman administration itself.

For most of 1949, another courtroom drama vied for public attention with the Hiss case. The eleven top leaders of the Communist Party were on trial for violation of the Smith Act of 1940, which outlawed conspiracy to advocate the violent overthrow of the government. A few liberals supported the prosecution. The prominent attorney, Morris Ernst, argued that the Communists were engaged in a secret conspiracy which had to be aborted, that the old "clear and present danger" test was outmoded. "When was there a 'clear and present danger' before the Communist coup in Czechoslovakia?" he asked. But a majority of progressives felt otherwise. The government evidence amounted to little more than proof that the defendants had reestablished the Communist Party of the United States in 1945 and had disseminated Communist propaganda. The trial was a sedition trial based on a questionable sedition statute, no less distasteful because of the totalitarian attitudes of the defendants.

The eventual guilty verdict in October caused serious concern. The *New Republic* admitted that the government had shown the Communist Party to be an unsavory organization from which genuine liberals should rigidly disassociate themselves, but it attacked the proceeding as a "political trial" conducted against a background of hysteria which made true justice impossible. In the *Nation,* Robert Bendiner ridiculed the idea that the Party as such, having lost half its membership in the past fifteen years and being on the verge of expulsion from the trade union movement, could constitute a danger. The Chicago *Sun-Times* compared the Smith Act to the Sedition Act of 1798, and the St. Louis *Post-Dispatch* warned that the verdict, if sustained by higher courts, would act as a virtual amendment to the Constitution severely circumscribing free speech.[10]

The federal loyalty program remained a constant problem

with its capricious suspensions and dismissals, its Kafkaesque atmosphere in which the accused could not even discover the identity of the accuser, and at times not even the charges against him. Some of the program's victims claimed that they were being persecuted for civil rights activities; others for reading left-wing literature or supporting the Communist Party's right to appear on the ballot. One inquiry after another by liberal investigators demonstrated that the program had a built-in right-wing bias, lacked procedural safeguards, and placed the burden of proof on the accused. Deeply symbolic of the excesses which were occurring was the case of William Remington. After he was charged with Communist Party membership and espionage by Elizabeth Bentley, the Commerce Department suspended him without pay and subjected him to a rigorous investigation. Miss Bentley refused to testify at his loyalty hearing; nevertheless, he and his counsel had to make what Wechsler described as an "almost superhuman effort" to secure his apparent vindication.

Some related security agencies and their programs were, if anything, worse. The armed forces established a loyalty apparatus to investigate all the civilian employees of firms with defense contracts and ordered firings without even giving an account of the charges brought against suspects. The immigration service refused to admit into the country an innocent-looking war bride named Ellen Knauff, held her on Ellis Island for more than three years while her attorneys fought in the courts, and leaked only nebulous charges that she was subversive.[11]

Some liberals felt that the loyalty program could be salvaged by reforms to give defendants safeguards against malicious gossip, prejudice, and anonymous informants. However, even some people who had initially felt the program necessary now advocated its termination. "There seems little justification for perpetuating the program in those agencies clearly unrelated to the national security," James Wechsler wrote in disgust, "it is becoming a boondoggle for intelligence agents." The St. Louis *Post-Dispatch* asserted that the program had done more harm than good. In 1949 and again in 1950, the ADA convention adopted resolutions urging the reform of the program and its limitation to sensitive agencies. By mid-1949 many liberals, including the ADA, were pressing for the appointment of a special presidential commission to investigate federal loyalty procedures.[12]

Samuel Grafton had commented at the beginning of 1949, that it might soon take a non-Communist affidavit to qualify for a subway ride. By midyear his prediction almost seemed on the way to fulfillment. In June, the National Education Association declared itself in favor of barring Communist Party members from teaching positions. By September, the Chicago *Sun-Times* was comparing the mounting anti-Communist hysteria to that which had attended the witch-hunts of Puritan Massachusetts, and the ACLU was warning that American civil liberties were facing their greatest danger since the era of A. Mitchell Palmer.[13]

Even the anti-Communist liberals could not escape smears. In April 1949, James Loeb and Roger Baldwin wrote to Attorney General Clark to protest the inclusion of the North American Committee to Aid Spanish Democracy (later the Spanish Refugee Relief Campaign) in the Justice Department's list of subversive groups. Both men had been members of the organization's executive committee and had in fact successfully forced out a pro-Communist clique. Harold Ickes had served as honorary chairman of the successor group. No doubt the issuance of the list was motivated by an effort to safeguard national security, conceded Loeb and Baldwin, but "it is becoming increasingly clear that this method of detection is not only unsuccessful but distinctly dangerous." [14]

By late 1949, the ADA itself was under increasing attack as pro-Communist from such right-wing pundits and politicians as Westbrook Pegler, George Sokolsky, and Karl Mundt. The charges seemed especially dangerous in Philadelphia, where the ADA-affiliated reform Democrats Richardson Dilworth and Joseph Clark were leading a strong drive to oust the Republican city administration. The Republicans charged that an unspecified "governmental report . . . based upon research into the files of the Congressional Record" demonstrated that two-thirds of the ADA leadership belonged to Communist-front organizations. The ADA and the local Democrats survived the accusation and won the election; the smears, however, continued. Perhaps the most remarkable incident came in February 1950, when Senator Homer Capehart of Indiana charged that the ADA was an outgrowth of the old PCA and then inserted into the *Congressional Record* a staff research paper which directly contradicted him! [15]

III

In that same month, anti-Communist demagoguery reached a new peak. Senator Joseph R. McCarthy bare-knuckled his way into the headlines with assertions that the State Department was honeycombed with Communist subversives. At first McCarthy seemed to be just another small-time demagogue, even more amateurish than Capehart. In a matter of days, his list of 205 Communists within the department dwindled to 81, then to 57. He refused to reveal the names to State Department security officials or to the FBI. His few concrete allegations had no supporting evidence, generally were absurd, and at times involved persons who had not even been connected with the State Department.

McCarthy's technique was not new, and he did not seem to be a very good practitioner of it. But he operated on a grander scale than others. No past Red-hunters had had the audacity to claim that there were 205, or 81, or 57 Communists in significant foreign policy posts; nor did they have McCarthy's persistence in dragging out one allegation after another. These factors alone compelled a Senate investigation, headed by Millard Tydings, a conservative Maryland Democrat who usually supported the administration on foreign policy issues. Many frightened and uncertain Americans were willing to believe that there might be some truth to McCarthy's shotgun charges. Many frustrated conservative Republican politicians supported McCarthy in the belief that anti-Communism was the only method that could return them to power. Once it was clear that McCarthy was drawing a public response, even Robert A. Taft moved behind him, and thereby added enormously to McCarthy's credibility and support.[16]

Nevertheless, most liberals believed that once McCarthy's charges were all examined and definitely refuted, he would fall back into obscurity. They believed, in short, that rationality still prevailed in American politics. "Anybody who stops to THINK, anybody who listens to REASON, must realize that the State Department and other agencies of government have already been loyalty-tested to death," commented the Chicago Sun-Times.[17]

Progressives tried to laugh McCarthy off and assumed that his demise was imminent. The St. Louis Post-Dispatch called his charges a "Mutt and Jeff farce." Thomas L. Stokes wrote that the senator's "house of 'Red' cards" was collapsing about his head. The Nation asserted that McCarthy's performance had been so sorry as to discredit the smear technique. By March 30, the New York Post was convinced that "with the ball game nearly over," the score was 9–0 against McCarthy. By the second week in April Max Lerner was commenting that Owen Lattimore's forceful reply to McCarthy's accusations had amounted to an "annihilation" which "swept like a tornado through the cluttered and dreary spaces of McCarthy's universe." A few days later, Willard Shelton felt that McCarthy had been forced on the defensive, and edged toward the past tense in discussing him ("It has been a miserable and repulsive business . . ."). As late as June 6, Max Ascoli asserted that McCarthy was likely to ruin the Republican Party, and even a month after the beginning of the Korean War, Arthur Schlesinger, Jr., wrote that the final report of the Tydings committee had destroyed the Wisconsin demagogue once and for all.[18]

McCarthy remained a significant figure, and some of these comments began to take on the strained quality of Herbert Hoover's assurances that prosperity was just around the corner. Slowly, liberals began to perceive that McCarthy and the forces which sustained him were far stronger and far more sinister than they had realized. The first analogy which came to the minds of many who analyzed McCarthy's technique, was the Big Lie; the first parallel was fascism—and, many added, Communism. Elmer Davis declared that in adopting the Big Lie, McCarthy was using the tactic employed by Hitler and Vishinsky. Freda Kirchwey wrote that the senator had revealed that Americans, as well as "Germans or Russians or Argentines" could be governed by slander and denunciation.[19]

Slowly, the liberals began to realize that McCarthyism— "dementia unlimited," the *Nation* called it—drew on irrational forces. The *New Republic,* which was among the first liberal publications to understand this lesson, commented that McCarthy was "moving in the realm not of politics but of pathology," attempting to initiate "vibrations of hatred and mob violence" among right-wing isolationists. His movement was "impossible to explain by rational argument and hard to deal with in rational ways." The issues in the fall elections required "thoughtful and searching debate," but if the McCarthyites were successful, the political campaigns would be dominated by "subterranean feelings of anxiety, bitterness and unreasoning fear." [20]

The *New Republic* expressed assumptions and apprehensions common among liberals. Politics, they felt, should be essentially a contest of ideas and issues with the people voting in a rational manner to promote the general welfare or at least their own self-interest. Most progressives believed they could cope with such a situation and that it would advance their cause. They feared a political climate dominated by emotion and the systematic distortion of truth; they knew only how to appeal to reason and could have no impact on the followers of unreason. And in the spring of 1950, even as many of them kept telling themselves that McCarthyism would soon cave in, they sensed the politics of irrationalism closing in on them.

By early April, T.R.B. was calling McCarthy the most formidable figure to appear in the Senate since Huey Long. Thomas L. Stokes wrote glumly of the way in which the tone of American politics and diplomacy was changing: "The proof of purity

has now become how many names one can call Russia and how
righteous one can get on that subject." The new approach to
Soviet-American relations which had seemed so necessary after
the H-bomb decision became more unlikely each day. By June,
Michael Straight was expressing the fear that McCarthyism
might be "the first incoherent demand for direct action in
place of the long, patient effort to overcome Communism without war." [21]

Even then, however, it was still possible to hope that the
McCarthy hysteria would ebb as the shock of the spy arrests
wore off and the nation learned to live with a nuclear-armed
Soviet Union and a Communist China. If excessively rational
liberals had underestimated the short-run impact which
McCarthy could make, they were probably correct in believing
that over the long run the people would reject his baseless
slanders—unless, of course, the politics of hysteria were fueled
anew by more crises in the U.S. struggle against Communism.

IV

The administration responded to the Red-hunters of 1949 and
then to McCarthy about as ineffectively as did the liberals.
Truman could produce his long, easily verifiable record of
anti-Communist policies. It was also apparent to anyone who
bothered to investigate that administration loyalty and internal
security activities were dominated by executive police agencies
such as the FBI and the Immigration Service, demonstrated insufficient regard for individual rights, and were extravagantly
suspicious of liberal viewpoints. Such facts, however, counted
for little. Truman found himself caught between the justifiable
liberal criticisms of the loyalty program and the groundless
onslaughts of the hysterical anti-Communist right.

Truman himself respected civil liberties, despite his tendency to dismiss the doubts being raised about the loyalty program. For example, he could have taken the course of prudence
when he saw the initial allegations against Harry Dexter White
and rescinded White's nomination to the International Mone-

tary Fund, but as Cabell Phillips has observed, the president liked to believe a man innocent until proven guilty. In early 1950 after refusing to renounce Alger Hiss, Dean Acheson offered his resignation. Truman rejected it, recalling that shortly after taking office as vice-president in January 1945 he had braved criticism to attend the funeral of "a friendless old man just out of the penitentiary," Tom Pendergast.[22]

One of the president's frequent advisers on libertarian questions was his old associate from the railroad investigation of the 1930s, Max Lowenthal, a disciple of Justice Brandeis and a dedicated believer in the Bill of Rights. In visits with Truman, in letters and memoranda, and in occasional work on special projects for the White House, Lowenthal pressed his conviction that individual liberty mattered above any and all requirements of the state. Truman himself read the manuscript of Lowenthal's book *The Federal Bureau of Investigation,* a broadside attack upon the FBI, with care and approval. "You certainly are doing a wonderful service to the country by writing a book of this sort," he told the author privately.

The regular members of the White House staff were not as outspoken or absolutist, but those involved with internal security—Stephen Spingarn, George Elsey, Clark Clifford, and Charlie Murphy—talked in terms of "balancing" security requirements with individual freedom and shared much of Lowenthal's concern. All agreed that the administration had to fight the Mundt-Nixon bill and other "sedition bills." "Reliance upon hysteria and repression as our weapons against totalitarian movements is self-defeating," commented Spingarn in a private memo to Clifford. Clifford, in a long memo to the president, warned of an "ominous trend" toward the curtailment of free expression and opinion, quoted Samuel Johnson's observation that patriotism was the last refuge of scoundrels, and expressed the fear that American liberty was in more danger than at almost any time in U.S. history.[23]

The presidential advisers also agreed that the loyalty program needed revision. Lowenthal had long argued against the program. Even Spingarn, who had helped devise it, realized by the spring of 1949 that it had serious flaws, and he endorsed the liberal demands for a special commission. By fall, or perhaps sooner, George Elsey was in agreement. The commission idea was kicked around the White House for over a year, but Truman refused to adopt it. Perhaps he felt that the criticisms of the program had been exaggerated, or perhaps he feared the political backfire that could develop from any move to "weaken" an anti-Communist program.[24]

By the spring of 1950, the White House staff was attempting to counter the Justice Department's lack of interest in individual rights. Spingarn and Charlie Murphy, who had succeeded Clark Clifford as Special Counsel, discovered that representatives of the department were still working for the Hobbs bill, which would allow administrative internment of aliens under deportation order, even though Truman had indicated his opposition to the deputy attorney general, Peyton Ford, months before. Murphy and Spingarn urged the president to take action not simply to end department lobbying for the Hobbs measure but also to order the department to institute procedures which would assure a proper balance between security requirements and individual rights. Truman agreed and sent Spingarn to confer with the attorney general, J. Howard McGrath. The conference, it seemed, was a great success. McGrath promised prompt action on all counts, including referral of internal security bills to the department's civil rights division.[25]

Actually, the talk changed little. Soon the Justice Department was advising the administration that the civil rights division fully approved of the alien deportation bill which the White House had found so objectionable. (Remarkably, Spingarn considered this development an indication of "demonstrable progress.") [26] Whatever McGrath's personal feelings, moreover, he was too much the easygoing Irish politician to bring his department into line on this or any other matter. It was actually run by his deputy, Ford, a holdover from the Tom Clark regime and a man of determination and independence. The situation soon became clear.

The St. Louis *Post-Dispatch* had crusaded for months in behalf of Ellen Knauff. In June, 1950, *Post-Dispatch* reporter Edward Harris wrote to his old associate Charley Ross, explained the case, and requested presidential intervention. Ross took the letter to Truman, who in turn ordered Spingarn to investigate. Despite one request after another, Spingarn could not even pry the files on the Knauff affair out of the Justice Department. When he left the White House on October 1, 1950, to become a member of the Federal Trade Commission, he had made no progress whatever.[27] Not until November 1951, when it appeared that Congress might pass a special law allowing Mrs. Knauff into the United States, did the Justice Department give up its stubborn fight.

Although Truman's intervention in the Knauff case proved abortive, his willingness to undertake it indicated a concern with justice and individual rights. Moreover, if the president was slow to acknowledge the flaws in his own loyalty program, he was easily aroused by the activities of Congressional demagogues. In mid-1949, he used press conferences to attack them as headline hunters and to compare the hysteria they were creating to that of the Alien and Sedition acts. (To some, however, his conclusion appeared a bit optimistic: "things straightened out, and the country didn't go to hell, and it isn't going to now.") [28]

The emergence of McCarthy called forth even more scathing denunciation. A few days after the Wisconsin senator made his initial accusations, Truman declared to a press conference that there was "not a word of truth" in them. At the end of March, he told reporters that McCarthy and his supporters were "the greatest asset the Kremlin had," and he characterized the charges against Owen Lattimore as "silly." When Senator Taft indignantly asserted that Truman had libeled McCarthy, the president asked a newsman, "Do you think that is possible?" In early May, after McCarthy had called General Marshall incompetent, Truman told a press conference that McCarthy's charges were not worth commenting on.[29]

The president's strategy during these early months of McCarthyism was clear. By using the press conference as a forum, he could denounce the man and his accusations without having appeared concerned enough to take the initiative. To devote a speech to the senator would magnify his importance; the press conference, on the other hand, allowed Truman to take a few tough jabs at McCarthy while downgrading his significance. (During the May whistle-stop tour, he said nothing about the senator.) Lowenthal and Spingarn meanwhile headed an unpublicized "task force" to provide administration Democrats and the press with instant rebuttals to McCarthy's charges.

Truman, like the liberals, had underestimated McCarthy's impact and staying power. The White House seems to have thought that a few sharp remarks accompanied by the facts would reassure the people and put an end to the senator's publicity splurge. The president and his staff, no less than the liberals, had made the mistake of assuming that McCarthy could be dealt with in a rational manner.[30]

In occasional press conferences and in a major address to the Federal Bar Association, Truman attempted to refute McCarthy by stressing his own efforts to halt the spread of Communism and root disloyalty from the government. He vehemently proclaimed his devotion to civil liberties. "We are not going to turn the United States into a rightwing totalitarian country in order to deal with a leftwing totalitarian threat. . . . We are going to keep the Bill of Rights on the books." Yet he also completely abandoned whatever doubts he might have been forming about the loyalty program; now he was praising its "democratic safeguards" and virtually celebrating its absolute perfection. He probably had no choice. In the atmosphere which had been created, McCarthy would have thrived on any admission that the loyalty procedures needed an overhaul, particularly if the changes were designed to provide more protection for those accused of disloyalty. For the time being, at least, Truman was chained to a loyalty program which was hardly consistent with his praise for the Bill of Rights.[31]

The continuing harassment of William Remington demonstrated the direction in which the administration was being driven. In the spring of 1950, right-wing congressmen again opened fire on Remington, although he had not only been cleared by the Loyalty Review Board but had obtained a substantial out-of-court settlement in his libel suit against Elizabeth Bentley. In June, Secretary of Commerce Charles Sawyer, apparently intimidated by Remington's Congressional enemies, fired him along with another official, Michael Lee, against whom even less substantial charges had been directed. Remington's intention of fighting the dismissal was aborted when a federal grand jury indicted him on the charge that he had perjured himself by denying Communist Party membership during the 1930s.* The *Nation* summarized the spectacle: "the whole concept of Anglo-Saxon law, with its rules of evidence, its protection against double jeopardy, and its statutes of limitations, is being wiped out before our very eyes by stupid and mean-spirited little men." [32]

By mid-1950, McCarthyism was submerging the entirely legitimate criticisms which liberals had once directed against the administration's internal security efforts. The Chicago *Sun-Times* even commended the Loyalty Review Board for its caution, prudence, and resistance to McCarthyite hysteria. It is probably true that most progressives remained concerned with the injustices which had occurred, but the *Sun-Times* editorial reflected a subtle intellectual reorientation. The anti-Communist upsurge of 1949, intensified by the emergence of McCarthy, created a climate in which any defense of the rights of Communists, alleged Communists, or so-called pro-Communists was suspect. Public opinion polls revealed overwhelming sentiment in favor of registering Communists and outlawing the Party. McCarthyism raised the specter of a loyalty program characterized by a mass purge rather than a relatively few injustices. Advocates of civil liberties now felt compelled to assert an aggressive anti-Communism, use anti-Communist rhetoric against even the McCarthyites, and compromise with lesser evils in an effort to stave off the larger ones.[33]

---

*Remington was convicted of perjury, sentenced to a federal penitentiary, and killed there under vague circumstances by another convict.

Liberals, for example, frequently argued that the Mundt-Nixon bill was bad because it actually would assist the Communist Party by allowing it to pose as a defender of civil liberties or by driving it underground and making FBI surveillance more difficult. After McCarthy became prominent, progressives commonly asserted that he was aiding Moscow. Harold Ickes, for example, declared that Stalin should give the senator the "biggest and shiniest medal" in the USSR.[34]

Other indications of the new climate were more serious than these relatively harmless debating tactics. The *New Republic* explained that its opposition to the Communist trials was based largely on its distaste for the Smith Act: "if the government had a good case against the Communists, it should have proceeded under the General Conspiracy Statute, or indicted them for failure to register as agents of a foreign principal." In effect, the most influential and widely read liberal journal had converted a matter of libertarian principle into a legal quibble. Even more ominous was the way in which a number of important progressives, including the prominent educators John L. Childs and Sidney Hook, joined the movement to oust Communist teachers from the classroom, arguing that Party membership in itself constituted proof of intellectual prostitution and commitment to a revolutionary conspiracy.[35]

The ADA, because of its efforts to work effectively in the political arena, had to make its own compromises. For instance, in October 1949, after the Communist leaders were convicted, federal judge Harold R. Medina refused to release them on bond pending the outcome of their appeal. The ADA leadership, prompted by an indignant Joe Rauh, quickly sent a telegram to Attorney General McGrath protesting this denial of a constitutional right. As a matter of principle, the telegram was commendable, even somewhat courageous; as a matter of politics, it was deplorable. Several ADA politicians complained that they had been hurt by the protest. It was hard enough to be a liberal on the clear-cut issues, warned Chester Bowles, telling the ADA leaders that their stand on the bail issue was just making political life more difficult for progressives. The Philadelphia ADA members, already under vicious attack as pro-Communist, admitted privately that the protest to McGrath was right in principle but said that any further declarations might destroy the chances of Richardson Dilworth and Joseph Clark in the November municipal election. As a result, the ADA remained silent even when a federal appeals court vindicated its position by overruling Medina and setting bail for the Communists.

By early 1950, there was even some debate within the ADA over remaining a part of the Emergency Civil Rights Mobilization. One consequence of staying in the mobilization would be association with the NAACP, which was assuredly non-Communist in its national leadership but Communist-dominated in some of its local branches. John J. Gunther, who worked on Congressional relations for the ADA, feared that even such an indirect taint might fatally compromise the organization.[36]

In the real world of politics, hypercaution and backtracking frequently are requisites for survival. The use of anti-Communist rhetoric against right-wing demagogues was natural enough and not particularly important in itself. What was important was the creeping development of a mood which the rhetoric partially reflected. Sensible anti-Communism was a negative principle but nevertheless necessary for a healthy liberlism. However, under the pressure of right-wing anti-Communism, too many progressives were beginning to compromise their affirmative principles. The loyalty program, for all its flaws, might not be so bad after all because McCarthy's techniques were worse. It was all right to bring the Communist Party into court if it could be done by "respectable" means. Party membership automatically branded an individual as a conscious participant in a conspiracy and justified his exclusion not just from jobs related to the national security but from many other opportunities.

The erosion was not yet serious. Few if any liberals were issuing blanket defenses of the loyalty program or the Communist trials; probably only a minority felt that Party membership alone disqualified a person as a teacher. Yet progressivism had bent at least a little. In years past, liberalism had compromised its moral integrity by accepting Communists and the Popular Front; now it was in danger of doing the same thing by conceding too much to the right-wing anti-Communists.

Some historians have felt that the Truman administration—and by implication anti-Communist liberalism—was caught in a trap of its own making by mid-1950. Having undertaken a commitment to the Cold War, having engaged in rhetoric and policies which underscored the Communist menace and brought it to the forefront of American politics and diplomacy, the administration and the anti-Communist liberals had cleared a path for demagogues who would seize the issue of anti-Communism and use it against those who had created it.[37] Such a view is tempting and superficially convincing if one selects his evidence to emphasize anti-Communist excesses and minimize the many doubts both inside and outside the administration about these excesses. Even so, it rests upon a naïve theory of causation, assuming that the Truman administration caused the Cold War and that it could have prevented the McCarthy upsurge by refraining from anti-Communist policies and rhetoric. It seems far more likely that an administration and a liberal movement clinging tenaciously to Popular Frontism would have suffered lethal right-wing assaults long before 1949. The historical situation in which Truman and the liberals found themselves by the middle of 1950 was complex in its nature and origins. Given the frailties of American democracy, which seems able to handle complicated issues of diplomacy in only the most simplistic, moralistic manner and is susceptible to demagoguery, the rise of McCarthyism was at least to some extent an inevitable tragedy. A rare mass leader in whom the people had a mystical faith, such as Roosevelt, might have blunted McCarthy's impact, but Truman was not such a person.

In the spring of 1950, McCarthyism seemed to show some political punch. Both Claude Pepper and Frank Graham lost their Senatorial primaries after campaigns filled with charges of pro-Communism. Yet race was probably a more important factor in these cases. In California, on the other hand, Helen Gahagan Douglas overcame charges of sympathy for the Communists to win the Democratic Senatorial primary. Her victory seemed to demonstrate that outside the South, voters still responded to a clear and aggressive advocacy of the Fair Deal. Truman's own whistle-stop tour in May provided convincing demonstrations of his popularity.

For most liberals then, the situation in June 1950 seemed difficult but not desperate, and McCarthy did not look invincible. Since the hysteria he had generated was largely irrational and based on artificial charges, it was reasonable to assume that the negative report soon to be issued by the Tydings committee might put the Wisconsin senator in great difficulty. In mid-June, the ADA National Board optimistically asserted that liberal candidates who refused to retreat would find the Fair Deal to be a winning issue.[38] Unfortunately, the ADA could not foresee a crisis which would eclipse the Fair Deal and make McCarthyism the most important factor in American politics.

Chapter 18

Korea and the Politics of Semiwar

As far as Truman was concerned, the North Korean attack paralleled the fascist aggressions of the 1930s. The lesson of history was clear: America had to fight, vindicate the principle of collective security, and thereby discourage future totalitarian aggressors.[1] The liberal movement agreed fully.

I

The conspicuously anti-Communist liberals, as one would expect, rallied behind the president's decision. Max Ascoli asserted that perhaps not even FDR had made "a decision so timely, so momentous, and so profoundly right." Walter Reuther told Truman that he had given "renewed hope and strengthened determination to the people of the world." The ADA praised the president for following in the tradition of Roosevelt's "quarantine" speech and scolded the Indian government for its refusal to give instant endorsement to the anti-Communist action.[2]

The support from others who had been less enthusiastic over the Cold War was equally strong. Thomas L. Stokes commended Truman for strengthening the United Nations. Frank Kingdon praised the president's refusal to "take the road to Munich." The *New Republic* warned that it was necessary above all else to uphold the U.N.'s authority. The *Nation* com-

pared the invasion to the aggressions of Hitler and warned that
unless it were stopped, "neither the United States nor the U.N.
will any longer be a barrier to the Communist conquest of
Asia." [3]

Even those who had been close to the pacifist movement
warmly approved of Truman's decision. The National Farmers
Union declared its strong support and began to move toward a
hard-line anti-Communism. (By late 1951, Jim Patton was even
talking of the need to help the Iron Curtain peoples "throw off
the ancient yoke of tyranny.") A. Philip Randolph declared vehemently that atomic warfare, if it came to that, would be preferable to Soviet domination of the world. "Given the naked
reality of Red aggression and the violation of international
agreement and the United Nations charter," wrote Morris
Rubin in the *Progressive,* "the only meaningful reply by the
rest of mankind could be armed resistance." [4]

Henry Wallace's resignation from the Progressive Party dramatically exemplified the massive liberal consensus—"I am on
the side of my country and the United Nations." By August,
Wallace was expressing his willingness to use the atomic bomb
if the battlefield situation necessitated it. By November, he was
advocating a large-scale American rearmament program, bitterly condemning the USSR, and abandoning his earlier support of the admission of Red China to the U.N.[5]

The invasion of South Korea seemed to substantiate the view
of the vital center that Communism and fascism, for all their
intellectual differences, were alike in practice. Liberals seeking
to come to grips with the situation invariably found parallels
in the fascist onslaughts of the 1930s. "This is where we came
in," said Elmer Davis, "say about 1938, when the pattern of totalitarian aggression had become clear." [6]

The decision to aid the South Korean resistance vindicated
the principles of peace and collective security. The sanction of
the U.N. provided a special justification, and even made American military action appear vital to the existence of the world
body. "The fall of South Korea, with the Russians and their
puppets defying the U.N., would deal the international organi-

zation a blow from which it might not recover," wrote Willard Shelton in the *Nation*.[7]

Praise for the decision to fight in Korea did not imply approval of a new departure in the administration's policy toward China. Truman announced that the United States Seventh Fleet would neutralize the Formosa Straits, block offensive action by either the Communists or the Nationalists, and thereby secure the U.N. force in Korea against action from a hostile, Communist-held Formosa. The president insisted that his only objective was to freeze the Chinese conflict and forestall a general Asian war. As liberals saw it, however, Truman's new policy could only lead to American identification with the fortunes of Chiang Kai-shek and thus discredit the U.S.-U.N. cause in Asia. "A Far Eastern defense can be organized without Formosa," protested the St. Louis *Post-Dispatch*. Others who felt that Formosa should remain non-Communist, the *Reporter* and the *New Republic*, among them, called upon the administration to force a free election, which surely would oust Chiang's tyrannical government. Progressives generally accepted Truman's sincerity when he claimed that the United States was not reembracing Chiang, but the very presence of the American fleet between the warring Chinese factions created a dangerous situation. Moreoever, even if the Communists shrank from a confrontation, American right-wingers might be successful in pushing the U.S. into a full-scale war with China.[8]

At the end of July, General Douglas MacArthur flew to Formosa, conferred with Chiang, and indirectly let it be known that he favored much stronger support of the generalissimo. An alarmed administration promptly dispatched Averell Harriman to Tokyo to impress upon MacArthur the need to keep Chiang at arm's length and specifically instructed MacArthur that Chiang was not to undertake any offensive operations. The general privately replied that he fully understood Washington's policy of protecting the Communists. A few days later, MacArthur released to the press without prior clearance a message to be read at the annual encampment of the Veterans of Foreign Wars. The lengthy communication amounted to a plea for a permanent commitment to the defense of Formosa and to the Chinese Nationalists.[9]

Liberals agreed that MacArthur had defied civilian policy-makers and advocated a policy which would alienate America's European allies, anger most Asian nations, and doom any chance of a diplomatic understanding with the Chinese Communists. "It seems clear that MacArthur's insubordination was a well-calculated gesture in an attempt to capture the leadership in American policy," commented the *New Republic,* adding that "Moments of crisis like the present are always those chosen by the military, in any country, to take over." Freda Kirchwey expressed the widespread progressive feeling that the general had undermined much of the American diplomatic position and had engaged in a provocation which might well lead to war with China.[10]

Truman ordered MacArthur to withdraw the VFW letter, but it was too late to prevent the document from being published all over the world. The president went on radio and television to make one of the most effective and eloquent addresses of his career, restating the limited objectives of the Korean conflict and specifically repudiating the idea of a wider war. "A lot of anxious, humble people got a real uplift," commented T.R.B. Eleanor Roosevelt said: "It was wonderful!" "It had the same right message for posterity that Lincoln gave at Gettysburg," declared the Chicago *Sun-Times*.[11]

Truman's speech amounted to a heartening repudiation of MacArthur and also of Secretary of the Navy Matthews, who had spoken ominously of the possibility of a "preventive war." Subsequently an air force general who boasted of America's ability to inflict atomic devastation upon the USSR was suspended. Then in mid-September the president dismissed Secretary of Defense Johnson, who was known to be in basic agreement with MacArthur and constantly at odds with Acheson. Johnson's replacement was the reliable, if unexciting, General Marshall. Thereafter, few liberals could doubt that Truman understood the issues and was determined to pursue a sane, limited course in Asia.[12]

The liberal quest for a geographical limitation to the war

did not preclude sweeping objectives in Korea itself. Progressives felt that Syngman Rhee and his supporters lacked the vision and will to goven their country successfully, that their conservative, ill-conceived policies had led to the weakness of the South Korean state, that they could not possibly muster the support to rule a postwar Korea. The U.N. should not only defeat the North Koreans but also should overthrow the Rhee government and initiate a process which would lead to free elections throughout Korea and the establishment of a democratic, reformist regime.[13]

Seduced by the lure of total victory, many liberals were calling for the destruction of the North Korean government. It was not enough to drive the aggressors back across the thirty-eighth parallel. The war had to extend democracy and liberal reform; it had to enlarge the authority and power of the United Nations. "Korea can be the beginning of a new era under a strengthened UN, in which our leadership can be notable," wrote Thomas L. Stokes in early August.

The successful American landing at Inchon in mid-September apparently placed such hopes within reach. "It is up to us and the U.N. to provide the Koreans with the national unity that they have been craving," declared Max Ascoli. The St. Louis *Post-Dispatch* called for an end to "the fiction of the thirty-eighth parallel" and for occupation of the entire peninsula. Elmer Davis discounted the danger of Chinese intervention and endorsed Syngman Rhee's demand for unconditional surrender. The *New Republic* bluntly observed that "the authority of the U.N. is identified with the unification of Korea and for that reason alone the restoration of the *status quo ante* is no longer a matter for negotiation with the USSR." Even after the initial skirmishes between U.N. forces and Chinese "volunteers" the journal continued to support an advance all the way to the Manchurian frontier. "War with China certainly would be a disaster for the West. Yet war cannot be averted by conceding to illegal aggression." [14]

Some liberals, it is true, had qualms about the dash toward the Yalu. The St. Louis *Post-Dispatch* hoped that Asiatic forces would handle most of the military burden north of the parallel. Conversely, Freda Kirchwey feared that the Chinese might throw themselves into the war if Rhee's troops advanced to the banks of the river and suggested "a general halt some distance south of the border, since the defeat of North Korea obviously does not require the physical conquest of every foot of its soil." But Max Lerner was almost alone in his warnings that the crossing of the parallel would surely lead to trouble with China and that a final settlement of the war would have to include Chinese assent.[15] Most liberals believed that China would accept American assurances of good will and remain passive. They had committed progressivism to a policy of liberation, to be accomplished under the U.N. flag and accompanied by democratic reform.

Near the end of September, the ADA issued a declaration on Asian policy which probably expressed the thinking of most liberals. It advocated the unification of Korea with democratic land reforms and general elections under U.N. supervision, recognition of Red China, upon the condition that the Chinese refrain from military action in Korea and Formosa, and U.N. settlement of the status of Formosa and Indochina. It backed large-scale economic aid, "boldly tied to the most explicit kind of reform programs," for the non-Communist areas of Asia, denounced the remnants of European colonialism, and rejected "a sterile anti-Communism that turns simply into defense of the unwanted and unworkable status quo." [16]

For some two months after the Inchon landing, it was reasonable to hope that the fighting—and with it the pressures for a reactionary policy—could be brought to a speedy conclusion. If the Communist aggression could be thrown back and the aggressors defeated, the outlook for the ADA approach in Asia might be fairly favorable. If the war persisted, it could only nourish the forces of reaction and negativism.

II

"McCarthyism will have a hollow sound when applied to the government that stood up to the Russians," commented the

Nation shortly after the beginning of the war. McCarthy himself seemed to be in trouble after the Democratic majority of the Tydings Committee issued a report effectively demonstrating the baselessness of his charges. Tydings delivered a scathing denunciation, thus writing, T.R.B. believed, "a punctuation point to a chapter of hysteria such as America has rarely known." The *Nation* even urged the Senate to begin expulsion proceedings.[17]

As usual, the liberals had logic, even common sense, on their side, but they failed to realize that the war underscored the existence of a Communist threat to America and thus refueled the irrational hysteria which McCarthy had exploited in the spring. Rather than revealing the strong anti-Communism of the Truman administration, the Korean War created a situation in which the most preposterous charges of Red subversion could gain attention. It had given McCarthyism a new lease on life.

Right-wing Republicans quickly realized the political potential of McCarthy's methods. Senator Andrew Schoeppel of Kansas accused Oscar Chapman of pro-Communism. Senator Styles Bridges of New Hampshire asserted that the National Farmers Union was friendly to the Reds, that it had developed the Brannan Plan, that the Brannan Plan was thus Communistic, and Secretary Brannan was thereby tainted with Communist affiliations. Representative George Dondero of Michigan asserted that Max Lowenthal had displayed sympathy for the Soviet Union throughout his career by attacking banks, railroads, and the FBI.

Schoeppel caved in as soon as Chapman issued a vigorous denial. The Farmers Union was so strong in the Plains states that even right-wing Republicans from the region rushed to repudiate Bridges. Lowenthal easily refuted the allegations made against him, but since he had few friends in Congress and could not influence large numbers of votes, he continued to be a favorite target of the McCarthyites. These were amateurish and relatively unimportant examples of demagoguery, but they seemed to indicate that the Republican Party had adopted

McCarthyism wholeheartedly. The *New Republic* warned its readers that the GOP had undertaken "a systematic drive to smear each member of the Truman Cabinet" before election day.[18]

Within a matter of weeks after the outbreak of fighting in Korea, there was irresistible pressure for the passage of some variant of the Mundt-Nixon bill. Congressmen rushed to attach their own anti-Communist provisions to the measure, and Pat McCarran, as chairman of the Senate Judiciary Committee, altered it to such an extent that his name displaced those of its originators.

Well aware of the situation and unwilling to consider joining the drive for drastic antisubversive legislation, Truman and his advisers on civil liberties searched for a counterstrategy. George Elsey, Charlie Murphy, and Stephen Spingarn continued to urge the appointment of a special commission on internal security. Following the axiom that it was impossible to beat something with nothing, they advised the president to offer mild internal security legislation of his own in the hope that an anti-Communist bill which had some concern for libertarian principles might be sold to the public.[19]

On August 8, Truman sent Congress a special message on internal security. The document was typical of Truman's utterances on the subject. Listing the laws against espionage, sabotage, and subversive activities, it reminded its readers of the Smith Act prosecutions and the federal loyalty program. It lost no opportunity to assert the administration's anti-Communism, and argued that the sedition proposals pending in Congress would only drive Communist conspirators underground and thereby make their control more difficult. Yet the message was filled with libertarian rhetoric: "extreme and arbitrary security measures strike at the very heart of our free society . . . we must be eternally vigilant against those who would undermine freedom in the name of security."

Truman asked for some clarification of existing espionage laws, extension of the statute of limitations for peacetime espio-

nage, greater presidential authority to establish security regulations around defense installations, and registration under the
Foreign Agents Registration Act of "persons who have received
instruction from a foreign government or political party in espionage or subversive tactics." In an effort to head off the
Hobbs bill, he requested registration of aliens under deportation order but specifically condemned the idea of internment
by administrative fiat.[20]

Some liberals questioned Truman's suggestions. The *Nation*
argued with some cogency that the president, for all his good
intention, was advocating "police state measures" akin to those
of the Mundt-Nixon bill in his deportable alien recommendation and his proposal to enlarge the Foreign Agents Registration Act. Most, however, felt, that Truman's objective was simply to guard against espionage and sabotage, not to punish
seditious opinion. The ADA praised the administration's "affirmative and realistic approach" to internal security. The Chicago *Sun-Times* commended the message's defense of "the great
All-American doctrine of free speech, free thought, free press,
and free political action." The *New Republic* approvingly contrasted Truman's moderation with the hysteria prevailing in
Congress.[21]

The McCarran bill, on the other hand, was an administrative monstrosity requiring the Justice Department to register
all members of the Communist Party, designate Communist-
front organizations, require disclosure of their finances, leadership, and membership, and order them to label all their
publicity and printed material as Communist. It barred Communists from employment by the federal government or
by defense plants and excluded from the United States all
aliens who advocated a totalitarian or one-party form of government. Its broad, vague provisions led to the fear that a conservative administration might use it to violate the liberties of
radicals and liberals as well as Communists. "It is a blunder-
buss bill which would entrap the innocent far more often than
the Communists, restrict dissenting opinion, establish intolera-

ble anti-immigration quotas and, in general, make all Americans suspect and fear one another," commented the New York *Post*.[22]

The White House found itself fighting not for the president's proposals but against the McCarran bill. Truman distributed to members of Congress, journalists, and other influential persons copies of an 18-page paper condemning " 'Witch Hunting' and Hysteria in the United States." Stephen Spingarn sent out dozens of letters and memoranda trying to enlist counterintelligence veterans and moderate, uncommitted public figures. Even the liberals in Congress, however, could not resist the immense pressure for the McCarran bill; almost as soon as Truman had sent his message to Congress, they were desperately searching for a "compromise."

In early September, they seized upon an idea which had been developed some two months before by Senator Warren Magnuson of Washington. Magnuson proposed that during periods of national emergency the president should be given the power to order the internment of individuals suspected of subversive activity. The liberal bloc in the Senate, including such stalwarts as Paul Douglas, Hubert Humphrey, Estes Kefauver, Herbert Lehman, and the bill's sponsor, Harley Kilgore, adopted the idea. In a meeting with Truman, they claimed that their bill contained adequate administrative and judicial safeguards, and that it offered the only possible way of beating McCarran.[23]

Some liberals outside of Congress were willing to support the alternative. The *New Leader,* which was strongly critical of the McCarran bill, argued that the substitute proposal "would have satisfied the country's demand for some 'anti-Communist' legislation and would have given us a standby act for use in an emergency." The New York *Post* commented that "in the event of war between America and Russia, the Communist parties throughout the world will serve as disciplined, secret Soviet battalions," so that some sort of legislation was desirable. Elmer Davis observed that a roundup of dangerous characters would almost certainly be necessary if full-scale war came.

Yet as plausble as such assumptions may have been, was it desirable to give legislative legitimacy to even a necessary violation of constitutional liberties? Most progressives thought not, and the White House was equally cool. Spingarn from the first had doubted the constitutionality of the internment idea and had called it a "concentration camp bill." Truman refused to commit himself to it.

However, Congress, looking toward the November elections, was in a panic. As expected, the Senate rejected the Kilgore bill. Then, Scott Lucas, who faced a strong challenge for his Senate seat from the McCarthy Republican Everett McKinley Dirksen, offered the Kilgore substitute as an amendment to the McCarran bill! With only seven liberals dissenting, the Senate approved an omnibus bill which Magnuson, Kilgore, and their allies had only made worse, and the tone of the debate was as bad as its results. So obsessive was the anti-Communism of the speeches that the *New Republic* found it "difficult to tell a liberal from a Mundt." The *Nation* commented that the liberals had given up valuable moral ground and had only made Truman's position more difficult. "These are times that call for a bold defense of principle, not for the kind of politics that trips on its own cleverness." [24]

In public and private, Truman for months had been expressing his opposition to sedition legislation in general and the Mundt-Nixon measure in particular. He was determined to defend the Bill of Rights as he understood it, and there was little doubt about his next move. As Spingarn observed, the president's signature on the bill "would represent an action of moral appeasement on a matter of highest principle." It would make it difficult for the White House to resist new repressive legislation from Congress and would encourage the passage of state and local sedition laws. Moreover, presidential approval, while doing little to mollify the anti-Communist extremists, would alienate the liberals. Principle and expediency thus pointed toward a veto, and the White House went to work on a message in the vain hope that somehow enough votes might be found in the Senate to sustain the president.[25]

On September 22, the president released his veto message. It rested on two bases. The first, meant to appeal to a Congress overwhelmed by anti-Communism, was the argument that the bill would help the Communists rather than hurt them. The second, essentially a statement of principle for the history books, consisted of an eloquent defense of the Bill of Rights. The message argued at length that the legislation would assist Communism by requiring the publication of a list of defense installations, by wasting the time and energy of the FBI and the Justice Department, by antagonizing some friendly governments, by discouraging enemy defectors; it characterized the bill as unrealistic, unworkable, and probably unconstitutional. But it was most eloquent and most memorable in its statement of libertarian principle: "In a free country, we punish men for the crimes they commit, but never for the opinions they have. . . . Let us not, in cowering and foolish fear, throw away the ideals which are the fundamental basis of our free society." [26]

"The President's veto message was magnificent," Joe Rauh told Spingarn. "Harry S. Truman stands up a bigger man than ever before in his life," said the St. Louis *Post-Dispatch*. Glenn Talbot of the Farmers Union said that Truman had written "a new Magna Carta of human and civil rights." The vast majority of liberals agreed.

The feeling in Congress was quite different. Truman had sent a copy of the veto to every legislator with a plea for careful deliberation, but, as Elmer Davis observed, the lawmakers were "in the mood of people in a theater stampeding for the nearest exit after somebody has yelled fire." Only 48 members of the House and just 10 senators voted to sustain the president. Among the important liberal politicians, Truman had been almost alone in his refusal to compromise, but he would have to look to the future for vindication. He and the cause of liberalism·had suffered a serious reversal.[27]

There was one course left—the appointment of a select presidential commission to study the problem of internal security and, the White House hoped, arrived at conclusions which would calm the public and even lead to reforms in the federal loyalty program. The McCarran Act seemed to make such a commission even more necessary than before, and many progressives urged the president to move ahead with it. Truman delayed, perhaps thinking it best to wait until after the Congressional elections. The liberals were left only with the realization that McCarthyism had become the dominant force in American politics.[28]

III

The outbreak of the Korean War instantly revived the fear of inflation. But despite a wave of scare buying and price increases, the administration moved slowly to meet the situation. On July 19, Truman asked Congress to enact a moderate economic program built around credit controls and government aid for the expansion of vital industries. He promised a request for higher taxes as soon as the government could develop a fair revenue program. He warned that if prices continued to rise, he would not hesitate to recommend price controls and rationing, but he did not ask for standby authority to impose such stringent measures.[29]

The president wanted to assure the Soviet Union that America was not preparing for all-out war. Moreover, he feared that a request for price controls would encounter stong opposition in Congress and delay passage of the rest of his economic program. Fundamentally, however, his approach was an outgrowth of Leon Keyserling's expansionary economics. Truman and Keyserling were gambling that the best way to fight inflation and provide for defense production was to enlarge the economy until it could meet total consumer and war demand. Price controls and rationing, they believed, would put the economy in a strait jacket, discourage economic growth, and subject the nation to intolerable social and political strains. Since the war was a small, limited conflict, it might be fit into an expanding economy in which a judicious application of fiscal and monetary policy would contain inflationary pressures.[30]

The liberal reaction demonstrated the small impact that

Keyserling's thinking had upon the progressive community. Most felt that Truman should have asked for at least standby authority to impose controls; yet they also recognized the need for economic expansion. Many sought a compromise solution with formulas involving selective controls and authority to decree a price rollback when the inflationary spiral reached an unacceptable point. Chester Bowles, still the major liberal pundit on inflationary problems, urged immediate selective controls on important basic commodities, a voluntary price-control program, and a stand-by law to go into effect if consumer prices rose more than 5 percent. Bowles and the many progressives who thought like him were willing to give the administration approach a chance, but if it failed they were ready to return to the tight restrictions of World War II. Bowles's standby proposal included rationing, wage controls, and a general price rollback to the level of June 15, 1950. Hubert Humphrey, the ADA, the *New Republic,* and the *Nation* advocated similar programs.[31]

A large number of progressives, in fact, advocated strong controls almost from the beginning. "Every week that passes will see further deterioration of the economic situation," declared the St. Louis *Post-Dispatch.* "The way to stop all this is to stop it." T.R.B. accused Truman of adhering to "the ancient fallacy" that the way to end inflation was to criticize it.[32]

Bernard Baruch provided support for those who wanted a quick imposition of controls. The old economic mobilizer, regarded with awe by many congressmen though not by Truman, urged an immediate freeze and rollback on prices and wages. Congress also felt heavy pressure from the public. Remarkably, the legislative branch gave Truman more power than he had requested. The president vigorously denied that freezes or strong controls were necessary but found himself virtually forced to accept standby authority.[33]

Truman did little to implement his new economic powers. Devoted to tidy administration, he hoped to avoid duplication of the maze of special agencies which had operated during World War II. He preferred to handle the domestic war effort through the regular bureaucracy. Most liberals, on the other hand, hoped for the establishment and staffing of a special agency which could immediately initiate controls and devote full time to their administration the minute they became necessary. An ideal solution seemed to be the elevation of the National Security Resources Board to the status of a central coordinating agency. Progressives had long respected the board's new chairman, Stuart Symington, for his vigor and administrative ability; and in September Truman granted him new powers to channel defense production. In addition, the president established an Economic Stabilization Agency to guide voluntary efforts at price restraint and prepare for the possibility of mandatory controls.[34]

Actually, however, Symington's authority was more limited than it appeared, and the NSRB was ill-staffed. The Economic Stabilization Agency existed almost entirely on paper, and Truman's appointment of the conservative Alan Valentine as its director was an unexpected shock. Arthur Schlesinger, Jr., called Valentine a bitter and unenlightened opponent of the New and Fair Deals. The New York *Post* sarcastically observed that the new ESA chief might be "exactly the man for the job of non-administering non-existent controls." [35]

The new tax program was also a disappointment. Most liberals realized that in order to avoid inflation, taxes would have to bite into the purchasing power of middle- and even low-income families; but they also believed that heavier corporation taxes, especially an excess-profits levy, were necessary to hold down prices and develop a balanced policy. The administration favored a postponement of the excess-profits issue, fearing that it would delay enactment of the entire tax bill. "We are waging a two-class war, in which men are drafted and money deferred," protested the *Progressive*. The *New Republic* scrutinized the legislation as it approached passage in Congress and discovered a dozen important loopholes favoring big business.[36]

As prices continued to creep higher in the fall, progressives called for faster and more decisive action. By the end of September, the *New Republic* was complaining of "galloping inflation" and urging the imposition of selective controls. A few weeks later, it was disturbed that inflation might become "sharp enough to jeopardize our whole business structure." Chester Bowles advocated a price rollback and the imposition of wage controls. In early November, *Nation* columnist Willard Shelton declared that "there should be no delay in imposing at least selective ceilings." During October, even Leon Keyserling began to warn of the possibility of controls, but he still stressed the administration's desire to avoid them. By the beginning of November, however, Alan Valentine's staff consisted of two experts on loan from another agency.[37]

Most liberals grasped the need to expand production, but many assumed that expansion was compatible with strong controls. Few agreed with Truman and Keyserling that even limited controls would act as a drag upon economic growth. The *New Republic,* for example, prodded the administration to conduct a highly planned program of productive expansion along with "at least limited controls over prices, wages and production." While not questioning the administration's ultimate objective of growth, the liberals feared that the Truman-Keyserling approach was self-defeating.[38]

However fumbling the administration may have looked to its liberal critics, it appeared well on the way to success by the end of October. The end of the Korean War seemed to be in sight as U.N. troops raced up the North Korean peninsula. A probable result would be an end to the war-induced inflationary spurt, then an orderly defense buildup within a steadily expanding economy, with inflation restrained by high taxes and credit controls. This was the prospect which Truman and Keyserling almost certainly anticipated. No one, least of all MacArthur's intelligence, foresaw the consequences of the advance to the Yalu River.

IV

"Politics is never a gentlemanly game," wrote Willard Shelton from Washington in mid-August, "but something particularly ugly is happening here this summer." Shelton was referring to the way in which so many Republicans were hurling charges of pro-Communism, even sexual perversion, at the administration. The Korean War had created a climate of anti-Communist hysteria in which McCarthyism could dominate the congressional campaign. In the fall, liberal Democrats, even some moderates and conservatives, faced wild but persistent accusations that they were soft on Communism. The situation, commented Elmer Davis, was "an affront not only to common decency but common sense." [39]

The war hindered the administration in other ways. It removed the Democratic Party's most effective campaigner, Truman himself, from the hustings. The president had proven his continuing appeal with his spring whistle-stop tour, and at some stops he had talked of returning in the fall. Given an extension of the springtime situation, Truman could have provided the Democratic campaign with leadership, given it unity, and helped many of its candidates enormously. But as the leader of a war effort, he was in a position in which excessive partisanship would appear unseemly and little time was available for election politics. Moreover, while the Fair Deal might have been a winning issue in a nation oriented toward domestic concerns and recovering from an economic recession, it had much less appeal in a country obsessed with Communist aggression and experiencing an inflationary war boom.

Throughout the Midwest, and even in Truman's own state, Democratic candidates shied away from the more controversial aspects of the administration program. The Democratic aspirant for the Senate in Indiana asked Oscar Ewing to stay out of the state. In Iowa, Albert Loveland, although he had won the Senatorial primary by advocating the Brannan Plan, avoided the issue. In Illinois, Scott Lucas attempted to appease the Farm Bureau and the AMA. In Missouri, Thomas Hennings's managers privately asked the White House to build Truman's only campaign speech around foreign policy rather than domestic issues. A few days before the election, Stewart Alsop returned from a tour through the region convinced that the country never had been more conservative. [40]

Nevertheless, Truman's political advisers, and probably Truman himself, felt that the Fair Deal issues still had appeal. With the turn of the tide in Korea, it seemed that the administration's foreign policy was secure also. "The Republican position will become more and more difficult to sustain as we approach success," David Lloyd predicted at the end of September. Kenneth Hechler, a Princeton political scientist who had joined the White House staff as a coordinator for political problems, was convinced that the Democrats could deliver a "devastating answer" to the charges that the administration had been "soft on Communism": "A very useful theme might be that we have bumbled, blundered, and slipped downhill to a point where we have the richest economy in history; and there has been so much fumbling with our foreign policy that we have beaten back communist aggression at every point." Two and a half weeks before the election, the Democratic National Committee and many local leaders were so confident of success that their main concern was simply to get out the vote.[41]

Truman's participation consisted only of a press conference comment defending Helen Gahagan Douglas against charges of tolerance toward Communism and one nationally broadcast speech a few days before the voting. The speech, delivered in St. Louis, was pure Truman, reminiscent of the 1948 campaign in its scathing denunciation of the Republicans. "The truth has been pressed to earth in this awful mudslinging campaign," he declared. "But the truth pressed to earth will rise again." The president denounced the GOP as the party of the isolationists who would abandon the struggle against Communism and of the special interests who would impartially wreck the prosperity of agriculture, labor, and business. He attacked the "false issue" of Communists in government and charged that those who employed it had "lost all proportion, all sense of restraint, all sense of patriotic decency." The major themes of the speech, however, were praise of Democratic prosperity and domestic reform and a claim that the Republicans were against both. Essentially, the address reflected a conviction that 1950 was 1948 all over again, that the people would vote basically on the issues of the New Deal and the Fair Deal.[42]

Some of Truman's rhetoric was extravagant and exaggerated, but in general he and his followers had reason on their side. The passage of the McCarran Act, however, had demonstrated the relative insignificance of reason in the political atmosphere of the Korean War. The Democrats dropped 28 seats in the House and 5 in the Senate. The numbers were small by traditional off-year election standards, and Truman pointedly reminded questioners that an incumbent party had rarely lost so few Congressional seats in a nonpresidential year. Hechler and Gus Tyler subjected the results to close scrutiny and all but announced a Democratic victory.[43]

All the same, statistical analysis could not overturn appearances. Hechler and Tyler brought some historical perspective to the results and discovered all sorts of extenuating circumstances, but political analysts can usually find extenuating circumstances, and the nature of the Democratic defeats was more important than their number. Among the Senatorial candidates who went under were Scott Lucas, who as Senate majority leader was a symbol of his party's fortunes; Francis Myers of Pennsylvania, the majority whip; Millard Tydings, McCarthy's antagonist; the liberal Coloradoan John Carroll; the respected Elbert Thomas of Utah; and Helen Gahagan Douglas. Most of the Democratic losses in the House were of dependable Fair Deal liberals such as Andy Biemiller and Chase Woodhouse.

It was true that Lehman had won reelection in New York, that McMahon had triumphed handily in Connecticut, and that Hennings had beaten the reactionary Forrest Donnell in Missouri, but the Republicans had made heavy gains in the Midwest, including a landslide reelection victory for Senator Taft. A close analysis of the Midwestern results, Hechler argued, revealed that the Democrats were still drawing a considerable farm vote and that their losses stemmed from urban defections. Perhaps so, but for all practical purposes, the returns from the corn belt spelled an end to the Brannan strategy of constructing a farm-labor coalition.[44]

Hechler also produced statistics to argue that McCarthyism had not been the controlling factor in the election. But again the statistics, even if accurate, meant little, and appearance was everything. McCarthyism, whether or not it had been decisive, had permeated the campaign, and there were several instances in which it seemed to pay off. In Illinois, the victorious Everett Dirksen had run as an unabashed follower of McCarthy. With the defeat of Tydings in Maryland, the Wisconsin senator had won a personal vendetta against the man who had tried to destroy him. In California, Richard Nixon defeated Helen Douglas by smearing her as pro-Communist. ("Mr. Nixon demonstrated how low a man can sink when his ambitions outrun his scruples," commented Harold Ickes. "Few would care to live with Mr. Nixon's conscience.") Elmer Davis told his radio audience about the Republican Congressional candidate who had privately admitted that McCarthy had proved nothing, and then proceeded to build a winning campaign around charges of Communism in the State Department. "If there is any man who is entitled to regard the election as peculiarly a triumph of his tactics and what may be called his principles, McCarthy is the man," Davis observed. T.R.B., who some four months before had believed that Tydings had put an end to McCarthyism, now called McCarthy "the most dangerous man to appear in public life for many a year." [45]

If the losses of the Democratic Party had been modest, the losses of the liberal movement had been great indeed. The returns from the Midwest had left the liberals without a political strategy. The new Congress would be weighted heavily against the Fair Deal. Worst of all, the elections demonstrated that although the Korean War was apparently near a successful conclusion, McCarthyism was still a potent force. The liberals hardly had time to analyze the election results before it became apparent that the Korean War was not ending in victory. By the end of November with MacArthur's offensive collapsing under the force of a massive Chinese counterattack, the outlook for progressivism was grim indeed.

Chapter 19

The Diplomacy of Stalemate

I

Chinese divisions rolled back MacArthur's "home-for-Christmas" offensive and moved southward with devastating force. As the president declared a national emergency, liberals found themselves forced to revise their hopes for the outcome of the Korean War. Unlike many Americans, they viewed the situation rationally, abandoned euphoric dreams of a total U.N.-reform victory, and began to consider global priorities. All agreed that it would be the greatest folly to carry the war beyond the Korean peninsula; full-scale war with China could only entail a massive commitment of American resources to an endless war on the Asian mainland.* Europe would be defenseless against a Soviet attack, which now seemed a real possibility. "The Soviets and Communist China are trying to make us turn a little war into a big war on the continent where they want

*As was frequently the case, the *New Leader* dissented from what appears to have been an extraordinarily wide liberal consensus on Asia. In its editorials and signed articles, the magazine advocated an aggressive and uncompromising policy toward Asian Communism, including the unification of Korea and the encouragement of Nationalist guerrillas on the Chinese mainland. Committed to the assumption of worldwide Communist unity, *New Leader* writers came to see Asia as a suddenly decisive battleground in the struggle against Stalin. After the dismissal of General MacArthur, the magazine expressed qualified endorsement of MacArthur's views about the importance of Asia and the need for tough tactics against the Communists, though it also supported Truman's decision to oust the general. (See note 1 for documentation.)

that big war fought," warned Frank Kingdon. "If we lose Western Europe we may have lost everything for our generation," declared the New York *Post*. It observed that there was an important difference between retreat and appeasement.[1]

Progressives rejected a total response to the Chinese attack; they also rejected the alternative of a total withdrawal from Korea. Concession of the peninsula to the aggressors would be an intolerable defeat for the West and the U.N. Many liberals still talked of winning the war, but realities compelled a grudging redefinition of the meaning of victory. Within months, progressives who once had hoped for a united, democratic Korea were accepting a stalemated conflict as a moral victory and advocating a truce which would restore the *status quo ante*.[2]

The administration perceived military-diplomatic imperatives in much the same way. By early 1951, Truman and Acheson had decided that a united Korea, if still "the ultimate political aim" of American policy, was impossible for the immediate future. They now sought only a military stalemate at a strategic position slightly north of the thirty-eighth parallel, and they were resigned to a negotiated settlement. For a time, however, it seemed to many liberals that the administration might be unable to adhere to a limited policy. In January, the United States pushed a resolution condemning Red China as an aggressor through the U.N. General Assembly. A few liberals, believing that the U.N. struggle in Korea was a deeply moral cause, supported the resolution; but most saw it as an act which simply made settlement of the war more difficult and bogged down the United States more deeply than ever in Asia. Truman himself evidently felt that it was politically impossible to be frank in stating the war's new limited objectives. Near the end of March, after the U.N. forces had resumed the offensive, he told a press conference only that military considerations would determine the limit of the advance.

With the administration apparently wavering, right-wing advocates of all-out war seemed especially menacing. "The War Party's influence is evident everywhere in Washington," wrote T.R.B. in mid-February. In the *Nation* Howard K. Smith sympathetically reported British fears that General MacArthur was planning full-scale war against China. By the end of March, MacArthur was publicly raising the possibility of attacks against the Chinese mainland.[3]

Truman resolved many fears by relieving MacArthur of his Far Eastern commands on April 10, 1951. The president went on the air to defend his decision: "I believe that we must try to limit the war to Korea for these vital reasons: to make sure that the precious lives of our fighting men are not wasted; to see that the security of our country and the free world is not needlessly jeopardized; and to prevent a third world war." Freda Kirchwey expressed the sentiments of the progressive community when she wrote that Truman had saved the Western alliance from a serious split and had "ended a very present threat of Bonapartism." One prominent liberal after another praised the president for what Max Lerner called "resolution and courage." The St. Louis *Post-Dispatch* declared that Truman's policy might avert World War III and rated his speech as possibly the highest achievement of his presidency.[4]

But if all the liberals could agree with the administration's dismissal of MacArthur, espousal of a limited war, and goal of a negotiated settlement, not all could approve of Truman's implementation of that policy. The progressives were significantly divided among themselves on the question of how to end the war while upholding the authority of the U.N.

Some, including the ADA, the *Reporter,* and usually the *New Republic,* were convinced that the Cold War could not be resolved in the foreseeable future. They advocated definition of priorities, supported a long-term mobilization effort, and affected a tough-minded Realism (although they did not always practice it). "The only way free nations can unite to avert war is to build up their military strength as well as their economic, moral and political strength," declared Arthur Schlesinger, Jr., in the fall of 1951. "In the ADA we know that we are no longer in a utopia. We are living in a jungle and we must do something about it." A few months earlier, the *New Republic* had warned that peace in Korea "could be a disaster for the entire democratic world" if it led the West to abort its mobilization program.[5]

Others, most consistently represented by the *Nation* and the *Progressive,* continued to hope that reason would prevail in international diplomacy. Reacting against the wasteful madness of destruction in Korea—"liberation by death," Freda Kirchwey called it—and against an arms race which absorbed funds needed for constructive international economic development, they assumed that the Communists would at least be receptive to settlements which protected their own interests. At bottom, moreover, they dared to hope that intelligent statesmanship on both sides could effect a complete escape from the morass of the Cold War and initiate a new era of peace.[6]

These two poles of liberal foreign policy thought corresponded roughly to Reinhold Niebuhr's division between the children of darkness and the children of light, and the occasional debates between them reflected a tension which existed within the minds of many liberals who seemed to move from one camp to another. This split, such as it was, did not parallel the controversies of 1945–1948; the "children of light" were not Popular Fronters. Most of the "children of darkness," moreover, found much to criticize in the administration brand of anti-Communist diplomacy.

Almost all liberals feared that Truman and Acheson were conceding too much to their right-wing critics. The needless U.N. condemnation of Red China and the increasingly harsh anti-Communist stance of the State Department in early 1951 drew criticism from liberals as far apart in their approaches to diplomacy as Morris Rubin and Arthur Schlesinger, Jr. Paradoxically, the MacArthur dismissal worsened the situation. The State Department seemed more determined than ever to prove to the public that it stood for hard-line anti-Communism. In Congressional testimony, Acheson expressed unalterable opposition to the admission of Communist China to the U.N. and declared that the United States would never permit the transfer of Formosa to the Reds. His assistant secretary for Far Eastern affairs, Dean Rusk, engaged in a startling eulogy of Chiang Kai-shek's regime and pledged "important aid and assistance" to it. "If MacArthur's disastrous policies are to be followed," commented the *New Republic*, "MacArthur should bear the responsibility as Secretary of State." The administration had scored debating points against its right-wing critics, Marquis Childs conceded, but at the cost of closing the door on a settlement of the Far Eastern conflict.[7]

The liberals could agree on the need to avoid identification with Chiang and to keep the war limited; but they were less certain about the nature of a desirable settlement with the Communists. The *Nation* and the *Progressive* favored a return to the China policy toward which the administration had been moving before the war—total disengagement from Chiang, diplomatic recognition of the Communist government, its admission to the U.N., and, probably, the eventual transfer of Formosa to the mainland regime. They felt that negotiations should strive for more than a shaky truce agreement, that the Korean conflict might provide the occasion for a general Far Eastern settlement.[8]

Yet the *Progressive* also argued that "while we are at war with the Chinese we should not recognize them, concede them any advantage we can deny them, or promise them anything outside of Korea in return for a Korean armistice." This contradictory attitude stemmed from what many liberals considered the moral importance of the war, the way in which it vindicated the United Nations and the principle of collective security against aggression. Owen Lattimore, who assuredly stood for conciliation of China, nevertheless wrote: "We have won a major point in preventing the Chinese from shooting their way into the United Nations." "We have been elected— by history," wrote Thomas L. Stokes, to help the U.N. "carry out its ordained task of keeping the peace and maintaining justice and upholding the law of nations." [9]

This moral dimension made it difficult for progressives to envision a peace settlement which would concede much to the aggressors. The *New Republic* talked in late 1950 of an agreement which would give diplomatic recognition and U.N. mem-

bership to the Red Chinese, but soon began to add qualifications. By the fall of 1951, its editors were convinced that the
Communists did not want a general peace agreement. They advocated simply a truce which would give the U.N. a defensible
line slightly above the thirty-eighth parallel. "There is almost
no common interest politically between China and Russia and
the West. There may be a common military interest in stopping the fighting." [10] The St. Louis *Post-Dispatch* was, if anything, tougher. When William O. Douglas advocated recognition of mainland China, the *Post-Dispatch* replied that it had
become unthinkable to recognize a state whose troops were
"engaged in killing troops of the U.N. in support of armed aggression." In the spring of 1951 the ADA national convention
adopted a foreign policy resolution which repudiated the hope
that "we can lure Peking away from Moscow" and endorsed
limited aid to Chiang.[11]

Even efforts to arrange a simple halt to the stalemated fighting provoked controversy. By early 1952, after both sides had
made compromises, the truce negotiations appeared deadlocked
on the issue of whether Communist prisoners of war should be
repatriated involuntarily. "It is an agonizing problem and involves a moral issue," observed T.R.B. For a time, some progressives who were anxious to end the killing, including the editors of the *Nation* and the St. Louis *Post-Dispatch,* hoped to
take refuge in the fact that the Geneva Convention made no
distinction between voluntary and involuntary repatriation.
The moral principle, however, was too powerful to ignore. The
Nation advanced exceptions to repatriation which would have
protected virtually every Communist prisoner who did not
choose to return, and the *Post-Dispatch* quickly decided that it
was, after all, impossible to compromise on the issue.[12]

By mid-1952, the truce talks were deadlocked, and there was
no foreseeable end. Most progressives, nevertheless, seemed to
agree with the *Post-Dispatch:* "History will say that with all its
costly agony and its inconclusiveness the Korean war was worth
fighting; for in fighting it the United Nations gave clear and

unmistakable warning that military aggression will be resisted." [13]

The challenge of Communism in the Far East, however, required something in addition to the military effort in Korea. It was more important than ever for the United States to seek identification with the revolutionary aspirations of the exploited Asian masses; the best and most convincing way of doing so would be through constructive economic aid. In the spring of 1951, Chester Bowles, soon to be appointed ambassador to India, urged the administration to undertake an Asian economic development program comparable in size and cost to the Marshall Plan. Early in 1952 Brien McMahon, speaking to an ADA gathering, suggested the recruitment of an "army" of young people to work in underdeveloped areas as "missionaries of democracy." That April, a surprisingly large attendance of over 1,200 persons came to Washington for a conference to promote Point Four.

As the liberals saw it, all Asia was on the edge of the abyss of Communism; only economic aid coupled with radical reform could save the non-Communist portions of the continent for democracy. T.R.B. compared the situation of India to that of China in 1945, described the Asian Cold War as "a struggle between the Kremlin and Point Four" with half the world at stake, and warned that "a plough is more important than a machine gun." The devastation of war and the passage of huge military appropriations underscored the necessity of an attempt to raise the living standards of the Asian common man. "We need today more than ever before the moral equivalent of the H-Bomb," declared Walter Reuther.

The results, however, were as disappointing as the expectations were high. Truman might be genuinely enthusiastic about Point Four, and Acheson might at least give it lip service, but it was so unpopular in Congress that the president merged it with his request for military aid. Financially weak, split among several agencies, narrowly conceived, frequently ignored or undermined by conservative ambassadors, Point Four limped along, its good works overshadowed by liberal disappointment at what might have been.[14]

The liberal push for Point Four proceeded from a belief that a democratic revolution built around the assumptions of the vital center represented a feasible policy in Asia. One testing ground was Indochina; yet the situation there only exemplified the way in which the vital center was being undermined by the facts of Asian politics and by the Korean War itself. Inevitably, Korea threw a new perspective upon the Communist-led insurgency in Southeast Asia, and the United States increased its aid to the French and their puppets. Even to most liberals, the Vietminh rebellion seemed a species of Communist aggression which had to be resisted.

Their solution to the Indochina situation was in the best interests of all except the Communists. While being encouraged to beat down the Vietminh, the French also had to be pressed to pledge true independence and form a genuine liberal-democratic government which, nurtured by the U.N. and by Point Four aid, would institute land reform and gain the allegiance of the masses. Such a government could force the Vietminh to come to a settlement or could organize the people against it. This plan, accepted in one variant or another by most liberals, was defective on all counts—the French could not beat the Vietminh; there was no third force of non-Communist democrats with the following to establish a viable government; it was doubtful even that the U.N., with its hands full in Korea, could manage a transition to Indochinese independence.

Some liberals, it is true, knew that the situation was difficult. In the fall of 1951, Robert Shaplen, a correspondent with considerable experience in Southeast Asia, drew a more realistic picture in the *Reporter*: the Vietnamese hated white imperialists, worshiped Ho Chi Minh, and fervently sought independence. In early 1952, Allen Griffin, a former government official who had managed U.S. aid programs in Southeast Asia, told the readers of the *New Republic* much the same story, adding that the French commanders who wanted only to end the war and go home had a greater interest in the people than

the reactionary landowners who ran the government. Yet neither man could face the inevitable. To Shaplen, it was necessary to funnel weapons to the French; like it or not, Indochina
had become part of the global struggle against Communism.
The American hope must be to convince the Vietnamese of
U.S. good will through constructive economic and social programs; it was a desperate hope perhaps, but it might provide a
happy ending. To Griffin, there still was a chance to beat the
Communists if the French could be made to grant independence and install a government with a real interest in the welfare of the masses. Both men—and the liberals in general—
believed that if at all possible Indochina had to be
non-Communist. It was impossible for progressives to support
French imperialism; yet the Red thrust in Korea made it appear equally impossible to acquiesce in a Vietminh triumph
and try to work out an accommodation with Ho. Instead, the
liberals grasped at insubstantial alternatives which were only
an escape from reality.[15]

Many progressives blamed the frustration of their Asian policy on the same elements which had undermined the Fair Deal.
A selfish special interest had to be responsible—in this case,
the China lobby. American foreign policy had been poisoned
by the irrationality of fanatical anti-Communists, neo-isolation-
ists, and demagogic McCarthyites who drew support and encouragement from a well-financed group representing the interests of Chiang Kai-shek and seeking to bend America's Far
Eastern policy toward the return of Chiang to the Chinese
mainland. There was only one way to achieve such a goal. The
China lobby was striving for total war between the United
States and Red China.

The Buchanan Committee had attempted to rout conservative opponents of the Fair Deal by exposing the selfish lobbyists. The liberals now hoped to achieve a sane Far Eastern policy by exposing the China lobby. Progressive-minded members
of the administration and of Congress—Charlie Murphy,
George Elsey, David Lloyd, Averell Harriman, Hubert
Humphrey and Wayne Morse—repeatedly pressed for an in-

quiry. In mid-1951, after efforts to secure a tough Congressional investigation had failed, Truman directed the Treasury and Justice departments to proceed on their own. In the meantime, the *Reporter* magazine devoted months to the preparation of a muckraking exposé.[16]

The investigations demonstrated some improper foreign influence in American politics, but they did little to change the tone of the debate over Asian policy. One reason, no doubt, was the success of McCarthyism in undermining rational foreign policy discussion. McCarthyism aside, however, an indictment of the China lobby was a political dead-end because most Americans could not believe that Chiang, in exile on the tiny island of Formosa, was in a position to run a massive operation which was bending the foreign policy of the United States to his will. Even worse, the investigations discouraged hard looks at other realities of the Far East and thus constituted an intellectual dead-end.

The progressives attempted to apply a basic postulate of Western liberalism to Asian politics—the belief that the democratic center naturally attracted the vast majority and would inevitably prevail unless submerged by desperate social conditions or repressive government. There were only a few dissenters from this belief. Reinhold Niebuhr, who seemed to take a grim delight in exposing unpleasant realities, argued that the democratic-reform groups in the Far East were too weak and divided to serve as a basis of American policy and warned against "the notion that we can create and organize adequate social forces in the vast convulsions of Asia." Albert Z. Carr, whose book *Truman, Stalin, and Peace* was a far more representative liberal view, accused Niebuhr of "tired negativism" and asserted that China could have been saved if the United States had possessed the will to organize the democratic forces there. Even in May 1951, the *New Republic* was writing seriously of the need to encourage the "third force" on the Chinese mainland in the belief that Mao might be ousted from power.[17]

The widespread progressive assumption that a constructive and successful Asian policy was being forestalled largely by the pressures of the China lobby and its right-wing minions was simply another reflection of liberal failure to grasp the nature of oriental culture and politics. As a general prescription, economic aid was sound enough, but the liberals did not understand the political context within which the aid would have to be administered and vastly exaggerated the results to be expected from it. Finally, their obsession with Asian reaction led them to overlook the possibility that Maoist Communism might be as great a barrier to success as Kuomintang nationalism. Attempting to combat the conspiratorial accusations of McCarthyism, the progressives had developed a conspiracy theory of their own. If it never approached the unreality and outright mendacity of McCarthyism, its blind spots prevented the liberals from formulating a truly viable Far Eastern policy.

II

The Korean War drove American policy toward the right in Europe as well as in Asia. "To contain the Red menace, it seems, we are courting undemocratic elements all over the globe," wrote one concerned liberal to Eleanor Roosevelt. "On the whole I agree," Mrs. Roosevelt told Truman as she forwarded the letter to him. "I would not dismiss his apprehensions lightly," admitted the president. He could only argue in a rather half-hearted fashion that the critique engaged in oversimplification and failed to consider "imponderables." [18]

After the Korean attack, the United States moved steadily toward an alliance with Spain. Nothing could have created more liberal indignation than the acceptance into the "free world" of the only surviving ally of the World War II fascist powers. By mid-1950, Generalissimo Franco had powerful support in the United States from much of the Catholic hierarchy, from Southern senators who had been assured that Spain needed dollars to buy American cotton, from military leaders seeking bases on the Iberian peninsula, and from some influential right-wing congressmen led by Senator McCarran, whom Harold Ickes dubbed "Don Pat McCarran, 'brevet grandee' of

Spain." The Korean conflict and the anti-Communist hysteria it engendered gave the same irresistible push to McCarran's efforts to aid Franco that it was giving to his sedition bill. By August 1950, all but the most reliable liberals in Congress had capitulated, and McCarran obtained passage of legislation requiring the extension of a $62,500,000 loan to the Franco regime.

Truman denounced the measure while it was being debated and after its passage declared that he regarded it only as an "authorization" which he was not required to follow. Moreover, he did not attempt to conceal his antipathy for the Spanish government. Acting, ironically, under authority given to the executive by the McCarran Internal Security Act, the administration barred members of the Spanish Falangist party from entry into the United States. In early November 1950, Truman informed reporters with relish that it would be "a long, long time" before he would send an ambassador to Madrid. In February 1952, he caustically remarked at a press conference that he had "never been very fond of Spain."

Yet by the end of 1950, the president had nominated an ambassador and the Export-Import Bank had begun to consider the Spanish request for aid. By mid-1951, Franco had received the full $62,500,000, and arrangements were under way for the establishment of American military bases. Few liberals blamed Truman personally, though they were reluctant to forgive the State Department. Nevertheless, the new entente with Franco was among the most demoralizing developments of postwar American foreign policy; indeed, many believed that only American assistance had saved the Spanish government from collapse. "We have exposed ourselves to the wrath of the Spanish people," declared Max Ascoli in August 1950. In mid-1951, Francis Biddle expressed the opinion of the ADA: "By identifying ourselves with Franco, we gain little and lose a great deal —our self-respect and the respect of democrats overseas." [19]

If assistance to Spain was humiliating, the prospect of German rearmament was terrifying. A remilitarized Germany, as American policy-makers saw it, was essential to the mobiliza-

tion of Europe, especially with French divisions tied down in
Indochina. A few liberals agreed. Was it more important, asked
Arthur Schlesinger, Jr., to stamp on the grave of a dead totalitarianism than to resist the real menace of Soviet Communism?
But most progressives were not convinced that the Germans
had renounced totalitarianism. "Armed or unarmed, they are
dangerous," commented Max Lerner, "only they are more dangerous when armed." Even the *Reporter* pictured West Germany as a nation moving toward rightist militarism and neo-
Nazism.

All the liberal fears seemed to be confirmed when the
occupation authorities, attempting to capture German public
opinion, cut the prison sentences of many war criminals. "The
bid for German support has become a futile competition for
the affection of Germany's most depraved and unreconstructed
elements," declared the New York *Post*. "It can only be hoped
that this process of appeasement will be stopped before we have
to apologize to the Germans for winning the war," said Elmer
Davis. "It will not be long," observed the *Nation*, "before mass
murder ranks with overtime parking as a minor misdemeanor."

A renascent, rearmed German state with fascist tendencies
and great industrial power, the liberals feared, would surely be
able to evade any restrictions placed upon its military forces.
As the dominant power of Western Europe, it might well
achieve a degree of independence and bargain with the East as
well as the West. The only way to avoid such a prospect was to
achieve a settlement of the Cold War in Europe. "Surely this is
the moment to 'try again,' " wrote Freda Kirchwey. "One honest effort should be made to come to an agreement on Germany
before its armed force is restored, before it is again equipped to
call the turn in Europe." The specter of Germany gave special
urgency to the quest for peace with the Soviet Union.[20]

The Korean conflict had hardened attitudes toward Russia,
but few liberals had renounced negotiation with the Communists. For those who were resigned to a long period of tension
between the U.S. and the Soviet Union, negotiation was part of
the game of diplomacy. Talks could serve as a substitute for

total war, perhaps even achieve limited understandings. In the wake of the initial Chinese victory in Korea, Max Ascoli advocated bargaining with Russia in an attempt to define a " 'No Trespassing' line" which both sides could observe. Whatever the possibility of agreement, moreover, the right diplomatic gestures could give the cause of the West moral vindication, unite Americans, and appeal to the skeptical and uncommitted portions of the world.[21]

For those whose commitment to the Cold War had been reluctant and provisional, negotiation embodied the hope of escape from a grim and intolerable future. To this group, whose attitudes were especially expressed in the *Nation* and the *Progressive,* the international situation was irrational. Rational men had to work for an agreement which would free the world from the peril of atomic war and release its energies for more vital matters; the task of diplomacy was to create a climate in which reason might prevail. Morris Rubin expressed this view when he argued that the U.S. and the USSR were suffering from a mutual paranoia which had to be cured "through patient discussion, mediation, negotiation, conciliation, [and] honorable compromise." Diplomacy became psychiatry attempting to restore balance to two demented and extremely dangerous patients.[22]

The administration agreed with neither Ascoli nor Rubin. Truman and Acheson felt a need to protect themselves against right-wing criticism. Moreover, they faced what they considered the urgent necessity of organizing a credible Western defense force. Until the West could deal from a position of strength, they believed, negotiation could only be a Soviet delaying tactic designed to perpetuate the weakness of NATO. East-West conferences which met in the glare of publicity to engage in vague discussions of peace settlements could only injure the interests of the West. The political and diplomatic objectives of the administration required a hard-line anti-Communism which would underscore the need for Western rearmament and rebut the criticism of the McCarthyites.

Among the progressives who demanded a more hopeful and constructive policy, none was more influential than Brien

McMahon. The Connecticut senator's motives and arguments typified those of many liberals; the eventual fate of his proposals exemplified the progressive frustration over Truman's diplomacy. Throughout the summer and fall of 1950, McMahon pressed for administration adoption of his plan for an effort at arms reduction, with the savings to be channeled into a world economic development fund. He probably was primarily concerned with the need to engage in gestures which would appeal to the uncommitted world, but like so many liberals he seems to have entertained a sneaking hope that a vigorous peace effort might lead to a measure of accommodation with the USSR and perhaps even to the settlement of the Korean War.

McMahon enlisted the support of Stephen Spingarn, Charlie Murphy, George Elsey, and Clark Clifford. Clifford, who still saw Truman frequently, handled special assignments, and wielded great influence, went to the White House in September and persuaded the president to build an important speech to the U.N. General Assembly around the McMahon program. However, the State and Defense departments immediately began to raise objections and qualifications. As a result, the address contained only a perfunctory plea for disarmament, and the administration did not follow through with concrete proposals.[23]

McMahon then moved in a different direction. Working with his Connecticut colleague, Representative Abraham Ribicoff, he secured passage in mid-1951 of a Congressional resolution expressing the American desire for peace and friendship with all the peoples of the world, including those of the USSR. Truman dutifully transmitted the resolution to the president of the Soviet Presidium, N. M. Shvernik, but attached a message which snidely dared the Soviet leadership to release the resolution to the Russian people. After a delay of a month, the government of the USSR authorized the printing and broadcasting of the McMahon-Ribicoff resolution, and the Presidium adopted an expression of good will toward America. Shvernik sent the Soviet document to Truman with a letter calling for atomic disarmament and a five-power conference (including Communist China) to discuss East-West differences.

Shvernik's response convinced few liberals that Russia had opted for an end to the Cold War. "We are forced to the reluctant conclusion that the Russian peace maneuver is not genuine," commented the *New Republic,* which once again seemed most finely tuned to the balance of progressive opinion. But liberals hoped also for a positive response and a continuing dialogue. Instead, Truman ridiculed the Presidium document and the Shvernik letter, telling the Congress: "These documents give no assurance that there will be any changes in the hostile and expansionist policies of the Soviet Union." Acheson issued a tough brush-off of his own, which the *Progressive* characterized as "the deadening legalisms of a stuffed-shirt lawyer." [24]

In subsequent months, as McMahon pressed for a White House reply to Shvernik or for some other dramatic gesture, the liberals became increasingly worried. In early October, the Russians underscored the dangers of war by exploding a second atomic bomb. "We are, all over the world, working up to a crazy state of mind which will find us tossing atom bombs . . . unless we hurry, hurry, hurry to do something about international control," wrote Thomas L. Stokes. In November, Truman announced a "new" disarmament initiative which, if successful, could underwrite a world development fund. But the American plan, personally presented by Acheson to the U.N. General Assembly in Paris, was modeled on the old Baruch formula and hardly a realistic basis for negotiation.

Some liberal cold warriors accepted the proposal as the propaganda device it was and hailed it as an effective blow. It would force the Kremlin to put up or shut up, declared ADA Executive Secretary Reginald Zalles as he called for a massive effort to communicate the plan to the people of the USSR. To most progressives, however, the propaganda intent was too transparent to deserve respect. The *New Republic* described the administration effort as a "sham battle for peace." Even the St. Louis *Post-Dispatch* felt compelled to call for a real peace effort.[25]

The Russians contemptuously rejected the American plan and put forth their own unacceptable suggestions. By the end of the year, serious negotiation was farther away than ever, and the rhetoric of Soviet-American relations had degenerated to new depths. Impartially condemning both Acheson and Soviet Foreign Minister Vishinsky, Harold Ickes coined the word "achinsky," which he defined as "discordance in managing negotiations between nations; hence, shouting down opposition in any negotiations; lack of artfulness in diplomacy." Throughout 1951, Truman himself employed increasingly tougher language. On July 4, he attacked "the constant efforts of the Soviet rulers to dominate the world by lies and threats and subversion." In March 1952, he declared: "The rulers of the Kremlin are trying to make the whole world knuckle under to the godless, totalitarian creed of communism." [26]

In such a climate, even liberals committed to a long struggle with the Communists felt a desperate psychological need for a real attempt to break through the diplomatic impasse. "It is essential to take refuge from despair in a world of *as if*," admitted the *New Republic*. The St. Louis *Post-Dispatch* praised the appointment of George Kennan as ambassador to the Soviet Union because: "Mr. Kennan believes in negotiation. He also believes that limited objectives are worth achieving."

Those who had never been comfortable with the Cold War felt an even greater urgency. Morris Rubin called upon Truman to request a summit meeting of the Big Four chiefs of state, to remain in session until actual agreements were achieved on universal disarmament and world development. "This is the last chance for sane men to check their guns at the door and sit down to seek . . . tolerance and understanding and good will." [27]

The prospect of German rearmament added more impetus to the liberal push for negotiations. In March 1952, the Russians appealed to progressive hopes by proposing talks aiming toward the unification and neutralization of Germany. In principle at any rate, the Soviet proposal was an appealing alternative to a militant West German republic. It was possible that the Russians were engaging in a strategy of delay, but most liberals felt that the West had to begin discussions with the USSR. Freda Kirchwey, as usual, went farther than a majority, but she expressed the deep fears of a growing number:

The real Western objection to the Moscow offers is not that they are phony but that they are almost certainly sincere—that Russia, in order to demolish the grand strategy of the Atlantic alliance, is actually ready to permit the reunion of Germany under a freely elected central authority. And this is something that the West will not tolerate for it would mean shifting the whole emphasis of Atlantic policy from military containment to diplomatic negotiation. For such a change, the American leaders of the Western coalition are not ready.[28]

The administration refused to budge from its timetable. On May 26, 1952, the NATO foreign ministers signed a "contractual agreement" with West Germany, integrating the republic into the Western alliance. To Acheson and doubtless also to Truman, the ceremony marked a triumph for Western diplomacy.[29] The liberal community could not share their enthusiasm.

Yet neither could the liberals mount a frontal attack against the administration's policies. Most agreed with its basic goals and major techniques. They accepted the need to contain Communism. They also wanted to limit the war in Asia. For the most part, they concurred with the policy of European rearmament. They were aware that public exasperation over the seemingly endless war in Korea and the onslaughts of a venomous right-wing opposition had created an enormously difficult situation for an administration trying to practice responsible diplomacy. Those who criticized Acheson generally felt compelled to begin with an apology for finding fault with the man who had been so shamelessly vilified by McCarthy.[30]

Liberal disenchantment with the foreign policy of Truman and Acheson did not reflect fundamental disagreement. In part, the matter was one of detail. But it had deeper roots also —in the unpleasant ramifications of the Cold War and the failure of some liberal foreign-policy formulas. In addition, it stemmed from the inability of the president and his secretary of state to provide a vision and an aura of hope which would have made their diplomacy not simply tolerable but inspiring.

Chapter 20

Political Pitfalls: The Political Economy of Mobilization

The Chinese victories in Korea created a national emergency, making the conduct of the war and the mobilization of the free world the first imperatives preempting the attention of the president and Congress. The early war against the North Koreans had already damaged the progressive cause severely. The new war against the Chinese demolished any faint hopes of liberal accomplishment which might have survived the Congressional elections. The Fair Deal might continue to exist, but it was now more an inspirational banner than a real political program.

I

This situation became evident as the new Congress convened. The House promptly repealed the 21-day rule, thereby reestablishing the near-absolute power of the conservative Rules Committee, and Senate Democrats selected as their new leader Ernest McFarland of Arizona, an amiable mediocrity and a tool of the Southern bloc. In comments which exemplified liberal disappointment, Elmer Davis called the House action an indication that the Eighty-second Congress was aiming to pattern itself after the Eightieth; Marquis Childs commented that the choice of McFarland underscored the need for some sort of guide which would enable observers to distinguish Senate Democrats from Republicans.[1]

The White House did nothing to block the conservative resurgence. Truman, for all his brave talk about the smallness of the Democratic Congressional losses, had read the election results. With Senator Vandenberg near death and resistance to administration diplomacy growing among the Republicans, Truman faced the collapse of the internationalist coalition which had supported his foreign initiatives. He had to choose between an almost certainly foredoomed attempt to build a Fair Deal majority in Congress and an effort, for which the odds were good, to salvage the internationalist coalition. Given the grim situation in Korea, the president opted for the second course. His primary line of action was to make peace with the Southern Democrats and unite his party behind the war. He even secretly asked Richard Russell of Georgia, the kingpin of the Southern conservatives, to assume the majority leadership. Russell, content with the substance of power, declined and gave the nod to McFarland.

Truman's State of the Union message reflected the reordering of priorities. Almost entirely devoted to foreign policy and defense mobilization, it mentioned the Fair Deal social welfare programs only as an afterthought. Subsequently, the president told a press conference that he supported the Fair Deal as strongly as ever but with the proviso that "first things come first, and our defense programs must have top priority." Many of the liberal Democrats in Congress seem to have agreed with Truman's basic approach, although they were disappointed by the lack of White House support for an effort to elect Joseph O'Mahoney as Senate majority leader. Even Hubert Humphrey and Paul Douglas admitted that the Fair Deal was a dead issue and endorsed cuts in domestic spending. Progressives outside of Congress tended to be more critical of the president's new tack. Willard Shelton argued in the *Nation* that, given the atmosphere of crisis, a majority of congressmen would support responsible internationalism and that the president could continue to fight for his domestic reforms. Writing in the *Reporter,* Douglass Cater complained that Truman was rejecting his staunchest supporters for the sake of an alliance with old opponents.[2]

The firing of MacArthur made Democratic unity more vital than ever and increased Truman's dependence upon the Southerners. In the weeks of investigation and accusation which followed MacArthur's return to America, Richard Russell and Robert Kerr emerged as two of the White House's strongest defenders. Playing the role of parliamentarian-statesman to the hilt, Russell chaired the Senate committee which investigated the MacArthur incident and saw to it that the administration had the opportunity to deliver a thorough rebuttal to the general. Kerr lashed out at MacArthur with a vehemence and effectiveness which no other Democrat could match.

Kerr's reward was especially sweet. In July 1951, the Federal Power Commission renounced the authority to regulate "independent" (non-pipeline-owning) natural gas producers. The FPC ruling amounted to an administrative enactment of the Kerr gas bill, which Truman had vetoed the year before, and the president's old crony Mon Wallgren cast the decisive vote.* Truman refused to admit that the new FPC direction had any relation to the Kerr veto and told reporters he assumed the commission had simply decided a case on its merits. The St. Louis *Post-Dispatch* demurred, warning that if the administration did not take steps to reverse the FPC decision "the consumers will know they were sold down a pipeline." [3]

All the same, Truman had not abandoned the Fair Deal ir-

---

*The state of Wisconsin promptly appealed the FPC edict through the federal courts, and in 1954 the Supreme Court restored to the agency the regulatory power which it had attempted to foreswear! Efforts to secure enactment of a new version of the Kerr bill during the Eisenhower era ran afoul of lobbying efforts so crude as to bring forth a veto from a president who had declared his sympathy with the legislation. Rowland Evans and Robert Novak, *Lyndon B. Johnson* (New York, 1966), pp. 153–54; Dwight D. Eisenhower, *Mandate for Change* (Signet ed.; New York, 1965), pp. 655–59. Emmette S. Redford and Charles B. Hagan, *American Government and the Economy* (New York, 1965), pp. 486–92, summarizes the controversy.

revocably. In May 1951, he met privately with a group of ADA leaders and was, Francis Biddle reported, "in a fighting liberal mood" as he urged his visitors to work for "the continuation of liberal government in America." His words and the meeting itself were off the record; nevertheless, they indicated the direction of his impulses. Speaking to a Democratic political gathering in September, the president came out with a militant, if general, affirmation of the Fair Deal. Truman had no illusions about overcoming Congressional opposition; he knew 1951 would have to be a year of postponement. However, he felt a strong personal identification with his reform program and was convinced that the Democratic candidate in 1952 would need to run on it. Even as he lowered the banner, he was planning to raise it again as soon as the time was right.[4]

The long-dormant health insurance program was put on the shelf temporarily in December 1951, when the president appointed a select commission to survey the medical needs of the nation. The group was about equally divided between noted physicians who were identified with neither the administration program nor its opponents and prominent liberals who were certain to back the Truman plan. At first the president had expected the commission to issue periodic interim reports during 1952 and thereby highlight the health problems of the nation; he had hoped that its final report would be released in time for the 1952 campaign. The commission, however, decided against both aspects of this strategy; it would reserve its final and only report until after the 1952 election. Truman acquiesced with the understanding that the administration was not committed to remain silent.[5]

The president even more noticeably soft-pedaled labor's demand for Taft-Hartley repeal. The 1951 State of the Union message avoided the term "Taft-Hartley" and simply asked for "improvement of our labor laws to help provide stable labor-management relations and to make sure that we have steady production in this emergency." Subsequently, the president spoke more directly in favor of revision of Taft-Hartley, but in the spring of 1952, he was ready to put the issue on ice by asking Congress to appoint a special bipartisan commission to study the law. The steel dispute of 1952 submerged the plan and made Congressional action so unlikely that the administration never submitted the request.[6]

The war also cut into the Fair Deal housing programs. Congressional conservatives saw the Korean emergency as an excuse to destroy public housing entirely. Truman was able to save a small public housing schedule only by arguing that the housing was needed for defense workers. By establishing the war effort as a new rationale, the administration was able to preserve the program, but only at the expense of diverting it from its original social reform purpose. Any hope of decent housing for slum dwellers was postponed for the duration of the conflict.[7]

The demand for civil rights proved less tractable. The war led to spectacular advances in the integration of the army, first in Korea, then in the United States and Europe. In addition, Truman made it clear that he was not about to reverse his civil rights record. In November 1951, he vetoed a bill to require segregation in federally constructed or operated schools located in the South. The veto did not amount to an unqualified endorsement of school integration, and its wording was mild. Nevertheless, it was a firm statement that the administration intended to preserve its identification with the civil rights movement: "We should not impair our moral position by enacting a law that requires a discrimination based on race. Step by step we are discarding old discriminations; we must not adopt new ones." [8]

Most liberals, however, expected more. World War II had provided a precedent for a federal attack against employment discrimination; black leaders demanded the creation by executive order of a new wartime FEPC. On June 25, 1951, the first anniversary of the North Korean attack and the tenth anniversary of Franklin D. Roosevelt's executive order establishing the old FEPC, civil rights advocates held meetings across the country, including a commemorative ceremony at FDR's grave presided over by Eleanor Roosevelt.

In February, the administration had issued an order requiring nondiscrimination clauses in government contracts, but it lacked enforcement machinery and attracted little attention. At the same time, the Labor Department had drafted an FEPC executive order, but because of legal difficulties and doubtless also political considerations, the White House took no action. In May, the president left the ADA leaders with the understanding that he would issue the order as soon as the foreign aid and defense production bills cleared Congress. Later, the White House told the ADA that the order had to wait for passage of the appropriation bills.

Finally, in December the president used his executive authority to create a Committee on Government Contract Compliance. The new body was weak and dependent upon persuasion and conciliation. Hubert Humphrey loyally called the order a step in the right direction, but it did not establish the FEPC for which the liberals had hoped. Some conceded that in the twilight war situation of Korea, Truman might have gone as far as he could, but all were disappointed. Civil rights, it seemed, had gone the way of the rest of the Fair Deal.[9]

II

The prospect of a larger, prolonged war not only eclipsed the Fair Deal, it also exposed the flimsiness of the administration's economic mobilization. Liberals feared that the inflation which had gathered momentum during the fall of 1950 would now assume frightening proportions. Drastic action seemed necessary, even high taxes for the low- and middle-income brackets, even a wage freeze, most assuredly price controls and levies which would bite deeply into corporate profits.[10]

In mid-December, the president proclaimed a national emergency. Asserting his determination to stop inflation and expand production, he created a new agency with broad authority, the Office of Defense Mobilization, headed by Charles E. Wilson, the president of General Electric. Functioning under Wilson's supervision, the existing Economic Stabilization Agency would work to halt the inflationary spiral. Implementation of the stabilization guidelines and in fact much of their formulation would be the responsibility of two agencies which on paper were subordinate to the ESA but actually enjoyed substantial autonomy—the Wage Stabilization Board, composed of nine members representing labor, industry, and the public, and the Office of Price Stabilization, run by the former mayor of Toledo, Michael DiSalle. The White House removed an important obstacle to meaningful action by forcing Alan Valentine's resignation from the ESA and replacing him with Eric Johnston. All the same, it was not until the end of January, after frustrating weeks of inaction, that the administration attempted to institute a general wage-price freeze.[11]

Part of the reason for the administration delay involved simple mechanics. There had been no price control structure worthy of the name before the Chinese had launched their attack; it took time to establish even a skeleton mechanism which could have some hope of enforcing government orders. In part also, the delay stemmed from a conflict between those in the administration who wanted a complex price control structure designed to provide the greatest possible equity for the businesses affected and those who desired a simple freeze even at the risk of benefiting firms which had ignored earlier requests for voluntary restraint. The first group was centered in the OPS under DiSalle; the leader of the second group was Leon Keyserling.

The price freeze order of late January represented an initial victory for the Keyserling viewpoint, but subsequent modifications came close to meeting the OPS position. The dispute itself was largely a squabble over detail since both sides agreed on the necessity for controls, but it was also an indication of Keyserling's attitude toward the economics of mobilization. Complex regulations might punish the profiteers but at the cost of diverting attention from the more central problem of economic expansion. The only way to combat inflation over the long haul was through an economic growth which would allow mobilization to fit comfortably into a larger economy.

Hoping at first that high taxes might contain inflation in the short run, Keyserling accepted controls with reluctance. "We'll never be able to out-control the Russians," he told a Senate committee in May, 1951, "but we can out-produce them." Speaking to an ADA economic conference that same month, he asserted that many liberals, in their opposition to tax breaks for large businesses which were expanding plant facilities and in their demands for stronger controls, were confusing the Korean situation with World War II and "engaging merely in hackneyed slogans out of the past." [12]

Most liberals disagreed with Keyserling's emphases. Seeing production as the first imperative, he was willing to take risks with inflation; the progressives visualized a halt to the wage-price spiral as the prime requirement not simply for economic growth but for social stability as well. "Unless we are willing seriously to endanger the basis of existence of the American middle class, we must stop prices from rising," wrote Hans Landsberg in the *Reporter*. In addition, the liberals assumed that economic expansion was possible within a framework of rigid, tightly administered controls. Some tended to believe, in fact, that Keyserling's denigration of controls arose from an attempt to protect himself politically, not from economics. Willard Shelton warned that Keyserling and Charles Wilson, who also emphasized economic expansion, were undercutting the struggle for effective stabilization. Chester Bowles indirectly answered Keyserling's criticism of liberals who looked to the past by observing that the controlled economy of World War II had turned out a twofold increase in industrial production.* John Kenneth Galbraith remarked that policies designed to strain productive capacity to the limit were in themselves inflationary if not tempered by high taxes, credit restraints, and wage-price controls. To most progressives the Keyserling approach seemed simplistic and even dangerous. [13]

---

*Bowles failed to mention that American productive capacity was underutilized at the beginning of World War II. Nevertheless, he was accurate in his observation that the government had successfully promoted genuine economic expansion within the complex control framework of the war years.

In early 1951, the way Charles Wilson was running the Office of Defense Mobilization appeared even more dangerous. Many liberals respected Wilson as a top-notch production expert with the ability to organize a well-planned defense program, but they questioned his political skills and his ability to work with nonbusiness groups. Wilson quickly confirmed their worst fears. Instead of drawing upon the services of liberal economists such as Robert Nathan or Chester Bowles, he surrounded himself with other businessmen and failed to appoint even a single liberal farm leader or labor union chief to a responsible policy-making position.

Speaking for the National Farmers Union, Jim Patton charged that Wilson was running mobilization exclusively in the interests of big business, bypassing Secretary of Agriculture Brannan, and seeking to drive farm prices below 100 percent of parity. In public letters to Wilson and Johnston, he called for a freeze on profits and tight restrictions on credit to combat inflation. In his organization's paper, he threatened the administration with a massive farm revolt. The NFU protests, for all their vehemence, went practically unnoticed, overshadowed as they were by the more drastic action of the labor movement. In mid-February, the unions, acting with rare unanimity, announced that they could no longer sanction or participate in the defense program and withdrew their representatives from the Wage Stabilization Board.

Labor's repudiation of the mobilization effort emphasized Wilson's single-interest outlook and his failure as a conciliator. By displaying an ill-disguised contempt for the labor leaders, by hinting that he favored antiunion policies, Wilson had created a serious labor-management clash. "The notion that 15,-000,000 American workers, highly organized, will consent over any prolonged period to have their most vital interests arbitrarily disposed of by a coterie of bankers and industrialists is patently absurd," commented the *Nation*. Even those liberals who questioned the labor tactics sympathized with the union grievances and had no doubt that the businessmen would have behaved in the same fashion had the situation been reversed.

The crisis underscored the basic liberal complaint with Wilson. "Republican big business has established a de facto government on the banks of the Potomac," asserted the *New Republic,* expressing a fear that Wilson and his associates were "likely to turn American capitalism into the mockery of democracy which the Communists wish it to become." The dominance of the managers led many to recall that under Roosevelt labor leaders had held prominent positions in war production programs. Truman's delegation of power to the industrialists caused many liberals to question anew his skill as a leader. "An adequate war president knows how to keep every social force in balance," wrote New York *Post* columnist Murray Kempton. "It is a measure of Mr. Truman's inadequacy that he has failed at this with people who were once his best friends."

After a month of dangerous and increasingly bitter deadlock, in early April Truman was able to attract labor back with a new special advisory board on mobilization which would report directly to the White House. Wilson himself, persuaded that his bull-it-through tactics were counterproductive, adopted a more conciliatory tone, began to rely on liberal-oriented government bureaucrats, and became a vociferous advocate of controls. With the dispute settled, the administration and the liberals could give undivided attention to the struggle against inflation—only to find that the enemy had disappeared from the field.[14]

From the outbreak of the war through February 1951, the cost-of-living index rose 8 percent (or at an annual rate of 12 percent). By early 1951, inflation appeared unstopable. This stiuation had contributed mightily to the bitterness of the labor revolt in February and March. Rewarding profiteers and apparently moving the country toward economic disaster, the unchecked price increases seemed to provide a statistical measure of the administration's failure at home. The stabilization program, declared Arthur Schlesinger, Jr., in early February, had become "a farce which may lead to a tragedy." [15]

Yet in March, the price increases suddenly abated; the cost-of-living increase for the remainder of 1951 would be less than

2.5 percent. In retrospect, the reasons for the sudden economic shift are clear. The waves of scare buying which followed the North Korean attack and the Chinese intervention had subsided. Higher taxes and restraints on consumer credit were beginning to take hold. The Federal Reserve System, after some opposition from the administration, had initiated a stringent monetary policy. The government stabilization program, although it failed to roll back prices, discouraged an inflationary psychology among both buyers and sellers. Tax write-offs to businesses expanding their plant facilities presaged increased productive capacity. The March lull indicated that serious inflation had been conquered.[16]

At the time, however, the situation seemed much more precarious. Many liberals even acted as if increases were continuing. At the beginning of April, Thomas L. Stokes asserted that inflation was "still at large like a ravenous wolf." In the middle of the same month, the ADA issued a strong condemnation of the "timid and confused anti-inflation program," and called upon the government "to do its job of stopping price increases instead of sanctioning them." Most economic observers assumed that the spring pause represented no more than a breathing spell and that prices would shoot up again in the fall as the impact of defense orders registered on the economy. The spring and summer of 1951, they feared, would provide a last chance to establish a strong, meaningful control program.[17]

The administration's perspective was much the same. Moreover, Truman and his advisers were doubtless aware of the political profit which could come from a strong stance against inflation. The government's basic mobilization law, the Defense Production Act was due to expire in the summer, and Truman moved to establish himself as the leader in the drive to extend and strengthen it. At the end of April, the president asked Congress for sweeping authority to control farm and industrial prices, rents, and credit. In addition, he requested the power to build and operate vital defense plants as the government had done during World War II. In the face of widespread Congressional and public apathy, Truman ostentatiously mounted an anti-inflation crusade. In a nationally broadcast speech, he read letters from ordinary people with limited incomes imploring him to continue the fight against inflation, and he lashed out at "special interests" which were undermining the national welfare. In a public letter to the Senate he warned that if Congress enacted a weak bill "the consumers in this country may be plundered by renewed inflation and our whole mobilization program threatened with disaster." [18]

Some liberals still rather ritualistically criticized Truman for his inability to mobilize the Congressional Democrats, but the president had largely reversed his weak image on the control issue. "Congress cannot now maneuver the President into the embarrassing situation of last fall," commented the *Reporter,* "for if it rejects the controls he demands, it will have to take the blame for runaway inflation."

As it turned out, Congress was willing to take the blame. With the price lull continuing, there was no strong demand for tough controls. At the end of July, the White House received a bill which was actually weaker than the original Defense Production Act. Truman signed it but issued a scathing condemnation, likening it to "a bulldozer, crashing aimlessly through existing pricing formulas, leaving havoc in its wake." Subsequently, Truman repeated his demand to Congress for more control authority, although it is inconceivable that he could have entertained hopes for real results.[19]

The experience of extending the Defense Production Act set the pattern for executive-Congressional relations on defense mobilization legislation. A few months later, Congress enacted a tax bill which failed to meet the government's revenue needs and thereby increased the danger of serious inflation. In addition, as the *Progressive* put it, the bill, filled with loopholes, was "an open grab-bag for every special interest." As in the case of the Defense Production Act, Truman announced that he was signing the measure only under the pressure of necessity and issued a sharp criticism of it.[20]

Well into the spring of 1952, most liberals continued to anticipate the second round of inflation and to call for stronger legislation to meet it. Yet inflation never developed, and in May the administration could even announce an easing of credit restrictions. Prices remained steady in large measure because defense production, hampered by multiple shortages and bottlenecks, lagged far behind its timetable. In late 1951, Truman decided to "stretch out" defense production schedules. Given the seemingly insoluble problems the production effort faced, the decision assumed an aura of necessity; moreover, it carried the dividend of economic stability.

Leon Keyserling disagreed. He argued that many shortages were imaginary, urged an all-out attempt to break the bottlenecks, and asserted that economic expansion was an all-important goal which justified the risk of inflation. Finding little support, he lost the struggle, just as he had been on the losing side in the battles to keep interest rates low and wage-price controls simple. Few members of the liberal community were prepared to accept the Keyserling theory; its offhand dismissal of the specter of inflation was unacceptable economically, politically, even morally. Those who criticized the slowness of defense production did so on grounds of national security, not economic expansionism. They gleefully charged that the production slowdown indicated the failure of Wilson and his big business associates. Unlike Keyserling, they bitterly denounced the tax benefits which underwrote plant expansion, calling them unjustified giveaways which only increased monopolistic concentration.[21]

But if Keyserling lost skirmishes over matters of technique, the Korean War nevertheless produced the essential economic result which he advocated. Before the war, the peak gross national product had been $285 billion in 1948; by the end of 1952, the GNP, measured in stable dollars, had reached a rate of $350 billion. The production index of durable manufactured goods had averaged 237 in 1950; by the last quarter of 1952, it had reached 313. Keyserling had advocated more, but it was still among the most breathtaking expansions in American history. Moreover, aside from the probably unavoidable inflation which accompanied the early months of the war, this remarkable growth had been carried through in a climate of economic stability. Using a somewhat more orthodox approach than Keyserling liked, the administration had achieved generally happy results.[22]

III

At the beginning of 1952, however, the success of mobilization seemed uncertain and doubtful, and the stabilization effort appeared to be in more danger than ever. The nation's most basic industry—steel—was on the verge of a nationwide strike which might disrupt defense production and culminate with an inflationary settlement. The United Steelworkers Union contract with the industry expired on December 31, 1951. At the president's request, the union agreed to postpone a walkout until the Wage Stabilization Board could consider the dispute and recommend a settlement.[23]

From the very start, the White House was inclined to distrust the steel managers and sympathize with the union, to believe that the workers had just grievances and that the companies would seek an exorbitant price increase for any wage concessions. Liberal-minded advisers, especially John Steelman's assistant, Harold Enarson, argued that the steel companies had profit margins large enough to absorb a reasonable wage increase and warned that the future of price stabilization was at stake. All indications are that Truman was receptive to such arguments.[24]

The Wage Stabilization Board recommendations, released on March 20, 1952, provided wage concessions and fringe benefits which most liberals thought reasonable. The steelworkers promptly accepted the proposed settlement, but the companies balked, arguing that they would require price increases of $10.00 to $12.00 a ton to finance the higher wages.

The administration accepted the WSB proposals. The Council of Economic Advisers privately told the president that steel profits were high enough to absorb most of the union gains, and recommended a price increase of about $2.50 per ton, perhaps as much as $4.00 if necessary to avoid a work stoppage. The Office of Price Stabilization, now headed by the Georgia liberal Ellis Arnall, was determined to hold the price line. Only one figure in the government inclined toward the industry position, Charles Wilson.

Concerned with maintaining production, sympathetic toward the steel executives, perhaps misunderstanding Truman's attitudes, Wilson publicly criticized the WSB recommendations. After the steelworkers refused to accept less, he embraced company demands for price increases. When Wilson discovered that he could not get presidential support, he submitted an angry letter of resignation charging the administration with capitulating to labor pressure and reneging on a promise of compensatory price increases. On March 30, the White House released a temperate letter from the president to Wilson accepting the resignation, rejecting Wilson's attack upon the wage settlement, pointedly observing that steel profits were "at extraordinarily high levels," and expressing a desire to protect the public interest by allowing only price increases which could be justified on the basis of fairness and equity.

This episode, as most progressives viewed it, had displayed what the *Nation* called "Wilson's bias and malevolent ignorance whenever he was forced to deal with a question involving labor." In broader perspective, they believed, Wilson's inept handling of the steel problem was yet another demonstration of his failure to mobilize the economy behind an effective, ongoing defense production effort. "Some 22 months after the opening salvo in the Korean War, our nation's productive might is still operating on a 'business as usual' basis," complained the *New Republic.* Conversely, Truman's firm stand indicated not simply support for the legitimate demands of labor, but also, as the ADA expressed it, "fighting determination to keep inflation from wrecking the national preparedness program." [25]

Whatever the meaning of the events leading to Wilson's resignation, the White House's main concern was the problem of finding a fair method of maintaining production. With the wage-price dispute stalemated, the long-delayed strike was imminent. A Taft-Hartley injunction seemed unfair, since the steel workers had already stayed on the job without a contract for longer than 80 days. The president even decided against the establishment of a Taft-Hartley fact-finding board because of a fear that any invocation of the act would alienate the union. There seemed to be only one course left.

On April 8, Truman went on the air to announce that the nation was facing a critical emergency. A prolonged steel strike "would bring defense production to a halt and throw our domestic economy into chaos"; it would threaten the very survival of American troops in Korea. Accordingly, he had directed the secretary of commerce "to take possession of the steel mills, and to keep them operating." The Taft-Hartley Act would solve nothing; it would simply mean further delay. The proposed WSB settlement was "fair and reasonable." The main barrier to continued defense production was the attitude of the companies. "If we granted the outrageous prices the steel industry wants, we would scuttle our whole price control program. . . . [T]he steel companies are recklessly forcing a shutdown of the steel mills. They are trying to get special, preferred treatment." [26]

For the liberals, the steel seizure raised new and disturbing questions. Most of them supported Truman's wage-price policy, but many could not repress concern over such a drastic exercise of presidential power without clear authority. Those who felt that production was vital generally defended the president, believing that he had struck a justifiable blow at an arrogant and unpatriotic corporate power. "The crisis is in this case unquestioned," declared Max Lerner. "There are times when the Constitution must bend or yield," wrote Thomas L. Stokes. The *New Republic* observed that no less a constitutional authority than Senator Wayne Morse had supported presidential seizure and called upon Truman to impose the WSB wage settlement. Elmer Davis, at first doubtful about the legality of the seizure, reluctantly accepted it as necessary to continue steel production—"it is a condition that confronts us, not a theory." [27]

Others, however, feared its long-range implications, especially after a bumbling assistant attorney general argued that the president had virtually unlimited "inherent powers." Truman did not have dictatorial ambitions, but he might be setting a precedent for some future chief executive with fewer scruples. "There doesn't seem to be a great difference between government seizure and court anti-strike injunction," remarked the *Reporter*. A few liberals, including the editors of the *Nation,* opposed seizure under any circumstances and denied that a real emergency existed. Most of those with qualms, however, admitted the existence of a crisis and were bothered more by the arbitrary exercise of presidential power. The ideal solution seemed to be an act of Congress which would establish clear conditions and procedures for government seizure of an industry and which would require equal sacrifice on all sides. It was, of course, unthinkable that Congress would assent to such legislation, and the liberals who criticized Truman's actions were for this reason generally more bitter toward the Congressional conservatives than toward the president himself. "Congress has passed legislation empowering the president to conscript men in the present emergency," commented the *Progressive*. "It has refused up to now to empower the President to conscript wealth." [28]

Whether or not its actions were justified, the administration met with defeat and frustration. First a federal district judge and then the U.S. Supreme Court ruled the seizure unconstitutional. Truman then requested authorization from Congress but got no action. Even some of his most trusted liberal advisers, including Clark Clifford and Sam Rosenman, favored a resort to the Taft-Hartley Act; but the president refused to budge. The seven-week strike which followed came to an end only when the government promised a price increase of $5.65 a ton. The final figure was only about half the original industry demand and not too far above the $4.00 level which the Council of Economic Advisers had considered tolerable; nevertheless, it had all the appearance of a business victory—even to Truman—and constituted a blow to the authority of the administration.

The steel settlement, together with some new holes that Con-

gress had knocked into price-control legislation, seemed to por-
tend a new spurt of inflation. "The price of the settlement
might be far greater than the cost of the strike itself," warned
Harry Conn in the *New Republic*. As it turned out, such fears
were exaggerated, the economy remained stable. Although it
was a serious political defeat for the administration, the steel
episode had not brought economic disaster.[29]

Despite the steel setback, despite the need to shelve the Fair
Deal in 1951, the Truman administration had handled the political-economic aspects of Korean mobilization about as well as
could be expected. The liberals did not hesitate to criticize
Truman's mistakes, but most appreciated the enormity of his
problems and the recalcitrance of Congress. Once the danger of
inflation had receded, few were prepared to be harsh with the
president. Yet throughout 1951 and into 1952, Truman's standing with both the general public and the liberals dropped. The
reasons for the president's declining popularity stemmed less
from his mobilization policy than from two other issues which
bedeviled and discredited both the administration and the liberal movement—corruption and communism.

Chapter 21

Political Pitfalls:
Corruption and Communism

One reason for Truman's low standing was the frequency—especially in the early months of the Korean War—with which he indulged in outbursts of temper against opposition congressmen, a music critic, even the U.S. Marine Corps.* At times, as in the Marine Corps incident, the president retrieved the situation with surprising grace, but all too often he behaved with a lack of dignity and a disturbing impulsiveness. "Makes me sick, and makes it harder and harder to stand up for him," David Lilienthal confided to his journal after Truman had struck out at a critic of daughter Margaret's singing voice. "I worry that one of these days that badly controlled temper might set off World War III." [1] Lilienthal and other liberals, however, appreciated the stresses to which the president was subjected, and his momentary lapses could not alienate them. What they

*In August 1950, Truman sent a curt letter to a Republican congressman who advocated separate representation on the Joint Chiefs of Staff for the Marine Corps. The document, promptly inserted in the *Congressional Record* by its recipient, declared: "For your information the Marine Corps is the Navy's police force and as long as I am President that is what it will remain. They have a propaganda machine that is almost equal to Stalin's."

A few days later, the president released a public apology to the Marine Corps and made a remarkably successful personal appearance before the annual convention of the Marine Corps League.

could not tolerate was the steadily growing evidence of corruption within the administration.

I

In early 1951, a Senate committee headed by J. William Fulbright revealed evidence that the Reconstruction Finance Corporation had dealt out loans to partisan favorites and had been receptive to improper influences. Chief among these influences had been pressure applied by White House aide Donald Dawson in behalf of applicants who had contributed heavily to the Democratic Party—and in some cases to Dawson's personal comfort. A few months later, the St. Louis *Post-Dispatch* exposed the successful efforts of Democratic National Chairman William Boyle on behalf of a client who twice before had been denied an RFC loan. In the meantime, Senator Estes Kefauver was staging a highly publicized investigation which uncovered a disturbing number of connections between organized mobsters and local Democratic machines.

As early as March 1951, the *New Republic* was claiming that corruption pervaded Washington. It made charges of bribery or favoritism against the Office of the Alien Property Custodian, the Federal Power Commission, the Antitrust Division of the Justice Department, the Maritime Commission, the Securities and Exchange Commission, and the Civil Aeronautics Board. It depicted the Democratic National Committee as a happy hunting ground for gamblers, racketeers, and unsavory special interests, linked Truman's appointments secretary, Matthew Connelly, to airlines which had profited from CAB decisions, and asserted that at least one federal collector of internal revenue had engaged in tax fixes. By the end of the year, dozens of individuals in the Bureau of Internal Revenue and the Tax Division of the Justice Department were involved in scandals.[2]

As the stories of malfeasance came out, liberals almost without exception reacted with anger and indignation. They still adhered to the values of nineteenth-century Mugwumps who had fought for the merit system, applauded the maxim that public service was a public trust, and idealized the honest nonpartisan government administrator. The federal bureaucracy belonged to all the people and was designed to serve their interests impartially. Any special influence was reprehensible and, if it involved outright dishonesty, was doubly so. A few did express doubts that the government could serve as a moral example on a higher level than the rest of American life—Marquis Childs caricatured this attitude as Cromwellian Puritanism—but most progressives seemed convinced that it could and should. All, of course, were convinced that crookedness had to be rooted out when it was discovered. The disclosures of corruption revealed the influence of antiliberal elements within a liberal administration, in a sense discrediting liberalism itself. "The Fair Deal and the ideals for which it once stood for millions of people have been tarnished by . . . cheap and shoddy political hucksters," wrote Thomas L. Stokes.[3]

Truman's erratic response raised disturbing doubts about his leadership and his concept of government. He first denounced and ridiculed Fulbright's charges about the RFC, but then implicitly admitted their accuracy by reorganizing the agency and appointing the capable Stuart Symington to clean it up. He allowed Donald Dawson to remain silent for weeks, then retained him even after his testimony only convinced most observers of his guilt. He stoutly, almost blindly, defended his aides. "My house is always clean," he told a press conference in March. During the last half of the year, the administration did purge several suspected tax fixers, and in September Truman asked Congress to enact tough conflict-of-interest legislation which would require government officials and party leaders to make regular disclosures of outside income. Yet, he also issued repeated defenses of Democratic Chairman Boyle, even after accepting his resignation in October. Moreover, he replaced Boyle with Frank McKinney of Indianapolis, also a machine politician.[4]

Truman did not mollify the liberals; in fact, the president

created an impression of White House complacency which obscured the practical constructive steps he was taking. Good government after all, as Thomas Stokes remarked, was a "very plain moral issue," and the liberals expected Truman to approach it as such. But instead of leading a crusade, the president acted as if he were being forced to do something about a matter he would prefer to ignore. Progressives realized that the Truman administration did not have a monopoly on corruption. The Republican national chairman, Guy Gabrielson, was generally considered as much an influence peddler as Boyle, and several prominent Republican congressmen had profited from very questionable connections. Nevertheless, the presidency was supposed to be the focus of moral leadership in the national government, and it was up to the president to set an example—Roosevelt, some observed, had done so. Instead, the St. Louis *Post-Dispatch* asserted, Truman was actually encouraging grafters and acting like a machine politician. The New York *Post* commented that Truman's "tolerance for amiable hacks has allowed the ethics of the precinct clubhouse to permeate his administration." "By not meeting the moral issue squarely the President has placed himself in a vulnerable political position," declared the *Nation*. Truman's measures had been too little and too late; by the fall of 1951, the liberals were convinced that only extraordinary action could clean up the government.[5]

With the Truman-MacArthur controversy dying down, with the danger of inflation receding, with the Fair Deal laid to rest, the issue of corruption increasingly preoccupied the liberals. "The seriousness of the situation cannot be exaggerated," Francis Biddle privately warned the president at the end of November. "The chief topic of conversation on all sides is the alleged dishonesty in the Bureau of Internal Revenue and, I regret to say, in the Department of Justice." The Justice Department, declared the St. Louis *Post-Dispatch* with reasonable accuracy, had been "unwilling, halting, delaying" in the fight against graft. Attorney General J. Howard McGrath, progressives believed, was an administrative lightweight interested only in sweeping political dirt under the rug. The *New Republic* advocated what seemed to be the only solution, "a special inquiry, directed by citizens of the highest character." The ADA urged the president to appoint two special prosecutors—one Republican, one Democrat—with extensive authority to expose wrongdoers.[6]

Truman's own attitude apparently had been a compound of personal indignation and mistaken political calculation. He seems to have genuinely believed that much of the outcry against corruption had been created by McCarthy-like senators seeking to embarrass the administration and grab publicity for themselves. He also probably felt that the dishonesty which did exist would raise the least political difficulties if it were handled quietly. Some of the president's aides, especially Charlie Murphy, disagreed; in fact, so did the new Democratic chairman McKinney. By late October, they seemed to have Truman's ear. The president announced that he would ask Congress to approve a reorganization placing all collectorships of the Bureau of Internal Revenue under the merit system. In December, he invited Federal Judge Thomas Murphy, who as a U.S. attorney had prosecuted Alger Hiss, to head a special investigation. By now also, Truman was ready to fire McGrath. These last two lines of action carried the promise of removing corruption as an actual problem within the government and as a political issue.

Both moves failed. Many liberals and other observers charged that it would be impossible for Judge Murphy to conduct a thorough investigation of an administration headed by the president who had appointed him to the bench. Perhaps because of such criticisms, Murphy backed out of the job after virtually accepting it. Truman then moved to replace McGrath. The president offered the attorney general's post to qualified men of independence and distinction, including Samuel I. Rosenman, Wayne Morse, Robert Patterson, and Chief Justice Vinson. Finally, Justin Miller, a veteran of the New Deal and former federal judge, accepted. On January 2, Truman had Clark Clifford ask McGrath to resign and accept appointment as ambassador to Spain. By now rumors about the attorney general's departure blanketed Washington, and Truman encouraged them by sidestepping questions at a press conference.

McGrath fought back, securing the support of his Rhode Island mentor, Senator Theodore F. Green, of Matt Connelly, and of prominent Catholic leaders, including Cardinal Spellman. He refused to go to Spain, making it clear that his ouster would be a nasty affair and that he would encourage his backers to depict it as evidence of anti-Catholicism. Faced with such a prospect, Truman kept McGrath in the Cabinet. On January 10, the president told surprised reporters that the attorney general, not a special commission, would handle whatever cleaning up needed to be done.[7]

"Coming even from Mr. Truman, this announcement is shocking," declared the St. Louis *Post-Dispatch*. "Public confidence in our Federal Government will not be restored by Democrats investigating Democrats," warned the ADA. Under the pressure of such protests, the White House resumed its quest for an outside investigator. On February 1, the New York reformer Newbold Morris accepted an appointment as special assistant to the attorney general with the duty of probing governmental corruption. As a maverick Republican from the La Guardia era, Morris had the respect of liberals; nevertheless, many doubted that his position as McGrath's assistant would allow for a meaningful investigation.

In fact, Morris was determined to conduct a thorough, nonpartisan investigation. He received private assurances of support from Truman and had Charlie Murphy as a firm friend at the White House. McGrath, however, rather obviously considered the Morris appointment as nothing more than political window-dressing. He refused to grant blanket access to Justice Department files and reacted in anger against a financial questionnaire which Morris proposed to distribute to top-level federal personnel.

Truman himself had mixed attitudes about investigating an individual's finances. In August 1951, he had looked over a questionnaire which a Congressional committee wanted to distribute to Bureau of Internal Revenue enforcement personnel and had scribbled an angry note to Charlie Murphy: "Attached documents are totalitarian. If one was sent to me for answer, I'd tell the sender to go to hell." Yet by early 1952 he had become convinced of the necessity of such measures and was advocating that all public officials making over $10,000 a year should be required to disclose their outside income. Such was the situation at the beginning of April when McGrath publicly denounced the Morris questionnaire, was observed in a heated conversation with Truman, then peremptorily fired Morris. Truman at once demanded McGrath's resignation and appointed federal judge James P. McGranery of Philadelphia as his successor.[8]

Truman made it clear that he had not sanctioned the dismissal of Morris, but he made no effort to bring the New Yorker back into the administration. Moreover, McGranery, a former congressman and longtime friend of the president, was, as the *New Republic* observed, "neither a nationally recognized lawyer, nor a man of proved technical competence." The liberal Philadelphia district attorney, Richardson Dilworth, was less restrained; he asserted that the appointment was "so bad as to be almost unbelievable" and predicted that the McGranery regime would feature "incompetence, bias, favoritism, and ward politics at its worst."

In the months that followed, however, McGranery and Truman undertook a quiet and fairly effective effort to weed out corruption, and they cooperated fully with a responsible Congressional committee headed by Frank Chelf of Kentucky. Belatedly attempting to depict himself as an opponent of patronage and a defender of the career civil service, Truman even submitted plans, all rejected by Congress, to extend the merit system to postmasters, customs collectors, and U.S. marshals. But in April 1952, Morris was gone, and the new attorney general was taking office under a cloud. The New York *Post,* which tried harder than most liberal organs to be kind to Truman, commemorated the seventh anniversary of Franklin Roosevelt's death by observing: "the way corruption and shabby mediocrity have taken hold of Washington since 1945 has made painfully obvious the degree to which at least in one respect FDR's personal qualities of leadership shaped his era." [9]

II

Throughout 1951 and 1952 the administration and the liberals also had to fight an increasingly futile battle against Senator Joe McCarthy and his associates. With the 1950 elections, with the firing of MacArthur and the Korean stalemate, McCarthyism became the dominant force within the Republican Party. Some liberals continued to hope that American politics would return to rationality and that the people would repudiate McCarthy. A few Senators, including William Benton and Thomas Hennings, conducted a form of guerrilla warfare against the Wisconsin demagogue. But McCarthy was stronger and more confident than ever. With the more or less open support of Senator Taft he continued to hurl one irresponsible accusation after another—at General Marshall, at the distinguished diplomat Philip Jessup, at Mrs. Leon Keyserling, and many others. "McCarthyism is a sickness," commented the St. Louis *Post-Dispatch* in the summer of 1951, "and the American people have not yet found the cure." [10]

The sickness, moreover, extended far beyond the Senate. McCarthyism was rapidly moving into every corner of American life as states and cities passed "little McCarran Acts," as schools, private industries, and entertainment media adopted loyalty programs. Inevitably such efforts smeared honest liberals. Even so anti-Communist a figure as Marquis Childs found himself barred from speaking at a District of Columbia teachers college because his name was "listed" in the files of the House Committee on Un-American Activities. "If our own doubts and fears have gone as far as this small incident illustrates," Childs commented, "then we have good reason to wonder about the future of democracy here in the United States." Writing an impassioned defense of civil liberties in 1951, Francis Biddle described the growth of McCarthyism as a "fear of freedom." [11]

The Supreme Court offered no encouragement as it issued one decision after another restricting free speech and upholding loyalty inquisitions. The most notable of these rulings, the *Dennis* decision, sustained the trial and conviction of the eleven top Communist leaders. To most liberals the decision was, as Max Lerner put it, "a monstrous backward step" which sanctioned punishment for the mere advocacy of subversive or unpopular opinion. Most liberals also observed that the only two dissenters were the old New Dealers Black and Douglas; the Court majority was built around what the *Nation* called "the Truman law firm of Vinson, Minton, and Burton." The Truman Court, wrote civil liberties attorney Eugene Gressman, was tipping the scales of freedom "in the direction of authoritarian oppression from which history teaches there is no return." [12]

One of the most objectionable abuses of civil liberties was the administration's loyalty program. After the 1950 elections, progressives renewed their appeals for a select committee to examine the program and to inquire into the entire cluster of problems connected with loyalty and subversion. Charlie Murphy continued to support the idea, arguing to Truman that a committee almost surely would recommend repeal of the McCarran Act, discredit Senator McCarthy, dampen the growing anti-Communist hysteria, and in general sustain the administration's approach to internal security. On January 23, 1951, Truman announced the establishment of a President's Commission on Internal Security and Individual Rights, headed by Admiral Chester Nimitz and authorized to "consider afresh, in all its present-day ramifications, the recurrent question of how a free people protect their society from subversive attack without at the same time destroying their own liberties." [13]

Liberals hailed the appointment of the Nimitz commission, but their hopes that it would strike a blow against McCarthyism were much too optimistic. In the first place, the body's membership, as a matter of political necessity, was very conservative and unlikely to make a last-ditch fight for civil liberties. In the second place, the McCarthyite bloc in Congress, fearing that the commission would take the Communist issue out of politics, moved to destroy the new group. Pat McCarran's Senate Judiciary Committee refused to report out a routine bill which would have exempted the commission members from conflict-of-interest statues. Since it was never able to begin work, the commission accomplished nothing.[14]

In the meantime, the administration had made the loyalty program even worse. In April 1951, Truman allowed the Loyalty Review Board to institute as a new basis for dismissal "reasonable doubt" of an employee's loyalty; the old standard had been "reasonable grounds exist for belief that the person involved is disloyal." The change involved more than semantics; in practice it more than ever placed the burden of proof on the accused and gave greater weight to hearsay evidence and flimsy accusations. In subsequent months, the board purged civil servants who had been cleared under the old rules. "The next step in the descent," wrote Alan Barth in early 1952, "must be to formalize what is already a fact—acceptance of any doubt whatever, no matter how capricious, as a basis for branding men disloyal to their country." [15]

Truman apparently had a genuine concern about such abuses. In May 1951, after ADA leaders had complained to him about the loyalty program, he directed Charlie Murphy to make an investigation: "I have been very much disturbed with the action of some of these Boards and I want to find some way to put a stop to their un-American activities." A year later, after McCarran's Senate Judiciary Committee had staged an investigation of China policy which featured sweeping attacks on Owen Lattimore and John Paton Davies, Truman wrote to Attorney General McGranery:

I do not want to prevent anyone from being prosecuted who deserves it; but from what I know of this case, I am of the opinion that Davies and Lattimore were shamefully persecuted. . . . If you find anything in the record that seems to indicate that the case should be laid before a grand jury, I wish you would let me know before that is done.[16]

The president also attacked Senator McCarthy and his followers more strongly than ever. Speaking in Detroit on July 28, 1951, he decried the atmosphere of fear and suspicion which was being created by "smearers and slanderers." On August 14, he used an American Legion gathering for a dramatic blast at "hate-mongers." "Character assassination is their stock in trade. Guilt by association is their motto." In May 1952, he delivered an address to the National Civil Service League denouncing "political gangsters" who used "innuendo and smear and just plain common, ordinary lies" to impugn the loyalty of government employees.[17]

The president's rhetoric was welcome, but his accomplishment was less satisfactory. Many liberals observed that the government all too frequently practiced McCarthyite tactics itself. The army refused to allow the distinguished Asian historian John K. Fairbank into Japan. The State Department delayed issuance of a passport to Owen Lattimore, and, however Truman felt about it, Lattimore was indicted for perjury. "Truman has made a bold and masterly attack upon the virus popularly known as McCarthyism," observed the *New Republic* in April 1952. "Yet every syllable of that attack applies with equal, if not more, pertinence to his own loyalty program." [18]

If Truman's words fell short of his actions, the same was true of many liberals who were likewise retreating before McCarthyism and even adopting some of its tactics. The progressive movement had by no means escaped infection by the virus of anti-Communist extremism. A substantial number of liberals supported the Supreme Court's *Dennis* decision. "We cannot take chances with the ringleaders of a conspiracy that, if successful, would pervert and destroy our institutions," declared Max Ascoli.[19]

The ADA experienced a serious split over the *Dennis* issue. Joseph Rauh and James Wechsler advocated a statement denouncing the ruling but were unable to muster a majority of the National Board. Then they proposed a declaration of opposition to further prosecutions under the Smith Act, but after two polls of the National Board this idea also failed. Some ADA leaders who were against attacking the *Dennis* ruling based their position upon political necessity. "I agree with you on principle," Chester Bowles told Jim Loeb, but he recalled that even Jefferson had once spoken of the need to "tread lightly at times in the presence of current opinion." Others simply adhered to a theory of judicial restraint. "The law is unwise and foolish," declared Francis Biddle. "But that does not mean that it is unconstitutional." Biddle and some other ADA leaders, moreover, feared that an attack upon the Supreme Court decision would, as Biddle put it, "cause a great many resignations to no purpose." Even Biddle, generally considered a staunch advocate of civil liberties, found himself arguing that the Communist leaders had been convicted for secret conspiracy, not public advocacy, that internal peril, not free speech, had been the central issue of the *Dennis* case.

The ADA finally achieved a consensus in opposition to the law under which the Communists had been tried, if not to the trials themselves. The leadership of the Communist Party might be engaged in a covert criminal conspiracy, but the Smith Act nevertheless was a broad and dangerous statute which could be used against public propaganda. In December 1951, the ADA issued a pamphlet, *Free Speech vs. the Communists—Let's Get Back Into Balance,* committing the organization to work for repeal of the Smith Act, opposing the prosecution of minor Communist functionaries, and even praising the dissents of Justices Black and Douglas from the *Dennis* ruling.

The broadside kept the ADA in the mainstream of the liberal tradition, but the equivocal and self-deceptive attitude which many ADA leaders had taken toward the *Dennis* case itself revealed the damaging impact which McCarthyism had inflicted upon liberalism. In effect, the ADA was seeking simply a more sanitary method of prosecuting Communists. Its position was but one or two steps removed from the assumption that the Communists were beyond the pale of civil liberty.[20]

The Korean War and the attendant growth of McCarthyism caused some liberals, frequently of a Communist or Marxist past, to become so committed in their anti-Communism that any equivocation on the issue became illegitimate, that any criticism of U.S. policy not coupled with a stronger anti-Red declaration became suspect. Their favorite and most natural target was the *Nation*. The journal, it is true, had refused to back Wallace in 1948 and had supported the Korean War, but it stopped far short of the Cold War mentality and was a persistent critic of the American role, which it depicted as support of conservatism and reaction in both Europe and Asia. A real basis existed for questioning the motives of its foreign editor, J. Alvarez del Vayo, an old Spanish Republican who was an ardent Popular Fronter, and of a few other contributors with histories of fellow traveling. The *Nation's* editorials on foreign policy, frequently signed by Freda Kirchwey, were open to serious and informed criticism, but they received something else.

The major occasion for attack upon the *Nation* was the publication of a special eighty-fifth anniversary edition in December 1950. It featured twenty five articles, most of them critical of U.S. foreign policy, written from a wide range of perspectives. The most notable critique came from Granville Hicks in the April 1951 issue of *Commentary*. For Hicks the *Nation's* anniversary number had not been a collection of diverse viewpoints with each article to be discussed on its own merits. Rather: "There is a pro-Soviet bias in enough of the twenty-five articles to color the entire issue." What was pro-Soviet? Isaac Deutscher's prediction that the Russian dictatorship might mellow over the years; del Vayo's belief that "rearming Germany is dangerous business"; Freda Kirchwey's assertion that America was failing in Asia because it had allowed the Communists to align themselves with popular revolutionary impulses. These articles, Hicks argued, had established the context of the magazine; hence articles by less "pro-Soviet" authors —Andrew Roth, Rayford Logan, Jesus Silva Herzog, James P. Warburg, Vera Micheles Dean, and Grenville Clark—might have been innocent in intention but were nevertheless items in "a bill of indictment against the democracies" or part of "an argument for appeasement." (Hicks did not extend the accusation to other writers in the issue, including the director of the

NAACP, the president emeritus of the Carnegie Endowment for International Peace, the president of the American Baptist Convention, the Methodist Bishop of New York, and the president of the Amalgamated Bank of New York.)

Hicks magnanimously admitted that there was "nothing sinister or subversive" about the *Nation's* practice of "pro-Soviet liberalism," but there was something sinister about his article. It might have been legitimate to criticize the *Nation* for shrillness, excessive simplification, and knee-jerk liberalism. Hicks demanded instead an unrelenting condemnation of the USSR and an uncritical celebration of U.S. foreign policy; anything less became "pro-Sovietism" through malice, self-deception, or guilt by association. Moreover, Hicks asserted that the *Nation* viewpoint was something of a menace, since if it were widely held it "would seriously weaken this country either in the maintenance of peace or the waging of war." The journal's attitudes "once were merely irresponsible but now are dangerous." [21]

There was a rather remarkable postscript to the Hicks article. In a letter of protest to *Commentary* Freda Kirchwey mentioned that President Truman's press secretary had acknowledged a complimentary copy of the anniversary issue with assurances that Truman appreciated the magazine's views and suggestions. Immediately, the former Marxist philosopher Sidney Hook wrote to White House press secretary Joseph Short demanding to know if Truman endorsed the *Nation*. ("This whole question has become something of a burning issue in literary and political circles in New York.") He described the journal as "a periodical which has not only been notoriously hostile to President Truman's position but a consistent advocate of the North Korean, Chinese Communist and Soviet Union's line." Short thereupon wrote an angry letter to Miss Kirchwey—"I would like to have your assurance that you will desist from any statements or implications that either the President or I endorsed your issue." A bit silly, yet also a bit frightening, Hook's communication revealed the inroads which McCarthyism had made among the liberals.[22]

Meanwhile, the *New Leader* printed a letter from the *Nation's* former art critic, Clement Greenberg, who leveled a tough attack against del Vayo and his magazine: "The *Nation* has the right to side with the Stalin regime when it holds itself compelled to by principle (though it does so so often that that constitutes another, if lesser, scandal), but not to put its pages at the regular disposal of one whose words consistently echo the interests of that regime. . . ." Greenberg's polemic was debatable at best, scurrilous at worst; in an atmosphere of McCarthyism, it was at the outer limits of legitimate liberal debate. The *Nation* nevertheless overreacted by instituting a libel suit, an action which only subjected it to further condemnation.* Reinhold Niebuhr and Robert Bendiner severed longstanding affiliations with the journal. The St. Louis *Post-Dispatch* criticized the suit. Arthur Schlesinger, Jr., attacked the *Nation* for printing "week after week, these wretched apologies for Soviet despotism," and Richard Rovere praised Greenberg for his "admirable restraint." Delighting in the controversy, the *New Leader* kept up the attack.[23]

The *New Leader* also carried on what can only be called a vendetta against Owen Lattimore and the organization with which he had been associated, the Institute of Pacific Relations, at a time when Lattimore had been accused of espionage by Senator McCarthy and the IPR characterized as a Communist front by Senator McCarran. Granville Hicks warned the liberals against a precipitate rush to defend Lattimore, hinting that he probably was guilty. Eugene Lyons in an article entitled "Lattimore: Dreyfus or Hiss?" concluded, on the basis of "symptomatic evidence" which fit a pattern, that the Far Eastern expert was probably the latter. David Dallin and William Henry Chamberlain tore into Lattimore's opinions, asserting

---

*The libel suit was finally settled in the fall of 1955 at no cost to either party with the *New Leader* disclaiming any intent to defame but still defending its motives in running the Greenberg letter. The outcome, as is the case with most such actions, could hardly have given the plaintiff much satisfaction. Richard Clark Sterne, "*The Nation* and Its Century," *N*, CCI (Sept. 20, 1965), 42–53, 241–334, 323.

that he was not only pro-Soviet but shared responsibility for the loss of China. Sidney Hook excoriated the professor's defense of the Moscow purge trials of the thirties and intimated that Lattimore had thereby forfeited any right to expect fair treatment from his accusers. In March 1952, a *New Leader* editorial described Lattimore's defenders, specifically the *Nation* and the *New Republic,* as "perverters of truth, justice, and morality," and the magazine devoted a 16-page special supplement to an attack upon Lattimore and the IPR.

That the evidence, mostly drawn from the 1930s, did not sustain such rhetorical overkill mattered little; the *New Leader* was determined to pillory Lattimore, more it seemed for past deviations than for contemporary sins. Clearly, Lattimore had been something of a fellow traveler during the thirties, but it was impossible to demonstrate that even then he had engaged in espionage or that he had regarded his primary mission as the advancement of Communist interests. Nor could there be any doubt that several members of the IPR research staff had been Communists; yet even by the criteria of the McCarran committee the vast bulk of IPR publications were non-Communist or anti-Communist. The thrust of the *New Leader* attack was not simply indictment of opinions, which the magazine had a perfect right to do. In McCarthy fashion, it blurred the distinction between advocacy of unpopular opinion and criminal subversion. Admitting that Lattimore had not been a spy, the *New Leader* found him guilty of a greater crime—he was a "LitAg," a literary agent of Moscow attempting to sabotage American foreign policy by deviously molding American opinion; as such, he was more valuable to Stalin than "a thousand Eugene Dennises." [24]

The *New Leader's* obsession with Stalinist Communism and practice of its own brand of McCarthyism naturally led the magazine to play down the dangers which McCarthyism posed to American life. The magazine and its writers insisted that, while McCarthy's charges might be partisan, exaggerated, and demagogic, he had failed to overcome libertarian institutions, he had seriously injured no one, and, moreover, his accusations contained a kernel of truth. McCarthyism might be bad, but it was not nearly so great a menace as Stalinism; hence, those liberals who stressed the fight against McCarthyism were establishing the wrong priorities, misrepresenting the state of American freedom, and, knowingly or otherwise, assisting the Communists. Correct in its claim that Stalin's totalitarianism was far more evil than McCarthy's demagoguery, the *New Leader* overlooked the obvious consideration that it was McCarthyism, after all, and not Stalinism which was actually being practiced in America.

In two articles with titles which accurately conveyed their tone—"The Hysteria of the Hisslings" and "The Phantom of McCarthyism"—Norbert Muhlen argued that the tactic of partisan Congressional investigation had been employed, and presumably legitimized, by liberals in past inquiries into big business. These investigations had possessed their share of irresponsibility. Why then the shock that the cycle was repeating itself with probes this time into "Great Dictatorship"? "Such investigations start rather late, are sometimes handled in unskilled, silly and worthless ways, and have a lot of regrettable accompaniments, yet few Americans can have any quarrel with their main purpose and effect: to keep this country from being turned into a concentration camp, and to save freedom from being submerged by fear."

What of the people whom McCarthy had attacked? Muhlen admitted in passing that the senator might have hit Millard Tydings "slightly below the political belt" but felt that in the main McCarthy had done no lasting harm to anyone. He had, it seemed, practically done Owen Lattimore a favor by giving Lattimore the chance to write a best-seller and increase his lecture bookings.

A basic *New Leader* assumption was that Communist subversion had been and continued to be a genuine problem. Muhlen contended that "almost one out of two Americans may at one time or another have been caught to some degree in the Communist web of lies" and thought Red infiltration so successful that there was "a great amount of pro-Soviet propaganda appearing in conservative and even reactionary newspapers and magazines." The magazine's editors and other contributors appear to have entertained a somewhat less expansive view of the peril, but they also had long contended that Communists or Communist sympathizers had influenced U.S. foreign policy. Hence, while McCarthyism might be demagogic and reactionary, McCarthy had a basis for his wild allegations; liberals could win the battle against him only if they themselves undertook the job of ejecting the Communists in a more responsible manner. In late 1951, an editorial hailed the dismissal of John Stewart Service from the State Department, notwithstanding the fact that Service had undergone and passed six previous loyalty hearings. Far from being a victory for McCarthy, the firing was merited and could be the start of a long overdue housecleaning: "Without naming further names, we can state —as we have many times before—that had Service and his kind been dismissed three years ago, there would have been no issue of pro-Communism in Government for McCarthy to howl about." [25]

Throughout 1952, with McCarthyism reaching a peak, *New Leader* reviews and articles denied the existence of a crisis in civil liberties. Irwin Ross, in a critique of Francis Biddle's *The Fear of Freedom,* argued that the situation was good compared to that of the post–World War I Red Scare; post–World War II America had experienced nothing like the Palmer raids. In the same vein, Diana Trilling attempted to discredit alarmists by reminding them that the United States had not become a police state. People accused of treason by demagogic congressmen still had a chance to refute the charges; teachers who refused to sign loyalty oaths were neither shot nor thrown into concentration camps—such points were so elementary that she felt embarrassed to have to make them. Richard Rovere, in an article which attacked a special *Nation* survey of the libertarian crisis, wrote that most institutions (other than those connected with the entertainment world, which was extremely vulnerable to pressure) had fought repression and that important political forces, including the presidency, still opposed McCarthyism;

writing in July 1952, he confidently asserted that the McCarthyites had failed to blur the distinction between liberalism and Communism.

It was, of course, fallacious to argue that in the absence of full-blown authoritarianism no crisis existed, but the *New Leader* had to deny that civil liberties were in urgent danger in order to support its attack against liberals who did not give anti-Communism the highest priority. From the *New Leader's* frame of reference, these other progressives could only be dupes of the Communists. Muhlen denounced the "non-Communists" and "anti-anti Communists" as crypto–Popular Fronters seeking a comfortable way to avoid the fight against Stalinism. Lucy S. Dawidowicz claimed that the Communist Party was trying to use anti-McCarthyism as the basis for a new version of the Popular Front and that "the CP line has been swallowed by many liberals, who then spew it forth with righteous indignation." "The idea that America is a terror-stricken country in the grip of hysteria," wrote Diana Trilling, "is a Communist-inspired idea." Richard Rovere declared that the *Nation's* alarmism over civil liberties would "encourage the world to accept Radio Moscow's view of the United States." A *New Leader* editorial, noting that Freda Kirchwey had described America as a counter-revolutionary force and had used the term "fascist" to describe developments in the United States, asserted that the *Nation* editor necessarily believed that the USSR was a "new democracy." [26]

Another telling indication of the way McCarthyism was affecting the liberal movement came in the March 1952 issue of *Commentary*. "Do we defend our rights by protecting Communists?" asked Irving Kristol. His answer was an emphatic "No." Liberalism was losing strength, Kristol declared, because too many liberals naïvely and uncritically defended the rights of Communists. "There is one thing that the American people know about Senator McCarthy; he, like them, is unequivocally anti-Communist. About the spokesmen for American liberalism, they feel they know no such thing. And with some justification." America's leading civil libertarians—Alan Barth, Henry

Steele Commager, Zechariah Chafee, Howard Mumford Jones, Ralph Barton Perry, William O. Douglas, even Francis Biddle —still thought in terms of the outmoded right-versus-left dualism which had characterized the Popular Front era. "A generation of earnest reformers who helped give this country a New Deal . . . find themselves in retrospect stained with the guilt of having lent aid and comfort to Stalinist tyranny."

The liberals, first of all, had to purge themselves of this guilt. One way to do so was to abandon all doubt about the culpability of Alger Hiss, Owen Lattimore, William Remington, and Harry Dexter White. (That Kristol lumped these four very different cases together was in itself a devastating comment on his concept of civil liberties.) Another, more important, way was to see the Communist Party for what it was—not a far-out extension of the left but a criminal conspiracy pure and simple, with virtually every member a conscious conspirator. The next step was simple—to realize that criminal conspirators had no claim to civil liberties, that universities had a right to get rid of Communist faculty members (although the loyalty oath might be a bad method for doing so), that there was nothing wrong with guilt by association so long as the concept was "soberly applied"—what could be wrong with declaring a person a Communist if he were "a member of three or more organizations officially declared subversive"?

A liberal "with clean hands and a clear mind"—and a reputation as a vociferous anti-Red—might defend the civil liberties of Communists strictly as a matter of pragmatic expediency, but it was foolish to take unpopular stands, to tell the citizens of Oshkosh, for example, that there was no harm in having their children taught to read and write by a Communist. "So long as liberals agree with Senator McCarthy that the fate of Communism involves the fate of liberalism, and that we must choose between complete civil liberties for everyone and a disregard for civil liberties entirely, we shall make no progress except to chaos." [27]

Purporting to present an anti-McCarthy strategy, Kristol actually agreed with the fundamental assumptions and tactics of McCarthyism. Yet the article won praise from, among others, the chairman of the Board of Directors of the ACLU ("I agree heartily with his thesis, while venturing to reserve judgment as to some of his comments on the particular citations.") and Norman Thomas ("It is high time that the case for civil liberties . . . should be stated by people who understand what civil liberties mean.").

Neither the *New Leader* nor Kristol appear to have spoken the thoughts of a majority of liberals. Elmer Davis published a reply to Granville Hicks's admonition that the liberals should not defend Lattimore: "Follow out his line of reasoning and it would mean that the anti-Communist Left must keep its mouth shut, leave the field to McCarthy, and regard everyone whom he accuses as guilty until he proves his innocence." Hicks himself found it impossible to swallow Muhlen's assertion that McCarthyism was a phantom. "I sometimes get an uncomfortable feeling in reading *The New Leader* that my name has been entered in a club whose only bond is a rejection of Stalinism," William E. Leuchtenburg told the magazine's readers, "and, as I look around at my fellow members, I feel certain that this is not enough of a bond for political fellowship." No other major organ of liberal opinion took up the attack on the *Nation* or Lattimore, and, despite the scattering of praise for Kristol, few liberals appear to have been willing to adopt the style of anti-Communism which he and the *New Leader* promoted. Kristol's article drew a wide range of hostile responses, and *Commentary* printed a full-length rebuttal by Alan Westin. A segment of the liberal movement had failed badly in the effort to cope with McCarthyism, but the classic civil libertarian position continued to display wide appeal and appears to have remained dominant.[28]

All the same, by early 1952, both the Truman administration and the liberal movement, their fortunes as intertwined as ever, were in retreat. The White House success in securing the combined objective of economic growth and stabilization was hardly noticed, overshadowed as it was by administration and liberal impotence against McCarthyism, by the way corruption was discrediting the ideals of the Fair Deal, by the administration's shelving of the Fair Deal programs, and by the steel stalemate. There remained little but hope for a liberal resurgence in the election campaign of 1952.

Chapter 22

Last Hurrahs and New Tomorrows

The presidential year offered the liberals the prospect of new leadership, a militant reassertion of progressive values in the campaign, and an electoral triumph which would return them to effective power in Washington. As in 1948, Truman contributed in an important way to the pursuit of all three objectives. Success in attaining the first two left the president with a feeling of vindication and the liberals with a new charismatic figure from whom they drew hope and inspiration. Failure to achieve the third, however, demonstrated that the liberals still were unable to master the forces which were overwhelming them.

I

Truman had always believed in the traditional two-term limit for presidents. His decision against running for reelection was firm enough by April 1950 that he committed it to paper in a memorandum for his private files and disclosed his intentions to a few associates. He felt that it was both his right and duty to name a successor, and from his perspective one individual stood above all others—Chief Justice Fred Vinson. Vinson had been a respected congressman and a first-class administrator. He was a loyal friend and adviser and a supporter of the administration's foreign and domestic policies. Like Truman, he combined practical political experience with a commitment to internationalism and liberalism. His health, however, was precarious; after protracted deliberation, he firmly refused the president's offer of support.

In the fall of 1951, Truman made approaches—it is impossible to say how serious—to General Eisenhower, then at the height of his prestige as commander of NATO. In a conversation with Truman on November 5, Eisenhower declared that it would be difficult for him to be a Democratic candidate since he disagreed with most of the party's domestic policies. The president nevertheless continued to respect Eisenhower's leadership and success in building support for NATO in both the United States and Europe. "My faith in him has never wavered nor ever will," he told Averell Harriman. On December 18, Truman wrote to the general, explaining that he hoped to leave the presidency and perhaps return to the Senate, but was determined to keep an isolationist out of the White House. He asked the NATO commander to declare his intentions. Eisenhower replied somewhat vaguely that he felt no "duty to seek a political nomination." Scarcely three weeks later, the general allowed his name to be entered on the Republican ballot in the New Hampshire presidential primary. From this point on, Truman expected Eisenhower to win the Republican nomination and feared that the politically inexperienced soldier would become a captive of right-wing isolationists.

The president had already begun to look elsewhere. David Lloyd, Jim Loeb, and other White House liberals had convinced him by the end of 1951 that the governor of Illinois, Adlai Stevenson, had ability, impressive diplomatic and administrative experience, and political appeal. On January 20, 1952, Truman called Stevenson to Washington and offered him the Democratic nomination. To Truman's surprise, Stevenson did not jump at the opportunity; instead, after almost two months of irritating silence, he told the president that he felt committed to stay in Illinois. A week later, Truman suffered a humiliating defeat, running behind the hard-campaigning Senator Estes Kefauver in the New Hampshire presidential primary. The president had a brief impulse to become a candidate after all and seek vindication; Democratic Chairman McKinney and other close advisers persuaded him to drop the idea. Unable to delay any longer, Truman publicly announced his decision to withdraw on March 29, 1952. He had only the hope that Stevenson might be induced to change his mind.[1]

Truman had no interest in the other candidates. He considered Kefauver a second-rate headline hunter whose highly publicized crime investigations had damaged the Democratic Party. He could not support Richard Russell, whose ability he respected, because Russell had become the candidate of the Southern conservatives. Robert Kerr, despite his services in the MacArthur controversy, despite the backing of Clark Clifford, was still very much a "special interest" oil-and-gas senator.

The candidacy of Averell Harriman provided an opportunity for a holding action. Truman admired Harriman's accomplishments as a diplomat but felt that the New Yorker's lack of electoral experience would prevent him from establishing a viable candidacy. The president apparently made it clear that Stevenson remained his first choice, but he encouraged Harriman to hold New York and provide a rallying point for anti-Kefauver Northerners. Harriman campaigned loyally and energetically, doubtless aware that his chances were slim and that the White House might pull the rug from under him at any time.[2]

Finding a candidate was only part of Truman's mission. He also intended to define the issues of the upcoming campaign in a way which would be both personally satisfying and best for the party. His own experience and the estimates of the professional pollsters led him in the same direction—toward a reassertion of the Fair Deal. In the months before the Democratic convention, Truman seized every opportunity to dramatize his advocacy of liberal principles and condemn Republican opposition to the New and Fair Deals. In one talk after another, he advocated more public housing and higher social security benefits, defended the Democratic agricultural and public power programs, and called for more progress in civil rights. "I think I have covered nearly every phase of the program of the Democratic Party for the last twenty years," he told Eleanor Roosevelt in June.

The high point of his effort came in mid-May when he addressed the ADA convention banquet, delivering a slashing attack against the Republican conservatives and a no-compromise defense of liberalism. "You made a great fighting speech," Jim Patton told the President. T.R.B. called Truman "about the most effective political speaker for liberalism in the country." The president was equally satisfied. "I don't believe I've had as much fun since the Campaign of 1948," he told Francis Biddle. The Fair Deal banner, if a bit tattered, was flying as high as ever.[3]

If Truman could not wring positive legislative results from Congress, he could wield a favorite and effective weapon. On May 29, he successfully vetoed a Congressional resolution allotting offshore oilfields to the adjacent states; he argued that the oil income should aid education throughout the nation. A month later, he issued a strongly worded veto of the McCarran-Walter immigration act. His tough message appealed to traditionally Democratic ethnic groups by attacking the bill's continuation of the discriminatory national-origins quota system; it attempted to reinforce civil liberties by condemning the vast grant of discretionary exclusion and deportation authority to immigration officials. The veto was not an unalloyed triumph —Congress overrode it by a narrow margin, partly because the State Department was too terrified of McCarran's power over appropriations to work against legislation bearing his name— but Truman drew praise for his affirmation of liberal principles. "Free men everywhere will be heartened by the President's fighting words," declared the New York *Post*. The episode was an effective culmination of the president's campaign to establish the political differences between his administration and the opposition.[4]

II

"I was greatly relieved," remarked David Lilienthal of Truman's decision to retire. Lilienthal's sentiments were those of most liberals, happy enough with the president's rhetoric and generally satisfied with his intentions but convinced that his administration had become tired and ineffective. At the beginning of February, the *New Republic* had urged Truman to withdraw "for the sake of his program and his party." The journal was blunt. Truman was "a spent force politically," incapable of winning reelection. Only the Negroes were solidly behind him. "Among other groups including labor's rank and file (if not its leadership) a general consciousness of the gap between the job and the man has sunk too deep for Truman to recover." A few weeks later, the liberal Philadelphia district attorney, Richardson Dilworth, warned that a ticket headed by Truman would lose Pennsylvania. The New Hampshire results underscored the lack of confidence in the president's leadership. After Truman announced his decision, a sympathetic Thomas L. Stokes remarked that he had done so "just in the nick of time, both for himself and for his party." [5]

A few liberals turned again to William O. Douglas. The *Nation* and the *Progressive* especially, both hoping for a candidate who would put forward a more positive non-Communist foreign policy, beat the drums for the justice. In a mail ballot conducted by the *Nation* two-thirds of the respondents chose Douglas. Beset by personal difficulties, however, Douglas did not express even the tentative interest he had shown in 1948, and there was no organization behind him. He was not a realistic alternative.[6]

Averell Harriman waged an unalloyed Fair Deal campaign and, largely because of his uncompromising advocacy of civil rights, won an enormous 80 percent of the vote in the District of Columbia primary. He was the most liberal of all the declared candidates; his staff included an impressive roster of progressives, among them Jim Loeb, who had concluded that Stevenson was out of the race. Harriman could count on New York and displayed some strength in the Mountain West because of his family railroad connections; but his personality was not suited for campaigning, and his lack of experience in elective politics made him seem, all his talent notwithstanding, a feeble contender with little chance of success.[7]

Kefauver, a strong and tireless campaigner, a crusader against crime and corruption, an ardent Fair Dealer on matters other than civil rights, was a superficially attractive choice. The *New Republic* was especially friendly, but his strength among the liberals was attained largely by default; many who respected his courage and integrity doubted that he was of presidential caliber. Within the Kefauver circle, there was bitterness over the coolness of so many leading progressives. From the beginning of 1952, most of the liberals had looked in the same direction as Truman—toward Adlai Stevenson.[8]

Stevenson had drawn some national attention and mention as a presidential possibility before 1952. Marquis Childs was boosting him as early as July 1951, and Arthur Schlesinger, Jr., listed him high among possibilities that November. In January 1952, several ADA leaders undertook an unofficial effort to draft Stevenson. The organization itself remained uncommitted, many of its members supporting Kefauver or Harriman, but most of those in top positions, including Biddle, Rauh, Niebuhr, Schlesinger, and political director Violet Gunther, worked to persuade Stevenson to declare his candidacy. The Independent Voters of Illinois issued a formal endorsement, and a small group affiliated with the IVI organized a Draft Stevenson Committee. The governor made no promises but allowed them to feel they had a green light to support him and remained in contact with them. As soon as Truman announced his withdrawal, the New York *Post* endorsed Stevenson to succeed him. By April, Stevenson was being besieged by a host of prominent progressives and by administration emissaries—and to the distress of all concerned he was refusing to give in.[9]

The increasing liberal interest in Stevenson developed along with an effort to wrest control of the Democratic convention from the Southerners and the party regulars. The contest did not center upon Stevenson, who, as it occurred, was acceptable to all factions, but upon the platform, specifically the civil rights plank. The issue carried great moral significance. It held the promise of cementing millions of Negro votes into the liberal electoral coalition. It focused squarely upon the Southern

conservatives who had been the prime force in obstructing the
Fair Deal. "Retreat here would be fatal," warned an ADA declaration. "The liberal-labor coalition will not support unprincipled compromisers."

The organization leaders felt differently. Near the end of
May, their spokesman and scheduled keynoter of the convention, Governor Paul Dever of Massachusetts, declared that he
considered the bland and evasive 1944 civil rights plank to be
as "satisfactory" as the one adopted in 1948. Francis Biddle immediately wrote a public letter of protest calling for a plank
even stronger than in 1948 and asserting that the Democratic
Party must demonstrate "whether it has the courage and vigor
to move forward." In subsequent letters to presidential con-
tenders and leading Democrats Biddle warned that a civil
rights compromise would alienate "the kind of fighting independent support that has insured Democratic victory for the
last twenty years." In the weeks before the convention, the
ADA spearheaded an effort to organize a liberal caucus for the
upcoming conflict.[10]

Truman wanted the convention to be an unequivocal affirmation of his leadership and his program. His spring speaking
effort was largely an attempt to control the platform, and his
candidate, Harriman, was an aggressive liberal. In a message
printed in the convention program, Truman declared: "There
must be no turning back or faltering on the great course our
party has pioneered. There must be no betrayal of the New
Deal and Fair Deal."

Yet having declared himself out of the race and having failed
to develop a credible replacement, the president was in no position to dominate the convention. His own choice for keynoter
reputedly had been Hubert Humphrey, but the party leaders
had insisted upon the less controversial machine politician
Dever. Publicly and privately, he insisted upon the necessity of
a strong civil rights plank, but Northern organization leaders
such as Frank McKinney and John McCormack joined with
Southern moderates in arguing for compromise. In the weeks
before the convention, with Stevenson still resistant to the

nomination, this group began to encourage the aspirations of the 74-year-old vice-president, Alben Barkley. Two weeks before the convention, Truman gave in and agreed with some misgivings to support Barkley. In doing so, he implicitly acknowledged the degree to which events had slipped from his control.[11]

III

When the Democrats assembled in Chicago at the end of July, two events dominated their convention, the confrontation of the liberals with the South and the irresistible movement to draft Adlai Stevenson. The progressive attack upon the South came in the form of a "loyalty resolution" which required all delegates to support the placement of the convention nominees under the symbol of the Democratic Party upon the state election ballots. The move, sponsored by the progressive Michigan senator, Blair Moody, amounted to a condemnation of the Dixiecrats, who had preempted the Democratic label for Thurmond in several Southern states four years earlier. The Kefauver forces, who could look only to the North for increased strength, supported the proposal. The machine leaders acquiesced. On the first day of the convention, the delegates whooped through the Moody resolution on a voice vote. The liberals, it seemed, had won an enormous victory similar to that of 1948.

Immediately, however, the organization men and the Southern moderates exerted enormous pressure for a compromise, and the White House made no effort to interfere. The very next day, the liberals felt forced to agree to a proviso that the Moody rule would not apply to delegates already bound by state party regulations. This blanket exemption in effect suspended the Moody resolution until 1956. When three diehard Southern states still withheld their assent, the regulars, desperately anxious to prevent a bolt, engineered their seating anyway—with the Illinois delegation casting a decisive bloc of votes. The regulars also successfully supported the seating of contested conservative delegations from Texas and Mississippi and secured the adoption of a civil rights plank which some thought was a shade weaker than that of 1948.

After these developments, even the most unreconstructed Dixiecrat had no excuse for walking out on the party, but many liberals were outraged. There was nothing wrong with an occasional compromise, observed an angry Joe Rauh, but the way one compromise after another had been forced upon the liberals was akin to rape. Feeling betrayed by the defection of the Illinois delegation, Rauh, Moody, Franklin Roosevelt, Jr., and a number of other liberals briefly considered an effort to block the impending nomination of Stevenson until the governor would give them assurances on civil rights and agree to accept Kefauver as his running mate. In the frenzied atmosphere of a 4:00 A.M. caucus, it appeared that many of the liberals who had been leaning toward Stevenson were ready to turn against him. A few hours later, in the light of day, it was clear that the liberal caucus had been little more than a futile temper tantrum, disowned by civil rights advocates as prominent as Hubert Humphrey and Walter Reuther. The nomination was moving irrevocably toward Stevenson—with or without the no-compromise liberals. They had little choice but to fall in line.[12]

The last barrier to a Stevenson draft collapsed when influential labor leaders declined to support Barkley's pathetic candidacy. The vice-president publicly withdrew, thereby relieving a somewhat disillusioned Truman of his commitment. Stevenson, still operating in an indirect and subdued manner, had decided to allow his supporters to place his name in nomination. On the eve of the balloting, he telephoned Truman to ask if such a move would embarrass the administration. "I replied with a show of exasperation and some rather vigorous words," Truman has written, but he promised his backing.

Truman's assistance facilitated the Stevenson nomination but probably was not decisive. Stevenson was the logical, al-

most perfect, candidate to unite the party, and his personality
had excited and enthralled the convention. The delegates were
determined not to let him escape.[13]

Despite the short-lived civil rights rebellion, moreover, no
group had been more captivated by Stevenson than the liberals. His address of welcome to the convention revealed rare ora-
torical gifts. He radiated wit, intelligence, humility, thoughtfulness, independence, and inspiration:

This is not the time for superficial solutions and endless elocution,
for frantic boast and foolish word. For words are not deeds and
there are no cheap and painless solutions to war, hunger, ignorance,
fear and to the new imperialism of Soviet Russia. . . .

Where we have erred, let there be no denial; where we have
wronged the public trust, let there be no excuses. Self-criticism is
the secret weapon of democracy, and candor and confession are
good for the political soul. But we will never appease, nor will we
apologize for our leadership in the great events of this critical century from Woodrow Wilson to Harry Truman!

Rather will we glory in these imperishable pages of our country's
chronicle. But a great record of past achievement is not enough.
There can be no complacency, perhaps for years to come. We dare
not just look back to great yesterdays. We must look forward to
great tomorrows.

There was, commented T.R.B., "an electric quality in his
prose that makes our spine tingle." The convention was
scarcely adjourned before the editors of the *New Republic*
were writing an editorial entitled "Toward the Great Tomorrows," declaring their wholehearted and unequivocal support.
Just after Stevenson's nomination, Marquis Childs wrote him:
"You made a great speech, a deeply moving speech, that immediately raised the whole tone of politics in your party. I want
you to know that my personal wish is to help you in any way
that I can." Stevenson's rhetoric and the qualities it suggested
had made him a hero overnight.[14]

For many progressives, the Stevenson personality and the
drama of a convention draft overshadowed or rendered insignificant the setbacks in the liberal confrontation with the

South. Analyzing the convention for the *Nation,* Willard Shelton argued that on balance the liberals had been successful in backing down the Dixiecrats, if not in running roughshod over them, that the wording of the civil rights plank amounted to a mere quibble. Some black leaders and civil rights advocates did express shock that Stevenson had given the vice-presidential nomination to Alabama Senator John Sparkman. The New York *Post* admitted that Sparkman was not a Dixiecrat, but called his designation "a symbolic defeat" for the cause of civil rights; the *Nation* even questioned Sparkman's liberalism in general. From the first, however, Sparkman had many defenders. David Lilienthal and Max Lerner expressed gratification at his nomination. Aubrey Williams defended his record to A. Philip Randolph. Thomas L. Stokes, himself a native Southerner, assured his readers that Sparkman represented "the decent and progressive leadership of the South." As the campaign progressed and liberals had a chance to compare Sparkman to his Republican opponent, even the *Nation* began to depict the Alabaman as an exemplar of liberal virtue.[15]

IV

The rise of Stevenson paralleled the declining reputation of another figure who had once been a liberal hope, Dwight D. Eisenhower. In command of NATO Eisenhower appeared to organize a Western European defense by the sheer force of his charismatic personality. As he prepared to assume his post in Europe in January 1951, T.R.B. called him "one of the country's precious national assets." Several months later, Elmer Davis returned from a trip to the continent to report that Eisenhower's presence had created and sustained European morale, that if such a post existed the general could easily win election as the president of all Western Europe. "We have a man whose ability to create and maintain courage and confidence in many different nations has been matched only by Winston Churchill in the darkest days of the war." Paul Douglas suggested that if Truman retired in 1952, both parties might nominate Eisenhower. ("With Senator Douglas as Vice President?" cracked Truman.) The *Reporter* endorsed Eisenhower as the one American capable of leading the non-Communist world. An ADA official commented privately that there was "a good deal of pro-Eisenhower sentiment" within the organization. Joseph Pulitzer, Jr., the publisher of the St. Louis *Post-Dispatch,* was prepared to back the general. When Eisenhower declared his availability for the Republican nomination, the *New Republic* urged him to come home and save the party from "the malignant and dark philosophy which McCarthyism, under Taft protection, has become." [16]

As in 1948, some liberals were not convinced. The *Nation* assailed the Eisenhower enthusiasm as a "neurotic need for a 'leader' " and expressed grave reservations about the possibility of a professional soldier, even one who had the best of intentions, in the White House. Thomas L. Stokes asserted that it would be an "admission of bankruptcy" if the American political system could not find a president from among its civilian politicians. But given the political stalemate at home and the overwhelming urgency of foreign problems, many progressives, although aware that Eisenhower was not a Fair Dealer, were willing to accept a degree of moderation if accompanied by unusually enlightened and capable foreign-policy leadership.[17]

Nevertheless, Eisenhower's return to America developed into a great disappointment for the liberals who had leaned toward him. It became increasingly apparent that the general was not just a bit conservative but actually well to the right of Taft. The New York *Post* and the *New Republic* were soon warning him that he could not win liberal votes by mouthing Coolidge-style clichés and tolerating McCarthy; the St. Louis *Post-Dispatch* was expressing dismay at his right-wing naïveté; and the *Nation* was asking "Who likes Ike now?" [18]

The circumstances of Eisenhower's nomination further contributed to the collapse of the general's reputation. He had enormous financial support. He let Thomas E. Dewey and the cold, efficient Dewey machine run his campaign. He and his backers did nothing to prevent the Republican convention from degenerating into an orgy of right-wing vituperation. "More treason screamers and poison-tongued character assassins were surely never before inflicted on a convention of one of our great parties," wrote Willard Shelton. "The theme was hate, hate, hate." The *New Republic* attacked the GOP platform as "distorted in its charges, dishonest in its promises." The selection of Richard Nixon as the vice-presidential candidate came as something of a shock and was an indication that the Republicans were going to use anti-Communism as a campaign issue. "The party selection seems to be the Ulysses S. Grant–Dick Tracy ticket," commented T.R.B.[19]

Even while describing his effort as a moral crusade, Eisenhower consented to support McCarthy and other unsavory right-wingers. He came to a "unity agreement"—the liberals considered it a surrender—with Senator Taft. He talked of the need to purge not only Communists but also "pinks" from the federal government. In a blatant bid for the Eastern European ethnic vote, he condemned the policy of containment and implicitly endorsed John Foster Dulles's cry for "liberation." ("The only alternative to containment that I can see is aggression," remarked Frank Kingdon.) To Marquis Childs, the general had become "a captive of the political Liliputians." "He stands down on a level to which no one would have expected him to descend," commented the St. Louis *Post-Dispatch*. "Can you remember way back when we thought it was going to be a dignified, high-level campaign?" Elmer Davis asked his radio audience. T.R.B. came to the conclusion that Eisenhower was actually a reactionary who even more than Taft wanted to turn the clock back to a simpler era—"He is a counter-revolutionist entirely surrounded by men who know how to profit by it." [20]

The incident which most symbolized the decay of the Eisenhower crusade developed from the revelation that Senator Nixon had benefited from a special fund raised by a large group of wealthy supporters. Liberals, who had already regarded Nixon as a demagogic reactionary, demanded that the Republicans apply the same moral standards to his case as to the Truman administration. The *New Republic* summed up their attitude: "Nixon is a kept man. He is also a phoney. He preaches one set of values, he practices another." Nixon delivered an emotional and effective, if factually evasive, television speech defending his position, and Eisenhower kept him on the ticket. The general had made his decision, the New York *Post* commented, not on the basis of morality and good government but rather on the basis of letters and telegrams and Nixon's support among Republican right-wingers. By the end of the campaign, Max Lerner was asking rhetorically: "Does anyone assert any more that Eisenhower has a shining integrity, or deep convictions, or is a man of clear principle?" [21]

Perhaps the most sinister aspect of the campaign was the systematic use of McCarthyism against Stevenson and his supporters. The Democratic candidate had scarcely assembled a staff before the Republican national chairman, Arthur Summerfield, denounced his campaign manager, Wilson Wyatt, as an advocate of "socialized housing" and living proof that Stevenson was controlled by "ultra left-wingers." "It is significant that Mr. Wyatt was formerly the head of Americans for Democratic Action, an organization dedicated to the promotion of Socialist schemes in America," Summerfield added. Senator Everett Dirksen joined in with an attack on Arthur Schlesinger, Jr., who was working as a speechwriter for Stevenson, and with a condemnation of ADA programs as "a definite threat to the American freedom for which we so proudly fought two world wars." In some states, especially Washington, attacks upon the ADA were a major feature of GOP campaigns against liberal candidates. Senator McCarthy's renomination by a large margin in the Wisconsin primary encouraged the use of the issue. Nixon lashed out at Stevenson for "belittling" the issue of Communists in government and for having testified to Alger Hiss's good reputation in 1949. Senators Francis Case and Karl Mundt charged that Schlesinger had a background of association with Communists and Communist organizations.[22]

Such accusations might be patently absurd, but they were by no means easy to handle. Wyatt lamely, although accurately, described himself as a former member of the "right wing" of the ADA and reminded the public that he had not been active in the organization for over three years. Subsequently, he and the new Democratic national chairman, Stephen Mitchell, decided that it was politically necessary to dismiss four trusted and valuable employees of the Democratic National Committee because of vague charges of Communist affiliations. Schlesinger aggressively asserted a militant anti-Communism, pointed to attacks which the *Daily Worker* had made upon him, and charged that Republican isolationists who wanted to undermine America's world position were the real helpers of the Communists. In the climate of irrationality which had made the original charges possible, however, there could be no meaningful response. A Wyatt or a Schlesinger could not sway those who accepted Dirksen or Mundt as exemplars of anti-Communism.

Alarmed and intimidated, many Stevenson supporters sought to disassociate themselves from the ADA. By the mid-point of the campaign, ADA chapters all over the country were complaining about being "frozen out" of the Volunteers for Stevenson movement. In late October, the ADA Executive Committee felt compelled to issue a refutation of charges that the organization was "left-wing" or "pro-Communist." Citing adverse comment from the *Daily Worker,* the document proclaimed devotion to "the principle of free and private competitive enterprise," and proudly observed that the organization had never been accused of Communist sympathies "by any committee of Congress or by any official agency." The statement was an intellectual disaster. A week later, the ADA canceled the charter of its Brown University student affiliate for sponsoring a talk by Mrs. Paul Robeson.[23]

On October 27, McCarthy went on national television to deliver a speech which hurled charges of pro-Communism at Stevenson, Wyatt, Schlesinger, James A. Wechsler, Archibald MacLeish, and the ADA. The address, with its spurious "documentation," and elusive examples of guilt by association, was a frightening example of the senator's demagoguery. The spectacle of a conservative party using an anti-Communist

bully boy led most liberals to an understandable, if rather pan-
icky analogy. "It was potential fascism," declared the St. Louis
Post-Dispatch. The ADA condemned the speech's " 'big lie'
technique" and "storm trooper mentality." Other liberals compared McCarthy to Hitler and Mussolini. "When I heard the
applause for McCarthy last night," declared a bitter and angry
Elmer Davis, "an echo of memory seemed to give it an
undertone—Sieg Heil, Sieg Heil, Sieg Heil." Eisenhower, the
liberals feared, might be not another Grant, but another Hin-
denburg.[24]

V

While the Eisenhower campaign angered, even shocked, the
liberals, the Stevenson campaign overwhelmed them. Eisenhower resorted to fuzzy and platitudinous demagoguery; Stevenson spoke out with eloquence, honesty, and thoughtfulness.
To a remarkable extent he appeared to be a living representation of the liberal ideal, the enlightened, disinterested public
servant refusing to pander to special interests, courageous in
his advocacy of the general welfare. He lectured the American
Legion on civil liberties, sternly denounced McCarthy, and
served notice upon every group to which he spoke that he
would consider their demands only in the light of the public
welfare. He ostentatiously divorced his campaign from the
Truman administration, ousting McKinney as party chairman,
maintaining his headquarters in Springfield, Illinois, choosing
a staff which had few ties to the White House. He would say
what he thought, no matter what the political consequences,
and do so in a rational, elevated way. He would "talk sense to
the American people."

The liberals responded with sheer veneration. "His speeches
are simply gems of wisdom and wit and sense," said David Lilienthal, who campaigned with all the enthusiasm of a student
volunteer. Marquis Childs called the candidate's addresses
"Lincolnian." Progressives gloried in Stevenson's rejection of
the witch-hunters, the special interests, the politicians. In deliv-

ering its endorsement, the *Reporter* praised him as "an independent first, a Democrat second." Liberals universally praised his "political courage and boldness" (Thomas L. Stokes), his "aristocratic contempt for the ignoble compromises that the unfortunate Ike is making" (T.R.B.), "his personal integrity" (the *Nation*). Max Lerner called him "the first figure of major stature to have emerged since Roosevelt." Richard Rovere quite deliberately and thoughtfully went farther: "his gifts are more imposing than those of any President or any major-party aspirant for the office in this century." The Farmers Union, while maintaining its tradition of formal independence, gave the Democratic candidate strong support. Papers and journals which had remained aloof from Truman in 1948—the New York *Post* and the St. Louis *Post-Dispatch,* the *Nation* and the *Progressive*—endorsed Stevenson with enthusiasm.[25]

To a remarkable extent, the liberal acclaim was an expression of confidence in Stevenson's character rather than joy over the substance of his campaign. His great tomorrows promised much in the way of leadership, little in the way of innovation. It was only after some hesitation that he came out for repeal of the Taft-Hartley Act with the proviso that a new and fairer modification of the Wagner Act was necessary. For a while he seemed to wobble on the offshore oil issue, although he eventually endorsed the administration position. T.R.B. found his declarations on public as against private electrical power alarmingly well balanced. He spoke frequently of the important role of the states in the federal system. He asserted the need for tight-fisted government economy and cited with pride his gubernatorial record of fiscal responsibility. Edwin Lahey called him the most conservative figure to head a Democratic ticket since John W. Davis in 1924.

Even on the issue of Communism, Stevenson's position was less than perfect civil libertarianism. He praised the Bill of Rights and denounced McCarthy. But he defended the removal of Communist teachers, the Smith Act prosecutions, and the federal loyalty program. As the campaign neared its end, he felt forced to devote an entire speech to an explanation of his deposition in support of Alger Hiss. He courageously asserted a citizen's duty to testify when called upon by the courts and legitimately observed that Eisenhower and Dulles had been among the Carnegie trustees who had maintained confidence in Hiss until his actual conviction. Yet Stevenson also embarrassingly felt compelled to minimize his association with Hiss and even recalled that he had after all only testified that Hiss's reputation was good, not very good.

Such equivocations, made under the enormous pressures of a presidential campaign, were understandable and no worse than Truman's past utterances, but Stevenson's position on civil rights was harder to explain. He endorsed a federal FEPC with reluctance and with the hope that effective state action would make a federal law unnecessary. Speaking in Richmond, Virginia, he all but waved the Confederate flag as he praised the culture and statesmanship of the South and attacked past Republican oppression of the region. He rejected as contemptible "the reckless assertion that the South is a prison in which half the people are prisoners and the other half are wardens," condemned anti-Southern prejudice, observed that racial and religious tensions were national in scope, and came extremely close to saying that economic progress was the real answer to Southern race problems. He possessed, as a New York *Times* journalist observed, more of the South in him than anyone had realized.[26]

A very few liberals were so disturbed by Stevenson's moderation on the race problem that they considered withholding their support. (In mid-August, 2 of the 71 members of the ADA National Board voted against an immediate endorsement.) Others, however, began to rethink the problem. Defending the selection of Sparkman, the *New Republic* argued that the vice-presidential candidate after all did represent the best of Southern liberalism and that there was something to be said for the Southern progressive emphasis on economic advance as a solution for racial difficulties. There was much to be said, moreover, for an all-out effort to isolate the Dixiecrats and liberalize the South. These considerations pointed toward a new direction: *"Now that the decision has been made to work with the best forces in the South, the proper endeavor becomes to seek a bridge between Northern and Southern liberalism."* The St. Louis *Post-Dispatch* agreed, asserting that Stevenson was taking a "sane, frank, rational approach" to civil rights. He was avoiding dogmatism and emotion, facing the issue for what it was, "a problem to be worked out by patient, constructive statesmanship, not a mere vote-catching flag to be waved at election time." Captivated by Stevenson, the liberals assumed that somehow he could impose a rational and honorable compromise upon the most irrational and intractable of American political problems.[27]

Aside from the civil rights issue, however, Stevenson's positions were substantively close to Truman's. His moderation was partly a matter of rhetoric. It is significant that in a speech which defended the welfare state and called for "better housing, better health, better schools, better security," Stevenson went on to call the Democrats "the truly conservative party" of the nation. Even his very manner of delivery, thoughtful and deliberate as it was, influenced his image. The public power speech which bothered T.R.B., who heard it in person, reads very differently than it must have sounded. In cold print, many of its passages seem almost Trumanesque in their denunciation of monopolistic utilities. To a large extent, the image of Stevenson as a moderate developed from his appearance as a calm, rational candidate who understood and brooded over the complexities of public issues, refrained from appeals to emotion, and refused to overpromise. His moderation, such as it was, disturbed few progressives because it grew so naturally out of the liberal virtues he embodied.

There could be little doubt in any case that the thrust of his campaign was in a liberal direction and that he had surrounded himself with prominent progressives. Given these circumstances, the important consideration was the caliber of Stevenson's leadership. As early as the beginning of the Democratic convention, Max Lerner had commented that "the exact degree of Stevenson's liberalism or moderateness of view

is less important than the skill and reflectiveness, the literate-
ness, the freshness of spirit he would bring into the White
House." Subsequently, Morris Rubin defended Stevenson's reluctance to be typed as a Fair Dealer, arguing that the governor had thereby gotten the attention of middle-of-the-roaders
and had gained "time to restate the issues in his own fresh language, and with his own modifications, free from President
Truman's clichés." The *Nation*, in delivering its endorsement,
criticized Stevenson's backtracking on the Communist issue,
but asserted: "we have confidence in his essential democracy
and liberalism, his passionate love for America, his concern for
human freedom." In the last analysis, most liberals believed
that the man himself was the deciding factor.[28]

One of the most prominent aspects of the Stevenson campaign was its disdainful aloofness from the White House. Early
in the campaign, Stevenson even promised to "clean up the
mess in Washington." His use of the phrase was inadvertent,
but it probably reflected his honest opinion. Truman was hurt
and angered. Some liberals, even while admiring Stevenson's independence from professional politicians, sympathized with the
president. The *New Republic* warned Stevenson that he was
decending from the heights of his acceptance address and going
too far in criticizing a basically sound administration. Thomas
L. Stokes wrote: "Harry Truman still stands for something very
valuable in his record and program with millions and millions
of plain people." [29]

Truman, however, for all his annoyance, still respected Stevenson's ability. Conversely, the Eisenhower campaign, which
embraced Taft and McCarthy, infuriated him. The president
felt driven by the indifference of his own candidate and the violent attacks of the opposition to seek vindication from the
people. At the end of September, despite a perceptible lack of
encouragement from the Stevenson camp, Truman set out
upon a whistle-stop tour even more arduous than the one he
had undertaken for himself in 1948.

He loyally eulogized Stevenson, but his major effort was directed toward defending the accomplishments and aspirations

of the New and Fair Deals. In one talk after another, he ticked off the Democratic record, ranging from social welfare to rural electrification and farm price supports. Far more than Stevenson, he carried the issue of immigration restriction to the ethnic groups and the issue of civil rights to the Negroes. He attacked the Republicans as a party of reactionary special interests, suggesting their slogan "Look ahead, neighbor" might appropriately be changed to "Look out, neighbor." Speaking in San Francisco, he declared: "My friends, we are dealing here with something beyond reason, something beneath reason. We are dealing with the herd instinct of the dinosaurs." Constantly as in 1948 he exorted his listeners to remember their own interests on election day: "Vote for yourselves. You are the Government." [30]

Nor was he hesitant to proclaim that the national monument who headed the GOP ticket was unfit for the presidency. In blunt language, he said that he had been mistaken in once thinking Eisenhower qualified for the White House, that Eisenhower had betrayed liberal and responsible Republicans, had played low politics with the Korean War, and had abandoned ordinary standards of decency and morality by joining hands with "moral pigmies" who had slandered General Marshall. After the Republican candidate endorsed Chapman Revercomb, a vicious immigration restrictionist whom Dewey had refused to touch in 1948, Truman asserted: "He has had an attack of moral blindness, for today, he is willing to accept the very practices that identified the so-called 'master race.' " [31]

The Republicans in turn charged Truman with mudslinging, dispatched hecklers to his talks, and assigned a "truth squad" to follow him around the country and refute his charges. (Speaking to a Columbus Day dinner in New York, Truman wondered aloud if the great admiral had once been followed by a truth squad proclaiming incessantly that the world was flat.) The president replied that he was just explaining the facts to the people. "When I stayed in Washington and took no part in the campaign, the Republican candidate and the one-party press felt free to vilify me as a traitor and a corruptionist," he said bitterly. "When I replied and carried a campaign of truth around the country, their only retort was to accuse me of slander and abuse." [32]

No aspect of Truman's effort was tougher and more uncompromising than his attack on McCarthy and McCarthyism. In Boston, where McCarthy had made inroads among normally Democratic ethnic groups, he devoted a major address to the issue. He compared accusations that the government was soft on Communism to the bigoted campaign against Al Smith in 1928. He accused the Republicans of using the Hitler technique of the big lie and condemned Eisenhower's toleration of the attack upon Marshall: "Most of us, I think, believe a man ought to be loyal to his friends when they are unjustly attacked; that he ought to stand up for them, even if it costs him some votes. At any rate, that is a rule of my life. I stand by my friends." To the surprise of the uneasy local politicians, the crowd booed the mention of McCarthy's name and enthusiastically cheered the president's defense of the Bill of Rights.[33]

A few liberals blanched at Truman's harsher language, especially the "master race" accusation, but most found his speeches exhilarating. His rhetoric provided a perfect counterpoint to Stevenson's lofty prose, his fighting qualities enlivened the campaign, and his crowd appeal was greater than ever. "This man, the subject of condescension so long, has become, at 68, almost an object of awe to the candidates who crowd his train and clasp his coattails," wrote New York *Post* reporter Murray Kempton. Freda Kirchwey offered her congratulations for "the superb fight you are making." "Give 'em hell, Mr. President," exhorted the New York *Post*. The *New Republic* expressed the wonderment of many liberals. Truman was going to the people and treating them as rational human beings, giving them the facts and assuming that they would decide accordingly. "The President is making the most sustained, earnest, intelligent struggle of his political career. . . . How odd that a Pendergast alumnus should be so wise and bold, but what a tribute to the American system." [34]

VI

Conceding the election to Eisenhower, Stevenson remarked that he felt like the little boy who had stubbed his toe and was too grown-up to cry but too hurt to laugh. "Thousands of us stubbed our toes with Stevenson," remarked the *New Republic*. For many, the disappointment seemed at first almost overwhelming. "We had suffered a disaster, for a great figure had come across the stage and we had missed him," wrote David Lilienthal. Reinhold Niebuhr wrote sadly of the irrationality of American electoral politics. Elmer Davis feared that it might be a hundred years before another presidential candidate could muster the courage to talk sense to the people.[35]

Yet a closer look at the results yielded plenty of encouragement. The voters had given Eisenhower a personal victory, but they had not endorsed right-wing reaction. Many liberal Democrats survived the presidential landslide. Conversely, Senator McCarthy had won only narrowly in Wisconsin, trailing every other GOP candidate on the state ballot. The country might believe it was time for a change, might be tired and frustrated over the Korean War, might have a transcendent faith in Eisenhower, but Democratic liberalism remained strong.

The liberals did not have Stevenson as a president, but they still had him as a leader. He had involved a new generation of reform-minded intellectuals in politics, and they sought only the privilege of following him in the battles yet to come. Some sensed with excitement that he was leading them toward a new liberalism which would go beyond the New and Fair Deals, not only in providing new answers but even in asking new questions. "It will be fun to be in opposition for a while," remarked T.R.B.[36] As Truman, now overshadowed by the new Democratic leader, prepared to leave office, the liberal anticipation of a new era obscured the realization that an old one was ending.

Chapter 23

Beyond the New Deal: Truman, the Liberals, and the Politics of Leadership

By 1952, American liberalism had moved far from the position it had held at the end of World War II. In 1945, the liberal movement, built around the charisma of Franklin D. Roosevelt and the aspirations he embodied, was fundamentally weak, yet hopeful of building a new world out of the wreckage of the old. The liberals sought an era of peace and prosperity at home and abroad as the logical and necessary culmination of the war. Caught up in the spirit of the wartime alliance, they accepted the Soviet Union and the American Communist Party as allies in a Popular Front against the common enemy, fascism. By 1952, the liberals subscribed to a "vital center" viewpoint, still advocating many of the same objectives as in 1945 but without utopian illusions. Rejecting the Popular Front, the vital center defined American liberalism as a movement which opposed the totalitarianism of the left as completely as it did the totalitarianism of the right. The vital center gave liberalism a definition more in line with its historical meaning and preserved it as an important, if not triumphant, force in American politics. The achievement, frequently denigrated because it failed to bring about international peace or to establish a new era of reform, was actually a substantial one.

Popular Frontism during World War II had been natural and to some degree salutary, for it helped focus American efforts on the greatest immediate threat to liberal values. But single-minded concentration upon the utter destruction of fascism encouraged the assumption that fascism was the only enemy which liberalism faced, that the end of the war would mean the beginning of a world moving toward peace and freedom. Popular Frontism, in addition, bred a selective morality which glossed over the fact that Stalin's totalitarianism was as grinding as Hitler's. Such blind spots were of little practical importance so long as the United States and the Soviet Union were united against a common enemy, but the Popular Front was less viable as the interests and aspirations of the two nations began to conflict.

On the ethical level, liberals found it increasingly difficult to maintain a complacent attitude toward a Soviet imperialism which appeared to be reaching beyond the limits required by Russian security and toward areas which had democratic traditions. For many liberals, the Czech coup served as a traumatic revelation of Soviet implacability and confirmed the argument that a democratic movement could not align itself with Communism. On the tactical level, Popular Frontism was political suicide. The failure of Henry Wallace and the Progressive Party exemplified the political and intellectual bankruptcy of a style of liberalism which had outlived its time.

New Left historians, who regret the demise of the Popular Front and frequently repeat its clichés, have tended to depict vital-center liberalism as a type of negative, monolithic anti-Communism. Actually, few of the vital-center liberals fit such a description. Many were *non*-Communist rather than *anti*-Communist. They constantly hoped that negotiation could resolve major differences between the United States and the USSR, that constructive world development could supplant Soviet-American conflict. Even the more pessimistic anti-Communist liberals, who saw the Cold War as an inescapable long-range struggle, sought constructive ways to wage it, opposed entanglements with foreign reactionaries, and shrank from MacArthur-Dulles style anti-Red crusades.

To the New Left, the vital center was illegitimate because of its complicity in the Cold War, but most adherents to the vital center came to the Cold War reluctantly. They were convinced that association with a totalitarian movement carried a greater burden of guilt. They were disillusioned with a Popular Front persuasion which increasingly shrank from any criticism of the USSR. By 1948, Popular Frontism had degenerated to the point that any hint of *some* Soviet responsibility for the Cold War—not the major responsibility but at least some small amount of blame—was routinely condemned as "Red-baiting." Thus with naïve disregard of the consequences the Progressive Party convention voted down the Vermont resolution, and its innocuous disclaimer of "blanket endorsement to the foreign policy of any nation." "The American public," Joseph Starobin has written, "grasped that the Cold War could not be halted by any movement which could not even approve the Vermont resolution and was largely unaware of its significance." [1]

Despite the New Left tendency to confuse all varieties of anti-Communism with McCarthyism, the vital center neither created McCarthyism nor encouraged it. Some liberal intellectuals behaved irresponsibly, and many liberal politicians gave in to pressures they thought too strong to resist; but most refrained from character assassination and defended fundamental liberties. Right-wing anti-Communism had been well established before the rise of the vital center and probably would have achieved its McCarthy-era strength earlier had the Popular Front continued to dominate the liberal movement. As it was, the isolation of Popular Frontism enabled the 1948 election to be fought out—and won—on the issues of liberal reform. The rise of the vital center made it impossible to smear the liberal movement until external events—the fall of China, the Soviet atomic bomb, the espionage cases, and especially the Korean War—created an irrational climate of hysteria and frustration. In such a situation even the vital-center liberals were vulnerable, but in the long run they were far safer than would have been the case had they clung to a Popular Frontism which would have given McCarthy's charges credibility in a rational political atmosphere.

Vital-center liberalism had significant shortcomings, but its accomplishments, if not dramatic, were genuinely important. The vital center's major organization, the Americans for Democratic Action, never attained great independent power. It was unable to transcend the progressive longing for charismatic leadership, and it failed to gain major reform breakthroughs. Yet it is hard to imagine that Popular Front liberalism would have fared better or even as well. The historian who sits in judgment must consider which style of progressivism best expressed the liberal spirit and which could best preserve the legitimacy of the liberal movement in American politics. With its impartial rejection of all brands of totalitarianism during the Cold War years, the vital center effected a happy merger of ethics and expediency which helped keep liberalism alive in a period of adversity.

The campaign of 1952 demonstrated anew the way in which Harry S. Truman had identified himself with the liberalism of the vital center. The president had not come to his position through a process of reflection and would have scorned any attempt to depict him as an "intellectual," although he had read widely in history and government and in many respects was more learned and perceptive than even his admirers understood. Essentially, he was a party man whose career reflected the course of the mainstream of the Democratic Party in the twentieth century. Born into a Southern Democratic family, he found himself from the time of his initial alignment with the Pendergast machine in a Northern urban Democratic political situation. His views changed accordingly, not because of simple political cynicism, but from a broadening of contacts and perspectives which, combined with the political pressures of the underprivileged and with his own sense of fairness and decency, impelled him toward liberalism. Doubtless, his career would have taken a different line had it centered around a rural courthouse, but it did not.

It was easy and natural for him to follow the national current of his party. To many, the New Deal of Franklin Roosevelt seemed but an extension of Woodrow Wilson's New Freedom, and it was a matter of course for a loyal Democrat to follow both. From the New Deal, it was only a few steps to the Fair Deal. As president—especially after 1948—Truman functioned with varying degrees of acceptance as a liberal leader, advocating a more far-reaching reform program than any chief executive before him, yet never able to win the devotion of his most natural constituency in the manner of an FDR or a Stevenson.

Whatever the motivations and forces which lay behind Truman's development, and whatever the moral strength of vital center liberalism, it appeared that both the president and the liberals failed to achieve the objectives they sought. As Truman left office, even observers sympathetic to him conceded that his domestic program had been unsuccessful and that his reputation would rest upon his foreign policy. Accepting the Cold War as a sad necessity, they assumed that Truman had at least approached greatness by mobilizing the free world against the threat of totalitarian aggression.[2]

A decade later, New Left historians viewed the Cold War quite differently—as a tragic blunder caused by the narrow-mindedness of Truman and his advisers. Explicitly or implicitly, they argued that this blunder, itself the major failure of the Truman administration, was the key to all the other failures—the blockage of the Fair Deal in Congress, the decline of civil liberties, the rise of McCarthyism, and the development of the climate of frustration which brought Truman himself down.[3] The New Leftists found it easy enough to demonstrate that Truman's diplomacy was at times crude and ill-considered. Their work, however, drew its impact and plausibility from the atmosphere of despair created by the Vietnam involvement (often justified by invocations of the Truman Doctrine) and from the shock of the enormous and explosive social problems which erupted in the sixties and were intensified by the Vietnam War.

For all its appeal, however, the New Left argument had many flaws. Perhaps the most fundamental was an apparent assumption that the natural order of human affairs was rationality, peace, and reform. In diplomacy, the New Leftists seemed to believe that nations normally found it possible to arrive at mutually acceptable arrangements on such difficult matters as spheres of influence and conflicting objectives; that cooperation, not conflict, was the usual state of international relations, or at least would be in a world uncorrupted by capitalistic institutions. Similarly, in assuming that the reform impulse was stifled by the Cold War, the New Leftists apparently believed that ongoing reform was the normal condition of American politics. The historical record refuted both assumptions, but the New Left point of departure, like that of all radicals, was a vision of what should have been rather than the human past as it had been. Unable to admit the fundamental irrationality of the way in which men and nations manage their affairs, the New Leftists found a convenient scapegoat in the Truman administration, just as did many liberals and radicals during the years 1945–1948.

All the same, indications are that the United States was more moved than the Soviet Union by millennial aspirations and dreams of international cooperation as World War II ended. Historians do not require access to the Kremlin archives to know that Stalin, far more than Truman, was wedded to the theory that struggle and force were the determinants of diplomacy. Perhaps Stalin would have been moved by such concessions as a generous loan and the sharing of atomic secrets, but the available evidence does not support such hopes; rather, his personality and his view of international relations appear to have convinced him that the USSR would have to go it alone in a hostile world.

Even the generally accepted judgment that the Cold War killed the Fair Deal requires reexamination. It is true, as Richard Neustadt has pointed out, that the Cold War occupied much of the administration's attention and that the key legislative measures associated with it necessarily claimed first priority when the president dealt with Congress.[4] Yet international hostilities, hot or cold, are not necessarily inimical to reform causes. The Cold War actually gave the civil rights movement greater impetus than it probably would have had otherwise, and it took the Korean conflict to make the army's desegregation policy a reality. There is little evidence that Truman's rather skillful construction of a bipartisan foreign-policy coalition during the early Cold War jeopardized domestic reform; as long as the president had substantial Republican support for his diplomacy, he found it practically unnecessary to mollify the right wing of his own party. It was only after bipartisanship collapsed under the pressure of Korea that he felt compelled to appease the conservative Democrats. In any event, historians should be wary of the assumption that an America with no international worries would have turned eagerly toward reform.

The Cold War and especially the Korean conflict placed new obstacles in the path of reform, but the barriers were formidable in any case. The New Deal had come to an end in 1938 before war or the threat of war had become the dominant force in American politics. World War II helped consolidate the New Deal and effected some limited advances in civil rights but failed to create a new liberal majority. A postwar depression might have opened the way for reform, but the inflationary-boom situation which actually developed appears to have had the reverse effect. Pollsters and analysts have drawn a convincing picture of a postwar public apathetic toward new reform breakthroughs but determined to protect the gains which they had secured from the New Deal and the war.

In examining the structure of the House of Representatives from 1947–1962, David R. Mayhew estimates that at any time during this period Democratic strength had to number at least 260 to insure the passage of urban-oriented reform legislation and that "the breaking point on the thornier labor questions —minimum wage and labor-management relations—lay well above the 280 mark." At the peak of their strength during the Truman years, in the Eighty-first Congress, the Democrats had a House delegation of 263; they enacted a correspondingly modest reform program. If Mayhew's figures are meaningful, the historian can assume that Truman functioned effectively as a legislative leader when he had the material to build a majority.[5]

Critics argue nevertheless that a stronger leader than Truman could have aroused public opinion and secured the election of a stronger reform majority. Americans regularly expect miracles from their presidents, and the innumerable assertions of presidential power in foreign policy since 1939 have been especially important in establishing a presumption of presidential omnipotence in other areas. Yet the Founding Fathers did not write the Constitution with the idea of such a carry-over. In structuring the American system of government, the Founding Fathers intended presidential dominance in foreign policy. Their design for domestic problems, however, was very different; it was based on a diffusion of power and responsibility designed to give important interests a veto over legislation which might affect them adversely. Throughout the history of the Republic, the system has functioned about as planned.

On occasion, reform-minded presidents coming to power on the crest of a wide demand for change have established mastery over public opinion and Congress, the most important examples being Woodrow Wilson from 1913 to 1916, Franklin D. Roosevelt from 1933 to 1938, and possibly Lyndon B. Johnson from 1964 to 1966. But such leadership is extremely difficult to sustain, even for the most talented and charismatic figure; in the case of Roosevelt the magic ran out with the nation still in a critical domestic situation. A president can provide leadership for reform legislation if the climate is right. He can mobilize a latent majority by gauging public opinion, doing what he can to mold it, and assuming leadership of it at the right moment. But his powers of manipulation are limited, and his efforts, if too crude or too obvious, may backfire. Above all, he cannot construct a majority if the building blocks are too few.

Truman's attempt to put over a legislative program rested on an effort to transform a mandate for continuation and consolidation into a mandate for change. The clearest and most ambitious phase of this effort was the attempt to build a farm-labor-consumer coalition around the Brannan Plan. The strategy failed, partly because of the Korean War, but more fundamentally because of the great gulf between farmers and workers. Truman's talents as a leader of the public and Congress never approached the brilliance of FDR, but Roosevelt's own failure to control the legislative branch after 1938 demonstrates the limits of such talent.

Measured against such a perspective, Truman's achievements are substantial. Realistic enough to perceive the limits of his personal appeal, he sought to identify himself with the reform issues which appealed to the most important segments of his party; in doing so, he defended and advanced the objectives of American progressivism. His course demonstrated that qualities other than charisma are important to constructive liberal leadership. If he waged the Cold War with a lack of finesse, he usually acted with an intelligence and moderation which in the main expressed liberal objectives—from the Marshall Plan to the Point Four program to the defense of the United Nations in the Korean War.

Truman's domestic accomplishments represent an important chapter in the history of American liberalism. First, he successfully defended and institutionalized the New Deal. The record of the Eightieth Congress had raised the specter of a new era of postwar normalcy and reversal of a substantial portion of the New Deal if the Republicans won the White House in 1948. Perhaps the reactionary intentions of the Eightieth Congress have been exaggerated—certainly Truman magnified them as much as possible—but there can be little argument that most of its leaders were not reconciled to the Roosevelt reforms and were perfectly willing to undo as many of them as possible. If Thomas E. Dewey was not a stark reactionary, his evasions in the campaign of 1948 nevertheless raised serious doubts as to whether he could have contained the Republican right-wingers, who would have taken his victory as a green light. As it was, Truman clearly and distinctly made the New Deal heritage the central issue between himself and Dewey. The Democratic victory insured that no sensible Republican candidate ever again would dare to be even evasive on the issue. (The Goldwater campaign of 1964 would confirm the rule.) Moreover, Truman demonstrated great skill in mobilizing the latent majority which was ready to support the New Deal, and he showed that, given the right issues, he could lead the public. He made the national consensus so clear that no politician could ignore it. Historians have tended to give Eisenhower credit for institutionalizing the New Deal, but Eisenhower had no choice. During the 1952 campaign, even the fantastically popular general felt compelled to issue a declaration stating his explicit adherence to the New Deal legacy.[6]

Truman also advanced and indeed added to the New Deal heritage with his management of the economy. Even during all the fumbling and mistakes of the postwar reconversion period, few doubted his acceptance of the New Deal assumption that government was responsible for the economy. The Employment Act of 1946 not only codified the principle but established important machinery for putting it into practice. The Council of Economic Advisers, although it might fluctuate in viewpoint and influence from one administration to the next, provided a central point in the bureaucracy for managing the economy. Even its more conservative members would be knowledgeable economists unwilling to accept the economic dogmas of the far right and unlikely to feel beholden to any special interest. The council's existence alone guaranteed a greater access to the White House for progressive economic ideas, even if it did not insure their acceptance. During the Truman era, the council became a launching pad for Leon Keyserling's program of economic expansion and for the growth policies of the Korean War. As a progressive Keyserling may have been somewhat iconoclastic, but he did influence the administration in a direction consistent with the goals of American liberalism.

Truman, moreover, could point to a legislative record more impressive than most observers realized. His failure to achieve such breakthrough legislation as national health insurance, a peacetime FEPC, Taft-Hartley repeal, and federal aid to education from the Eighty-first Congress obscured important "piecemeal" advances, such as the substantial enlargement of social security and public power. Although usually remembered for the proposals it rejected, the Eighty-first was the most liberal Congress in a decade [7] and surely demonstrated that Truman was less than a total failure as a legislative leader.

Truman also moved more vigorously on the problem of civil rights than any president before him. Unable to secure the legislation he had requested, he nevertheless spoke out with increasing forthrightness and militance. His determination was the decisive factor in forcing the army to abandon its segregation policy. The Justice Department briefs in civil rights cases threw the moral weight of the federal government behind black legal efforts as never before. After the election of 1952, when there was no more political advantage to be wrung from the issue, the solicitor general submitted a brief to the Supreme Court in behalf of elementary and secondary school desegregation. At about the same time, Clark Clifford and Charlie Murphy were working to change the Senate rules so as to stifle future Southern filibusterers. "As you leave the White House," Roy Wilkins wrote to Truman in January 1953, "you carry with you the gratitude and affectionate regard of millions of your Negro fellow citizens who in less than a decade of your leadership, inspiration and determination, have seen the old order change right before their eyes." [8]

Thrown into partnership by a whim of history, Truman and the liberals coexisted uneasily but in a manner which reinforced each other's tendency toward increasingly advanced progressivism. Truman responded to liberal pressures, and in doing so provided an example which foreclosed any slackening of progressive goals and spurred the liberals on to demand new gains. The subtle creative tension which characterized their relationship was a healthy one. Their accomplishments may have been limited—vanguard movements rarely enjoy instant success—and their programs were not necessarily applicable to the problems of the next generation; yet they successfully defended and reinforced liberalism, moving it beyond the New Deal and keeping it in confrontation with the crises of postwar America. It was by no means an inconsiderable record. Truman and the liberals had served their nation, their party, and their tradition better probably than they themselves realized.

Abbreviations

ADA   Americans for Democratic Action
ALP   American Labor Party
AVC   American Veterans Committee
CIOPAC Congress of Industrial Organizations Political Action Committee
COHC   Columbia University Oral History Collection
CR   *Congressional Record*
CS   Chicago *Sun*
CST   Chicago *Sun-Times*
EP   Editorial paragraph
FDRL   Franklin D. Roosevelt Library
FEPC   Fair Employment Practices Committee
HST   Harry S. Truman
HSTL   Harry S. Truman Library
ICCASP Independent Citizens Committee of the Arts, Sciences, and Professions
LC   Library of Congress
MSS   Manuscript Collection
N   *Nation*
NCPAC National Citizens Political Action Committee
NFU   National Farmers Union
NL   *New Leader*
NR   *New Republic*
NUF   *National Union Farmer*
NYP   New York *Post*
NYS   New York *Star*

NYT   New York *Times*
OF   Official File
P   *Progressive*
PCA   Progressive Citizens of America
PP   Progressive Party
PPF   President's Personal File
R   *Reporter*
SLPD   St. Louis *Post-Dispatch*
UDA   Union for Democratic Action

Notes

CHAPTER 1 : SIXTY MILLION JOBS AND THE
PEOPLE'S REVOLUTION

1. The pioneer statement of the thesis that there were two New Deals is Basil Rauch, *The History of the New Deal* (New York, 1944). The most elaborate version, however, was developed by Arthur M. Schlesinger, Jr., in the *Coming of the New Deal* (Boston, 1958), esp. chs. 21 and 22. James MacGregor Burns accepts a modified version of the thesis in *Roosevelt: The Lion and the Fox* (New York, 1956), chs. 10 and 11. Rexford Tugwell discusses the problem in his study, *The Democratic Roosevelt* (Garden City, N.Y., 1957), esp. ch. 16. Otis L. Graham, Jr., "The Historian and the Two New Deals: 1944–1960," *Social Studies*, LIV (April 1963), 133–40, thoroughly surveys the debate.

2. The major critic is William E. Leuchtenburg, *Franklin D. Roosevelt and the New Deal* (New York, 1963), pp. 162–66. See also William H. Wilson, "The Two New Deals: A Valid Concept?" *Historian*, XXVIII (Feb. 1966), 268–88.

3. The literature on World War II and social reform is unfortunately still quite thin. A pioneering effort was Eric F. Goldman, *Rendezvous with Destiny* (New York, 1952), ch. 16. J. Joseph Huthmacher, *Senator Robert F. Wagner and the Rise of Urban Liberalism* (New York, 1968), ch. 16, is valuable. Thomas A. Kreuger, *And Promises to Keep: The Southern Conference for Human Welfare, 1938–1948* (Nashville, 1967), is a significant case study of one liberal organization; chs. 5 and 6 cover the war years. Richard Polenberg, *War and Society* (Philadelphia, 1950), ch. 3, is useful and well done.

4. Lewis Corey, *The Unfinished Task* (New York, 1942), p. 3.

5. Stuart Chase, "The Fear of Peace," *P*, VIII (Nov. 20, 1944), 1–2; "Warning—Harding Ahead," *Common Sense*, XII (Jan. 1943), 450–451; George Soule, "That Post-War Depression," *NR*, CVII (July 20, 1942),

74–76; E. D. Kennedy, "Post-War Inflation," *ibid.*, CVII (Sept. 28, 1942), 375–77; Paul A. Samuelson, "Unemployment Ahead," *ibid.*, CXI (Sept. 11, 18, 1944) 297–99, 333–35; "Lindbergh's Nazi Pattern," *ibid.*, CV (Sept. 22, 1941), 360–61; "The Same Old Coughlin," *ibid.*, CVI (Jan. 5, 1942), 7–8; Heinz H. F. Eulau, "False Prophets in the Bible Belt," *ibid.*, CX (Feb. 7, 1944), 169–71; Will Chasan and Victor Riesel, "The Reverend Gerald L. K. Smith," *N*, CLIV (May 16, 1942), 566–68; Riesel, "Fascist Pie for Veterans," *ibid.*, CLVI (April 17, 1943), 554–56; Charles G. Bolte, "When the Soldiers Return," *ibid.*, CLIX (Oct. 21, 1944), 493–94; Frank Kingdon, *"That Man" in the White House* (New York, 1944), pp. 11–15, 32–38; Max Lerner, *Public Journal: Marginal Notes on Wartime America* (New York, 1945), pp. 59–145. See also the many other articles in the *New Republic* and the *Nation* on native fascists and fascist-leaning politicians. John Roy Carlson [Arthur Derounian], *Under Cover* (New York, 1943), influenced many liberals.

6. William L. Shirer, "The Poison Pen," *Atlantic Monthly*, CLXIX (May 1942), 548–52; Freda Kirchwey, "Curb the Fascist Press," *N*, CLIV (March 28, 1942), 357–58; "Free Speech in Wartime," *NR*, CVI (April 27, 1942), 559–60; Kreuger, *And Promises to Keep*, pp. 101–102. Cf. Roger N. Baldwin, "Free Speech for Native Fascists," *NR*, CVI (April 27, 1942), 574–75; and Milton Mayer, "How Liberalism Disappears," *P*, VII (Jan. 18, 1943), 5.

7. Chester Bowles to Henry Wallace, September 15, 1944, Henry Wallace MSSP FDRL. "Industrial Treason at Home," VI (April 18, 1942), 1; Robert La Follette, Jr., "Breeding the Next War," *ibid.*, VIII (May 22, 1944), 1–2; Homer T. Bone, "Munition Frauds Imperil the War Effort," *ibid.*, VII (July 26, 1943), 1–2; Richard J. Davis and Wesley McCune, "Capitol Letter," *Common Sense*, X (Oct., 1941), 310–11; T.R.B., "The Fight for Production," *NR*, CVI (Jan. 19, 1942), 84; I. F. Stone, "Production Politics," *N*, CLIV (Jan. 10, 1942), 27–28.

8. T.R.B., "The Tories and the Dynamic Lie," *NR*, CVI (March 30, 1942), 428; "Obstruction by Privateers," *P*, VI (Dec. 21, 1942), 12; I. F. Stone, "All-Out Against Labor," *N*, CLIV (March 28, 1942), 358–60; Victor G. Reuther, "Labor in the War—and After," *Antioch Review*, III (Fall 1943), 311–27; Victor H. Bernstein, "The Antilabor Offensive," *ibid.*, pp. 328–40.

9. Daniel Bell, "Monopoly Can Lead to Fascism," *Common Sense*, X (Sept. 1941), 267–69, 280; Maury Maverick, "Economic Democracy for Postwar America," *P*, VIII (May 1, 1944), 1–2; Thurman Arnold, "The Coming Economic Conflict," *ibid.*, VIII (July 17, 1944), 1, 10; James Burnham, *The Managerial Revolution* (New York, 1941); Robert A. Brady, *Business as a System of Power* (New York, 1943), p. 320. See also Malcolm Cowley's review of *The Managerial Revolution*, *NR*, CIV (April

28, 1941), 607–608, and C. Wright Mills's review of *Business as a System of Power, ibid.,* CVIII (April 12, 1943), 482–83.

10. Robert F. Wagner, "Social Security Lifts Its Sights," *Survey Graphic,* XXXII (July 1943), 283–84, 301–302; James E. Murray, "Medical Care for All Americans," *NR,* CXI (July 10, 1944), 39–41; Richard Lee Strout, "The Beveridge Report," *ibid.,* CVII (Dec. 14, 1942), 784–86; "A Beveridge Plan for America," *ibid.,* CVII (Dec. 21, 1942), 810–11; Huthmacher, *Senator Robert F. Wagner,* pp. 292–93.

11. Leslie H. Fishel, Jr., "The Negro in the New Deal Era," *Wisconsin Magazine of History,* XLVIII (Winter 1964–1965), 111–26.

12. Carey McWilliams, *Brothers under the Skin* (Boston, 1944), surveys the entire range of minority group problems and presents its author's ideas for remedial legislation. For the Japanese-Americans, see also Charles Iglehart, "Citizens Behind Barbed Wire," *N,* CLIV (June 6, 1942), 649–51; and John Larison, " 'Jap Crow' Experiment," *ibid.,* CLVI (April 10, 1943), 517–19. For the Negro: Frank Winn, "Labor Tackles the Race Question," *Antioch Review,* III (Fall 1943), 341–60; Earl Brown, "American Negroes and the War," *Harper's,* CLXXXIV (April 1942), 545–52; Oswald Garrison Villard, "Negroes Not Allowed," *Common Sense,* X (July 1941), 199–201; Alfred D. Lewis, "Racism at Home," *ibid.,* XI (June 1942), 194–95; Common Sense Spotter, "Louder than Words," *ibid.,* XI (Aug. 1942), 277; "The Negro: His Future in America," *NR,* CIX (Oct. 18, 1943), 535–50; Thomas Sancton, "Race Fear Sweeps the South," *ibid.,* CVIII (Jan. 18, 1943), 81–83; "A Plea to the President," *N,* CLIX (Sept. 9, 1944), 285–86; Richard M. Dalfiume, "The 'Forgotten Years' of the Negro Revolution," *Journal of American History,* LV (June 1968), 90–106.

13. James G. Patton, "A Plan for Prosperity," *NR,* CXI (Nov. 6, 1944), 586–88. Other significant explorations of full employment and the postwar economy are Harry W. Laidler, "Platforms to the Left," *Common Sense,* XIII (Aug. 1944), 269–72; Stuart Chase, ed., "From War to Work," *Survey Graphic,* XXXII (May 1943).

14. Mordecai Ezekiel, "Lines of Action in Economic Reconstruction," *Antioch Review,* I (Fall 1941), 328–42.

15. Corey, *Unfinished Task, passim.* See also Corey's review of Burnham's *The Managerial Revolution* in *N,* CLII (April 26, 1941), 505–506. Accounts of Corey's fascinating life are in Esther Corey, "Lewis Corey (Louis C. Fraina), 1892–1953: A Bibliography with Autobiographical Notes," *Labor History,* IV (Spring 1963), 103–31; and Theodore Draper, *The Roots of American Communism* (Compass ed.; New York, 1963), *passim.*

16. Rovere, "Warning to the Liberals," *Common Sense,* XI (Aug. 1942), 266–68.

17. Richard Lee Strout, "Hansen of Harvard," *NR*, CV (Dec. 29, 1941), 888–90; Robert L. Heilbroner, *The Worldly Philosophers* (rev. ed.; New York, 1961), pp. 263–66; John Kenneth Galbraith, "Came the Revolution," *NYT Book Review*, May 16, 1965, pp. 1, 34–39; Daniel Bell, *The End of Ideology* (rev. ed.; New York, 1962), ch. 4; Alvin H. Hansen, *Full Recovery or Stagnation?* (New York, 1938); Hansen, *Fiscal Policy and Business Cycles* (New York, 1941); Hansen and Guy Greer, "The Federal Debt and the Future," *Harper's*, CLXXXIV (April 1942), 489–500.

18. Hansen, *After the War—Full Employment* (Washington, 1942), pp. 1–5 and *passim*. See also Hansen, "Our Coming Prosperity," *Common Sense*, XI (June, 1942), 186–89; Hansen, "Social Planning for Tomorrow," in Hansen, et al., *The United States after the War* (Ithaca, N.Y., 1945); Hansen and Harvey S. Perloff, *State and Local Finance in the National Economy* (New York, 1944).

19. National Resources Planning Board, *National Resources Development: Report for 1943; Part I: Postwar Plan and Program* (Washington, 1943), pp. 2–8, 27–30, and *passim*; "Editorial," *Antioch Review*, III (Summer 1943), 147–52; "A New Bill of Rights," *N*, CLVI (March 20, 1943), 401–402; Bruce Bliven, Max Lerner, George Soule, "Charter for America," *NR*, CVIII (April 19, 1943), 523–42. The New Bill of Rights originally appeared in the Board's 1942 report, but at that time it attracted little attention. *National Resources Planning Board, National Resources Development: Report for 1942* (Washington, 1942), p. 3.

20. Samuel I. Rosenman, ed., *The Public Papers and Addresses of Franklin D. Roosevelt*, 1944–1945 (New York, 1950), pp. 40–43, 369–78; Huthmacher, *Senator Robert F. Wagner*, p. 293.

21. Goldman, *Rendezvous with Destiny*, pp. 374–85; James A. Wechsler, *The Age of Suspicion* (New York, 1953), pp. 168–69; "Should We Declare War?" *NR*, CV (July 21, 1941), 72–73; "For a Declaration of War," *ibid.*, CV (Aug. 25, 1941), 235–38; *ibid.*, CV (Sept. 1, 1941), 279–81; *ibid.*, CV (Sept. 15, 1941), 341–43; Freda Kirchwey, "Shall We Declare War?" *N*, CLIII (July 26, 1941), 64–65. For the antiwar viewpoint, see Stuart Chase, "Ideologies for Export," *P*, V (May 31, 1941), 5.

22. Richard Hofstadter, *The Age of Reform: From Bryan to F.D.R.* (New York, 1955), ch. 7, pts. 3 and 4; Leuchtenburg, *Roosevelt and the New Deal*, ch. 14; and Otis L. Graham, *An Encore for Reform* (New York, 1967), esp. ch. 2, all depict New Deal liberals as more hard-boiled and less principled than the reformers of the progressive era. Freda Kirchwey, "Program of Action," *N*, CLVIII (March 11, 1944), 300–305.

23. The statements on war goals are innumerable. The following declarations are representative. Alvin H. Hansen, *America's Role in the World Economy* (New York, 1945); J. Donald Kingsley, "The Defense of Democracy," *Antioch Review*, I (Spring 1941), 5–20; James B. Carey, "Labor's Interest in the Peace," *ibid.*, III (Fall 1943), 361–71; "Standards of Living

and of Life," *NR*, CIII (Dec. 9, 1940), 777–79; "Alternative to Fascism," *ibid.*, CIII (Dec. 23, 1940), 857–61; "Ground Plan for a Post-War World," *ibid.*, CIV (Feb. 10, 1941), 169–71; "What Comes After the War," *ibid.*, CIV (May 26, 1941), 718–20; "Substitute for Imperialism," *ibid.*, CV (Sept. 8, 1941), 297–300; Milo Perkins, "The Future We Fight For," *ibid.*, CVI (June 15, 1942), 820–22; "Cartels: The Menace of Worldwide Monopoly," *ibid.*, CX (March 27, 1944), 427–47; Freda Kirchwey, "Program of Action," *N*, CLVIII (March 11, 1944), 300–305; Fiorello H. La Guardia, "A New Peace for a New Era," *Free World*, V (Jan. 1943), 21–23; "Program for Victory," *Common Sense*, XI (Jan. 1942), 18–19; "Program for Europe," *ibid.*, XII (Oct. 1943), 366–67; Max Lerner, *Ideas for the Ice Age* (New York, 1941), pp. 3–79.

24. Bruce Bliven, Max Lerner, and George Soule, "America and the Postwar World," *NR*, CIX (Nov. 29, 1943), 763–90; "Have We Lost the Peace?" *N*, CLVIII (June 10, 1944), 669; "The Peace Plans," *ibid.*, CLIX (Sept. 2, 1944), 257; Louis Fischer, "The Big Power Peace," *ibid.*, CLIX (Sept. 16, 1944). 315–17; *SLPD*, June 18, 1944; *CS*, June 17, Aug. 25, Sept. 30, 1944. Robert A. Divine, *Second Chance: The Triumph of Internationalism in America during World War II* (New York, 1967), surveys the debate over the extent and nature of postwar internationalism.

25. Frank A. Warren, III, *Liberals and Communism: The "Red Decade" Revisited* (Bloomington, Ind., 1966), intelligently and convincingly surveys Popular Front attitudes in the thirties. "Party Zigzag," *NR*, CV (July 7, 1941), 4; T.R.B., "Why the CP is Dying," *ibid.*, CVII (Nov. 23, 1942), 677; "Communists and the ALP," *ibid.*, CIX (Aug. 9, 1943), 181.

26. Robert Kenny to Martin Popper, June 23, 1945, Robert Kenny MSS, Bancroft Library, University of California (Berkeley); Bruce Bliven, Oral History Memoir, pp. 52–53, COHC.

27. Clifton Brock, *Americans for Democratic Action* (Washington, 1962), pp. 43–45; David A. Shannon, *The Decline of American Communism* (New York, 1959), p. 86; Adam Clymer, "Union for Democratic Action; Key to the Non-Communist Left" (Unpublished senior honors thesis, Harvard University, 1958), pp. 81–82, 89–90; James Loeb, Jr., in *SLPD*, June 16, 1946; Walter Davenport, "Ruddy Rodeo," *Collier's*, CXVII (June 1, 1946), 14–15; *Liberal Party Declaration and Platform* (New York, [1944]).

28. "The Soviet-Nazi Partnership," *NR*, CIV (May 26, 1941), 715–16; Max Lerner, "Homage to a Fighting People," *ibid.*, CV (Nov. 17, 1941), 643–44; John Dewey, "Can We Work with Russia?" *Frontiers of Democracy*, VIII (March 15, 1942), 179–80; Margaret Marshall, "Mr. Davies's Revelations," *N*, CLIV (Jan. 31, 1942), 118–19; Granville Hicks to Max Lerner, Jan. 12, 1942, Granville Hicks MSS, Syracuse University Library.

29. Lerner, *Public Journal*, pp. 270–74; Freda Kirchwey, "Stalin's Choice," CLVIII (Jan. 22, 1944), 89–90; "Russia's Western Claims," *NR*,

CX (Jan. 17, 1944), 72; Jerome Davis, "Russia's Postwar Aims," *ibid.*, CXI (Sept. 4, 1944), 276–78; J. L. Childs, "Comments by John L. Childs on Mr. Dewey's Letter," *Frontiers of Democracy,* VIII (March 15, 1942), 181–82; "Our Bolshevik Friends," *Common Sense,* XI (Dec., 1942), 414–15.

30. Niebuhr's attitudes toward the Soviet Union and Communism found expression in the following writings: "Russia and the West," *N,* CLVI (Jan. 16, 23, 1943), 82–84, 124–125; "Great Britain's Post-War Role," *ibid.*, CLVII (July 10, 1943), 39–40; "World War III Ahead?" *ibid.*, CLVIII (March 25, 1944), 356–58; "The Basis of World Order," *ibid.*, CLIX (Oct. 21, 1944), 489; "Will America Back Out?" *ibid.*, CLX (Jan. 13, 1945), 42–43; "Is This 'Peace in Our Time'?" *ibid.*, CLX (April 7, 1945), 382–84; *The Children of Light and the Children of Darkness* (New York, 1944), p. 183; Niebuhr to John L. Childs, July 14, 1944, Reinhold Niebuhr MSS, LC. Leuchtenburg's observation was made in a conversation with the author.

31. Raymond Clapper, *Watching the World,* ed., Mrs. Raymond Clapper (New York, 1944), pp. 317–21; Harry Paxton Howard, "How to Mobilize the Far East," *Common Sense,* XI (March, 1942), 79–82; "A New Order for Asia," *NR,* CVI (March 9, 1942), 320; Milton Mayer, "We Have Got to Lick Churchill Too," *P,* VI (Nov. 23, 1942), 1. Cf. Carl L. Becker, *How New Will the Better World Be?* (New York, 1944), ch. 4.

32. Freda Kirchwey, "Mr. Hull Should Resign," *N,* CLIV (Jan. 3, 1942), 1–2; EP, *ibid.*, CLIX (July 22, 1944), 86; Harry Paxton Howard, "France —Republic or Fascist Empire?" *P,* VI (Dec. 7, 1942), 1, 5; Fred Rodell, "Shall It be a New Holy Alliance?" *ibid.*, VII (Nov. 8, 1943), 1; Morris H. Rubin, "The Time is Now, Mr. Roosevelt," *ibid.*, IX (Feb. 5, 1945), 1, 8; Irwin Ross, "What Price American Foreign Policy?" *Antioch Review,* III (Summer 1943), 209–22; David Dempsey, "War for Democracy—Or Restoration?" *ibid.*, pp. 271–82; Walter Millis, "American Foreign Policy: A Symphony Without A Score," *Free World,* I (Oct. 1941), 29–33; Francis P. Locke, "Retreat from the Four Freedoms," *ibid.*, V (March 1943), 201–207; "United for What?" *NR,* CVI (June 15, 1942), 814–15; Sumner Welles, *World of the Four Freedoms* (New York, 1943).

33. Frank Kingdon, *An Uncommon Man: Henry Wallace and Sixty Million Jobs* (New York, 1945), ch. 1; interview with Henry A. Wallace, Dec. 16, 1964. See also Russell Lord, *The Wallaces of Iowa* (Boston, 1946); Edward L. and Frederick H. Schapsmeier, *Henry A. Wallace of Iowa: The Agrarian Years, 1910–1940* (Ames, Iowa, 1968); Schapsmeier and Schapsmeier, *Prophet in Politics: Henry A. Wallace and the War Years, 1940–1965* (Ames, Iowa, 1970); Dwight MacDonald, *Henry Wallace: the Man and the Myth* (New York, 1948); Schlesinger, *Coming of the New Deal,* 28–35; Gardner Jackson, "Henry Wallace: A Divided Mind," *Atlantic Monthly,* CLXXXII (Aug. 1948), 27–33. The COHC con-

tains several memoirs which have valuable observations on Wallace, including those of Paul Appleby, Samuel Bledsoe, Rudolph Evans, Mordecai Ezekiel, Fred Henshaw, John B. Hutson, Howard Tolley, and Rexford G. Tugwell. Wallace's own memoir is closed, as are those of several persons connected with the 1948 Progressive Party.

34. Lord, *Wallaces of Iowa*, pp. 432–40; Kingdon, *Uncommon Man*, ch. 8; Henry A. Wallace, *Democracy Reborn*, ed., Russell Lord (New York, 1944), pp. 62, 66–76, 94, 102, 125–27, 139–40; Wallace, *Sixty Million Jobs* (New York, 1945), pp. 1–2, 81–83.

35. Wallace, *Statesmanship and Religion* (New York, 1934), pp. 29, 35, 103; Norman Thomas, Oral History Memoir, I, 94, II, 180–81, COHC.

36. Wallace interview; Bledsoe, Oral History Memoir, pp. 120, 126, COHC; Curtis MacDougall, *Gideon's Army* (New York, 1965), I, ch. 6.

37. Wallace interview; Don S. Kirshner, "Henry A. Wallace as Farm Editor," *American Quarterly*, XVII (Summer 1965), 187–208; Schlesinger, *Coming of the New Deal*, pp. 77–80; Richard S. Kirkendall, "Commentary on the Thought of Henry A. Wallace," *Agricultural History*, XLI (April 1967), 139–42; Appleby, Oral History Memoir, pp. 166–83 COHC; Roland [Wolseley] to Curtis MacDougall, Aug. 20, 1953, PP MSS, State University of Iowa. The evidence concerning Wallace's attitude toward government spending during the recession of 1937–1938 is somewhat contradictory. Schapsmeier, *Henry A. Wallace* pp. 239–41, shows that Wallace spoke in favor of government spending, and Appleby, Oral History Memoir, p. 149, COHC, has a similar recollection. However, Professor Robert E. Burke, who has kindly shared his research with the author, has discovered indications that on other occasions Wallace recommended a conservative approach.

38. This speech, reprinted in many places was published separately as *The Price of Free World Victory* (New York, 1942).

39. "Vice President Wallace," *NR*, CVI (May 25, 1942), 717; Childs, *I Write from Washington* (New York, 1942), p. 317.

40. Wallace, *The Century of the Common Man*, ed., Russell Lord (New York, 1943), p. 13 and *passim*.

41. *Ibid.*, ch. 6, 13. Wallace received many invitations to speak to Councils of American-Soviet Friendship or to send messages to their meetings. See the relevant files in the Wallace MSS, FDRL, and the Henry A. Wallace MSS at the University of Iowa.

42. Wallace, *Democracy Reborn*, pp. 37–38, 238–45, 259–63.

43. *Ibid.*, pp. 17–40, 119–28, 249–53, 264–73; Wallace, *Century of the Common Man*, ch. 10; Wallace, *Sixty Million Jobs*.

CHAPTER 2: WALLACE, TRUMAN, THE LIBERALS,
AND THE POLITICS OF WORLD WAR II

1. *NYT*, June 16, July 1, 5, 6, 13, Sept. 5, 1943.

2. Such, at least, was the liberal view of Jones, expressed in such articles as I. F. Stone, "Why Wallace Spoke Out," *N*, CLVII (July 10, 1943), 34–36. For a friendly view, see Bascom Timmons, *Jesse H. Jones* (New York, 1956), esp. pp. 285–361. Richard F. Fenno, Jr., *The President's Cabinet* (Vintage ed.; New York, n.d.), pp. 234–47, discusses Jones's influence with Congress.

3. Timmons, *Jones*, pp. 317–30; Lord, *Wallaces of Iowa*, pp. 496–514; *NYT*, June 30, July 1, 6, 16, 17, 1943.

4. Robert E. Sherwood, *Roosevelt and Hopkins* (New York, 1950), p. 741; Jonathan Daniels, *The Man of Independence* (New York and Philadelphia, 1950), p. 235; EP, *Antioch Review*, III (Fall 1943), 458–59; James M. Landis, Oral History Memoir, pp. 350–51, COHC.

5. Wallace, *Democracy Reborn*, p. 254; Karl M. Schmidt, *Henry A. Wallace: Quixotic Crusade, 1948* (Syracuse, N.Y., 1960), pp. 5–6; Robert Kenny to Mary Morris, March 7, 1946, Kenny MSS; "Keep Vice-President Wallace!" *NR*, CXI (July 17, 1944), 62–63; Freda Kirchwey, "The People Want Wallace," *N*, CLIX (July 22, 1944), 89; Francis Biddle, *In Brief Authority* (Garden City, N.Y., 1962), pp. 355–58.

6. Lord, *Wallaces of Iowa*, pp. 525–37; *Proceedings of the Democratic National Convention, 1944* (n.p. [1944]), pp. 79–80.

7. Jo Davidson to Mary Huss, Aug. 9, 1944, Jo Davidson MSS, LC; Charles Bolte to Wallace, Aug. 5, 1944, Wallace MSS, FDRL; "The Democratic Winner," *NR*, CXI (July 31, 1944), 116–17; Ickes to Wallace, July 24, 1944, Wallace MSS, Iowa.

8. Louis Bean, Oral History Memoir, p. 255, COHC; Lord, *Wallaces of Iowa*, pp. 543–44; Wallace interview; Wallace, Excerpts from remarks to NCPAC luncheon, Sept. 22, 1944, Davidson MSS.

9. "Dewey: The Man and His Record," *NR*, CXI (Sept. 25, 1944), 387–407; "The Home Stretch," *ibid.*, CXI (Nov. 6, 1944), 579–80; "Why F.D.R.?" *N*, CLIX (Oct. 28, 1944), 503–504; Lerner, *Public Journal*, pp. 205–11; Goldman, *Rendezvous with Destiny*, p. 404.

10. William P. Tucker, "Populism Up-To-Date: The Story of the Farmers Union," *Agricultural History*, XXI (Oct. 1947), 198–208; Tucker, "The Farmers Union: The Social Thought of a Current Agrarian Movement," *Southwestern Social Science Quarterly*, XXVII (June 1946), 45–53; "James G. Patton," *Current Biography, 1945* (New York, 1946), pp. 450–53; Stephen K. Bailey, *Congress Makes a Law* (New York, 1950), pp. 23–25; Grant McConnell, *The Decline of Agrarian Democracy* (Berkeley,

1953), pp. 37–39, 108; Christiana McFadyen Campbell, *The Farm Bureau and the New Deal* (Urbana, Ill., 1962), pp. 169–74; Richard S. Kirkendall, *Social Scientists and Farm Politics in the Age of Roosevelt* (Columbia, Mo., 1966), pp. 233–34; John A. Crampton, *The National Farmers Union: Ideology of a Pressure Group* (Lincoln, Neb., 1965), *passim*; Patton, "Farmers for Freedom," *NL*, XXVIII (May 26, 1945), 4–5.

11. Matthew Josephson, *Sidney Hillman* (Garden City, N.Y., 1952), pp. 595–635; I. F. Stone, "The P.A.C. at Work," *N*, CLIX (Oct. 14, 1944), 425–27; Samuel Lubell, *The Future of American Politics* (3d ed., rev.; New York, 1965), pp. 58–59.

12. Josephson, *Hillman*, pp. 626–28; NCPAC advertisement in *NR*, CXI (Aug. 7, 1944), 168; Freda Kirchwey, "A New Popular Front?" *N*, CLIX (Dec. 2, 1944), 677–78; Clark Foreman, "Statement of the National Citizens Political Action Committee," *Antioch Review*, IV (Fall 1944), 473–75; *NYT*, March 24, May 12, 1945.

13. "Calvin B. Baldwin," *Current Biography, 1943* (New York, 1944), pp. 18–20; Will W. Alexander, Oral History Memoir, pp. 474–87, and Jackson, Oral History Memoir, pp. 352–53, both in COHC; Jackson to Elizabeth Donahue, March 30, 1948, ADA MSS, State Historical Society of Wisconsin.

14. *NYT*, July 22, Dec. 20, 22, 1944, Feb. 19, 1945; Walter Davenport, "Ruddy Rodeo," *Collier's*, CXVII (June 1, 1946), 14–15, 61–63; Jo Davidson to Babette Deutsch, July 28, 1945, Davidson MSS.

15. Wechsler, *Age of Suspicion*, pp. 211–12; Bailey, *Congress Makes a Law*, p. 81; Brock, *Americans for Democratic Action*, p. 49; Thomas Amlie to Howard Y. Williams, Sept. 28, 1942, Amlie MSS, State Historical Society of Wisconsin; James Loeb, Jr., to Howard Y. Williams, Oct. 12, 1942, Williams MSS, Minnesota State Historical Society; Adam Clymer, "Union for Democratic Action," (honors thesis, Harvard College, 1958), pp. 38, 67, 72, 73, 85–88; Loeb to A. Powell Davies, Jan. 24, 1950, ADA MSS; interview with Loeb, Dec. 28, 1969. The characterization of Loeb draws heavily upon the author's conversations with William E. Leuchtenburg.

16. Freda Kirchwey, "A New Popular Front?" *N*, CLIX (Dec. 2, 1944), 677–78; "Progressives Must Organize," *NR*, CXI (Nov. 27, 1944), 678–79; Clymer, "Union for Democratic Action," pp. 52–65, 89–95; Reinhold Niebuhr to Roy Jacobson, Jan. 11, 1943, Niebuhr MSS; James Loeb, Jr., to Albert A. Blum, Oct. 21, 1947, ADA MSS.

17. James G. Patton and James Loeb, Jr., "Challenge to Progressives," *NR*, CXII (Feb. 5, 1945), 185–208.

18. Timmons, *Jones*, pp. 351–61; *NYT*, Jan. 25, 26, 1945; Lord, *Wallaces of Iowa*, pp. 543–55; "Wallace's World—or Jones's?" *NR*, CXI (Feb. 5, 1945), 167.

19. *NYT*, Jan. 30, 1945; Wallace speech, Jan. 29, 1945, ADA MSS. For

expressions of support, see Wyatt to Wallace, Jan. 24, 1945; Porter to Wallace, Jan. 25, 1945; Bowles to Wallace, Jan. 26, 1945; Loeb to Wallace, Feb. 1, 1945; Alfange to Wallace, Feb. 1, 1945, and attached speech —all in Wallace MSS, Iowa.

20. "The Crimean Charter," *NR*, CXII (Feb. 26, 1945), 278–80; *SLPD*, Feb. 13, 1945; "More Perfect Union," *N*, CLX (Feb. 17, 1945), 169–70; Reinhold Niebuhr, "The Conference of the 'Big Three,'" *Christianity and Crisis*, V (March 5, 1945), 1–2.

21. I. F. Stone, "This Is What We Voted For," *N*, CLX (Feb. 17, 1945), 174–75.

22. Among the most important sources for Truman's early career are his own *Memoirs:* Volume I, *Year of Decisions* (Garden City, N.Y., 1955) [hereafter cited as *Memoirs*, I]; Alfred Steinberg, *The Man From Missouri* (New York, 1962); William P. Helm, *Harry Truman: A Political Biography* (New York, 1947); and especially Daniels, *Man of Independence*. The more scholarly work of Lyle Dorsett, Franklin Mitchell, and Gene Schmidtlein, all cited below, is indispensable. I have drawn freely and with great gratitude upon Richard S. Kirkendall's incomparable knowledge and insight. His "Truman's Path to Power," *Social Science*, XLIII (April 1968), 67–73, and "Truman and the South" (paper delivered at the Southern Historical Association meeting, 1969) are especially relevant to a study of Truman's early career. J. Joseph Huthmacher's work on the connection between modern liberalism and urban machine politics, especially *Senator Robert F. Wagner*, has also greatly influenced me.

23. HST, *Memoirs*, I, 149; Franklin D. Mitchell, "'Who Is Judge Truman?': The Truman-for-Governor Movement of 1931," *Mid-Continent American Studies Journal*, VII (Fall 1966), 3–15; Lyle W. Dorsett, "Truman and the Pendergast Machine," *ibid.*, pp. 16–27. See also comments on these two articles by Gene Schmidtlein, *ibid.*, pp. 28–35, and Richard S. Kirkendall, *ibid.*, pp. 36–39. Dorsett's article is somewhat elaborated in Dorsett, *The Pendergast Machine* (New York, 1968).

24. Gene Schmidtlein, "Truman's First Senatorial Election," *Missouri Historical Review*, LVII (Jan. 1963), 128–55; Childs, *I Write From Washington*, pp. 97–98; EP, *N*, CXXXIX (Nov. 21, 1934), 576.

25. Gene Schmidtlein, "Truman the Senator" (Ph.D. dissertation, University of Missouri, 1962), is the best source for Truman's Senate career; HST, *Memoirs*, I, 151; *NYT*, Feb. 10, April 20, 1937.

26. Schmidtlein, "Truman the Senator," pp. 150–83; Daniels, *Man of Independence*, pp. 184–87.

27. *CR*, 75 Cong., 2 Sess. (Dec. 20, 1937), pp. 1912–24.

28. *Ibid.*, 75 Cong., 3 Sess. (Feb. 15, 1938), pp. 1962–64; Steinberg, *Man from Missouri*, pp. 130–32, 157–60; HST, *Memoirs*, I, 142–58.

29. Schmidtlein, "Truman the Senator," pp. 214–16; Harold L. Ickes, *The Secret Diary of Harold L. Ickes*, III (New York, 1954), 205–206.

30. Schmidtlein, "Truman the Senator," pp. 131, 218–20.

31. *CR*, 76 Cong., 3 Sess. (Appendix), pp. 4546–47.

32. HST, Speech to the National Colored Democratic Association, *ibid.*, pp. 5367–69; Roy Wilkins, Oral History Memoir, pp. 95–96, COHC; Schmidtlein, "Truman the Senator," pp. 222–23; Richard M. Dalfiume, *Desegregation of the United States Armed Forces: Fighting on Two Fronts, 1939–1953* (Columbia, Mo., 1969), pp. 135–37.

33. Schmidtlein, "Truman the Senator," pp. 243, 266–69, 275–77, 284, 290–97, 300–304; *Senate Report 10*, Part 12, 78 Cong., 1 Sess. (Nov. 5, 1943); "The Rail Wage Fight," *NR*, CIX (Nov. 29, 1943), 733–34; HST, "Big Business Advertises At Your Expense," *P*, VII (Sept. 20, 1943), 1–2; *CR*, 78 Cong., 1 Sess. (July 3, 1943), pp. 7081–88; Donald H. Riddle, *The Truman Committee: A Study in Congressional Responsibility* (New Brunswick, N.J., 1964), p. 36 and *passim*.

34. Ickes, *Diary*, III, 631; Kingdon interview. Examples of the liberal image of the Truman Committee as a collective entity are I. F. Stone, "Nelson and Guthrie," *N*, CLIV (June 27, 1942), 731–32; and "Can Congress Run the War?" *NR*, XVIII (March 8, 1943), 302–303.

35. *NYT*, June 24, 1941, March 20, 1943; "Last Week," *NR*, CIV (June 30, 1941), 874; "Fumbling with Peace," *ibid.*, CIX (Nov. 8, 1943), 638–39; "International Economic Collaboration," *ibid.*, CX (March 20, 1944), 365; HST, Speech to United Nations Forum, Jan. 17, 1944, *CR*, 78 Cong., 2 Sess. (Appendix), pp. A265–66; Divine, *Second Chance*, pp. 92, 128, 148.

36. *NYT*, March 27, 1944.

37. *NYP*, July 21, 1944; "A Fourth Term with Whom?" *NR*, CX (Jan. 31, 1944), 134–35; Philadelphia *Record*, July 22, 1944; *CS*, July 23, 1944; *NYT*, July 23, 1944; Freda Kirchwey, "The Battle of Chicago," *N*, CLIX (July 29, 1944), 118–20; George W. Norris to Henry A. Wallace, July 31, Aug. 19, 1944, Wallace MSS, Iowa.

38. Grace and Morris Milgram, "The Man from Missouri," *Common Sense*, XIII (Oct., 1944), 347–51.

39. Kingdon interview.

40. *NYT*, Aug. 1, Sept. 1, Oct. 17, Nov. 1, 1944.

41. *Ibid.*, Sept. 5, Oct. 13, 14, 20, 27, 31, 1944.

42. "The Home Stretch," *NR*, CXI (Nov. 6, 1944), 579–80. See also *PM*, Oct. 27, 1944.

43. *NYT*, Nov. 1, 1944.

44. "Vice President Truman," *NR*, CXI (Nov. 13, 1944), 611; "Aubrey Williams and the Senate," *ibid.*, CXII (March 12, 1945), 350; "The Vice President Didn't," *ibid.*, CXII (March 19, 1945), 374; T.R.B., "FDR's Opening Gambit," *ibid.*, CXII (March 12, 1945), 359; Smith in *NUF*, March 1, 1945; "Washington Calling," *P*, IX (April 9, 1945), 6, 16; *NYT*, March 4, 1945; Williams to HST, June 7, 1945, HST MSS, PPF 1726.

45. William Hillman, *Mr. President* (New York, 1952), p. 115.

CHAPTER 3: TRUMAN, THE LIBERALS, AND THE
POLITICS OF ALIENATION

1. "Washington Memo" column in *NYP*, April 14, 1945; *ibid.*, April 17,
1945; *PM*, April 15, 1945; Max Lerner in *ibid.*, April 22, 1945; Philadelphia *Record*, April 14, 18, 1945; *SLPD*, April 15, 1945; Marquis Childs in
ibid., April 23, 1945; *CS*, April 17, 1945; Willard Shelton in *ibid.*, April
18, 1945; Samuel Grafton in *ibid.*, April 21, 1945; Thomas L. Stokes in
ibid., May 31, 1945; "President Truman's First Task," *NR*, CXII (April
23, 1945), 539–41; T.R.B., "Mr. Truman's First Week," *ibid.*, CXII (April
30, 1945), 586; Irving Brant, "Harry S. Truman," *ibid.*, CXII (April 30,
May 7, 1945), 577–79, 635–38; Freda Kirchwey, "End of an Era," *N*, CLX
(April 21, 1945), 429–30; I. F. Stone, "Farewell to F.D.R.," *ibid.*, pp.
436–37; Margaret Marshall, "Portrait of Truman," *ibid.*, pp. 438–40;
"Washington Calling," *P*, IX (May 14, 1945), 7; David E. Lilienthal, *The
Journals of David E. Lilienthal:* Volume I, *The TVA Years, 1939–1945*
(New York, 1964), p. 690 [hereafter cited as *Journals*, I]; Francis Biddle,
In Brief Authority, p. 364; unsigned partial copy of a letter to Robert
Kenny, attached to Kenny to George Killion, May 31, 1945, Kenny MSS.

2. Alan Barth, "Truman: A Trial Balance," *N*, CLX (May 19, 1945),
563–564; "Washington Calling," *P*, IX (May 14, 1945), 7, 16; "Mr. Truman Measures Up," *ibid.*, p. 16; *EP*, *ibid.*, IX (June 18, 1945), 3; "People
in the Limelight: David Lilienthal," *NR*, CXII (May 14, 1945), 662;
"More Truman Appointments," *ibid.*, CXII (June 18, 1945), 829; Lilienthal, *Journals*, I, 698; Bartley C. Crum to Rosenman, June 4, 1945, Samuel I. Rosenman MSS, HSTL.

3. "The Presidential Appointments," *P*, IX (June 4, 1945), 12; "New
Blood in the Cabinet," *NR*, CXII (June 4, 1945), 773; "New Faces in
Washington," *ibid.*, CXIII (July 16, 1945), 60; T.R.B., "Capital House-
cleaning," *ibid.*, p. 77; "The Cabinet Changes," *N*, CLX (June 2, 1945),
616–17; *EP*, *ibid.*, CLX (June 16, 1945), 662; *NUF*, June 1, 1945; Biddle,
In Brief Authority, pp. 364–66.

4. T.R.B., "Congress Discovers the World," *NR*, CXIII (July 2, 1945),
21–22; "Pork-Barreling the Courts," *ibid.*, CXIII (Sept. 24, 1945), 364–65;
Helen Fuller, "Big Business Buys the Air," *ibid.*, pp. 370–71; T.R.B.,
"Mr. Truman's Challenge," *ibid.*, p. 373.

5. Alan Barth, "Truman: A Trial Balance," *N*, CLX (May 19, 1945),
563–64; "Appointments for Reaction," *NR*, CLIV (Jan. 28, 1946), 110;
PM, Feb. 11, 1946; Jonathan Daniels, *Frontier on the Potomac* (New
York, 1946), pp. 43, 141–42.

6. *PM*, April 18, Nov. 4, 1945; Philadelphia *Record*, April 18, 1945;
NYP, April 20, 1945; Robert Kenny to Manchester Boddy, Aug. 2, 1945,
Kenny MSS; Helen Fuller, "Hot Seat for Snyder," *NR*, CXIII (Aug. 13,

1945), 183–85; "An Injustice to Mr. Davis," *ibid.*, CXIII (Oct. 1, 1945), 421–22; EP, *N*, CLXI (Sept. 1, 1945), 194.

7. "Washington Calling," *P*, IX (June 18, 1945), 9; Helen Fuller, "The Pauley Puzzle," *NR*, CXIII (Aug. 6, 1945), 156–58; "An Injustice to Mr. Davis," *ibid.*, CXIII (Oct. 1, 1945), 421–22; *PM*, Sept. 19, 20, 1945; *NYT*, Sept. 22, 1945; *Public Papers of the Presidents of the United States: Harry S. Truman, 1945* [volumes in this series are hereafter cited as *Public Papers* with the appropriate year], p. 327; Davis, Oral History Memoir, pp. 199–203, COHC; HST to Davis, Sept. 19, 1945, HST MSS, PPF 829; David E. Lilienthal, *The Journals of David E. Lilienthal:* Volume II, *The Atomic Energy Years, 1945–1950* (New York, 1964), p. 2 [hereafter cited as *Journals*, II]; Harold Smith, Conference with the president, Sept. 18, 1945, Smith MSS, Bureau of the Budget, Washington, D.C. (Dr. Mary Blewett kindly made this last item available from her notes on the Smith MSS.)

8. T.R.B., "The Challenge to the Old Order," *NR*, CXII (June 11, 1945), 813–14; T.R.B., "Echoes from the Past, Hope for the Future," *ibid.*, CXII (June 18, 1945), 843; Jonathan Daniels, Diary, Sept. 24, 1945, Jonathan Daniels MSS, Southern Historical Collection, University of North Carolina; EP, *N*, CLXI (Aug. 4, 1945), 100; Crum to Rosenman, Dec. 7, 1945, Rosenman MSS; *PM*, Dec. 10, 1945; author's interview with Robert Nathan, Sept. 20, 1967.

9. T.R.B., "Peacetime Miscellany," *NR*, CXIII (Sept. 10, 1945), 315; Crawford, "The Test for Mr. Truman," *P*, IX (June 4, 1945), 1–2; "Washington Calling," *ibid.*, IX (Dec. 24, 1945), 9; Stokes in *CS*, Feb. 5, 1946; Curtis MacDougall, *Gideon's Army*, I, 24.

10. *PM*, Jan. 30, 1946.

11. "Harold, With All Thy Faults," *P*, IX (May 28, 1945), 12; Kenneth Crawford, "The Test for Mr. Truman," *ibid.*, IX (June 4, 1945), 1–2; T.R.B., "Capital Housecleaning," *NR*, CXIII (July 16, 1945), 77; "Cabinet Changes," *N*, CLXI (July 14, 1945), 23–24; ICCASP to HST, undated copy of a telegram, Oscar L. Chapman MSS, HSTL.

12. "A Timely Warning," *P*, IX (April 23, 1945), 12; Bolte, "Labor, Vets, and Jobs," *N*, CLXI (Aug. 4, 1945), 104–106; EP, *ibid.*, CLXI (Sept. 22, 1945), 271.

13. *Public Papers, 1945*, pp. 28–29, 72–75; "Reconversion—the Human Side," *NR*, CXII (June 11, 1945), 807.

14. Stephen K. Bailey, *Congress Makes a Law*, pp. 3–79; Heinz Eulau, Mordecai Ezekiel, Alvin H. Hansen, James Loeb, Jr., George Soule, "The Road to Freedom: Full Employment," *NR*, CXIII (Sept. 24, 1945), 395–415; EP, *N*, CLX (June 9, 1945), 634; "Speed the Murray Bill!" *ibid.*, CLXI (Aug. 25, 1945), 169–70; Stuart Chase, "Mr. Wallace and the Wise Boys," *ibid.*, CLXI (Sept. 29, 1945), 313–16; *Public Papers, 1945*, p. 225; Adam Clymer, "Union for Democratic Action," pp. 98–107.

15. *NYT*, July 8, 31, Aug. 13, 1945; Reuther, "Are War Plants Expend-

able?" *P*, IX (July 23, 1945), 5; I. F. Stone, "Washington Faces Peace," *N*, CLXI (Aug. 18, 1945), 151–52; T.R.B., "Atomic Anxieties," *NR*, CXIII (Aug. 20, 1945), 222; "Transition to Peace," *ibid.*, CXIII (Aug. 27, 1945), 239–40.

16. EP, *N*, CLX (May 12, 1945), 531.

17. *Public Papers, 1945*, pp. 104–105; "Save the FEPC!" *N*, CLX (June 16, 1945), 663; *SLPD*, June 6, 1945; Williams to HST, June 7, 1945, HST MSS, PPF 1726; Analysis of FEPC Mail, *ibid.*, OF 40.

18. *Public Papers, 1945*, pp. 263–309.

19. Daniels, Interview with HST, Nov. 12, 1949, Daniels MSS; *SLPD*, Sept. 9, 1945; Stokes in *CS*, Sept. 9, 1945; "Mr. Truman's Challenge," *NR*, CLIII (Sept. 24, 1945), 335–36; EP, *P*, IX (Sept. 17, 1945), 3.

20. *UDA Congressional Newsletter*, Sept. 15, 1945; "Which Way, Mr. Truman?" *P*, IX (Oct. 8, 1945), 12; Helen Fuller, "Is Truman Licked?" *NR*, CXIII (Oct. 15, 1945), 488–90; Richard O. Davies, *Housing Reform During the Truman Administration* (Columbia, Mo., 1966), p. 43.

21. *UDA Congressional Newsletter*, Oct. 1, 1945; "Administration Sit-down," *NR*, CXIII (Oct. 1, 1945), 421; T.R.B., "Back to Normalcy," *ibid.*, CXIII (Oct. 22, 1945), 527; "Six Months of Mr. Truman," *P*, IX (Oct. 22, 1945), 12; Kenneth Crawford, "America Adrift without a Compass," *ibid.*, IX (Oct. 29, 1945), 1; "Washington Calling," *ibid.*, p. 7; *CS*, Oct. 19, 1945; Stokes in *ibid.*, Oct. 5, 1945; Goldman, *Rendezvous with Destiny*, p. 80.

22. *UDA Congressional Newsletter*, Nov. 1, 1945; T.R.B., "The World Moves to Washington," *NR*, CXIII (Dec. 10, 1945), 797.

23. William Withers, "How Much Unemployment?" *NR*, CXIII (Oct. 15, 1945), 490–93; *UDA Congressional Newsletter*, Dec. 15, 1945 (supplement); "Phony Jobs Bill Passes," *P*, IX (Dec. 24, 1945), 3; Bailey, *Congress Makes a Law*, pp. 164–77.

24. EP, *P*, IX (Dec. 17, 1945), 3; Houston to HST, Dec. 3, 1945, HST MSS, OF 40; HST to Houston, Dec. 7, 1945, *ibid.*; S.I.R. [Samuel I. Rosenman], Memo to HST, Dec. 3, 1945, *ibid.*; HST to Heads of all government departments, agencies and independent establishments, Dec. 18, 1945, *ibid.*; FEPC, Memo to HST, Dec. 17, 1945, *ibid.*; Executive Order 9664, 10 *Federal Register*, 15301. Louis Ruchames, *Race, Jobs, and Politics: The Story of the FEPC* (New York, 1953), pp. 132–34, argues erroneously that the Executive Order was intended to undermine the agency.

25. Eleanor Roosevelt to HST, Dec. 18, 1945; HST to Eleanor Roosevelt, Dec. 21, 1945; HST to Tom Clark, Dec. 21, 1945; Clark, Memo to HST, Jan. 10, 1946; HST, Memo for the Attorney General, Jan. 17, 1946—all in HST MSS, OF 197.

26. "A Fine Appointment," *NR*, CXIV (Jan. 14, 1946), 38; HST to Brant, March 29, 1946, HST MSS, OF 465-B; David K. Niles, Memo to HST, April 11, 1946, *ibid.*; John Haynes Holmes and Roger Baldwin, ACLU, to HST, April 9, 1946, *ibid.* See also the White House files of

Philleo Nash (FEPC file) in the HST MSS for many communications urging HST to denounce the filibuster.

27. Joseph Davies, Diary, June 25, 1945, Davies MSS, LC; *NYT*, Oct. 1, 1945; Thomas L. Stokes in *CS*, Aug. 1, 1945; "That Wave of Strikes," *NR*, CXIII (Oct. 1, 1945), 420; "Plotting a New Depression," *ibid.*, CXIII (Dec. 17, 1945), 819–20; "G.M. Strike, '46 Model," *N*, CLXI (Dec. 1, 1945), 567–68; Irving Howe and B. J. Widick, *The UAW and Walter Reuther* (New York, 1949), ch. 6; Barton J. Bernstein, "The Truman Administration and Its Reconversion Wage Policy," *Labor History*, VI (Fall 1965), 214–31; Bernstein, "Walter Reuther and the General Motors Strike of 1945–46," *Michigan History*, XLIX (Sept. 1965), 260–77.

28. *Public Papers, 1945*, pp. 441–49; *NYT*, Dec. 2, 1945; Bernstein, "Reconversion Wage Policy," *Labor History*.

29. *Public Papers, 1945*, pp. 516–23; *NYT*, Dec. 5, 9, 1945.

30. Philadelphia *Record*, Dec. 6, 1945; Kenneth Crawford, "Labor's Dilemma," *P*, IX (Dec. 17, 1945), 5; "Labor Says No," *N*, CLXI (Dec. 15, 1945), 648.

31. *Public Papers, 1945*, pp. 533–39, 563–64, 569, 579–83; "Men in the Streets," *N*, CLXI (Dec. 22, 1945), 676–77; "Housing," *NR*, CXIII (Dec. 24, 1945), 858; "What's Back of the GM Strike," *ibid.*, CXIII (Dec. 31, 1945), 884–85; *CS*, Dec. 23, 1945; Philadelphia *Record*, Dec. 26, 1945; *Public Papers, 1946*, pp. 1–8.

32. Eleanor Roosevelt to HST, Nov. 1, 1945, HST MSS, OF 264; Bailey, *Congress Makes a Law*, pp. 162–64.

33. *NYT*, Dec. 17, 1945; *NYP*, Dec. 6, 1945; Lerner in *PM*, Dec. 17, 18, 1945; Sherwood to Rosenman, Jan. 5, 1946, Rosenman MSS.

34. Max Lerner in *PM*, Dec. 19, 1945; Helen Fuller, "Has Truman Lost the Left?" *NR*, CXIII (Dec. 17, 1945), 825; *UDA Congressional Newsletter*, Oct. 1, 1945; Victor Riesel in *NYP*, Dec. 11, 1945; Robert Lasch in *CS*, Dec. 17, 1945; Stokes in *ibid.*, Dec. 20, 1945.

35. EP, *N*, CLXII (Feb. 16, 1946), 181–82; John J. Carson, "Men Against Unemployment," *ibid.*, CLXIII (Aug. 10, 1946), 151–52; "Is It Full Employment?" *NR*, CXIV (Feb. 18, 1946), 240; "Full Employment Stalled," *ibid.*, CXIV (June 3, 1946), 789–90; "Washington Calling," *P*, X (Aug. 12, 1946), 12; Smith in the *NUF*, Aug. 15, 1946.

36. *NYP*, Dec. 6, 1945; "Washington Memo" column in *ibid.*, Dec. 5, 1945; Grafton in *ibid.*, Jan. 31, 1946; Potomacus, "The Hole in Your Pocketbook," *NR*, CXIV (Feb. 11, 1946), 182–84; *PM*, Feb. 10, 1946; Chester Bowles to HST, Dec. 17, 1945 (Memo), Feb. 6, 1946, and Bowles to William Benton, April 16, 1946, all in Bowles MSS, Yale University.

37. Smith, Conference with the president, May 15, 1946, Smith MSS.

38. *PM*, Feb. 15, 17, 1946; *NYP*, Feb. 16, 1946; I. F. Stone, "Mr. Truman Wavers," *N*, CLXII (Feb. 23, 1946), 214–15; *Public Papers, 1946*, pp. 119, 122–24; Bowles to HST, Feb. 13, 1946, Bowles MSS; Bowles to Jona-

than Daniels, Feb. 18, 1946, Daniels MSS; Bowles to Ralph Ingersoll, April 16, 1946, Ralph Ingersoll MSS, Boston University; "Wage-Price Policy," *NR*, CXIV (Feb. 25, 1946), 267–68; Barton J. Bernstein, "The Truman Administration and the Steel Strike of 1946," *Journal of American History*, LII (March 1966), 791–803; Chester Bowles, *Promises to Keep: My Years in Public Life, 1941–1969* (New York, 1971), pp. 137–42.

39. Schlesinger, *Coming of the New Deal*, pp. 282–83; Jonathan Daniels, Diary, Jan. 31, 1945, Daniels MSS; Daniels, *Man of Independence*, p. 304; interview with Oscar L. Chapman, Dec. 30, 1964.

40. HST, *Memoirs*, I, 553–54; HST, Memo to Charles G. Ross, Ross MSS, HSTL; Daniels, *Man of Independence*, pp. 305–306; *SLPD*, Feb. 5, 1946; "Appointments for Reaction," *NR*, CXIV (Jan. 28, 1946), 110; *CS*, Feb. 3, 1946.

41. *NYT*, Feb. 2, 6, 14, 17, 1946; *Public Papers, 1946*, pp. 111, 119; HST, *Memoirs*, I, 554; HST to Eleanor Roosevelt, March 19, 1946, Eleanor Roosevelt MSS, FDRL.

42. Freda Kirchwey, "The Harding Aura," *N*, CLXII (Feb. 23, 1946), 213; *CS*, Feb. 14, 1946; *SLPD*, Feb. 13, 1946; Childs in *ibid.*, Feb. 14, 1946.

43. Howard Y. Williams to his family, Feb. 16, 1946, Williams MSS; James G. Patton to HST, Feb. 19, 1946, HST MSS, OF 555; Walter Millis, ed., *The Forrestal Diaries* (New York, 1951), p. 134; EP, *N*, CLXII (March 9, 1946), 273–74; Richard L. Neuberger, "Secretary for the West— Wisconsin's Krug," *P*, X (March 18, 1946), 8.

44. *NYT*, Feb. 14, March 1, 11, June 13, 1946.

45. *Public Papers, 1946*, pp. 185, 192–93; "Washington Calling," *P*, X (April 15, 1946), 5, 12; National Lawyers Guild Resolution, July 5, 1946, Kenny MSS.

46. "Revolution on the Right," *NR*, CXIV (Jan. 28, 1946), 107–108; Alfred Friendly, "American Industry's Grand Strategy," *N*, CLXII (Jan. 19, 1946), 62–63; EP, *ibid.*, CLXII (Jan. 26, 1946), 85; Max Lerner in *PM*, Jan. 21, 1946; Wechsler in *ibid.*, Feb. 1, 1946.

47. I. F. Stone, "Salute to Symington," *N*, CLXII (Jan. 28, 1946), 90–91; "Big Business Gets Bigger," *NR*, CXIV (July 1, 1946), 917–18; "Time for Action," *P*, X (May 13, 1946), 16; "Washington Calling," *ibid.*, X (Aug. 5, 1946), 4; Robert L. Branyan, "Antimonopoly Activities during the Truman Administration" (Ph.D. dissertation, University of Oklahoma, 1961), ch. II.

48. Allen Matusow, *Farm Policies and Politics in the Truman Years* (Cambridge, Mass., 1967), chs. 1–4; Kirkendall, *Social Scientists and Farm Politics*, pp. 230–54.

49. *NUF*, Dec. 15, 1945, Jan. 15, Feb. 1, 15, March 1, April 1, May 1, 15, June 15, 1946; Patton to Anderson, Oct. 4, 1945, mimeographed copy filed with press releases NFU MSS; Patton, press release, July 10, 1946,

ibid.; Patton to HST, May 2, 1946, and HST to Patton, May 4, 1946, Anderson MSS, HSTL; "Washington Calling," *P*, X (July 22, 1946), 5; Hutson, Oral History Memoir, pp. 477–78, 482–92, COHC; Matusow, *Farm Policies and Politics*, p. 72.

50. Millis, *The Forrestal Diaries*, p. 143; HST to Wallace, Feb. 18, 1946, Wallace MSS, Iowa.

51. HST, Handwritten speech [May 1946], Clark Clifford MSS, HSTL.

52. *Public Papers, 1946*, pp. 274–80; Cabell Phillips, *The Truman Presidency* (New York, 1966), pp. 115–18.

53. *SLPD*, May 26, 1946; Philadelphia *Record*, May 31, 1946; "The Labor Crisis," *N*, CLXII (June 1, 1946), 641–43; "Truman's Blunder," *NR*, CXIV (June 3, 1946), 787–88; Helen Fuller, "Has Truman Lost Labor?" *ibid.*, CXIV (June 10, 1946), 826–28; *NUF*, June 1, 1946; Max Lerner in *PM*, May 28, 1946; ICCASP press release, May 28, 1946, Vito Marcantonio MSS, New York Public Library; *NYT*, May 29, 1946; J. David Stern to HST, June 20, 1945, and other communications in HST MSS, PPF 1638; Eleanor Roosevelt to HST, May 27, 1946, *ibid.*, PPF 460.

54. Philip Jones, Chairman, ALP, to HST, June 6, 1946, HST MSS, OF 1016; *NYT*, June 5, 1946; Eric Sevareid, news commentary, May 26, 1946, Sevareid MSS, LC; Fuller, article cited in n. 53.

55. *Public Papers, 1946*, pp. 289–97; EP, *N*, CLXII (June 22, 1946), 734; EP, *P*, X (June 17, 1946), 3; Chester Bowles, Memo of interview with HST, June 10 [1946], Bowles MSS.

56. HST to Henry Wallace, July 2, 1946, Wallace MSS, Iowa; Hubert Dalton and Joseph Welsh, Greater Kansas City CIOPAC, to HST, Aug. 6, 1946; Hassett to Dalton and Welsh, Aug. 9, 1946; Jack Kroll to HST, Aug. 8, 1946; Matthew J. Connelly to Kroll, Aug. 12, 1946—all in HST MSS, OF 300. Kroll is not listed in the Truman Library's master index for the 1946 White House appointment book.

57. Tris Coffin, "Murder by Amendment," *N*, CLXII (April 27, 1946), 500–501; Coffin, "Counter-Attack in Washington," *ibid.*, CLXII (June 29, 1946), 774–75; "Last Chance to Stop Inflation," *ibid.*, CLXII (June 15, 1946), 708; "The Senate Votes for Inflation," *NR*, CXIV (June 24, 1946), 884.

58. *Public Papers, 1946*, pp. 319, 322–34; Bowles to HST, June 28, 1946, and Bowles to William Hassett, June 28, 1946, HST MSS, OF 96.

59. Fiorello La Guardia, WJZ radio broadcasts, June 30, July 14, 1946, La Guardia MSS, New York City Municipal Archives and Records Center; Tris Coffin, "Showdown on Inflation," *N*, CLXIII (July 7, 1946), 5–6; "After the OPA," *NR*, CXV (July 8, 1946), 3–4; "What Salvage from the OPA?" *ibid.*, CXV (July 29, 1946), 92.

60. William Hillman, *Mr. President*, p. 235; EP, *N*, CLXII (July 20, 1946), 58–59; Padover in *PM*, July 18, 1946; Daniels, *Man of Independence*, pp. 184–85.

61. *Public Papers, 1946*, pp. 350–52; Philadelphia *Record*, Aug. 8, 1946; EP, *N*, CLXIII (Aug. 17, 1946), 169–70; *SLPD*, Sept. 30, 1946.

62. Helen Fuller, "Truman Minus Ickes," *NR*, CXIV (Feb. 25, 1946), 273–75; "The New Treasury Secretary," *ibid.*, CXIV (June 17, 1946), 853–54; John J. Carson, "Men Against Unemployment," *N*, CLXIII (Aug. 10, 1946), 151–52; "Washington Calling," *P*, X (Aug. 12, 1946), 12; Stokes in *CS*, June 11, 1946.

63. "Washington Memo" in *NYP*, Feb. 1, 1946; Robert L. Riggs in the Louisville *Courier-Journal*, Feb. 3, 1946; Joseph P. Lash, *Eleanor Roosevelt: A Friend's Memoir* (Garden City, N.Y., 1964), pp. 296–316.

64. Richard S. Kirkendall, "Truman's Path to Power," *Social Science*, XLIII (April 1968), 67–73.

65. HST, *Memoirs*, I, 325.   66. Lilienthal, *Journals*, II, 434.

67. HST to Eleanor Roosevelt, Nov. 6, 1945, HST MSS, OF 264; Monte M. Poen, "The Truman Administration and National Health Insurance" (Ph.D. dissertation, University of Missouri, 1967), pp. 229–32.

68. Hillman, *Mr. President*, p. 127. See also on Truman's attitude about the need for a liberal party, Daniel Hoan to Fiorello La Guardia, Jan. 7, 1946, and La Guardia to Hoan, Feb. 14, 1946, La Guardia MSS.

69. Neuberger to Ross, Jan. 16, 1946, HST MSS, PPF 1648; "Six Months of Mr. Truman," *P*, IX (Oct. 22, 1945), 12.

70. I. F. Stone, "Where There Is No Vision," *N*, CLXII (Feb. 2, 1946), 118–19.

71. Thomas L. Stokes in *CS*, Nov. 22, 1945; Max Lerner in *PM*, Dec. 18, 1945.

72. Philadelphia *Record*, Dec. 19, 1945; San Francisco *Chronicle*, Aug. 1, 1946.

CHAPTER 4: TRUMAN, THE LIBERALS, AND THE
ORIGINS OF THE COLD WAR

1. Philadelphia *Record*, April 14, 18, 1945; *SLPD*, April 18, 1945; Lerner in *PM*, April 22, 1945; Reinhold Niebuhr and James Loeb, Jr., UDA, to HST, April 23, 1945, HST MSS, PPF 453.

2. *NYP*, April 28, 1945; Grafton in *ibid.*, May 15, 1945; Thomas L. Stokes in *CS*, May 22, 1945; I. F. Stone, "Pie in the Frisco Sky," *N*, CLX (May 19, 1945), 561–63; Stone, "Trieste and San Francisco," *ibid.*, CLX (May 26, 1945), 589–90; Stone, "Truman and the State Department," *ibid.*, CLX (June 9, 1945), 637–39; Bruce Bliven, "Golden Gate Round-Up," *NR*, CXII (May 14, 1945), 665–67; "Rift in the Big Three," *ibid.*, CXII (June 4, 1945), 771–72; Thomas F. Reynolds, "The U.S.A. at San Francisco," *ibid.*, CXII (June 11, 1945), 809–11.

3. *CS*, June 26, 1945; Philadelphia *Record*, June 25, 1945; *SLPD*, June 24, 1945; Freda Kirchwey, "Mirror of Our World," *N*, CLXI (July 7, 1945), 5; Thomas F. Reynolds, "San Francisco Finale," *NR*, CXIII (July 2, 1945), 16–17.

4. "A Purge Needed in State," *NR*, CXIII (July 9, 1945), 38–39; T.R.B., "New Faces in the Capital," *ibid.*, CXIII (Aug. 27, 1945), 254; "Cabinet Changes," *N*, CLXI (July 14, 1945), 23–24; "The State Department Reorganization," *ibid.*, CLXI (Sept. 15, 1945), 245; EP, *P*, IX (Aug. 27, 1945), 3; *SLPD*, June 17, 1945.

5. Helen Fuller, "Politics and Europe's Hunger," *NR*, CXIII (Oct. 1, 1945), 428–29; "The World Needs Our Help," *ibid.*, CXIII (Dec. 10, 1945), 779–81; Childs in *SLPD*, Oct. 30, 1945; Bowles to HST, Nov. 2, 1945, copy attached to Bowles to Samuel I. Rosenman, Nov. 2, 1945, Rosenman MSS.

6. "Lehman Resigns in Disgust," *NR*, CXIV (March 25, 1946), 398; T.R.B., "We Eat and Others Starve," *ibid.*, CXIV (April 22, 1946), 568; "Famine: America's Duty," *ibid.*, CXIV (April 29, 1946), 595–97; A. Powell Davies, "Let Them Eat Statistics," *ibid.*, CXIV (June 3, 1946), 801; "Act Now on Famine," *N*, CLXII (April 20, 1946), 451–52; *NUF*, May 15, 1946; Allen Matusow, *Farm Policies and Politics*, p. 37.

7. M.H.R. [Morris H. Rubin], "The Last Column," *P*, IX (Nov. 5, 1945), 12; EP, *N*, CLXI (Dec. 29, 1945), 723.

8. EP, *ibid.*, CLXI (Aug. 25, 1945), 167; Freda Kirchwey, "British Policy Breaks Down," *ibid.*, CLXI (Nov. 24, 1945), 540–41; Freda Kirchwey, "Palestine and Bevan," *ibid.*, CLXII (June 22, 1946), 737–39; EP, *ibid.*, CLXIII (Oct. 12, 1946), 393; "Nowhere to Lay Their Heads," *NR*, CXIII (Oct. 29, 1945), 556–57; Samuel I. Rosenman to Bartley Crum, Dec. 13, 1945, Rosenman MSS; *Public Papers, 1945*, pp. 228, 355–57, 402, 467–70; *NYT*, Aug. 22, 24, Oct. 29, 1946; *Public Papers, 1946*, pp. 442–44.

9. "Germany: East and West," *NR*, CXII (June 18, 1945), 827–28; Joachim Joesten, "AMG—the Soviet Way," *N*, CLXI (July 28, 1945), 77–79; Saul K. Padover, "What Happened in Bavaria," *ibid.*, CLXI (Oct. 20, 1945), 397–99; "Wanted: an American Policy," *P*, IX (July 2, 1945), 12.

10. Lillie Shultz, Nation Associates, to Fiorello La Guardia, Feb. 27, 1946, La Guardia MSS; Freda Kirchwey, et al., to HST, Feb. 26, 1946, *ibid.*; "Franco Before the Security Council," *N*, CLXII (April 13, 1946), 428–29; "Memorandum on Spain," *ibid.*, pp. 429–37; *SLPD*, May 22, 1946; "Americans for Franco," *NR*, CXIV (May 13, 1946), 675–76.

11. Saul Padover in *PM*, Sept. 3, 1946; *SLPD*, Sept. 4, 1946; Daniels, press release [Sept. 1946], Daniels MSS (filed with Jan. 1946 correspondence); EP, *N*, CLXIII (Oct. 5, 1946), 365.

12. Freda Kirchwey, "Old Game, New Rules," *N*, CLXI (Dec. 29, 1945), 725–726; *SLPD*, Nov. 26, 1945; "What Is Happening in Iran," *NR*, CXIII

(Dec. 3, 1945), 731–32; "Behind the Scenes in Iran," *ibid.*, CXIII (Dec. 31, 1945), 887–88.

13. Maxwell S. Stewart, "China's New Danger," *N*, CLXI (Aug. 25, 1945), 172–73; "Get Our Troops Out of China," *ibid.*, CLXI (Nov. 10, 1945), 483; Sevareid, News commentary, Oct. 29, 1945, Sevareid MSS; *Public Papers, 1945,* pp. 543–45; "New Hope for China," *NR*, CXII (Dec. 24, 1945), 856.

14. EP, *N*, CLXII (Feb. 9, 1946), 154–55; EP, *ibid.*, CLXIII (Dec. 28, 1946), 742–43; "Propping Up Chiang Kai-Shek," *ibid.*, CLXIII (Sept. 14, 1946), 284; "Storm Clouds Over China," *NR*, CXIV (May 13, 1946), 677–78; Irving Brant, "What Russia Wants," *ibid.*, CXIV (June 3, 1946), 794–96; "Danger in China," *ibid.*, CXV (Sept. 2, 1946), 243–44; Richard Watts, Jr., "An American Policy for China," *ibid.*, CXV (Sept. 23, 1946), 344–45; Theodore H. White, "Lost: American Policy in China," *ibid.*, CXV (Dec. 16, 1946), 796–98; *SLPD*, Aug. 1, 1946; *PM*, Sept. 6, 1946; *Public Papers, 1946,* pp. 499–505; Carlson, Statement for National Committee to Win the Peace, July 24, 1946, in *CR*, 79 Cong., 2 Sess. (Appendix), p. A4750; Carlson to Vito Marcantonio, Aug. 21, 1946, Marcantonio MSS; Elmer Davis, News commentary, July 22, 1946, Davis MSS; Sabath to HST, Aug. 17, 1946, HST MSS, OF 150-Misc.

15. These judgments are drawn primarily from Tang Tsou, *America's Failure in China* (Chicago, 1963), and HST, *Memoirs: Volume II, Years of Trial and Hope* (Garden City, N.Y., 1956) [hereafter cited as *Memoirs, II*], esp. pp. 61–92.

16. *SLPD*, April 29, 1945; "Russia Returns from Isolation," *NR*, CXII (May 7, 1945), 630–31; "Progress in the Balkans," *ibid.*, CXIII (Sept. 10, 1945), 301; Freda Kirchwey, "Russia and the West," *N*, CLX (June 23, 1945), 684–86; "Churchill Bearing Gifts," *ibid.*, CLXI (Aug. 25, 1945), 167–68; Elmer Davis, News commentary, Dec. 18, 1945, Davis MSS.

17. "The Bomb Is No Secret," *NR*, CXIII (Oct. 8, 1945), 451–53; Freda Kirchwey, "Russia and the Bomb," *N*, CLXI (Nov. 17, 1945), 511–12; Walter Millis, "Share and Share Alike," *ibid.*, CLXI (Dec. 22, 1945), 707–708; *Public Papers, 1945,* p. 382; HST, *Memoirs*, I, 524–28; Elting E. Morison, *Turmoil and Tradition* (Boston, 1960), p. 642; Richard G. Hewlett and Oscar T. Anderson, Jr., *The New World, 1939–1946* (University Park, Pa., 1962), pp. 418–21; Joseph P. Lash, *Eleanor Roosevelt*, p. 296. Reinhold Niebuhr, however, expressed deep pessimism about the chances *both* for agreement with Russia and for international control. Niebuhr, "The Atomic Issue," *Christianity and Crisis*, V (Oct. 15, 1945), 5–7.

18. "Horse-Trading at London," *NR*, CXIII (Oct. 8, 1945), 455–56; *SLPD*, Oct. 7, 1945.

19. *Public Papers, 1945,* pp. 290, 404–13; *NYT*, Oct. 25, 1945; "What Does Mr. Truman Mean?" *NR*, CXIII (Nov. 5, 1945), 587–88; Robert

La Follette, Jr., "The Military's Drug for Democracy," *P*, IX (Nov. 19, 1945), 1.

20. *Public Papers, 1945*, pp. 431–38; "Are We Planning War?" *N*, CLXI (Nov. 3, 1945), 447–48; *SLPD*, Oct. 28, 1945.

21. *Public Papers, 1945*, pp. 511–13; Grafton in *NYP*, Dec. 3, 1945; Eric Sevareid, News commentary, Oct. 10, 1945, Sevareid MSS; Thomas F. Reynolds, "Pulmotor Needed for UNO," *NR*, CXIII (Dec. 17, 1945), 827–29.

22. ICCASP Resolution, Dec. 4, 1945, attached to Jo Davidson to HST, Dec. 7, 1945, HST MSS, PPF 471; *NYT*, Dec. 5, 1945.

23. "Good News from Moscow," *NR*, CXIV (Jan. 7, 1946), 3–4; *NYP*, Dec. 28, 1945.

24. *NYT*, March 6, 1946.

25. Churchill's "Union Now," *N*, CLXII (March 16, 1946), 303–304; Curtis MacDougall, *Gideon's Army*, I, 30; Stokes to Ralph Ingersoll, May 4, 1946, Ingersoll MSS.

26. *NYT*, April 1, 1946; James Loeb, Jr., in *SLPD*, June 16, 1946; Sabath in *CR*, 79 Cong., 2 Sess. (Appendix), p. A2387; Adam Clymer, "Union for Democratic Action" (honors thesis, Harvard, 1958), pp. 113–15; Loeb to Joseph P. Lash, May 7, 1946, ADA MSS; *Program* of the Win the Peace Conference, copy in *ibid.*, unsigned, undated memo on the Win-the-Peace Conference, *ibid.* This last document points out that many non-Communist liberals—Eleanor Roosevelt, Freda Kirchwey, Bruce Bliven, and Max Lerner, among others—refused to give the conference their support; the many who did, however, seem more impressive.

27. "Declaration of Principles. . . ." in *CR*, 79 Cong., 2 Sess. (Appendix), pp. A2388–89.

28. *NYT*, May 2, 1946; *NUF*, Aug. 15, 1946; Lerner in *PM*, Oct. 20, 21, 22, 1946; "The Military Clique and the War Party" (unsigned mimeographed document [April? 1946]), Chapman MSS. Mr. Chapman declined to reveal the author of the last document. Apparently it originated within the Interior Department and was circulated among younger liberals in the administration.

29. Robert L. Riggs in the Louisville *Courier-Journal*, Sept. 22, 1946.

30. Pepper, speeches in *CR*, 79 Cong., 2 Sess. (Appendix), A517–18, A4179–83.

31. "A World Made for War," *NR*, CXIV (March 4, 1946), 299–300; "Trouble in Manchuria," *ibid.*, CXIV (March 11, 1946), 334–35; Uhl in *PM*, July 1, 1946; *NYT*, Feb. 9, 13, Nov. 9, 1946.

32. *Public Papers, 1946*, pp. 105–106, 157–58; Tris Coffin, "Washington's Atomic War," *N*, CLXII (Feb. 16, 1946), 187–89; "The Fruits of Suspicion," *ibid.*, CLXII (March 2, 1946), 247–48; "Russia and the Atom," *ibid.*, CLXIII (Aug. 3, 1946), 116–17; Freda Kirchwey, "Roots of Suspicion," *ibid.*, CLXIII (Aug. 31, 1946), 228–29; Frank Kingdon, NCPAC, to

HST, March 2, 15, 1946, HST MSS, OF 692 Misc.; Helen Gahagan Douglas in *CR*, 79 Cong., 2 Sess. (July 18, 1946), pp. 9350–53; "A World Made for War," *NR*, CXIV (March 4, 1946), 299–300; "Three Cheers," *ibid.*, CXIV (April 8, 1946), 461–62; "Evatt, Gromyko and the Bomb," *ibid.*, CXV (July 22, 1946), 61; "Atomic Front Door to Peace," *ibid.*, CXV (Aug. 5, 1946), 115–16; Hewelet and Anderson, *The New World*, chs. 13–16; Lilienthal, *Journals* II, 60–61.

33. "Bargain at Yalta," *NL*, XXVIII (Feb. 17, 1945), 1; "The World This War Has Made," *ibid.*, XXVIII (Aug. 11, 1945), 3; "The Irrepressible Conflict," *ibid.*, XXIX (Aug. 10, 1946), 1; Jonathan Stout, "Acheson Tries to Muzzle MacArthur," *ibid.*, XXIX (Sept. 7, 1946), 1, 3; Stout, "The Irrepressible Conflict Sharpens," *ibid.*, XXIX (Dec. 14, 1946), 1, 3; Stout, "Communist Influence in Washington," *ibid.*, XXVIII (Aug. 11, 1945), 3; Liston M. Oak, "American Intervention in Chinese Internal Affairs," *ibid.*, XXVIII (Nov. 10, 1945), 2; "Alert: The Institute of Pacific Relations and American Far Eastern Policy," *ibid.*, XXVIII (Dec. 15, 1945), 5; "China Moves Toward Democracy," *ibid.*, XXIX (Aug. 17, 1946), 1; Liston Oak, "Trends," *ibid.*, XXIX (Dec. 14, 1946), 2; Max Nomad, "American Pseudo-Liberalism," *ibid.*, XXVIII (Dec. 22, 1945), 3; "Is the ICCASP a Communist Front?" *ibid.*, XXIX (Jan. 26, 1946), 5; Ferdinand Lundberg, "How *PM* Gives Totalitarianism a 'Liberal' Camouflage," *ibid.*, XXIX (July 20, 1946), 5. For Chamberlain's obsession with Yalta, see, e.g., his exchange with Joseph and Stewart Alsop in *ibid.*, XXXIV (Sept. 10, 1951), 19–21.

34. M.H.R. [Morris H. Rubin], "The Last Column," *P*, IX (May 28, 1945), 12; Robert La Follette, Jr., "Russia, Britain, and Peace," *ibid.*, IX (June 18, 1945), 1; Kenneth Crawford, "The Peacemakers at Potsdam," *ibid.*, IX (July 23, 1945), 1–2; Louis Fischer, "How to 'Stop' Stalin," *ibid.*, X (March 18, 1946), 4; Fischer, "Imperialism Threatens the Peace," *ibid.*, X (May 13, 1946), 4; Fischer, Letters to the Editor, *N*, CLX (June 2, 23, 1945), 631–32, 706–708; "The Fischer-Nation Debate," *ibid.*, CLX (June 30, 1945), 728; James A. Wechsler, *The Age of Suspicion*, pp. 179–81; *NYT*, June 16, 1946.

35. Davis, "Clash Between Britain and Russia," *NL*, XXIX (March 2, 1946), 9.

36. *NYT*, June 16, 1946.

37. UDA foreign policy statement, reprinted in *CR*, 79 Cong., 2 Sess. (Appendix), p. A3513.

38. Niebuhr and James Loeb, Jr., Letter to the Editor, *NYT*, April 18, 1946; *ibid.*, April 6, June 9, Oct. 8, 1946; Niebuhr, "American Liberals and British Labor," *N*, CLXII (June 8, 1946), 682–84; Niebuhr, "Europe, Russia, and America," *ibid.*, CLXIII (Sept. 14, 1946), 288–89; Lash, *Eleanor Roosevelt*, pp. 298–300.

39. *SLPD*, May 17, June 16, 1946.

40. Lasch, *CS* column reprinted in *CR,* 79 Cong., 2 Sess. (Appendix), p. A2383.

41. Johnson in the *Bell-Ringer,* April 1946.

42. Helen Douglas in *CR,* 79 Cong., 2 Sess. (Appendix), pp. A119–21.

43. John L. Gaddis, *The United States and the Origins of the Cold War, 1941–1947* (New York, 1972), pp. 198–206.

44. MacDougall, *Gideon's Army,* I, 23.

45. HST, Diary entries, May 22, June 7, 1945, in William Hillman, *Mr. President,* pp. 114–16, 121; Joseph C. Grew, *Turbulent Era: A Record of Forty Years in the U.S. Diplomatic Service,* ed., Walter Johnson, 2 vols. (Cambridge, Mass., 1953), II, 1453. The Joseph Davies MSS, LC, contain several items that are very significant to an understanding of Truman's attitudes especially HST to Davies, April 19, 1945; Davies, Memos or notes on conversations with HST, April 30, Sept. 18, 1945, Sept. 10, 1946; Davies, Diary and journal entries on meetings with HST, April 30, May 13, 21, July 16, Dec. 8, Dec. 19, 1945. See also HST to Eleanor Roosevelt, May 10, 1945, Eleanor Roosevelt MSS.

46. HST, Diary entries, May 22, June 7, June 13, 1945, in Hillman, *Mr. President,* pp. 114–16, 121–22.

47. Burton K. Wheeler, *Yankee from the West* (Garden City, N.Y., 1962), p. 397; HST, *Memoirs,* I, 341–42, 350, 411–12; Walter Millis, ed., *The Forrestal Diaries,* p. 78; Jonathan Daniels, *Man of Independence,* p. 23. See also HST to Henry Wallace, July 27, 1945, Wallace MSS, Iowa.

48. Daniels, *ibid.,* p. 266; Harold Smith, Conference with the president, Oct. 5, 1945, Smith MSS.

49. HST, *Memoirs,* I, 552.

50. *Ibid.;* Byrnes, "American Policy on Germany," *Vital Speeches,* XII (Sept. 15, 1946), 706–709. Gaddis, *The United States and the Origins of the Cold War,* argues persuasively that administration attitudes had crystallized by early 1946.

51. Arthur Krock, *Memoirs: Sixty Years on the Firing Line* (Popular Library ed.; New York, 1968), Appendix A.

CHAPTER 5: DEMORALIZATION AND DEFEAT

1. Humphrey to Wallace, April 12, 1945, and Eleanor Roosevelt to Wallace, April 17, 1945, Wallace MSS, Iowa.

2. Karl Schmidt, *Henry A. Wallace,* p. 7; "Speech of Helen Gahagan Douglas for Smaller Industries Day . . . October 23, 1945," Helen Douglas MSS, University of Oklahoma; Louis Bean, Oral History Memoir, p. 262, COHC; *PM,* Sept. 11, 1945; Willard Kiplinger to Wallace, May 22, 1946, Wallace MSS, Iowa. Wallace's original plans for the Department of

Commerce are in [Wallace] "The Department of Commerce" [Nov. 29, 1944], *ibid.*

3. *NYT*, May 25, June 5, Aug. 29, Dec. 5, 1945, Feb. 1, 17, 20, March 13, 16, April 13, Aug. 21, 22, 1946; *PM*, Sept. 24, Nov. 2, Dec. 5, 1945, Feb. 10, 1946; Hansen, "The Wallace Goal," *NR*, CXIII (Sept. 17, 1945), 353–55; Williams to his family, Nov. 15, 1945, Williams MSS; Barton J. Bernstein, "Walter Reuther and the General Motors Strike of 1945–1946," *Michigan History*, XLIX (Sept. 1965), 260–77.

4. *NYT*, Sept. 14, 1945, Feb. 7, 16, March 19, 20, April 11, 23, 1946; *NYP*, Feb. 18, 1946; "Statement by F. H. La Guardia Endorsing Mr. Johannes Steel, February 15, 1946," La Guardia MSS; David A. Shannon, *The Decline of American Communism* (New York, 1959), p. 116; *Public Papers, 1946*, p. 164; Wallace, "How to Elect a Progressive Congress," *N*, CLXIII (Aug. 31, 1946), 231–32.

5. I. F. Stone in *PM*, Sept. 22, 1946; Byrnes, *All in One Lifetime* (New York, 1958), p. 373; Jonathan Daniels, *Frontier on the Potomac* (New York, 1946), p. 238; Daniels, *Man of Independence*, pp. 313, 316; HST, *Memoirs*, I, 560; Wallace interview; Harold Smith, Conference with the president, Dec. 11, 1945, Smith MSS; Howard Tolley, Oral History Memoir, p. 648, COHC; Wallace to Hubert Humphrey, April 21, 1945, Wallace MSS, Iowa, is typical of Wallace's efforts to praise Truman.

6. *PM*, April 19, 1945; *NYP*, April 19, 1945; "Washington Memo," *ibid.*, Dec. 17, 1945; T.R.B., "Five Hurdles for Mr. Truman," *NR*, CXIII (Nov. 12, 1945), 638; *NYT*, Feb. 17, March 24, 1946; [Wallace], two letters to HST, Dec. 18, 1945, HST MSS, OF 264, copies in Wallace MSS, Iowa; "Washington Calling," *P*, X (June 10, 1946), 12; Joseph Lash, *Eleanor Roosevelt*, pp. 295–96; Thomas L. Stokes in *CS*, Dec. 20, 1945; Wallace to Robert O. Bland, June 20, 1946, and Wallace to Eda Cummings, June 28, 1946, both in Wallace MSS, Iowa.

7. *NYT*, Feb. 19, March 8, 13, 20, 22, April 29, May 8, 1946; Wallace interview; Cohen interview; Wallace, Address to the Liberal Voters League of St. Louis and the NCPAC, June 14, 1946, Alfred Schindler MSS, HSTL; Millis, *Forrestal Diaries*, pp. 133, 154–55; interview with Harold Young, April 1953, PP MSS, University of Iowa. Wallace also states his attitudes in letters to Anna T. Davis, May 5, 1945; James LeCron, May 23, 1945; Edgar R. Smothers, June 13, 1945; Warner K. Herz, June 23, 1945; Manuel Avila Camacho, March 21, 1946; Frank Sterrett, April 26, 1946; Edward Stinnes, April 3, 1946—all in Wallace MSS, Iowa.

8. Wallace to HST, Sept. 24, 1945, *ibid.*

9. HST, *Memoirs*, I, 555–56; HST to Wallace, March 20, 1946, and Wallace to HST, March 15, 21, 1946, all in Wallace MSS, Iowa.

10. HST, *Memoirs*, I, 556–57; HST to Wallace, Aug. 8, 1946, and Clark Clifford, Memo to the Secretary of State, July 26, 1946, Clifford MSS; Lord, *The Wallaces of Iowa*, p. 561; Wallace, "The Path to Peace with

Russia," *NR*, CXV (Sept. 30, 1946), 401–406; Bean, Oral History Memoir, p. 257, COHC.

11. *Public Papers, 1946*, pp. 426–27; "Washington Memo," *NYP*, Sept. 12, 1946; Doris Fleeson in *SLPD*, Sept. 12, 1946; MacDougall, *Gideon's Army*, I, 59–61. Joseph Davies, Diary, Sept. 10, 1946, Davies MSS, in a passage obviously written at a later date indicates that Wallace did not read the speech to the president. On the other topics discussed, which may have required only a couple of minutes, see Wallace to Walter Thurston, Sept. 10, 1946, Wallace MSS, Iowa.

12. *PM*, Sept. 13, 1946; *NYT*, Sept. 13, 1946; Shannon, *Decline of American Communism*, pp. 119–20; Wallace to Norman Thomas, Oct. 2, 1946, Thomas MSS, New York Public Library.

13. *NYT*, Sept. 15, 1946.

14. *SLPD*, Sept. 14, 1946; *PM*, Sept. 13, 1946; Kenneth Crawford, "Suffering World," *P*, X (Sept. 30, 1946), 1–2; "Wallace Is Wrong," *ibid.*, p. 12; Davis, News commentary, Sept. 14, 1946, Davis MSS; "Wallace's Threat to US Foreign Policy," *NL*, XXIX (Sept. 21, 1946), 1; Niebuhr, "Europe, Russia, and America," *N*, CLXIII (Sept. 14, 1946), 288–89; Niebuhr, "The Fight for Germany," *Life*, XXI (Oct. 23, 1946), 65–72; Niebuhr, "Mr. Wallace's Errors," *Christianity and Crisis*, VI (Oct. 28, 1946), 1–2.

15. *NYP*, Sept. 16, 1946; "The Wallace Speech," *N*, CLXIII (Sept. 21, 1946), 311–12; Stokes in *CS*, Sept. 17, 1946; "Wallace—a World Leader," *NR*, CXV (Sept. 23, 1946), 339–40; Harrison to Wallace, Sept. 13, 1946, Wallace MSS, Iowa.

16. *Public Papers, 1946*, p. 427n; *PM*, Sept. 16, 17, 1946; "The Wallace Speech," *N*, CLXIII (Sept. 21, 1946), 311–12; Davis, News commentary, Sept. 14, 1946, Davis MSS.

17. HST, *Memoirs*, I, 557–60; Hillman, *Mr. President*, p. 128; *NYT*, Sept. 21, 1946; Phillips, *Truman Presidency*, p. 153.

18. Kenneth Crawford, "Suffering World," *P*, X (Sept. 30, 1946), 1–2; "Wallace Is Wrong," *ibid.*, p. 12; "Union for Democratic Action Statement on Henry Wallace," in "Remarks of Dr. James Loeb, Jr. . . . Sept. 29th, 1946," ADA MSS; *PM*, Sept. 22, 1946; Freda Kirchwey, "The Challenge of Henry Wallace," *N*, CLXIII (Sept. 28, 1946), 337–39; "Crisis in Foreign Policy," *NR*, CXV (Sept. 30, 1946), 395–96; "What the Liberals Should Do," *ibid.*, CXV (Oct. 14, 1946), 470; La Guardia, WJZ Radio Broadcast, Sept. 22, 1946, La Guardia MSS; Davis to Wallace, Sept. 20, 1946, Wallace MSS, Iowa.

19. *CS*, Sept. 24, 1946.

20. EP, *N*, CLXII (May 18, June 22, 1946), 585–86, 734; EP, *ibid.*, CLXIII (July 20, 27, Aug. 10, 31, 1946), 58, 86–87, 143–44, 226–27; Carey McWilliams, "The Lesson of California," *ibid.*, CLXII (June 22, 1946), 742–44; "La Follette's Folly," *ibid.*, CLXIII (Aug. 24,

1946), 200–201; "The GOP v. Liberalism," *NR*, CXV (July 22, 1946), 89; "Education for Politics," *ibid.*, CXV (July 15, 1946), 35; Carroll Kilpatrick in *CS*, Aug. 11, 1946; Uhl in *PM*, Aug. 18, 1946.

21. *NYT*, Sept. 27, 28, Oct. 2, 3, 4, 8, 13, 1946; *PM*, Oct. 9, 25, 31, Nov. 3, 4, 5, 1946; Hewlett and Anderson, *The New World*, pp. 601–606; "Baruch v. Wallace," *NR*, CXV (Oct. 14, 1946), 468.

22. *NYT*, Sept. 22, 25, Oct. 12, 1946; *PM*, Sept. 22, 30, 1946; Allan Nevins, *Herbert H. Lehman and His Era* (New York, 1963), pp. 303–307; Jack Bell in *CS*, Oct. 31, 1946; Robert Kenny to Mrs. Harvey C. Evans, June 11, 1946, and Kenny to Martin Popper, July 29, 1946, Kenny MSS; Harold Young to Paul de Kruif, Nov. 26, 1946, Wallace MSS, Iowa.

23. "Anderson Lifts the Lid," *NR*, CXV (Sept. 9, 1946), 277–78; "Riding for a Crash," *ibid.*, CXV (Oct. 28, 1946), 534–36; *Public Papers, 1946*, pp. 433–35, 451–55; *PM*, Sept. 30, 1946; Bowles to HST, Oct. 15, 1946, HST MSS, PPF 2687; "Meat and Politics," *N*, CLXIII (Oct. 26, 1946), 459–60; Philadelphia *Record*, Oct. 16, 1946; *NYT*, Oct. 17, 1946.

24. Stokes in *CS*, Nov. 9, 1946; Myra Lee Houck, Memo to Connelly, Ross, Hassett, and Steelman, Oct. 17, 1946, Clifford MSS; Clifford to Hannegan [Oct. 1946] and Hannegan to Clifford [Oct. 1946], *ibid.*

25. "We Were Licked," *NR*, CXV (Nov. 18, 1946), 656–57; *CS*, Nov. 14, 1946; *NYT*, Nov. 11, 1946.

26. Perry in *PM*, Nov. 7, 1946; *NYP*, Nov. 7, 1946.

27. Tris Coffin, "Confusion in the GOP," *N*, CLXIII (Nov. 23, 1946), 574–75; *Public Papers, 1946*, pp. 475–79; *NYT*, Nov. 7, 1946; *CS*, Nov. 7, 1946; *NYP*, Nov. 11, 1946; Ickes in *ibid.*

28. Rauh interview; I. F. Stone, "Some News to Cheer," *N*, CLXII (Feb. 16, 1946), 186–87; Bryant Putney, "Obituary for Veterans' Housing," *ibid.*, CLXIII (Dec. 21, 1946), 722–23; Richard O. Davies, *Housing Reform during the Truman Administration*, pp. 43–57; Davis R. B. Ross, *Preparing for Ulysses: Politics and Veterans during World War II* (New York, 1969), pp. 249–74.

29. "Liberals and the Labor Crisis," *NR*, CXIV (June 10, 1946), 830–31; "What the Liberals Should Do," *ibid.*, CXV (Oct. 14, 1946), 470; *NYT*, May 5, June 29, Nov. 5, Dec. 6, 21, 1946; *PM*, Nov. 5, 1946; Shannon, *Decline of American Communism*, p. 114; interview with Ben Davidson, Dec. 11, 1964; *CS*, June 30, 1946; John Cort, "Third Party?" *Commonweal*, XLIV (July 26, 1946), 350–53; "Ideas for a New Party," *Antioch Review*, VI (Fall 1946), 449–72; "Ideas for a New Party—A Symposium," *ibid.*, VI (Dec. 1946), 602–24; MacDougall, *Gideon's Army*, I, 46–47; Arnold Beichman, "Is Third-Party Talk Merely Political Escapism?" *NL*, XXIX (July 6, 1946), 8; Samuel Shore, "A Labor-Liberal Alliance Can Rescue US from Paralysis," *ibid.*, XXIX (July 6, 1946), 9; John L. Childs, "America Needs Political Realignment," *ibid.*, XXIX (Aug. 24, 1946), 3,

14; Pearl Willen, "America Needs New Political Party," *ibid.*, XXIX (Nov. 30, 1946), 6, 15. William E. Leuchtenburg generously shared his notes on the National Educational Committee with me.

30. La Guardia, WJZ Radio Broadcast, Jan. 26, 1947, La Guardia MSS.

31. Gardner Jackson in *NUF*, Feb. 1, 1946; Henry Zon, "The Melody Is Gone," *N*, CLXIII (Oct. 12, 1946), 404–405; Wechsler in *PM*, Feb. 14, 1946; Cabell Phillips, "The New Dealers—Where Are They Now?" *NYT Magazine*, Sept. 29, 1946, pp. 12–13; interviews with Leon Keyserling and Robert Nathan, Sept. 20, 1967.

32. Grafton in the Louisville *Courier-Journal*, April 12, 1946.

33. Elliott Roosevelt, *As He Saw It* (New York, 1946), p. 115 and *passim*.

34. *Ibid.*, ch. 11, pp. 254, 256.   35. *CS*, Nov. 15, 1946.

36. Daniels, "The FDR Legend—True and False," *Saturday Review*, XXIX (Oct. 5, 1946), 9–11.

37. *(Proposal) National Roosevelt Clubs*, Harley Kilgore MSS, FDRL; Nichols to Kilgore, May 17, 1946 and George Killion to Kilgore, May 21, 1946, *ibid.*; unsigned and undated memorandum, Chapman MSS, "1948 Campaign, Miscellaneous"; Hannah [Dorner] and May [?] to Jo and Florence Davidson, July 30, 1946, Davidson MSS; Chapman interview.

CHAPTER 6: THE POLARIZATION OF THE
LIBERAL MOVEMENT

1. Walter Davenport, "Ruddy Rodeo," *Colliers*, CXVII (June 1, 1946), 14–15, Hannah Dorner, ICCASP form letter to members and accompanying report [Oct. or Nov. 1945], PP MSS; James Loeb, Jr., to Nathalie Panek, Feb. 20, 1947, ADA MSS; William Cochran to Reinhold Niebuhr, May 28, 1946, Niebuhr MSS; MacDougall, *Gideon's Army*, I, 53. Kreuger, *And Promises to Keep*, pp. 82–92, attributes anti-Communist sentiments to Foreman during the years 1939–1942; in the postwar years, however, Foreman was clearly a Popular Fronter.

2. Max M. Kampelman, *The Communist Party vs. the C.I.O.* (New York, 1957), pp. 35–60; John J. Rooney to Philip Murray, Aug. 16, 1946, and Murray to Rooney, Aug. 20, 1946, Philip Murray MSS, Catholic University of America; "Progressives in the CIO," *P*, X (Oct. 14, 1946), 12; John C. Cort, "The Labor Beat," *ibid.*, X (Oct. 21, 1946), 5; "Washington Calling," *ibid.*, X (Dec. 23, 1946), 1, 12; Edwin Lahey, Oral History Memoir, pp. 104–105, COHC.

3. Jackson to Patton, Aug. 3, 1946; Elmore to Patton, Sept. 9, 1947; Elmore, "Communist Foot in the Farmer's Door"—all in *CR*, 81 Cong., 2

Sess. (Sept. 7, 1950), pp. 14287–92. *SLPD*, Sept. 15, 1947; MacDougall, *Gideon's Army*, III, 608–10; Patton to Chester Bowles, Jan. 28, Feb. 14, 1947, Bowles MSS.

4. *NYT*, June 16, 17, Nov. 11, 1946; *PM*, June 26, 1947; Thomas L. Stokes in *CS*, June 18, 1946, July 1, 1947; "Statement on Communism . . ." AVC Press Release in Melvyn Douglas MSS, University of Oklahoma; AVC Press Release, April 26, 1947, *ibid.*; Ed Logue, " 'Citizens First, Veterans Second,' " *P*, X (Dec. 16, 1946), 4, 11; "Washington Calling," *ibid.*, XI (Jan. 27, 1947), 12; L. A. Nikloric, "AVC—Innocent No More," *ibid.*, XIII (May 1949), 11–13; Robert L. Tyler, "The American Veterans Committee: Out of a Hot War and Into the Cold," *American Quarterly*, XVIII (Fall 1966), 419–36.

5. Childs in *SLPD*, Feb. 19, 1946; Philadelphia *Record* editorial, reprinted as "American Liberalism: A Faith to Fight For," *P*, X (May 27, 1946), 12; "Washington Calling," *ibid.*, X (June 24, 1946), 12; La Follette, "Look Out, Liberals!" *ibid.*, X (Nov. 4, 1946), 1–2; Schlesinger, "The U.S. Communist Party," *Life*, XXI (July 29, 1946), 84–96; Freda Kirchwey, "Liberalism at Los Angeles," *N*, CLXIII (Oct. 5, 1946), 369–70.

6. Eleanor Roosevelt in the Philadelphia *Record*, June 11, 1945; *NYT*, April 6, Oct. 8, 1946; Clymer, "Union for Democratic Action" (honors thesis, Harvard College, 1958), pp. 116, 120–26; Bruce Bliven to James Loeb, Jr., April 9, 1946, and Loeb to Bliven, April 11, May 1, 1946, ADA MSS; Loeb to the Editor, *NR*, CXIV (May 13, 1946), 699; Minutes, National Board of Directors Meeting, UDA May 22, 1946, and "Memorandum: Proposed National Conference of Democratic Progressives," July 1, 1946, Niebuhr MSS.

7. Isaacs to the Editor, *NR*, CXIV (May 20, 1946), 733; Valtair to the Editor and Foreman to the Editor, *ibid.*, CXIV (June 10, 1946), 837; MacDougall to the Editor, *ibid.*, CXIV (July 1, 1946), 936; Loeb to Howard Y. Williams, May 21, 1946, and Williams to Bruce Bliven, May 25, 1946, Williams MSS; Isaacs to Reinhold Niebuhr, April 11, 1946, Niebuhr MSS.

8. Bailey to the Editor, *NR*, CXIV (May 27, 1946), 771; Arthur to the Editor, *ibid.*, CXIV (July 1, 1946), 935–36; and *ibid.*, CXV (July 15, 1946), 48; Lewis to the Editor, *N*, CLXIII (Sept. 14, 1946), 308.

9. Neuberger, "Washington's Strange Election," *P*, X (July 22, 1946), 9.

10. Milburn P. Akers in *CS*, Sept. 28, 1946.

11. "Unity on the Left," *NR*, CXIV (May 13, 1946), 681; "Excitement Down South," *ibid.*, CXIV (May 20, 1946), 721; "The Democrats and the PAC," *ibid.*, CXIV (May 27, 1946), 753; *NYT*, May 12, 1946.

12. *NYT*, Sept. 29, 1946; *CS*, Sept. 29, 30, 1946; *NYP*, Sept. 28, 1946; Helen Fuller, "Report from Chicago—Progressives' Progress," *NR*, CV (Oct. 7, 1946), 433; *Report of Conference of Progressives. Hotel Continental, Chicago, Sept. 28–29, 1946* [New York, 1946], *passim*; Ickes, Speech

to Conference of Progressives, Sept. 28, 1946, ADA MSS; MacDougall, *Gideon's Army*, I, 106–109.

13. *NYT*, Oct. 16, 1946; Loeb to Joseph P. Lash, Sept. 2, Oct. 10, 15, 1946, and [Loeb] draft of a letter to Murray, written for Altman, ADA MSS; Charles Weinstein to Philip Murray, Nov. 14, 1946, Murray MSS; MacDougall, *Gideon's Army*, I, 109–10.

14. Davis, News commentary, Nov. 11, 1946, Davis MSS; Neuberger, "The People Spin the Wheel Full Circle," *P*, X (Nov. 25, 1946), 4; M.H.R. [Morris H. Rubin], "The Last Column," *ibid.*, X (Dec. 16, 1946), 12; Wechsler, "Liberals Without Reds," *ibid.*, XI (Jan. 13, 1947), 1–2; Philadelphia *Record*, Nov. 7, 1946; Childs in *SLPD*, Dec. 2, 1946.

15. Lerner in *PM*, Nov. 19, 20, 25, 1946; Stokes in *CS*, Nov. 16, 1946.

16. Ickes to Kenneth Crawford, Jan. 9, 1947, ADA MSS; Hannah [Dorner] and May [?] to Jo and Florence Davidson, July 30, 1946, Davidson MSS; "Glamour Pusses," *Time*, XLVIII (Sept. 9, 1946), 23–25; *NYT*, July 15, Oct. 4, 8, Nov. 12, 1946; Chapman interview; Ickes to Norman Thomas, Nov. 26, 1946, Thomas MSS.

17. *NYT*, Nov. 8, 1946.

18. Cooke to Jo Davidson, Nov. 21, 1946, and Cooke to Jo Davidson and Frank Kingdon, Dec. 17, 1946, Davidson MSS, Kenneth E. Trombley, *The Life and Times of a Happy Liberal: A Biography of Morris Llewellyn Cooke* (New York, 1954), pp. 231–36.

19. *PM*, Oct. 15, Nov. 13, 1946; NCPAC-ICCASP joint press release, Nov. 14, 1946, PP MSS; MacDougall, *Gideon's Army*, I, 113, 117–18.

20. *NYT*, Dec. 29, 30, 1946; *PM*, Dec. 30, 31, 1946; James A. Wechsler, "Liberals Without Reds," *P*, XI (Jan. 13, 1947), 1; PCA letterhead, Kingdon and Davidson to Helen Gahagan Douglas, March 14, 1947, Helen Douglas MSS; *Progressive Citizen*, July 1947; Wallace, "Unity for Progress," *NR*, CXVI (Jan. 20, 1947), 3, 46; MacDougall, *Gideon's Army*, I, 114–20; "Program for Political Action Adopted at First National Convention of Progressive Citizens of America," PP MSS.

21. Wechsler, *Age of Suspicion*, pp. 213–16; "Committee of the Whole as of Jan. 9, 1947," ADA MSS; *NYT*, Jan. 5, 1947; Rauh interview; Loeb interview; John W. Edelman, Note to staff, Jan. 16, 1947, Edelman MSS, Labor History Archives, Wayne State University.

22. *NYT*, Jan. 4, 5, 1947; *PM*, Jan. 6, 1947.

23. Loeb to the Editor, *NR*, CXVI (Jan. 27, 1947), 3, 46.

24. Loeb, Reports to National Board, Sept. 20, Dec. 3, 1947; Loeb to Joseph P. Lash, Nov. 5, 1946; Loeb to James Rowe, Jr., Oct. 5, 1948; ADA press release, Jan. 23, 1947—all in ADA MSS. *ADA World*, March 29, May 15, 30, July 24, Sept. 23, Oct. 10, 31, Nov. 21, 1947; Loeb interview; Wallace, "The Enemy Is Not Each Other," *NR*, CXVI (Jan. 27, 1947), 22–23.

25. Davidson, Undated speech, Davidson MSS.

26. *CS*, Jan. 8, 1947; Ickes in *SLPD*, Jan. 3, 1947; Ickes to Kenneth Crawford, Jan. 9, 1947, ADA MSS.

27. G. W. Jacobson to Loeb, Sept. 26, 1947; Loeb to Jacobson, Oct. 9, 1947; Loeb to Eugenie Anderson, Jan. 19, 1948; Andrew J. Biemiller, Memo, July 14, 1947; Arnall to Wilson Wyatt, Nov. 3, 1947; Loeb to William Rosenblatt, Jan. 14, 1948; Loeb to Carl Auerbach, March 8, 1948; David Lloyd to Auerbach, March 12, 1948; Schlesinger, Memo to Wyatt and Leon Henderson, Feb. 21, 1947; Straight to Loeb, June 5, 1947; Loeb to Bliven, Oct. 7, 1947; Straight to Loeb, Oct. 10, 1947; Bliven to Loeb, Oct. 14, 1947—all in ADA MSS. Helen Douglas to Dorothy W. Stein, May 14, 1947, Helen Douglas MSS; P.B. [Paul Bixler], "Let's Make Up Our Minds," *Antioch Review*, VII (March 1947), 151–55; Lewis Corey, "Toward a Liberal Program for Prosperity and Peace," *ibid.*, VII (June 1947), 291–304.

On Chester Bowles, see, e.g., James Loeb, Jr., to Bowles, Oct. 21, 1946; Bowles to Raymond Swing, Oct. 21, 1946; Bowles to Henry Wallace, Jan. 2, May 29, Sept. 17, 1947; Bowles to Gael Sullivan, Feb. 17, 1947; Bowles to Robert Hannegan, Oct. 14, 1947; Bowles to William Benton, March 6, 1947; Bowles to James Krug, June 10, 1947; Bowles to Max Lerner, May 29, 1947; Bowles to James Patton, March 13, 1947; Bowles to Chase Woodhouse, April 24, 1947; Bowles to A. F. Whitney, July 28, 1947—all in Bowles MSS.

28. Helen Fuller, "The Liberals—Split as Usual," *NR*, CXVI (Jan. 13, 1947), 26–27; Arthur Schlesinger, Jr., to Loeb, Jan. 18, 1947, and Harry W. Schacter to Loeb, Feb. 16, 1948, ADA MSS; Catherine Bauer to Harlow Shapley, Oct. 8, 1947, Helen Douglas MSS; Lasch to Mr. Dimitman, Jan. 16, 1947, Robert Lasch MSS, State Historical Society of Wisconsin.

29. Lerner in *PM*, Jan. 9, 1947; Freda Kirchwey, "Mugwumps in Action," *N*, CLXIV (Jan. 18, 1947), 61–62.

30. Kampelman, *Communist Party vs. the C.I.O.*, pp. 102–104; *NYT*, Feb. 19, 28, March 7, 15, June 16, 1947; Baldwin to Murray, Jan. 31, 1947, Murray MSS; *ADA World*, March 29, 1947.

CHAPTER 7: THE POLITICS AND DIPLOMACY
OF CONTAINMENT

1. Grafton in *CS*, Dec. 31, 1946, Jan. 10, 1947; T.R.B., "For the Record," *NR*, CXVI (Jan. 20, 1947), 11.

2. Willard Shelton in *PM*, Feb. 9, 1947; Lerner in *ibid.*, March 7, 1947; Eccles to Clark Clifford, Nov. 27, 1946, Clifford MSS.

3. *NYT*, March 12, 30, 1947; Davis, News commentary, March 13, 1947, Davis MSS; "The Anti-Totalitarian Broom," *NL*, XXX (March 29, 1947),

1; *NYP*, March 27, 1947; *SLPD*, March 23, 1947; Helen Douglas to Norman Cousins, March 28, 1947, Helen Douglas MSS; *EP*, *N*, CLXIV (March 29, 1947), 346–47; Robert Kenny in the *Progressive Citizen*, May 1947; Wechsler, "Pray for the President!" *P*, XI (March 31, 1947), 1–2; Murray to HST, April 14, 1947, HST MSS, OF 252-K; PCA press release, March 30, 1947, PP MSS; Stokes in *CS*, March 27, 1947; Alan D. Harper, *The Politics of Loyalty: The White House and the Communist Issue, 1946–1952* (Westport, Conn., 1969), pp. 20–46. On Truman's attitude toward the FBI, see [George Elsey] Handwritten memo, May 2, 1947; Elsey, Draft memo to Clark Clifford, May 2, 1947; Clifford, Memos to HST, May 7, 9, 23, 1947—all in Elsey MSS.

4. *Public Papers, 1947*, pp. 211–16; *NYT*, April 23, 1947.

5. *NYT*, May 16, 1947; James Loeb, Jr., to HST, May 13, 1947, HST MSS, OF 396; Keyserling to Loeb, May 22, 1947, ADA MSS.

6. *NYT*, May 12, June 8, 1947.

7. Coffin, *Missouri Compromise* (Boston, 1947), *passim;* Coffin to Jonathan Daniels, Oct. 22, 1945, Daniels MSS.

8. "Defeat in China," *NR*, CXVI (Jan. 20, 1947), 9; *CS*, June 7, 1947; "The Palestine Problem," *N*, CLXIV (May 17, 1947), 585–613; "A Bad Practice," *P*, XI (Jan. 20, 1947), 12.

9. *NYT*, Jan. 10, 1947; *Public Papers, 1947*, pp. 176–80; Barnett, *Intervention and Revolution*, ch. 6; Dean Acheson, *Present at the Creation: My Years in the State Department* (New York, 1969), pp. 198–200, 217–23; Joseph M. Jones, *The Fifteen Weeks (February 21–June 5, 1947)* (New York, 1955), pp. 39–77, 148–57; [George Elsey] Memo, Aug. 15, 1947, Elsey MSS.

10. *PM*, March 13, 1947; Lerner in *ibid.*, March 18, 1947; PCA Executive Board Statement, attached to Frank Kingdon and Jo Davidson, PCA, to Vito Marcantonio, March 14, 1947, Marcantonio MSS; Freda Kirchwey, "To the Greeks Bearing Gifts," *N*, CLXIV (March 29, 1947), 347–49.

11. Pepper in *CR*, 80 Cong., 1 Sess. (April 10, 1947), pp. 3278–90; Taylor in *ibid.* (April 15, 1947), pp. 3403–3407; Williams to Pepper in *ibid.* (April 18, 1947), p. 3703; Helen Douglas in *ibid.* (May 8, 9, 1947), pp. 4809–10, 4933–34; *CS*, March 13, 26, 1947; Stokes in *ibid.*, March 22, 1947; Lasch, Memo to Field, March 26, 1947, Lasch MSS; Eleanor Roosevelt, newspaper column in ADA MSS; La Guardia, WJZ Radio Broadcast, March 16, 1947, La Guardia MSS; Elliott Roosevelt, "A Plea to America," *N*, CLXIV (March 29, 1947), 352; *NUF*, April 1, 1947; Grafton in *NYP*, March 12, 1947; Bolte, Statement on Greece and Turkey, Helen Douglas MSS; Rubin, "The People Speak!" *P*, XI (April 7, 1947), 1–2; Jones, *The Fifteen Weeks*, pp. 180–84. For White House awareness of the liberal criticism, see J. Donald Kingsley, Undated memo to Clark Clifford, HST MSS, Clifford files.

12. *SLPD*, March 4, 13, 14, 1947; Marquis Childs in *ibid.*, March 22,

1947; *NYP*, March 13, 1947; Fischer, "The U.S. and the U.N.," *P*, XI (April 7, 1947), 5; Paul Porter, "The Pursuit of Peace," *ibid.*, XI (June 23, 1947), 1–2; ADA Foreign Policy Platform, March 30, 1947, ADA MSS; ADA National Board Minutes, Sept. 20, 1947, *ibid.*; James Loeb, Jr., to Philip Dunne, Nov. 27, 1948, *ibid.*; Dunne to Melvyn Douglas, June 23, 1947, Melvyn Douglas MSS; Speech by Wilson Wyatt, April 8, 1947, HST MSS, OF 1231; *PM*, April 9, 1947; Charles Bolte, "A Democratic Assembly," *N*, CLXIV (April 12, 1947), 424; Ickes in the Washington *Evening Star*, March 19, 1947; Davis, News commentary, March 3, 1947, Davis MSS; "A Positive Policy at Last," *NL*, XXX (March 15, 1947), 2; Schlesinger interview; Leuchtenburg interview.

13. Ingersoll in *PM*, Jan. 24, 1947; Ingersoll, Address to Spanish Refugee Appeal Dinner, March 25, 1947, Ingersoll MSS.

14. *CS*, June 6, 1947; "Hungarian Outburst," *NR*, CXVI (June 16, 1947), 8–9; Freda Kirchwey, "Behind the Hungarian 'Coup,'" *N*, CLXIV (June 21, 1947), 731–32.

15. *NYT*, June 13, 1947; Carey McWilliams, "Wallace in the West," *N*, CLXV (July 5, 1947), 6–8; Andrew Biemiller, Memo, July 14, 1947, ADA MSS; A. M. Donaher to Matthew J. Connelly, June 11, 1947; Los Angeles County Democratic Central Committee to HST, June 11, 1947; Victor G. Hall to Robert Hannegan, June 20, 1947; Hall to HST, June 20, 1947—all in HST MSS, OF 300.

16. HST, Handwritten notes on relations with Congress, n.d., and James Rowe, Jr., " 'Cooperation'—or Conflict?" both in Clifford MSS; HST to Eleanor Roosevelt, Nov. 14, 1946, Eleanor Roosevelt MSS. The data on HST's meeting with the Republican senator (Hugh Butler of Nebraska) were kindly made available to me by Dr. Susan Hartmann.

17. "Agenda for Discussion of the January Messages to Congress," Dec. 5, 1946, Elsey MSS.

18. Phillips, *Truman Presidency*, pp. 162–65; Irwin Ross, *The Loneliest Campaign* (New York, 1968), pp. 27–29; interview with George Elsey, Sept. 19, 1967; Oscar Ewing, Oral History Memoir, esp. pp. 67–69, HSTL.

19. Lilienthal, *Journals*, II, 144; *NUF*, March 1, 1947; James A. Wechsler, "The Washington Story," *P*, XI (March 3, 1947), 1, and "Congress Digs a Grave," *ibid.*, XI (July 21, 1947), 5; Richard L. Neuberger, "Is the GOP Hell-Bent on Political Suicide?" *ibid.*, XI (May 5, 1947), 1–2; *SLPD*, June 22, 1947; T.R.B., "Neanderthal Men," *NR*, CXVII (Aug. 4, 1947), 3–4; "15 Major Problems Ignored by the 80th Congress," *ibid.*, pp. 18–19; "Congress, Late and Lamentable," *N*, CLXV (Aug. 2, 1947), 115–16; Patton, Radio talk, Aug. 2, 1947, NFU MSS.

20. *Public Papers, 1947*, pp. 263–64, 279–81.   21. *Ibid.*, pp. 288–301.

22. *Ibid.*, pp. 309–10, 313–17, 342–44, 371–72.

23. *CS*, June 17, 1947; EP, *N*, CLXIV (June 28, 1947), 755; "Rent and Politics," *ibid.*, CLXV (July 12, 1947), 31; *NYP*, June 21, 1947; T.R.B.,

"Well-Concealed News," *NR*, CXVI (June 30, 1947), 3–4; James A. Wechsler, "New Law, New Crisis," *P*, XI (July 7, 1947), 1–2; Wilson Wyatt, et al., to HST, June 10, 1947, Clifford MSS.

24. *ADA World*, July 24, 1947; *CS*, June 11, 1947; Grafton in *ibid.*; Lerner in *PM*, June 17, 1947; "The Marshall Plan," *N*, CLXIV (June 21, 1947), 729–31; "The Marshall Program," *NR*, CXVI (June 16, 1947), 5.

25. PCA Foreign policy statement, June 28, 1947, PP MSS.

26. ADA press release, Sept. 20, 1947, ADA MSS; NFU press release, Oct. 15, 1947, NFU MSS; "The Case for Price Control," *NR*, CXVII (Oct. 20, 1947), 26; Chester Bowles to the Editor, *NYT*, Oct. 12, 1947.

27. *Public Papers, 1947*, pp. 465–69; Kingdon in *NYP*, Oct. 21, 1947; Thomas L. Stokes in *CS*, Oct. 16, 1947.

28. *Public Papers, 1947*, pp. 475–79, 492–98; *SLPD*, Nov. 18, 19, Dec. 11, 1947; Helen Fuller, "Truman Speaks Out at Last," *NR*, CXVII (Nov. 24, 1947), 6; Lerner in *PM*, Nov. 18, 1947; NFU press release, Nov. 19, 1947, NFU MSS; unsigned note on telephone conversation with Charles Ross, Nov. 14, 1947, Chapman MSS; David Lloyd to Leon Henderson, Dec. 31, 1947, ADA MSS.

29. *Public Papers, 1947*, pp. 515–29; *PM*, Dec. 21, 1947; *CS*, Dec. 23, 1947; *CR*, 80 Cong., 1 Sess. (Dec. 5, 1947), pp. 11098–99.

30. Charles R. Bush, "The Truman Civil Rights Program" (unpublished honors thesis, Harvard University, 1964), pp. 24–25; *Public Papers, 1947*, pp. 31–32, 311–13; "So Deep the Roots," *NR*, CXVI (June 9, 1947), 5–6; Eleanor Roosevelt, newspaper column dated July 2, 1947, Elsey MSS; Niles, Memo to Matthew J. Connelly, June 16, 1947, *ibid.*; William C. Berman, *The Politics of Civil Rights in the Truman Administration* (Columbus, Ohio, 1970), pp. 58–64.

31. Berman, *The Politics of Civil Rights*, pp. 66–70; *CS*, Nov. 2, 1947; Newman, "Examination of Freedom," *NR*, CXVII (Nov. 17, 1947), 24–28; Frank Watts Ashley, "Selected Southern Liberal Editors and the States' Rights Movement of 1948" (Ph.D. dissertation, University of South Carolina, 1959), pp. 58–63, 146.

32. *Public Papers, 1947*, p. 482; Berman, *The Politics of Civil Rights*, pp. 72–74; George Elsey, Memo, Oct. 29, 1947, and other material on the civil rights message, Elsey MSS; Perlman to Joseph Rauh, Jr., Jan. 28, 1948, ADA MSS; interview with Philip Elman, Sept. 14, 1967.

33. Wechsler, "Congress Digs a Grave," *P*, XI (July 21, 1947), 5; Freda Kirchwey, "Twenty Years After," *N*, CLXV (Aug. 23, 1947), 173–74; *SLPD*, Nov. 3, 1947; ACLU statement on loyalty program, Melvyn Douglas MSS; Cohen to the Editor, Washington *Post*, Dec. 18, 1947; Fortas to the Editor, *ibid.*, Jan. 17, 1948; *Public Papers, 1947*, pp. 489–91; Leon Henderson to Robert Lovett, Nov. 3, 1947, and James Loeb, Jr. to James Forrestal, Sept. 22, 1948, ADA MSS; Walter White to HST, Nov. 26, 1948, HST MSS, OF 252-K; John Thurston, Memo to John Steelman, Nov. 13,

1947, *ibid.*, OF 596-A; Davidson to Clark Clifford, Dec. 29, 1947, *ibid.*, Charles Murphy Files.

34. "Truman's Helper," *NR*, CXVII (Aug. 18, 1947), 7; T.R.B., "For a Special Session," *ibid.*, CXVII (Sept. 15, 1947), 3–4; "Mopping-Up Operation," *ibid.*, CXVII (Oct. 6, 1947), 5; Richard L. Neuberger to Charles G. Ross, Sept. 8, 1947, HST MSS, OF 299-A; *SLPD*, Dec. 20, 1947; Stokes in *CS*, Dec. 31, 1947.

35. *Public Papers, 1947,* pp. 532–34; *SLPD*, Dec. 20, 1947; Eleanor Roosevelt to HST, Dec. 23, 1947, HST MSS, PPF 460; Edmund G. Brown to Matthew J. Connelly, Dec. 29, 1947, *ibid.*, OF 300.

36. PCA advertisement in *NR*, CXVI (April 7, 1947), 4; *PM*, April 1, 11, 1947. Contrast the bulging "Greek Proposal—Anti" folder with the slim "Greek Proposal—Pro" file in the Helen Douglas MSS.

37. *NYT*, May 16, June 30, Oct. 5, 1947; EP, *N*, CLXIV (May 24, 1947), 616–17; *PM*, June 12, 1947; Max Lerner in *ibid.*, May 21, 1947; Corey, "Toward a Liberal Program for Prosperity and Peace," *Antioch Review*, VII (June 1947), 291–304.

38. *Progressive Citizen*, July, 1947; *PM*, Oct. 6, 1947; "PCA Domestic and Foreign Program," *NR*, CXVII (Oct. 13, 1947), 8; PCA Press Release, June 24, 1947, PP MSS. Glen Taylor and Claude Pepper endorsed the U.N. alternative. The Popular Frontist Eastern Division of the Farmers Union issued a strong denunciation of the Marshall Plan. *CR*, 80 Cong., 1 Sess. (Dec. 1, 1947), pp. 10970–76; Marshall Plan Resolution, Jan. 31, 1948, HST MSS, OF 555.

39. *ADA World*, Oct. 10, 1947, Dec. 16, 1947; Kingdon interview. James Loeb, Jr., Report to National Board, Dec. 13–14, 1947; Joseph Rauh, Jr., to Mrs. Dwight Davis, Jan. 27, 1948; Loeb, Memo to Harold Stein, Jan. 2, 1948; Loeb to the Editor of the *Nation*, Oct. 3, 1947—all in ADA MSS.

40. "The ADA Policy Statement," *NR*, CXVII (Dec. 22, 1947), 10–11; *ADA World*, Oct. 10, 31, 1947; *NYT*, Nov. 13, Dec. 7, 1947; Loeb interview. Mrs. Mortimer Hays to Loeb, Dec. 8, 1947; Keyserling to Loeb, May 22, 1947; Davidson to Loeb, Oct. 29, 1948—all in ADA MSS.

41. James Loeb, Jr., to Mrs. Mortimer Hays, Jan. 6, 1948, *ibid.*

CHAPTER 8: TOWARD A GIDEON'S ARMY

1. Wallace, "Jobs, Peace, Freedom," *NR*, CXV (Dec. 16, 1946), 785–89.

2. "Wallace Splits the Liberal Movement" (unsigned, undated memo), and Schlesinger, Memo to Wilson Wyatt and Leon Henderson, Feb. 21, 1947, both in ADA MSS; Bruce Bliven, Oral History Memoir, pp. 32–33, 49, COHC; MacDougall, *Gideon's Army*, I, 209–11; William Harlan

Hale, "What Makes Wallace Run?" *Harper's*, CXCVI (March 1948), 241–48; Straight, "Fixing the Blame for the Cold War," *NR*, CXVII (Sept. 15, 1947), 10–12; Straight, "1948: Point of Departure," *ibid.*, CXVII (Dec. 29, 1947), 8–9; Straight, "Days with Henry Wallace," *ibid.*, CLIII (Dec. 4, 1965), 9–11.

3. "A New Deal with Russia," *ibid.*, CXV (Dec. 16, 30, 1946), 806–14, 901–907, CXVI (Jan. 27, 1947), 26–31; "Oil—Inflammable," *ibid.*, CXVI (Feb. 10, 1947), 26–30; William Walton, "Men Around Marshall," *ibid.*, CXVII (Sept. 22, 1947), 15–19.

4. Wallace to Donald Bruce, Oct. 23, 1946, Wallace MSS, Iowa; Wallace, "Churchill's Crusade," *NR*, CXVI (Jan. 13, 1947), 22–23, and "The Moscow Conference Can Succeed," *ibid.*, CXVI (March 10, 1947), 20–21; *NYT*, Jan. 23, 1947; "A Cable to Bevin," *NL*, XXX (Jan. 25, 1947), 1, 19; Max Lerner in *PM*, Jan. 23, 1947; *ibid.*, April 7, 1947.

5. Wallace, "A Bad Case of Fever," *NR*, CXVI (April 14, 1947), 12–13; Wallace to Wallace D. McLay, Feb. 8, 1947, Wallace MSS, Iowa.

6. Wallace, Speeches reprinted in the Washington *Post*, March 20, April 15, 1947.

7. *PM*, April 7, 1947; *NYT*, April 10, 25, 1947; *ADA World*, April 26, 1947; Elmer Davis, News commentary, April 11, 1947, Davis MSS.

8. *NYT*, May 3, 13, 15, 16, 18, 20, 22, June 10, 17, 1947; Alexander Uhl in *PM*, May 28, 1947; Richard L. Neuberger, "Henry Wallace Comes to Town," *P*, XI (June 16, 1947), 4; *NYP*, June 5, 1947; Marquis Childs in *SLPD*, June 12, 1947; Stokes in *CS*, June 21, 1947; Baldwin in the *Progressive Citizen*, June 1947.

9. Cabell Phillips in *NYT*, April 20, June 1, 1947, and news reports in *ibid.*, April 6, 12, 13, 14, 28, May 18, 31, June 6, 10, 1947; MacDougall, *Gideon's Army*, I, ch. 8; Joseph and Stewart Alsop in *CS*, June 2, 1947; James A. Wechsler, "Showdown in Washington," *P*, XI (June 16, 1947), 1, 12.

10. *NYT*, April 16, 1947; *PM*, April 11, 1947; *Public Papers, 1947*, p. 203; Allen in the Denver *Post*, May 28, 1947; HST to Louis Starr, April 16, 1947, HST MSS, OF 1170.

11. Alsop brothers in the Louisville *Courier-Journal*, July 3, 1947; Sullivan, "Memo Re. Wallace Situation," June 2, 1947, Clifford MSS.

12. Hale, "What Makes Wallace Run?" *Harper's*, CXCVI (March 1948), 241–48; MacDougall, *Gideon's Army*, I, 192; Wallace interview.

13. Wallace, "The Sellout," *NR*, CXVII (Aug. 4, 1947), 15–16, and "Come Out Fighting," *ibid.*, CXVII (Sept. 1, 1947), 13–16; Wallace, Speech at Detroit, Sept. 1, 1947, ADA MSS; Wallace, Speech reprinted in *PM*, Sept. 12, 1947; Wallace, Speech at Baltimore, Oct. 15, 1947, PP MSS; *NYT*, Dec. 12, 1947; Shannon, *Decline of American Communism*, pp. 103, 170; Kingdon interview.

14. Hale, "What Makes Wallace Run?" *Harper's*, CXCVI (March 1948),

241–48; *NYT,* June 23, July 21, Dec. 5, 1947; Wallace, "Bevin Muddies the Waters," *NR,* CXVI (June 30, 1947), 11–12, "What We Must Do," *ibid.,* CXVII (July 14, 1947), 13–14, and "Too Little, Too Late," *ibid.,* CXVII (Oct. 6, 1947), 11–12.

15. *NYT,* July 21, 27, Aug. 15, 25, Oct. 17, 1947; PCA press release, June 24, 1947, PP MSS.

16. *NYT,* May 19, 25, June 9, 1947; Neuberger, "Curtain Raiser for '48," *N,* CLXIV (June 7, 1947), 682–83; ADA National Board Minutes, n.d., ADA MSS; Sweetland in the *ADA World,* June 18, 1947; Childs in *SLPD,* June 10, 1947.

17. *ADA World,* July 24, 1947; *NYT,* July 24, Aug. 15, 1947; "Condiments," *NR,* CXVII (Aug. 25, 1947), 7.

18. *Progressive Citizen,* July, 1947; Robin Kinkhead, "Liberal Democrats in Fresno," *NR,* CXVII (July 28, 1947), 9; "Third Party Stirrings," *ibid.,* CXVII (Aug. 18, 1947), 8; "California Progressives," *ibid.,* CXVII (Sept. 1, 1947), 8; *NYT,* July 4, 20, 27, Sept. 19, 24, Nov. 10, 19, 22, 1947; William R. Burke, "Report of the Fresno Conference . . ." ADA MSS; "Report of Palace Hotel Meeting of Wallace Democrats [October 11, 1947]," n.d., J. Howard McGrath MSS, HSTL; Schmidt, *Wallace,* pp. 125–26; Ernest S. Griffith, Library of Congress, to Marcantonio, July 28, 1947, Marcantonio MSS; PCA Statement on Political Policy, June 29, 1947, PP MSS.

19. *NYT,* Sept. 2, 11, 12, 20, 23, Oct. 1, 5, 18, 23, 1947; MacDougall, *Gideon's Army,* I, ch. 11.

20. *NYT,* Dec. 5, 10, 11, 13, 1947; *PM,* Dec. 12, 1947; Kingdon interview.

21. Helen Douglas to Wallace, Dec. 10, 1947, Helen Douglas MSS; Williams to Wallace, Dec. 26, 1947, Chapman MSS; Williams to John Coe, April 21, 1959 [1949?], Williams MSS; Straight, "Days with Henry Wallace," *NR,* CLIII (Dec. 4, 1965), 9–11; Walsh to Wallace, Dec. 18, 1947, Wallace MSS, Iowa.

22. *NYT,* Dec. 17, 18, 19, 1947.   23. *Ibid.,* Dec. 19, 20, 22, 23, 30, 1947.

CHAPTER 9: TRUMAN AND THE LIBERAL QUEST
FOR LEADERSHIP

1. Clifford, Memo to HST, Nov. 19, 1947, Clifford MSS; Batt, Oral History Interview, pp. 2–5, 28–29, HSTL; Ross, *Loneliest Campaign,* p. 29.

2. *Public Papers, 1948,* pp. 1–10; Batt, Oral History Interview, pp. 11–12, HSTL; George Elsey, Memo attached to ninth draft of the message, Elsey MSS.

3. *CS,* Jan. 9, 1948; *SLPD,* Jan. 8, 1948; Thackrey in *NYP,* Jan. 8, 1948;

EP, *N*, CLXVI (Jan. 17, 1948), 58; Loeb to Wilson Wyatt, Jan. 8, 1948, ADA MSS; Ross, *Loneliest Campaign*, p. 62.

4. Harold Ickes in *NYP*, Jan. 7, 1948; Estabrook, "Last of the Brain-Trusters," *N*, CLXVI (Jan. 17, 1948), 68–70; Louise Levitas, "Wrapped Up in Himself and the World's Evils," *New York Star Picture News*, Oct. 17, 1948, pp. 11–12; Landis, Oral History Memoir, pp. 549–56, COHC.

5. *Public Papers, 1948*, pp. 108, 113–14, 116; *ADA World*, Jan. 29, 1948; *NYP*, Jan. 29, 1948; Eccles, *Beckoning Frontiers* (New York, 1951), pp. 434–56.

6. Dorothy Gobelle to HST, Feb. 1, 1948, HST MSS, OF 90-Misc; Chester Bowles to David Williams, Feb. 10, 1948, Bowles MSS.

7. *Public Papers, 1948*, pp. 121–26.

8. *NYT*, Feb. 20, 27, 1948; Charles Bush, "The Truman Civil Rights Program" (honors thesis, Harvard, 1964), pp. 35–36; "A Daring Program," *P*, XII (March 1948), 4–5; EP, *N*, CLXVI (Feb. 14, 1948), 169; *CST*, Feb. 8, 1948; George Elsey, Handwritten notes on civil rights message, Elsey MSS.

9. Walter White, NAACP, to HST, April 7, 1948, HST MSS, OF 413; William I. Batt, Jr., Memo to Gael Sullivan, April 20, 1948, Clifford MSS; Ross, *Loneliest Campaign*, pp. 64–67.

10. *NYT*, Nov. 30, Dec. 6, 1947; Freda Kirchwey, "Plots and Counterplots," *N*, CLXIV (Jan. 17, 1948), 60–61; "Failure in Palestine," *NR*, CXVIII (Feb. 9, 1948), 7; Stone in *PM*, Jan. 28, 1948.

11. *NYT*, Jan. 17, 18, 29, 1948.

12. *Ibid.*, Dec. 30, 31, 1947; *ADA World*, Jan. 8, April 17, 1948; Richard L. Neuberger, article reprinted in *CR*, 80 Cong., 2 Sess. (Appendix), p. A736; National Educational Committee press release [Dec. 30, 1947], ADA MSS; *"Henry Wallace Will Merely Destroy the Very Things He Wishes to Achieve"—Mrs. Roosevelt* (n.p. [1948]), copy in *ibid.;* Franklin D. Roosevelt, Jr. to Elmer J Holland, Feb. 5, 1948, Murray MSS; Leonard Lyons in the Boston *Herald*, March 29, 1948.

13. *CS*, Jan. 2, 1948; Stokes in *ibid.*, Dec. 22, 1947; Lerner in *PM*, Dec. 30, 1947; Freda Kirchwey, "Wallace: Prophet or Politician?" *N*, CLXVI (Jan. 10, 1948), 29–31.

14. Kampelman, *Communist Party vs. the C.I.O.*, pp. 141–47; *NYT*, Feb. 7, March 6, April 29, 1948; Murray, *No Third Party in '48* (n.p. [1948]); Jack Kroll to Saul Mills, April 21, 1948, Murray MSS; Shannon, *Decline of American Communism*, pp. 154–57; MacDougall, *Gideon's Army*, II, 320–22; *CR*, 80 Cong., 2 Sess. (Appendix), pp. A3977–78.

15. *NYT*, Jan. 21, 25, 1948; *NUF*, Jan., Feb. 1948; Joseph K. Howard, "The Rockies," *P*, XII (April 1948), 38; James Patton to Chester Bowles, Aug. 4, 1947, Bowles MSS; Michael Straight, "The NR and the Third Party," *NR*, CXVIII (Jan. 19, 1948), 22–23; A. F. Whitney to C. B. Baldwin, Jan. 16, 1948, ADA MSS; Whitney to Wilson Wyatt, Jan. 16, 1948,

ibid.; James Loeb, Jr., to Whitney, Jan. 19, 1948, *ibid.;* Tugwell to Leon Henderson, Jan. 21, 1948, *ibid.;* Thomas L. Stokes in the Washington *Evening Star,* Jan. 16, 1948; Robert Bendiner, "Politics and People," *N,* CLXVI (Jan. 31, 1948), 118; "Proceedings: State Executive Committee, American Labor Party. January 7, 1948," Marcantonio MSS. On the fear of fascism, see Frederick Schuman to Max Lerner, Jan. 18, 1948, Max Lerner MSS, Yale University.

16. Bean, Oral History Memoir, pp. 258–60, COHC; Wallace to Donald Murphy, Jan. 13, 1948, and Wallace to Anita McCormick Blaine, April 2, 1948, both in Wallace MSS, Iowa.

17. Schmidt, *Wallace,* pp. 67–71; *NYT,* Feb. 15, 17, 1948; Wallace, "Palestine: Civilization on Trial," *NR,* CXVIII (Feb. 16, 1948), 9–10; EP, *N,* CLXVI (Feb. 14, 1948), 171; Gus Tyler, Memo on the Bronx election, ADA MSS.

18. James Hagerty in *NYT,* Feb. 23, 1948; Robert Bendiner, "Politics and People," *N,* CLXVI (Feb. 28, 1948), 229–30; Dale Kramer, "Must It Be Truman?" *ibid.,* CLXVI (March 13, 1948), 295–97.

19. The text of Taylor's speech is in the *Daily Worker,* Feb. 24, 1948.

20. Freda Kirchwey to J. Howard McGrath, Feb. 25, 1948, McGrath MSS; Daniels, *Man of Independence,* pp. 317–18; *Public Papers, 1948,* pp. 190–91; Steinberg, *Man from Missouri,* p. 307; Henderson in the *ADA World,* March 31, 1948; *CST,* March 25, 1948; *CR,* 80 Cong., 2 Sess. (March 22, 1948), p. 3241; [Clifford] Memo to HST, March 8, 1948, Clifford MSS; Eleanor Roosevelt to HST, March 22, 1948, and HST to Eleanor Roosevelt, March 25, 1948, both in Eleanor Roosevelt MSS.

21. Thackrey in *NYP,* June 3, 1948; Freda Kirchwey to HST, June 19, 1948, McGrath MSS; New York *Star,* June 24, 28, 1948; [Niebuhr] EP, *Christianity and Crisis,* VIII (April 12, 1948), 42.

22. Davis, News commentary, Feb. 24, 1948, Davis MSS.

23. *Public Papers, 1948,* pp. 182–86; Chester Bowles to David Williams, March 5, 1948, Bowles MSS; Freda Kirchwey, "Prague—a Lesson for Liberals," *N,* CLXVI (March 6, 1948), 265–66, and "The President's Message," *ibid.,* CLXVI (March 27, 1948), 341–42; Straight, "Aid to Peace . . . or Road to War?" *NR,* CXVIII (March 15, 1948), 11–12, and "There Are Great Fears," *ibid.,* CXVIII (March 22, 1948), 6–7; Murrow, "Jan Masaryk," *ibid.,* p. 7; *CST,* March 19, 1948; Grafton in *ibid.,* March 24, 1948; Stokes in the Washington *Daily News,* March 18, 1948; *SLPD,* April 4, 1948; Chat Patterson, AVC, to HST, March 22, 1948, HST MSS, OF 1142; Niebuhr, "Amid Encircling Gloom," *Christianity and Crisis,* VIII (April 12, 1948), 41–42.

24. *Public Papers, 1948,* pp. 147–51, 186–90; MacDougall, *Gideon's Army,* II, 337–41.

25. *Public Papers, 1948,* pp. 156–63, 196–97, 200–203, 205–206, 272–77; *SLPD,* Feb. 24, 1948; Davies, *Housing Reform,* pp. 75–77.

26. *NUF*, May 1, 1947, Dec. 1947, April–June, 1948; Patton to Anderson, March 17, 1948, Anderson MSS; interview with Brannan, Sept. 21, 1964.

27. *NYT*, May 8, 1948; William L. Batt, Memo to Clark Clifford, April 22, 1948, Clifford MSS; *Public Papers, 1948*, p. 236.

28. Dale Kramer, "Must It Be Truman?" *N*, CLXVI (March 13, 1948), 295–97; Doris Fleeson in *SLPD*, Feb. 25, 1948; Loeb to Richard Heldt, May 24, 1948, ADA MSS.

29. Bowles to Henderson, March 5, 1948; Loeb, Memos on conversations with Reuther and Dubinsky, March 15, 1948; Humphrey to Loeb, March 24, 1948; Loeb to Frank McCulloch, March 9, 1948—all in ADA MSS.

30. Freda Kirchwey, "A Word to Mr. Wallace," *N*, CLXVI (March 13, 1948), 294–95; *NYT*, March 27, 30, April 2, 1948; Straight, "Truman Should Quit," *NR*, CXVIII (April 5, 1948), 1, 5; MacDougall, *Gideon's Army*, II, 472.

31. *ADA World*, April 17, 1948; *NYT*, April 13, 28, 29, 1948; Loeb interview.

32. Wechsler, "What Hit Harry Truman?" *P*, XII (May 1948), 9–11.

33. "The Sad Democrats," *P*, XII (May 1948), 3–4; Morris Rubin, "State of the Union," *ibid.*, XII (Aug. 1948), 28–29; Childs in *SLPD*, Nov. 17, 1947; Davis, News commentary, March 30, 1948, Davis MSS; New York *Star*, July 13, 1948; Lilienthal, *Journals*, II, 378–79; Stokes in the Atlanta *Constitution*, April 7, 1948. In the ADA MSS, see Niebuhr to Loeb, April 9, 1948; Loeb to Eleanor Roosevelt, June 15, 1948; Eugenie Anderson to Loeb, April 4, 1948; Biemiller, Memo, April 4, 1948; Carl Auerbach [?] to ?, March 27, 1948; Granger to Loeb, June 14, 1948. Elmer Davis did, however, want to keep Eisenhower in the picture since the threat of his candidacy might force the Republicans to name a first-rate nominee, "a Vandenberg rather than a Martin or a Bricker." Davis to Milton Eisenhower, May 4, 1948, Davis MSS.

34. Robert Nathan to Chester Bowles, April 5, 1948, and Hubert Humphrey to Bowles, May 4, 1948, both in Bowles MSS; Bowles to Eleanor Roosevelt, June 18, 1948, Eleanor Roosevelt MSS; Schlesinger, Rauh, and Loeb interviews; Doris Fleeson in *SLPD*, June 23, 1952.

35. "Washington Memo" in *NYP*, May 17, 1948; Loeb to Richard Heldt, May 24, 1948, ADA MSS.

36. Chester Bowles to Leon Henderson, March 5, 1948, Carl Auerbach to Joseph Rauh, Jr., April 3, 1948, and James Loeb, Jr., to Eleanor Roosevelt, June 15, 1948—all in ADA MSS; Lasch, Memo, ribbon copy dated April 16, 1948, carbon copy dated April 23, 1948, Lasch MSS; Douglas, "Liberal Leadership," *NR*, CXVIII (June 14, 1948), 11; Douglas speeches in *CR*, 80 Cong., 2 Sess. (Jan. 16, 1948, and Appendix), pp. 275–77, A2133–36, A3666–68, A3883–84.

37. *NYT*, Feb. 25, April 4, 20, June 7, 1948; Wallace, "Buying Foreign Elections," *NR*, CXVIII (April 5, 1948), 10; Elmer Davis, News commentary, Feb. 25, 1948, Davis MSS; Morris Rubin, "State of the Union," *P*, XII (March 1948), 30–32; Rubin, "State of the Union," *ibid.*, XII (April 1948), 36–37; Neuberger, "The Northwest," *ibid.*, XII (March 1948), 19–20; Wallace speeches, e. g., Jan. 17, March 19, 1948, PP MSS; Wallace, *The Wallace Plan vs. the (Hoover) (Dulles) Marshall Plan* (New York, 1948), copy in *ibid.*

38. *NYT*, Feb. 28, March 16, 1948; Schmidt, *Wallace*, pp. 73–75; National Wallace-for-President Committee press release, March 17, 1948, PP MSS. For Wallace's defense of his Czechoslovakian position, see Wallace to Gregory Zilboorg, March 23, 1948; Wallace to Arthur Hays Sulzberger, March 24, 1948; Wallace to Julia C. Welden, April 2, 1948—all in Wallace MSS, Iowa.

39. James Wechsler, Memo to Charles Van Devander, May 7, 1948, ADA MSS; Bean, Oral History Memoir, pp. 260–61, COHC; Bliven, Oral History Memoir, pp. 47–49 COHC; *NYT*, Feb. 2, May 22, 1948; Wallace interview; Shannon, *Decline of American Communism*, pp. 159–60.

40. *NYT*, July 22, 1948.   41. *Ibid.*, May 12, 1948.

42. *Ibid.*, May 12, 18, July 8, 1948; *NYP*, May 19, 1948; "Washington Memo" in *ibid.*, May 20, 1948; Freda Kirchwey, "Moves Toward Peace," *N*, CLXVI (May 29, 1948), 592–93; "Editorial: If Not Truman, Who?" *NR*, CXVIII (May 17, 1948), 27; *CST*, May 20, 1948; Samuel Grafton in *ibid.*, May 17, 1948.

43. Schmidt, *Wallace*, pp. 79–80; *NYT*, May 25, 1948.

44. Ross, *Loneliest Campaign*, pp. 77–79; Sullivan, "Victory in 1948 . . ." attached to Memo to Clifford, Aug. 19, 1947, and William L. Batt, Jr., Memo to Clifford, May 17, 1948, Clifford MSS; Lilienthal, *Journals*, II, 317.

45. *Public Papers, 1948*, pp. 284–379; Lucey in the Washington *Daily News*, June 14, 1948; Denver *Post*, June 13, 1948.

46. *Public Papers, 1948*, pp. 330–32, 344–46, 354–55.

47. *Ibid.*, pp. 382–86, 388–91.   48. *Ibid.*, pp. 399–401.

49. *NUF*, June, 1948; *NYP*, June 24, 1948; Henderson in the *ADA World*, July 1948; "Congress Is the Issue," *N*, CLXVI (June 26, 1948), 703–704; *CST*, June 13, 1948.

50. Unsigned memo, June 29, 1948, Rosenman MSS. On the origins of this document and other suggestions for a special session, see R. Alton Lee, "The Turnip Session of the Do-Nothing Congress: Presidential Campaign Strategy," *Southwestern Social Science Quarterly*, XLIV (Dec. 1963), 256–67; John E. Meaney to Matthew J. Connelly, June 22, 1948, HST MSS, OF 300; Dean Alfange to Harry Vaughn, June 25, 1948, *ibid.*, PPF 1746; Aubrey Williams to HST, July 14, 1948, *ibid.*, PPF 1726; Batt, Oral History Memoir, pp. 5–8, 10–11, HSTL; Batt, Memo to Clifford [June

1948], Clifford MSS; *CST*, June 24, 30, 1948; Samuel Grafton in *ibid.*, July 2, 1948; Louis Brownlow, Memo to James E. Webb, June 28, 1948, Webb MSS, HSTL; Ross, *Loneliest Campaign*, pp. 129–31.

51. Loeb to Mrs. Churchill Murray, May 20, 1948; Loeb, Memo to Henderson and Joseph Rauh, Jr., May 22, 1948; Bowles to Loeb, June 9, 1948; Niebuhr to Loeb, June 28, 1948—all in ADA MSS. *ADA World*, June 5, 1948; *NYT*, June 13, 1948.

52. T.R.B., "Washington Wire," *NR*, CXVIII (June 28, 1948), 3–4; Stokes in the Atlanta *Constitution*, June 15, 18, 1948; Payne, Undated memo on Truman's Seattle visit, ADA MSS; EP, *N*, CLXVI (June 19, 1948), 673; Karr, "Trekking with Truman," *ibid.*, CLXVI (June 26, 1948), 707–708; Davis, News commentary, June 10, 1948, Davis MSS; Wechsler, "Washington on the Eve," *P*, XII (July 1948), 10–12.

CHAPTER 10: CAMPAIGN FOR LIBERALISM

1. Lerner in *NYS*, June 24, 26, 1948; Kelly cartoon in *ibid.*, Oct. 10, 1948; Bendiner, "The Nominee Nobody Loves," *N*, CLXVII (July 3, 1948), 6 8; *CST*, June 25, 1948.

2. "Bill Douglas Has What It Takes," *P*, XII (July, 1948), 3–4; *NYP*, July 8, 1948; Thackrey in *ibid.*, July 9, 1948; "Truman's Big Chance," *N*, CLXVII (July 10, 1948), 33–34; "The Democrats' Last Chance," *NR*, CXIX (July 12, 1948), 11–20; Lerner in *NYS*, July 6, 1948; Frank McCulloch, IVI, to HST, July 9, 1948, HST MSS, OF 299-D; *NYT*, July 4, 6, 7, 1948; Brock, *Americans for Democratic Action*, pp. 92–93; *CST*, July 7, 1948; John Tucker to Hubert Will, July 22, 1948, ADA MSS; telegram signed by Bowles, Henderson, and Reuther in *CR*, 80 Cong., 2 Sess. (Appendix), p. A4872.

3. *NYT*, July 6, 10, 12, 1948; Thackrey in *NYP*, July 12, 1948; *NYS*, July 12, 1948; Perry in *ibid.*, July 13, 1948; James Loeb, Jr., to Charles Engvall, July 28, 1948, and Loeb to Leo Rosten, Oct. 4, 1948, ADA MSS.

4. James Loeb, Jr., Memorandum to Executive Committee, March 16, 1948, ADA Executive Committee Minutes, March 18, 1948, Loeb to Frank McCulloch, April 24, 1948, Hubert Humphrey to William O'Dwyer, April 29, 1948—all in ADA MSS; Loeb to Helen Gahagan Douglas, April 29, 1948, Helen Douglas MSS; *NYT*, July 5, 1948; *NYP*, July 15, 18, 1948; Wechsler, "The Men Nobody Wanted," *P*, XII (Aug., 1948), 5–8.

5. *Public Papers, 1948*, pp. 406–10; *NYS*, July 16, 1948: Lerner in *ibid.*, July 18, 1948; T.R.B., "Washington Wire," *NR*, CXIX (July 26, 1948), 3–4; Michael Straight, "Turnip Day in Washington," *ibid.*, p. 7; Yvonne Guilbert to HST, July 14, 1948, HST MSS, OF 299-D; Lloyd in the *ADA World*, Aug. 7, 1948; Bendiner, "Rout of the Bourbons," *N*, CLXVII (July 24, 1948), 91–93.

6. Loeb in the *ADA World*, Aug. 7, 1948; James A. Wechsler, "The Philadelphia Pay-Off," *P*, XII (Sept. 1948), 8–10; Shannon, *Decline of American Communism*, pp. 167, 175; *NYT*, July 25, 1948; Davis, News commentary, July 26, 1948, Davis MSS; Lerner in *NYS*, July 25, 1948; EP, *N*, CLXVII (July 31, 1948), 113; Howard K. Smith, "The Wallace Party," *ibid.*, CLXVII (Aug. 7, 1948), 145–47; *CST*, July 29, 1948. For quite different versions of the Progressive convention, see Schmidt, *Wallace*, ch. 8, and MacDougall, *Gideon's Army*, II, chs. 22–25. Schmidt and MacDougall notwithstanding, even some of Wallace's best friends were disturbed by the evidence of Communist influence. Lee Fryer to Louis Adamic, July 10, 1948, PP MSS; Aubrey Williams to James Patton, July 26, 1948, Williams MSS.

7. *NYT*, April 1, July 17, 18, 1948; Leon Henderson, ADA, to HST, July 22, 1948, McGrath MSS; Daniel James, AVC, to HST, July 26, 1948, HST MSS, OF 596-A; Berman, *Politics of Civil Rights*, pp. 116–20; *NYS*, July 28, 1948; Dalfiume, *Desegregation of the U.S. Armed Forces*, pp. 170–74.

8. *Public Papers, 1948*, pp. 416–21.

9. *Ibid.*, pp. 421–22, 436–38; *SLPD*, Aug. 9, 1948; *NUF*, Aug. 1948; *CST*, Aug. 9, 1948.

10. Anthony Leviero in *NYT*, Aug. 1, 1948; Ross, *Loneliest Campaign*, pp. 163–66. William L. Batt, Jr., Memo to Clifford, Aug. 11, 1948, and [Clifford], Memo to HST, Aug. 17, 1948, are perhaps the most important of many documents in the Clifford MSS illustrating the important role of the Research Division and the administration liberal caucus.

11. *Public Papers, 1948*, pp. 550, 743.   12. *Ibid.*, pp. 518, 534.

13. *Ibid.*, pp. 615, 799; *NYT*, Sept. 3, Nov. 2, 1948; Brannan interview; W. E. Kenworthy, "Corn Cribs and Ballot Boxes," *P*, XIII (Jan. 1949), 9–12; M.J.C. [Matthew J. Connelly], Memo to Clark Clifford, Sept. 17, 1948, Clifford MSS; Charles Murphy, Memo to Clifford and George Elsey, Sept. 18, 1948, Elsey MSS; W. McNeil Lowry, Oral History Memoir, HSTL.

14. *Public Papers, 1948*, p. 903.

15. *Ibid.*, pp. 852, 923–25; *NYT*, Oct. 9, 14, 1948; HST to Hastie, Nov. 9, 1948, HST MSS, PPF 2583; Memo on Hastie, n.d. [1949], Stephen Spirngarn MSS, HSTL.

16. *Public Papers, 1948*, pp. 685, 722.   17. *Ibid.*, pp. 804, 807.

18. *Ibid.*, pp. 609–14, 787–92.

19. *Ibid.*, pp. 558–59, 770–74; Margaret Truman, *Harry S. Truman* (New York, 1972), pp. 8–10, 15, 26.

20. *Public Papers, 1948*, pp. 505, 847–48, 866, 880.

21. *Ibid.*, pp. 502, 601; Norman Podhoretz, "Truman and the Idea of the Common Man," *Commentary*, XXI (May 1956), 469–74.

22. "UN Comes Through," *N*, CLXVII (Oct. 16, 1948), 415–16; "The

East-West Crisis," *NR*, CXIX (Oct. 11, 1948), 5–6; *CST*, July 8, Sept. 16, 29, Oct. 7, 1948; Grafton in *ibid.*, July 3, 1948; Wallace-for-President Committee Fact Sheet on the Berlin Crisis and the UN, Oct. 1948, PP MSS; Patton to Aubrey Williams, July 21, 1948, Williams MSS; Drew Pearson in the Washington *Post*, July 27, 1948; Batt, Memo to Clark Clifford, July 22, 1948, Clifford MSS.

23. HST, *Memoirs*, II, 212–19; Daniels, *Man of Independence*, pp. 361–62.

24. Davis, News commentary, Oct. 11, 1948, Davis MSS; EP, *N*, CLXVII (Oct. 16, 1948), 413; Lerner in *NYS*, Oct. 12, 1948; *SLPD*, Oct. 10, 1948.

25. "The Truth About the Vinson Mission," *NR*, CXIX (Oct. 25, 1948) 5–6; *NYS*, Oct. 11, 1948; Perry in *ibid.*, Oct. 13, 1948; Stokes in the Atlanta *Constitution*, Oct. 15, 1948; *CST*, Oct. 13, 1948; Elsey, Remarks on 1948 Campaign to Politics 203, Princeton University, Jan. 11, 1949, Elsey MSS; *Public Papers, 1948*, p. 817; Ross, *Loneliest Campaign*, p. 202.

26. Freda Kirchwey, "Will Murder Pay Off?" *N*, CLXVII (Oct. 2, 1948), 360–61; Crum in *NYS*, Oct. 7, 1948; *Public Papers, 1948*, pp. 843–44, 913; Dorothy Thackrey in *NYP*, Oct. 31, 1948; Rauh interview; HST, *Memoirs*, II, 166–68; Eleanor Roosevelt to HST, Sept. 12, 1948, HST MSS, OF 280; Bowles to Clifford, Sept. 23, 1948, Crum to Clifford, Oct. 20, 1948, Draft of memo to Secretary Marshall, Sept. 11, 1948, and Clifford, Memo to HST, Oct. 23, 1948, all in Clifford MSS.

27. *NYS*, Sept. 2, 1948; Perry in *ibid.*, Oct. 26, 1948; *CST*, Oct. 10, 25, 1948; Eleanor Roosevelt to HST, Oct. 4, 19, 1948, HST MSS, PPF 460; Eleanor Roosevelt to Frances Perkins, Oct. 4, 1948, Eleanor Roosevelt MSS.

28. Childs in *SLPD*, Oct. 1, 1948; Shelton in *NYS*, Oct. 10, 1948; Uhl in *ibid.*, Oct. 17, 1948; T.R.B., "Washington Wire," *NR*, CXIX (Nov. 8, 1948), 3–4; Robert G. Spivack, " 'Harry Don't Fight Orthodox,' " *N*, CLXVII (Oct. 9, 1948), 396–97.

29. Brannan interview; *NUF*, Oct. 1948; *NYT*, Sept. 1, 2, 11, Oct. 29, 1948.

30. ADA National Board Resolution, Aug. 29, 1948; "Henry A. Wallace—the Last Seven Months of His Presidential Campaign" (ADA Press Release); Margaret McSweeney to Evelyn Dubrow, Aug. 2, 1948; John F. P. Tucker to David Dubinsky, Oct. 19, 1948; Tucker to Richard Gilbert, Sept. 28, 1948; James Loeb, Jr., to Babette Deutsch, Sept. 14, 1948; Loeb to Reginald Zalles, Oct. 1, 1948; Loeb to William E. Leuchtenburg, Sept. 21, 1948; Leuchtenburg to Loeb, Oct. 29, 1948—all in ADA MSS. See also *ADA World*, Nov. 10, 1948.

31. Michael W. Straus to Chapman, Sept. 5, 1948, Chapman MSS; Chapman interview; Address by Ickes, Oct. 14, 1948, HST MSS, OF 931; *NYT*, Oct. 5, 12, 1948; James Loeb, Jr., to Ickes, Oct. 15, 1948, ADA MSS;

Elmer Davis, News commentary, Oct. 19, 1948, and Ickes to Davis, Oct. 24, Nov. 2, 1948, Davis MSS.

32. "1948: The New Beginning," *NR*, CXIX (Sept. 27, 1948), 32; Johnson in *NYS*, Sept. 12, 1948; Grafton in *NYP*, Oct. 27, 1948; Kingdon in *ibid.*, Nov. 1, 1948.

33. "Issues and Platitudes," *N*, CLXVII (Oct. 9, 1948), 387–88; Stone in *NYS*, Oct. 6, 1948; "The Race Ends," *P*, XII (Nov. 1948), 3; Davis, News commentary, Nov. 1, 1948, Davis MSS; Lilienthal, *Journals*, II, 424; Niebuhr, "The Presidential Campaign," *Christianity and Crisis*, VIII (Nov. 1, 1948), 137–38.

34. Freda Kirchwey, "How Are You Going to Vote?" *N*, CLXVII (Oct. 23, 1948), 452.

35. Dorothy Thackrey in *NYP*, Oct. 31, 1948; *SLPD*, Oct. 12, 1948.

36. T. O. Thackrey in *NYP*, Oct. 24, 1948; Stone in *NYS*, Oct. 6, 1948; Perry in *ibid.*, Oct. 28, 1948.

37. *NYT*, Sept. 7, 15, 27, Oct. 15, 25, 1948; Wallace, *Increase Wages Out of Profits!* (n.p. [1948]). See also the Wallace speech file in PP MSS.

38. *NYT*, Aug. 30, 31, Sept. 1, 2, 1948; Wechsler, "My Ten Months with Wallace," *P*, XII (Nov. 1948), 4–8; "Wallace in the South," *N*, CLXVII (Sept. 11, 1948), 277–78.

39. *NYT*, Sept. 1, 1948; Schmidt, *Wallace*, pp. 86–88, 219–21; *NYS*, Sept. 3, 1948; MacDougall, *Gideon's Army*, III, 789–92.

40. Davis, News commentary, March 31, 1948, Davis MSS; *NYP*, June 11, 1948; *NYT*, Sept. 22, 23, Oct. 1, 1948; "Progressive Policy Change," *NR*, CXIX (Oct. 11, 1948), 6–7; MacDougall, *Gideon's Army*, III, 748.

41. "Humphrey in Minnesota," *NR*, CXIX (Oct. 18, 1948), 8.

42. "The Choice for President," *P*, XII (Sept. 1948), 3–4; "Split in Colorado," *NR*, CXIX (Aug. 30, 1948), 8; Shannon, *Decline of American Communism*, pp. 164–65, 176; MacDougall, *Gideon's Army*, III, 767, 798; William E. Leuchtenburg, "Wallace in the Rockies," *NL*, XXXI (Sept. 25, 1948), 5; Dewey, "Wallace vs. a New Party," *ibid.*, XXXI (Oct. 30, 1948), 1, 14. See also Lewis Corey's polemical articles run under the general title "What Is Henry Wallace?" in *ibid.*, XXXI (Oct. 2, 1948), 8–9, 15, (Oct. 9, 1948), 4, 15 (Oct. 16, 1948), 7.

43. Baltimore *Sun*, Aug. 20, 25, 27, 1948; *NYT*, Sept. 8, Oct. 16, 1948; Kenny, "A Californian Looks Ahead," *N*, CLXVII (Oct. 23, 1948), 460–61; "Wallace and the UE," *NR*, CXIX (Sept. 20, 1948), 7; MacDougall, *Gideon's Army*, III, 632–34; Tugwell, Oral History Memoir, p. 15, COHC; Tugwell, "Progressives and the Presidency," *P*, XIII (April 1949), 5–7.

44. Kingdon interview; James Wechsler, Memo to Charles Van Devander, May 7, 1948, ADA MSS; Wechsler, "My Ten Months with Wallace," *P*, XII (Nov. 1948), 4–8.

45. Lerner in *NYS*, Oct. 10, 1948; "The Choice for President," *P*, XII (Sept. 1948), 3–4.

46. *NYT*, May 25, June 18, 1947, Oct. 18, Nov. 1, 1948; "Heptisax" in the New York *Herald-Tribune*, May 2, 1948; *NYS*, July 14, 1948; Widick and Howe, *UAW and Walter Reuther*, pp. 276–77; Houston Irvine Flournoy, "The Liberal Party in New York State" (Ph.D. dissertation, Princeton University, 1956), p. 130; Davidson interview; Reuther, Radio speech, Oct. 24, 1948, Donald Montgomery MSS, Labor History Archives, Wayne State University; Thomas, Oral History Memoir, p. 142, COHC; Thomas to Richard S. Childs, Feb. 15, 1949, Thomas MSS; Loeb to Eleanor Roosevelt, June 15, 1948, and Arthur Schlesinger, Jr., Memo to James Loeb, Joseph Rauh, Jr., and James Wechsler, Nov. 1, 1948, ADA MSS; Corey to Norman Thomas, Nov. 3, 1947, Feb. 4, 1948, Lewis Corey MSS, Columbia University; Thomas, "Do Left-Wing Parties Belong in Our System?" *The Annals*, CCLIX (Sept. 1948), 24–29.

CHAPTER 11: THE QUEST FOR IDENTITY AND
THE STRUGGLE AGAINST NORMALCY

1. Samuel Lubell, *The Future of American Politics* (3rd ed., rev.; New York, 1965), pp. 156–59; W. H. Lawrence in *NYT*, Nov. 29, 1948; "It Was Not Magic That Won," *NR*, CXIX (Nov. 15, 1948), 6–8; Ross, *Loneliest Campaign*, pp. 237–45.

2. *NUF*, Nov. 1948; Robert Bendiner, "Two and Two Make Four," *N*, CLXVII (Nov. 13, 1948), 540–42; "Damn the Torpedoes," *NR*, CXIX (Nov. 15, 1948), 1, 5–6; T.R.B., "Washington Wire," *ibid.*, pp. 3–4.

3. Freda Kirchwey, "Mr. Truman on His Own," *N*, CLXVII (Nov. 13, 1948), 535–37; Stone in *NYS*, Nov. 5, 1948; Stokes in the Atlanta *Constitution*, Nov. 5, 1948; *ADA World*, Nov. 10, 1948; Rauh to George Edwards, Nov. 5, 1948, ADA MSS.

4. *ADA World*, Nov. 10, 1948; Brock, *Americans for Democratic Action*, ch. 8; Robert E. Tehan and Julia H. Boegholt to HST, Nov. 15, 1948, HST MSS, OF 300.

5. "What Now?" *P*, XII (Dec., 1948), 3–4; Norman Thomas, "A Test for the Democrats," *ibid.*, pp. 10–12; *NYS*, Nov. 5, 1948; Widick and Howe, *UAW and Walter Reuther*, p. 277; Robert Bendiner, "Labor's Triple Choice," *N*, CLXVIII (Feb. 12, 1949), 177–78; A. H. Raskin, "Reuther Explains the 'Reuther Plan,'" *NYT Magazine*, March 20, 1949, pp. 17, 62–63; David Dubinsky, "What Now for the Liberals?" *NL*, XXXII (Jan. 1, 1949), 6, 12.

6. Schmidt, *Wallace*, ch. 12; MacDougall, *Gideon's Army*, III, ch. 35.

7. *NYT,* Sept. 26, Oct. 27, 1948; Wallace interview; Baldwin, Report to Progressive Party national committee, Nov. 13, 1948, PP MSS.

8. Davis, News commentary, Nov. 3, 1948, Davis MSS.

CHAPTER 12: THE VITAL CENTER

1. Leland Stowe, *Target: You* (New York, 1949), p. 164 and *passim.*

2. Max Ascoli, *The Power of Freedom* (New York, 1949), pp. xiii, 8, 70–71, and *passim.*

3. Irwin Ross, *Strategy for Liberals* (New York, 1949), p. 45 and *passim.*

4. Jonathan Daniels, "Ready to Be Radical," *Saturday Review of Literature,* XXXII (Sept. 10, 1949), 11–12.

5. Arthur M. Schlesinger, Jr., *The Vital Center* (Boston, 1949), pp. 223–24 and *passim.*

6. Seymour Harris, ed., *Saving American Capitalism* (New York, 1948).

7. Schlesinger, *Vital Center,* pp. 208–209.

8. *NYP,* April 6, 1949; James A. Wechsler, *The Age of Suspicion* (New York, 1953), pp. 238–41.

9. Loeb to Edith Fountain, Feb. 2, 1949, ADA MSS, State Historical Society of Wisconsin; "The Court, the Communists and the Liberals," *NR,* CXX (June 20, 1949), 5–6.

10. M. A. [Max Ascoli], "What We Stand For," *R,* I (Dec. 20, 1949), 2; "Our Liberalism," *ibid.,* II (March 28, 1950), 1.

11. Max M. Kampelman, *The Communist Party vs. the C.I.O.* (New York, 1957), p. 256 and chs. 11–13; David J. Saposs, *Communism in American Unions* (New York, 1959), chs. 17–20.

12. Lerner, *NYP,* Nov. 1, 1949; "The Purge in the CIO," *NR,* CXXI (Nov. 14, 1949), 5–7; Bendiner, "Showdown in the C.I.O.," *N,* CLXIX (Oct. 15, 1949), 361–63.

13. *CST,* April 9, 1949; T.R.B., "Washington Wire," *NR,* CXX (April 18, 1949), 3–4; Charles La Follette, "A.D.A. Reports," *A.D.A. Annual,* II (1950 Roosevelt Day Issue), copy in Oscar Chapman MSS, HSTL. Joseph Rauh, Jr. to George Edwards, Nov. 5, 1948; "Minutes of Meeting of Subcommission on Political Policy," Nov. 7, 1949; James Loeb, Jr. to Mortimer Smith, Feb. 13, 1950; "Fair Deal Conferences Resolution," April 21, 1949—all in ADA MSS.

14. Loeb to Mortimer Smith, Feb. 13, 1950; Loeb to Eugenie Anderson, June 8, 1950; Loeb to Albert Hilliard, June 22, 1950—all in ADA MSS. David Lloyd, Memorandum on ADA Convention, April 12, 1949, HST MSS, PPF 4752, HSTL.

15. Lloyd memo, *ibid.;* Loeb to Milton Farber, April 13, 1949, ADA MSS; Ickes to Loeb, Sept. 29, 1949, *ibid.;* Rauh to Ickes, Oct. 3, 1949,

ibid.; Robert Bendiner, "A.D.A. and the Democrats," *N,* CLXVIII (April 23, 1949), 461–62.

16. Childs in *SLPD,* Feb. 2, 1950; *ibid.,* April 15, 1950; *NYP,* April 3, 1950; Schlesinger in *ibid.,* April 9, 1950; *NYT,* April 25, 1950; Daniel James, "ADA Three Years Later," *NL,* XXXIII (March 25, 1950), 8–9; Gus Tyler, "New Trends in ADA," *ibid.,* XXXIII (April 15, 1950), S-1, S-4.

17. Clifton Brock, *Americans for Democratic Action* (Washington, D.C., 1962), pp. 128–30; *NYT,* Jan. 22, Aug. 1, 1949; "The ADA Convention," *NR,* CXXII (April 17, 1950), 15; La Follette to HST, Aug. 1, 1949, HST MSS, PPF 4752; Loeb to Albert Hilliard, June 22, 1950, ADA MSS; La Follette to Byrnes, Dec. 5, 1949, *ibid.;* Loeb to Patton, March 16, 1951, *ibid.*

18. Lloyd Memo, April 12, 1949, HST MSS, PPF 4752. Loeb to David Williams, May 20, 1949; Loeb to Alden Hopkins, Jan. 11, 1950; William Sturdevant to David Koonce, Dec. 7, 1950; Loeb to Harriet Doar, March 19, 1951; Loeb to A.D.G. Cohn, April 16, 1951; Koonce to Sturdevant, Nov. 26, 1950; Schlesinger, Memo to Joseph Rauh and James Loeb, Jan. 25, 1950— all in ADA MSS.

CHAPTER 13: THE POLITICAL ECONOMY
OF THE FAIR DEAL

1. *Public Papers of the Presidents: Harry S. Truman, 1949,* pp. 1–7 (volumes in this series hereafter cited as *Public Papers* with appropriate year); "The President Charts the Course," *NR,* CXX (Jan. 17, 1949), 5–6. See also *CST,* Jan. 6, 1949; *SLPD,* Jan. 5, 1949; EP, *N,* CLXVIII (Jan. 15, 1949), 57; Thomas Sancton, "Second Chance For the New Deal?" *ibid.,* pp. 61–63.

2. Straight, "Harry Truman on His Own Now," *NR,* CXX (Jan. 24, 1949), 5–7; T.R.B., "Washington Wire," *ibid.,* CXX (Jan. 17, 1949), 3–4; Marquis Childs in *SLPD,* Jan. 6, 1949.

3. Lloyd, Memo to Charles Murphy, Dec. 16, 1948, Murphy MSS, HSTL; HST to Helen G. Rotch, Nov. 9, 1948, HST MSS, PPF 65-G; Lloyd, Memorandum on ADA Convention, April 12, 1949, and HST-ADA correspondence, *ibid.,* PPF 4752; HST-Humphrey correspondence, *ibid.,* PPF 4232; *Public Papers, 1949,* p. 552.

4. Stewart Alsop in *SLPD,* Jan. 7, 1949; George Hall in *ibid.,* June 19, 1949; William Walton, "Only Superman Could Do It," *NR,* CXX (Feb. 7, 1949), 11–14.

5. *NYT,* June 2, Sept. 14, 1945, Feb. 3, March 17, April 13, 1946, Dec. 3, 1947, Jan. 28, 1948, Jan. 10, Feb. 19, May 20, Aug. 17, 1949; Ewing

speeches in *CR*, 81 Cong., 2 Sess. (Appendix), pp. A1844–45, A4071–73; *Current Biography, 1948,* pp. 193–96; Monte M. Poen, "The Truman Administration and National Health Insurance" (unpublished Ph.D. dissertation, University of Missouri, 1967), pp. 104–42, 145–50, 155–56, 176, 188–89; Arthur M. Schlesinger, Jr., *The Coming of the New Deal* (Boston, 1958), p. 554.

6. *Current Biography, 1948,* pp. 352–55; interview with Keyserling, Sept. 20, 1967; J. Joseph Huthmacher, *Senator Robert F. Wagner and the Rise of Urban Liberalism* (New York, 1968), pp. 147, 163–64, 190, 192, 211, 224–25, 296–97.

7. Charles La Follette to HST, Oct. 20, 1949, and La Follette to William Green, Oct. 27, 1949, both in ADA MSS; "Toward Full Employment," *NR*, CXXII (May 22, 1950), 8.

8. Robert S. Allen and William V. Shannon, *The Truman Merry-Go-Round* (New York, 1950), pp. 79–81.

9. Keyserling, "Deficiencies of Past Programs and Nature of New Needs" in *Saving American Capitalism,* pp. 81–94.

10. Keyserling to Clifford, Dec. 20, 1948, and Jan. 3, 1949, both in Clifford MSS, HSTL; *NYT*, Jan. 19, Feb. 28, April 21, 1949.

11. Keyserling in *Saving American Capitalism,* pp. 81–94; "For A National Prosperity Budget," *NYT Magazine,* Jan. 9, 1949, pp. 42–43, 45; "The Middle Way for America," *P*, XIII (May 1949), 5–9; "A Policy for Full Employment," *NR*, CXXI (Oct. 24, 1949), 13–15.

12. Keyserling, Address in San Francisco, Sept. 18, 1949, Clifford MSS; "Memorandum Relating to $4000 Minimum Standard of Living," Sept. 30, 1949, George Elsey MSS, HSTL; "Planning for a $300 Billion Economy," *NYT Magazine,* June 18, 1950, pp. 9, 24–27.

13. *Public Papers, 1949,* p. 494.

14. Richard Lester, "Truman Economics—1950 Model," *NR*, CXXII (Jan. 23, 1950), 11–13.

15. Allen J. Matusow, *Farm Policies and Politics in the Truman Years* (Cambridge, Mass., 1967), pp. 170–85; Shannon and Allen, *Truman Merry Go-Round,* pp. 114–16.

16. Grafton in *CST*, Jan. 26, 1949.

17. Loeb to George Jacobson, Feb. 5, 1949; Loeb to James Patton, Feb. 7, 1949; Loeb to Hubert Humphrey, Feb. 17, 1949; Loeb to Joseph P. Lash, April 15, 1949; Loeb, Radio speech, March 8, 1949—all in ADA MSS.

18. Matusow, *Farm Policies and Politics,* pp. 115–19, 194–200.

19. Grafton in *CST*, April 20, 1949; *SLPD*, April 8, 1949; McDonald, "The Fair Deal's Farm Program," *NR*, CXX (May 2, 1949), 11–13; EP, *N*, CLXVIII (April 16, 1949), 429–30; Patton in *NUF*, April 1949.

20. Matusow, *Farm Policies and Politics,* pp. 199–201, 204–19; *Public Papers, 1949,* pp. 292–93.

21. *NUF,* June, Aug. 1949.

22. Brannan, Talk in Chicago, Sept. 5, 1949, Clifford MSS; Paul E. Fitzpatrick to Maurice Tobin, May 3, 1950, HST MSS, OF 300; Fitzpatrick to Brannan, May 8, 1950, *ibid.;* Matusow, *Farm Policies and Politics,* pp. 199–200; *Public Papers, 1949,* pp. 460, 467–68.

23. Mezerik, "The Brannan Plan," *NR,* CXXI (Nov. 28, 1949), 11–13; Matusow, *Farm Policies and Politics,* pp. 218–21; McGrath to Kroll, June 20, 1949, Kroll MSS, LC.

24. Loeb, Radio speech, March 8, 1949, ADA MSS; Milburn P. Akers in *CST,* June 15, 1949; Lauren Soth, "Democrats in Des Moines," *R,* I (July 19, 1949), 4–7.

25. Loeb to J. M. Kaplan, Nov. 1, 1949, ADA MSS; *CST,* July 12, 1949; "New Farm Plan Needed," *N,* CLXVIII (June 11, 1949), 649–50; *NYT,* April 4, 1950.

26. Loeb to David Williams, May 20, 1949; Loeb to Brannan, June 15, 1949; Violet Gunther to Wilbur Hitchcock, May 10, 1950—all in ADA MSS.

27. Matusow, *Farm Policies and Politics,* pp. 202–204, 220–21.

28. HST to Williams, Nov. 18, 1950, Williams MSS, FDRL; Herblock in *SLPD,* Sept. 1951.

CHAPTER 14: THE FAIR DEAL, THE ANATOMY
OF STALEMATE

1. Stokes in the Atlanta *Constitution,* Nov. 10, Dec. 6, 1948; Loeb, Radio speech, Dec. 14, 1948, ADA MSS.

2. Bendiner, "End of an Era," *N,* CLXVIII (Jan. 15, 1949), 60–61.

3. *SLPD,* Jan. 4, 1949; Childs in *ibid.,* Jan. 6, 1949; Davis, News commentary, Jan. 6, 1949, Davis MSS, LC; Thackrey in *NYP,* Jan. 6, 1949; T.R.B., "Washington Wire," *NR,* CXX (Jan. 17, 1949), 3–4; Grafton in *CST,* Jan. 26, 1949; Sancton, "Hearings on the Hill," *N,* CLXVIII (Feb. 12, 1949), 175–77.

4. *Public Papers, 1949,* p. 147; *CST,* March 2, 1949; "Time for a Showdown," *N,* CLXVIII (March 12, 1949), 292.

5. Violet Megrath to Mrs. Charles Muehlstein, Jan. 31, 1949, ADA MSS; James Loeb, Jr., to David Williams, March 18, 1949, *ibid.;* Rauh to Lucas, Feb. 16, 1949, *ibid.; Public Papers, 1949,* pp. 158–59; Stokes in the Atlanta *Constitution,* March 8, 1949; *NYP,* March 1, 1949; T.R.B., "Washington Wire," *NR,* CXX (March 14, 1949), 3–4; Charles Murphy, Memos to HST, March 8, 1949, and HST to Murphy, March 9, 1949, Murphy MSS.

6. Loeb, Radio speech, March 15, 1949, ADA MSS.

7. *Public Papers, 1949*, pp. 170, 237–38, 439; EP, *N*, CLXVIII (May 21, 1949), 569; "Starting a New Democratic Party," *NR*, CXXI (Sept. 5, 1949), 5–6.

8. *Public Papers, 1949*, pp. 174, 208–13, 226–30.

9. Rauh, Statement, May 24, 1949, ADA MSS.

10. *Public Papers, 1949*, pp. 268–69; "The Lucas Fiasco," *N*, CLXVIII (June 4, 1949), 627; Richard E. Neustadt, "The Fair Deal: A Legislative Balance Sheet," *Public Policy*, V (1954), 349–81.

11. *SLPD*, March 17, 1949; "No Time to go Fishing," *NR*, CXX (March 21, 1949), 5–6; Loeb to David Williams, March 18, 1949, ADA MSS.

12. Kingdon in *NYP*, March 22, 1949; "The Fair Deal Falters," *NR*, CXX (Feb. 21, 1949), 5–6; Childs in *SLPD*, March 9, April 15, 1949; *ibid.*, May 29, 1949; Kenneth Hechler, Memo, Jan. 5, 1951, Murphy MSS.

13. "Break-up of the Parties?" *N*, CLXVIII (March 26, 1949), 345–46; Grafton in *NYP*, May 24, 1949.

14. Sancton, "Our House of Lords," *N*, CLXVIII (March 19, 1949), 322–24; Lerner in *NYP*, May 31, 1949.

15. "Break-up of the Parties?" *N*, CLXVIII (March 26, 1949), 345–46; Loeb, Radio speech, March 15, 1949, ADA MSS; Rowland Evans and Robert Novak, *Lyndon B. Johnson: The Exercise of Power* (New York, 1966), ch. 3, perceptively discusses power in the Senate during the Truman years.

16. "No Surrender," *P*, XIII (July 1949), 3; Stokes in the Atlanta *Constitution*, April 4, 1949; "Break-up of the Parties?" *N*, CLXVIII (March 26, 1949), 345–46; Thomas Sancton, "New Congress, Old Factions," *ibid.*, CLXVIII (May 14, 1949), 548–49.

17. "Where Are We Now?" and "The People vs. the People," *R*, I (May 10, 1949), 3–7; Schlesinger, "A Sense of Necessity," *ibid.*, I (April 26, 1949), 26–27, and "The Shade of John C. Calhoun," *ibid.*, I (June 7, 1949), 37–39; Burns, "Truman's One Way Out," *ibid.*, I (July 19, 1949), 17–19.

18. Grafton in *NYP*, May 27, 1949; "The Lucas Fiasco," *N*, CLXVIII (June 4, 1949), 627.

19. T.R.B., "Washington Wire," *NR*, CXXI (Sept. 12, 1949), 3–4; "Responsible Party Government," *ibid.*, CXXII (May 29, 1950), 5–6; Burns, "Truman's One Way Out," *R*, I (July 19, 1949), 17–19.

20. Burns, *ibid.*; "Whose Mandate?" *NL*, XXXII (May 14, 1949), 1.

21. See Mildred Strunk, ed., "The Quarter's Polls," *Public Opinion Quarterly*, XIII (1949), 154–76, 346–71, 537–61, 709–32.

22. "The Administration Must Fight," *NR*, CXX (March 14, 1949), 5.

23. Loeb to Milton Farber, April 13, 1949, ADA MSS. See also above, ch. 12.

24. See, e.g., editorial comment in *CST*, June 29, 1949.

25. "Damn the Torpedoes," *NR*, CXIX (Nov. 15, 1948), 6; *Public Papers, 1948*, pp. 951, 965; Stokes in the Atlanta *Constitution*, Nov. 24, 1948, Jan. 31, 1949. This section relies heavily upon Linda S. Webb, "The Buchanan Committee on Lobbying: The Politics of Investigation" (unpublished seminar paper, Ohio University, 1969).

26. Reuther to HST, March 11, 1949, and attached memo, HST MSS, OF 967; HST to Reuther, April 4, 1949, *ibid.*

27. *SLPD*, July 25, 1949; Murphy, Memo to HST, Sept. 12, 1949, Murphy MSS.

28. Allen and Shannon, *Truman Merry Go-Round*, p. 352; EP, *N*, CLXX (June 24, 1950), 603–604.

CHAPTER 15: THE FAIR DEAL, PROMISE
AND PERFORMANCE

1. Council of Economic Advisers, Memo to HST, Dec. 7, 1948, and Edwin Nourse, Memo to HST, Dec. 21, 1948, both in Clifford MSS. William O. Wagnon kindly facilitated my use of his "The Politics of Economic Growth. The Truman Administration and the 1949 Recession" (Ph.D. dissertation, University of Missouri, 1970). It is a valuable work which did much to clarify my own thinking on its topic.

2. *NYT*, Feb. 9, 1949.

3. Keyserling, "The Middle Way for America," *P*, XIII (May 1949), 5–9. See also *NYT*, April 21, 1949.

4. "The Club in the Closet," *N*, CLXVIII (March 5, 1949), 265.

5. *NYT*, June 10, 16, July 12, 1949; Dewey Anderson, Wilfred Lumer, and John Shott, "Unemployment: It's Here. Let's Stop It Now!" (Mimeographed, Public Affairs Institute, June 1949), copy in HST MSS, Office of the Assistant to the President File; Bowles to HST, July 7, 1949 and attached letter to Nourse, July 6, 1949, *ibid.*, PPF 2687; "Recession Progress," *N*, CLXVIII (June 25, 1949), 696–97; "Plan Now or Pay the Piper Later," *NR*, CXXI (July 4, 1949), 5–6; "To Head Off the Coming Depression," *ibid.*, p. 12; ADA press release, June 12, 1949, ADA MSS.

6. *SLPD*, June 19, 1949; Murray, "A Plan to Maintain Prosperity," *NR*, CXXI (July 11, 1949), 12–14; *CST*, June 28, 1949.

7. *Public Papers, 1950*, pp. 356–67, 369–75.

8. *NYT*, July 20, 1949; ADA press release, July 19, 1949, ADA MSS.

9. Wagnon, "The Politics of Economic Growth," chs. 7–8.

10. *Ibid.*, pp. 146–47; *Public Papers, 1949*, p. 518; Allen and Shannon, *Truman Merry Go-Round*, p. 81.

11. *SLPD*, June 17, 1949; Marquis Childs in *ibid.*, July 5, 1949; Davis, News commentary, Oct. 3, 1949, Davis MSS; Democratic National Committee Press Release, Oct. 5, 1949, and Tucker to James Loeb, Oct. 8,

1949, both in ADA MSS; *NYT*, Oct. 9, 1949; EP, *N*, CLXIX (Oct. 15, 1949), 358–59; HST to Eleanor Roosevelt, Oct. 5, 1949, and Oct. 17, 1949, HST MSS, OF 235; Olds to HST, Nov. 4, 1949, *ibid.*, PPF 5142; *Public Papers, 1949*, pp. 496–97, 502–503; Evans and Novak, *Lyndon B. Johnson*, pp. 35–39; Joseph P. Harris, "The Senatorial Rejection of Leland Olds," *American Political Science Review*, XLV (Sept. 1951), 674–92.

12. Ickes, "Farewell, Secretary Krug," *NR*, CXXI (Nov. 28, 1949), 17; Biemiller to Murphy, Dec. 28, 1949, and Goldberg to Murphy, Jan. 4, 1950, Murphy MSS.

13. Richard L. Neuberger, "Hail Fellow Well Met," *N*, CLXVIII (March 12, 1949), 303–305; Davis, News commentary, Oct. 18, 1949, Davis MSS.

14. *SLPD*, May 20, 1949; Marquis Childs in *ibid.;* Daniels, Oral History Memoir, pp. 13, 91, HSTL.

15. T.R.B., "Washington Wire," *NR*, CXXI (Aug. 8, 1949), 3–4; Ickes, "Tom Clark Should Say 'No, Thanks,'" *ibid.*, CXXI (Aug. 15, 1949), 11–12; *SLPD*, July 29, 1949; Marquis Childs in *ibid.*, Aug. 4, 1949; *CST*, Aug. 1, 1949.

16. *SLPD*, Sept. 16, 1949; *CST*, Sept. 19, 1949; "The New Appointments," *P*, XIII (Oct. 1949), 3; Stokes in the Atlanta *Constitution*, Aug. 2, 1949; "Second-Class Government," *NR*, CXXI (Aug. 8, 1949), 5–6; "Mr. Justice Minton," *ibid.*, CXXI (Sept. 26, 1949), 9; Bendiner, "Politics and the High Court," *N*, CLXIX (Sept. 24, 1949), 292–93.

17. *SLPD*, Nov. 6, 1949; *CST*, Feb. 28, 1950; "The Truman Court," *NR*, CXXII (March 6, 1950), 7; Ickes, "Star Chamber Comes to America," *ibid.*, CXXII (June 12, 1950), 17; Finley, "Truman's Judges," *ibid.*, CXXVI (March 10, 1952), 10–11; *NYP*, Feb. 22, 1950.

18. *Public Papers, 1949*, pp. 135, 142–43, 420; *CST*, Sept. 6, 1949; EP, *N*, CLXIX (Sept. 10, 1949), 241; Elmer Davis, News commentary, Aug. 19, 1949, Davis MSS; "General Vaughn and His Friends," *NR*, CXXI (Aug. 22, 1949), 5–7.

19. Ernest Kirschten, "Truman in Missouri," *N*, CLXX (April 1, 1950), 297–98; Schlesinger in *NYP*, April 23, 1950; Childs in *SLPD*, March 31, 1950.

20. T.R.B., "Washington Wire," *NR*, CXXI (Oct. 17, 1949), 3–4; Stokes in the Atlanta *Constitution*, Oct. 3, 1949; *SLPD*, Oct. 20, 1949; EP, *N*, CLXIX (Oct. 29, 1949), 405–406.

21. "The Meaning of the Elections," *NR*, CXXI (Nov. 21, 1949), 5–6; Davis, News commentary, Nov. 9, 1949, Davis MSS; Lerner in *NYP*, Nov. 9, 1949; *CST*, Nov. 10, 1949; *SLPD*, Nov. 9, 1949; Robert Bendiner, "G.O.P.—Nothing to Sell," *N*, CLXIX (Nov. 19, 1949), 486–87.

22. "Half-Time Score," *N*, CLXIX (Oct. 8, 1949), 339–40; "The Future of the Fair Deal," *NR*, CXXI (Nov. 14, 1949), 32; Marquis Childs in *SLPD*, July 1, 1949; editorial in *ibid.*, Jan. 1, 1950.

23. *Public Papers, 1950*, pp. 2–11.

24. Rauh to HST, Jan. 4, 1950, ADA MSS; "Policies and Politics," *P*, XIV (Feb. 1950), 3; "The President's Message," *NR*, CXXII (Jan. 9, 1950), 5–7; Bruce Catton, "Congressional Calendar," *N*, CLXX (Jan. 7, 1950), 5; "President and Congress," *ibid.*, CLXX (Jan. 14, 1950), 25–26; Charles Van Devander, "Fair Deal Prospects," *ibid.*, CLXX (Jan. 21. 1950), 54–55.

25. *Public Papers, 1950*, pp. 110, 164–69.

26. Charles La Follette to HST, Oct. 1, 1949, ADA MSS; *NYT*, Oct. 3, 1949; *Public Papers, 1949*, pp. 501, 562; *SLPD*, Nov. 11, 1949; Richard M. Dalfiume, *Desegregation of the U.S. Armed Forces* (Columbia, Mo., 1969), pp. 175–96.

27. Dalfiume, *ibid.*, pp. 196–201, 216–19; *NYT*, Feb. 15, 1950; Clifford, Memo to HST, n.d. [Jan. 23, 1950], HST MSS, Phillco Nash Files; David K. Niles, Memo to HST, May 22, 1950, *ibid.*

28. John Gunther to Stephen Spingarn, April 27, 1950; Gunther, Memo to Spingarn, May 11, 1950; La Follette to Roy Wilkins, April 14, 1950—all in ADA MSS.

29. S.J.S. [Stephen J. Spingarn], Memo to Charles Murphy, Dec. 10, 1949, Clifford MSS; ADA press release, Dec. 17, 1949, ADA MSS; Henry Lee Moon, "FEPC Rally in Washington," *NR*, CXXII (Jan. 30, 1950), 14–15; *Public Papers, 1950*, p. 115.

30. Marquis Childs in *SLPD*, Jan. 23, Feb. 27, 1950; EP, *N*, CLXX (Feb. 4, 1950), 97; *Public Papers, 1950*, p. 134; "Design for Decency," *P*, XIV (April, 1950), 3–4; *CST*, Feb. 24, 1950.

31. *Public Papers, 1950*, p. 253; *NYP*, April 13, 1950; Willard Shelton, "Battle in a Paper Bag," *N*, CLXX (May 20, 1950), 467; ADA press release, June 5, 1950, ADA MSS.

32. Charles La Follette to Roy Wilkins, April 14, 1950, ADA MSS; Roy Wilkins to Spingarn, Feb. 16, 1950, Spingarn MSS, HSTL; Spingarn, Memos to Charles Murphy, March 16, May 22, July 3, 1950, *ibid.*; Spingarn, Memo for the FEPC file, July 5, 1950, *ibid.*

33. "The Housewife's Friend," *NR*, CXXII (April 10, 1950), 11; Harold L. Ickes, "Kerr's Asphyxiation Bill," *NR*, CXXII (April 17, 1950), 25; Donald Montgomery to John Gunther, Feb. 15, 1950, ADA MSS; Charles La Follette et al. to Gray Leslie, March 6, 1950, Murphy MSS.

34. La Follette to HST, April 6, 1950, *ibid.*; Murphy, Memo to HST, April 13, 1950, *ibid.*; Allen and Shannon, *Truman Merry Go-Round*, p. 98.

35. *Public Papers, 1950*, pp. 257–58; *NYP*, April 17, 1950; "Votes Before Dollars," *NR*, CXXII (April 24, 1950), 7; *SLPD*, April 16, 1950; Davis, News commentary, April 17, 1950, Davis MSS.

36. *Public Papers, 1950*, pp. 296–314, 321–416; Carleton Kent, "Harry Goes A-Hunting," *N*, CLXX (May 20, 1950), 466–67.

37. *CST*, May 15, 1950; "Reports to the People," *NR*, CXXII (May 22, 1950), 7; "Election Overture," *N*, CLXX (May 27, 1950), 514–15.

38. "Middle-Housing's Death," *NR*, CXXII (April 3, 1950), 12–13; S.J.S. [Stephen J. Spingarn], Memo for the files on aid to medical education, June 29, 1950, Spingarn MSS; Legislative summary, May 29, 1950, Elsey MSS; *Public Papers, 1950*, pp. 288–94; Richard E. Neustadt, "The Fair Deal: A Legislative Balance Sheet," *Public Policy*, V (1954), 349–81.

39. *Public Papers, 1950*, pp. 480–83; Spingarn, Memo for the File on the Basing Point Bill, June 16, 1950, Spingarn MSS; *SLPD*, June 17, 1950; Thomas L. Stokes in the Atlanta *Constitution*, June 20, 1950.

40. Neustadt, "Fair Deal."

CHAPTER 16: TRUMAN, THE VITAL CENTER, AND AMERICAN FOREIGN POLICY

1. *Public Papers, 1949*, pp. 112–16.

2. "Mr. Truman's Chance," *P*, XIII (Feb. 1949), 3–4; Freda Kirchwey, "Cold War Inaugural," *N*, CLXVIII (Jan. 29, 1949), 117; Sancton, "Truman's Big Parade," *ibid.*, pp. 120–21.

3. "President Truman's Global Plans," *NR*, CXX (Jan. 31, 1949), 5–6.

4. *CST*, Jan. 21, 1949; *SLPD*, Jan. 20, 1949; Lilienthal, *The Journals of David E. Lilienthal: The Atomic Energy Years, 1945–1950* (New York, 1964), p. 448 (hereafter cited as *Journals*, II).

5. Davis, News commentary, Jan. 7, 1949, Davis MSS; *CST*, Jan. 11, 1949; Loeb to Acheson, Jan. 17, 1949, ADA MSS; "Dean Acheson Takes Over State," *NR*, CXX (Jan. 17, 1949), 7.

6. Loeb to David Williams, March 18, 1949, ADA MSS; Marquis Childs in *SLPD*, March 5, 1949; Elmer Davis, News commentary, March 3, 1949, Davis MSS; "Secretary Johnson," *NR*, CXX (March 21, 1949), 6–7.

7. Paul Blanshard, "Pork Barrels in the Pentagon," *N*, CLXVIII (June 4, 1949), 632–34; Samuel Grafton in *NYP*, Jan. 17, 1949; *CST*, Aug. 27, 1949.

8. *NYT*, March 19, 28, May 6, 1949; Glen Taylor in *CR*, 81 Cong., 1 Sess. (April 8, 1949), pp. 4141–42; Blatnik in *ibid.* (Appendix), pp. A5399–A5402; T. O. Thackrey and I. F. Stone in *NYP*, March 21, 1949; *NUF*, April 1949; Stokes in the Atlanta *Constitution*, July 17, 1949; "Pacts or Pax?" *P*, XIII (April 1949), 3; "The Basic Question," *ibid.*, XIII (May 1949), 3–4; Freda Kirchwey, "Questions about the Pact," *N*, CLXVIII (March 26, 1949), 348–49, and "The Pact and the Charter," *ibid.*, CLXVIII (April 9, 1949), 403–405.

9. *CST*, March 20, April 4, 14, July 24, 1949; "The North Atlantic Pact," *NR*, CXX (Feb. 14, 1949), 5–6; "If Not ADA, Then Who?" *ibid.*,

CXX (April 18, 1949), 8; Helen Gahagan Douglas, "Why I Voted for Arms for Europe," *ibid.*, CXXI (Aug. 29, 1949), 9–10; ADA press releases, May 13, Aug. 5, 1949, ADA MSS; Loeb, Radio speech, April 5, 1949, *ibid.*; Eleanor Roosevelt in *CST*, March 22, 1949; *SLPD*, March 18, July 26, 1949; Paul Douglas in *CR*, 81 Cong., 1 Sess. (Appendix), pp. A4554–56; "The Psychology Behind the Pact," *R*, I (May 24, 1949), 11–13; Niebuhr, "The North Atlantic Pact," *Christianity and Crisis*, IX (May 30, 1949), 65–66.

10. *NYT*, Jan. 15, Feb. 20, Dec. 1, 4, 1949; Kingdon in *NYP*, Jan. 18, 1949; Lerner in *ibid.*, May 23, 1949; Stokes in the Atlanta *Constitution*, e.g., Dec. 1, 1948, Dec. 1, 1949; Davis, News commentary, Dec. 9, 1949, Davis MSS; Freda Kirchwey, "Playing with Fire," *N*, CLXIX (Dec. 3, 1949), 531–32.

11. *CST*, March 13, 1949; *SLPD*, April 21, 1950; "Can There Be a Four-Power Agreement?" *NR*, CXX (May 9, 1949), 5–6.

12. *SLPD*, Jan. 18, 1949; Childs in *ibid*.

13. Loeb to David Williams, May 20, Nov. 30, 1949, ADA MSS; Loeb to Acheson, Jan. 26, 1950, *ibid.*; ADA press releases, Jan. 27, June 14, 1950, *ibid.*; *NYT*, April 2, 1950; *Public Papers, 1949*, p. 380; *Public Papers, 1950*, pp. 569 70, 594, 616; S.J.S. [Stephen J. Spingarn], Memo for the record, Aug. 2, 1950, Spingarn MSS.

14. *Public Papers, 1949*, pp. 277–79, 286–91, 324–25, 285–89, 295–400, 555–57; *CST*, July 21, 1949.

15. *Public Papers, 1949*, p. 519; Lilienthal, *Journals*, II, 464, 501, 527; HST, Handwritten notes, June 7, 1949, Clifford MSS.

16. Davis, News commentary, Feb. 1, 1949, Davis MSS; *SLPD*, Jan. 31, 1949; *NYP*, March 21, 1949; "The Need Is for a Democratic International," *NR*, CXX (March 28, 1949), 5–6.

17. *CST*, Feb. 6, 1949; Freda Kirchwey, "Stalin and Truman," *N*, CLXVIII (Feb. 12, 1949), 169–70; Stokes in the Atlanta *Constitution*, Feb. 9, 1949.

18. "Mr. Truman's Chance," *P*, XIII (Feb. 1949), 3–4.

19. *CST*, June 22, 25, 1949; Freda Kirchwey, "The Paris Conference," *N*, CLXVIII (June 18, 1949), 675–76.

20. "Post-Mortem on Paris," *NR*, CXX (June 27, 1949), 5–6.

21. Freda Kirchwey, "As Others See Us," *N*, CLXIX (Oct. 29, 1949), 407–408, and "Soviet Tactics and Soviet Fears," *ibid.*, CLXIX (Dec. 10, 1949), 559–61; "Creative Bargaining," *P*, XIII (Sept. 1949), 3–4; Talbot quoted in "Notes on Peace," HST MSS, OF 555.

22. *SLPD*, Jan. 1, 5, 22, 1950; Niebuhr, "Streaks of Dawn in the Night," *Christianity and Crisis*, IX (Dec. 12, 1949), 162–64, and "A Protest Against a Dilemma's Two Horns," *World Politics*, II (April 1950), 338–44; La Follette to Acheson, Nov. 5, 1949, ADA MSS; George F. Kennan, *Memoirs: 1925–1950* (Boston 1967), pp. 406–14. See also A. A. Berle,

Jr., "George Kennan, Kindly Machiavellian," *NL*, XXXIV (Nov. 5, 1951), 20–22.

23. See, e.g., Samuel Grafton in *NYP*, Jan. 3, 4, 1949; T. O. Thackrey in *ibid.*, Jan. 17, 1949; *NYT*, April 11, 1949; Stewart Meacham, "Crisis in Korea," *P*, XIII (Aug. 1949), 20–22; *SLPD*, July 13, 1949, March 15, 1950.

24. *CST*, Nov. 11, 1948, Jan. 15, 1949; Grafton in *ibid.*, Dec. 3, 1948, Jan. 15, 1949; "The U.S. and Red China," *N*, CLXIX (July 30, 1949), 100; Franklin Wallick, "The Tragedy of China's Liberals," *P*, XIII (April 1949), 24–25; Robert Root, "The New Regime for Old China," *ibid.*, XIII (July 1949), 18–19; *SLPD*, Oct. 20, 1949; "Next Steps in China," *NR*, CXX (May 2, 1949), 5–6; "A New Policy in Asia," *ibid.*, CXXI (Sept. 26, 1949), 5–7; Niebuhr, "Streaks of Dawn in the Night," *Christianity and Crisis*, IX (Dec. 12, 1949), 162–64.

For Dallin and the *New Leader*, see Dallin, "The Debacle in China," *NL*, XXXI (Nov. 27, 1948), 1, 15; Dallin, "Mao No Tito; U.S. Must Act," *ibid.*, XXXII (May 7, 1949), 1–2; "Recognizing Mao," *ibid.*, XXXII (Nov. 5, 1949), 3; Dallin, "Myth of Chinese 'Titoism' Revisited," *ibid.*, XXXIV (Aug. 27, 1951), 13. For critical responses, see Robert Shaplen, "The China Debacle: A Reply to David J. Dallin," *ibid.*, XXXI (Dec. 11, 1948), 14; Joseph and Stewart Alsop to the Editor, *ibid.*, XXXIV (Oct. 8, 1951), 26.

25. Lilienthal, *Journals*, II, 525; "The Mess in China," *NR*, CXXI (Aug. 15, 1949), 7; John K. Fairbank, "America and the Chinese Revolution," *ibid.*, CXXI (Aug. 22, 1949), 11–13; *CST*, Aug. 9, 1949; *SLPD*, Aug. 12, 1949.

26. *SLPD*, Jan. 4, 1950; Freda Kirchwey, "China: Blunder upon Blunder?" *N*, CLXX (Jan. 7, 1950), 1–2; "China Muddle (cont'd)," *NR*, CXXII (Jan. 9, 1950), 7; Harold L. Ickes, "Truman's Formosa Policy," *ibid.*, CXXII (Jan. 23, 1950), 17.

27. *Public Papers, 1950*, pp. 11–12, 33; *NYP*, Jan. 17, 1950; "No Time for Secret Diplomacy," *NR*, CXXII (Jan. 16, 1950), 5; "The Truman Doctrine Is Dead," *ibid.*, CXXII (Jan. 23, 1950), 5–7; "The Lesser Risk," *P*, XIV (Feb. 1950), 4.

28. *NYT*, April 2, 1950; Kingdon in *NYP*, Feb. 1, 1950; "What Sort of Help for Indo-China?" *NR*, CXXII (May 22, 1950), 5–6; *CST*, May 10, 1950.

29. "Arithmetic and Higher Mathematics," *R*, I (April 26, 1949), 3–4; "China, Asia, and the U.S.," *NR*, CXXI (July 18, 1949), 5–6.

30. Thomas Sancton, "Truman's Colonial Experiment," *N*, CLXVIII (Feb. 5, 1949), 146–48; "A Bold New Program . . ." *NR*, CXXI (July 11, 1949), 5–6. On the origins of Point Four, see George Elsey, Memo to Clark Clifford, July 17, 1963, and Clifford to Herbert Feis, July 16, 1963, both in Clifford MSS.

31. Ezekiel, "Point Four and the United Nations," *NR*, CXXII (May 15, 1950), 11–14; *CST*, Jan. 30, 1949.

32. HST, *Memoirs,* II, 227–39; David Lloyd, Memo to George Elsey, Nov. 29, 1949, Lloyd MSS, HSTL; Lilienthal, *Journals,* II, 475.

33. Helen Fuller, "Point Four Whittled Away," *NR,* CXXII (April 10, 1950), 15–17; Kingsley to Clifford, May 9, 1949, Clifford MSS; Lloyd Memo to Walter Salant, June 22, 1949, and Lloyd, Memo to Elsey and Charles Murphy, Jan. 19, 1950, Lloyd MSS; Elsey, Memo to Clifford, April 13, 1950, and R.E.N. [Richard E. Neustadt], Memo for the files, July 11, 1950, Elsey MSS.

34. *Public Papers, 1950,* pp. 596–97; Charles Murphy, Memos to HST, June 19, July 7, 1950, and Elsey, Memo to Murphy, June 17, 1950, all in HST MSS, Murphy files; Elsey, Memo to Clifford, Jan. 9, 1950, Elsey MSS; Elsey, Memos to Lloyd, Jan. 9, 1950, Feb. 23, 1951, *ibid.;* Elsey, Memos to Murphy, July 6, 1950, May 21, 1951, *ibid.;* Elsey, Memo on Point Four, Nov. 14, 1950, *ibid.;* Lloyd, Memo to Elsey, Aug. 9, 1950, *ibid.*

35. Schlesinger, in *NYP,* Dec. 25, 1949; Schlesinger to Loeb, Jan. 6, 1950, ADA MSS.

36. *CST,* Sept. 25, Oct. 22, 1949, March 18, 1950; Thomas L. Stokes in the Atlanta *Constitution,* Sept. 29, 1949; *NYP,* Sept. 23, 1949; *SLPD,* Sept. 24, 1949; "The Only Hope," *P,* XIII (Nov. 1949), 3–4.

37. Lerner in *NYP,* Feb. 1, 1950; Kingdon in *ibid.,* Feb. 5, 1950; Thomas L. Stokes in the Atlanta *Constitution,* Feb. 7, 1950.

38. Davis, News commentary, Feb. 7, 1950, Davis MSS; *NYP,* Feb. 1, 1950; Schlesinger in *ibid.,* Feb. 5, 1950; Niebuhr, "Utilitarian Christianity and the World Crisis," *Christianity and Crisis,* X (May 29, 1950), 66–69.

39. *NYP,* Feb. 1, 1950; *SLPD,* Feb. 1, 1950; *CR,* 81 Cong., 2 Sess. (Feb. 2, 1950), pp. 1338–41.

40. Humphrey, "The Moral Alternative to Chaos," *P,* XIV (April 1950), 5–7; *NYT,* March 6, July 19, 1950. For sympathetic critiques, see *SLPD,* Feb. 3, 1950; Freda Kirchwey, "Some Other Choices," *N,* CLXX (Feb. 11, 1950), 120–21.

41. *Public Papers, 1950,* pp. 151–53; [Wallace Carroll], Memo attached to George Elsey, Memo to Murphy, Lloyd, and Bell, May 26, 1950, Elsey MSS; Walter La Feber, *America, Russia, and the Cold War* (New York, 1967), pp. 90–91.

42. "The Acheson Approach," *P,* XIV (April 1950), 3; "An Open Letter to Secretary Acheson," *ibid.,* XIV (May 1950), 3–4; "Diplomacy of Reprisal," *N,* CLXX (Feb. 18, 1950), 148.

43. Stokes in the Atlanta *Constitution,* Feb. 9, 1950; T.R.B., "Washington Wire," *NR,* CXXII (Feb. 20, 1950), 3–4; Ickes, "Let the President Lead," *ibid.,* pp. 16–17.

44. "The Hydrogen Bomb," *NR,* CXXII (Feb. 13, 1950), 5–8; "Breaking the Atomic Deadlock," *ibid.,* CXXII (April 3, 1950), 5–11; "Who Prevents Atomic Agreement?" *ibid.,* CXXII (April 10, 1950), 5–10; "Atomic Peace and Atomic Politics," *ibid.,* CXXII (April 17, 1950), 5–13; "Mr. Lie

Goes to Moscow," *ibid.*, CXXII (June 5, 1950), 5–6. For the Kennan article itself see "X" [George F. Kennan], "The Sources of Soviet Conduct," *Foreign Affairs*, XXV (July 1947), 566–82.

45. *NYP*, March 20, 1950; *CST*, March 19, April 26, 1950; *SLPD*, March 13, 29, 1950; *NYT*, April 2, 1950; James Loeb, Jr., to David Williams, April 12, 1950, ADA MSS; Ascoli, "The World Civil War," *R*, II (May 9, 1950), 5–7.

46. Elsey, Memo to Murphy, April 7, 1950, and Memo to [Elmer] Staats, Aug. 9, 1950; Unsigned memo for HST, March 9, 1950; Unsigned memo on McMahon's resolution, June 20, 1950–all in Elsey MSS.

CHAPTER 17: THE VITAL CENTER AND THE POLITICS OF ANTI-COMMUNISM

1. Cabell Phillips, *The Truman Presidency* (New York, 1966), pp. 354–60, 365–73, has a good basic chronology of these developments. See also Earl Latham, *The Communist Controversy in Washington; From the New Deal to McCarthy* (Cambridge, 1966) and Alistair Cooke, *A Generation on Trial: U.S.A. v. Alger Hiss* (New York, 1950).

2. Liberal Party press release, April 8, 1948, PP MSS, University of Iowa; [Elsey], "Random Thoughts 26 August" and Elsey, Memo to Clark Clifford, Aug. 27, 1948, Elsey MSS; *Public Papers, 1948*, pp. 432–34, 609–14.

3. "An American Creed," *NR*, CXIX (Aug. 23, 1948), 7; Wechsler, "The Remington Loyalty Case," *ibid.*, CXX (Feb. 28, 1949), 18–20; *SLPD*, Aug. 20, 1948.

4. Wechsler, "The Trial of Our Times," *P*, XIII (Feb. 1949), 10–12; Ralph de Toledano, "Hiss Must Face New Ordeal, but Great Drama Is Now Over," *NL*, XXXII (July 16, 1949), 1; William E. Bohn, "Hiss Conviction Victory for Clear Thinking," *ibid.*, XXXIII (Jan. 28, 1950), 1–2; *CST*, Dec. 14, 1948; Marquis Childs in *SLPD*, Dec. 9, 1948; Eleanor Roosevelt in *CST*, Dec. 27, 1948.

5. "Who's Lying?" *P* XIII (Aug. 1949), 3–4; Davis, News commentary, July 12, 1949, Davis MSS; R.K.B. and M.A. [Bingham and Ascoli], "The Case of Alger Hiss," *R*, I (Aug. 30, 1949), 4–7; *CST*, July 14, 1949; "The Unsolved Mystery," *NR*, CXXI (July 18, 1949), 7–8; Rovere to Granville Hicks, June 7, 1949, Hicks MSS, Syracuse University.

6. Bliven, Oral History Memoir, p. 52, COHC; Schlesinger, "Espionage or Frame-up?" *Saturday Review of Literature*, XXXIII (April 15, 1950), 21–23; Wechsler, "The Trial of Our Times," *P*, XIV (March 1950), 5–6.

7. Bendiner, "The Ordeal of Alger Hiss," *N*, CLXX (Feb. 11, 1950), 123–25; Miller, "The Second Hiss Trial," *NR*, CXXII (Feb. 6, 1950), 11–14; Arnold, et al., Letter to the editor, *NYP*, Feb. 1, 1950.

8. Lerner in *NYP*, Jan. 30, 1950; *CST*, Jan. 24, 1950; Eleanor Roosevelt in *ibid.*, Jan. 26, 1950; *SLPD*, Jan. 22, 1950; Childs in *ibid.*, Jan. 24, 1950. In 1952, Lerner and the *Post-Dispatch* were among those who supported Hiss's motion for a new trial. Lerner in *NYP*, June 5, 1952; *SLPD*, April 25, 1952. By the fall of 1950, however, Childs was conceding Hiss's probable guilt. Childs, "The Hiss Case and the American Intellectual," *R*, III (Sept. 26, 1950), 24–27.

9. "Pressure for Mundt-Nixon," *NR*, CXXII (April 3, 1950), 13; *NYT*, March 29, 1950.

10. Morris Ernst and Roger Baldwin, "Liberals and the Communist Trial," *NR*, CXX (Jan. 31, 1949), 7–8; "The Court, the Communists and the Liberals," *ibid.*, CXX (June 20, 1949), 5–6; "After the Communist Trial," *ibid.*, CXXI (Oct. 24, 1949), 5–6; Robert Bendiner, "Marx in Foley Square," *N*, CLXIX (Oct. 22, 1949), 388–90; *CST*, Oct. 17, 1949; *SLPD*, Oct. 16, 1949.

11. "Letters to and From the Editor of Time," *P*, XIII (May 1949), 27; L. A. Nikoloric, "New Victims for Old Witches," *ibid.*, XIII (Oct. 1949), 15–16; Joseph L. Rauh, Jr., "Informers, G-Men, and Free Men," *ibid.*, XIV (May 1950), 9–11; Thomas L. Stokes in the Atlanta *Constitution*, March 7, 1950; Wechsler, "The Remington Loyalty Case," *NR*, CXX (Feb. 28, 1949), 18–20; "The Knauff Scandal," *N*, CLXX (May 27, 1950), 515–16; Walter White to HST, Nov. 26, 1948, HST MSS, OF 252-K.

12. Elmer Davis, News commentary, Jan. 24, 1949, Davis MSS; Wechsler, "The Remington Loyalty Case," *NR*, CXX (Feb. 28, 1949), 18–20; *SLPD*, June 26, July 8, 1949; Marquis Childs in *ibid.*, July 8, 1949; *NYT*, April 11, 1949, April 3, 1950; Leon Henderson to HST, Sept. 27, 1948, HST MSS, OF 252-K; Stephen J. Spingarn, Memo to Clark Clifford, May 5, 1949, Spingarn MSS.

13. Grafton in *NYP*, Jan. 27, 1949; EP, *N*, CLXIX (July 23, 1949), 69; *CST*, Sept. 11, 1949; *NYT*, Sept. 25, 1949.

14. Loeb and Baldwin to Clark, April 28, 1949, ADA MSS.

15. Charles La Follette to J. Howard McGrath, Nov. 1, 1949, and La Follette to Robert Kintner, Nov. 3, 1949, *ibid.; CR*, 81 Cong. 2 Sess. (Feb. 7, 1950); pp. 1565–68.

16. Richard Rovere, *Senator Joe McCarthy* (paperback ed.; New York, 1960), pp. 119–53; *NYT*, Feb. 28, 1950.

17. *CST*, March 12, 1950; Willard Shelton, "The McCarthy Method," *N*, CLXX (May 6, 1950), 417.

18. *SLPD*, March 21, 1950; Stokes in the Atlanta *Constitution*, March 23, 1950; EP, *N*, CLXX (March 25, 1950), 261–62; *NYP*, March 30, 1950; Lerner in *ibid.*, April 10, 1950; Schlesinger in *ibid.*, July 23, 1950; Shelton, "McCarthy's Vicious Retreat," *N*, CLXX (April 15, 1950), 341–42; Ascoli, "The G.O.P.'s Choice," *R*, II (June 6, 1950), 4.

19. Max Lerner in *NYP*, April 5, 1950; Freda Kirchwey, "The McCar-

thy Blight," *N*, CLXX (June 24, 1950), 609; Davis, News commentary, May 15, 1950, Davis MSS.

20. "Dementia Unlimited," *N*, CLXX (April 29, 1950), 388; "Vibrations of Hatred," *NR*, CXXII (April 10, 1950), 10–11.

21. T.R.B., "Washington Wire," *ibid.*, CXXII (April 10, 1950), 3–4; Michael Straight, "The Mood of America," *ibid.*, CXXII (June 26, 1950), 10–12; Stokes in the Atlanta *Constitution*, April 4, 1950.

22. Phillips, *Truman Presidency*, p. 360; Dean Acheson, *Present at the Creation* (New York, 1969), p. 360.

23. [Lowenthal], "The Sedition Bills of 1949," Spingarn MSS; Spingarn, Memo to Clifford, April 19, 1949, *ibid.*; Clifford, Memo to HST, April 29, 1949, Clifford MSS; HST to Lowenthal, June 17, 1950, HST MSS, PPF 2791.

24. Spingarn, Memo to Clifford, May 5, 1949, Spingarn MSS; Spingarn, Memo to Donald Dawson, June 17, 1949, *ibid.*; Elsey, Memo to Clifford and attached note, Sept. 19, 1949, Clifford MSS; David Bell, Memo to Charles Murphy, June 14, 1950, HST MSS, OF 2750; Ward Canaday to Phillip Graham, June 5, 1950, and HST to Canaday, June 12, 1950, HST MSS, OF 2750-A.

25. Murphy and Spingarn, Memo to HST, May 16, 1950, and HST, Memo to McGrath, May 19, 1950, HST MSS, OF 2750; [Spingarn], "Notes for 5/19/50 Talk with Attorney General," May 18, 1950, and Memo for the files, May 20, 1950, Spingarn MSS.

26. S.J.S., Memo to Murphy, June 16, 1950, *ibid.*

27. Harris, Memo to Ross, June 15, 1950, and HST, Memo to Spingarn, June 17, 1950, *ibid.* Spingarn's losing fight with the Justice Department is amply documented in *ibid.*

28. *Public Papers, 1949*, pp. 280, 294.

29. *Public Papers, 1950*, pp. 163, 234–36, 252, 287.

30. Phillips, *Truman Presidency*, p. 392.

31. *Public Papers, 1950*, pp. 235, 267–73.

32. Helen Fuller, "Remington and Lee: New Loyalty Purge," *NR*, CXXII (June 19, 1950), 13–15; EP, *N*, CLXX (May 13, 1950), 433. For Sawyer's incredible justification of the Remington incident, see Sawyer, *Concerns of a Conservative Democrat* (Carbondale and Edwardsville, Ill., 1968), pp. 182–83.

33. *CST*, May 29, 1950; "The Administration Replies to McCarthy," *NR*, CXXII (May 8, 1950), 5–6; Mildred Strunk, ed., "The Quarter's Polls," *Public Opinion Quarterly*, XIII (1949), 156, 540, 712.

34. *NYT*, March 29, 1950; Ickes, "A Decoration for McCarthy," *NR*, CXXII (April 10, 1950), 17–18.

35. "After the Communist Trial," *ibid.*, CXXI (Oct. 24, 1949), 5–6; Childs, "Communists and the Right to Teach," *N*, CLXVIII (Feb. 26, 1949), 230–33; Hook, "Heresy, Yes—But Conspiracy, No," *NYT Magazine*, July 9, 1950, pp. 12, 38–39.

36. Charles La Follette to McGrath, Oct. 21, 1949; James Loeb, Jr., to Alfred Baker Lewis, Nov. 8, 1949; John Gunther, Memo to La Follette, Oct. 27, 1949; Rauh to executive committee members, Nov. 3, 1949; John Gunther, Memo to Violet Gunther, Jan. 25, 1950—all in ADA MSS.

37. Athan Theoharis, "The Rhetoric of Politics: Foreign Policy, Internal Security, and Domestic Politics in the Truman Era," in Barton J. Bernstein, ed., *Politics and Policies of the Truman Administration* (Chicago, 1970), pp. 196–241.

38. ADA press release, June 18, 1950, Spingarn MSS; "Exit Senator Pepper," *N*, CLXX (May 13, 1950), 436–37; *SLPD*, May 3, June 26, 27, 1950.

CHAPTER 18: KOREA AND THE POLITICS
OF SEMIWAR

1. HST, *Memoirs*, II, 333; *Public Papers, 1950*, pp. 527–37.

2. Ascoli, "Where We Left Off," *R*, III (July 18, 1950), 4–5; Reuther to HST, July 15, 1950, in *CR*, 81 Cong., 2 Sess. (Appendix), p. A5247; ADA press release, June 28, 1950, ADA MSS.

3. Stokes in the Atlanta *Constitution*, June 29, 1950; "Korea: Final Test of the UN," *NR*, CXXIII (July 3, 1950), 5–6; EP, *N*, CLXXI (July 1, 1950), 1; Kingdon in *NYP*, June 30, 1950.

4. *NUF*, Aug. 1950, Aug., Nov. 1951; Glen Talbot, Annual report to the North Dakota Farmers Union, Nov. 15, 1950, pp. 3–4, HST MSS, OF 555; Randolph to the Editor, *NYT*, July 1, 1950; Rubin, "The Consequences of Korea," *P*, XIV (Aug. 1950), 2–4; Laurence S. Wittner, *Rebels Against War: The American Peace Movement, 1941–1960* (New York and London, 1969), pp. 201–203.

5. *NYT*, July 16, Aug. 11, Nov. 13, 1950.

6. Davis, News commentary, June 26, 1950, Davis MSS.

7. *SLPD*, June 28, 1950; Shelton, "Notes from Capitol Hill," *N*, CLXXI (July 1, 1950), 6–7.

8. *Public Papers, 1950*, pp. 492, 531–32; Max Lerner in *NYP*, June 28, 1950; *SLPD*, Sept. 6, 1950; Max Ascoli, "Formosa: The Test," *R*, IV (Feb. 6, 1951), 4.

9. John Spanier, *The Truman-MacArthur Controversy and the Korean War* (2d ed.; New York, 1965), pp. 70–76.

10. "MacArthur Tries to Make Policy," *NR*, CXXIII (Sept. 4, 1950), 7; Freda Kirchwey, "Into a Russian Trap?" *N*, CLXXI (Aug. 12, 1950), 139–40.

11. T.R.B., "Washington Wire," *NR*, CXXIII (Sept. 11, 1950), 3–4; Eleanor Roosevelt to HST, Sept. 2, 1950, HST MSS, PPF 460; *CST*, Sept. 3, 1950; *Public Papers, 1950*, pp. 609–14.

12. Harold Ickes, "Harry S. Truman Is President," *NR*, CXXII (Sept.

11, 1950), 17; Max Lerner in *NYP*, Sept. 13, 1950; Thomas L. Stokes in the Atlanta *Constitution*, Sept. 15, 1950 ; *CST*, Sept. 14 , 1950.

13. ADA press release, Sept. 25, 1950, ADA MSS; Freda Kirchwey, "A Plan for Korean Peace," *N*, CLXXI (Aug. 26, 1950), 177–78; "Korea: Two Kinds of Defeatism," *NR*, CXXIII (Aug. 7, 1950), 5; "Peace Aims for Korea," *ibid.*, CXXIII (Sept. 25, 1950), 5–7; "The Next Step in Korea," *P*, XIV (Nov. 1950), 3–4.

14. Stokes in the Atlanta *Constitution*, Aug. 9, 1950; Ascoli, "The Dismal Summer," *R*, III (Oct. 10, 1950), 4–5; *SLPD*, Sept. 28, 1950; Davis, News commentaries, Sept. 26, 27, 28, 1950, Davis MSS; "Peace Aims for Korea," *NR*, CXXIII (Sept. 25, 1950), 5–7; "Korea: Will China Fight the UN?" *ibid.*, CXXIII (Nov. 20, 1950), 5–6; "Unite Korea!" *NL*, XXXIII (Sept. 30, 1950), 30.

15. *SLPD*, Oct. 7, 1950; Freda Kirchwey, "Unanswered Questions," *N*, CLXXI (Oct. 28, 1950), 376–77, and "Threat Out of China," *ibid.*, CLXXI (Nov. 11 , 1950), 423–25; Lerner in *NYP*, Sept. 18, 1950.

16. ADA press release, Sept. 25, 1950, ADA MSS; "For a New Asiatic Policy," *NR*, CXXIII (Oct. 9, 1950), 6.

17. "The Washington Front," *N*, CLXXI (July 8, 1950), 25; "McCarthy to Trial," *ibid.*, CLXXI (July 29, 1950), 99–100; T.R.B., "Washington Wire," *NR*, CXXIII (July 31, 1950), 3–4.

18. Willard Shelton, "The Waning Congress," *N*, CLXXI (Sept. 16, 1950), 241–42; T.R.B., "Washington Wire," *NR*, CXXIII (Sept. 18, 1950, 3–4; "The Big Lie in Washington," *ibid.*, p. 7; *NYT*, Sept. 2 , 8, Nov. 19, 20, Dec. 1 , 1950; *NUF*, Sept., Oct. 1950.

19. Murphy, Elsey, and Spingarn, Memo to HST, July 11 , 1950; Spingarn, Memo on proposed commission, July 12, 1950; Spingarn, Memo to Murphy, Elsey, and Donald Dawson, July 20, 1950; Spingarn, Memo on proposal for presidential leadership, July 21, 1950; Spingarn, Memo on conference with HST, July 22 , 1950—all in Spingarn MSS.

20. *Public Papers, 1950*, pp. 571–76.

21. "Excess of Zeal," *N*, CLXXI (Aug. 19, 1950), 158–59; ADA press release, Aug. 9, 1950, ADA MSS; *CST*, Aug. 11, 1950; "For Internal Security," *NR*, CXXIII (Aug. 21, 1950), 7–8.

22. *NYP*, Sept. 14, 1950; "Personal Freedom in Wartime," *NR*, CXXIII (Sept. 4, 1950), 5–7.

23. HST, Memos to Alben Barkley, Sam Rayburn, Scott Lucas, and John McCormack, Aug. 28, 1950; William Hassett to Spingarn, Aug. 28, 1950; Elsey letters to Mark Ethridge, Erwin Canham, Philip Reed, Mark May, and Justin Miller, Sept. 2, 1950; Charles Ross to Norman Thomas, Aug. 28, 1950—all in HST MSS, OF 2750-B. Among the many letters and memoranda in the Spingarn MSS, see, e.g., Spingarn to Stanley Goodrich, Aug. 18, 1950; Spingarn to J. Edgar Hoover, Aug. 22, 1950; Spingarn to William J. Donovan, Aug. 23, 1950; Spingarn to Matthew J. Connelly,

Aug. 23, 1950; Spingarn to Kenneth Royall, Aug. 30, Sept. 15, 1950. On the internment proposal, see Spingarn, Memoranda for the file, July 12, Aug. 11, Sept. 6, 1950, Spingarn MSS; Willard Shelton, "Notes From Capitol Hill," *N*, CLXXI (Sept. 2, 1950), 202.

24. Spingarn, Memoranda for the file, July 12, Sept. 6, 1950, Spingarn MSS; *NYP*, Sept. 14, 1950; Davis, News commentary, Sept. 12, 1950, Davis MSS; " 'Unwise, Unworkable,' " *NR*, CXXIII (Sept. 25, 1950), 7–8; "Liberals Outsmarted," *N*, CLXXI (Sept. 23, 1950), 260–61; "Internal Panic Act," *NL*, XXXIII (Sept. 30, 1950), 30.

25. *Public Papers, 1950*, pp. 561, 620; Spingarn, Memoranda, Sept. 19, 20, 25, 1950, Spingarn MSS; Spingarn, Memoranda, Sept. 19, 25, 1950, Elsey MSS.

26. *Public Papers, 1950*, pp. 645–53.

27. Rauh to Spingarn, Sept. 28, 1950, Spingarn MSS; *SLPD*, Sept. 24, 1950; Talbot, Annual report to the North Dakota Farmers Union, Nov. 15, 1950, p. 13, HST MSS, OF 555; "Congress Aids the Communists," *NR*, CXXIII (Oct. 2, 1950), 6–7; Spingarn, Memo for the internal security file, Sept. 25, 1950, Elsey MSS; Davis, News commentary, Sept. 25, 1950, Davis MSS.

28. Helen Douglas to HST, Sept. 20, 1950, HST MSS, OF 2750-C; Lehman, Murray, and Kefauver to HST, Sept. 20, 1950, *ibid.;* Kilgore to HST, Sept. 14, 1950, *ibid.;* Francis Biddle to HST, Dec. 5, 1950, *ibid.*

29. *Public Papers, 1950*, pp. 527–42.

30. Richard Neustadt, Memo to Kenneth Hechler, April 28, 1952, Elsey MSS; *NYT*, Aug. 4, 10, 1950; interview with Keyserling, Sept. 20, 1967.

31. Bowles to Burnet R. Maybank in *CR*, 81 Cong., 2 Sess., (Aug. 4, 1950), pp. 11825–26; ADA Mobilization Program, *ibid.*, pp. 11826–27; Humphrey in *ibid.* (Appendix), pp. A5647–49; ADA press release, July 27, 1950, ADA MSS; Helen Fuller, "How Much Mobilization Now?" *NR*, CXXIII (July 17, 1950), 10–11; "Mobilization Now Is the Price," *ibid.*, CXXIII (July 24, 1950), 5–6; EP, *N*, CLXXI (July 29, 1950), 97; EP, *ibid.*, CLXXI (Aug. 19, 1950), 157; "Washington Fiddles," *ibid.*, CLXXI (Aug. 26, 1950), 178–79.

32. *SLPD*, July 28, 1950; T.R.B., "Washington Wire," *NR*, CXXIII (July 31, 1950), 3.

33. Edward S. Flash, Jr., *Economic Advice and Presidential Leadership: The Council of Economic Advisers* (New York, 1965), pp. 43–44; *Public Papers, 1950*, pp. 561–64, 568–69, 589–90.

34. "Who Will Be the War Boss?" *NR*, CXXIII (Aug. 7, 1950), 6–7; EP, *N*, CLXXI (Sept. 9, 1950), 217; Willard Shelton, "Truman's New Team," *ibid.*, CLXXI (Sept. 23, 1950), 261–62; Elmer Davis, News commentary, Sept. 11, 1950, Davis MSS.

35. *NYP*, Oct. 10, 1950; Schlesinger in *ibid.*, Oct. 15, 1950; Flash, *Economic Advice and Presidential Leadership*, pp. 55–57.

36. *Public Papers, 1950,* pp. 580–81; Helen Fuller, "How to Pay for the War," *NR,* CXXIII (Aug. 28, 1950), 12–14; "Full of Loopholes," *ibid.,* CXXIII (Sept. 18, 1950), 7; "Money Deferred," *P,* XIV (Oct. 1950), 3.

37. "Galloping Inflation," *NR,* CXXIII (Oct. 2, 1950), 5–6; "The Conditions of Peace at Home," *ibid.,* CXXIII (Oct. 23, 1950), 6–7; Shelton, "Remobilization GHQ," *N,* CLXX (Nov. 11, 1950), 425–26; *NYT,* Sept. 29, Oct. 3, 23, 1950.

38. "Production: The Answer to Inflation," *NR,* CXXIII (Nov. 6, 1950), 5–6.

39. Shelton, "Notes From Capitol Hill," *N,* CLXXI (Aug. 26, 1950), 181–82; *SLPD,* Nov. 5, 1950; Arthur Schlesinger, Jr., in *NYP,* Nov. 5, 1950; Davis, News commentary, Nov. 7, 1950, Davis MSS.

40. Alsop in *SLPD,* Nov. 4, 1950; George Elsey, Memo to Charles Murphy, Oct. 30, 1950, Elsey MSS.

41. Lloyd, Memo to Charles Murphy, Sept. 28, 1950, Lloyd MSS; Hechler, Memoranda, Aug. 30, Oct. 24, Oct. 27, 1950, Elsey MSS.

42. *Public Papers, 1950,* pp. 697–703.

43. *Ibid.,* p. 713; HST to Aubrey Williams, Nov. 18, 1950, Williams MSS; Hechler, Memo on the 1950 elections, Nov. 15, 1950, Murphy MSS; Tyler, "The Mid-Term Paradox," *NR,* CXXIII (Nov. 27, 1950), 14–15. In much the same vein, see Daniel James, "Did the GOP Win?" *NL,* XXXIII (Nov. 20, 1950), 2–3; and Louis Hollander, "Labor Didn't Lose the Election," *ibid.,* XXXIV (Jan. 1, 1951), 18–19.

44. Hechler, Memo cited above, note 43; Matusow, *Farm Policies and Politics,* pp. 220–21; Thomas L. Stokes in the Washington *Evening Star,* Nov. 13, 1950; W. McNeil Lowry, "Frustration in the Corn Belt," *P,* XIV (Dec. 1950), 14–16; James Patton in *NUF,* Nov. 1950.

45. Hechler, Memo cited above, note 43; Davis, News commentary, Nov. 8, 1950, Davis MSS; T.R.B., "Washington Wire," *NR,* CXXIII (Nov. 20, 1950), 3–4; Ickes, "Fear Rides Herd," *ibid.,* p. 17. For comment in the same vein, see *NYP,* Nov. 8, 1950; Arthur Schlesinger, Jr., in *ibid.,* Nov. 12, 1950; Marquis Childs in *SLPD,* Nov. 10, 1950; "McCarthy Wins," *NR,* CXXIII (Nov. 20, 1950), 7; James Loeb, Jr., to David Williams, Nov. 13, 1950, ADA MSS; ADA press release, Nov. 8, 1950, *ibid.;* Richard Bolling to HST, Dec. 18, 1950, HST MSS, PPF 4379. The influence of McCarthyism is minimized in "The Meaning of the Month," *P,* XIV (Dec. 1950), 3–4; and "The Elections," *N,* CLXXI (Nov. 18, 1950), 451–52.

CHAPTER 19: THE DIPLOMACY OF STALEMATE

1. Kingdon in *NYP,* Dec. 8, 1950; *ibid.,* Dec. 11, 1950; *SLPD,* Dec. 4, 1950; Reinhold Niebuhr to the Editor, *NYT,* Dec. 23, 1950; Thomas L.

Stokes in the Washington *Evening Star,* Jan. 8, 1951; ADA press release, Dec. 10, 1950, ADA MSS.

For the *New Leader,* see "The World Situation," *NL,* XXXIII (Dec. 11, 1950), 30–31; "Peace Plan for Korea," *ibid.,* XXXIV (Feb. 19, 1951), 30; "Neither MacArthur Nor Truman," *ibid.,* XXXIV (April 16, 1951), 30–31; "For a New Far Eastern Policy," *ibid.,* XXXIV (April 23, 1951), 2–3, 30; Lewis Corey, "We Must Free All Korea," *ibid.,* XXXIV (June 18, 1951), 2–4, and "Containment Is Not Enough," *ibid.,* XXXIV (July 2, 1951), 18–20; David J. Dallin, "No Ceasefire At the 38th!" *ibid.,* XXXIV (June 25, 1951), 11; Christopher Emmet, "Appeasement in Korea," *ibid.,* XXXIV (Sept. 10, 1951), 2–4; "The Panmunjom Trap," *ibid.,* XXXV (Jan. 28, 1952), 30; William Henry Chamberlain, "Why Is Red China Untouchable?" *ibid.,* XXXV (March 24, 1952), 19; "How to Make a Truce," *ibid.,* XXXV (May 12, 1952), 30.

2. Thomas L. Stokes in the Washington *Evening Star,* June 25, 1951; *SLPD,* June 24, 1951; *NYP,* June 12, 1951; "Korea: Trial and Achievement," *NR,* CXXIV (June 25, 1951), 9–10. Compare, e.g., Elmer Davis, News commentaries, Nov. 21, 1950, and April 17, 1951, Davis MSS.

3. Acheson, *Present at the Creation,* pp. 517–20; Spanier, *Truman-MacArthur Controversy,* pp. 187–202; *Public Papers, 1951,* pp. 205–206; Paul Douglas, quoted in *NYT,* Jan. 29, 1951; *SLPD,* Jan. 31, 1951; Smith, "Equal Among Equals?" *N,* CLXXII (Feb. 3, 1951), 103–104; Freda Kirchwey, "After the U.N. Vote," *ibid.,* CLXXII (Feb. 10, 1951), 120–21; T.R.B. "Washington Wire," *NR,* CXXIV (Feb. 12, 1951), 3–4; *NYP,* March 26, 1951; Elmer Davis, News commentary, March 26, 1951, Davis MSS.

4. *Public Papers, 1951,* pp. 223–27; Freda Kirchwey, "Next Moves," *N,* CLXXII (April 21, 1951), 360–61; Lerner in *NYP,* April 11, 1951; *SLPD,* April 11, 12, 1951; *NYP,* April 11, 1951; Frank Kingdon in *ibid.,* April 13, 1951; Thomas L. Stokes in the Washington *Evening Star,* April 11, 1951; ADA press release (Francis Biddle to HST), April 11, 1951, ADA MSS; Eleanor Roosevelt to HST, April 12, 1951, HST MSS, OF 584.

5. *NYT,* Sept. 16, 1951; "The Communists Accept," *NR,* CXXV (July 9, 1951), 6.

6. Freda Kirchwey, "Liberation by Death," *N,* CLXXII (March 10, 1951), 215–16.

7. M.H.R. [Morris Rubin], "The Man Who Stayed Too Long," *P,* XV (March 1951), 3–4; "The Locked Door," *ibid.,* XV (July 1951), 3–4; "Has Acheson Surrendered?" *NR,* CXXIV (May 28, 1951), 5–6; Childs in *SLPD,* June 27, 1951.

8. "The Locked Door," *P,* XV (July 1951), 3–4; "Korea: Stop! Look! Listen," *N,* CLXXII (March 24, 1951), 264–65; Freda Kirchwey, "Peace: Rumor and Reality," *ibid.,* CLXXII (June 2, 1951), 505–506.

9. "The Locked Door," *P*, XV (July 1951), 3–4; Lattimore, "Korea: We Win a Round," *N*, CLXXIII (July 21, 1951), 44; Stokes in the Washington *Evening Star*, Jan. 31, 1951.

10. "The Chances for Peace in Korea," *NR*, CXXV (Oct. 22, 1951), 5. See also "Peace Without Appeasement," *ibid.*, CXXIII (Dec. 18, 1950), 5–8; "The Choice in Korea," *ibid.*, CXXIV (April 30, 1951), 5–6.

11. *SLPD*, Sept. 2, 1951; "ADA Convention," *NR*, CXXIV (March 5, 1951), 6.

12. T.R.B., "Washington Wire," *NR*, CXXVI (Feb. 4, 1951), 3–4; "Korea Kaleidoscope," *N*, CLXXIV (June 21, 1952), 595–96; *SLPD*, April 26, May 8, 1951.

13. *Ibid.*, June 24, 1952.

14. Freda Kirchwey, "Democracy's Way Out," *N*, CLXXI (Dec. 16, 1950), 622–25, 645; "Break and Freedom," *P*, XVI (June 1952), 3–4; "A Tragic Blunder: A Vital Program," *NR*, CXXIV (June 4, 1951), 5–6; T.R.B., "Washington Wire," *ibid.*, CXXVI (Feb. 4, 1952), 3–4; "Letter to the President—Subject: Point Four," *ibid.*, CXXVI (March 10, 1952), 6–7; "Rally for Point Four," *ibid.*, CXXVI (April 21, 1952), 6; *NYP*, Sept. 13, 1951; *NYT*, Jan. 26, 1952; ADA press release, Dec. 9, 1950, ADA MSS; Bowles, Memo to Clark Clifford, May 2, 1951, Murphy MSS.

15. "The Choice in Indo-China," *NR*, CXXIII (Oct. 30, 1950), 5; Griffin, "Must Indo-China Be Lost?" *ibid.*, CXXVI (March 31, 1952), 16–17; Shaplen, "Indo-China: the Eleventh Hour," *R*, V (Oct. 2, 1951), 6–10; *SLPD*, Jan. 12, 1952.

16. Willard Shelton, "Acheson Foils the Wolves," *N*, CLXXII (June 16, 1951), 553–54; Elsey, Memo to HST, March 28, 1951, Elsey MSS; Elsey. Memos to Theodore Tannenwald, April 30, May 25, June 5, 1951, *ibid.*; Elsey, Memos to Murphy, July 5, 6, 1951, *ibid.*; Lloyd, Memo, June 9, 1951, *ibid.*; HST, Memos to Secretary of the Treasury, Attorney General, and Collector of Internal Revenue, all dated June 11, 1951, *ibid.* The *Reporter* exposé appeared in a series of articles in *R*, VI (April 15, 29, 1952), 2–24, 4–24.

17. Carr and Niebuhr, Letters to the Editor, *N*, CLXXI (Nov. 11, 1950), 447; "Has Acheson Surrendered?" *NR*, CXXIV (May 28, 1951), 5–6; Niebuhr, "The Two Dimensions of the Struggle," *Christianity and Crisis*, XI (May 28, 1951), 65–66.

18. Eleanor Roosevelt to HST, Feb. 28, 1951 (partial copy of Robert Hamlisch to Eleanor Roosevelt attached) and HST to Eleanor Roosevelt, March 7, 1951, HST MSS, PPF 460.

19. *Public Papers, 1950*, pp. 569–70, 594, 616, 680, 697, 712, 762; *Public Papers, 1952*, pp. 141, 144; Acheson, *Present at the Creation*, p. 169; *SLPD*, Aug. 3, 4, 1950; *NYT*, July 18, 1951; T.R.B., "Washington Wire," *NR*, CXXIII (Aug. 14, 1950), 3–4; "Making Friends with Franco," *ibid.*,

CXXV (July 30, 1951), 6–7; Ickes, "McCarran Holds Another Prisoner," *ibid.*, CXXV (Aug. 13, 1951), 17; Willard Shelton, "The Surrender to Franco," *N*, CLXXI (Aug. 12, 1950), 141–42; Alexander Uhl, "Franco at the Front Door," *ibid.*, CLXXIII (July 28, 1951), 70–72; EP, *ibid.*, CLXXIV (Jan. 12, 1952), 21; Ascoli, "Rules of Thumb for Foreign Aid," *R*, III (Aug. 29, 1950), 4–5; Theodore Draper, "Franco: A Dependable Ally?" *ibid.*, V (Aug. 21, 1951), 7–10; Violet Gunther to James Loeb, Jr., Aug. 4, 1950, ADA MSS; ADA press release [Joseph L. Rauh, Jr., to Scott Lucas, incorrectly dated "1950, June"], *ibid.*; Stephen J. Spingarn, Memo for the record, Aug. 2, 1950, Spingarn MSS.

20. Schlesinger in *NYP*, Sept. 10, 1950; Lerner in *ibid.*, Sept. 12, 1950; *ibid.*, Feb. 9, 1951; Hans Simons, "If Germany Is Unchecked . . ." *R*, V (Dec. 11, 1951), 9–11; EP, *N*, CLXXII (Feb. 10, 1951), 117–18; Freda Kirchwey, "The Issue Is Germany," *N*, CLXXIII (Sept. 22, 1951), 224–25; Davis, News commentary, Feb. 15, 1951, Davis MSS.

21. Ascoli, "The Bitter Lesson of Retreat," *R*, III (Dec. 26, 1950), 3–5; Arthur Schlesinger, Jr., in *NYP*, Dec. 24, 1950.

22. Rubin, "The Meaning of the Month," *P*, XIV (Dec. 1950), 3–4.

23. *Public Papers, 1950*, pp. 683–87; Elsey, Memo on HST's speech to the U.N., Nov. 10, 1950, Elsey MSS.

24. *Public Papers, 1951*, pp. 377, 455–56, 475–77; "Russia's 'Peace Offensive,'" *NR*, CXXV (Aug. 20, 1951), 6; "Who's Trapping Whom?" *P*, XV (Sept. 1951), 3–4; *SLPD*, Aug. 22, 1951; Freda Kirchwey, "Proof of the Pudding," *N*, CLXXIII (Aug. 18, 1951), 122–23.

25. *Public Papers, 1951*, pp. 623–27; Acheson, *Present at the Creation*, pp. 576–83; "Sham Battle for Peace," *NR*, CXXV (Nov. 19, 1951), 5–6; "Disarmament: How to Get Off Dead Center," *ibid.*, CXXV (Dec. 3, 1951), 5; Stokes in the Washington *Evening Star*, Oct. 5, 1951; *SLPD*, Nov. 12, 1951; David Lloyd, Memo to Charles Murphy, Oct. 4, 1951, Elsey MSS; ADA press release, Nov. 8, 1951, ADA MSS.

26. Ickes, "Diplomacy with an Ax," *NR*, CXXV (Dec. 3, 1951), 17; *Public Papers, 1951*, pp. 370–74; *Public Papers, 1952*, pp. 178–79. See also Elsey, Memo on May 17 speech, May 29, 1951, Elsey MSS.

27. "Disarmament: How to Get Off Dead Center," *NR*, CXXV (Dec. 3, 1951), 5; *SLPD*, Nov. 24, 1951; Rubin, "A Time for Greatness," *P*, XV (Dec., 1951), 5–8.

28. Freda Kirchwey, "A Time to Bargain," *N*, CLXXIV (May 3, 1952), 416–17; *NYP*, March 26, 1952; *SLPD*, May 2, 1952; "The Month in Foreign Affairs," *P*, XVI (May, 1952), 4.

29. Acheson, *Present at the Creation*, pp. 647, 650.

30. See, e.g., Max Lerner in *NYP*, Jan. 3, 1952, and James R. Newman, "The Case for Acheson: A Deferential and Discreet Defense," *NR*, CXXVI (Feb. 25, 1952), 17–18.

CHAPTER 20: POLITICAL PITFALLS, THE POLITICAL
ECONOMY OF MOBILIZATION

1. Davis, News commentary, Jan. 3, 1951; Childs, *SLPD*, Jan. 5, 1951; "Domestic Retreat," *P*, XV (Feb. 1951), 3–4; John Gunther, Memo to Mary Alice Baldinger, Jan. 17, 1951, ADA MSS.

2. Shelton, "The 'Do-less' 82d," *N*, CLXXII (Jan. 6, 1951), 5–6; Cater, "The New Congress: Where Are the Leaders?" *R*, IV (Feb. 6, 1951), 25–27; *SLPD*, Dec. 19, 1950; Violet Gunther to Monroe Sweetland, Dec. 19, 1950, ADA MSS; John Gunther, Memo to Francis Biddle on Jan. 16th Dinner Meeting with Senators, n.d., *ibid.;* Evans and Novak, *Lyndon B. Johnson*, pp. 41–43; *Public Papers, 1951*, pp. 6–13, 18, 22; *NYT*, Feb. 5, 1951.

3. Marquis Childs in *SLPD*, May 2, 1951; *ibid.*, July 20, 22, 1951; Douglass Cater, "A Parliamentarian, a Hatchet Man, an Inquisitor," *R*, IV (June 12, 1951), 31–32; Willard Shelton, "Presidential Appointments;" *N*, CLXXIV (Feb. 16, 1952), 149; "Costly Alliance," *P*, XV (Dec. 1951), 3; *Public Papers, 1951*, p. 402.

4. Biddle to HST, May 22, 1951, ADA MSS; Biddle to Emil Rieve, June 14, 1951, *ibid.; Public Papers, 1951*, pp. 500–503; Thomas L. Stokes in the Washington *Evening Star*, Jan. 15, 1951.

5. David Stowe, Memo to HST, April 24, 1951, Murphy MSS; Stowe, Memo to Charles Murphy, May 28, 1951, Elsey MSS; Stowe, Memo to HST, Oct. 12, 1951, and HST, Memo to Stowe, Oct. 15, 1951, Stowe Files, HST MSS; "Mr. Truman Versus A.M.A.," *N*, CLXXIV (Jan. 12, 1952), 24–25; Poen, "The Truman Administration and National Health Insurance," pp. 214–19; *Public Papers, 1951*, pp. 655–56; *Public Papers, 1952–53*, pp. 3–4.

6. *Public Papers, 1951*, pp. 11, 590–91; *Public Papers, 1952–53*, p. 16; For the commission plan, see the several memoranda in the "Taft-Hartley—1952" File, David Stowe MSS, HSTL.

7. Davies, *Housing Reform*, pp. 130–32.

8. Dalfiume, *Desegregation of the U.S. Armed Forces*, ch. 10; *Public Papers, 1951*, 616–17.

9. Herbert Garfinkle, *When Negroes March* (New York, 1969), pp. 176–77; *Public Papers, 1951*, pp. 640–41; *NYT*, July 18, 1950, Dec. 4, 1951; National Council for a Permanent FEPC press release, July 10 [1950], ADA MSS; ADA press release, Dec. 3, 1951, *ibid.;* Clarence Mitchell, Memo to Walter White, Dec. 8, 1950, *ibid.;* Walter White to Charles La Follette, April 20, 1951, *ibid.;* Violet Gunther, Memo to Reginald Zalles, n.d. [early Nov. 1951], *ibid.;* John F. P. Tucker to Francis Biddle, Aug. 16, 1951, *ibid.;* Fred Lawton, Memo for the record, Feb. 1, 1951, Lawton

MSS, HSTL; Charles Murphy, Memo to HST, Dec. 1, 1951, HST MSS, OF 40; Patrick Murphy Malin, et al., to HST, June 24, 1951, *ibid.*, OF 40 Misc.; "FEPC for Defense," *NR*, CXXV (Dec. 17, 1951), 6.

10. *SLPD*, Nov. 29, Dec. 9, 1950; Elmer Davis, News commentary, Dec. 8, 1950; ADA press release, Dec. 3, 1950, ADA MSS; Willard Shelton, "Dream's End," *N*, CLXXI (Dec. 23, 1950), 669–70; Charles E. Noyes, "Taxes Versus Controls," *ibid.*, CLXXII (Jan. 13, 1951), 28–30; "81st Congress—The Last Mile," *NR*, CXXIII (Nov. 27, 1950), 5–6; "Inflation Can Be Stopped," *ibid.*, CXXIV (Jan. 29, 1951), 5–6.

11. *Public Papers, 1950*, pp. 744–45; *SLPD*, Jan. 14, 28, 1951; EP, *N*, CLXXII (Jan. 27, 1951), 69; "Inflation Can Be Stopped," *NR*, CXXIV (Jan. 29, 1951), 5–6; Chester Bowles, "To Stop Inflation," *NYT Magazine*, Jan. 28, 1951, pp. 8, 34–35.

12. Flash, *Economic Advice and Presidential Leadership*, pp. 69–76; *NYT*, Nov. 30, Dec. 11, 12, 1950, May 10, 1951; Keyserling, Speech to ADA conference, May 18, 1951, ADA MSS; Keyserling interview; Harold Enarson, Memo to David Stowe, April 11, 1951, Enarson Papers, HSTL.

13. Landsberg, "Who Pays for Mobilization?" *R*, IV (March 20, 1951), 6–8; Galbraith, "The Taxonomy of Inflation Control," *ibid.*, V (July 10, 1951), 9–11; Shelton, "Confusion on the Potomac," *N*, CLXXII (May 26, 1951), 486–87; *SLPD*, Dec. 12, 1951; Bowles, public letter to Paul Douglas, May 31, 1951, copy attached to Bowles to Charles Murphy, June 6, 1951, HST MSS, Murphy files.

14. "Mobilizing Short of War," *NR*, CXXIII (Dec. 25, 1950), 5–6; "Labor's Break with Truman," *ibid.*, CXXII (March 12, 1951), 5–6; "Masters of Defense," *ibid.*, CXXIV (April 16, 1951), 11; "Senator Truman was Right," *ibid.*, p. 25; T.R.B., "Washington Wire," *ibid.*, CXXIV (Feb. 26, 1951), 3–4; "The Squeeze on Labor," *N*, CLXXII (Feb. 24, 1951), 166–67; Willard Shelton, "Wilson's One-Man War," *ibid.*, CLXXII (March 3, 1951), 197–98; Claire Neikind, "Labor Declares Wilson the Aggressor," *R*, IV (April 3, 1951), 32–34, and "Change in Charley," *ibid.*, V (Aug. 7, 1951), 12–13; *SLPD*, Dec. 16, 1950, Feb. 26, March 1, 2, 1951; Kempton in *NYP*, Feb. 19, 1951; *ibid.*, March 1, 2, 1951; *NYT*, March 12, April 2, 1951; Elmer Davis, News commentary, Feb. 16, 1951, Davis MSS; Richard Neustadt, Memo to Charles Murphy, Feb. 16, 1951, Elsey MSS; Andrew Biemiller, Memo to Oscar Chapman, March 26, 1951, Chapman MSS; *NUF*, March, April, 1951.

15. Schlesinger in *NYP*, Feb. 11, 1951; *ibid.*, Feb. 22, 1951; "It's Serious, Mr. President," *NR*, CXXIV (April 2, 1951), 5–6.

16. Arthur Viner, "What Happened to Inflation?" *R*, VI (April 15, 1952), 32–34; *Statistical Abstract of the United States, 1953* (Washington, 1953), p. 307.

17. Stokes in the Washington *Evening Star*, April 4, 1951; ADA press release, April 16, 1951, ADA MSS; Chester Bowles, Public letter to Paul

Douglas, May 31, 1951, attached to Bowles to Charles Murphy, June 6, 1951, HST MSS, Murphy files; "Are We Licking Inflation?" *NR*, CXXIV (April 30, 1951), 6; *SLPD*, June 12, 1951.

18. *Public Papers, 1951*, pp. 244–53, 320–21, 333–38, 364, 369; Richard Neustadt, Memo to Charles Murphy, April 16, 1951, HST MSS, Murphy files; Chester Bowles, Memo to Clark Clifford, May 2, 1951, Murphy MSS; Kenneth Hechler, Memo to John Carroll, June 7, 1951, Elsey MSS; "The End of Price Control?" *NR*, CXXIV (June 11, 1951), 5–6.

19. *Public Papers, 1951*, pp. 435–37, 478–83; "Convertible Mobilization," *R*, V (July 10, 1951), 5; *SLPD*, June 25, July 31, 1951; Marquis Childs in *ibid.*, July 6, 1951; Elmer Davis, News commentary, July 6, 1951, Davis MSS; "The Great Gold Rush of 1951," *NR*, CXXV (July 23, 1951), 5; "Congress Will Decide," *ibid.*, CXXV (July 30, 1951), 5–6; "Guaranteed: Profits and Deprivations," *ibid.*, CXXV (Aug. 13, 1951), 5; "Defense with Inflation," *N*, CLXXIII (Aug. 11, 1951), 104; Thomas L. Stokes in the Washington *Evening Star*, June 13, Sept. 24, 1951.

20. "Neglected Instrument," *P*, XV (Nov. 1951), 3–4; Arthur A. Elder, "The Great Tax Fraud," *NL*, XXXIV (Nov. 26, 1951), 2–4, (Dec. 3, 1951), 8–10, (Dec. 10, 1951), 8–10; *Public Papers, 1951*, p. 590.

21. Flash, *Economic Advice and Presidential Leadership*, pp. 85–99; "The Human Costs of Leadership," *NR*, CXXVI (Jan. 14, 1952), 14–16; Harry Cohn, "How Mobilization Failed," *ibid.*, CXXVI (April 14, 1952), 13–15; Matthew K. Amberg, "The Raid on Price Controls," *ibid.*, CXXVI (June 2, 1952), 10–12; EP, *N*, CLXXIV (Jan. 26, 1952), 69; "Easy Credit for Consumers," *N*, CLXXIV (May 17, 1952), 463; John Gunther, Congressional testimony, May 6, 1952, ADA MSS.

22. *Public Papers, 1952–53*, p. 1179; *Statistical Abstract of the United States, 1953*, p. 786.

23. For accounts of the steel controversy, see Grant McConnell, *The Steel Seizure of 1952* (University, Alabama, 1960); HST, *Memoirs, II*, 465–78; Sawyer, *Concerns of a Conservative Democrat*, pp. 255–77; Richard E. Neustadt, *Presidential Power: The Politics of Leadership* (New York, 1960), pp. 13–16, 21–25, 28–29, 31.

24. Enarson, Memo to Steelman, Jan. 9, 1952, David Stowe MSS; Enarson, Memo to Stowe and Murphy, Jan. 30, 1952, *ibid.*

25. Willard Shelton, "Fair Offer on Steel," *N*, CLXXIV (March 29, 1952), 293–94; "The Wilson Fiasco," *ibid.*, CLXXIV (April 5, 1952), 311–12; "Wilson: A Failure Bows Out," *NR*, CXXVI (April 7, 1952), 6–7; *SLPD*, March 21, April 1, 1952; Marquis Childs in *ibid.*, April 3, 1952; ADA press release, April 1, 1952, ADA MSS; *Public Papers, 1952–53*, pp. 226–27; Council of Economic Advisers, Memo to HST, March 28, 1952, Stowe MSS; Harold Enarson, "Analysis of Report and Recommendations of Wage Stabilization Board in the Steel Case," March 27, 1952, *ibid.*

26. *Public Papers, 1952–53*, pp. 246–50.

27. *NYP*, April 10, 1952; Lerner in *ibid.;* Stokes in the Washington *Evening Star*, April 28, 1952; "Steel: What Next, Mr. President?" *NR*, CXXVI (April 21, 1952), 5; Davis, News commentaries, April 10, 22, 29, 1952, Davis MSS.

28. "The President and Il Duce," *R*, VI (June 10, 1952), 6–7; "Steel Seizure—Threat Against Labor," *N*, CLXXIV (May 10, 1952), 443–44; "Congress, the Court, and the Country," *P*, XVI (July 1952), 3; *SLPD*, April 13, May 4, June 11, 1952; Marquis Childs in *ibid.*, May 27, June 10, 1952; *Public Papers, 1952–53*, pp. 410–14.

29. Sawyer, *Concerns of a Conservative Democrat*, p. 272; HST, *Memoirs, II*, p. 477; Conn, "Steel and the Price of Peace," *NR*, CXXVII (July 28, 1952), 8–9; Harold Enarson, Memo to John Steelman, June 24, 1952, Stowe MSS.

CHAPTER 21: POLITICAL PITFALLS,
CORRUPTION AND COMMUNISM

1. Lilienthal, *The Journals of David E. Lilienthal: The Venturesome Years, 1950–1955* (New York, 1966), p. 41 [hereafter Journals, III]; *CST*, Sept. 7, 1950; Elmer Davis, News commentary, Dec. 12, 1950. For the Marine episode, see George Elsey, Memo for the files, Sept. 1950, Elsey MSS; and *Public Papers, 1950*, pp. 617–19.

2. "Truman Is to Blame," *NR*, CXXIV (March 26, 1951), 5–6; Marquis Childs in *SLPD*, Feb. 8, 1951; James Loeb, Jr., to Harold Ickes, Feb. 7, 1951, ADA MSS. The corruption issue is surveyed in Phillips, *Truman Presidency*, pp. 402–14, and in Jules Abels, *The Truman Scandals* (Chicago, 1956).

3. Stokes in the *Washington Evening Star*, Nov. 2, 1951; Childs, " 'How Ethical Can You Get?' " *R*, V (Aug. 21, 1951), 22–25; W. McNeil Lowry, "Ethics and Cost-Plus," *P*, XV (Sept. 1951), 6–8.

4. *Public Papers, 1951*, pp. 144–46, 158–60, 175, 191–92, 454–58, 530–31, 540–42, 564–67, 587, 631, 639; Elmer Davis, News commentaries, Feb. 8, March 7, 15, May 10, June 25, 1951, Davis MSS; T.R.B., "Washington Wire," *NR*, CXXIV (May 21, 1951), 3–4; Arthur Schlesinger, Jr. in *NYP*, Nov. 4, 1951.

5. Stokes in the Washington *Evening Star*, March 7, 1951; *SLPD*, April 8, July 28, Sept. 16, 21, 1951; Marquis Childs in *ibid.*, Sept. 25, 1951; "Mr. Truman and the Collectors," *N*, CLXXIII (Oct. 27, 1951), 341–42; "Corruption and the Truman Campaign," *NR*, CXXV (Sept. 24, 1951), 5; *NYP*, Oct. 15, 1951; ADA press releases, Aug. 4, Oct. 6, 1951, ADA MSS.

6. *SLPD*, Oct. 18, 28, 1951; "Boyle Bows Out," *NR*, CXXV (Oct. 22, 1951), 6; "The Democrats—Cancer and Cure?" *ibid.*, CXXV (Dec. 10,

1951), 5; "Use a Broom, Mr. Truman!" *N,* CLXXIII (Dec. 8, 1951), 491–92; Elmer Davis, News commentary, Dec. 6, 1951, Davis MSS; Biddle to HST, Nov. 30, 1951, Clifford MSS; ADA press release, Nov. 27, 1951, ADA MSS.

7. *SLPD,* Dec. 17, 22, 1951, Jan. 30, 1952; Marquis Childs in *ibid.,* April 8, 1952; Harold Ickes, "Surgeon's Knife or Soothing Syrup," *NR,* CXXV (Dec. 31, 1951), 17; EP, *N,* CLXXIV (Jan. 26, 1952), 50; *Public Papers, 1952–53,* pp. 4, 20–21; Arthur Krock, *Memoirs: Sixty Years on the Firing Line* (Popular Library ed.; New York, 1968), pp. 242–45; A. Robert Smith, *The Tiger in the Senate: The Biography of Wayne Morse* (Garden City, N.Y., 1962), pp. 132–34; Richard E. Neustadt, "Notes on the White House Staff Under President Truman" (mimeographed paper; copy at HSTL), p. 23; Elsey, Memo to Clark Clifford, Dec. 12, 1951, Clifford MSS; Elsey, Confidential memo to HST, Aug. 2, 1951, Elsey MSS; Rosenman, Oral History Memoir, pp. 35–37, HSTL; Joseph Davies, Diary, Dec. 19, 1951, Davies MSS.

8. *SLPD,* Jan. 11, Feb. 2, 1952; ADA press release, Jan. 11, 1952, ADA MSS; Richard H. Rovere, *The American Establishment and Other Reports, Opinions, and Speculations* (New York, 1962), pp. 85–112; HST, Memo to Murphy, c. Aug. 24, 1951, Murphy MSS; Murphy, Memo to HST, April 1, 1952, *ibid.;* Hillman, *Mr. President,* pp. 61–62. Harold Seidman, Oral History, pp. 26–37, HSTL, emphasizes Morris's shortcomings as an investigator.

9. "Firing the Villain," *NR,* CXXVI (April 14, 1952), 6; "Morris, McGrath, and Hoover," *N,* CLXXIV (April 12, 1952), 338–40; "Government by McCarran," *ibid.,* CLXXIV (May 31, 1952), 509; *NYP,* April 4, 13, 1952; Thomas L. Stokes in the Washington *Evening Star,* April 7, 1952; *SLPD,* April 4, 5, Aug. 10, Sept. 13, 1952; Stephen A. Mitchell, Memo to Harry Barnard, March 21, 1955, Mitchell MSS, HSTL; *Public Papers, 1952–53,* pp. 251–58, 310–15.

10. *SLPD,* Feb. 18, Aug. 24, 1951; Elmer Davis, News commentaries, April 27, June 14, 1951, Davis MSS; Max Lerner in *NYP,* Aug. 8, 1951; "Expel McCarthy," *NR,* CXXV (Aug. 20, 1951), 5–6; "Attacking an Abuse," *P,* XV (Nov. 1951), 4; W. McNeil Lowry, "Ebbing Tide for McCarthy," *ibid.,* pp. 12–15; *NYT,* April 22, 1952.

11. Childs in *SLPD,* Feb. 1, 1951; Biddle, *The Fear of Freedom* (Garden City, N.Y., 1952).

12. Frank Logue, "Retreat from Freedom," *P,* XV (May 1951), 17–18; Fred Rodell, "Black and Douglas Affirming," *ibid.,* XV (Nov. 1951), 9–11; "What the Court Has Destroyed," *NR,* CXXIV (June 18, 1951), 5–6; "Communism and the Court," *ibid.,* p. 7; Gressman, "The Tragedy of the Supreme Court," *ibid.,* CXXV (Sept. 3, 1951), 10–13; "The Outlawing of Academic Freedom," *ibid.,* CXXVI (March 17, 1952), 5; "Strait-Jacketing Free Speech," *N,* CLXXII (June 16, 1951), 552–53; Freda Kirchwey,

"Communism in the Schools," *ibid.,* CLXXIV (March 15, 1952), 243–44; *SLPD,* June 5, 1951; Lerner in *NYP,* June 6, 1951.

13. Francis Biddle to HST, Dec. 5, 1950, ADA MSS; Benjamin Kaplan to Murphy, Nov. 9, 1950, Murphy MSS; Max Kampleman to Murphy, Nov. 20, 1950, *ibid.;* Murphy, Memo to HST, Nov. 15, 1950, HST MSS, Murphy files; *Public Papers, 1951,* pp. 119–21, 152–53.

14. Francis Biddle to HST, Jan. 24, 1951, ADA MSS; Elmer Davis, News commentaries, Jan. 24, May 14, 1951, Davis MSS; A. Philip Randolph to HST, Jan. 24, 1951, HST MSS, OF 2750-A, Misc.; Patrick Murphy Malin, ACLU, to HST, Jan. 24, 1951, *ibid.; SLPD,* Jan. 25, 27, 1951; "Mr. Truman Dallies with Evil," *P,* XVI (Jan. 1952), 3–4; Harper, *Politics of Loyalty,* ch. 8.

15. Athan Theoharis, "The Escalation of the Loyalty Program," in Bernstein, *Politics and Policies of the Truman Administration,* pp. 258–59; EP, *N,* CLXXIII (Dec. 22, 1951), 537; Barth, "The Age of Doubt," *P,* XVI (Feb. 1952), 6–8.

16. Francis Biddle to HST, May 22, 1951, and attached memo, HST MSS, OF 2750-A; HST, Memo to Murphy, May 24, 1951, *ibid.;* HST, Memo to the Attorney General, July 5, 1952, Murphy MSS.

17. *Public Papers, 1951,* pp. 433, 462–63; *Public Papers, 1952–53,* pp. 314–15.

18. Thomas L. Stokes in the Washington *Evening Star,* Aug. 31, 1951; "This Terrible Business," *N,* CLXXIII (Aug. 25, 1951), 142–43; " 'Loyalty' and Human Freedom," *NR,* CXXVI (April 14, 1952), 5–6; "Midsummer-Night Madness," *ibid.,* CXXVI (June 30, 1952), 5; Joseph Rauh, Jr., to George C. Marshall, Sept. 7, 1951, ADA MSS; *SLPD,* June 30, 1952.

19. Ascoli, "The American Politboro," *R,* V (July 10, 1951), 4–5.

20. Arthur Schlesinger, Jr., to James Loeb, Jr., June 7, 1951; Biddle to Jim [Loeb?], June 11, 1951; Loeb to ADA Board, June 12, 1951; Schlesinger, Jr., Memo to Rauh and Wechsler, June 22, 1951; Bowles to Loeb, June 28, 1951; Biddle to Jo [Rauh?], June 30, 1951; Biddle to ADA board, July 17, 1951; ADA press release, Dec. 14, 1951—all in ADA MSS.

21. Hicks, "The Liberals Who Haven't Learned," *Commentary,* XI (April 1951), 319–29; Irving Kristol to Hicks, Jan. 31, 1951, Hicks MSS; Hicks to Kristol, Feb. 4, 1951, *ibid.;* Kristol to Hicks, March 2, 1951, *ibid.*

22. Freda Kirchwey to the Editors, *Commentary,* XI (May 1951), 495–97; Hook to Short, May 10, 1951, HST MSS, PPF 5540; Short to Kirchwey, May 19, 1951, *ibid.;* Kirchwey to Short, May 22, 1951, *ibid.* See also Kirchwey, "The Cohorts of Fear," *N,* CLXXII (April 14, 1951), 339–41.

23. "The *Nation* Censors a Letter of Criticism," *NL,* XXXIV (March 19, 1951), 16–18; "The *Nation* Sues Us," *ibid.,* XXXIV (April 2, 1951), 2; Rovere to the Editor, *ibid.,* XXXIV (April 9, 1951), 27; Schlesinger to Freda Kirchwey, March 26, 1951, in *ibid.,* XXXIV (April 30, 1951), 27; Lewis Corey to the Editor, *ibid.,* XXXIV (May 14, 1951), 28; Daniel

James, "The Liberalism of Suicide," *ibid.*, XXXIV (Aug. 27, 1951), 14–17; Rovere, "How Free Is the *Nation?*" *ibid.*, XXXV (July 14, 1952), 12–14; "The 'Nation's' Fear," *ibid.*, 22–23; "Why *The Nation* Sued," *N*, CLXXII (June 2, 1951), 504–505; *SLPD*, Aug. 26, Sept. 22, 1951; Reinhold Niebuhr to Freda Kirchwey, April 26, 1951, and Evans Clark to Niebuhr, May 23, 1951, Niebuhr MSS.

24. Hicks, "Owen Lattimore and Louis Budenz," *NL*, XXXIII (May 6, 1950), 15; Dallin, "Writings of Owen Lattimore Reflect Pro-Soviet Views," *ibid.*, XXXIII (May 13, 1950), 11; Lyons, "Lattimore: Dreyfus or Hiss?" *ibid.*, XXXIII (Sept. 2, 1950), 16–19; Chamberlain, "Owen Lattimore— On the Record," *ibid.*, XXXV (March 17, 1952), 21, and "Conclusive Verdict on the IPR," *ibid.*, XXXV (July 28, 1952), 14; "Lattimore: Whose Ordeal?" *ibid.*, XXXV (March 17, 1952), 30–31; "Lattimore and the IPR," *ibid.*, XXXV (March 31, 1952), S1–S16; Hook, "Lattimore on the Moscow Trials," *ibid.*, XXXV (Nov. 10, 1952), 16–19; "The LitAgs," *ibid.*, XXXV (July 21, 1952), 30–31.

25. Muhlen, "The Hysteria of the Hisslings," *ibid.*, XXXIII (May 13, 1950), 16–18, and "The Phantom of McCarthyism," *ibid.*, XXXIV (May 21, 1951), 16–18; "A Loss for McCarthy," *ibid.*, XXXIV (Dec. 24, 1951), 30–31.

26. Ross, "Is It Hysteria?" *ibid.*, XXXV (Feb. 11, 1952), 16–17; Dawidowicz, "Liberals and the CP Line on McCarthyism," *ibid.*, XXXV (April 21, 1952), 16–18; Trilling, "Mr. Russell, Communism and Civil Liberties," *ibid.*, XXXV (April 28, 1952), 16–18; Rovere, "How Free Is the *Nation?*" *ibid.*, XXXV (July 14, 1952), 12–14; "The 'Nation's' Fear," *ibid.*, XXXV (July 14, 1952), 22–23. In an even less temperate vein, see J. C. Rich, "Justice Douglas and His 'Black Silence of Fear,'" *ibid.*, XXXV (March 17, 1952), 12–13, and Merlyn S. Pitzele's exchange with Merle Miller, "Is 'The Judges and the Judged' an Honest Book?" *ibid.*, XXXV (June 16, 1952), 12–18.

27. Kristol, "'Civil Liberties,' 1952—A Study in Confusion," *Commentary*, XIII (March 1952), 228–36.

28. Davis and Hicks, "Lattimore and the Liberals," *NL*, XXXIII (May 27, 1950), 16–18; Hicks, "Is McCarthyism a Phantom?" *ibid.*, XXXIV (June 4, 1951), 7; Leuchtenburg, "Liberals Must Again Learn to Kindle Men's Souls," *ibid.*, XXXV (May 12, 1952), 18–19; Westin, "Our Freedom and the Rights of Communists," *Commentary*, XIV (July 1952), 33–40; "Letters from Readers," *ibid.*, XIII (May 1952), 491–500, and *ibid.*, XIV (July 1952), 83–86.

CHAPTER 22: LAST HURRAHS AND NEW TOMORROWS

1. Eisenhower, *Mandate for Change*, pp. 45–46; Krock, *Memoirs*, 252–54; Phillips, *Truman Presidency*, pp. 414–19; HST, *Memoirs*, II,

488–92; HST to Harriman, Nov. 30, 1951, HST MSS, PPF 1191; Gerald Johnson to HST, April 1, 1952, *ibid.*, PPF 65-F (Pro); *SLPD*, March 12, 1952.

2. HST, *Memoirs, II,* 493–94; Loeb interview; Clifford to HST, March 15, 1952, Clifford MSS; interview with Harriman, July 20, 1971.

3. *Public Papers, 1952–53,* pp. 319–21, 331–34, 341–47, 374–78, 419–24, 456–61; *NYT,* May 18, 1952; Joseph and Stewart Alsop in *SLPD,* May 23, 1952; Jim Lanigan, Memo to Charles Murphy, Nov. 26, 1951, HST MSS, Lloyd files; HST to Eleanor Roosevelt, June 20, 1952, *ibid.*, PPF 460; Patton to HST, May 19, 1952, *ibid.*, OF 56-F; HST to Biddle, May 22, 1952, *ibid.*, PPF 4752; T.R.B., "Washington Wire," *NR,* CXXVI (May 26, 1952), 3–4.

4. *Public Papers, 1951–53,* pp. 379–84, 441–47; Hyman, *William Benton,* pp. 472–73; David Lloyd, Memo to HST, May 3, 1952, HST MSS, Lloyd files; Oscar Ewing, Memo to HST, June 23, 1952, *ibid.;* "No More Melting Pot," *NR,* CXXVII (July 7, 1952), 8; *NYP,* June 26, 1952.

5. Lilienthal, *Journals,* III, 305; *Public Papers, 1952–53,* p. 174; "President Truman Should Withdraw," *NR,* CXXVI (Feb. 4, 1952), 5; "The Pressures on the President," *ibid.,* CXXVI (March 24, 1952), 5; John P. Mallan, "New Hampshire Reviewed," *N,* CLXXIV (March 22, 1952), 267–69; Max Lerner in *NYP,* March 13, 1952; Frank Kingdon in *ibid.,* March 14, 1952; Arthur Schlesinger, Jr., in *ibid.,* March 16, 1952; Stokes in the Washington *Evening Star,* March 31, 1952.

6. Harry Barnard to Stephen A. Mitchell, Jan. 4, 1951 and March 12, 1951, Mitchell MSS; Aubrey Williams to Barnard, March 22, 1952, Williams MSS; "Justice Douglas *Is* Available," *N,* CLXXIV (Jan. 26, 1952), 73; "Our Readers Prefer Douglas," *ibid.,* CLXXIV (May 10, 1952), 444–45; "First Choice," *P,* XVI (April 1952), 3; Richard L. Neuberger, "Northwest Revives Boom for Douglas," *ibid.,* pp. 29–30.

7. Elmer Davis, News commentaries, April 18, 22, 1952, Davis MSS; Marquis Childs in *SLPD,* May 22, 1952; Harriman interview.

8. David Lilienthal, *Journals,* III, 361; "Rip Tide for the Democrats," *NR,* CXXVI (April 28, 1952), 5; T.R.B., "Washington Wire," *ibid.,* CXXVI (May 5, 1952), 3; Marquis Childs in *SLPD,* Jan. 28, May 12, 1952; Doris Fleeson in *ibid.,* May 15, 1952; Thomas L. Stokes in the Washington *Evening Star,* March 14, 1952; Max Lerner in *NYP,* March 13, 1952.

9. Robert Lasch, "Stevenson's First Year," *R,* I (Aug. 30, 1949), 23–25; Childs in *SLPD,* July 24, 1951; Schlesinger in *NYP,* Nov. 4, 1951, Jan. 20, 1952; *ibid.,* March 31, 1952; *NYT,* May 17, 1952; Jonathan Daniels, Oral History Memoir, p. 95, HSTL. For the ADA effort, see Rauh to Schlesinger, Jan. 7, 1952; Schlesinger, Memo to Stevenson Strategy Board, n.d.; Violet Gunther to Stevenson, Feb. 2, 1952; Violet Gunther to Mrs. Robert Sorenson, Feb. 8, 1952; Monroe Sweetland to Richard Nelson, March 11, 1952; Niebuhr to Biddle, April 9, 1952; Violet Gunther to Monroe Sweetland, Jan. 9, 1952; Violet Gunther to Schlesinger, Jan. 30, 1952; Violet

Gunther to Robert Trentlyon, Feb. 19, 1952; Reginald Zalles to chapter chairmen, Feb. 25, 1952; Zalles to Mary A. Bachelder, June 23, 1952—all in ADA MSS. Walter Johnson, *How We Drafted Adlai Stevenson* (New York, 1955), overstresses the importance of the Illinois committee and shows no awareness of the ADA behind-the-scenes interest.

10. ADA press releases, March 31, May 18, 1952; Biddle to Dever, May 27, 1952; Biddle to Stevenson, May 29, 1952, and similar letters to others; Violet Gunther to Monroe Sweetland, June 10, 1952; Violet Gunther to Biddle, June 24, 1952—all in ADA MSS. See also *NYT*, July 5, 17, 1952; Alan Barth, "The Democrats and FEPC," *R*, VII (Aug. 5, 1952), 13–16.

11. *NYT*, July 10, 1952; *SLPD*, July 17, 1952; Joseph and Stewart Alsop in *ibid.*, May 16, 23, 1952; Doris Fleeson in *ibid.*, June 26, 1952; Charles Murphy, Memo to HST, July 16, 1952, Murphy MSS; HST, *Memoirs*, II, 495.

12. Oscar Handlin, "Party Maneuvers and Civil Rights Realities," *Commentary*, XIV (Sept. 1952), 197–205; Douglass Cater, "How the Democrats Got Together," *R*, VII (Aug. 19, 1952), 6–8; Joseph and Stewart Alsop and Marquis Childs in *SLPD*, July 28, 1952; Drew Pearson in *ibid.*, July 29, 1952; Doris Fleeson in *ibid.*, July 30, 1952.

13. HST, *Memoirs*, II, 496–97; Bert Cochran, *Adlai Stevenson: Patrician Among the Politicians* (New York, 1969), pp. 206–207; Kenneth Davis, *A Prophet in His Own Country: The Triumphs and Defeats of Adlai E. Stevenson* (Garden City, N.Y., 1957), pp. 399–405; Sawyer, *Concerns of a Conservative Democrat*, pp. 278–82.

14. Adlai Stevenson, *Major Campaign Speeches of Adlai E. Stevenson, 1952* (New York, 1953), pp. 3–10; T.R.B., "Washington Wire," *NR*, CXXVII (Aug. 4, 1952), 3–4; "Toward the Great Tomorrows," *ibid.*, p. 5; Childs to Stevenson, n. d., Chapman MSS.

15. "The Democrats Meet," *NR*, CXXVII (Aug. 4, 1952), 6–7; Shelton, "Adlai Was Available," *N*, CLXXV (Aug. 2, 1952), 85–87; "Sparkman's 'Liberalism,'" *ibid.*, CLXXV (Aug. 9, 1952), 101; "Running Mates and Their Records," *ibid.*, CLXXV (Oct. 25, 1952), 371; Shelton, "The Number One Number Two Man," *P*, XVI (Sept. 1952), 9–12; *NYP*, July 28, 1952; Lerner in *ibid.*, July 29, 1952; Lilienthal, *Journals*, III, 332; Randolph to Williams, Aug. 5, 1952, Williams MSS; Stokes in the Atlanta *Constitution*, July 29, 1952; *SLPD*, July 28, Oct. 29, 1952.

16. T.R.B., "Washington Wire," *NR*, CXXIV (Jan. 15, 1951), 3–4; "Eisenhower or McCarthy?" *ibid.*, CXXVI (Feb. 18, 1952), 7; Davis, News commentary, Aug. 31, 1951, Davis MSS; *Public Papers, 1951*, p. 323; Max Ascoli, "The Decisive Election," *R*, V (Sept. 27, 1951), 5–6; "The Deadly Gap," *ibid.*, VI (Feb. 5, 1952), 1; John Hoving to Francis Henson, May 28, 1951, ADA MSS.

17. "Eisenhower; Silent Symbol," *N*, CLXXIV (Jan. 19, 1952), 51–52; "Eisenhower As Symbol," *ibid.*, CLXXIV (Feb. 23, 1952), 168–69; Stokes in the Washington *Evening Star*, May 12, 1952.

18. "Mr. Eisenhower States His Views," *NR*, CXXVI (June 16, 1952), 5–6; *SLPD*, June 17, 21, 1952; "Who Likes Ike Now?" *N*, CLXXIV (June 14, 1952), 567; *NYP*, July 8, 1952.

19. "Financing Eisenhower," *NR*, CXXVII (July 7, 1952), 7; T.R.B., "Washington Wire," *ibid.*, CXXVII (July 21, 1952), 3–4; "The Dilemma of Candidate Eisenhower," *ibid.*, pp. 5–6; "The Platform Was the Payoff," *N*, CLXXV (July 19, 1952), 42–43; "Pitfalls Ahead for Eisenhower," *ibid.*, 48–50; William V. Shannon, "The Eisenhower Blitz," *P*, XVI (Aug. 1952), 6–8.

20. *SLPD*, Sept. 14, 1952; Childs in *ibid.*, Aug. 14, 1952; T.R.B., "Washington Wire," *NR*, CXXVII (Oct. 20, 1952), 3–4; Elmer Davis, News commentaries, Sept. 2, Oct. 6, 1952, Davis MSS; Max Lerner in *NYP*, Sept. 3, 1952; Kingdon in *ibid.*, Sept. 5, 1952; Morris H. Rubin, "The Clinching Question," *P*, XVI (Nov. 1952), 3–5.

21. Ralph M. Blayden and Robert K. Bingham, "Who Is Richard Nixon?" *R*, VII (Aug. 19, 1952), 16; Ernest Brashear, "Who Is Richard Nixon?" *NR*, CXXVII (Sept. 1, 1952), 9–12; "II. Who Is Richard Nixon?" *ibid.*, CXXVII (Sept. 8, 1952), 9–11; "Sir Mordred," *ibid.*, CXXVII (Sept 29, 1952), 5–6; Norman Redlich, "A Handbook for Demagogues," *N*, CLXXV (Oct. 4, 1952), 290; *SLPD*, Sept. 19, 1952; *NYP*, Sept. 25, 1952; Lerner in *ibid.*, Oct. 29, 1952; Reinhold Niebuhr to the Editor, *NYT*, Oct. 2, 1952.

22. *NYT*, Aug. 3, 20, Oct. 2, 5, 12, 1952; Violet Gunther to David Lloyd, Sept. 29, 1952, ADA MSS; James B. Wilson, Urgent memo to national ADA board, Sept. 22, 1952, *ibid.*; Violet Gunther, Memo to national board, Dec. 13–14, 1952, *ibid.*; "The Reluctant Mr. Nixon," *R*, VII (Sept. 30, 1952), 1; *SLPD*, Oct. 14, 1952.

23. *NYT*, Aug. 7, Oct. 20, 1952; Violet Gunther to Harry Girvetz, Aug. 28, 1952, and Reginald Zalles to Mrs. Philip Taft, Oct. 29, 1952, ADA MSS; ADA press release, Oct. 22, 1952, *ibid.*; [Violet Gunther] "Report on Political Activity to the National Board of ADA," Sept. 27, 1952, and Violet Gunther to Schlesinger, Sept. 29, 1952, *ibid.*; Mitchell, Memo to Harry Barnard, Nov. 1 and 5, 1958, Mitchell MSS.

24. *NYT*, Oct. 28, 29, 30, 1952; *SLPD*, Oct. 28, 1952; ADA press release, Oct. 28, 1952, ADA MSS; Statement attached to Reinhold Niebuhr to Otto Spaeth, Oct. 23, 1952, Niebuhr MSS; Davis, News commentary, Oct. 28, 1952, Davis MSS.

25. Lilienthal, *Journals*, III, 337, 340, 343; *NYP*, July 27, 1952; Lerner in *ibid.*, Sept. 9, 1952; *SLPD*, Sept. 28, 1952; Childs in *ibid.*, Sept. 16, 1952; Stokes in the Atlanta *Constitution*, Aug. 29, 1952; "The Stake in Stevenson's Victory," *N*, CLXXV (Oct. 18, 1952), 341–43; T.R.B., "Washington Wire," *NR*, CXXVII (Sept. 22, 1952), 3–4; "The Man for the Job —Part II," *R*, VII (Oct. 14, 1952), 5; Morris H. Rubin, "Adlai, Warts and All," *P*, XVI (Oct. 1952), 3–5; Richard Rovere, "The Stevenson Story," *ibid.*, XVI (Nov. 1952), 6–9; *NUF*, Sept., Oct. 1952.

26. Lahey, "Labor, Adlai, and Ike," *NR,* CXXVII (Aug. 25, 1952), 8; T.R.B., "Washington Wire," *ibid.,* CXXVII (Sept. 22, 1952), 3–4; Stevenson, *Major Campaign Speeches,* esp. pp. 12–13, 17–22, 25–29, 46–52, 83–90, 125–33, 149–56, 173–80, 213–19, 235–44, 269–75; Cochran, *Adlai Stevenson,* pp. 221–23; William C. Berman, "Presidential Politics and Civil Rights: 1952" (paper delivered to Organization of American Historians, April 1970).

27. Charles Mahone to Stanley Girwitz, [late July or early August 1952], ADA MSS; ADA press release, Aug. 18, 1952, *ibid.;* "John Sparkman and the Civil Rights Issue," *NR,* CXXVII (Aug. 18, 1952), 5–6; *SLPD,* Aug. 30, Sept. 22, 1952.

28. Stevenson, *Campaign Speeches,* 83–90, 204–205; Lerner in *NYP,* July 22, 1952; *SLPD,* Aug. 3, 11, 1952; T.R.B., "Washington Wire," *NR,* CXXVII (Aug. 11, 1952), 3–4; Rubin, "Adlai, Warts and All," *P,* XVI (Oct. 1952), 3–5; "The Stake in Stevenson's Victory," *N,* CLXXV (Oct. 18, 1952), 341–43.

29. "The Campaign," *NR,* CXXVII (Sept. 1, 1952), 7; Stokes in the Atlanta *Constitution,* Aug. 15, 1952.

30. HST, *Memoirs,* II, 497–503; *Public Papers, 1952–53,* pp. 601, 703, 729.

31. *Ibid.,* pp. 737–41, 863.   32. *Ibid.,* pp. 804, 989.

33. *Ibid.,* pp. 854–59; Murray Kempton in *NYP,* Oct. 24, 1952.

34. Elmer Davis, News commentary, Oct. 20, 1952, Davis MSS; Kempton in *NYP,* Oct. 20, 1952; *ibid.,* Sept. 30, 1952; Freda Kirchwey to HST, Oct. 15, 1952, HST MSS, OF 299-K; "The Truman Train," *NR,* CXXVII (Oct. 13, 1952), 8.

35. "Stubbed Toes and Hardening Arteries," *NR,* CXXVII (Nov. 17, 1952), 5–6; Lilienthal, *Journals,* III, 369; Niebuhr, "The Republican Victory," *Christianity and Crisis,* XII (Nov. 24, 1952), 153–54; Davis, News commentary, Nov. 5, 1952, Davis MSS.

36. *SLPD,* Nov. 5, 6, 1952; *NYP,* Nov. 5, 7, 1952; Max Lerner in *ibid.,* Nov. 6, 1952; "The Meaning of the People's Mandate," *P,* XVI (Dec. 1952), 3–5; Arthur Schlesinger, Jr., "Which Road For the Democrats?" *R,* VIII (Jan. 20, 1953), 31–34; Aubrey Williams to Stevenson, Nov. 6, 1952, Williams MSS; T.R.B., "Washington Wire," *NR,* CXXVII (Nov. 17, 1952), 3–4.

CHAPTER 23: BEYOND THE NEW DEAL: TRUMAN,
THE LIBERALS, AND THE POLITICS OF LEADERSHIP

1. Joseph R. Starobin, *American Communism in Crisis, 1943–1957* (Cambridge, Mass., 1972), pp. 193–94.

2. See, e.g., Elmer Davis, "Harry S. Truman and the Verdict of History," *R*, VIII (Feb. 3, 1953), 17–22.

3. See, e.g., Barton J. Bernstein, "America in War and Peace: The Test of Liberalism," in Bernstein, ed., *Towards a New Past: Dissenting Essays in American History* (Vintage ed.; New York, 1968), pp. 289–321, and the essays in Bernstein, ed., *Politics and Policies of the Truman Administration*. The most important New Left interpretations of early Cold War diplomacy are Gabriel Kolko, *The Politics of War* (New York, 1968); Gabriel and Joyce Kolko, *The Limits of Power* (New York, 1972); and Lloyd Gardner, *Architects of Illusion* (Chicago, 1970). The best critiques of New Left diplomatic history are Robert W. Tucker, *The Radical Left and American Foreign Policy* (Baltimore, 1971); Charles S. Maier, "Revisionism and the Interpretation of Cold War Origins," *Perspectives in American History*, IV (1970), 313–47; Alfred Eckes, "Open Door Expansionism Reconsidered," *Journal of American History*, LIX (March, 1973), 909–24; and John L. Gaddis, "A Revisionist Monolith: American Foreign Policy and the Origins of the Cold War" (paper presented at a session of the American Historical Association, Dec., 1970).

4. Richard E. Neustadt, "The Fair Deal: A Legislative Balance Sheet," *Public Policy* V (1954), 349–81.

5. Mayhew, *Party Loyalty among Congressmen: The Difference between Democrats and Republicans, 1947–1962* (Cambridge, Mass., 1966), p. 167. On electoral attitudes see Samuel Lubell, *The Future of American Politics*, (3d ed., rev.; New York, 1965), and the many polls reproduced in the *Public Opinion Quarterly*.

6. See, e.g., Eisenhower speech in *NYT*, Nov. 1, 1952.

7. Neustadt, "The Fair Deal: A Legislative Balance Sheet."

8. Anthony Lewis, *Portrait of a Decade* (Bantam ed.; New York, 1963), p. 21; Murphy to Clifford, Dec. 30, 1952, and Clifford to Murphy, Jan. 5, 1953, Murphy MSS; Wilkins to HST, Jan. 12, 1953, HST MSS, OF 596.

Bibliographical Note

The purpose of this essay is not to recapitulate the notes but rather to discuss the major sources I have employed.

MANUSCRIPT COLLECTIONS

When I started Part One of this project as a doctoral dissertation, I wanted to examine every manuscript collection which might be relevant. I quickly discovered that many contributed little or nothing to what I was doing. The twentieth-century revolutions in transportation and communication appear to have reduced the importance of the private written document as a basic historical source; at the same time, this type of material is more frequently duplicated and more widely preserved than in precontemporary eras—when it had greater value to scholars. When I began work on Part Two, I had come to the conclusion that I should confine my manuscript research to collections of obvious importance and look at others only if it was convenient to do so. In a few cases, I took the word of colleagues, archivists, or archival finding aids that a collection would not be particularly helpful to my work. In a number of other cases, I felt it was unnecessary to return to collections I had consulted in Part One.

A. The Truman administration: President Truman retained personal possession of his private files until his death. These

MSS were deeded to the Harry S. Truman Library in the president's will and will be available to scholars after the usual archival processing. State Department restrictions will necessitate the closing of much material on foreign policy, as is the case with other HSTL holdings. Nevertheless, the collections at the Truman Library are extremely valuable to the researcher who is willing to take the time involved in working his way through large quantities of routine papers to find useful documents. Especially significant were the Harry S. Truman MSS (including the "Files" of several White House aides), Clark M. Clifford MSS, Stephen J. Spingarn MSS, George Elsey MSS, Charles Murphy MSS, and David Lloyd MSS. I also examined and found some useful information in the Oscar Chapman MSS, Samuel I. Rosenman MSS, Clinton Anderson MSS, William Boyle MSS, Harold Enarson MSS, J. Howard McGrath MSS, Stephen A. Mitchell MSS, Richard Neustadt MSS, Edwin Nourse MSS, John Redding MSS, Charles Ross MSS, Harold Smith MSS (also at FDRL), David Stowe MSS, Theodore Tannenwald MSS, and Fred Lawton MSS.

The Joseph Davies MSS, LC, are useful for Davies's diary, provided they are used with great caution. Admiral William Leahy's diary in the Leahy MSS, LC, is disappointing. The Jonathan Daniels MSS, University of North Carolina, contain Daniels's notes taken for his biography of Truman (copies available also at HSTL), but most of this material comes out in the finished book, *The Man of Independence* (Philadelphia and New York, 1950).

B. Wallace and the Progressives: The two basic collections are the Progressive Party MSS and the Henry Wallace MSS, both at the University of Iowa. The Progressive Party MSS are a large and valuable group of materials donated by Professor Curtis MacDougall, who used them for his book, *Gideon's Army* (3 vols.; New York, 1965). The Henry Wallace MSS, Iowa, contain extensive personal correspondence and a file of speeches; Wallace's diary and oral history (original at COHC) remain closed. Other Wallace MSS are at FDRL, covering the vice-presidential years, and LC, which has no special material on the problems covered in this study. All three Wallace MSS collections will shortly be available on microfilm. The Alfred Schindler MSS, HSTL, contain a complete file of Wallace's speeches and press releases during his tenure as Secretary of Commerce. The Robert Kenny MSS, University of California—Berkeley, the Vito Marcantonio MSS, New York Public Library, and the Ralph Ingersoll MSS, Boston University, contained little which I could use for this project, although substantial additions are anticipated for the Ingersoll MSS. The Jo Davidson MSS, LC, have a number of worthwhile items. I was unable to secure permission to use the Rexford Tugwell MSS, FDRL.

C. The ADA and liberals associated with it: The major source is the ADA MSS, State Historical Society of Wisconsin. I first saw these papers in a somewhat disorganized state at the ADA National Headquarters in Washington, D.C., while doing research for Part One. When I used them for Part Two, they had been transferred to Wisconsin and superbly arranged for scholars. This is an extremely important and meaty collection. Also at Wisconsin are the Thomas R. Amlie MSS, good for the UDA, William H. Davis MSS, and Marquis Childs MSS. The Eleanor Roosevelt MSS, FDRL, are extensive but yield little information not available in Joseph P Lash, *Eleanor: The Years Alone* (New York, 1972). The Elmer Davis MSS, LC, are valuable for Davis's radio scripts, but the Reinhold Niebuhr MSS, LC, are disappointingly thin. The Chicago Historical Society has a few boxes of Independent Voters of Illinois MSS and a massive collection of Paul Douglas MSS, but the Douglas MSS have very little concerning my period of interest. The Howard Y. Williams MSS, Minnesota Historical Society, and the Helen Gahagan Douglas MSS and Melvyn Douglas MSS, both at the University of Oklahoma, were at best of marginal value. The Chester Bowles MSS, Yale University, contain speeches and valuable correspondence on Bowles's variegated and productive postwar career.

D. Other collections: The National Farmers Union (Denver, Colorado) allowed me to examine press releases and other non-confidential material from its files. Neither the Merlin Hull MSS, State Historical Society of Wisconsin, nor the Robert La Follette, Jr., MSS, LC, were useful in getting at the attitudes of the old Wisconsin Progressives. The Aubrey Williams MSS, FDRL, had some items of interest. The Fiorello La Guardia MSS, New York City Municipal Archives, contain correspondence and radio scripts. The following collections were of little importance for this project: Robert Lasch MSS, Dore Schary MSS, Morris Rubin MSS, all at the State Historical Society of Wisconsin; Frank Murphy MSS and Blair Moody MSS, University of Michigan; John W. Edleman MSS, Paul Sifton MSS, and Donald Montgomery MSS, all at Wayne State University; Harley Kilgore MSS, FDRL; Harley Kilgore MSS, University of West Virginia; Philip Murray MSS, Catholic University of America; Robert F. Wagner MSS, Georgetown University; Lewis Corey MSS, Columbia University; Granville Hicks MSS, Syracuse University; Eric Sevareid MSS and Joseph Alsop MSS, LC; Max Lerner MSS, Yale University; Norman Thomas MSS, New York Public Library.

PERSONAL INTERVIEWS

Between 1964 and 1971, the following people kindly took time to talk with me: William L. Batt, Jr., Charles F. Brannan, Oscar L. Chapman, Clark M. Clifford, Benjamin V. Cohen, Ben Davidson, Philip Elman, George Elsey, W. Averell Harriman, Leon Keyserling, Frank Kingdon, Charles Murphy, Robert Nathan, Joseph L. Rauh, Jr., Arthur M. Schlesinger, Jr., Henry A. Wallace.

ORAL HISTORY INTERVIEWS

In general, I found these most useful for forming impressions of personalities, but I was wary of relying very heavily upon them for factual information. While I read a few oral histories at the University of California and at Wayne State, those which were useful to me came either from the COHC or the HSTL. Several of the Columbia interviews, done by Dean Albertson, are among the finest examples of the craft. Regrettably, a number of transcripts which touch on the Progressive Party are closed. At COHC, I examined interviews with Will Alexander, Paul Appleby, Joseph Clark Baldwin, Louis Bean, Samuel Bledsoe, Bruce Bliven, William H. Davis, Rudolph Evans, Mordecai Ezekiel, Fred Henshaw, John B. Hutson, Gardner Jackson, Edwin Lahey, James M. Landis, Norman Thomas, Howard Tolley, Rexford G. Tugwell, and Roy Wilkins. At HSTL, I gleaned bits and pieces of information from the oral histories of George Allen, John Barriere, William L. Batt, Jr., Kenneth Birkhead, Samuel Brightman, John Franklin Carter, Jonathan Daniels, Harry Easley, Oscar Ewing, Joseph Feeney, Martin Friedman, Donald Hansen, Frederick Lawton, Max Lowenthal, W. McNeil Lowry, Edward McKim, Charles Murphy, Irving Perlmeter, J. Leonard Reinsch, Samuel I. Rosenman, Walter Salant, Harold Seidman, James L. Sundquist, Roger Tubby, and Harry Vaughn.

PERIODICALS

As its zigs and zags indicated, the *New Republic* was the most sensitive indicator of liberal opinion during this period; it also was the most widely read liberal magazine. The *Nation* had a somewhat smaller following and was more Popular Frontist in tone. The *Progressive* was a tabloid weekly which functioned as the personal organ of Robert La Follette, Jr., until its reorganization as an independent monthly at the beginning of 1948; it voiced the La Follette brand of Midwestern liberalism —pacifism, isolationism (until the end of World War II), anti-Communism, independence from the Democratic Party. It appears to have been estranged from the main body of liberalism during World War II, but indications are that it moved back into the progressive mainstream after the war. Beginning in

1949, the *Reporter,* was an important voice of anti-Communist liberalism. The *ADA World* was a useful supplement to the ADA MSS, and the *National Union Farmer* provided basic information about the Farmers Union. The *UDA Congressional Newsletter* was a good source for the ADA's predecessor organization. The *New Leader* served as an outlet for the most vehemently anti-Communist liberals and socialists. Its vocal hostility toward most of the rest of the liberal press reflected its peripheral status, but some of its writers were important and influential. In researching the war years, I used *Common Sense* (which ceased publication in 1946), *Free World* (which also ceased publication in 1946), and the *Antioch Review,* which began in 1941 as mainly a political magazine and increasingly became a literary and scholarly publication.

NEWSPAPERS

Like all historians of twentieth-century America, I used the New York *Times* as a basic factual source. For various shades of editorial opinion, I examined the Chicago *Sun* (later the *Sun-Times*) during the period that the elder Marshall Field was publisher, the New York *Post, PM* (ceased publication in 1948), its successor, the New York *Star* (ceased publication in 1949), the Philadelphia *Record* (ceased publication in 1947), and the St. Louis *Post-Dispatch.*

Among the liberal newspaper columnists of the period, Thomas L. Stokes was unique in having a mass readership for his strongly progressive articles. Eleanor Roosevelt was also widely syndicated, but her personal correspondence is frequently more revealing than her newspaper articles.

OTHER PRIMARY SOURCES

I have attempted to use the full range of memoirs, autobiographies, and documentary collections with the hope that I have exercised the caution which such material demands. To cite only the most obvious instances, the *Memoirs* of Harry S. Truman are more useful for insights into their author's character and attitudes than for an account of what actually happened, and William Hillman, ed., *Mr. President* (New York, 1952), published while Truman was still in office, is a highly selective compilation from private papers not yet available to scholars. The historian can learn much from such material, but he must handle it with care.

Although the main focus of this study is outside Congress, I have used the *Congressional Record* for the attitudes of some key liberal politicians and have also discovered a surprising amount of other relevant material inserted into it.

SECONDARY SOURCES

I have relied heavily on the work of other historians in seeking to understand a wide range of issues and have attempted to indicate in the footnotes the books and articles which were most important to me. I discuss the political historiography of the period at some length in an essay scheduled for publication in Richard S. Kirkendall, ed., *The Truman Period as Research Field,* 2d ed. As I was writing a history of responses to the Cold War rather than analyzing the Cold War itself, I did not feel obligated to undertake the extensive manuscript research which has characterized recent writing on the topic. In making my way through the secondary accounts, I have been most impressed by William H. McNeill, *America, Britain, and Russia* (New York, 1953); Louis J. Halle, *The Cold War as History* (New York, 1967); Norman Graebner, *Cold War Diplomacy* (Princeton, 1962), a brief but important essay; Tang Tsou, *America's Failure in China, 1941–50* (Chicago, 1963); and John L. Gaddis, *The United States and the Origins of the Cold War, 1941–1947* (New York, 1972).

Index